WITHDRAWN
HARVARD LIBRARY
WITHDRAWN

INTRODUCTORY READINGS IN CANON LAW

Andrew J. Cuschieri, O.F.M.

INTRODUCTORY READINGS IN CANON LAW

Andrew J. Cuschieri, O.F.M.

Roman Catholic Studies
Volume 3

The Edwin Mellen Press
Lewiston/Queenston
Lampeter

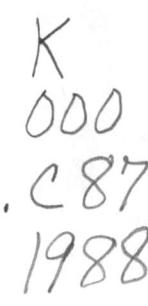

Library of Congress Cataloging-in-Publication Data
Cuschieri, Andrew
    Introductory readings in canon law / by Andrew Cuschieri.
      p. cm.
    Bibliography: p.
    Includes index.
    Contents: Church and the creation of human consciousness--Philosophy of law--The concept of equity and its relation to epikeia and dispensation--The juridical concept of custom--The concept of public authority--Personhood as endorsed in the code of canon law--The person as member of the common priesthood--The parochial community--Episcopal conference in the life of the church--Diocesan consultors/Senate of priests--Ecumenism in the new code of canon law.
    ISBN 0-88946-210-0
    1. Canon law. I. Title
LAW ‹CANON Cush 1988›   87-29820
262.9--dc19   CIP

This is volume 3 in the continuing series
Roman Catholic Studies
Volume 3 ISBN 0-88946-210-0
RCS Series ISBN 0-88946-240-2

© 1988 The Edwin Mellen Press. All rights reserved.

For information contact **The Edwin Mellen Press**

Box 450   **Box 67**
Lewiston, New York   **Queenston, Ontario**
U.S.A. 14092   **CANADA L0S 1L0**

Mellen House
Lampeter, Dyfed, Wales
UNITED KINGDOM SA48 7DY

Printed in the United States of America

ACKNOWLEDGEMENT

I wish to express my heartfelt thanks to Rev. Fr. Joseph Lynch, Rev. Fr. Brian Colbert, and Mr. Frank Kinlin, who generously corrected, and sometimes edited, the manuscript.

CHURCH AND THE CREATION OF HUMAN CONSCIOUSNESS

Christ, as the Formal and final cause of creation -- thus head of the Church -- in the primordial and absolute will of God	1

PHILOSOPHY OF LAW

Christ: the eternal Wisdom incarnate which expresses itself as:	19
A. the fundamental law of creation;	21
B. the law of the sensitive world;	22
C. the law of the spirit:	
I. *Natural Law*:	22
1. the concept of Natural law in Roman philosophy	26
2. the concept of natural law in *Corpus Iuris Civilis*	33
3. The concept of natural law in Christian literature	36
4. the concept of natural law in canonical and civil authors	45
5. towards a comprehensive understanding of natural law:	52
a. natural law, the foundation of koinonia -- *Ius gentium*;	58
b. natural law is *diakonia* -- justice as principle and as virtue;	62
c. natural law is *martyrion*	70
II. *Ius divinum*	73
III. *Ius humanun:*	
1. law as conceived by the Roman jurist	79
2. *ius humanum* in Christian philosophy of law	84
IV. *Ius ecclesiasticum*	96
The understanding of canon law in the context of the present study	99

THE CONCEPT OF EQUITY AND ITS RELATION TO EPIKEIA AND DISPENSATION

I.	Equity understood as principle and as virtue	109
II.	Equity as fundamental criterion of legal justice:	123
	a. equity as mitigation of legal justice;	124
	b. equity as rectification of legal justice:	128
	1. epikeia;	129
	2. interpretation;	132
	3. dispensation.	135
	c. equity as substitution of legal justice	142

THE JURIDICAL CONCEPT OF CUSTOM

I.	Definition of custom of fact	149
II.	Definition of custom of law	153
III.	Custom of Roman law	154
IV.	Custom in ecclesiastical codification	157
V.	Juridical analysis of custom	160
	Distinction between private and public custom;	
	1. public custom of fact in general;	166
	2. public custom of fact, and custom of law in the Code of canon law:	172
	a. *consuetudo praeter legem*	175
	b. *consuetudo contra legem*	177
	c. *consuetudo secundum legem*	180
VI	Conclusion	181

THE CONCEPT OF PUBLIC AUTHORITY

I.	The understanding of public authority in Roman law	183
II.	The concept of authority in the Judeo-Christian religion	186
III.	The concept of authority in patristic literature	191
IV.	The concept of authority in juridical literature	209
V.	The concept of authority in Thomas Aquinas	217

VI.	The concept of public authority in the context of the present study;	219
	The concept of Ecclesiastical authority	224

PERSONHOOD AS ENDORSED IN THE CODE OF CANON LAW

The three essential components of personhood:

I.	Rationality	235
II.	Conscientiousness	242
III.	Sociability:	245
	Right to Life	251
	Right to embrace the faith	251
	Right to freedom of conscience	251
	Right to privacy	252
	Right to good reputation	253
	Right to protect oneself from grave burden	254
	Right to assume a state of life	254
	Right to obtain personal documents	255
	Right to just remuneration	255
	Right to equality among spouses	257
	Right of spouse and children to financial support by the other spouse after separation or dissolution of marriage	257
	One's rights in ecclesiastical courts	257
	One's rights of defence against administrative decrees	259
	The right of one accused of a criminal act	260
	Respect shown towards the penalized person	261
IV	Conclusion	263

THE PERSON AS MEMBER OF THE COMMON PRIESTHOOD

I.	Historical introduction		266
II.	Rights in general of the common priesthood:		277
	1.	Rights of the faithful to Christian education	278
	2.	Right of the faithful to receive the sacraments	280

III.	The involvement of the faithful in the liturgical life of the Church	281
IV.	The involvement of the common priesthood in the pastoral life of the Church:	288
	the role of the faithful in the diocese	291
V.	Conclusion	297

THE PAROCHIAL COMMUNITY

I.	The parochial community in historical perspective	299
II.	The concept of parish in the doctrine of Vatican Council II	310
III.	Towards a further understanding of the parochial community in the light of the teaching of Vatican II:	314
	1. The ministerial priesthood and common priesthood as essential components in the formation of the parochial community	314
	2. The parochial community is *koinonia*	316
	3. The parochial community is diakonia:	318
	a. the office of pastor in the context of *diakonia*	320
	b. the faithful in the context of *diakonia*	321
	4. The parochial community is *martyrion*	324

EPISCOPAL CONFERENCE IN THE LIFE OF THE CHURCH

I.	Theology of Episcopal Conference	326
II.	History of the Episcopal Conference:	328
	1. the Vatican model of the Church in antithesis to the manorial model of the Medieval Church	330
	2. the episcopal college as viewed by the Medieval Church and by Vatican Council II	332
III.	The theologico-juridical understanding of episcopal college in the new Code of canon law	335
IV.	Episcopal conference as juridical person:	340
	1. nature and purpose of the episcopal conference	341

	2.	ecclesiastical province and ecclesiastical region -- plenary council	345
	3.	episcopal conference and the Holy See	346
	4.	episcopal conference and *Ecclesia*	347
	5.	episcopal conference and diocese:	348
		a. clergy	349
		b. sacraments	351
		c. liturgy	353
		d. pastoral activity	356
		e. the judiciary	359
		f. the administration	361
		g. diocesan synod	362
	6.	episcopal conference and institutes of consecrated life	363
	7.	episcopal conference and ecumenism	364
V.	Conclusion		366

DIOCESAN CONSULTORS -- SENATE OF PRIESTS

I.	Introduction	369
II.	Council of priests	370
III.	College of diocesan consultors	375
IV.	Personal reflections on the subject	381

ECUMENISM IN THE NEW CODE OF CANON LAW

I.	Introduction		384
II.	Holy See and ecumenism		387
III.	Episcopal conference and ecumenism		388
IV.	Local Ordinary and ecumenism		389
V.	The Code of canon law and ecumenism		391
VI.	Different dimensions of ecumenism:		392
	1.	ecclesiological aspect	392
	2.	sociological aspect	394
	3.	educational aspect	395

4.	spiritual aspect:		399
	a.	*communicatio in spiritualibus*	402
	b.	*communicatio in sacris*	403
		baptism	405
		penance, eucharist, anointing of the sick	407
		confirmation	411
		marriage	411
	c.	penalties concerning ecumenism	414
5.	the right to stand as plaintiff in an ecclesiastical court		417
VII. Conclusion			417

BIBLIOGRAPHY 421

INDEX 435

FOREWORD

This series of papers may serve as a form of commentary on Canon Law. Some of these papers were read in seminars, but all have been presented as lectures in my introductory course in canon law at the Toronto School of Theology. Admittedly, a paper on the general norms would have enriched and integrated the compilation. Cognizant of the importance of such an exposition, I believe, nevertheless, the existing commentaries on the Code substitute more than adequately for this lacuna. It should be acknowledged, moreover, that references are often made to some of these basic norms. Other important subjects, v.g., the office of Bishop, priest, and deacon, the sacraments, etc. are left out since they form the content of other courses.

These papers are addressed to an audience which, presumably, has some acquaintance with the Latin language. However, I have availed myself of the English translation whenever this was feasible for the convenience of the reader. The Latin text can serve merely to corroborate what is being said in the text.

PREFACE

My intention, when compiling these eleven essays, was that each should stand on its own. However, they form, collectively, a development of a fundamental idea: Christ is the *causa formalis* and the *causa finalis* of human consciousness. It is extremely important that one should start with the first essay for a clear understanding of this theologico-juridical curriculum.

The first study, "Church and the Creation of human Consciousness" serves as a premise to the present compilation. It is incomplete by itself since it contains certain fundamental ideas which have to be expounded and clarified in subsequent papers. Christ is presented in this essay as the all-embracing and unifying force of creation, Lord of creation and head of the human family. The premise of Christ being the *causa formalis* and the *causa finalis* of human consciousness leads to the perception of the intrinsic inter-relatedness between Church and human consciousness. The Church, as the perpetuation of Pentecost, has no reason to be if not to enlighten, purify, and to energize human consciousness in the pursuit of self-discovery and self-unfolding, which ultimately leads to the explication of its Christological nature.

The study of the philosophy of law presents Christ as the revelation of the Wisdom of God manifesting itself in the threefold law of nature. Only in human consciousness is Christ supremely revealed as the *causa formalis* of creation. Natural law is nothing other than the image of Christ being implanted in the human consciousness, by virtue of which human consciousness, whether as individual or universal spirit, is destined to become ever more rational, conscientious, and sociable. This innate law has been crystallized, solidified, and vivified, even moreso after the Fall, through the redemptive merits of the Lord. The ultimate self-fulfillment of human consciousness is delineated in the Gospel. Human laws ought to be perceived in this perspective. They spring from human consciousness itself; they are instruments by which it expresses itself; they signal at what stage human consciousness has arrived in the christolization of itself. In light of this exposition, natural law, divine positive law, human law, not only share ultimately the same divine source, but they also appear to be mere modes by which divine Wisdom manifests itself in and through human consciousness. Ecclesiastical law is human law imbued with the Spirit of Pentecost. In the manner of human laws, ecclesiastical laws emerge ultimately from the christianized human consciousness; they demonstrate that the Church is indeed alive, moving forward in the explication of itself; they therefore register at what stage the Church has arrived in the authenticity of herself, and her ability to permeate human consciousness, in order that the latter may expediently actualize its christological nature as its ultimate finality.

The basic presupposition on the study of equity is the subordination of the human justice to eternal justice. The ongoing process of human consciousness in becoming explicitly what it is implicitly bespeaks of its own mediocrity. The understanding of eternal justice implanted in the human heart will ever remain defective, and consequently its correct application through human law cannot be accomplished to the full. Equity, understood as principle, is nothing other than divine justice. As virtue, it is the anguish of human consciousness to actualize eternal justice. In this sense, equity serves as mitigation, rectification, and substitution of legal justice. It becomes apparent that *epikeia*, interpretation, and dispensation intrinsically flow from equity, and that, the more civilized a legal system is, the more impelling becomes their existence in the administration of human justice.

Custom is *l'esprit de corps* in actuality. This constitutes the theme of the fourth paper. Custom of fact germinates from the individual human consciousness, which by its very nature explicates itself in a communal spirit. Custom seeks, by intrinsic necessity, the authentication of itself through the recognition of public authority, since both are the realization of human consciousness. By virtue of the endorsement of public authority, custom of fact assumes the force of law -- hence the custom of law. The Code of canon law acknowledges three manners by which custom may relate to law: apart from, against, and in consonance with, the law.

The fifth essay concentrates on the nature and origin of public authority. An endeavour is made to interpret the Pauline doctrine on the divine origin of public authority. Rather than being an imposition upon human freedom, public authority is at once emanation from and complete fruition of the universal inwardness of human consciousness; the three qualities of human consciousness -- rationality, conscientiousness, and sociability -- attain their full expression in the establishment of public authority. The Christo-centric understanding of creation enables us to see civil authority as proceeding remotely and indirectly from Christ as *causa formalis* through human consciousness, whereas ecclesiastical authority flows proximately and directly from Christ as the *causa finalis* of human consciousness.

The presentation on personhood in the Code of canon law presupposes the conviction that the Church is human consciousness enlightened by the Gospel and vivified by the divine Spirit. The Church thus stands out as the most genuine expression of the law implanted *ab initio* in human consciousness. Upon this assumption, the human being, *qua talis*, is indeed a member of the Church in matters pertaining to fundamental and inalienable human rights; as such, the human being is entitled to the solicitude and succour of the Church in what concerns the temporal and spiritual welfare of his or her being.

The Second Vatican Council marks the emergence of the common priesthood from passive to active participation in the life of the Church. The seventh paper is an exposition of the Conciliar doctrine on the subject as it is implemented by the Code of Canon law. It cannot be denied that the faithful, throughout history, enjoyed fundamental rights concerning, particularly, their Christian education, and the reception of the sacraments and sacramentals. The great achievement of the Council was that it decreed a formal involvement of the common priesthood in the liturgical ministries, and fostered a deeper sense of belonging through participation of the same on different levels and in different spheres of the Church's pastoral activity. The emancipation of the common priesthood ensued from the transformation of a concept of Church defined as an institution, as a highly legalized and impersonal society, into an understanding of Church as being rooted in human consciousness, that is a community of humans who share one baptism, one faith, one Lord.

The exposition on the parochial community follows as a corollary of the preceding paper. Nowhere do the faithful feel so deep a sense of belonging as within the parochial community; within its perimeter the

Christian identifies himself or herself with the universal ecclesial community, becomes an active participant in the life of this community, and comes to the realization of the supreme worth of the human person. The common priesthood constitutes an essential component, together with the ministerial priesthood, in the formation of the parochial community, which is the Church in miniature. The same realities which are attributed to natural law, and consequently to the Church -- *koinonia, diakonia, martyrion* -- should, by nature of the thing itself, be applied to the parochial community.

One would have expected a study on the office of Bishop in the context of the general theme. The office of Bishop, as an authority established by divine institution in the Church, has been expounded in its substantiality in the essay on authority. The fundamental concept of this authority is also presented in this paper. The revelance of the presentation on Episcopal Conference derives from the newness of the institution in the constitution of the Church. In this exposition the office of the Bishop is further clarified. The Episcopal Conference is indeed a realization of the collegial nature of the episcopal order in contradiction to the seigneurial conceptualization of the episcopal office.

The senate of priests enjoys special attention since, in my opinion, it follows from the doctrine on episcopal collegiality. This paper has this belief as its presupposition. The institution of this senate in every diocese signals a growing awareness of the collegial nature of the presbyterate, and, to some extent, of its participation in the episcopal college. In spite of the persistent presence of the diocesan consultors, the relationship between the Bishop and the presbyterate is moving from an extremely hierarchial stratification of the ministerial priesthood, characteristic of the Medieval Church, to the realization of a community between Bishop and priests.

The last paper concentrates on ecumenism. The Church, with its increasing awareness of her intimacy with human consciousness, is able to realize her close relationship with other Christian Churches and non-Christian Religions. This same awareness forces her to reach out from her traditional insular existence into a realm of communication, recognizing that a certain amount of truth exists outside herself.

Ecumenism is the outcome of the Church's self-evaluation, self-purification, and her identification with the rest of the human family.

This preface had a twofold objective. I hope I have succeeded in presenting a synthesis of each paper, and in demonstrating that the whole compilation is the development of a central idea announced in the first essay. It must be said, however, that only through the reading of all these papers can one acquire a better idea of my approach to canon law.

ABBREVIATIONS

AAS -- *Acta Apostolicae Sedis*
Mansi -- *Sacrorum Conciliorum Nova, et Amplissima Collectio a Joanne Dominico Mansi*, Florentiae -- Venetiis.
P. G. -- *Patrologiae Cursus Completus Omnium SS. Patrum, Doctorum Scriptorumque Ecclesiasticorum*, Series Graeca, Accurante J.-P. Migne, Parisiis.
P. L. -- *Patrologiae Cursus Completus Omnium SS. Patrum, Doctorum Scriptorumque Ecclesiasticorum*, Series Latina, accurante J.-P. Migne, Parisiis.

The English translation of the documents of Vatican Council II is the Abbot -- Gallagher translation, Guild Press -- New York, 1966.

Church and the Creation of Human Consciousness

Protagoras believed "man is the measure of all things."[1] Vatican Council II acknowledges the growing universal awareness that "all things on earth should be related to man as their center and crown."[2] The Christian contention on the nature of the human being helps lay down the conviction that any philosophical theory, psychological hypothesis, political ideology, or sociological doctrine may be valid only if the significance it manages to construct is interpreted as the result of the acknowledgement of the human being as of supreme worth. Thus, within the Christian spectrum the single human being is placed as the ultimate reality, the be-all and the end-all of human society, the focal point in the understanding of the cosmos.

While acknowledging the human being as the centrality of the cosmos, an inner force is undeniably experienced in the human individual, as well as in the universal human spirit, which results from a perennial discontent in the face of the highest achievement of self-actualization. The absolute fulfillment of humanization, whether as individual or as universal consciousness, is a myth. It remains nonetheless a reality, for, although unattainable, it is indeed approachable. In the Christian perspective, humanity in its forward march to self-fulfillment boasts of its ideal as a historic reality -- the Word made flesh. Christ is the ultimate destiny of the individual and global humanization; he is at the same time the formal and final cause of the individual and universal human unfolding unto full

---

[1] *The Dialogues of Plato*, trans. B. Jowett, New York, 1895, Vol. III, *Theaetetus*, pp. 316, 321.

[2] *Gaudium et spes*, n. 12, p. 210. Abbot translation is being used in this study.

actualization. The teaching of St. Paul offers to the searching mind sufficient insight into the Christological nature of humanity.

For Protagoras the measure of all things is man; for Paul, Christ, "the image of the unseen God."[3] In the eternal will of God the Incarnation preceded creation, for "before anything was created, he existed."[4] Decreed by the Divine Will as the central idea of creation, Christ is indeed "the beginning,"[5] "the first born of all creation."[6] It is only because of him that creation has reason to be, "for in him were created all things in heaven and on earth: everything visible and everything invisible."[7] Thus the will of God was that Christ be the all-embracing and unifying force in order that anything created bears his image. All were created in him,[8] "all things were created through him and for him."[9] Creation must find its absolute and ultimate significance in Christ as its centripetal force. "He would bring everything together under Christ, as head, everything in the heavens and everything on earth,"[10] so that Christ "holds all things in unity."[11] All the more, human existence finds its ultimate meaning in the creation of Christ since "before the world was made, he chose us, chose us in Christ."[12] It follows that by reason of its nature and aim the destiny of creation is to explicate its "Christological" nature. In its forward march in self-development, creation moves towards its own christological ontology,

---

[3] Col 1:15.

[4] Col. 1:17.

[5] Col. 1:18.

[6] Col. 1:15

[7] Col. 1:16.

[8] Col. 1:16.

[9] Col. 1:16.

[10] Eph. 1:10.

[11] Col. 1:17.

[12] Eph. 1:4.

since "God wanted all perfection to be found in him."[13] The unfolding of human consciousness, whether as a universal spirit or as a unique and individual reality, *a fortiori*, has as its ultimate aim the "christolization" of its nature.

The vision of Christ by St. Paul as the *causa formalis* and *causa finalis* of creation induces one to a deeper understanding of Genesis on the creation of the first man.

The Book of Genesis presents in its first two chapters the creation of the human being as a unique enterprise, one which is thereby essentially distinct from the rest of living creatures. Upon a cursory survey of the two chapters one is likely to realize a repetitious and ill-featured account of the creation of the first man. It is indeed this very characteristic that instigates investigation into the issue and the attempt to grasp the rationale for such a presentation. The two chapters have each a specific theme of the same truth, and together form the whole truth.

Biblical scholars have pointed out two traditions involved in the formation of Genesis, viz., the *Priestly* and the *Yahwist* Traditions. The *Priestly* Tradition seems to be responsible for the first chapter, whereas the *Yahwist* Tradition takes care of the second. Each Tradition has its own story to tell on the creation of the human being and each tradition by itself ought to be acknowledged as integral. However, for the complete picture of the creation of Adam -- which, after all, was the intention of the Redactor of the Canonical Bible -- both schools are bound to form one single dissertation. The two schools each present a different human creature: the *Priestly* Tradition concerns itself with the creation of the spiritual man; the *Yahwist* Tradition knows only of the creation of the corporal man, which partly belongs to the earth.[14] It behooves us to understand the doctrine contained in each Tradition in order to acquire a clear understanding of "the man" as the measure of all things.

---

[13] Col. 1:19.

[14] Gn. 2:7.

The divine origin cannot be denied to the man of the *Yahwist* Tradition for the Lord God "breathed into his nostrils the breath of life."[15] The same Tradition, however, places its full attention on the somatic Adam, and makes a strong point that in the creation of this man a *compositum* was applied together with the breath of the Supreme: "The Lord God formed man out of the dust of the ground."[16] The difference of the sexes comes to the foreground in such a manner that it also becomes the central idea of the second chapter of Genesis. The human creature acquires a somatic individuality and a psychological identity; thereby a name is given according to sex: Adam, Eve -- names based mainly on gender. This creature is presented as a historic reality in absolute manner endowed with feelings who administers, controls, plans, rules, discerns, communicates and enters into interpersonal relationship. The man of the *Yahwist* Tradition is master of his own destiny. In fact, the Tradition takes pains to hand over the story of his tragedy.

The whole theme of the *Priestly* Tradition centres around the idea of the human being formed in the image of the Creator. In spite of the difference of sexes mentioned,[17] the concept of *creatio ex nihilo* is so powerful that the corporal aspect is overshadowed by the divine likeness of the same creature: "Let us make man in our own image, in the likeness of ourselves";[18] "God created man in the image of himself, in the image of God he created him."[19] In contrast with the *Yahwist* Tradition, the man of the *Priestly* Tradition is presented outside historical context, in purely ontological perspective.

In the study of both chapters of Genesis an exclusive concentration by the *Priestly* tradition on an archetype of the human family cannot be

---

[15] Gn. 2:7.

[16] Gn 2:7.

[17] Gn. 1: 27.

[18] Gn. 1: 26.

[19] Gn. 1:27.

amiss-"The Man"-who indeed was intended by God as his own masterpiece and in the image of whom the man of the *Yahwist* Tradition was to be formulated. The man of the *Priestly* Tradition, being the *causa formalis* and *causa finalis* of the Yahwist man, remains nameless since he is the most perfect creature, the most authentic image of God. This interpretation, however speculative, throws new light on the immortal utterance of God, "Let us make man in our own image, in the likeness of ourselves." In this phrase we understand God had Christ in mind, in whom, through whom and for whom Adam and Eve were created.

This particular interpretation of the creation of man was not unknown to the *Patristica*. Tertullian maintains that God in uttering the words, "Let us make man in our own image, in the likeness of ourselves," had in mind his masterpiece, which is "the Word was made flesh",[20] God in breathing into the lime of the earth fashioned Adam upon Christ, His primordial idea. Thus the human being is created in the likeness of Christ who is the most genuine reflection of God. Tertullian writes: "Imagine God wholly employed and absorbed in it -- in His hand, His eye, His labour, His purpose, His wisdom, His providence, and above all, in His love, which was dictating the lineaments (of this creature). For, whatever was the form and expression which was then given to the clay by the Creator, Christ was in His thoughts as one day to become man, because the Word, too, was to be both clay and flesh, even as the earth was then. For so did the Father previously say to the son: "Let us make man in our own image, after our likeness." And God made man, that is to say, the creature which He moulded and fashioned; after the image of God, that is of Christ, did He make man."[21] Hilarius Pictaviensis also helps one to appreciate the idea

---

[20] Jhn. 1:14.

[21] QUINTUS SEPTIMIUS FLORENS TERTULLIANUS, *De Resurrectione Carnis*, cap. VI *Opera Omnia*, Tomus II, P.L., Tomus 2, Parisiis, 1844, col. 802. "Recogita totum illi Deum occupatum ac deditum, manu, sensu, opere, consilio, sapientia, providentia, et ipsa imprimis affectione, quae liniamenta ducebat. Quodcumque enim limus exprimebatur, Christus cogitabatur, homo futurus, quod et limus, et caro sermo, quod et terra tunc. Sic enim praefatio Patris ad Filium: 'Faciamus hominem ad imaginem et similitudinem nostram. Et fecit hominem Deus.' Id utique quod finxit, ad imaginem Dei fecit illum, scilicet Christi."

that Christ is the most authentic image of God and that he was willed by God from all eternity to be the *causa formalis* in the creation of the human being.[22] One may also quote Irenaeus, although his views are not clear on the score. In his treaty *Adversus haereses* Irenaeus seems to rebut Tertullian's interpretation when he writes: "Si enim non haberet caro salvari, nequaquam Verbum Dei caro factum esset. Et si non haberet sanguis justorum inquiri, nequaquam sanguinem habuisset Dominus." In another place, however, he seemingly concurs with Tertullian on the Christocentrism of creation when he states: "in semetipsum fabricator omnium Verbum praeformaverat."[23]

The above Scriptural and theological exposition on the raison d'être for the creation of the human family not only brings into focus the christocentrism of creation, but it also recognizes and endorses the Church and the human family, in the primordial and sinless state of creation, as one interlocked reality. Our Lord, Jesus Christ, is thus acclaimed as lord of creation and head of the human family-Church, independently of sin. The aim of the Incarnation after the Fall was precisely intended to correct the distortion provoked by sin between the man of the *Priestly* Tradition and the man of the *Yahwist* Tradition. Sin changed the Incarnation of Logos from an event of glorification into a role of redemption. "He was first to be born from the dead, so that he should be first in every way,"[24] as was the primordial plan of God. The Incarnation was meant for the restoration of the human family in and for Christ, through Christ himself, that is "all things to be reconciled through him and for him, everything in heaven and everything on earth, when he made peace by his death on the cross."[25]

---

[22] HILARIUS PICTAVIENSIS, *Tractatus Super Psalmos*, Psalmus CXVIII, Litt,n.7, *Opera Omnia*, Tomus I, P.L., Tomus 9, Parisiis, 1844, col. 566: "Incorporale est, quidquid illud tum de consilii sententia inchoatur: fit enim ad imaginem Dei. Non Dei imago; quia imago Dei est primogenitus omnis creaturae: sed ad imaginem Dei, id est, secundum imaginis et similitudinis speciem."

[23] *Contra Haereses Libri Quinque*, Liber V, cap. 14, n.1, Tomus unicus, P.G., Tomus 7, Parisiis, 1857, col. 1161; ibid., Liber III, cap. 22, n.3, col. 958.

[24] Col. 1:18.

[25] Col. 1:20; cf. Eph. 1:10.

Church and the Creation of Human Consciousness

The Incarnation and death of the Lord thus brought about the restoration of the human family of whom Christ is the archetype, and the transformation of the human family into the Church of whom Christ is the head.

Christ is God who became human. In the *unio hypostatica* the divine and eternal love manifested itself by itself outside itself. The Creator created himself outside himself. Christ, as the second person of the triune God, is self-subsistent, infinitely omnipotent and incomprehensible. He created himself human, subject to his own law, the law of nature. Out of his own free will he experienced the bitterness of a fallen humanity, except for sin. The Son of Man appeared in history as the epitome of human maturation, in whom resided the primordial and perfect equilibrium between spirit and matter, characteristic of the sinless stage of humanity. As the prototype of the human race, he presented himself as the rational, conscientious and social creature in the most absolute manner. By word and action he proved to be the embodiment of absolute, objective freedom, the perfectly human and unblemished freedom, in his unconditional obedience to the will of the Father, and in his complete self-bestowal to his fellow, but inferior, humans. The Son of Man stands as the ultimate aspiration of the human mind in its forward march of self-discovery and self-completion.

The human being, created in the image of Christ, was bound to be created a spiritual, as well as physical, being. Thus sin could never obliterate the essence of the human creature. In spite of the Fall the human being will ever remain a spiritual being. The human individual in the recesses of his being forever knew himself to be the receptacle of the eternal Spirit. Anthropology has furnished us with enough data that the human being has always been a religious and conscientious creature, endowed with glimmer of truth. The Spirit of God, the glimmer of truth, was transposed and translated into human consciousness. St. Paul in his letter to the Romans teaches that the eternal law was implemented in the heart of the human individual.[26] St. Augustine repeats the same idea in a different manner: "In search of truth you should not look outside yourself

---

[26] Rom. 2:15.

but rather you should delve into your own innermost being for truth dwells within there."[27] Man, in returning to his inmost inwardness, finds the eternal truth, which is his authentic self absorbed in Christ. By so doing, he actualizes his authentic humanity, namely, that of being a rational, conscientious and social creature. "In the depths of his conscience, man detects a law which he does not impose upon himself, but which holds him to obedience. Always summoning him to love good and avoid evil, the voice of conscience can when necessary speak to his heart more specifically: do this, shun that. For man has in his heart a law written by God. To obey it is the very dignity of man; according to it he will be judged."[28] "Therefore, this sacred Synod proclaims the highest destiny of man and champions the godlike seed which has been sown in him."[29]

What happened by the first disobedience was the disruption of the inner equilibrium between spirit and matter in human reality. Since that event human consciousness has been in search of that primordial equilibrium in the human *compositum* lost by sin.

In spite of political and social movements throughout history in search of the ideal humanization, human consciousness still groans under the yoke of its creation. Socio-political ideologies were bound to provoke social upheavals and turmoil, culminating in barricades of resistance and great loss of human life. The so-called civilized society is still divided into those who rule and those who serve. Social injustice, human exploitation, discrimination of classes still afflict society at large. The universal human consciousness still endorses the law of the jungle, the supremacy of the fittest, in its performance for its own stability, welfare and development. The influence of humanitarian movements on the humanization of the human consciousness has been relatively small in comparison with the sacrifice endured by the individual. Their principles and ideals, however valid they

---

[27] *De Vera Religione Liber Unus*, cap.39, n.72, *Opera Omnia*, Tomus III, P.L., Tomus 34, Parisiis, 1841, col.154. "Noli foras ire, in teipsum redi; in interiore homine habitat veritas."

[28] *Gaudium et spes*, n.16, p. 213; cf. n.17, p.214.

[29] Loc. cit., n.3, p.201.

may be, shall forever remain an imposition on the human will. The individual self, insofar as it operates in subjective freedom, reacts to any outside interference with savage resistance. Subjective freedom is characteristic of the brute; it is instinctualistic, individualistic, and wild. In the human self, subjective freedom assumes the spirit of destructiveness, chaos and anarchy. Total subjective freedom registers complete alienation of the self from itself since the self alienates itself from its essence-being, from its ontological nature; it contradicts its being rational, conscientious and social in its fullness. Humanitarian movements, per se, signal infantilism of the human consciousness. If and when the universal human spirit attains the absolute and objective freedom of itself, humanitarian movements would automatically become *contradictio in terminis*.

The more the human mind is centripetally oriented and the more the human will is self-centered and individualistic, the greater is the alienation and estrangement of the christological self. The person, whose insight and foresight do not venture beyond the realm of natural and materialistic survival, which is crude being, deprives his own consciousness from attaining the maturation of the universality of his christological nature. Christian ethics enables the human mind to go against its own estrangement. In doing so, it goes against the contingent otherness. By suppressing its instinctual inwardness the human self is at the same time breaking loose from materialistic externality within itself. In detaching from the inner-outer materialistic self, human consciousness attains complete freedom of itself within itself. While having nothing of its own, the christianized mind becomes master of the inner and outer worlds-complete, objective and absolute freedom. The more deeply oriented the human will is towards the universal good, which is also an ontological reality in itself, the less it is restrained by itself. Once the human mind reaches out to objective-eschatological externality, deeper becomes the grasp of the human inwardness in itself, of its substantial and solid independence, as its ultimate and absolute reality. In losing oneself, one finds oneself. The human consciousness emerges outside itself, suspends itself, negates its crude, materialistic being, only to return unto itself more true to itself, alive and more complete in the fulfillment of its own universality; thus it approaches all the more its own christological authenticity.

Human progress emerged from an idea imposed on the subjective human freedom. In antithesis to this historical reality stands Christianity. Unlike human movements, Christianity reaches out directly at the core of individual human consciousness. In Christian philosophy the individual self constitutes the ultimate reality. Thus the one and sole destiny of Christianity is the transformation of subjective and instinctualistic freedom into objective and absolute freedom of the human will. This transformation stems from inner conviction of one's rationality, conscientiousness and sociability. In opposition to primitive religions, the Judeo-Christian religion holds that humanization of the human self, and therefore authentic civilization, can ever be achieved only if it results from internal morality- "To obey (the law written by God in the human heart) is the very dignity of man; according to it he will be judged."[30] In this precisely consists the christianization of the human mind; from this emerges authentic humanization of the human mind; in this consists true civilization and progress. The Church is there so that the self comes to know itself, its christological self. Indeed, revelation "discloses the dignity of the human person in its full dimensions."[31]

The Church traces its beginning in the eternal and divine decree in willing "the first-born of all creation."[32] Since everything was created through him, in him and for him,[33] Church and the human family, in the primordial and sinless stage, formed one interlocked reality. In the

---

[30] Loc. cit., n.16, p.213.

[31] *Dignitatis humanae*, n.9, p.688.

[32] Col. 1:15.

[33] Col. 1: 16.

redemptive economy the being and not-being of the Church as humanity is mere contingence, caused by accident -- the Fall.[34]

The redemptive Church personifies the human race in the process of inner rectification of itself. The glimmer of eternal truth transposed and translated into human consciousness at the time of its creation, which has been obscured by sin, is being revitalized, enlightened and crystalized by a second breathing of God into human consciousness which started at Pentecost. The breath of God which vivified the dust into Adam is the same divine breath which took hold of the disciples' personhood at Pentecost and which perpetuates in the administration of Baptism and Confirmation. In this perspective, Pentecost assumes the aspect of revival and rejuvenation of the christological nature of human consciousness; thus Pentecost signifies the end of times when Christ became the historic finality of creation- "When the times had run their course to the end: that he would bring everything together under Christ as head"[35] and that "all perfection to be found in him."[36] "The renovation of the world has been irrevocably decreed and in this age is already anticipated in some real way. For even now on this earth the Church is marked with a genuine though imperfect holiness. However, until there is a new heaven and a new earth where justice dwells (cf. 2 Pet. 3:13), the pilgrim Church in her sacraments and institutions, which pertain to this present time, takes on the appearance of this passing world. She herself dwells among creatures who groan and

---

[34] Vatican Council II does not go so far as to identify the Church with the human family. It does, however, acknowledge and endorse an intimate relationship between the two. Thus the Constitution, *Gaudium et spes*, declares: "... this Council can provide no more eloquent proof of its solidarity with the entire human family with which it is bound up, as well as its respect and love for that family, than by engaging with it in conversation about these various problems" (n.3, p.201). "That is why this community (the Church) realizes that it is truly and intimately linked with mankind and its history" (n.1, p.200).

[35] Eph. 1:10.

[36] Col. 1:19.

travail in pain until now and await the revelation of the sons of God (cf. Rom. 8:19-22)."[37]

Pentecost is the beginning and completion of human transformation from subjective to objective, absolute freedom. The messianic age started at Pentecost,[38] when the redemptive Church came into being, alive, dynamic, compact, sealed by the Spirit. The perpetuation of the Pentecostal mystery was soon felt in the salvific activity of the Church in the individual member for the messianic gift's intent was to purify, intensify, and transform into oneness, thus creating a bond of unity and profound solidarity among the many.

The historic event of Pentecost devolved in two phases: the partition of the Spirit into different tongues of fire; the emergence of one-mindedness of the disciples. From these two events one can envisage the true meaning of the humanization of the human mind and perceive the Church, the perpetuation of Pentecost, as the epitome of this same humanization.

The breath of God parted in the shape of tongues of fire resting upon each member of Christ's fellowship. The partition of the Spirit according to the number of disciples points to the acknowledgement by the Spirit of the presence of the individual member; it endorses the supreme worth of the individual, the intrinsic validity of the human being, *qua* unique personhood, with subjective individuality. It reveals God Himself breathing in each individual soul; it manifests the working of divine grace being directed essentially and exclusively to the subjectivity of human personality, accommodating itself to individual idiosyncrasies. The Spirit's intent was to perfect each member, to intensify self-interiorization, and to vivify the human will in absolute freedom with its fortifying virtue. Thus the christolization of human personhood was achieved. From the transformation of human personhood the Church was born, and presented herself to the world alive and dynamic in testimony of the one Spirit. The

---

[37] *Lumen gentium*, n.48, p.79.

[38] Acts 2:1-47.

interiorization of the self by the Spirit resulted in exteriorization of the self in a bond of unity and profound solidarity among the many. In unison with legitimate diversity of individual minds, for nothing was amiss in the personal individuality of the member, the group emerged as brotherhood solidified in one-mindedness in the belief of the one truth. In this transformation the human self negated itself in order to find the authenticity of itself; it lost its subjective, instinctualistic freedom only to gain objective, absolute freedom; the individualistic human will was sublimated into a truly rational and social will, oriented towards the universal and eternal good; thus the human will was enlightened and led back to the primordial, authentic freedom which was lost through the Fall.

In the *unio hypostatica* the human nature cloaked the eternal and divine nature. In the image of his prototype the human being likewise enshrines the union of spirit and matter, soul and body. The Church, the synthesis of the relationship between Christ and the human creature, partakes of the twofold nature of her head, that is to say, she is both divine and human, visible and yet invisibly endowed.[39]

As divine, the Church stands on an immovable and irreducible basis; she is the embodiment of absolute and perennial values; she is the manifestation and actualization of the eternal idea of God in willing Christ as the alpha and omega of creation. The presence of the Church in the world marks the return back of human consciousness to its very foundation, Christ. "The final age of the world has already come upon us (cf. 1 Cor. 10:11). The renovation of the world has been irrevocably decreed and in this age is already anticipated in some real way."[40] "Therefore, the promised restoration which we are awaiting has already begun in christ, is carried forward in the mission of the Holy Spirit, and through Him continues in the Church."[41] Revealed truth is still an imposition on the subjective human will due to its own alienation. The further the human will

---

[39] *Sacrosanctum concilium*, n.2, p.137.

[40] *Lumen gentium*, n.48, p.79.

[41] Ibid.

proceeds in explicating its true inner humanity, the more it verifies its christological nature. Thus the Church signals the ultimate aspiration of human consciousness in the process of its own maturation.

The Church, as part of the human consciousness, is likewise in search of herself through groan and travail in pain. It is her destiny, as part of the fallen humanity, to succumb to historical vicissitudes. She is forever adapting to, and influenced by,[42] the gradual development of the universal human consciousness. By her inherent nature she endlessly moves forward in self-discovery, self-actualization and self-completion in Christ, her head. The eternal spirit of God makes itself gradually manifest in the process of the Church's self-purification; thus she is always becoming the embodiment of the "Word made flesh." "Christ summons the Church, as she goes her pilgrim way, to that continual reformation of which she always has need, insofar as she is an institution of men here on earth."[43]

This inner process of self-explication is the most intensive (self-purification) as well as the most extensive (identification with the human family) exercise of its own reality. The perennial process of self-discovery in the pursuance of its own authenticity entails simultaneously the fusion of the Church with the human family as its ultimate finality. The Church through the twofold process-that of self-explication and that of the christianization of the human consciousness-brings about the gradual humanization of the human family in view of the parousia. As divine-human reality, the Church is human consciousness heightened, enlightened, fortified, and crystalized by the breath of the divine at Pentecost in the pursuance of its own eschatological fulfillment.

The above theological exposition shows the distinction between Church and the human family based on contingency-a disruption caused by

---

[42] The Church acknowledges that there is wisdom in the world from which she benefits in the process of her own self-discovery and self-actualization. It is worth reading apropos *Gaudium et spes*, n.44, pp. 245-247. It suffices here to quote the first sentence which synthesizes the whole theme: "Just as it is in the world's interest to acknowledge the Church as a historical reality, and to recognize her good influence, so the Church herself knows how richly she has profited by the history and development of humanity."

[43] *Unitatis redintegratio*, n.6, p.350; cf. *Lumen gentium*, n.9, p. 26.

sin. The fundamental identification of Church and the human family in Christ induces one to depart from the traditional conceptualization of the Church as a segregated group antagonistic to the world at large. The present theological position helps one realize the intrinsic relationship between the natural and supernatural orders of things; indeed the two orders of things are essentially the same by reason of their source, nature and aim. Through Baptism, rather than separating oneself from the world, the person becomes more involved with the universal human consciousness in the ongoing process of its own christolization. The baptismal grace introduces the person into the plenitude of humanity, that humanity which before its beginning belonged to Christ.

Consequential to the above theological contention follows the endorsement that the person, by the very fact of his humanity, belongs to the People of God; he is a member of the Church through mystical Baptism brought about through the global redemption of our Lord, Jesus Christ. In all human beings, whether baptized or unbaptized, "grace works in an unseen way. For, since Christ died for all men, and since the ultimate vocation of men is in fact one, and divine, we ought to believe that the Holy Spirit in a manner known only to God offers to every man the possibility of being associated with this paschal mystery."[44]

The well-known statement of Boniface VIII, "extra quam (Ecclesiam) nec salus est nec remissio peccatorum,"[45] should be interpreted in the light of the above theological exposition. Catholic doctrine always held that nothing else is needed to obtain justification than an act of perfect charity and of contrition. A person who elicits these acts receives immediately the gift of sanctifying grace, and is numbered, in a mystical manner, among the children of God. Thus it should be observed that those who are outside the visible boundaries of the Church, not of their own fault, in some real sense belong to the Church. The desire to live up to one's own conscience-that

---

[44] *Gaudium et spes*, n.22, pp. 221-222; cf. *Lumen gentium*, n.9, p. 24.

[45] Bulla, *Unam sanctam*, 18 novembris 1302, in *Enchiridion Symbolorum Definitionum et Declarationum de Rebus Fidei et Morum*, Ed. Denzinger-Schonmetzer, 34, Barcinone-neo-Eboraci, 1967, n.870, p.279.

conscience which is the spirit of God breathing through the nostrils of Adam, namely that eternal law transplanted in the recesses of the human heart-implicity entails the desire for incorporation into the Church as an institution. Thus a person, who lives according to the dictates of that glimmer of truth, may be said to belong, and rightly so, to the visible Church by reason of baptism of desire-"*voto baptismi.*" This doctrine has been sanctioned by Vatican Council I when it teaches: "Certainly not all those who are in invincible ignorance of Christ and his Church are to be eternally damned solely on account of this ignorance. For it bears no guilt in the eyes of the Lord who wants all men to be saved and to attain to knowledge of the truth. To all who do their best he gives his grace so that they may attain justification and eternal life."[46] "Whosoever, therefore, knowing that the Catholic Church was made necessary by God through Jesus Christ, would refuse to enter her or to remain in her could not be saved."[47]

The foregoing scriptural and doctrinal exposition assists us to define the juridical status of the human being, *qua* human being, as a member of the Church. Before we proceed further, however, we must emphatically insist that no real distinction exists between the institutional Church and the mystical Church; they merely form two aspects of the same reality. In this manner there is eliminated once and for all the legalistic conceptualization of the Church and her laws. Having this clarification established, we feel confident in translating the aforesaid theological exposition into juridical perspective. From the juridical point of view, the following criteria have to be maintained if we really desire to maintain an all-embracing and unifying vision of the Church in its relationship with the human family:

1. every human being, *qua* human being, that is by virtue of natural

---

[46] *The Teaching of the Catholic Church as contained in her Documents*, Ed. Karl Rahner, New York, 1967, n. 365, pp. 216-217; cf. Allocution of Pius IX, *Singulari quadam* (1854), eodem loco, n. 351 (2865*), p. 207.

[47] *Lumen gentium*, n. 14, pp. 32-33; cf. *Ad gentes divinitus*, n. 7, p. 593.

law, is a member of the Church just as much as the individual is a member of the human family;
2. the person is thus subject to the Church's authority when she interprets natural law;
3. the Church, essentially being the human race, is the embodiment of natural law; thus she has full authority in interpreting and explicating natural law according to the stage of human maturation;
4. the Church thus has the most sacrosanct right and duty to defend the fundamental and inalienable rights of the human person;
5. divine positive law defines and explicates natural law obscured by the Fall. Only in this sense, divine positive law is considered as revealed truth. The Church, being the embodiment of revealed truth, is empowered to interpret this further clarification of natural law for those who through baptism belong to this ulterior state of humanization;
6. the Church, as human community, strives to safeguard and interpret revealed truth on a par with the degree of maturation of the universal Christian consiousness by her own disciplinary laws.

The Code of Canon Law

The Code of Canon Law thus appears in the aforesaid theological spectrum as a synthesis of the Church in all her diverse dimensions. This statement certainly requires clarification:
- the Church, it was contended, is essentially the human family. In this aspect, the Code of Canon Law enshrines laws which defend and enhance human dignity;
- the Church is said to be the expression of revealed truth. In this respect, the Code constitutes manifestation, confirmation and implementation of a faith;
- the Church, as the perpetuation of the *unio hypostatica*, partakes of the divine and human nature. As divine, the Church is the embodiment of absolute and perennial truths. For this reason, the Code of the Church must ensure that the purity of *depositum fidei* be

maintained. The Code, in fact, concerns itself with divine positive laws pertaining to the constitutional structure of the Church, the sacraments, and the office of sanctifying, teaching and ruling in the Church;

- At the same time, the Church is a human community. Disciplinary laws enacted by the church manifest and confirm the human aspect of the Church. The ensemble of these laws constitutes the object-matter of canon one of the Code. In this respect, the Code illustrates at what stage of development the Church has arrived in the revelation of her own inwardness. The disciplinary laws of the Code are thereby the laws which the universal Christian consciousness is capable of understanding and embracing in the condition in which it presently finds itself in the ongoing process of crystalization of its "christological" nature.

Philosophy of Law

"With you is Wisdom, she who knows your works, she who was present when you made the world; she understands what is pleasing in your eyes and what agrees with your commandments."[1] The author of the Book of Wisdom defines Wisdom as the spirit of the Divine; "a breath of the power of God, pure emanation of the glory of the Almighty; . . . she is a reflection of the eternal light, untarnished mirror of God's active power, image of his goodness."[2] She willed, and creation emerged in a process of self-unfolding and of becoming. In the midst of all-inclusive harmony, she inscribed phenomena in the heart of creation, while she remains the foundation, the immutable and irreducible law of being and not being. "She deploys her strength from one end of the earth to the other, ordering all things for good."[3] As from a flowing font, the human mind drinks from God's eternal wisdom.

The eternal Wisdom unfolded itself intensively in willing the Incarnation and extensively in universal creation. Christ, begotten of the divine Wisdom, emerges as the primordial idea and epitome of creation, the objective externality of the eternal harmony, the most authentic manifestation of the eternal truth, the revelation of eternal justice. Christ remains the basis, the all-inclusive and unchanging idea and the fundamental raison d'être of creation. Christ is "the image of the unseen God";[4] "before anything was created he existed";[5] indeed, he is "the

---

[1] Wis. 9:9

[2] Loc. cit. 7:25-26

[3] Loc. cit. 8:1

[4] Col. 1:15.

[5] Loc. cit., 1:17.

beginning,"[6] "the first born of all creation";[7] "in him were created all things in heaven and on earth: everything visible and everything invisible";[8] "all things were created through him and for him";[9] he "holds all things in unity."[10] The eternal Wisdom expressed itself outside itself in Christ, by whom creation had its beginning, in whose image it was formed, in whom it finds its ultimate significance, and to whom it moves in search of self-fulfillment. To know this one truth is the starting point and the end of philosophy: to understand Christ as the fountain from which all laws of nature, all phenomena of nature and consciousness spring.

The eternal, divine Wisdom expresses itself outside itself in three perennial laws of nature, all of which lead to universal good: the law of being in universal unification, constancy and perpetuation of all that is; the law of becoming which reveals itself in evolution and productivity; the law of the Spirit which unfolds itself in human consciousness. The human being, remarks Thomas Aquinas, is the embodiment of these three laws of nature.[11] The contention that human nature is indeed the synthesis of the threefold law of nature must, by force of reason, uphold Christ as the most authentic expression and the ultimate fulfillment of the law, in whom all things were created,[12] who "holds all things in unity,"[13] in whom "God

---

[6] Loc. cit., 1:18.

[7] Loc. cit., 1:15.

[8] Loc. cit., 1:16.

[9] Loc. cit., 1:16.

[10] Loc. cit., 1:17.

[11] *Summa Theologica*, Ia-IIae, q. 94, art. 2, Resp., *American Edition in Three Volumes*, New York, vol. 1, 1947, p. 1009.

[12] Col. 1:16.

[13] Loc. cit., 1:17.

wanted all perfection to be found,"[14] since the eternal Will decreed, "in the dispensation of the fullness of times, to re-establish all things in Christ that are in heaven and on earth."[15] In dying, Christ absorbed creation so that in him everything on earth identifies itself, receives significance and comes to perfection; in giving his life, Christ transformed crude productivity into spiritual generation of human nature; through incarnation and redemption Christ discloses the ultimate aspiration of human consciousness in its forward march of self-discovery and self-completion.

The Fundamental Law of Creation

"In man there is first of all an inclination to good in accordance with the nature which he has in common with all substances, inasmuch as every substance seeks the preservation of its own being, according to its nature; and by reason of this inclination, whatever is a means of preserving human life, and of warding off its obstacles, belongs to the natural law."[16] The divine Wisdom reveals itself, in a primeval mode of expression, as an all-embracing and unifying force of nature. It has always been the Christian contention that nothing in creation is drawn to action by sheer innate compulsion of its own; divine Providence is at the helm of creation's destiny. The Christian consciousness believes that behind creation there is the eternal mind which permeates all things, by virtue of which everything subsists, and under its guidance natural phenomena explicate their innate potentiality towards perfection. Of this perennial law of nature, Blessed Prosper writes: "Lex aeterna, Dei stabili regit omnia nutu, nec mutat vario tempore consilium."[17]

---

[14] Loc. cit., 1:19.

[15] Eph. 1:10.

[16] *Summa Theologica*, Ia-IIae, q. 94, art. 2, Resp., *American* . . ., p. 1009.

[17] Quoted by Hincmarus Rhemensis in *Expositiones ad Carolum Regem pro Ecclesiae Libertatem Defensione, Opera Omnia*, Tomus I, P.L., Tomus CXXV, Parisiis, 1879, Expositio I, col. 1055.

The Law of the Sensitive World

The law of the sensitive world is traditionally termed as *"ius naturale,"* which Thomas Aquinas defines as "inclination."[18] This law is common to humans and beasts as Ulpianus points out: "natural law is that which nature teaches to all beasts; thus it cannot be said that natural law is the prerogative of man alone."[19] The existence of this law and its comprehension are of modest interest to the student of philosophy of law; they serve only as a point of reference without any direct relation to the juridical disquisition.

The Law of the Spirit

"Natural law is nothing other than the impression of divine light in us; thus natural law is nothing other than a participation of the eternal law by the rational creature."[20] By virtue of this law, the human being stands out as a unique creature and lord over creation. It is the law that causes creation to divide itself into two main blocks: the crude being and consciousness. The eternal wisdom is objectivized in a body of principles of justice and reason which the human mind can rationally apprehend, and which forms the ideal norm or standard of right conduct. Reason is common to all, and there is no resemblance in nature so great, there is no equality so complete, as that between one human individual and another. As one

---

[18] *Summa Theologica*, Ia-IIae, q. 94, art. 2, Resp., *American* . . . p. 1009: "There is in man an inclination to things that pertain to him more specially, according to that nature which he has in common with other animals: and in virtue of this inclination, those things are said to belong to the natural law."

[19] Ulpianus, L. *Iuri operam*, 1, D., *De iustitia et iure*, 1, 1, §3. "Ius naturale est, quod natura omnia animalia docuit: nam ius istud non humani generis proprium, sed omnium animalium, quae in terra, quae in mari nascuntur, avium quoque commune est."

[20] *Summa Theologica*, Ia-IIae, q. 91, art. 2, Resp., *American* . . ., p. 997. "Ius naturale nihil aliud est, quam impressio divini luminis in nobis: unde patet, quod lex naturalis nihil aliud est, quam participatio legis aeternae in rationali creatura."

would expect, the question of natural law attracts the attention of the philosopher, the theologian, and the jurist.

Now more than ever before in history human consciousness is becoming increasingly aware of its own nature as being rational, conscientious and social, and with equal proportion is escalating the awareness of and respect for its own dignity. The universal acknowledgement and endorsement of fundamental and inalienable rights demonstrate the existence of natural law engraved in human nature. The conscious world is earnestly seeking a universal charter of social justice. However, the cardinal question so far has not been addressed. So far nothing has been decided on what criterion of truth justice should be conceptualized. It is undeniably true that human consciousness is discovering itself more convincingly as the receptacle of a perennial law of justice. It is equally true, however, that human consciousness will ever remain in a perpetual process of self-discovery and self-authentication; the unfolding of its inwardness already suggests obscurity, limitedness, incompleteness, relativity, imperfection, mediocrity. The remark of the Aquinatis suits the purpose: "I answer that, besides the natural and the human law it was necessary for the directing of human conduct to have a Divine law . . . because, on account of the uncertainty of human judgment, especially on contingent and particular matters, different people form different judgments on human acts; whence also different and contrary laws result."[21]

The innate destiny of human nature in self-explication deprives the same nature of the right of self-authentication; it needs to resort to authority outside itself. This was precisely the reason for presenting the Book of Wisdom as the *status quaestionis* of our disquisition. The eternal Wisdom crystalised human nature in the Incarnation; Christ stands in history as the full revelation of the truth, the ultimate aspiration of the human consciousness in becoming rational, conscientious and social.

Total repudiation of natural law is the theory of the "*contract social*" of which Carneades was forerunner. The human being, according to

---

[21] *Summa Theologica*, Ia-IIae, q. 91, art. 4, Resp., *American* . . . , p. 998.

Carneades, is deprived of an innate and immutable law which reflects eternal justice, and which forms the fundamental raison d'être for the universal equality and solidarity among humans. The human family is united out of necessity; laws arise out of the experience of utility; the only measure of what is right and wrong is human agreement; justice is thus conceived of as mere expediency and immediacy.[22]

The theory of Carneades found credibility among scholars at the end of the eleventh century. Flaccus Albinus, among others, maintained that, in the primeval stage of existence, human individuals roamed the land in the manner of wild beasts -- "bestiarum more vagabantur" -- without any rational or moral principle or rule of life, but motivated by sheer instinct -- "caeca et temeraria cupiditas." At a point in time a wise man appeared who managed to tame these savages, group them together, and made them live peaceably and humanely in communities.[23] The mind of the author on the subject can further be envisaged if one accepts his understanding of *ius naturale* as being sheer instinct, the instinct of self-preservation and self-defence.[24]

A similar story is told by Rabanus Maurus. In defining the word "town," *oppidum*, the author presents human beings as not being by nature social. At first, they lived, in the manner of wild beasts, in solitude, naked and unarmed; finally, they came together in order to protect themselves from wild beasts, entered into relationship with each other, and formed communities.[25]

In both stories the human family is conceived of as a formless mass, the movement and action of which is elementary; its decision to live a community life is imposed upon it by mere brute force and natural instinct.

---

[22] Quoted by Lactantius, *The Divine Institutes*, Trans. Sr. Mary Francis McDonald, Book V, chap. 17, *The Fathers of the Church*, Washington, D.C., 1964, vol. 49, pp. 370, 371.

[23] *Dialogus de Rhetorica et Virtutibus*, in *Opera omnia*, Tomus II, P.L., Tomus CI, Parisiis, 1851, coll. 920-921.

[24] Loc. cit., col. 921.

[25] *De Universo Libri Viginti Duo*, *Opera Omnia*, Tomus V, Liber XIV, cap. 1. P.L., Tomus CXI, Parisiis, 1864, col. 375.

Justice is not thought of as the revelation of eternal Wisdom in human nature, but rather it arose out of necessity. Justice is not thereby considered a virtue in human conduct, but rather a matter of convenience.

Aristotle does not recognize the divine origin of justice, but believes that it is a mere human characteristic, and accepts it on his own terms. He stands in open confrontation with the Christian position on natural law. There is only one valid assumption for all humankind: reason is common to all. The human individual enshrines in his innermost being a law which is right reason, commanding and forbidding. This Aristotle denies in his advocacy of the natural inequality of human nature. According to him, the human creature is a political animal, *zoon politikon*.[26] This term was taken by later generations of thinkers to mean "social animal." With such an interpretation of the term, Aristotle thus appears to posterity as the herald of human dignity. In veracity, he is being accredited with a concept which he *a priori* rejected. The Aristotelian assumption of human recognition depends entirely on the political recognition, specifically, of the Hellenic state.[27] This means that, to be human, one first has to be a political being of Hellas. Apart from the *polis*, the human creature is "either sub-human or super-human";[28] thus one's humanity does not follow from its own intrinsic nature. The Aristotelian position relies on the hypothetical suppositum that "the state is both natural and prior to the individual."[29] Such a contention leads one to conclude that the human being is essentially a hording animal, devoid of individual identity, a mere political symbiosis, deprived of inner autonomy and conviction; one's social status is the sole criterion for self-identification and self-actualization. The Aristotelian aberration reaches its

---

[26] *The Politics*, Trans. T.A. Sinclair, Middlesex, England, 1978, Bk. I, chap. 2, p. 28, "Man is by nature a political animal; it is his nature to live in a state."

[27] Loc. cit., pp. 26-27, "It is proper that Hellenes should rule over barbarians, meaning that barbarian and slave are by nature identical."

[28] Loc. cit., p. 28.

[29] Loc. cit., p. 29.

logical conclusion in its belief in slavery as a natural institution;[30] it is human nature which decrees the discrimination between human beings as to who should be the free-man and rule, the true human being, and who should be the slave and be possessed as a piece of property by somebody else.[31] In synthesis, the human being is not the embodiment of natural law by reason of his own intrinsic nature; there are indeed individuals who are naturally dispossessed, *hoi polloi*, and therefore they are expected to subordinate themselves and render unconditional obedience to the developed reason of others.

It was his disciple, Alexander the Great, who really fostered the universal awareness of the homogeneity of the human race. With the extension of the Macedonian empire, the universal human consciousness became increasingly aware that in each human person there is something absolutely non-subordinate to history, but something intrinsically eternal and divine, an innate law which is common to all, a body of moral principles which is always and everywhere recognized by human reason as binding. And this was precisely the philosophy of Socrates who considered the human individual as being his own centre. By assigning the determination of one's action to insight and conviction, he posited the individual as capable of a final moral decision. In the Socratic view, the human soul can only know the divine, so far as it knows itself.

Roman Philosophy on Natural Law

Any philosophy, states Clement of Alexandria, -- not necessarily

---

[30] He rebuts, in fact, the opinion of those who contend "that it is contrary to nature to rule as master over slave, that the distinction is one of convention only, since in nature there is no difference, and that this form of rule is based on force and therefore wrong:, loc. cit., chap. 3, p. 31. The thinking of the philosopher is unequivocally found in chapters IV, V.

[31] Loc. cit., chap. 4, p. 32, "Any human being that by nature belongs not to himself but to another is by nature a slave; and a human being belongs to another whenever he is a piece of human property, that is a tool or instrument having a separate existence and useful for the purposes of living": cf. loc. cit., chap. 5, pp. 33-34.

Christian -- entails a glimmer of the eternal wisdom of God.[32] In the writings of great minds who preceded Christianity, so much can be found which bears witness to the revealed truth. "For we shall find that very many of the dogmas that are held by such sects as have not become utterly senseless, and are not cut out from the order of nature . . . though appearing unlike one another, correspond in their origin and with the truth as a whole. For they coincide in one, either as a part, or a species, or a genus."[33] We do not know of any Roman philosopher who came so close to the Christian doctrine on natural law as did Cicero, Seneca and emperor M. Aurelius Antoninus.

Marcus Tullius Cicero rebuts the Carneadian view on human nature, natural law, and justice. It was not necessity caused by human weakness[34] that brought humans to live and function as a community. Cicero acknowledges a supreme Being as the artificer of justice: "there was never a time when the human race was not governed by a perennial and immutable law which appears as the master, ruler and God."[35] Notwithstanding human frailty and propensity to evil, the eternal law of God reveals itself in the individual human consciousness "(the human person) in its totality, constitution and mind, is overwhelmingly permeated by the divine fire."[36] This innate law constitutes a perennial and absolute

---

[32] *The Miscellanies (Stromata)*, vol. 1, Bk. 1, chap. 13, Trans. William Wilson, *Ante-Nicene Christian Library*, Edinburgh, vol. IV, 1880, p. 389: "So the sects both of barbarian and Hellenic philosophy have done with truth, and each vaunts as the whole truth the portion which has fallen to its lot. But all, in my opinion, are illuminated by the dawn of light. Let all, therefore, both Greeks and Barbarians, who have aspired after the truth,-both those who possess not a little, and those who have any portion,-produce whatever they have of the word of truth."

[33] Ibid.

[34] *De Re Publica*, liber I, cap. 25, n. 40, *Opera Omnia*, edidit Carolus Fridericus Augustus Nobbe, Lipsiae, 1850, p. 1178; cf. Liber III, cap. 14, n. 23, p. 1192.

[35] Loc. cit., Liber III, cap. 22, n. 33.16, p. 1193: "Omnes gentes et omni tempore una lex et sempiterna et immutabilis continebit, unusque erit communis quasi magister et imperator omnium deus"; cf. *De Legibus*, lib. II, cap. 4, nn. 8,9, pp. 1210-1211.

[36] Loc cit., lib. III, cap. 1, n. 1, p. 1190. "In quo tamen inesset tamquam obrutus quidam divinus ignis ingenii et mentis."

norm of justice,[37] a law which has preceded the institution of the state,[38] and allows no discrimination among races, nations, states.[39] The natural equality and the universal solidarity among humans emerge from this essential characteristic.[40] By virtue of this innate law, the human creature excels the beast[41] in that the human individual is a moral creature, capable of discerning good from evil.[42] It is precisely this law that renders the learned and the illiterate alike; because of it every human being is capable of knowing in doing wrong and thereby feels guilty.[43] "Ex natura vivere summum bonum" (to abide by natural law is supreme good).[44] Nature is taken to mean "recta ratio" (right reason), the sole criterion of justice and goodness.[45] The human creature is born not to live in solitude or in misanthropy; "recta ratio" is there to guide the individual in right and just

---

[37] Loc. cit., lib. III, cap. 22, n. 33.16, p. 1193: "Huic legi nec abrogari fas est, neque derogari ex hac aliquid licet, neque tota abrogari potest: nec vero aut per senatum aut per populum solvi hac lege possumus: neque est quaerendus explanator aut interpres eius alius."

[38] *De legibus*, lib. I, cap. 6, n. 19, p. 1205.

[39] *De Re Publica*, lib. III, cap. 22, n. 33.16, p. 1193: "Nec erit alia lex Romae, alia Athenis, alia nunc, alia posthac." However, when it comes to the social stratification within the state, Cicero seems to change his view: "Quum omnia per populum geruntur, quamvis iustum atque moderatum, tamen ipsa aequabilitas est iniqua, quum habet nullos gradus dignitatis," loc. cit., lib. I, cap. 27, n. 43, p. 1178.

[40] Loc. cit., lib. I, cap. 25, n. 39, p. 1178, "Eius autem prima caussa coeundi est non tam imbecillitas, quam naturalis quaedam hominum quasi congregatio . . . (n. 40) itaque inter se congregatos, quod natura hominum solitudinis fugiens et communionis ac societatis appetens esset."

[41] *De Legibus*, lib I, cap. 10, n. 30, p. 1206.

[42] Loc. cit., lib. I, cap. 6, n. 18, p. 1205, "Lex est ratio summa, insita in natura, quae iubet ea, quae facienda sunt, prohibetque contraria" cf. lib. I, cap. 12, n. 33; lib. I, cap. 15, n. 42, p. 1207; lib. II, cap. 4, nn. 8,9, pp. 1210-1211; *De Re Publica*, lib III, cap. 22, n. 33.16, p. 1193.

[43] Loc. cit., lib. I, cap. 14, n. 41, p. 1207. "O rem dignam, in qua non modo docti, verum etiam agrestes erubescant."

[44] Loc. cit., lib. I, cap. 21, n. 56, p. 1209.

[45] Loc. cit., lib. I, cap. 6, n. 19, p. 1205, "ea est enim naturae vis, ea mens ratioque prudentis, ea iuris atque iniuriae regula"; cf. lib. I, cap. 15, n. 42, p. 1207.

Philosophy of Law

conduct[46] in order that the human community may live peaceably.[47] Without the virtue of justice, human society cannot stand firm and flourish.[48] All positive ordinances of human society, all customs, if they are to have any truth and validity, must conform to this divine norm implanted in human consciousness.[49]

Lucius Annaeus Seneca, the most Christian among the pagan philosophers, has enjoyed great esteem among Christian authors of all times. The stoic doctrine of the universal equality of humans, by reason of an innate law of justice common to all, is adhered to by Seneca. By the term "nature," he understands this immanent, perpetual and irreducible law[50] which forms the *radix* of human justice.[51] Like Cicero, he maintains that nature is the criterion of proper human conduct,[52] and to live according to nature is the command of reason.[53] It is nature which draws the human

---

[46] Loc. cit., lib. I, cap. 14, n. 41, p. 1207, "noster quidem hic natura iustus vir ac bonus etiam colloquetur, iuvabit, in viam deducet"; lib. I, cap. 10, n. 28, p. 1206, "nos ad iustitiam esse natos, neque opinione, sed natura constitutum esse ius. Id iam patebit, si hominum inter ipsos societatem coniunctionemque perspexeris"; *De Finibus Bonorum et Malorum ad Brutum*, lib. II, cap. 18, n. 59, p. 1010.

[47] Loc. cit., lib. I, cap. 15, n. 43, p. 1207, "nam haec nascuntur ex eo, quia natura propensi sumus ad diligendos homines: quod fundamentum iuris est"; n. 42, "Est enim unum ius, quo devincta est hominum societas, et quod lex constituit una"; cf. lib. I, cap. 12, n. 33.

[48] *De Re Publica*, lib. II, cap. 44, n. 71, p. 1189, "non modo falsum illud esse, sine iniuria non posse, sed hoc verissimum esse, sine summa iustitia rem publicam geri nullo modo posse."

[49] *De Legibus*, lib. I, cap. 15, n. 42, p. 1207; *De Re Publica*, lib. III, 50.41, p. 1195.

[50] *Ad Marciam De Consolatione*, Liber VI, VIII, *Seneca, Moral Essays*, Trans. John W. Basore, vol.2, London, 1935, p.24, "quod naturale est non decrescit mora."

[51] *Ad Serenum De Otio*, Liber VIII, 1, 4, loc. cit., vol.2, p.182, "Usque ad ultimum vitae finem in actu erimus, non desinemus communi bono operam dare, adiuvare singulos, opem ferre etiam inimicis senili manu."

[52] Loc. cit., Liber VIII, 5, 8, p.194, "Ergo secundum naturam vivo, si totum me illi dedi, si illius admirator cultorque sum."

[53] Loc. cit., V, 1, P. 188, "Solemus dicere summum bonum esse secundum naturam vivere. Natura nos ad utrumque genuit, et contemplationi rerum et actioni."

person to love other fellow humans through mutual service or helpfulness.[54] The human individual is a social animal, born to serve the common good.[55]

What makes the philosophy of Seneca unique is his belief in a primeval state of blissful living among humans. There was a period in human history when people lived in perfect understanding and harmony, and possessed a penetrating knowledge of all natural laws and of intellectual truth. This primitive state of innocence, happiness, and wisdom, however, did not indicate a complete explication of human nature: the human consciousness is born to virtue, but not in possession of it -- "non est adhuc bonus, sed in bonum fingitur."[56] This human condition was, in fact, lost, and corruption in human consciousness ensued which necessitated the establishment of a coercive authority to control the unruliness of human conduct.[57] Thus, according to Seneca, the present socio-juridical configuration of society is not so much a consequence of the true nature of things as a contingency, the consequence of human corruption.[58] In this precarious stage of rebellion, human consciousness nonetheless retains its inherent authenticity; it still enshrines in its inwardness the germ of rationality, conscientiousness, and sociability. The human individual is still drawn to virtue, and has the ability to attain it, whether one is a free

---

[54] *Ad Novatum De Ira,* Liber III, Liber I, 5, loc.cit., vol.1, London, 1963, p.118, "Beneficiis enim humana vita constat et concordia, nec terrore sed mutuo amore in foedus auxiliumque commune constringitur."

[55] *Ad Neronem Caesarem De Clementia,* Liber I, 3, 2, loc.cit., vol.1, p.364.

[56] *Ad Lucilium Epistulae Morales,* Trans. Richard M. Gummere, Vol. II, London, 1930, Epistula 92, n. 29, p. 464.

[57] *De Clementia,* Liber I, 1, loc. cit., pp. 356, 358.

[58] *Epistulae Morales,* Vol. II, Epist. 75, n. 16, p. 144, "Ad virtutem contendimus inter vitia districti."

citizen, a freedman, a slave, a king, or an exile[59] -- "The body may belong to a master, the mind is its own."[60]

The philosophy of Marcus Aurelius Antoninus never did enjoy popularity among Christian authors. In verity, his philosophy is not immune from certain ambiguity or obscurity. The lack of clarity particularly involves the question as to whether the main thrust of his philosophy is pantheistic; in some instances the deity is conceived of as being essentially distinct from the material universe; in other instances the all-pervading, ever-present, and ever-active energy of Zeus is such in creation that the universal substance is presented as the one-and-all reality endowed with an inherent self-evolving power. This difficulty, however, does not diminish the validity of the emperor's thoughts on human nature.

Underlying the seeming confusion and dispersion of natural phenomena,[61] there exists, in the estimation of Antoninus, an immanent law which governs and unites all creation in a harmonious orchestration.[62] Upon attentive analysis of the material universe, one is able to envisage a primordial unison of phenomena which, from its part, demonstrates an all-embracing and unified method in the working of Zeus.[63] But the same ruling principle, which pervades all things and unites them in a holy bond, reveals itself most wonderfully in the conscious world, a world of pure

---

[59] *Ad Aebutium Liberalem De Beneficiis*, Liber III, 18,2, loc. cit., vol. 3 London, 1935, p. 160, "nulli praeclusa virtus est; omnibus patet, omnes admittit, omnes invitat, et ingenuos et libertinos et servos et reges et exules; non eligit domum nec censum, nudo homine contenta est." Cf. *De Clementia*, Liber I, 3, 2, loc.cit., p. 364.

[60] Loc. cit., Liber III, 20, p. 164, "interior illa pars mancipio dari non potest."

[61] *The Thoughts of the Emperor M. Aurelius Antoninus*, Trans. George Long, New York, VI, n. 10, p.95.

[62] Loc. cit., VII, n.9, p. 109, "For there is one universe made up of all things, and one God who pervades all things, and one substance, and one law, (one) common reason in all intelligent animals, and one truth"; cf. VI, n.1, p. 94.

[63] Loc. cit., IV, n.45, p. 77, "In the series of things those which follow are always aptly fitted to those which have gone before; for this series is not like a mere enumeration of disjointed things, which has only a necessary sequence, but it is a rational connection: and as all existing things are arranged together harmoniously, so the things which come into existence exhibit no mere succession, but a certain wonderful relationship."

reason and truth.[64] The human being is the most authentic revelation of divine existence; "the deity which is planted within him"[65] renders the human being a unique creation. The human being is a mere reflection of the divinity, and not an extension or a portion of the divinity; the eternal wisdom does not metamorphosize into the human mind, but it inserts a glimmer of its truth in the human individual together with the ability to recognize the truth and follow its dictates; in obedience to this inherent law the person becomes "like a priest and minister of the gods using too the (deity) which is planted within him";[66] thus the human mind is capable of virtue. Human creatures, being the receptacles of eternal wisdom, are all equally rational, conscientious, and social. The human mind is rational for "it sees itself, analyzes itself, and makes itself such as it chooses,"[67] "and values nothing more than itself."[68] The rational soul enshrines a code of morality which enables the soul to act by conviction or belief, rather than by instinctual compulsion -- a code "which commands us what to do, and what not to do,"[69] and which induces us to "venerate the gods and bless them."[70] But the inner destiny of the human soul, being thus rational and conscientious, is to find its ultimate fulfillment of itself in suspending itself and to reach out of itself to similar otherness. For the human person is also by nature social. Thus the human consciousness can only make itself as it is and such as it wills to be insofar as it approaches the universality of its nature, the attainment of objective and absolute freedom through the social dimension of its existence. It is the firm conviction of Antoninus

---

[64] Loc. cit., VII, n. 9, p.109.

[65] Loc. cit., III, n. 4, p. 60; cf. n.5, p. 61.

[66] Ibid.

[67] Loc. cit., XI, n. 1, p. 166.

[68] Ibid.

[69] Loc. cit., IV, n.4, p.69; cf. VIII, nn.8, 16, p.126, n.16, p.127; IX, n.1, p.138; XI, n.29, p. 177.

[70] Loc. cit., V, n. 33, p. 92.

that "men exist for the sake of one another"[71] that it is the property of the rational soul to love one's neighbour,[72] and "in no way to injure one another,"[73] but rather "to do good to men, and to practice tolerance and self-restraint."[74] It is precisely this essential quality of the human soul that aggregates all humans in one, sole family; thus the conscious world is conceived of as one political society, one state[75] -- "But my nature is rational and social; and my city and country, so far as I am Antoninus, is Rome, but so far as I am a man, it is the world. The things then which are useful to these cities are alone useful to me."[76] It is the Christian conviction that divine justice reaches out of itself and imprints itself in the human heart only to lead the soul back to eternity. The eschatological dimension of justice is likewise advocated by the emperor: "For neither wilt thou do anything well which pertains to man without at the same time having a reference to things divine; nor the contrary."[77] The one who defiles this inner sacred law "is clearly guilty of impiety towards the highest divinity."[78]

The Concept of Natural Law in Corpus Iuris Civilis

In *Corpus iuris civilis* the term *ius naturale* is applied both to the instinctual world and the conscious world, but with substantially different connotations. In the first conceptualization of natural law, no distinction is

---

[71] Loc. cit., VIII, n. 59, p. 137; cf. VI, n.14, p. 96, nn. 21, 23, p. 99.

[72] Loc. cit., XI, n. 1, p. 166; III, n. 4, p. 61.

[73] Loc. cit., IX, n. 1, p. 138.

[74] Loc. cit., V, n. 33, p. 92; cf. X, n. 4, p. 152.

[75] Loc. cit., IV, n. 4, p. 69.

[76] Loc.cit., VI, n.44, p. 104.

[77] Loc. cit., III, n.13, p.65; cf. n.5, p.61.

[78] Loc. cit., IX, n.1, p. 138.

made between the human and the brute; both are drawn by mere instinct. In reference to this first connotation, mention has been made in an earlier part of the study. It is the second connotation of the term that now holds our attention.

In the latter sense, *ius naturale* denotes a rational system of order uniquely characteristic of human nature. The same traditional belief in the divine origin of human justice is endorsed by the *Institutiones;* thus natural law is conceived of as "impressio divini luminis in humanam creaturam." The divine origin of these moral and ethical principles constitutes the raison d'être for their intrinsic validity which surpasses time and space. In this context should the content of the Institutions be understood when they maintain that natural law, which has always been universally observed, was established by some divine providence; thus they remain forever firm and irrevocable.[79] It is precisely by reason of its source that this code inherent to human nature is at the same time a force converging all human beings into a homogeneous group -- "cum inter nos cognationem quandam natura constituit."[80] Ulpianus thus reaches the conclusion on the universal equality of human beings, namely "that as far as natural law is concerned, all human beings are born equal."[81] A definition of natural law is volunteered by Paulus: natural law enshrines all that is just and good.[82] What is just and good is further specified in the *Institutiones*: "the precepts of law are the following: to live honestly, not to cheat others, to recognize the right of others";[83] thus Florentinus concludes: that never should deceit be

---

[79] *Inst., De iure naturali et gentium et civili*, 1, 2, §1. "Sed naturalia quidem iura, quae apud omnes gentes peraeque servantur, divina quadam providentia constituta semper firma atque immutabilia permanent."

[80] Florentinus, L. *Ut vim*, 3, D., *De iustitia et iure*, 1,1.

[81] Ulpianus, L. *Quod attinet*, 32, D., *De diversis regulis iuris antiqui*, 50,17. "quod ad ius naturale attinet, omnes homines aequales sunt."

[82] Paulus, L. *Ius pluribus*, 11, D., *De iustitia et iure*, 1,1. "Ius pluribus modis dicitur: uno modo, cum id quod semper aequum ac bonum est ius dicitur, ut est ius naturale."

[83] *Inst., De iustitia et iure*, 1,1,§3: "Iuris praecepta sunt haec: honeste vivere, alterum non laedere, suum cuique tribuere"; cf. Ulpianus, L. *Iustitia*, 10, D., *De iustitia et iure*, 1,1,§1.

justified for any reason whatsoever.[84] Celsus concurs with the concept of natural law as being that which is just and good; however, he rather concentrates on the subjective aspect of the idea, and defines *ius* as art, the very observance of what is good and just; thus *ius* is taken to mean the virtue of justice.[85] Marcus Aurelius Antoninus ascertains that the observance of justice renders one a priest and minister of the gods.[86] The same idea recurs in the writings of Celsus -- "cuius merito quis nos sacerdotes appellet."

It is evident from the literature just quoted that Roman law acknowledged a law superior to it, a law which is perennial and immutable. It was also cognizant of the reality of human nature as the embodiment of the fundamental and irreducible principles of justice and humanity. Human beings are not drawn to action by compulsion, but it is their intellectual ability to discern the just from the unjust and their autonomous and free will that enable them to reach a final moral decision. It is in the nature of the human person to discover and recognize in oneself what is the right and the good. In this sense, natural law may rightly be defined: reasonableness and freedom. By freedom is meant objective and absolute freedom, in contrast to subjective freedom, for the right and the good are in nature universal. Thus true, human freedom, the virtue of justice, can only be attained in the ethical or social world which is the absolute unity of subjective and objective freedom: "honeste vivere, alterum non laedere, suum cuique tribuere."

---

[84] Florentinus, L. *Ut vim*, 3, D., *De iustitia et iure*, 1,1. "hominem homini insidiari nefas esse."

[85] Ulpianus, L. *Iuri operam*, 1, D., *De iustitia et iure*, 1, 1, §1: "Celsus definit, ius est ars boni et aequi. Cuius merito quis nos sacerdotes appellet: iustitiam namque colimus et boni et aequi notitiam profitemur, aequum ab iniquo separantes, licitum ab illicito discernentes, bonos non solum metu poenarum, verum etiam praemiorum quoque exhortatione efficere cupientes, veram nisi fallor philosophiam, non simulatam affectantes."

[86] Loc. cit., III, n. 4, p. 60.

The Concept of Natural Law in Christian Literature

If indeed Pentecost is nothing else but the revitalization, crystalization and rejuvenation of the wisdom of God engraved in the man of the Yahwist tradition, but obscured by sin, it stands to reason that the question of natural law claims special interest in Christian awareness. It goes without saying that St. Paul was the first among Christian authors to write on natural law as the glimmer of eternal truth engrafted in the human nature. The divine wisdom reflected in human nature seeks not self-fulfillment in outwardness, for what is not itself, is mere contingency; by its own intrinsic nature it fulfills itself, by itself, in itself. Thus divine justice appears in the human creature only to go back from where it started -- itself. It is precisely for this reason that it is not possible ever to acquire a solid and comprehensive understanding of natural law, human justice, human conduct, if human nature is not placed in an eschatological perspective not only with regard to its source but also in respect of its finality. In this sense the human mind, by virtue of its own nature and ultimate aim, is judge and judgment of its own actions in its accountability to the divine Wisdom. On this point St. Paul writes: "Pagans who never heard of the law but are led by reason to do what the law commands, may not actually 'possess' the law, but they can be said to 'be' the law. They can point to the substance of the law engraved on their hearts -- they can call a witness, that is, their own conscience -- they have accusation and defence, that is, their own inner mental dialogue."[87]

The patristic Fathers left to posterity a prolific literature on the subject of natural law. The main thrust of this literature is the belief that the inner destiny of the individual human consciousness is to discover itself and unfold its eternal harmony implanted in it by divine Providence; by reaching out to similar otherness and to its creator, it explicates ever more its inwardness which is the universality of its nature. While this general consensus is maintained throughout the patristic literature, each author,

---

[87] Rom. 2:14-15.

Philosophy of Law

however, contributes to a further clarification of the subject with personal insights and nuances.

Clement of Alexandria exquisitely defines natural law as "illumination." "Illuminated by the dawn of light," human beings, whether Greeks or Barbarians, have aspired for, and indeed succeeded in acquiring some knowledge of the eternal wisdom.[88] However, for Clement, divine truth engraved in the human soul does not intrinsically entail the virtue of justice. His position is similar to that of Seneca in distinguishing the state of virtue from the state of innocence in which the Yahwist man was created. Adam, endowed with a spiritual soul, was thereby created with an aptitude to attain virtue, with an ability to select what is noblest. However, neither the illumination of the eternal wisdom in the human soul, nor the ability of the soul to move of itself towards perfection, is itself virtue, which is the actual implementation of the inner goodness of the human soul. In synthesis, natural law is the source of human, moral conduct, by virtue of which goodness resides *in potentia* in the human soul; the inner destiny of human nature has been from the moment of its creation the unfolding of itself into its own perfection. "For they shall hear from us that he (Adam) was not perfect in his creation, but adapted to the reception of virtue. For it is of great importance in regard to virtue to be made fit for its attainment. And it is intended that we should be saved by ourselves. This, then, is the nature of the soul, to move of itself. Then, as we are rational, and philosophy being rational, we have some affinity with it. Now an aptitude is a movement towards virtue, not virtue itself. All, then, as I said, are naturally constituted for the acquisition of virtue."[89]

Tertullian does not seem preoccupied with making a distinction between the natural and supernatural order of things; for him, everything is sacred, everything proclaims the majesty of God's wisdom. The eternal

---

[88] *The Miscellanies (Stromata)*, vol. 1, Bk. 1, chap.13, p.389.

[89] Loc. cit., vol. 2, Bk 6, chap. 12, vol. 12, pp.359-360.

wisdom has engraved itself on natural tablets[90] as the first rule of all[91] in order that it may present itself to the human creature as an authoritative teacher of God's wisdom.[92] The human soul is capable of witnessing the divine Wisdom outside itself and of verifying it in its innermost being. Nowhere in all creation does the wisdom of God reveal itself so manifestly and marvelously as in the individual human consciousness. The human soul, being the receptacle of "the secret deposit of an inborn knowledge,"[93] the more deeply it moves introspectively into itself, towards its authentic inwardness, the more clearly the knowledge of God, the eternal justice approaches. "The soul is not a boon from heaven to Latins and Greeks alone. Man is the one name belonging to every nation upon earth . . . There is not a soul of man that does not, from the light that is in itself, proclaim the very things we are not permitted to speak above our breath. Most justly, then, every soul is a culprit as well as a witness: in the measure that it testifies for truth, the guilt of error lies on it."[94]

The teaching of Origen on natural law is representative of the common consensus of the Patristic Fathers. In his response to Celsus, the identification of natural law with the divine positive law cannot be denied. Origen insists that there is only one law which deservedly should be acknowledged and endorsed as "king of all things," and this is the law instilled in the human heart.[95] It is thus the sacrosanct commitment of the human soul to follow the dictates of its inner law. Since, however, no

---

[90] Quintus Septimius Florentinus Tertullianus, *On the Soldier's Chaplet (De Corona)*, vol. 1, XIII, 6, *Ante-Nicene Christian Library*, Trans. Alexander Roberts and James Donaldson, vol.11, Edinburgh, 1882, p.339.

[91] Loc. cit., 5, p. 338.

[92] *On the Testimony of the Soul, (De Testimonio Animae)*, vol. 1, III, 5, *Ante-Nicene Christian Library*, Trans. Alexander Roberts and James Donaldson, vol.11, Edinburgh, 1882, pp. 42-43; cf. *On the Soldier's Chaplet*, 6, p.340.

[93] Loc. cit., 5, p. 43.

[94] Loc.cit.,5, p.45.

[95] *Against Celsus*, Bk V,Chap.40, *The Ante-Nicene Fathers*, Trans. Frederick Crombie, vol. 4, Grand Rapids, Michigan, 1979, p. 561.

Philosophy of Law

distinction exists between natural law and divine law, but both reflect the same eternal truth, Christians, by following the Gospel, far from denying the intrinsic validity of natural law, are indeed observing it in a more perfect manner. "We Christians, then, who have come to the knowledge of the law which is by nature "king of all things," and which is the same with the law of God, endeavour to regulate our lives by its prescriptions, having bidden a long farewell to those of an unholy kind."[96]

Lactantius, in his exposition on natural law, resorts to the authority of Cicero.[97] In conformity with the Ciceronian position, Lactantius maintains that humans are bound together by reason of their humanness.[98] In this one family all humans are born equal since each one of them proceeds from one heavenly seed -- "to all that same one is Father."[99] Whoever destroys this sacred bond should be regarded as nefarious and a parricide.[100]

Behind human action there lies a perennial and unchangeable law, the expression of the command and sovereignty of God over the human soul,[101] a universal principle of justice,[102] which constitutes the greatest and most profound solidarity among humans -- "justice is peace with all men."[103] By virtue of this inherent law, the human soul is at the same time the accuser, the judge, and the accused in its accountability to its creator. This, we

---

[96] Ibid.

[97] *The Divine Institutes*, Bk 6, chap.8, *The Fathers of the Church*, Trans. Sr. Mary Francis McDonald, vol.49, Washington, D.C., 1964, pp.412-413.

[98] Loc.cit., Bk 6, chap.10, pp.417, 419.

[99] Loc. cit., p. 418.

[100] Loc. cit., p. 417.

[101] Loc. cit., Bk. 5, chap. 17, p.370, "Justice has its source in eternity, otherwise is folly."

[102] Ibid., "Justice, because it is the singular good of man, will not receive the name of folly."

[103] Loc. cit., p. 370.

believe, Lactantius has in mind when he states that justice, which proceeds from eternity, ends in eternity.[104]

Hilarius Pictaviensis concurs with the common consensus of the Fathers in maintaining that human nature is endowed with a natural code of morality which dictates abstention from any immoral behaviour.[105] The purpose of this code is not to inflict fear; it rather helps the human individual to act out of love, for whatever human nature is endowed with is intended for the individual's own sake -- "Whatever the human being is endowed with is there for his own benefit."[106] Therefore, human conduct should proceed from the love for justice rather than from fear of it.[107]

The major contribution of Hilarius to the present study is his doctrine on the christological ontology of human nature. If we are interpreting the author's mind correctly, he, like Tertullianus, teaches that the man of the Yahwist Tradition was not, strictly speaking, created in the image of God, but in the image of Christ who is the most authentic image of God, the first born of all creatures.[108]

There is stamped in the human heart, says Saint Ambrose, a holy law which "is not written, but inborn; it is not acquired by reading, but springs up in each one as from the flowing font of nature, and men's minds drink from it."[109] The human individual carries in his heart justice, a code of

---

[104] Loc. cit., p. 371.

[105] *Tractatus super Psalmos,* psalmus CXVIII, litt. XV, n. 11, col.604-605, *Opera Omnia,* Tomus I, P.L. Tomus IX, Parisiis, 1844.

[106] Loc. cit., litt. X, n.1, col. 564. "In homine autem quidquid est, sibi proficit."

[107] Loc. cit.,litt. XX, n.9, col. 655. "Et quamquam amor legis potior quam metus sit."

[108] Loc.cit.,X,n.7, col.566, "Incorporale est, quidquid illud tum de consilii sententia inchoatur: fit enim ad imaginem Dei. Non Dei imago; quia imago Dei est primogenitus omnis creaturae: sed ad imaginem Dei, id est, secundum imaginis et similitudinis speciem. Divinum in eo et incorporale condendum, quod secundum imaginem Dei et similitudinem tum fiebat: exemplar scilicet quoddam in nobis imaginis Dei est, et similitudinis institutum."

[109] *Letters, Letter to Irenaeus,* 83, (73), *The Fathers of the Church,* Trans. Sr. Mary Melchior Beyenka, vol.26, New York, 1954, p.464; cf. *Letter to Simplicianus* 54 (37), loc.cit., p. 297; *Seven Exegetical Works, Jacob and the Happy Life, (De Iacob et Vita Beata),* (5.17), (6.20), *The Fathers of the Church,* Trans. Michael P. McHugh, vol.65, Washington, D.C., 1972, pp.131, 132;

Philosophy of Law

morality, so that human conduct can be brought to the test even in contravention of one's own instincts; the rational soul is capable of judging and condemning itself in the eyes of God even of things known to none but itself.[110] It was the sole intent of the divine Will that, by the observance of this law alone, the human soul could attain its inner integrity and self-fulfillment.[111] Just as in the physical body the spirit coordinates all organs in perfect harmony towards wholeness of the same, so it is with the whole human family: the spirit of God expressed in natural law unites all human beings in profound solidarity.[112] There would have been no need for the Mosaic law had natural law not been neglected through human corruption caused by the Fall.[113] Saint Ambrose remarks that not even the law of Moses could remedy the dilapidation of the human soul caused by sin.[114] The only redeeming hope layed in the Incarnation which brought about the reconciliation of the two opposing forces in fallen humanity, a harmony between the inner, spiritual realm and the exterior, materialistic realm in human personality.[115]

---

loc. cit., *Flight from the World, (De Fuga Saeculi)*,(3.15),p.292.

[110] *Letter to Irenaeus*, 83, (73), loc. cit., pp.464-465; *Jacob and the Happy Life*, (5.17), loc.cit., p.131; *Flight from the World*, (3.15), loc.cit.,p.292.

[111] *Letter to Simplicianus*, 54, (37), loc.cit., pp.291,297; *Jacob and the Happy Life*, (5.17), loc.cit., p. 131.

[112] *De Officiis Ministrorum Libri Tres*, Lib.III, cap.3, n.19, col.159, *Opera Omnia*, Tomus II, pars prior, P.L., Tomus 16, Parisiis, 1866; loc.cit.,Lib.I, cap.28, n.132, col. 67; n.135, col. 67-68.

[113] *Letter to Irenaeus*, 83, (73), loc.cit.,pp.465,467; *Jacob and the Happy Life*, (6.20), loc.cit., p.132.

[114] *Flight from the World*, (3.15), loc.cit., p.292.

[115] *Enarrationes in XII Psalmos Davidicos, In Psalmum XXXVI Enarratio*, n.64, col. 1047, *Opera Omnia*, Tomus I, pars prior, P.L., Tomus 14, Parisiis, 1866, "Duo sunt enim homines in singulis: unus interior, alter exterior; interior cogitat quae mentis sunt, quae mentis sunt loquitur; exterior quae sunt corporis. Tamen adveniens Dominus utrumque conjunxit: et duos in uno homine condidit; ne diversis sese impugnent mentibus, sed invicem sibi voluntatem suarum unitate socientur . . . Jam enim et ipse exterior homo justi in interioris hominis transfusus est disciplinam: et in ejus conformatus naturam, ipsius exercet officia, ut caro meditetur quod mentis internae est."

Lex universa, natural law, finds its complete significance in love, without which there is no charity. When love and charity are lacking, the human family turns into a band of brigands ready to destroy or devour each other. This is how Eusebius Hieronymus perceives the necessity of natural law as the source of justice among humans.[116] Upon this presupposition one may also envisage the raison d'être for the distinction between subjective, individualistic freedom, characteristic of the beast, and the objective and authentic freedom which flows from the rationality, conscientiousness, and sociability of the human soul. This also means that the ethical, social world is the absolute unity of subjective and objective good which the human soul, by its very nature, is deemed to attain as its self-fulfillment. Saint Jerome, interestingly enough, defines natural law as "foedus sempiternum" (everlasting covenant):[117] a covenant between the Creator and creature, and between creatures themselves.[118] The corruption of human nature in observing this universal law necessitated the enactment of the Mosaic law in order to enforce the primordial one given to each and every human being,[119] in view of the promised incarnation of justice itself.[120]

None of the Patristic Fathers surpasses Aurelius Augustinus in beauty of style and clarity of expression in his teaching on natural law. The *cardo* of his teaching is that nothing in the conscious world can be acclaimed just and good unless it proceeds from the eternal justice of God.[121] And nowhere can this divine justice be apprehended more assuredly than in the

---

[116] *Commentariorum in Epistolam ad Galatas Libri Tres,* lib.3, cap.5,vers.11, *Opera Omnia,* Tomus VII, P.L.,Tomus 26, Parisiis, 1866, col.440.

[117] *Commentariorum in Isaiam Prophetam Libri Duodeviginti,* lib. 8, cap.24, vers.6, *Opera Omnia,* Tomus IV, P.L., Tomus 24, Parisiis, 1865, col. 292.

[118] Ibid. "universae primum gentes totusque orbis naturalem acceperit legem."

[119] *Commentariorum in Epistolam . . . ,* lib. 2, cap.3, vers.19, col. 391; *Commentariorum in Isaiam . . . ,* lib.8, cap. 24, vers.6, col. 292.

[120] *Commentariorum in Epistolam . . . ,* lib. 2, cap. 3, vers. 19, 20, col. 392-393.

[121] *De Libero Arbitrio Libri Tres,* lib. I, cap.6, n.15, *Opera Omnia,* Tomus I, P.L., Tomus 32, Parisiis, 1845, col. 1229, "in illa temporali nihil esse justum atque legitimum, quod non ex hac aeterna sibi homines derivarint."

recesses of one's being; the human mind cannot know itself unless it goes within itself; in the search of its own inwardness, it realizes itself to be the receptacle of divine justice, although in limited manner; in the depth of its being, it finds the chart and compass to be followed for the journey, a march backward into its shrouded self, towards its own veiled authenticity, where it finds itself in close proximity with the eternal wisdom. In search of truth, states Saint Augustine "you should not look outside yourself but rather you should delve into your own innermost being for truth dwells within there. And remember that when you transcend into the infinite it is the rational soul within you that transcends your mind."[122] This eternal truth clustered in human consciousness is a law most sacred which no human mind can ignore without guilt; the human soul must abide by it;[123] it is the law *par excellence* from which all virtues flow as from a spring.[124] The human person has to discover and recognize in himself what is the right and the good, and that this right and good is in its nature universal. This mental process leads one to the realization of the universal equality of human beings; thus emerges the profound awareness that each individual, by the very nature of his being, is born to live in justice and peace with others.[125] This law is the fountain from which human justice springs; it constitutes an absolute and fundamental criterion for what is

---

[122] *De Vera Religione Liber Unus*, cap. 39, n.72, *Opera Omnia*, Tomus III, P.L. Tomus 34, Parisiis, 1845, col. 154: "Noli foras ire, in teipsum redi; in interiore homine habitat veritas; et si tuam naturam mutabilem inveneris, transcende et teipsum. Sed memento cum te transcendis, ratiocinantem animam te transcendere"; cf. *The City of God*, Bk 19, chap.12, *Fathers of the Church*, Trans. Gerald G. Walsh and Daniel J. Honan, vol.24, New York, 1954, p.215, "No man's sin is so unnatural as to wipe out all traces whatsoever of human nature. Anyone, then . . . is rational enough to prefer right to wrong and order to disorder."

[123] Loc. cit., cap. 31, n.58, col. 148, "Aeternam igitur legem mundis animis fas est cognoscere, judicare non fas est."

[124] *De Diversis Quaestionibus LXXXIII Liber Unus*, Quaestio 31, n 1, *Opera Omnia*, Tomus VI, P.L., Tomus 40, Parisiis, 1841, col.20, "Natura jus est, quod non opinio genuit, sed quaedam innata vis inseruit, ut religionem, pietatem, gratiam, vindicationem, observantiam, veritatem . . ."

[125] *The City of God*, Bk 19, chap. 12, loc.cit., p.215, "By the very laws of his nature, he (man) seems forced into fellowship and, as far as in him lies, into peace with every man"; cf. *The Good of Marriage (De Bono Coniugali)*, chap. 1, *The Fathers of the Church*, Trans. Charles T. Wilcox, vol. 27, New York,1955, p.9.

proper, correct, and just in the temporal order of things.[126] It is the foundation of society; without it society is reduced to a mere multitude, a formless mass, wild and terrible, or a throng of humans living a degenerated life of blind and unconditional compliance to an organized brigandage.[127] The rational soul is master of its own destiny; one's aspirations stem from personal autonomous conviction or belief. The conscious world, the most approximate reflection of the divine, thus stands as an ornament to the global creation.[128]

Hincmarus Rhemensis, Ratherius Veronensis, Jonas Aurelianensis, Rabanus Maurus, and Magnus Aurelius Cassiodorus, have not bequeathed posterity with a thorough exposition on the subject. In unison, however, with the common consensus of the Fathers, they ascertain the eternal law of God being implanted in the human heart, which forms the absolute and unchangeable norm or standard of right conduct, and is thereby binding in conscience.[129] They maintain the doctrine that no human community can subsist without having the eternal law of God as the foundation of its own justice; in conformity with it, human ordinances must be enacted and by it they are to be tested; these ordinances represent the human attempt to

---

[126] *De Libero Arbitrio Libri Tres,* lib.I, cap. 6, n.15, loc. cit., col. 1229.

[127] *The City of God,* Bk II, chap. 21, loc.cit., pp.107-108; Bk IV, chap. 4, p.195; Bk XIX, chap. 21, pp.232-234, vol.24.

[128] *De Genesi ad Litteram Libri Duodecim,* Lib. IX, cap.9, *Opera Omnia,* Tomus III, P.L., Tomus 34, Parisiis, 1841, col. 398, "An vero ita quis caecus est mente, ut non cernat quanto terris ornamento sit genus humanum, etiam cum a paucis recte laudabiliterque vivatur; quantumque valeat ordo reipublicae, in cujusdam pacis terrenae vinculum coercens etiam peccatores? Neque enim tantum depravati sunt homines, ut non etiam tales pecoribus et volatilibus antecellant; quorum tamen omnium generibus hanc infimam mundi partem pro sui loci sorte decoratam, quem non considerare delectet?"

[129] HINCMARUS RHEMENSIS, *Expositiones ad Carolum Regem pro Ecclesiae Libertatum Defensione,* Expositio I, *Opera Omnia,* Tomus I, P.L., Tomus 125, Parisiis, 1879, col. 1055; MAGNUS AURELIUS CASSIODORUS, *Variarum Libri Duodecim,* lib III, epistola 17, *Opera Omnia,* Tomus I, P.L., Tomus 69, Parisiis, 1865, col. 585.

apply the eternal and absolute principle of justice to the circumstances of human life.[130]

The Concept of Natural Law in Canonical and Civil Authors

A cursory survey suffices for one to realize the modest influence the teaching of the Fathers had upon canonical, and, more so, civil authors on the subject of natural law. With the exception of *Decretum Gratiani*, canonical and civil authors seem to have given exclusive attention to the authority of Roman law. This does not mean that substantial discrepancies transpire between patristic and canonical literature, in particular. On the contrary, the Christian doctrine on the score is maintained throughout the canonical and civil traditions.

The survey of canonical literature on the theme is initiated with our concentration on *Decretum Gratiani*. Gratianus quotes verbatim the description given by Saint Isidore of Seville on natural law.[131] It is clear, however, from other passages of the *Decretum* that for Gratianus the Isidorian description with its instinctualistic connotation remains unsatisfactorily indicative of human nature. He therefore elaborates on a concept in consonance with the teaching of the Fathers. Natural law is thus presented as the prerogative of human nature; being the eternal wisdom translated into human consciousness, it holds primacy over all human ordinances; indeed it is the absolute, irreversible and unchangeable source of justice. Natural law, one reads in *Decretum Gratiani*, "takes precedence over any human law by reason of time and dignity. It had its beginning in the creation of the rational creature; it never changes with the passage of

---

[130] RATHERIUS VERONENSIS, *Praeloquiorum Libri Sex*, Tit.I, n.2; Tit.II, n.4, *Opera Omnia*, Tomus Unicus, P.L., Tomus 136, Parisiis, 1853, col. 220, 221; RABANUS MAURUS, *De Universo Libri Viginti Duo*, Lib.16, cap.3, *Opera Omnia*, Tomus V, P.L., Tomus 111, Parisiis, 1864, col. 445, JONAS AURELIANENSIS, *Opusculum de Institutione Regia*, Cap. VI, *Opera Omnia*, Tomus unicus, P.L., Tomus 106, Parisiis, 1851, col. 294; HINCMARUS RHEMENSIS, loc. cit., Exp.I, col. 1055; MAGNUS AURELIUS CASSIODORUS, loc. cit., lib.IV, ep. 33; lib. V, ep. 39, col. 630, 671.

[131] *Decretum*, Pars I, Dist.I, c.7; ISIDORUS, *Etymologiarum Libri XX*, Lib.V, cap.4, nn. 1, 2, *Opera Omnia*, Tomus III, P.L., Tomus 82, Parisiis, 1878, col. 199.

time, but remains forever immutable."[132] The term, *ius naturale,* for Gratianus assumes a more comprehensive meaning than traditionally understood: it is taken to mean both the law enshrined in human nature as well as the law of the Gospel, commonly defined as divine positive law;[133] thus it appears that according to Gratianus *distinctio formalis* is the only distinction admissible between the two categories of law -- a view which offers more depth of insight into the subject.

A fundamental question is raised by Gratianus which has excruciated the minds of the canonist and theologian of later generations: natural law is the embodiment of absolute truth, eternal and divine, irresistible to historic contingency; hence it can never be abrogated, obrogated or derogated, and its binding force on human conscience can never be dispensed with[134] although conditions of life actually exist which rebut the indiscriminatory nature of its injunction.[135] Gratianus realizes that one has to choose the lesser of two evils in such circumstances.[136]

The *Corpus iuris civilis* was the main point of reference for canon and civil lawyers on the doctrine of natural law. Nevertheless, their doctrine may rightfully be considered as re-iteration of the basic teaching of the Patristic Fathers on the theme. In the Roman fashion, these authors endorsed the double connotation of natural law. In its primitive sense, the term indicates the law of nature in its pure form, identical to humans and

---

[132] Pars I, Dist.V, pars I, §1: "Naturale ius inter omnia primatum obtinet et tempore et dignitate. Cepit enim ab exordio rationalis creaturae, nec variatur tempore, sed immutabile permanet"; cf. Pars I, Dist.VI, c.3, §1; Pars I, Dist. VIII, pars. II.

[133] Pars I, Dist.V, pars I, §2, "Sed cum naturale ius lege et evangelio supra dicatur esse comprehensum . . ."

[134] Pars I, Dist. XIII, pars I.

[135] Pars I, Dist. V, pars I, §2.

[136] Pars I, Dist. XIII, pars 1, c.1.

Philosophy of Law

beasts.[137] However, major concentration is given to the second meaning, concerning exclusively human consciousness.

The eternal wisdom of God descended and took hold of the human creature in the very moment of creation. Divine justice is likened by Badus De Ubaldis to the stars the light of which illuminate all human beings alike.[138] Upon this premise Azo refrains from laying down a distinction between natural law and divine positive law; for him all ordinances contained in the Mosaic law and all norms found in the Gospel constitute one sole law which is natural law.[139] The divine law implanted in human nature would have sufficed in the pursuance of right human conduct, had not the Fall enticed the escalation of human evil which in turn necessitated the enactment of the Mosaic Law.[140]

The presentation of Antonius A Butrio on the concept of natural law deserves particular attention since it has certain nuances not shared by other authors. Antonius ratifies the belief that natural law is divine. He then moves on in classifying natural law according to the human *compositum*, namely the rational and sensitive aspects of the human

---

[137] HENRICUS DE SEGUSIO, *In Primum Decretalium Librum Commentaria, De Summa Trinitate, et Fide Catholica*, cap.1, *Firmiter*, n.28, fol.6r., Venetiis, 1581; JOANNES ANDREAE, *In Primum Decretalium Librum Novella Commentaria, De Summa Trinitate et Fide Catholica*, cap. *Firmiter*, n.32, fol.8r., Venetiis, 1581; AZO, *Summa Institutionum*, Liber I, *De Iure Naturali Gentium et Civili*, P. 348, col. 2, Papiae, 1506.

[138] BALDUS UBALDI PERUSINUS, *In Decretalium Volumen Commentaria, Super Primo Decretalium, De Electione et Electi Potestate*, cap. 34, *Venerabilem*, n.13, fol. 78v., Venetiis, 1595: "Astraea id est iustitia quae de caelo descendit, dicta est ab astris id est a stellis quia lumen suum naturaliter communicat universae creaturae."; cf. *Super Secundo Decretalium, De Iudiciis, prooemium, Post.*, n.10, fol. 147 v; HENRICUS DE SEGUSIO, *In Primum . . .*, nn. 28, 29, fol. 6r; JOANNES ANDREAE, *In Primum . . ., De Constitutionibus*, cap. *Postquam*, n.1, fol. 11r; CYNUS PISTORIENSIS, *In Digesti Veteris Libros Commentaria*, Rubrica I, *De Justitia et Iure*, n.10, fol. 3v., Francoforti ad Moenum, 1578.

[139] *Summa Institutionum*, Liber I, *De Iure Naturali . . . , p.348*, col.2: "Item dicitur ius naturale quod in lege mosaica vel in evangelio continetur ut legitur in decretis"; cf. *Summa Super Codicem*, Liber I, *De Ignorantia Iuris et Facti*, p.11, col.2, Papiae, 1506; ALBERICUS DE ROSATE BERGOMENSIS, *Dictionarium Iuris tam Civilis, quam Canonici*, v. *Ius*, p.412, Venetiis, 1573.

[140] HENRICUS DE SEGUSIO, *In Primum . . . , De Summa Trinitate, et Fide Catholica*, cap. 1. n.32, fol.6.r; JOANNES ANDREAE, *In Primum . . . , De Constitutionibus*, cap. *Postquam*, nn.1,2, fol.11r; *De Summa Trinitate et Fide Catholica*, cap. *Firmiter*, nn. 35, 36, fol. 8r.

person.[141] In reference to the spiritual aspect, three kinds of law are encountered in accordance with the various situations in which humankind found itself in relation to the Divinity.[142] The first natural law was enacted when the human being still enjoyed the state of innocence; a prohibition was imposed to eat from the tree of knowledge.[143] In creation itself another law was also given to the human being, a law common to both humans and beasts. After the Fall, this same law stemmed from instinct, although it still remained guided by reason.[144] The third kind of law found its way into human consciousness after the Fall, when rationality, being weakened, fell prey to concupiscence. This third type of law consists partly of human agreement and partly of human rationality; thus this third law may be defined *ius gentium,* as well as *ius naturale.*[145]

The indelibility of the divine law in fallen humanity has been endorsed by the unanimous consensus of canon and civil lawyers throughout the Middle Ages. This body of moral principles still forms the ideal norm or standard of right conduct, always and everywhere recognized by human

---

[141] *Super Prima Primi Decretalium Commentarii Tomus Primus,* Liber I, *De* Constitutionibus, prooemium, n.8, fol. 9r., Venetiis, 1578, "Ius divinum multiplex: quoddam ius divinum ad hominem determinatum, secundum partem rationis: quoddam determinatum ad hominem, et equum secundum consonantiam etiam partis sensitivae."

[142] Ibid., "Primum determinatum ad hominem secundum partem rationis, est multiplicis speciei, secundum variationem temporum in homine."

[143] Ibid., "Ab exordio creaturae rationalis fuit data lex Adae, ne comederet de ligno scientiae boni, et mali."

[144] Ibid., "Secunda species iuris, etiam ab exordio, fuit ex instinctu post peccatum, quo homines solo instinctu communi animantibus, rationabili tamen moventur ad id, ad quod etiam animalia absque ratione moventur: ut ad procreationem liberorum, educationem . . . et hoc etiam appellatur ius naturale: quia a naturante in naturae exordio, et ex naturae instinctu proditum est."

[145] Ibid., "Tertia species iuris divini est, quod etiam appellatur naturae: fuit post pactum: quia iam ratione captivata, et concupiscentiae subiecta, a qua peccatum surrexit, et intellectus hominis captivus factus est, et legi concupiscentiae subiectus: et secundum hoc ut convenirent homines, hoc solum eis remansit pro iure . . . Dicebam secundo, quod erat dare ius humanum, et hoc multiplex. Quoddam primaevum, et generale hominum: ut illud in particularibus exortum a traditionibus illis generalibus: ut, Facies alteri, quod tibi vis fieri, . . . et hoc appellatur ius gentium, et quod pereque ab hominibus custoditur: et hoc potest dici naturale, altero respectu: quia determinatur ex aspectu rationis naturalis."

Philosophy of Law

reason as binding. In the pursuit of clear conceptualization, various terms and remarks have been suggested by authors. Natural law is defined as *"naturalis ratio"* by Hostiensis,[146] Joannes Andreae,[147] and Antonius A Butrio.[148] The attribute, *aequissimum* is given to natural law by Azo[149] and Albericus De Rosate.[150] Cynus Pistoriensis[151] and Antonius a Butrio[152] define natural law simply as *aequitas*. For Baldus De Ubaldis natural law is *veritas* ;[153] Hostiensis concurs with his remark that "natural law insists more on truth rather than on subtleties."[154] Justice of the conscious, according to Baldus De Ubaldis, is the human soul itself as though it were inscribed with divine letters. This justice is at the same time witness and judge of itself. Thus human conscience is nothing other than the mind conscious of itself and the flower of the intellect. Conscience may also be defined as the capacity of the mind to judge itself.[155] Human conscience is consciousness itself endowed with an ability to be judge of its own actions.

---

[146] *In Primum . . . , De Summa Trinitate, et Fide Catholica,* cap. 1, n.32, fol.6r.

[147] *In Primum . . . , De Summa Trinitate et Fide Catholica,* cap. *Firmiter,* n.36, fol. 8r.

[148] *Super Prima . . . ,* Liber I, De *Constitutionibus,* prooemium, n.8, fol. 9r.

[149] *Summa Institutionum,* Liber I, *De Iure naturali gentium et civili,* p.348, col.2.

[150] *Dictionarium . . . ,* v. *Ius,* pp. 410, 411.

[151] *In Digesti Veteris . . . ,* Rubrica I, *De Iustitia et Iure,* n. 3, fol. 3r.

[152] *Super Prima . . . ,* Liber I, *De Constitutionibus,* prooemium, n.8, fol. 9r.

[153] *In Decretalium . . . , Super Secundo Decretalium, De Sententia et Re Judicata,* cap. 11, *Consanguinei,* n.3, fol. 280 v.

[154] *In Quartum Decretalium . . . , De eo, qui duxit in matrimonium, quam polluit per adulterium,* cap. 5, *Cum haberet,* n. 10, fol. 20 v. "naturale nempe ius . . . magis insistit veritati, quam subtilitati."

[155] *In Decretalium . . . , Super Secundo Decretalium, De Iudiciis,* prooemium, *Post.,* n. 10, fol. 147 v: "Iustitia conscientiae est ipsa anima, ac si scripta esset literis divinis . . . et unus et idem est testis et iudex . . . Nihil aliud est conscientia nisi mens subipsi conscia, et est flos intellectus, vel conscientia est mentis qualitas seipsam dijudicans"; cf. *Consiliorum, sive Responsorum Volumen Primum,* cons. 271, n. 1, fol. 81 v; *Volumen Tertium,* cons. 371, n.1, fol. 105r.-v., Venetiis, 1575.

The description of natural law by Ubaldus, however, focuses exclusively on the subjectivity of human conscience, leaving aside the universality of human inwardness which renders the human person ethical just as much as he is moral. Thus for a more complete comprehension of natural law it is necessary to insert in addition the concept of *iustitia commutativa*, which Hostiensis in somewhat poetic style verbalizes: "Whatever you expect of me, do the same to me, and what you dislike in my relationship with you, don't do likewise to me. It is precisely this law which governs and unites the whole human race."[156]

It was the constant conviction that natural law forms the *cardo* of any legal system; from natural law all human ordinances proceed and by it they are to be tested. Natural law is thought to be a body of principles which is sacred, and thereby supreme, incontestable, permanent and immutable.[157] In confrontation with this ontological truth, authors were cognizant of the insurmountable dilemma that conditions in life do exist which deprive the endorsement of natural law of its intrinsic and absolute validity. Circumstances may arise where principles or values of natural law come in conflict with one another. The assumption unanimously upheld is

---

[156] *In Primum . . . , De Summa Trinitate, et Fide Catholica,* cap. 1, *Firmiter,* n.29, fol. 6r: "Quod tibi vis fieri, mihi fac, quod non tibi, noli. Sic polis in terris vivere iure poli"; cf. *In Quartum . . . , De eo, qui duxit in matrimonium, quam polluit per adulterium.,* cap. 5, *Cum haberet,* nn.10, 11, fol. 20 v; IOANNES ANDREAE, *In Primum.., De Summa Trinitate et Fide Catholica,* cap. *Firmiter,* n. 33, fol. 8r; ALBERICUS DE ROSATE, *Dictionarium . . . ,* v. *Lex,* p. 422; ANTONIUS A BUTRIO, *Super Prima . . . ,* liber I, *De Constitutionibus,* prooemium, n.8, fol. 9r; AZO, *Summa super Codicem,* liber I, *De Ignorantia Iuris et Facti,* p. 11, col.2; *Summa Institutionum,* liber 1, *De Iusticia et Iure,* p. 347, col. 2; *De iure Naturali Gentium et Civili,* p. 348, col. 2; PLACENTINUS, *In Summam Institutionum sive Elementorum D. Iustiniani Libri IIII_,* Liber I, tit. I, *De Iustitia et Iure,* p.1, *Moguntiae,* 1535; CYNUS PISTORIENSIS, *In Digesti Veteris . . . ,* Rubrica I, *De Iustitia et Iure,* n.5, fol. 3r; n. 10, fol. 3v.

[157] HENRICUS DE SEGUSIO, *In Quartum . . . , De eo, qui duxit in matrimonium, quam polluit per adulterium,* cap. 5, *Cum haberet,* n. 10, fol. 20 v; JOANNES ANDREAE, *In Primum . . . De Consuetudine,* cap. 11, *Cum tanto,* nn.1,2,11, fol. 59 v; n.23, fol 60 r; n. 46, fol. 61 v; BALDUS DE UBALDIS, *In Decretalium . . . , Super Secundo Decretalium, De iudiciis,* prooemium, *Post.,* n. 13, fol.148r; *Consiliorum . . . ,* vol. I, cons. 267, n. 9, fol. 59v; ALBERICUS DE ROSATE, *Dictionarium . . . ,* v. *Ius,* p. 412; AZO, *Summa Institutionum,* Liber I, *De Jure Naturali Gentium et Civili,* p. 349, col.1; *Ad Singulas Leges XII, Librorum_ Codicis Iustinianei Commentarius,* Liber VIII, tit. 53, *Quae sit longa consuetudo,* lex 2, n.7, p.672, Parisiis, 1577; PLACENTINUS, *In Summam Institutionum . . . ,* Liber I, tit.II, *De Iure Naturali Gentium, et Civili,* p. 3; CYNUS PISTORIENSIS, *In Digesti Veteris . . . ,* Rubrica XIV, *De Officio Praetoris,* n. 7, fol. 13 v.

Philosophy of Law

that in such cases natural law be waived "ad maius malum vitandum."[158] Situations of lesser validity are also allowed to exist which contradict the principles of natural law; it seems feasible that human law and custom sometimes prevail over natural law -- "ius naturale seu divinum est mutabile per consuetudinem, vel ius positivum."[159]

The perenniality and immutability of natural law, due to its divine origin, induces Antonius A Butrio to reach out for a solution of the dilemma: how could ever a human law or custom conflicting with natural law be justified?[160] He resorts to the authority of the *Glossa* in classifying natural law into divine counsels and divine precepts. Whenever it concerns divine counsels, natural law tolerates an inferior law or custom contrary to it since divine counsels do not proceed out of necessity; whereas divine precepts resist any contrary human law or custom due to their intrinsic validity and absolute necessity, "ex toto genere suo." There are, nevertheless, dictates of nature which are not moral precepts; they are simply statutes and, as such, they are immutable only "ex genere suo"; this means that, although they are not enforced in an absolute manner, these statutes cannot be abrogated in their integrity. In the event that a human law or custom contradicts the divine statute, or adds something to it, one may presume that either the statute in question is not of divine origin, or that it entails a mere statement. In the case where the statute is a mere divine statement, three alternative conclusions could be sought: in the first case, if the existence of the human law or custom is justified, and the introduction of either one excludes sin, the validity of the human law or custom should be maintained; in the second case, if there is no reason for the existence of either one, or there can be no justification without danger

---

[158] ALBERICUS DE ROSATE, *Dictionarium..*, v. *Ius*, p.412.

[159] JOANNES ANDREAE, *In Primum . . . , De Consuetudine*, cap. 11, *Cum tanto*, nn. 1,2,11, fol. 59 v; n.23, fol. 60r; nn. 43,46, fol. 61r; ALBERICUS DE ROSATE, *Dictionarium . . . ,* v. *Ius*, p.411; AZO, *Summa Institutionum*, Liber I, *De Iure Naturali Gentium et Civili*, p.349, col. 1; *Summa Super Codicem*, Liber IV, *De Usuris*, p. 141, col. 2.

[160] *In Sextum Decretalium Volumen Commentaria, De Constitutionibus*, cap. 1, *Licet Romanus*, n.49, fol. 3r., Venetiis, 1575; *Super Prima Primi . . . ,* Tomus I, *De Consuetudine*, cap. 11, *Cum tanto*, n. 25, fol. 79r.

of sinning, the human law or custom is devoid of its intrinsic validity; in the third case, if the reason itself for the existence of either one is doubtful, the existence of human law or custom is inadmissable.[161] In trying to solve the quandary, Antonius, we believe, demotes natural law from its eminency of being the sole foundation of human justice.

Gregory IX unequivocally ascertains the indispensability of natural law. No one in his right mind, says the Pontiff, would ever deny that the transgression of natural law jeopardizes one's eternal felicity. No contrary custom, whatever its longevity, could ever waive the binding force of natural law.[162]

Towards a Comprehensive Understanding of Natural Law

The perusal so far accomplished enables us to acquire an all-embracing and unified philosophy of natural law. Our present objective is to envisage natural law in three dimensions: natural law is in essence human consciousness, and thereby the source of *koinonia* (community); human response to natural law gives rise to *diakonia* (service); *koinonia* and *diakonia* complementing each other give rise to *martyrion* (witnessing) which is nothing other than the christolization of human consciousness.

To Judeo-Christian Religion is assigned the greatest achievement of acknowledging the human individual as the receptacle of the eternal wisdom. It has been our constant contention that Christ is the tangential reality with which the human consciousness identifies and in which it finds its ultimate significance and self-completion; thus Christ appears as the *causa formalis* and the *causa finalis* of human consciousness, the epitome of human maturation. Upon this presupposition we endeavour to understand natural law, defined by the Aquinatis as "participatio aeterni luminis" in the threefold spectrum of *koinonia, diakonia,* and *martyrion*.

---

[161] *Super Prima Primi* . . . , Tomus I, *De Consuetudine,* cap. 11, *Cum tanto,* n. 25, fol. 79r.

[162] Liber X, lib. I, tit. IV, *De Consuetudine,* cap. 11.

It has always been the universal conviction that in human consciousness there is something absolute, non-subordinate, to historical evolution, but something intrinsically eternal and divine: a perennial law, absolutely potent and uncompromising, which constitutes the sole criterion for what is good or evil in human conduct. Natural law, understood, as "impressio aeterni luminis," thus appears as being its own premise and presupposition; its end is the absolute finality of the humanization of human consciousness. Nothing is revealed in the conscious world except this law, its grandeur and its authority. Natural law, it must be said, constitutes the immovable, irreducible basis and the starting point in the understanding of human consciousness.

Natural law is the Foundation of Koinonia

The basic presupposition that natural law is equally implanted in all human beings posits the conviction of the fundamental, absolute, and irreducible similarity of all humans. By reason of this similarity, all human beings are recognized substantially equal, all individually entitled to the same fundamental human rights. However, the endorsement of similarity and equality among human individuals succeeds only in forming a togetherness, a formless mass, a multitude. This seems to have been in the mind of Cicero when he availed himself of the definition of *populus* by Africanus, according to whom by the term "populus" is not meant a throng, any multitude assembled for any reason, a formless mass; it is rather a community aggregated by legal consent and communality of convenience.[163] In verity, the concept of similarity and equality may rightfully be applied also to living creatures, other than humans, so long as they belong to the same species. The mere fact of similarity does not reveal the real nature of human consciousness, the universality of human inwardness; it deprives the universal human consciousness of its intrinsic and most fundamental bond

---

[163] *De Re Publica*, Lib. I, cap. 25, n. 39, p. 1178. "Populus autem non omnis hominum coetus quoquo modo congregatus, sed coetus multitudinis iuris consensu et utilitatis communione sociatus."

within itself, and thereby ignores, *a priori,* natural law as the source of *koinonia.* The concept of natural law must therefore entail the most intensive and at once the most extensive comprehension, such that it renders itself one and the same thing with human consciousness.

One speaks of natural law without being able to precisely state what its essential content is; the concept is still indeterminate and ambiguous, liable to many misunderstandings, confusion, and errors. This fact alone is indicative of its nature. The vagueness of the concept, in fact, lends itself to a plausible exposition of our own. Natural law is taken to mean human consciousness itself, and the identity of the two concepts forms the central idea of the present study.

It has been pointed out by Seneca and Clement of Alexandria that the initial phase of human history, known in Judeo-Christian Tradition as the state of innocence, does not signify the plenitude of humanization. The man of the Yahwist Tradition should by no means be acclaimed as the fullness of humanness, as the human consciousness in ultimate fruition of itself, the personification of virtue *par excellence.* With the creation of the Yahwist man, the human consciousness was rather endowed with the aptitude, the ability to approach perfection of itself; the human consciousness is born to virtue, but not in possession of it. It is thus the inner destiny of human consciousness, thus equipped, to explicate what it is implicitly. What the human consciousness wants to discover is itself, its true, authentic self; in unfolding itself, it acquires more depth of insight into its rationality, conscientiousness, and sociability. This is precisely the absolute and ultimate aspiration of human consciousness: to understand and comprehend itself; it is its inner destiny and the root of its existence. Natural law, conceived of as human consciousness, is thus alive, dynamic, always unfolding its own authenticity.

We define human consciousness in its crude and simplistic apprehension as *ecceitas,* denoting self-identity by exclusion of anything other than the self-pure being-for-self. Such a conceptualization of human consciousness remains very restrictive and defective since it merely vouches for the similarity and equality among humans. In a more intensive and comprehensive understanding, human consciousness reveals itself as an inner drive, an impetus in itself and for itself, breaking through the bonds of being the bare and negative fact of self-identical consciousness, moving out of the shell of subjective independence, in order to reach out of itself in common consort with similar others. It must be said that a proclivity for socialization is encountered as well in the animal kingdom; the herd instinct is witnessed particularly in the migration of many species. One may, on this same premise, contend that what the beast does instinctively, the human individual does consciously. In fact, with all due respect to Cicero and Africanus, the definition of *populus*, as "coetus multitudinis iuris consensu et utilitatis communione sociatus" (an aggregate of persons joined by a legal consent and by reason of expediency), can well be understood on the same line of thought. Neither does this definition rebut the Carneadean theory that utility and expediency are the foundation of human society.

Therefore the sociability of human consciousness must indicate something more intrinsic, more substantial, more intensive and extensive, than mere grouping and togetherness solely out of convenience and expediency, or even by agreement. The ultimate reason for being social must be sought in the depth of human psychological and spiritual configuration. Being social in a human context is to be of one-mindedness, to experience a deep feeling of belonging, to be fully aware of one's inner universality. What therefore distinguishes human sociability from the herd instinct is precisely that inner, insatiable craving for genuine change for the better, the more perfect, that perennial discontent in the face of the very highest achievement of self-actualization. The inner destiny of the human consciousness is to unfold itself, to discover itself; in doing so, it moves inwardly, reflecting upon itself, enlightening and heightening itself into a higher plane of understanding of itself; the more the human consciousness turns into the recesses of itself, the more it becomes convinced of itself as universality; in the growing awareness of its inner universality, the human consciousness is at once identifying itself and arraying itself with the general human consciousness which is itself universality.

The essential similarity between Pentecost and the creation of the Yahwist man has been pointed out earlier. It was ascertained as a basic assumption that since God is one, the Spirit, which overshadowed the Apostles, was the same that pervaded and vivified the Yahwist man. In order to acquire more depth of insight into the nature of human consciousness, it seems incumbent to bring back into focus the personal interpretation of the Pentecostal event. The messianic age started at Pentecost, when the Church, the profound solidarity of all human beings in Christ, came into being, alive, dynamic, compact, sealed by the Spirit. The intent of the Pentecostal Spirit was to purify, intensify and transform into one-mindedness all believers in the Risen Christ. But the Spirit achieved this through the interiorization of the individual human consciousness. In the parting of tongues of fire, we envisage the acknowledgement and the endorsement of the individual human consciousness, and of its dignity, by God; indeed, we witness the recognition of the Yahwist man by God as already the receptacle of the eternal wisdom. Pentecost thus appears as the rejuvenation, revitalization, intensification, re-enforcement and heightening of the Spirit of God which was transposed and translated once and for all in the Yahwist man. What happened in Pentecost, the emergence of all humans in a bond of unity and profound solidarity in Christ, was nothing but the ultimate aspiration of the human consciousness in explicating what it is implicitly; in Pentecost the universality of human inwardness was brought to full fruition. The "Word made flesh" presented itself in Pentecost as the epitome of the humanization of the human consciousness.

It is only because the two modes of human consciousness of itself -- simple existence for self -- and absolute universality of self are distinct but not separate that the human consciousness forms an interlocked reality of two opposing forces, an innate contradiction within itself. This self-estrangement of human consciousness remains the basis and the all-inclusive and unchanged reality because of which human consciousness is in nature dynamic; it agitates within itself, develops itself; thus it appears as its own activation and production from inside itself into actuality of itself. This inner contradiction posits the volitive faculty as the decisive factor in the destiny of itself to become fully and vividly developed, to explicate what is still shrouded in the obscurity of itself. In this process, the reconciliation of the two opposing modes of experience is also being attained. The human will, albeit faced with this inner contradiction, has nonetheless an enormous strength that, while it allows the self to express itself to itself as individualistic and subjective self-identical consciousness, has also the capacity to suspend the first mode of being-for-self in order that the universality of its own inwardness may emerge as the ultimate authenticity of being. In other words, what the human consciousness wants to achieve is equilibrium and harmony of itself: to resolve the contradiction between the subjectivity and objectivity within itself, to pass from mere immediacy, from subjective freedom and personal utility, over to a higher mode of experience which constitutes the substantial content of the self, since by this renunciation the human consciousness arrives at the universality of its own nature.

The parable of the good Samaritan is didactic of the present theme. Three persons appear on the scene: Priest, Levite and the Samaritan -- three individual human consciousnesses, separate but identical in content. Being equally receptacle of the divine truth, their inwardness is universal; thus, ontologically speaking, all three formed a community with the unfortunate victim long before they ever met him; in fact, each and every one of them at once recognized his relationship with the victim and his duty towards him. What made the Samaritan more humane than the Priest and the Levite was his response to his own universal inwardness. In that act of duty, the Samaritan responded to his inner authenticity, objectified his inherent universality and actualized his true and wholesome self, for duty limits only the caprice of subjectivity, and comes in conflict only with the abstract good to which subjectivity clings. Duty in the Samaritan was the gaining of affirmative freedom -- the complete actualization of the self and the most authentic manifestation of the self to itself and to the world outside itself.

In conclusion, "community," rather than being an actuality resultant of human agreement, is in essence the externality of human consciousness itself; more specifically, it is the human response to its own inherent universality. And only when it flows from the universality of the self does human agreement emerge as the valid and authentic foundation of the community, whatever form it may assume. The community, as the externality of the universality of human inwardness, is thus the realm where the struggle between the two extremes of human consciousness -- the subjective and the objective, the substantial and the particular -- is solved. In the ongoing process of humanization of the human consciousness, the unification of opposites, an equisposei, is being registered; a solution is being reached by the self within itself between being and not being for itself since, while being itself, it gives itself to otherness only to return back to itself; thus it discovers itself more, becomes more assured of itself; it explicates more its inherent universality, approaches more the fulfillment of itself, attains affirmative freedom of itself -- to lose oneself, one finds oneself.

Natural law thus appears as human consciousness in its substantial rationality and immediate actuality in the process of humanization, the objectivization of the universality of human inwardness, the transformation from subjective to absolute, affirmative freedom. In this sense, natural law is in essence the foundation of *koinonia*.

Ius Gentium

The concept of natural law as *koinonia* finds confirmation in the ancient recognition of a body of laws known as *ius gentium*. We are cognizant of the fact that there has always been a divergency of views as to the distinction between *ius naturale* and *ius gentium*.

The first view sharply distinguished *ius gentium* from *ius naturale*. This distinction seems to have been related to the distinction between the primitive state of nature and the conventional configuration of the human community. Among the Roman jurists who cherished this view were Ulpianus,[164] Tryphoninus,[165] Florentinus,[166] and Hermogenianus.[167] A quotation from *Institutiones* suffices for the purpose of clarification: *"ius*

---

[164] Ulpianus, L. *Manumissiones*, 4, D., *De iustitia et iure*, 1,1.

[165] Tryphoninus, L. *Si quod*, 64, D., *De condictione indebiti*, 12, 6.

[166] Florentinus, L. *Libertas*, 4, D., *De statu hominum*, 1, 5.

[167] Hermogenianus, L. *Ex hoc*, 5, D., *De iustitia et iure*, 1,1.

gentium is common to all the human race. It was out of exigency and neccesity that the human race emerged into different nations. Wars eventually took place, and captivity and slavery ensued which are contrary to natural law. Initially, however, all human beings, by natural law, were born free. It is precisely by virtue of *ius gentium* that all different types of contract were introduced."[168] This position was seconded by some Fathers of the Church among whom are enumerated Sanctus Isidorus[169] and Ivo Carnotensis.[170] The *Decretum Gratiani* seems to pertain to this school of thought. Gratian defines *ius gentium* as the customary law of mankind, which came long after natural law.[171] Among Medieval authors, Joannes Andreae, for one, lays down a sharp distinction between *ius naturale* and *ius gentium*.[172] Albericus de Rosate Bergomensis in his *Dictionarium* points out the imprecision of concepts: sometimes *ius gentium* is taken to mean *ius naturale;* other times a distinction is made between the two terms.[173]

The second position concurs more closely with our conceptualization of natural law as *koinonia*. We tend to believe Cicero is on our side since law, according to him, should be conceived of as the expression of the universal and natural reason and sense of justice. We are not aware either of any distinction made by Cicero between *ius naturale* and *ius gentium*. Among Roman jurists Gaius, Paulus and Pomponius adhere to this position.

---

[168] Inst., *De iure naturali et gentium et civili* 1, 2, §2. "Ius autem gentium omni humano generi commune est. nam usu exigente et humanis necessitatibus gentes humanae quaedam sibi constituerunt: bella etenim orta sunt et captivitates secutae et servitutes, quae sunt iuri naturali contrariae. iure enim naturali ab initio omnes homines liberi nascebantur. ex hoc iure gentium et omnes paene contractus introducti sunt, ut emptio venditio, locatio conductio, societas, depositum, mutuum et alii innumerabiles."

[169] *Etymologiarum Libri XX*, Liber V, cap. 6, n.1, loc.cit., col. 199-200.

[170] *Decretum*, Pars IV, cap. 178, *Opera Omnia*, Tomus 1, P.L.,Tomus 161, Parisiis, 1855, col. 305.

[171] Pars I, Dist. I, c.9.

[172] *In Primum Decretalium . . . , De Summa Trinitate et Fide Catholica*, cap. Firmiter, nn.35,36, fol. 8r.

[173] *Dictionarium . . .*, v. *Ius*, p. 411: "Interdum ponitur ius gentium pro iure naturali. eo. c. ius gentium, aliquando econtra."

Gaius defines *ius naturale* and *ius gentium* alike: *naturalis ratio*.[174] Thus in his opinion *ius gentium* is nothing but that body of principles or laws which human beings have always learned from their reason to recognize as the basis of rectitude and justice. Paulus[175] and Pomponius[176] seem to ignore any distinction between the two systems of law. This understanding of *ius gentium* is endorsed by Saint Clement of Alexandria[177] and Saint Augustine[178] according to whom *ius gentium* constitutes a body of laws which human beings come to acquire by *naturalis ratio* alone.

Nor were there lacking medieval Canonists and Civilists who perpetuated the identity of concepts. For Baldus Ubaldi Perusinus[179] and Antonius A. Butrio[180] both systems of law form one and the same reality. Among the Civilists, Azo[181] and Placentinus[182] follow suit. Both authors appear at first hand to be inconsistent in their conceptualization of *ius gentium;* at times they seem to sharply distinguish *ius gentium* from *ius*

---

[174] Gaius, L. *Omnes*, 9, D., *De iustitia et iure*, 1,1: ". . . quod vero naturalis ratio inter omnes homines constituit, id apud omnes peraeque custoditur vocaturque ius gentium, quasi quo iure omnes gentes utuntur"; cf. *Institutionum Gai Commentarius Primus*, Tit. *De Iure Civili et Naturali*, §1, *Institutionum et Regularum Iuris Romani Syntagma*, Edidit Rudolphus Gneist, Lipsiae, 1880, p.6.

[175] Paulus, L. *Ius pluribus*, 11, D., *De iustitia et iure*, 1,1.

[176] Pomponius, L. *Veluti* 2, D., *De iustitia et iure*, 1,1.

[177] *The Miscellanies (Stromata)*, vol. 1, Bk 1, chap.13, loc.cit., p. 389.

[178] *Contra Faustum Manichaeum Libri Triginta Tres*, Lib. XIX, cap. 2, *Opera Omnia*, Tomus VIII, P.L., Parisiis, 1841, Tomus 42, col. 347, 348.

[179] *In Decretalium . . .*, *Super Primo Decretalium, De Summa Trinitate, et Fide Catholica*, cap. *Summum*, n. 40, fol. 8r; *Super Secundo Decretalium, De Sententia et Re Iudicata*, cap. 11, *Consanguinei*, n. 3, fol. 280 v.

[180] *Super Prima Primi . . .*, Lib. I, *De Constitutionibus*, prooemium, n.8, fol. 9r.

[181] *Brocardica Aurea*, Rubrica 17, *De Verbo Effectu et Significatione*, fol.51 v., Neapoli, 1568; *Summa Institutionum*, Lib. I, *De Iure Naturali Gentium et Civili*, p. 348, col. 2; Lib.II, *De Rerum Divisione et Acquisitione*, p.353, col. 2.

[182] *In Summam Institutionum . . .*, Lib.I, Tit. II, *De Iure Naturali Gentium, et Civili*, pp.2, 3.

naturale. However, upon accurate attention, one realizes that for Azo and Placentinus *ius naturale* means *instinctum naturae,* natural instinct.

In answer to the theory which implies a contrast between the primitive conditions of human life and the conventional organization of society, it remains an undeniable fact that these so-called conventional laws were contemporarily and universally recognized and endorsed. This fact by itself is indicative of a usage which spontaneously emerged from a consciousness identical to all human beings. Gratian classified *ius gentium* as the customary law of mankind; indeed it was. It is precisely the customary nature of these laws that reveals their universal spontaneity and accounts for the fact that these laws are taught equally to all human beings by *naturalis ratio,* and not by any kind of agreement. Although we detest the shamefully hypocritical reasons brought forward in justification of slavery,[183] we agree with what Thomas Aquinas has to say on the nature of *ius gentium:* "Since natural reason dictates matters which are according to the right of nations, as implying a proximate equality, it follows that they need no special institution, for they are instituted by natural reason itself . . ."[184] He also considers *ius gentium* as deriving from *ius naturale,* as conclusion from premise.[185] We rather define *ius gentium* as *ius naturale,* revealing itself as human consciousness adapting itself according to a specific phase of its own explication, of its own humanization. One should find no difficulty in accepting the Gratian contention that *ius gentium* came after the law of nature, once the assumption is laid down that the inner destiny of human consciousness is to ever disclose its own authenticity. Upon this premise, it cannot be said that *ius gentium* is an addition to *ius naturale,* as the Aquinatis points out.[186] To add something to a thing means that the thing is in itself incomplete, and that this added something is physically distinct to the thing. *Ius gentium,* like *ius naturale,*

---

[183] *Summa Theologica,* IIa-IIae, qu. 57, art. 3, ad 2 um, *American . . .* , p. 1433.

[184] Ibid., ad 3um.

[185] *Summa Theologica,* Ia-IIae, qu. 95, art. 4, Resp., *American . . .* , p. 1016.

[186] *Summa Theologica,* Ia-IIae, qu. 94, art. 5, ad 3um, *American . . .* , p. 1012.

should be considered rational, primordial, spontaneous, and universal; *ius gentium* is *ius naturale* in operation at that specific phase in the process of its own crystalization. Thus *ius gentium,* being in essence *ius naturale,* is nothing but the earnest endeavour of human consciousness to disclose itself as one-mindedness, one universal spirit; it is the revelation of the inner universality of human consciousness which burgeons into the universal esprit de corps at a determined phase in the process of the perennial unfolding of human consciousness. This is the reason why *ius gentium* is that body of laws which "apud omnes populos peraeque custoditur."

Natural Law is Diakonia

Koinonia is human consciousness in its substantial rationality. Had it not been for the universality inherent in human consciousness, the arbitrariness of the human will would have been the principle of right, and personal convenience the sole criterion of justice. Because of its own intrinsic universality, the human consciousness imposes upon itself a struggle to suppress the caprice of its own subjectivity in order to unfold itself into substantial rationality and objective freedom. *Koinonia* is the realm of actualized rational freedom, since human consciousness finds its true universal content in and with the conscious world. The universality of inwardness must first lead the human consciousness to the acknowledgement of the substantiality of another human consciousness -- a fundamental presupposition without which the integration of the individual human consciousness, first within itself and then outside itself, can never be achieved. At this stage, however, human consciousness arrives only at the knowledge and recognition of the equality among similars. In the pursuit of the fulfillment of its intrinsic universality, the self moves forward to a further and deeper involvement, that of active interpenetration; thus the human consciousness passes from a condition of passivity, of mere awareness, conviction, and affirmation, into a phase of active participation, holistic integration, and self-bestowal. In reflecting upon itself and moving into the profundity and intimacy of itself, the human consciousness realizes that trust and loyalty shown to others similar do not in themselves satisfy and complete its inner substantiality; activation, or actualization, is further needed. Its authentic inwardness draws the human consciousness towards the virtue of justice, which calls for rectitude, probity, service, duty and sacrifice of the self. The Good Samaritan is a classical example of the inner universality of human consciousness blossoming itself into actuality. By this it is not meant that the self is drawn to action by some inner compulsion, or to a blind and unconditional compliance with another human will. Autonomous conviction and insight must correspond with the universality which the self embodies in order that its objective be rational and authentically free. It is only when the determination of human action is assigned to insight and conviction that the individual self becomes capable of a final moral decision, and capable of virtue. Justice not based on internal morality is nothing else but travesty, hypocrisy, expediency, capriciousness, and tyranny. When justice flows from moral conviction, it is virtue; and only when understood in this perspective, does *koinonia* become dynamic, alive, active, and compact. Only then does it denote the realm of sociability, of absolute spiritual unity of the essence of selves; only then does it indicate the arrival of affirmative freedom of the self; only then does the universality of human inwardness, as an ontological reality, pass into historic actuality. Natural law, when put into action by the human will, becomes the virtue of justice.

Justice

Integral to the reality of natural law as *diakonia* is the virtue of justice. One must be aware, however, of the different connotations which the term assumes in juridical literature. A summary of the diverse meanings is indeed useful and necessary for a better comprehension of the theme.

Baldus De Ubaldis considers three connotations of justice: "iustitia conscientiae, iudicii, compositionis seu concordiae." *Iustitia conscientiae* denotes justice inscribed in the human heart; thus it signifies natural law; *iustitia iudicii* is justice which ensues from a judicial sentence; *iustitia compositionis* finds its source in human agreement.[187] In another place, the author uses the term to indicate human law in general.[188] In this last nuance, the term "justice" seems to be adopted by other authors.[189]

It should not surprise anybody that the term is also used to mean *iustitia divina*. In this context, we interpret the mind of Saint Ambrose when he states: "that the law is just not for reason of its pure being but because it traces its roots in justice; the justice of law is empty if devoid of the Christian spirit since Christ is the fullness of the human law."[190] Baldus De Ubaldis seems to have had in mind this significance of justice when he defined it as *astraea* -- like the stars, its radiance enlightens the human mind.[191] The same meaning of the term is found in Azo[192] and in Placentinus.[193]

As pointed out earlier, Baldus De Ubaldis adopts the term to mean natural law, *iustitia conscientiae*. It seems that this is what Seneca also understood by the term when he wrote: "Justice is not of our own making,

---

[187] *In Decretalium. . . , Super Secundo Decretalium, De iudiciis*, prooemium, *Post*, n. 10, fol. 147v.

[188] *Consiliorum . . . Volumen Quintum*, cons. 184, n.4, fol. 51r.

[189] MAGNUS AURELIUS CASSIODORUS, *Variarum Libri Duodecim*, loc. cit., Lib. IV, epistola 33, col. 630; HENRICUS DE SEGUSIO, *In Primum . . . , De Officio Iudicis Ordinarii*, cap. 2, *Si sacerdos*, n. 4, fol. 159r; CYNUS PISTORIENSIS, *In Digesti Veteris . . .* , Rubrica I, *De Iustitia et Iure*, n. 3, fol.3r.

[190] *Expositio Evangelii Secundum Lucam Libris X Comprehensa*, Lib. V, cap. 5, n. 21, *Opera Omnia*, Tomus I, pars posterior, P. L., Tomus 15, Parisiis, 1866, col. 1726. "Est igitur in lege iustitia, sed non est per legem iustitia . . . iustitia enim legis sine Christo vacua est, quia plenitudo legis Christus est."

[191] *In Decretalium . . . , Super Primo Decretalium, De Electione et Electi Potestate*, cap. 34, *Venerabilem*, n. 13, fol. 78v: "Astraea id est iustitia quae de caelo descendit, dicta est ab astris id est a stellis, quia lumen suum naturaliter communicat universae creaturae"; cf. Loc. cit. *De Officio Iudicis Ordinarii*, cap. 12, *Licet*, n. 1, fol. 127r.

[192] *Summa Super Codicem*, Liber I, *De Summa Trinitate et Fide Catholica ut Nemo publice contendere audeat*, p. 3, col. 1.

[193] *In Summam Institutionum . . .* , Liber I, tit. I, *De Iustitia et Iure*, p. 1: " . . . iustitia, utpote ex qua omnia iura emanant, tanquam ex fonte rivuli."

it is divine law, the bond of human society."[194] In a similar connotation, the term is used by Azo[195] and by Albericus De Rosate, according to whom God is the author of justice, whereas man is the author of right (ius).[196]

The term posits a serious difficulty of comprehension when applied in a general and indeterminate manner. This occurs when the use of the term refers to the principle of justice. The ambiguity becomes more stringent when one tries to discern the principle from the virtue of justice. Principles, ideals, and values are something general and inward; they form the content of the *nous,* and are thereby outside the existential world; what is by itself, exists only *in potentia.* The content of the mind cannot force itself by itself; it needs the human will to activate and actualize it in the real life. Thus natural law by intrinsic necessity requires human response in order that it be human consciousness itself. This very actualization of natural law is nothing less than the virtue of justice. The distinction therefore between principle and virtue pertains only to the metaphysical realm; what in ontology is called principle, is defined as virtue in existentiality; a principle, whether moral or ethical, not existentialized is totally meaningless. This intrinsic relatedness between principle and virtue convinces us all the more that natural law is human consciousness itself.

Thus justice understood as virtue becomes most illustrative of the nature of natural law and confirmation of our contention that natural law is in essence *diakonia*. A definition of justice, as virtue, which received the approval of posterity is that of Ulpianus which reads as follows: "Justice is the constant and perpetual will to give to each one what belongs to him or her."[197] For a better comprehension of the concept, one must also include

---

[194] Cf. ALBERICUS DE ROSATE, *Dictionarium* . . . , v. *Iustitia*, p. 413. "Iustitia non est constitutio nostra, sed divina lex, et vinculum societatis humanae."

[195] *Summa Institutionum*, Liber I, *De Iure Naturali Gentium et Civili*, p. 348, col. 2.

[196] *Dictionarium* . . . , v. *Iustitia*, p. 414.

[197] Ulpianus, L. *Iustitia*, 10, D., *De iustitia et iure*, 1, 1: "iustitia est constans et perpetua voluntas ius suum cuique tribuendi"; cf. Inst., *De iustitia et iure*, 1,1; AZO, *Summa Institutionum*,, Liber I, *De Iusticia et Iure*, p. 347, col. 2; *De Iure Naturali Gentium et Civili*, p. 348, col. 2; PLACENTINUS, *In Summam Institutionum* . . . , Liber I, tit.I, *De Iustitia et Iure*, p.1; HENRICUS DE SEGUSIO, *In Secundum Decretalium*,.., *De testibus et Attestationibus*, cap. 25, *Cum venisset*,

what Ulpianus names as the precepts of law, which are: to live honestly, to hurt nobody, to give each one his due.[198] Celsus, who adopts the word *ius* in lieu of *iustitia*, defines justice as "ars boni et aequi."[199] Justice is usually conceived of as virtue by Cicero.[200] There is no substantial difference between the Ulpianian and the Ciceronian definition of the virtue of justice. However, the definition given by Cicero stands out as being more explanatory and comprehensive than the one offered by Ulpianus. Cicero first states what he understands by virtue: "Virtus est enim habitus naturae modo atque rationi consentaneus."[201] The intrinsic relatedness between virtue and reason, which is natural law, or human nature, is attested in this definition. From this definition one can easily deduce the intrinsic dependency of the concept of justice, as virtue, in its existential reality on the dictates of reason; thus justice in this perspective is nothing less than perfect reason -- "virtus perfecta ratio."[202] According to Cicero justice is a habit of the mind, retained by common convenience, which ascribes to each and everyone his or her own dignity -- "Iustitia est habitus animi, communi utilitate conservata, suam cuique tribuens dignitatem."[203] Significant is the use of the term *habitus*, in lieu of *voluntas* albeit *constans et perpetua*, a term which more explicitly denotes constancy of resolution; *ius suum* in the definition of Ulpianus is replaced

---

nn 2,3, fol. 90 v; *In Quintum Decretalium* . . . , *De Verborum Significatione*, cap. 10, Forus, n. 10, fol. 124v; IOANNES ANDREAE, *In Primum Decretalium*. . .,prooemium,*Rex*, n. 13, fol. 6r.

[198] Ulpianus, L. *Iustitia.*, 10, §1, D., *De iustitia et iure*, 1, 1: "Iuris praecepta sunt haec: honeste vivere, alterum non laedere, suum cuique tribuere."

[199] Ulpianus, L. *Iuri operam*, 1, D., *De iustitia et iure*, 1, 1.

[200] *De Finibus Bonorum et Malorum ad Brutum*, Liber II, cap. 18, n.59, loc. cit., p.1010; *De Re Publica*, Liber III, cap. 14, n. 23, p. 1192; cap. 50, 41, p.1195, loc.cit; Liber II, cap. 43, n.70; cap. 44, n.71, loc.cit., p. 1189; *De Legibus*, Liber I, cap. 10, nn.28,29,30,31, p. 1206; cap. 15, n. 42, p. 1207; cap. 16, n. 45, p. 1208, loc.cit.

[201] *Rhetoricorum vel De Inventione Rhetorica Libri Duo*, Liber II, cap. 53, n. 159, loc. cit., p. 69.

[202] *De Legibus*, Liber I, cap. 16, n. 45, loc. cit., p. 1208.

[203] *Rhetoricorum* . . . , Liber II, cap. 53, n. 159, p. 69.

by the phrase *suam dignitatem;* in this manner there should be no reason to believe that the observance of justice is directed only towards those who enjoy the full rights of citizenship; the object of the virtue of justice must entail the fundamental human rights identical to all human beings. He inserts, moreover, the phrase, "communi utilitate conservata," in order to indicate that in the exercise of justice a balance ought to be maintained between the good of the commonweal and the good of the individual. Justice, regardless of whether its object is understood as *ius suum* (Ulpianus) or *sua dignitas* (Cicero), must be exercised towards the individual human being only within the reality of the community, and never outside it. In this vision, we maintain that natural law is at once the source of *koinonia* and, in essence, *diakonia;* and natural law has no reason to be human consciousness itself, and thereby *diakonia,* if it were not for its ultimate goal, the ever building-up and the solidification of the *koinonia.*

Among the Fathers of the Church the term signifies most frequently the virtue of justice.[204] Lactantius relates justice to peace, and defines it as humanity or kindness.[205] But in their treatises on justice many patristic writers, including Saint Augustine, simply adopted the definition given by Cicero.[206]

Civil and canonical writers, while retaining the definition given by Ulpianus as the premise in their understanding of justice, endeavoured to clarify the basic concept by diverse nuances. Justice is conceived of by

---

[204] LACTANTIUS, *The Divine Institutes,* Bk V, chap.17, loc.cit., p.372; Bk VII, chap. 15, pp. 512-513; CATULFUS, *Instructio Epistolaris ad Beatum Carolum Regem, Opera Omnia,* Tomus unicus, P.L., Tomus 96, Parisiis, 1851, col. 1365; IONAS AURELIANENSIS, *De Institutione Laicali Libri Tres,* Liber II, cap. 24, *Opera Omnia,* Tomus unicus, P. L., Tomus 106, Parisiis, 1851, col. 218-219; RABANUS MAURUS, *De Universo Libri Viginti Duo,* Liber XVI, cap. 3, *Opera Omnia,* Tomus V, P.L., Tomus 111, Parisiis, 1864, col.445-446; IOANNIS SARESBERIENSIS, *Polycraticus sive de Nugis Curialium et Vestigiis Philosophorum,* Liber IV, cap.1, *Opera Omnia,* Tomus unicus, P.L., Tomus 199, Parisiis, 1855, col. 513.

[205] *The Divine Institutes,* loc. cit., Bk V, chap. 17, p. 370; Bk VI, chap. 10, p. 417.

[206] *De Diversis Quaestionibus LXXXIII Liber Unus,* Quaestio 31, loc. cit., n.1, col. 20; FLACCUS ALBINUS, *Dialogus de Rhetorica et Virtutibus, De Virtutibus,* loc. cit., col. 944; MAGNUS AURELIUS CASSIODORUS, *De Anima,* cap. 5, Tomus posterior, P.L., Tomus 70, Parisiis, 1847, col. 1290; RATHERIUS VERONENSIS, *Praeloquiorum Libri Sex,* tit. II, loc. cit., n.5, col. 222.

Cynus Pistoriensis as goodness and equity;[207] Baldus De Ulbaldis defines justice as faith;[208] Hostiensis considers justice as the highest good;[209] for Albericus De Rosate, justice is a laudable attitude.[210]

The definition of justice by Cicero seems to have attracted the attention of many scholars, particularly patristic Fathers. However, we believe that in addition to it one must include the understanding of justice by Seneca for a further comprehension of natural law as *diakonia*. He writes that to be just does not mean only that one should not harm another person, but it also entails the duty to impede one person from not inflicting harm on others. Not to harm anyone is not a virtue of justice, but is abstaining from what is not yours.[211] In the statement of Seneca, the virtue of justice entails more than willingness, which accords to each and everyone fundamental human rights; it insists on protecting and defending human dignity by personal involvement. That was precisely what the Good Samaritan did. Only in the understanding of Seneca does the virtue of justice assume its full significance, and natural law disclose itself most authentically as human consciousness.

All definitions and descriptions of the virtue of justice vouch for the human endeavour in search of its own inner truth. Concepts entertained by pagan and Christian authors alike enshrine the truth; thus they resist the historic development of the human spirit; they are not subordinate to history, but they remain perennially valid. The concepts expressed by Cicero, Ulpianus, Seneca, and others are as valid to the modern mind as when they were first conceived by these great minds. Our admiration,

---

[207] *In Digesti Veteris . . .*, Rubrica I, *De Iustitia et Iure*, n.3, fol. 3r.

[208] *Consiliorum . . .*, Volumen I, Cons. 271, n.1, fol.81v; Volumen II, Cons.371, n.1, fol. 105v.

[209] *In Secundum Decretalium . . .*, *De Testibus et Attestationibus*, cap. 25, *Cum venisset*, nn 2, 3, fol. 90v.

[210] *Dictionarium . . .*, v. *Iustitia*, p. 413.

[211] Cf. ALBERICUS DE ROSATE, *Dictionarium . . .*, v. *Iustitia*, p. 413. "Iustus ut sis non solum non nocebis: sed etiam nocentes prohibetis. Nam nulli nocere non est iustitia: sed abstinentia alieni."

however, should not lessen the fact that none of these notions by itself embraces the whole truth of the nature of justice. One may even dare say that the total ensemble of learning on the subject throughout history can never help us reach the profundity of the meaning of justice. Twenty centuries have passed, and the human mind still waits for an answer to the question put forward by Pontius Pilate: Quid est veritas? Quid est iustitia?

According to Saint Thomas Aquinas, justice "denotes a kind of equality, as its very name implies; indeed we are wont to say that things are adjusted when they are made equal, for equality is in reference of one thing to some other."[212] He tried nonetheless to accommodate a justification for the universal acceptance of slavery.[213] The ultimate aim of justice, according to Cicero, is to uphold human dignity, while he felt at ease in postulating discrimination of classes -- "the very equality is unjust since it ignores different grades of dignity."[214] None of the pagan philosophers and jurists or Christian Doctors saw any conflict between their teaching on justice and the socio-political conditions of their times, conditions which appear degrading and appalling to the modern mind. Neither Ulpianus nor any other scholar, in conceptualizing justice as one's obligation to accord to another person his right, had in mind fundamental human rights, as acknowledged and endorsed by the General Assembly of the United Nations on December 10, 1948. In all probability, posterity will ask how the twentieth-century human consciousness failed to recognize and advocate human rights which will then stand out to human awareness as natural, valid, fundamental, vital, and integral to the notion of human dignity.

The notion of justice and of truth is eternal; it exists beyond time and space; the phrases, "ius suum cuique tribuens," "suam cuique tribuens dignitatem," "nocentes prohibebis," form a metaphysical truth, an idea

---

[212] *Summa Theologica*, IIa-IIae, q. 57, art. 1, *American* . . . , vol. 2, p.1431.

[213] Loc. cit., art. 3, ad 2um, p. 1433.

[214] *De Re Publica*, Liber I, XXVII, n.43, loc.cit., p. 1178. ". . . ipsa aequabilitas est iniqua, quum habet nullos gradus dignitatis."

which is in itself unchangeable and irreducible. What is subject to historic reality is its content; the externality of the idea, of the truth, reveals and registers at what stage human consciousness stands in the process of its own humanization; the gradual intensity and extensity of the content are nothing other than the on-going disclosure of the human consciousness of itself to itself. The ultimate aspiration of human consciousness is precisely to know the entirety of the content, which is its inner universality, which is itself in full.

Natural Law is Martyrion

The intimate relatedness, indeed identity, between Christianity and humanity, between divine revelation and natural law, is lucidly taught by Saint Augustine: "For what is now called the Christian religion existed even among the ancients and was not lacking from the beginning of the human race until "Christ came in the flesh." From that time, true religion, which already existed, began to be called Christian."[215] That there is one truth is at the bottom of the Christian philosophy. The Christian Church set out on its history with a conception of human nature which the Yahwist man had received in its substantiality directly from his Creator. Revelation does nothing but disclose what human consciousness embraced, indeed has always been, *ab initio*. It has been stated earlier that the intent of the Spirit in Pentecost was to vivify, crystalize, fortify and energize the divine truth transposed and translated in the human soul. The glimmer of truth implanted in the human heart formed the blue-print which human consciousness received in being created in the pursuit of the ultimate fulfillment of itself. The blue-print was actualized in its entirety in the Incarnation: "those who strive for justice and truth do indeed follow Christ."[216] From its very creation human consciousness was destined to

---

[215] *One Book on the True Religion (De Vera Religione Liber Unus). The Retractations*, chap. 12 (3), *The Fathers of the Church*, Trans. Sister Mary Inez Bogan, Washington, D.C., 1968, p. 52.

[216] IONAS AURELIANENSIS, *De Institutione Laicali* . . . , Liber II, cap. 24, loc. cit., col. 219. ". . . illi qui iustitiae et veritati student, Christo adhaerent."

bear a perennial inner discontent with itself in the face of the very highest achievement of self-actualization in Christ.

Natural law, being the reflection of the eternal wisdom, is its own premise and presupposition; its end is absolute and final. As premise, natural law is not subordinate to history in its substantiality; it is the absolute truth which is at the bottom of all the process of humanization. In view of its finality, natural law is subject to evolution in the explication of itself; it is thereby at the same time its own activation and production from inside itself. This means that natural law is present in fullness of itself, but just as necessarily it is becoming, it progresses in its development; natural law is perennial, irreducible and absolute, not explicitly, but implicitly; the passage from being implicitly present to explicity of itself denotes the immanent unfolding of itself as its inherent destiny. Natural law will ever remain in restless activity and in endless struggle within itself until it reaches the full explication of itself.

What the human consciousness wants to discover and actualize within itself is this immanent law which is itself. This pursuit constitutes the ultimate aspiration of human consciousness and the root of its existence: to understand and comprehend itself. In this respect the history of humankind is the history of the humanization of the human consciousness; it presents the phases in the development of human consciousness towards absolute, objective freedom of itself, its eternal harmony as its immanent law. This affirmative freedom, this eternal harmony within the human consciousness itself will ever remain indeterminate, ambiguous and obscure in definition unless Christ is posited as the *causa formalis* and *causa finalis* of human consciousness; thus the spirit of the Lord is acknowledged as the root and at once the absolute finality of human consciousness: the fundamental premise and presupposition as well as the millennium in the humanization of human consciousness.

The human consciousness, having Christ as its *causa formalis,* in its forward march in self-discovery, self-explication, and self-actualization, is doing nothing but returning to its foundation, to the source of wisdom for, as Lactantius says: "Virtue joined with knowledge is wisdom."[217] This moving back to the primordial source and archetype can also be perused as a cycle of the human consciousness returning upon itself, since the human consciousness in so doing is unfolding into a faithful resemblance of its *causa formalis*. By inherent necessity, the human consciousness breaks through the estrangement of itself, the bare living for itself, and arrives at the authenticity of itself, that is in imitation of Christ. For this same reason, Christ stands also as the finality of the humanization of human consciousness. Human consciousness, whether considered as universal or individual reality, in unfolding itself in accordance with the *causa formalis* and in view of the ultimate fulfillment of the *causa finalis* within itself, is increasingly gaining insight into itself and into its christological ontology. It is for this reason that we contend that the humanization of human consciousness is nothing other than the christolization of human consciousness. Human history is the rational and necessary way of understanding the idea of Christ as the substance of history: the idea is one and always the same, which explicates itself in human history. This idea has been in the process of being actualized and unfolding since the creation of the Yahwist man. While burgeoning in history, the idea is outside of time, it is eternal; thus it has centuries at its disposal in actualizing itself as human consciousness. Upon this assumption, human consciousness by inherent necessity can discover no point in the aspiration of self-fulfillment, if not in the identification of itself with the idea of Christ by whom, in whom, and for whom everything subsists. In conclusion, natural law, the idea of Christ humanized into the human self, finds itself in perennial evolution in explicating what it is implicitly; and what it is, implicit in itself, is contained in the evangelical script; and the total explication of natural law is nothing but the complete christolization of human consciousness. Natural law is *martyrion*, for the more it unfolds itself as human consciousness, the more human consciousness witnesses within itself and to itself its own inherent authenticity in the image of Christ in view of the *parousia*. Thus Saint Thomas Aquinas concludes that

---

[217] *The Divine Institutes*, Bk. III, chap. 8, loc. cit., p. 181.

the ultimate aim of human consciousness is not to live according to virtue, but rather that through a virtuous life human conscousness arrives at divine fruition.[218]

Ius Divinum

The Jewish religion marked a new era in the relation between God and the human creature. After the Fall, for sure, the only link that was left between the Creator and His creature was the glimmer of truth implanted once and for all in the Yahwist man. Sin obscured, but never deleted, the ontological semblance of Christ in the human being. The voice of God made itself heard in the recesses of the human consciousness; in one's own inwardness one met the Creator; in turning back into his innermost being, the human individual apprehended self-authenticity featured on Christ, the prototype of humanness. With the call of Abraham from Mesopotamia, God took a further step in His relationship with human beings: Jehovah, the pure One, comes in direct contact with the Yahwist man; God presents Himself personified; he insists on establishing a covenant with His creature in preparation for the fullness of time. The divino-human consortium was aimed at a process of crystalization and invigorization of that glimmer of truth implanted in the Yahwist man, until the primordial idea, because of which creation was decreed, the "Man" of the priestly Tradition, became a historic reality. The "Word" becoming flesh signalled and realized the millennium of the desired restoration by God of his intimacy with the Yahwist man. In the Incarnation, the christological ontology of the human being became history.

An integral part of this divino-human consortium is *ius divinum*, divine positive law, which forms part of the revealed truth. Saint Thomas Aquinas defines *ius divinum* in the traditional manner: "The Divine right is

---

[218] *Opusculum XXXI De Regimine Principum ad Regem Cypri*, Liber I, cap. 14, *Sancti Thomae Aquinatis Opuscula Philosophica et Theologica*, edidit A. Michaele De Maria, Vol. II, Tiferni Tiberini, 1886, p. 32. "non est ergo ultimus finis multitudinis congregatae vivere secundum virtutem, sed per virtuosam vitam pervenire ad fruitionem divinam."

that which is promulgated by God."[219] This promulgation of divine law was necessitated by sin -- "disobedience to the first law necessitated the Mosaic law."[220]

Before proceeding any further on the subject of divine right, it seems incumbent to discuss the relatedness between the Mosaic law and the Evangelical law. Saint Augustine seems to advocate a *distinctio realis* between the Mosaic and the Evangelical laws: the former, he calls, in the manner of St. Paul, the law of sin and death,[221] the latter, he defines as the law of truth.[222] The essential identity of the Mosaic law with the Evangelical law was authoritatively endorsed by the Council of Trent with the acknowledgement of the Canonical Books of the Old Testament.[223] Upon this premise, no distinction between the Mosaic law and the Evangelical law can retain any validity other than *distinctio formalis*. Only in this context is *ius divinum* understood in the present exposition.

Back to the central theme, we endeavour to illustrate the intrinsic relationship between natural law and divine positive law by reason of their source, nature, and aim. The identity of natural law and divine positive law by reason of their source has amply been demonstrated in the preceding part of this study. It suffices here to quote Saint Thomas Aquinas on the score. "The Divine and natural laws (proceed) from the reasonable will of

---

[219] *Summa Theologica*, IIa-IIae, q. 57, art. 2, ad 3um, *American* . . ., p. 1432.

[220] EUSEBIUS HIERONYMUS, *Commentariorum in Isaiam* . . ., Liber 8, cap.24, vers.6, loc.cit., col. 292: "lex data est per Moysen, quia prima lex dissipata est"; cf. ST. AMBROSE, *Seven Exegetical Works, Flight from the World*, (3.15), loc. cit., p. 292; *Letters, Letter to Irenaeus*, 83, (73), loc. cit., pp. 465, 467; HENRICUS DE SEGUSIO, *In Primum Decretalium* . . ., *De Summa Trinitate, et Fide Catholica*, cap. 1, n. 32, fol. 6r; JOANNES ANDREAE, *In Primum Decretalium* . . ., *De Summa Trinitate et Fide Catholica*, cap. *Firmiter*, n. 37, fol. 8r.

[221] *Contra Faustum Manichaeum* . . ., Liber 19, cap. 2, loc.cit., col. 347.

[222] Ibid., col. 348.

[223] Sessio IV, *Decretum de canonicis Scripturis*, in *El Sacrosanto y Ecumenico Concilio De Trento*, Madrid, 1798, p.34. "omnes libros tam veteris, quam novi Testamenti, cum utriusque unus Deus sit auctor."

God."[224] This twofold law forms in essence the manifestation of the eternal wisdom to the human creature.

It is, however, difficult to peruse the mind of the Fathers, canonists and civilists regarding the identity of both laws. It is not clear whether these authors are advocating a *distinctio realis* between natural law and divine positive law so as to constitute two categories of law essentially distinct from each other, or whether they consider both laws essentially the same, recognizing, however, a *distinctio formalis* between the two. Saint Ambrose and Saint Augustine seem to adhere to the first hypothesis. According to Ambrose, the reason for the enactment of the Mosaic law was that natural law "was corrupted and blotted out by disobedience";[225] he thus considers the Mosaic law an addition,[226] even a replacement of natural law.[227] Saint Augustine recognizes three types of law essentially distinct from one another, namely, natural, Mosaic, and Evangelical laws.[228] As stated earlier, he even lays down a *distinctio realis* between the Mosaic and the Evangelical law. The views of Eusebius Hieronymus lack clarity; in our opinion he tends to advocate the identical nature of both laws.[229] Azo is much more specific in his views on the identical nature of both laws. He writes: "Natural law is contained both in the Mosaic law and in the law of the Gospel."[230]

---

[224] *Summa Theologica*, Ia-IIae, q. 97, art. 3, resp., *American* . . . , p. 1024.

[225] *Letters, Letter to Irenaeus*, 83 (73), loc. cit., p. 465.

[226] *Seven Exegetical Works, Jacob and the Happy Life*, (6.20), loc.cit., p. 132.

[227] *Letters, Letter to Irenaeus*, 83, (73), loc. cit., p. 467.

[228] *Contra Faustum Manichaeum* . . . , Liber 19, cap. 2, loc. cit., col. 347.

[229] *Commentariorum in Isaiam* . . . , Liber 8, cap. 24, vers. 6, loc. cit., col. 292, "Audiant Iudei, qui se solos legem accepisse Domini gloriantur, quod universae primum gentes totusque orbis naturalem acceperit legem, et idcirco postea lex data sit per Moysen, quia prima lex dissipata est . . . Qui igitur has leges observaverint, praemia consequuntur."

[230] *Summa Institutionum*, Liber I, *De Iure Naturali Gentium et Civili*, p. 348, col. 2. "Item dicitur ius naturale quod in lege mosaica vel in evangelio continetur."

An exhaustive exposition on the subject is found in the *Summa Theologica*. *Inter alia,* Saint Thomas Aquinas writes: "The written law is said to be given for the correction of the natural law, either because it supplies what was wanting to the natural law; or because the natural law was perverted in the hearts of some men, as to certain matters, so that they esteemed those things good which are naturally evil; which perversion stood in need of correction."[231] The logical sequence of this *status quaestionis* has to lead to the admittance of *distinctio realis* between *ius naturale* and *ius divinum.*

In contrast with the view contending a *distinctio realis* between *ius divinum* and *ius naturale,* it is our fundamental stipulation that natural law -- "impressio divini luminis in anima"- could never be so blotted out, corrupted, or perverted, as to be in want of correction; such terms are *contradictio in terminis.* The divine positive law was indeed necessitated by sin; this law should not thereby be considered as an addition, replacement or substitution of natural law. To add, to replace, or to substitute something indicates that the thing is faulty, imperfect, incomplete. There was nothing wanting in natural law itself even after the Fall; the Yahwist man received the glimmer of truth in its fullness, albeit implicitly, as divinely decreed, and he retained it in spite of sin; sin indeed eclipsed the brightness, but the eternal light never faded out in the human heart. The content of the truth, which is the spirit itself, remained integral in itself, by itself, within itself; the inherent eternal law, the spirit itself, was forever the living movement within itself, despite the inner turmoil caused by sin.

The intrinsic validity of natural law remained intact in spite of sin; its authority never diminished. What sin debilitated was the human will, through the awakening of concupiscence, as Antonius A Butrio rightfully points out: "reason fell into captivity and became vulnerable to concupiscence from which sin arises, and the human intellect became

---

[231] Ia-IIae, q.94, art.5, ad 1um, *American* . . . , p.1012; cf. IIa-IIae, q.57, art.2, ad 3um, loc.cit., p. 1432.

captive and subject to the law of concupiscence."²³² No mortal would ever doubt the truthfulness of Our Lord's acclamation: "The spirit is willing but the flesh is weak."²³³ Because of the primordial rebellion, a clarification of natural law and its re-endorsement was necessary. Indeed, in the process of this rejuvenation the divine law was felt as an external imposition on the freedom of the human will,²³⁴ which had become a subjective, individualistic and instinctualistic will.

Divine positive law was not intended to substitute what was deleted, to correct what was imperfectly done, to replace what was perverted, or to add what was wanting in natural law. The reason is simple: natural law and divine positive law are identical in nature; they form essentially one law; they are equally the manifestation of the eternal wisdom of God to the human being; thus natural law enjoys the same intrinsic validity, the same supreme authority, the same inherent irreducibility, the same perennity, as the divine positive law. No distinction between natural law and divine positive law is admissible other than *distinctio formalis*. It has been stated earlier that the Yahwist man received in embryo the eternal truth. The inner destiny of this eternal truth, the spirit itself, was to explicate itself into full humanization of the human consciousness. Sin disrupted this gradual and harmonious unfolding of the innate law of itself into human consciousness. Direct divine intervention was needed to re-endorse what natural law was in substantiality, to crystalize its authenticity, to re-enforce its authority, to heighten its supremacy. Through this outward direction of God, the human consciousness was at the same time invigorated and animated to face its internal turmoil adroitly, was brought into major clarity of itself and of its universal inwardness, and was given the golden

---

[232] *Super Prima Primi Decretalium* . . . , Liber 1, *De Constitutionibus*, prooemium, n. 8, fol. 9r. "quia iam ratione captivata, et concupiscentiae subiecta, a qua peccatum surrexit, et intellectus hominis captivus factus est, et legi concupiscentiae subiectus."

[233] Mk 14:38. "Spiritus promptus est, caro autem infirma."

[234] EUSEBIUS HIERONYMUS, *Commentariorum in Epistolam ad Galatas Libri Tres*, Liber 2, cap. 3, vers. 19, 20, *Opera Omnia*, Tomus 7, P.L., Tomus 26, Parisiis, 1866, col. 392,"sed etiam illa (praecepta) quae per Moysen duro populo quasi jugum legis imposita sunt."

rule to expedite and facilitate its inherent destiny of self-explication and self-meaningfulness; thus it passed from crude being and subjective freedom to moral and ethical existence and objective and absolute freedom of itself within itself -- "so our soul is always in motion, and the more ardent it is, the greater its motion and activity."[235]

Distinctio formalis between *ius divinum* and *ius naturale* is endorsed by reason of their origin as well as by reason of their nature: they constitute essentially the same eternal truth, the same divine law; they express the same primordial idea of God in creating; they are the manifestation of the *causa formalis* of creation, Christ, the Alpha and Omega of creation, whose image finds its most genuine expression in the Yahwist man. *Ius naturale* came out of the divine will *ex ipsa natura rei,* out of intrinsic necessity -- the human being had to be a recipient of natural law if he had to be created in the image of Christ. *Ius divinum* was given *per accidens,* because of sin, as re-invigoration of the one and the same truth instilled in the human heart. Thus, *ius naturale* and *ius divinum* being identical by reason of their nature as well, *ius divinum* may be apprehended as the ontological explicity of what is implicit in natural law. *Ius divinum* indeed constitutes the final realization of natural law in the process of explication of itself. In this sense, *ius divinum* stands out as the ontology, the normativity, the absoluteness and the finality of natural law actualized and translated in human consciousness.

The aim of both natural law and divine positive law is the same; both aim at the absolute fulfillment of the individual human consciousness in the *parousia.* Thus natural law and divine positive law indicate, per se, modes by which God expresses His will to humankind: through natural law God reaches out to the human individual with an innate law identical to all humans; in this manner God sets the universal inwardness of the individual consciousness as the pivotal point in the establishment of profound and universal solidarity among humans, in view of the full achievement of one-mindedness of all in Christ. Through divine positive law God approaches

---

[235] SENECA,L.A., *Epistulae Morales,* Vol IV Epistula 39, n. 3, p. 260. "ita noster animus in motu est, eo mobilior et actuosior quo vehementior fuerit."

the human family as a whole with the sole intent of becoming more intimate with the individual human consciousness, in order that the self unfolds itself more expediently, more authentically as a true semblance of Christ. Thus Christ, through natural law and divine positive law, presents Himself as the tangential point of the individual human consciousness and the universal human consciousness, the converging point of subjective and objective freedom, the equipoise between the irreducible dignity of the human individual and the substantiality of the common good, the finality of the humanization process of both the individual human consciousness and the universal human consciousness.

Ius Humanum
Law as Perceived by the Roman Jurist

An exposition on the theme remains incomplete without, at least, a cursory survey of how the law was defined by the Roman jurist. The influence of Roman law on the philosophy of law, particularly on canon law, down to our times can never be over-estimated. The two most important sources for a comprehensive understanding of law are the *Digesta*, which preserves fragments of the philosophy of law expounded by great jurists of the second century and the early years of the third century, and *Institutiones*, compiled by a commission of lawyers from the Court of Justinian in the sixth century.[236] In both sources, the term *ius humanum* is not used; this term was adopted by Christian writers in order to distinguish human law, whether canonical or civil, from divine law, whether natural or divine positive law. In *Corpus iuris civilis*, the term *ius civile*, or simply *ius*, is used to indicate the *ius humanum* of the Christian writer. Thus in Roman law three categories of law are acknowledged: *ius naturale, ius gentium, ius civile.*

---

[236] Another source of paramount importance in the study of Roman law is the *Corpus*, also known as *Codex*, a collection of imperial constitutions issued during the period from Hadrian to Justinian. Although it is not of as much usefulness for the present theme as the *Digesta* and *Institutiones*, it nevertheless serves as illustration of the principles of law contained in the two other collections.

A distinction must be made between *ius civile* and *lex*, terms which, although intimately related to each other, have specific nuances of their own. *Ius civile* is a more comprehensive term than *lex;* the former constitutes the *genus,* the latter the *species;* the term *ius civile* includes *lex,* but not vice versa.

In line with the central idea of the present study, attention must first be given to the relationship between *ius civile* on one side and *ius naturale* and *ius gentium* on the other, in the context of the Roman philosophy of law. Ulpianus contends that the subordination of *ius civile* to *ius naturale* and *ius gentium* must be maintained in principle, however, with some qualifications. According to him *ius civile* cannot antagonize the two former types of law, but neither is it expected that *ius civile* adapt itself, *in toto,* to them. In the former clause, *ius civile* is said to be an addition, and more correctly, an application of the two superior forms of law to particular circumstances. In the second clause, *ius civile* may sometimes militate against the authority of either one.[237] Without entering into such details, Hermogenianus concurs with the view that *ius civile* is an addition to *ius gentium* in consonance with the exegencies of a particular community.[238] Paulus does not seem to acknowledge any relationship between the two categories of law; his advocacy is for the sovereignty of the *ius civile,* and thereby the law of the State does not recognize a superior authority besides itself. According to him the raison d'être of the law is its usefulness to the welfare of the community as a whole or to the majority of its members; thus *ius civile* results from mere utility and expediency without any consideration of the principle of justice.[239] It is

---

[237] Ulpianus, L. *Ius civile,* 6, D., *De iustitia et iure,* 1, 1, "Ius civile est, quae neque in totum a naturali vel gentium recedit nec per omnia ei servit: itaque cum aliquid addimus vel detrahimus iuri communi, ius proprium, id est civile efficimus"; cf. Ulpianus, L. *Iuri operam,* 1, D., *De iustitia et iure,* 1, 1, §4.

[238] Hermogenianus, L. *Ex hoc,* 5, D., *De iustitia et iure,* 1, 1.

[239] Paulus, L. *Ius pluribus,* 11, D., *De iustitia et iure,* 1, 1, ". . . ius pluribus modis dicitur: . . . altero modo, quod omnibus aut pluribus in quaque civitate utile est, ut est ius civile."

Philosophy of Law

worth noting that this view is the one upheld in today's philosophy of law -- the sovereignty of state laws, "la statualita' del diritto."

As one would expect, *ius naturale* and *ius gentium* belong to the unwritten law, whereas *ius civile* is a written law. With regard to *ius civile*, this was not necessarily so; *ius civile* comprises also unwritten law, known as customary law, which bears the same force as the written law.[240] Under the term *ius civile* were included laws, plebiscites, decrees of the senate, imperial ordinances, and opinions of jurists.[241] To the *ius civile* also pertained *ius honorarium,* or *ius praetorium*.[242] These juridic institutions differed from each other by reason of source and of *ambitus iurisdictionis*. However, philosophically speaking, they are essentially the same since they share the same constitutive elements of the law. And precisely the nature of the law in general, as conceived of by the Roman jurist, is what constitutes our objective.

In the study of the Roman philosophy of law, one cannot disregard two Greek philosophers, Demosthenes and Chrysippus, who contributed considerably to the understanding of law by the Roman jurist. Their definition of law caught the attention of Marcianus because of whom these definitions were included in *Digesta*. In the definition of Demosthenes,[243] three concepts emerge which serve as points of reference in further

---

[240] Inst., *De iure naturali et gentium et civili*, 1, 2, §3; Pomponius, L. *Necessarium*, 2, D., *De origine iuris et omnium magistratuum et successione prudentium*, 1, 2, §5, 12; Ulpianus, L. *Ius civile*, 6, D., *De iustitia et iure*, 1, 1; CICERO,M.T., *De Legibus*, liber 1, cap. 15, n. 42, loc. cit., p. 1207.

[241] Papinianus, L. *Ius autem*, 7, D., *De iustitia et iure*, 1, 1, "Ius autem civile est, quod ex legibus, plebis scitis, senatus consultis, decretis principum, auctoritate prudentium venit."

[242] This type of law may rightly be called *iurisprudentia praetorialis*. The praetor was empowered to give a decision based on natural equity when an express provision of the law was lacking, or even to correct the law -- Papinianus, L. *Ius autem*, 7, D., *De iustitia et iure*, 1, 1, §1; Marcianus, L. *Nam*, 8, loc. cit; Inst., *De legitima adgnatorum successione*, 3, 2, §3a, §7.

[243] Marcianus, L. *Nam et*, 2, D., *De legibus senatusque consultis et longa consuetudine*, 1,3. "Haec lex est, cui omnes homines convenit obtemperare cum propter alia pleraque tum maxime, quod omnis lex inventum est et donum dei, placitum vero sapientium hominum coercitioque peccatorum tam voluntariorum quam non voluntariorum, civitatis autem pactum commune, secundum quod convenit vivere quicunque in ea sunt."

development of this study: law is the gift of God, *donum dei,* and thereby law is considered as a particular application of the principles of universal reason and justice; law is the product of the wisdom of the community; law binds all members of the community for the correction of offences. Chrysippus[244] speaks of the law as the queen of divine and human knowledge; law is said to be the leader and teacher of anything that pertains to the social nature of the human being; it thereby constitutes the norm or standard of what is just or unjust. Both authors concur in envisaging law as the result and at the same time the re-enforcement of the sociability of human consciousness. Any interpretation of what Chrysippus meant by law being the queen of divine and human knowledge remains highly speculative. If by this Chrysippus meant that human law is the result of *recta ratio,* which for its part reflects eternal wisdom and so ought to be acknowledged as queen of divine and human knowledge, his understanding of law in its substantiality does not differ from that of Demosthenes. In this case, both definitions allude to a superior and divine law from which human law traces its origin and to which it is subordinate; both lend themselves to the apprehension of human law as the interpretation and implementation of supreme, divine will manifested through the law inherent to human consciousness.

Cicero belongs also to this school. He acknowledges the validity of human law insofar as it is based on the absolute and unchangeable principle of justice. The mind of Cicero on the score has been exposed earlier. It may be re-iterated that justice, in his opinion, is the manifestation of eternal wisdom implanted in the human being. Human law, being the reflection and deduction of this eternal law, is defined as "right reason commanding or prohibiting, a reason when ignored renders the person unjust."[245] On this presupposition, Cicero stands very forcefully against the

---

[244] Ibid. "Lex est omnium regina rerum divinarum humanarumque, oportet autem praeesse eam tam bonis quam malis, et ducem et magistram esse animalium quae natura civilia esse voluit, indeque normam esse iusti et iniusti, quae iubeat fieri facienda, vetet fieri non facienda."

[245] *De Legibus,* Liber 1, cap. 15, n. 42, loc.cit., p. 1207: "recta ratio imperandi atque prohibendi: quam qui ignorat, is est iniustus"; cf.*De Re Publica,* Liber 3, cap. 22, n.33.16, loc. cit., p. 1193.

opinion of those jurists, like Paulus, who maintain that expediency and convenience of those in power are the raison d'être for the justification of a law.[246]

The majority of Roman jurists seems to ignore any relationship between *ius humanum* and *ius divinum,* and thereby denies any subordination of the former to the latter. This is not to say that for them the law does not emerge from the sociability of the human consciousness and that it does not reflect l'esprit de corps, the actual universal human consciousness. One can easily peruse this doctrine in the definition of law given by Gaius: "Lex est quod populus iubet atque constituit" (Law is that which the people order and establish).[247] According to him, the community is the primordial source of law in the State. Any law, whatever its proximate origin, assumes its validity ultimately from the authority of the people. In like manner, the law is defined by Papinianus. He defines law as a precept binding all members of the community, enacted by the common consort of wise men in defense against abuses for the guarantee of the Republic.[248] In different terms the same notion of law is fostered by *Institutiones:* "Lex est, quod populus Romanus senatore magistratu interrogante, veluti consule, constituebat."[249]

Other statements are found, particularly in *Institutiones,* which are extremely useful in formulating a wholesome notion of law. The power of law, as Modestinus points out, is to order, prohibit, permit, or to punish.[250]

---

[246] *De Legibus,* Liber 1, cap. 15, n. 42, loc.cit., p.1207, "Ita fit, ut nulla sit omnino iustitia, si neque natura est, et ea, quae propter utilitatem constituitur, utilitate alia convellitur."

[247] *Institutionum Gai Commentarius Primus,* Titulus, *De iure civili et naturali,* §3, in *Institutionum et Regularum Iuris Romani Syntagma,* edidit Rudolphus Gneist, Lipsiae, 1880, p. 7; cf. §1, p.6; Gaius, L. *Omnes,* 9, D., *De Iustitia et iure,* 1, 1.

[248] Papinianus, L. *lex est,* 1, D., *De legibus senatusque consultis et longa consuetudine,* 1, 3, "Lex est commune praeceptum, virorum prudentium consultum, delictorum quae sponte vel ignorantia contrahuntur coercitio, communis rei publicae sponsio."

[249] Inst. *De iure naturali et gentium et civili,* 1, 2, §4.

[250] Modestinus, L. *Legis,* 7, D., *De legibus senatusque consultis et longa consuetudine,* 1, 3. "Legis virtus haec est imperare vetare permittere punire."

The power of law, *legis virtus*, is not limitless; its authority should remain within the limits of reasonableness and moderation; thus, the severity of the law can be corrected by the *praetor*.[251] The jurisdiction of the law embraces all members of the community equally, without discrimination. In this manner, the law leads to the attainment of the common good in absolute manner.[252] By the very fact that law is the product of l'esprit de corps in view of its own guarantee, stability should form an integral part of the nature of the law. This characteristic of the law, however, should not be understood in an absolute manner; just as much as human consciousness, expressed in l'esprit de corps, by its inherent destiny is forever in a forward march of self-discovery and self-humanization, so the law, the authentic expression of l'esprit de corps, by its intrinsic necessity is destined to develop apace with the humanization process of human consciousness. All allusion to this is found in the *Institutiones:* "That which the social community establishes for itself is bound to change either by the consent of the same community or by a subsequent law enacted on the same subject matter."[253]

Ius Humanum in Christian Philosophy of Law

Ius humanum is a term introduced by Christian writers to indicate human law in distinction to *ius divinum*, whereas the term *ius civile* is meant to signify State law as opposed to ecclesiastical law, known also as canonical law.

---

[251] Inst., *De legitima adgnatorum successione*, 3, 2, §3a, §7.

[252] Impp. Theodosius et Valentinianus, L. *Leges*, 3, C., *De legibus et constitutionibus principum et edictis*, 1, 14.

[253] Inst., *De iure naturali et gentium et civili* 1, 2, §11. ". . . ea vero quae ipsa sibi quaeque civitas constituit, saepe mutari solent vel tacito consensu populi vel alia postea lege lata."

Ius Civile

The study of *ius humanum* suggests a partition of the theme into two sub-headings. Our attention is first focussed on *ius civile* in the context of Christian philosophy of law. Our second enquiry will concentrate on *ius ecclesiasticum*. In reference to *ius civile*, we intend to expound the presentation in three main segments, namely the subordination of *ius civile* to *ius divinum;* the reason for and the purpose of civil law; the nature of civil law.

A general consensus seems to have prevailed among the patristic Fathers that a certain continuity exists between *iustitia divina* and *iustitia humana*, between *ius divinum* and *ius civile*, between God and the temporal ruler. The relatedness of these two types of law posits the question as to whether civil law should be considered subordinate to divine law, whether natural or divine positive law. An impressive majority of the Fathers denies to human law absolute supremacy. Such denial necessarily implies that human law can never be acknowledged as a source of justice.

The continuity between the two types of law, and more so the subordination of civil law to divine law, fostered by patristic literature has already been discussed in general in the section on the meaning of justice. It appeared then quite clearly that the main thrust of the patristic doctrine referred to the belief that no comunity can survive, and no law enjoys binding force, unless the configuration itself of the community and its laws trace their roots in eternal justice. The patristic doctrine on the subject is magisterially synthetized in the statement of Saint Augustine: "I think that you also see that it is from this eternal law that men have obtained whatever is just and lawful in the temporal law."[254] He insists that the State "can in no way exist without justice,"[255] and he forcefully denounces "the falsity of the view that the State cannot be governed without

---

[254] *De Libero Arbitrio Libri Tres*, Liber I, cap.6, n.15, *Opera Omnia*, Tomus I, P.L., Tomus 32, col. 1229. "Simul etiam te videre arbitror in illa temporali nihil esse justum atque legitimum, quod non ex hac aeterna sibi homines derivarint."

[255] *The City of God*, Bk II, chap. 21, *Fathers of the Church*, p. 107.

86   Readings on Canon Law

injustice, and, secondly, [insists upon] the solidity of the truth that it cannot be governed without absolute justice."[256] Saint Ambrose expresses the same idea succinctly when he writes "the justice of the law does not derive from the mere existence of the law; rather the law flows from justice."[257] John of Salisbury bases the distinction between a tyrant and a prince worthy of the name precisely on this same doctrine.[258] In addition, he states: "Censure of human laws would have been futile had human laws not been a reflection of divine law; and human ordinances would have been devoid of meaning unless they conformed with the laws of the Church."[259] In the estimation of Clement of Alexandria, the worst thing that can befall a State is that the promptings of the ruler's passions overrun justice.[260] According to Catulfus, Civil rule must be based on jusctice as contained in the gospel.[261] Identical doctrine is advocated by Sanctus Irenaeus,[262] S.

---

[256] Ibid; cf. loc.cit., Bk 19, chap.21, p. 232; *De Vera Religione -- Liber Unus*, cap. 31, n.58, *Opera Omnia*, Tomus III, P.L., Tomus 34, col. 148; *De Libero Arbitrio Libri Tres*, Liber I, cap. 6, n.14, loc.cit., col.1229; *Expositio quarumdam propositionum ex epistola ad Romanos -- Liber Unus*, LXXII, *Opera Omnia*, Tomus III, P.L., Tomus 35, col. 2083; *In Psalmum CXLV Enarratio* (Sermo ad plebem), n.15, *Opera Omnia*, Tomus IV, pars altera, Tomus 37, Parisiis, 1841, col. 1894.

[257] *Expositio Evangelii secundum Lucam Libris X Comprehensa*, Liber V, cap.5, n. 21, *Opera Omnia*, Tomus I, pars posterior, P.L., Tomus 15, col. 1726: "Est igitur in lege justitia, sed non est per legem justitia"; cf. *Letters, Letter to Valentinian*, (21), 9, *Fathers of the Church*, vol.26, p.54; *De Officiis Ministrorum Libri Tres*, Liber I, cap. 28, n. 136, *Opera Omnia*, Tomus II, P.L., Tomus 16, col. 67.

[258] *Polycraticus sive de Nugis Curialium et Vestigiis Philosophorum*, Liber IV, cap. 1, *Opera Omnia*, Tomus Unicus, P.L., Tomus 199, col. 513; loc.cit., Liber VIII, cap. 17, col. 777.

[259] Loc.cit., Liber IV, cap. 6, coll. 522-523. "Omnium legum inanis est censura, si non divinae legis imaginem gerat; et inutilis est constitutio principis, si non ecclesiasticae disciplinae sit conformis."

[260] *The Miscellanies (Stromata)*, vol. 1, Bk 1, chap.24, *Ante-Nicene Christian Library*, vol. 4, pp.455-456.

[261] *Instructio Epistolaris ad Beatum Carolum Regem*, Tomus Unicus, P.L., Tomus 96, col. 1364.

[262] *Contra Haereses Libri Quinque*, Liber V, cap. 24, n.2, Tomus Unicus, P.G., Tomus 7, Parisiis, 1857, col. 1187.

Hieronymus,[263] S. Isidorus,[264] Ivo Carnotiensis,[265] Hincmarus Rhemensis,[266] and Sedulius Scotus.[267] Nobody in his right senses can deny the truth of the Augustinian statement: "In the absence of justice, what is sovereignty but organized brigandage?"[268] Saint Ambrose joins in with the remark that "the petty, occult stealing of the slave has its counterpart in the public pillage of the wealthy."[269]

In discussing the concept of law, one cannot entirely dismiss its correlation with the concept of authority. A correct and complete understanding of one reality cannot be acquired without the other. However, the topic of authority is intentionally left to a later part of the study, with the exception of some reference to the subject when necessary.

In the question on the raison d'être and the purpose of civil law, a stream of thought among the patristic Fathers runs counter to the central idea of the present thesis. Some, like Sanctus Irenaeus, express a pessimistic view of human nature; they see nothing in human nature other than indomitable corruption which can only be curbed by fear of the sword; the human being is a vicious creature who obeys only with secret malice, and waits in silence ready to burst out in rebellion. Upon this

---

[263] *Commentariorum in Epistolam ad Galatas Libri Tres,* Liber III, cap.5, vers.11, *Opera Omnia,* Tomus VII, P.L., Tomus 26, col. 440.

[264] *Etymologiarum Libri XX,* Liber V, cap. 3, n.4, *Opera Omnia,* Tomus III, P.L., Tomus 82, col. 199.

[265] *Decretum,* Pars IV, cap.178, *Opera Omnia,* Tomus I, P.L., Tomus 161, col. 306.

[266] *De Divortio Lotharii Regis et Tetbergae Reginae,* Quaestio VI, *Opera Omnia,* Tomus Prior, P.L., Tomus 125, Parisiis, 1879, col. 757; *Expositiones ad Carolum Regem pro Ecclesiae Libertatem Defensione,* Expositio I, *Opera Omnia,* Tomus Prior, P.L., Tomus 125, col. 1055; *Ad Proceres Regni, pro Institutione Carolomanni Regis et de Ordine Palatii,* cap. 9, *Opera Omnia,* Tomus Prior, P.L., tomus 125, coll. 996-997; *De Coercendo et Exstirpando Raptu Viduarum, Puellarum ac Sanctimonialium* cap. 12, *Opera Omnia* Tomus Prior, loc.cit., col.1026.

[267] *Liber de Rectoribus Christianis ad Carolum Magnum vel Ludovicum Pium,* cap. II, *Opera Omnia,* Tomus unicus, P.L., Tomus 103, Parisiis, 1851, col. 295.

[268] *The City of God,* Bk 4, chap. 4, *Fathers of the Church,* p. 195: "Remota itaque justitia, quid sint regna nisi magna latrocinia?"

[269] *De Officiis Ministrorum Libri Tres,* Liber III, cap. 3, n. 22, *Opera Omnia,* Tomus II, pars prior, P.L., Tomus 16, col. 160. "servorum tamen occulta furta, divitum rapinae publicae."

presupposition, they peruse the reason and purpose of authoritative power and of the law. In such a degrading conception of human nature, one can comprehend why authoritative power was coined *gladius*. "For since man," writes Saint Irenaeus, "by departing from God, reached such a pitch of fury as even to look upon his brother as his enemy, and engaged without fear in every kind of restless conduct, and murder, and avarice; God imposed upon mankind the fear of man, as they did not acknowledge the fear of God, in order that, being subjected to the authority of men, and kept under restraint by their laws, they might attain to some degree of justice, and exercise mutual forbearance through dread of the sword suspended full in their view."[270] Pope Silvester II,[271] Optatus Afri. Milevitanus,[272] Flaccus Albinus[273] share the same views. Saint Ambrose speaks of the authority of rulers as an imposition by God on the foolish man, and of the law as bridle for his unruliness;[274] "The law is not made for the just but for the unjust."[275] To this group also belong Sanctus Isidorus and Hincmarus Rhemensis. According to the former, "Laws are made so that in fear of them human audacity may be curbed, human innocence be safeguarded from the impious, and a criminal intention be refrained for fear of punishment."[276] The latter joins in by stating "The law is not enacted for

---

[270] *Against Heresies*, Bk 5, Chap.24, n.2, Trans. Alexander Roberts and W.H. Rambaut, vol. II, *Ante-Nicene Christian Library*, vol. 9, Edinburgh, 1880, pp. 119-120.

[271] *Epistola XI ad Monasteria Stabulense et Malmundartense, Opera Omnia*, Tomus unicus, P.L., Tomus 139, Parisiis, 1880, coll. 282-283.

[272] *De Schismate Donatistarum adversus Parmenianum*, Liber III, cap. 3, *Opera Omnia*, Tomus Unicus, P.L., Tomus 11, Parisiis, 1845, coll.1001-1002.

[273] *Dialogus de Rhetorica et Virtutibus, Opera Omnia*, Tomus II P. L., Tomus 101, coll. 920-921.

[274] *Letters, Letter to Simplicianus*, 54 (37), *The Fathers of the Church*, vol. 26, p. 288.

[275] Ibid., p. 292.

[276] *Etymologiarum Libri XX*, Liber V, cap. 20, n.1, *Opera Omnia*, Tomus III, P.L., Tomus 82, col. 202: "Factae sunt leges ut earum metu humana coerceatur audacia, tutaque sit inter improbos innocentia, et in ipsis improbis, formidato supplicio, refrenetur nocendi facultas"; cf. *Sententiarum Libri Tres*, Liber III, cap.47, nn. 1, 3, *Opera Omnia*, Tomus VI, P.L., Tomus 83, Parisiis, 1862, col. 717.

the just, but for the unjust, for the unruly, the impious and the sinners."[277]

Other Fathers look upon human nature in a more dignified, humane, and positive manner; they recognize the nobility of human nature and extol its potentiality for self-betterment in spite of its sinfulness. Thus they look at law as a means which by its nature leads human consciousness towards self-fulfillment; only by exception does it become an instrument of subjugation of human freedom and destruction of human life. Although he argues strongly for the death penalty, Clement of Alexandria sees law, in principle, in this light: "For the law, in its solicitude for those who obey, trains us to piety, and prescribes what is to be done, and restrains each one from sins, imposing penalties even on lesser sins."[278] For Saint Augustine, the reason for the law to be is the very sociability of human consciousness. The law is there in order that human nature explicate its "capacity for friendship as a great and natural good."[279] No other expression reveals more clearly the mind of Augustine than the following: "Who is so blind as not to see that the human race is a distinguished ornament for the earth even when only a few men live good and praiseworthy lives, and that public order is of great importance when it keeps even sinners within the limits set by a certain kind of earthly peace?"[280] With this view concur Sedulius Scotus,[281] Joannis

---

[277] *De Divortio Lotharii Regis et Tetbergae Reginae*, Quaestio VI, loc. cit., col. 757. "Lex non est posita justo, sed injustis, et non subditis, impiis et peccatoribus, sceleratis."

[278] *The Miscellanies, (Stromata)*, vol.1, Bk.1, Chap.27, loc.cit., vol.4, p.464; cf. p.465.

[279] *The Good of Marriage, (De Bono Coniugali)*, Chap.1, Trans Charles T. Wilcox, *The Fathers of the Church*, vol.27, New York, 1955, p.9.

[280] *De Genesi ad Litteram Libri Duodecim*, Liber IX, cap.9, *Opera Omnia*, Tomus III, P.L., Tomus 34, col. 398: ; cf. *De Libero Arbitrio Libri Tres*, Liber I, cap.6, nn.14,15, *Opera Omnia*, Tomus I, P.L., Tomus 32, col.1229; *Expositio Quarumdam Propositionum ex Epistola ad Romanos, Liber Unus*, LXXII, *Opera Omnia*, Tomus III, P.L., Tomus 35, coll.2083-2084; *The City of God*, Bk 19, chap.12, *Fathers of the Church*, vol. 24, p.215.

[281] *Liber de Rectoribus Christianis ad Carolum Magnum vel Ludovicum Pium*, Caput II, *Opera Omnia*, Tomus unicus, P.L., Tomus 103, col.296.

Saresberiensis,[282] according to whom law is "a gift of God, dogma for the wise, correction of the arbitrariness of the will, foundation of the community, and a remedy for all crimes,"[283] and Magnus Aurelius Cassiodorus, who acknowledges laws as "solace to human life, assistance to the weak, restraint of the powerful."[284]

The subject of the nature of the law in the patristic literature has already been introduced with the exposition on the reason and purpose of the law. There remains, however, the gist of the issue, namely the understanding of the nature of law, as such, as viewed by the patristic Fathers. With the exception of Sanctus Isidorus,[285] Ivo Carnotensis[286] and few others, there is a general and total disregard among the Fathers for the Roman philosophy of law.[287] Such definitions, "Ius civile est, quod quisque populus, vel civitas sibi proprium, humana divinaque causa constituit,"[288] and "Lex est constitutio populi, qua majores natu simul cum plebibus aliquid sanxerunt"[289] are completely alien to the patristic literature. In contrast to the Roman doctrine, the law is not conceived of as the authentic expression of l'esprit de corps, as the deliberate and

---

[282] *Polycraticus sive de Nugis Curialium et Vestigiis Philosophorum*, Liber IV, cap.2, *Opera Omnia*, Tomus unicus, P.L., Tomus 199, coll.514-515.

[283] Ibid., col.515. "donum Dei, dogma sapientum, correctio voluntariorum excessuum, civitatis compositio et totius criminis fuga."

[284] *Variarum Libri Duodecim*, Liber III, epistola 17, *Opera Omnia*, Tomus Prior, P.L., Tomus 69, col. 585. "humanae vitae solatia, infirmorum auxilia, potentum frena."

[285] *Etymologiarum Libri XX*, Liber V, in toto, *Opera Omnia*, Tomus III, P.L., Tomus 82, coll. 198-203.

[286] *Decretum*, Pars IV, capp. 168, 169, 194, *Opera Omnia*, Tomus I, P.L., Tomus 161, coll. 303-308.

[287] Cicero and Seneca were the most respected by the Fathers. Cicero had a tremendous influence on Saint Augustine.

[288] *Etymologiarum Libri XX*, loc. cit., Liber V, cap. 5, n.1, col. 199.

[289] Ibid., Liber V, cap.10, n.1, col. 200.

conscious will of the *populus* in whom legislative authority primordially resides. Law was no longer considered as the human consciousness bound together by virtue of the sociability of human nature into one-mindedness. The theory of the condescending theocratic form of government, so vigorously inculcated by the patristic literature, despised the masses. Civil authority is of divine institution; it is bestowed directly by God upon his anointed -- "quaedam divinae majestatis imago" (a certain image of divine majesty),[290] "quia quidquid est supra homines, jam quasi Deus est" (because whoever stands above human beings is already almost God).[291] The monarch thus was acclaimed the "pater omnibus sapientior," and *hoi polloi* became his supposedly beloved children. In correlation to the paternalistic figure of the monarch, the concept of *potestas iurisdictionis*, which had reached an astounding stage of clarity in Roman law, assumed quite noticeable nuances of *potestas dominativa*. By force of logic, the concept of law had to accommodate itself to this juridic vision of authority; thus law was rather envisaged as a precept; observance of the law turned into filial obedience to a paternal surrogate. "Consensus populi" was not required; indeed, it did not exist. There was only one mind, the most perfect, the most knowledgeable, the most wise, and one will, the most absolute among humans -- this was the monarch, God's anointed. The theory of absolute monarchy found its full meaning in the well-known assertion: "Quod principi placuit, legis habet vigorem" (the wish of the ruler has the force of law).[292] Rather than intrinsically flowing from the sociability of human nature, law was perceived as the result of sin, an external imposition upon a rebellious human nature. Thus Saint Ambrose concludes that God, the God of love, places the monarch, addressed by antonomasia the "Wise," to subjugate the foolishness of the crowd; the plebeian, fool and unruly, must

---

[290] IOANNIS SARESBERIENSIS, *Polycraticus sive de Nugis Curialium et Vestigiis Philosophorum*, Liber IV, cap. 1, *Opera Omnia*, Tomus unicus, P.L., Tomus 199, col. 513.

[291] OPTATUS AFRI. MILEVITANUS, *De Schismate Donatistarum adversus Parmenianum*, Liber III, cap. 3, *Opera Omnia*, Tomus unicus, P.L., Tomus 11, col. 1003.

[292] Inst., *De Iure Naturali et Gentium et Civili*, 1, 2, §6.

be denied liberty and live by the sword of the wise.[293] For this reason, the fundamental assumption in the understanding of the nature of the law accepted by some of the Fathers was that the law is given to the unjust, and not to the just; the law is there not because human nature is a rational, conscientious, and social creature, but because man is a dangerous brute to be kept in check by the sword.

The same repertoire of views on *ius civile* is encountered among canonists and civilists. In conjunction with the previous exposition on the principle of justice, one is bound to expect an over-riding opinion defending the supremacy of divine law over human law. The following excerpt from *Decretum Gratiani* illustrates the common opinion on the subject: "Natural law surpasses in dignity custom and human ordinances. Therefore any norm of law introduced through usage or by enactment of the ruler which goes against natural law should be held useless and void."[294]

No jurist of either school, as far as we know, has ever promoted the doctrine that human nature is intrinsically evil, devoid of inner potentiality for self-amelioration. Nevertheless, in their doctrine a humanity is projected which seems to be still operating in a stage of savagery; it needs therefore to be brought to submission. Upon this assumption, any philosophy of law, to be valid and coherent, must fundamentally relate to human tragedy caused by sin. In this perspective, law is thus necessarily conceived of as subjugation intended to curtail the unruliness of the human will which is, if

---

[293] *Letters, Letter to Simplicianus*, 54 (37), *The Fathers of the Church*, vol. 26, p. 288.

[294] Pars I, Dist. VIII, II pars: "Dignitate vero ius naturale simpliciter prevalet consuetudini et constitutioni. Quecumque enim vel moribus recepta sunt, vel scriptis comprehensa, si naturali iuri fuerint adversa, vana et irrita sunt habenda"; cf. Pars I, Dist. I, c.5, §2; Pars I, Dist. V, I pars, §1,2; Pars I, Dist. VI, c. 3, §1; Pars I, Dist. X, II pars; ALBERICUS DE ROSATE, *Dictionarium*, v. *Lex*, pp. 422, 423, 424, 425; BALDUS UBALDI, *In Decretalium Volumen . . . Super Primo Decretalium, De Constitutionibus*, cap. 1, *Canonum*, n. 66, fol. 11 v; *Consiliorum sive Responsorum Volumen Quartum*, Venetiis, 1575, cons. 19, n.3, fol. 8r; ANTONIUS A BUTRIO, *Super Prima Primi . . .*, Tomus I, *De Consuetudine*, cap.11, *Cum tanto*, n. 25, fol. 79r; n.13, fol. 80r; *In Librum Quartum Decretalium Commentarii Sextus Tomus*, Venetiis, 1578, *De Secundis Nuptiis*, cap. 4, *Super illa*, n. 3, fol. 63 v; AZO, *Summa super Codicem*, liber IV, *De Usuris*, p. 141, col. 2; PLACENTINUS, *In Summam Institutionum sive Elementorum . . .*, Liber I, tit. 2, *De Iure Naturali Gentium et Civili*, p.3; CYNUS, *In Digesti Veteris Libros . . .*, Rubrica I, *De Iustitia et Iure*, n. 2, fol. 3r.

not intrinsically, at least, highly prone to evil.[295] It must be pointed out that it is not always easy to decipher where a particular author stands on the matter; in one place he might appear cherishing a positive understanding of human nature, believing in its inner strength and ability to unfold its inherent authenticity, only to contradict himself in another place.[296] There are others, however, who are more explicit and coherent in their affirmation of the inherent goodness of human nature; although weakened by sin, human consciousness never lost sight of its immanent, eternal law and was never deprived of its ability to improve itself and to become morally what it is ontologically; thus the human being is acknowledged as a social being in the full sense of the word. Upon this assumption, these authors understood the nature of the law. To this group belong Placentinus,[297] Cynus Pistoriensis[298] and most of all Albericus De

---

[295] *Decretum, Pars I, Dist. IV*, c.1, I pars: "Causa vero constitutionis legum est humanam cohercere audaciam et nocendi facultatem refrenare"; HENRICUS DE SEGUSIO, *In Primum Decretalium . . .* , prooemium, §*Rex*, n.21, fol. 4r; Loc. cit., *De Maioritate et Obedientia*, cap. 6, *Solitae*, n. 3, fol. 170 v; *In Quintum Decretalium Librum Commentaria*, Venetiis, 1581, *De privilegiis et Excessibus Privilegiatorum*, cap. 2, *Sicut*, nn. 6, 7, fol. 79v; BALDUS UBALDI, *In Decretalium Volumen . . .* , *Super Primo Decretalium, De Electione et Electi Potestate*, cap. 62, *Quia Propter*, n. 15, fol. 81r.

[296] This seems to be the case with Azo. In *Summa super Codicem* he does not seem to have much trust in human nature (Liber I, *Incipit Materia ad Codicem*, p. 1, col. 2; p. 2, col.1), whereas in *Summa Institutionum* he seems to recognize implicitly a potentiality in human nature for self-improvement: "Unde et leges dicuntur sacratissime boni et equi notitiam profitentur equum ab iniquo seperantes licitum ab illicito discernentes bonos non solum metu penarum verum etiam premiorum exortatione efficere cupientes" (Liber I, *De Iustitia et Iure*, p. 347, col. 2). We find the same problem with Antonius A Butrio: in one place he talks on "crescente malitia, cupiditas effrenata" of humans (*Super Prima Primi Decretalium . . .* , Tomus I, Liber I, *De Constitutionibus*, prooemium, n. 4, fol. 8v; cf. Loc. cit., Liber I, *De Constitutionibus*, cap. 4, *Nam concupiscentiam*, nn. 6, 15, fol. 12 v; loc. cit., Tomus II, *De Officio Ordinarii*, cap. 8, *Ad reprimendam*, n. 18, fol. 74 v.); in another place, however, he has this to say: "Nota quod inter homines est quoddam foedus, et quaedam naturalis obligatio ex charitate procedens, ut velit pacem, et alterius odiat molestationem, et velit in alium, quod appetit in se" (Loc. cit., Liber I, prooemium, cap. *Rex pacificus*, n. 7, fol. 4 v.). To this group belongs Ioannes Andreae; cf. *In Primum Decretalium Librum . . .* , prooemium, *Rex*, n. 12, fol. 5r; loc.cit., *De Constitutionibus*, cap. *Postquam*, n. 2, fol. 11r; *In Secundum Decretalium Librum . . .* , *De Foro Competenti*, cap. 12, *Si diligenti*, n.19, fol. 23r.

[297] *In Summam Institutionum sive Elementorum . . .* , Liber I, tit. 1, *De Iustitia et iure*, p. 1.

[298] *In Digesti Veteris Libros . . .* , prooemium, n. 8, fol. 2 v; Rubrica 1, *De Iustitia et Iure*, n. 6, fol. 3 v.

Rosate.²⁹⁹ A definition of law more descriptive than the ones given by John of Salisbury and by Magnus Aurelius Cassiodorus is found in his *Dictionarium*, a definition which indeed reveals the author's understanding of law: "Law is a gift of God, a form of equity, a norm of justice, an image of divine will, custodian of relations among persons, alliance of peoples, a rule for duties, extermination of criminal behaviour, penalty for violence and many types of injury."³⁰⁰

The Roman definition of law, in which *populus* is acknowledged as the source of law, is still retained in canonical and civilistic literature.³⁰¹ It remains, however, extremely difficult for us to relate such a definition with a philosophy of law advocating a condescending theocratic form of government. In the time of the Empire, and before the Peace of Constantine, the emperor enjoyed incontestable and absolute powers of authority. This notwithstanding, the juridic doctrine never did lose sight of the assumption that the ruling power of the emperor was handed over

---

299 *Dictionarium* . . . , v. *Lex*, p. 422, "finis quem intendit lex humana, est pax humani generis"; "ut proinde humanae societatis conciliatio, tuta pacis tranquillitate sub custodia iustitiae laetaretur."

300 Ibid. Albericus mentions *Inventarium Universi Orbis* of Aristotle as the source of this definition. It is apparent that John of Salisbury availed himself of this same source. "lex est donum Dei: aequitatis forma: norma iustitiae: imago divinae voluntatis: custodia salutis: unio populorum: regula officiorum: exterminatio vitiorum violentiae et totius iniuriae poena."

301 *Decretum Gratiani*, Pars I, Dist. I, c. 8, "Ius civile est, quod quisque populus vel civitas sibi proprium divina humanaque causa constituit"; Pars I, Dist. II, c.1, "Lex est constitutio populi, qua maioresnatu simul cum plebibus aliquid sanxerunt"; Pars I, Dist. I, c.1 (Gratianus), "nomine vero legis humanae mores iure conscripti et traditi intelligantur"; IOANNES ANDREAE, *In Primum Decretalium Librum* . . . , *De Constitutionibus, Quae in ecclesiarum*, nn. 26, 27, fol. 15r; loc. cit., *De Consuetudine*, cap. 11, *Cum tanto*, n. 42, fol. 61r; ALBERICUS DE ROSATE, *Dictionarium* . . . , v. *Lex*, p. 423; ANTONIUS A BUTRIO, *Super Prima Primi Decretalium* . . . , Tomus I, Liber I, *De Constitutionibus*, prooemium, n. 9, fol. 9r; AZO, *Summa Super Codicem*, Liber I, *De legibus et Constitutionibus Principum et Edictis*, p. 8, col. 2; *Summa Institutionum*, Liber I, *De Iure Naturali Gentium et Civili*, p. 348, col. 2; loc. cit., Liber II, *De Rerum Divisione et Acquisitione*, p. 353, col. 2; PLACENTINUS, *In Summam Institutionum sive Elementorum* . . . , Liber I, tit. II, *De Iure Naturali Gentium, et Civili*, p. 3; CYNUS PISTORIENSIS, *In Digesti Veteris Libros* . . . , Rubrica III, *De Legi. et Sena. et Long. Consu.*, nn. 12, 13, 14, foll. 7 v -- 8r; Rubrica XIV, *De Officio Praetoris*, n. 6, fol. 13 v.

Philosophy of Law 95

initially by the people; thus *populus* remained, at least in theory, as the recognized ultimate source of law. This Roman doctrine came in open confrontation with Christian philosophy which acclaimed the ruler God's representative on earth whose authority comes directly from God: "Note from this law that laws consider the emperor God, or a divine person, and rightly so since the ruling power comes from God";[302] "Legislators received the power of enacting laws from God";[303] "Laws are divinely promulgated through the mouth of the prince";[304] "The emperor is the living law on this earth, he is the father and the soul of the law";[305] consequently, "Since the emperor is the source of justice, and the fountain from which rights emerge, it is impossible that his laws could ever be considered unjust."[306]

This confrontation between the two positions becomes even sharper when one relates the Roman understanding of law with the contention of those who express serious reservations on the humanness of human nature. Depending on the vision one cherishes of human nature, not only the

---

[302] CYNUS PISTORIENSIS, *In Digesti Veteris Libros* . . . , Rubrica IV, *De Constitutionibus Principum*, n.1, fol. 8r: "Nota ex lege ista, quod iura reputant Imperatorem Deum, seu personam divinam, et hoc merito: quia imperium est a Deo"; cf. *In Codicem Commentaria*, Francoforti ad Moenum, 1578, Liber I, tit. 2, *De Sacrosancta Ecclesia*, n. 3, fol. 6r.

[303] ALBERICUS DE ROSATE, *Dictionarium* . . . , v. *lex*, p. 419. "Leges proferendi licentiam acceperunt a Deo legislatores."

[304] CYNUS PISTORIENSIS, *In Digesti Veteris Libros* . . . , prooemium, n.9, fol.2v: "Item per ora Principum leges divinitus promulgatae sunt"; cf. HENRICUS DE SEGUSIO, *In Secundum Decretalium Librum* . . . , *De Iureiurando*, cap. 30, *Nimis*, n. 3, fol. 137r; IOANNES ANDREAE, *In Secundum Decretalium* . . . , *De Iureiurando*, cap. 30, *Nimis*, n. 2, fol. 199r. However, in another work Cynus seems to contradict himself. He states: "Et decretum dicit, quod leges sunt divinitus, etc. sed de hoc derident nos laici, arguendo sic. Aut dicis, quod leges sunt factae a Deo immediate, et hoc est falsum de legibus civilibus: aut dicis quod mediate, et tunc idem est in quibuscunque rebus . . . ," *In Codicem Commentaria*, Liber VII, tit. 33, *De Praescriptione longi Temporis decem vel viginti Anno*, n. 2, fol. 444 v.

[305] ALBERICUS DE ROSATE, *Dictionarium* . . . , v. *Lex*, p. 421. "Lex animata est Imperator in terra . . . et est pater legum et anima."

[306] BALDUS UBALDI, *Consiliorum, Sive Responsorum Volumen Tertium*, cons. 359, n. 5, fol. 101 v: "Nam cum Imperator sit fons iustitiae, et fons orientali unde iura oriuntur, impossibile est, quod oriantur iniuriae"; cf. ANTONIUS A BUTRIO, *In Sextum Decretalium Volumen* . . . , *De Constitutionibus*, cap. 1, *Licet Romanus*, n. 49, fol. 3r.

definition of law, but also the nature of authority, assume a corresponding conceptualization. If human nature requires the law to protect itself from itself, authority, by force of logic, is understood by the Christian philosophy as a reality external to human consciousness itself, a supra-imposition caused by sin, an indispensable tool willed by Divine Providence to control an irrational and self-destructive humanity. In this perspective, authority is bound by necessity to assume the nature of paternalism in all its plenitude -- "The intention of the ruler is to teach with authority those who go astray and to restrain the obstinate."[307] The conceptualization of a paternalistic authority can easily develop, as history amply testifies, into dictatorship which not rarely leads to tyranny, especially if the ruler concurs with the following statement: "Merum imperium consistit in gladii potestate" (The ruling power consists exclusively of the power of the sword).[308]

Ius Ecclesiasticum

With the Peace of Constantine the State acknowledged the right of the Church to legislate its own laws. This is not to say that this prerogative of the Church emerged by the approval of the State. The Church, being a perfect and independent society, has the innate right to enact laws for its members. Already in the Acts of the Apostles the Church is presented as fully conscious of this inherent legislative power.[309] The ensemble of laws, which the Church throughout its history enacts and revises in the process of its own evolution, is known as *ius ecclesiasticum* or *ius canonicum*.

The philosophy of law expounded in the preceding section cannot be transposed, *in integro,* to the study of *ius canonicum*. By reason of the

---

[307] AZO, *Summa Super Codicem,* Liber I, *Incipit Materia ad Codicem,* p.2, col. 2. "Auctoritate docent errantes, potestate cohercent contumaces. hec est communis omnium principum intentio."

[308] CYNUS PISTORIENSIS, *In Digesti Veteris Libros* . . . , Rubrica I, *De Iurisdictione omnium Iudicum,* n. 2, fol. 23r.

[309] Acts VI: 3; XV: 6-10, 20.

Philosophy of Law

specific nature of both societies, Church and State, a distinction ought to be made between State law and Church law, although such a distinction is based on mere contingency. Thus the nature of the Church itself forced jurists, whether canonists or civilists, to recognize *ius canonicum* as *divinum*,[310] more so than *ius civile,* and thereby acknowledge the supremacy of the former over the latter.[311] Some, however, take exception to this doctrine. Baldus De Ubaldis[312] and Antonius A Butrio[313] do not recognize *ius canonicum* as essentially *ius divinum.* Placentinus goes on to deny the subordination of civil law to ecclesiastical law.[314] Baldus insists that *ius canonicum* is *ius civile,* unless it entails evangelical precepts. The position of Baldus and Antonius presupposes a *distinctio realis* between *ius canonicum* and *ius divinum,* a position from which one is able to more readily peruse the inferiority of the former to the latter. It is worth noting that in the *Decretum Gratiani* one encounters an extensive *casuistica* where

---

[310] HENRICUS DE SEGUSIO, In Secundum Decretalium Librum . . . , *De Iuramento Calumniae,* cap. 1, *Inhaerentes,* n.7, fol. 28 v; Loc. cit., *De Iureiurando,* cap. 30, *Nimis,* nn. 1, 2, foll. 136v-137r., IOANNES ANDREAE, *In Secundum Decretalium Librum* . . . , *De Iuramento Calumniae,* cap. 1, *Inhaerentes,* n. 9, foll. 46v-47r; loc. cit., *De Iureiurando,* cap. 30, *Nimis,* n. 2, fol. 199r; ALBERICUS DE ROSATE, *Dictionarium* . . . , v. *Ius,* p. 411; v. *Lex,* p. 422; ANTONIUS A BUTRIO, *Super Prima Secundi Decretalium Commentarii Tomus Tertius,* Venetiis, 1578, *De Iuramento Calumniae,* cap. 1, *Inhaerentes,* n. 11, fol. 78r.

[311] *Decretum,* Pars I, Dist. X, c.4, "Constitutiones contra canones et decreta Presulum Romanorum, vel bonos mores, nullius sunt momenti"; Pars I, Dist. X, II pars (Gratianus); HENRICUS DE SEGUSIO, *In Primum Decretalium Librum* . . . , *De Electione et Electi Potestate,* cap. 44, *Nihil est,* n. 12, fol. 69 v; *In Quintum Decretalium Librum, De Privilegiis et excessibus Privilegiatorum,* cap. 2, *Sicut,* n.10, fol. 79 v; loc. cit., cap. 27, *Super Specula,* n. 1, fol. 88 v; ALBERICUS DE ROSATE, *Dictionarium* . . . , v.*Lex,* p. 422, p. 425; ANTONIUS A BUTRIO, *Super Prima Secundi Decretalium* . . . , Tomus III, *De Restitutione Spoliatorum,* cap. 19, *Saepe,* n. 7, fol. 140 v; CYNUS, *In Codicem Commentaria,* Liber I, tit. 2, *De Sacrosancta Ecclesia,* n. 2, fol. 6 r; BALDUS DE UBALDIS, *In Decretalium Volumen* . . . , *Super Secundo Decretalium, De Iudiciis,* prooemium, *Post.,* n. 13, fol. 148r.

[312] *In Decretalium Volumen* . . . , *Super Secundo Decretalium, De Testibus,* cap. 23, *Licet universis,* n. 4, fol. 221 v.

[313] *In Librum Quartum Decretalium* . . . , Tomus VI, *De Consanguinitate, et Affinitate,* cap. 4, *De infidelibus,* n. 3, fol. 36 v; *In Librum Quintum Decretalium* . . . , Tomus VII, *De Sententia Excommunicationis,* cap. 44, *Inquisitioni,* n. 2, fol. 131 v., "Nota quod ubi Dei iudicium et ecclesiae discrepant, amplectendum est Dei iudicium, et ecclesiae relinquendum."

[314] *In Summam Institutionum sive Elementorum* . . . , Liber III, tit. 12, *De Obligationibus,* p. 47.

the conclusion of each case follows as the application of the subordination of *ius canonicum* to *ius divinum* as fundamental principle.[315] Innocent III makes it very clear that the judgment of the Church is not the judgment of God, and is liable to error -- "The judgment of God, which can never deceive nor be deceived, ensues from the eternal truth, whereas the judgment of the Church sometimes adheres to an opinion which, as it happens, may turn out to be erroneous, and thus the Church is deceived."[316]

It goes without saying that this distinction between *ius divinum* and *ius canonicum* does not diminish the indispensibility of ecclesiastical law. As Antonius A Butrio remarks, the ultimate aim of canon law is eternal salvation of the human soul -- "Canon law has as its ultimate aim the eternal good; thus it is a guidance of the pilgrim soul to the eternal happiness."[317] On the other hand, it is also believed that canon law and State law share similarity in respect to their raison d'être: both types of law were provoked "crescente malitia, effrenata cupiditas" (ever-growing malice and unbridled greed),[318] and thus they are intended to restrain human lawlessness.

---

[315] Pars II, Causa XI, q.3, cc.1,30,40,43,46,64,65,72,77,86,90, VII pars, 101; Pars II, Causa XXV, q. 1, I pars, (Gratianus).

[316] Liber X, Liber V, tit.XXXIX, *De Sententia Excommunicationis*, cap. 28. "iudicium Dei veritati, quae non fallit, nec fallitur, semper innititur; iudicium autem ecclesiae nonnunquam opinionem sequitur, quam et fallere saepe contingit et falli."

[317] *Super Prima Primi Decretalium* . . . , Tomus I, *De Consuetudine*, cap. 11, *Cum tanto*, n. 6, fol. 77 v; cf. *Super Secunda Primi Decretalium* . . . , Tomus II, *De Tregua, et Pace*, cap. 1, *Treguas*, n. 12, fol. 93 v. "finis canonicus est etiam propter finem boni aeterni, et directivus est animae viatoris in bonum aeternum."

[318] IOANNES ANDREAE, *In Primum Decretalium Librum* . . . , *De Constitutionibus*, cap. *Postquam*, n.2, fol. 11r; ANTONIUS A BUTRIO, *Super Prima Primi Decretalium* . . . , Tomus I, Liber I, *De Constitutionibus*, prooemium, n.4, fol. 8 v.

The Understanding of Canon Law in the Context of the Present Study.

Saint Isidore, *Decretum Gratiani*, and others, make a distinction between *ius* and *lex* -- "Ius generale nomen est, lex autem juris est species . . . omne autem jus legibus et moribus constat" (*Ius* is a general term; the term law is a species of *ius*; *ius* consists of laws and customs).[319] According to Placentinus, "*Ius* and law relate to each other as the premise, or *status quaestionis*, and the development of the same."[320] Thus *ius* is taken to mean *genus*, a body of laws, an ensemble of laws and customs conceived "en bloc"; *lex* is understood as a particularity, a specification of the same, an individual component of the legal *corpus*. The distinction between *ius* and *lex* is maintained in the present study, but with a different connotation.

A reiteration of the fundamental assumptions is incumbent for an understanding of canon law in the light of the present dissertation. A primordial premise has been laid down that, acknowledging Christ as the *causa formalis,* and *causa finalis* of creation, Church and creation substantially form one and the same reality; what makes them differ from each other is mere contingency, caused by sin. This presupposition leads to the second assumption that since God is one, the Spirit of God, which pervaded the individual human being at Pentecost, was the same Spirit of God that vivified the Yahwist man. Pentecost, in this perspective, stands out as rejuvenation, invigoration, heightening of that glimmer of truth and divine life translated and transposed once and for all in the Yahwist man. Thus the Church, the perennial unfolding of Pentecost, is nothing other than the crystallization of the "christologicity" of human nature in history.

Christ being the *causa formalis* of human nature means that human nature has been featured in the semblance of the *unio hypostatica;* the human being forms a union of spirit and matter, constitutes a synthesis of

---

[319] ISIDORUS, *Etymologiarum* . . ., Liber V, cap. 3, loc.cit., n.1, col. 199; *Decretum,* Pars I, Dist. I, c. 2.

[320] *In Summam Institutionum* . . ., Liber I, tit. 1, *De Iustitia et Iure*, p. 1. "ius et lex ita se habent ut argumentum et argumentatio."

the eternal and the temporal orders, is a compositum of soul and body. It is in the nature of the Church, being in essence human consciousness itself, to cluster in itself this duality of reality; thus the Church is divine and human visibly and invisibly endowed; while rooted in eternity, it unfolds in history, profiting at the same time from the ongoing process of the humanization of human consciousness.[321] The Church is "a visible assembly and a spiritual community."[322] But also, as the perpetuation of Pentecost, the Church must by intrinsic necessity assume the semblance of the *unio hypostatica*.

As a divine reality, the Church is the embodiment of absolute and eternal principles and values; it is the living Gospel, "the Gospel which is the source of all saving truth and moral teaching."[323] Divine revelation in its entirety subsists in the Church; its *magisterium* stands on an immovable and irreducible basis. "Sacred tradition and sacred Scripture form one sacred deposit of the word of God, which is committed to the Church. Holding fast to this deposit, the entire holy people united with their shepherds remain always steadfast in the teaching of the Apostles, in the common life, in the breaking of the bread, and in prayers (cf. Acts 2, 42, Greek text), so that in holding to, practicing, and professing the heritage of the faith, there results on the part of the bishops and faithful a remarkable common effort."[324]

In this study, the term *ius* expresses that which pertains to the divine aspect of the Church; the term thereby entails all that constitutes the deposit of faith which is to be maintained by the Church in all its entirety and integrity until the end of time. By its very nature the Church is thus endowed with the authority of teaching and the power of sanctifying. In reference to the teaching office, *ius canonicum* indicates what precisely canon 750 endorses: "Those things are to be believed by

---

[321] *Gaudium et spes* n. 44, pp. 245-247.

[322] Ibid., n. 40, p. 239.

[323] *Dei Verbum*, n. 7, p. 115.

[324] Ibid., n. 10, p. 117.

divine and catholic faith which are contained in the word of God as it has been written or handed down by tradition, that is, in the single deposit of faith entrusted to the Church, and which are at the same time proposed as divinely revealed either by the solemn *magisterium* of the Church, or by its ordinary and universal *magisterium,* which is manifested by the common adherence of Christ's faithful under the guidance of the sacred *magisterium.* All are therefore bound to shun any contrary doctrines."[325] In matters concerning the sanctifying office of the Church, the term, *ius canonicum,* signifies that which constitutes the "unchangeable elements divinely instituted"[326] of liturgy, namely, that which pertains to the essence of each sacrament. Once *ius canonicum* is envisaged in this perspective, one may willingly subscribe to the opinion of Hostiensis and others that *ius canonicum* is essentially *ius divinum*. This contention leads to a further affirmation that no distinction is admissable between *ius canonicum* and *ius naturale* other than *distinctio formalis*. Thus the ultimate intent of *ius canonicum* appears to be the re-endorsement of natural law in its substantiality, the crystalization of its authenticity, the re-enforcement of its authority, the heightening of its supremacy. *Ius canonicum* may most appropriately be defined as the ever-actualization of Pentecost in history, the very apostolicity of the Christian community, since through *ius canonicum,* thus understood, the Church proves to be the perennial and absolute truth incarnate; it maintains its bond of unity with the Apostolic college and preserves the genuine doctrine of Christ. *Ius canonicum* is the forever present *digitus Dei* enabling the human consciousness more adroitly to explicate its innate authenticity and to unfold its true nature *ab aeterno* modelled on the "Word made flesh."

The Church, while being divine revelation throughout the ages, is at the same time humanity itself; it is, in essence, human consciousness. On the one hand, the Church stays anchored in the perennity of the Gospel truth, and therefore its *magisterium* is complete within itself, absolutely

---

[325] Cf. *Lumen gentium,* n. 25, pp. 48-50; *Dei Verbum,* n. 10, pp. 117-118.

[326] *Sacrosanctum Concilium,* n. 21, p. 146.

self-contained. On the other hand, the Church by its very nature is subject to the same law, and thereby shares the same destiny, which was allotted to human consciousness from the moment of its creation. It is precisely because of the Church's being human consciousness itself that in Pentecost, together with the manifestation of eternal truth, the spirit of the divine pervaded human consciousness. Thus grace -- *virtus, robur, fortitudo* -- was bestowed in Pentecost to energize, invigorate, and strengthen human consciousness crippled by sin, and to enlighten, solidify, endorse, and heighten in human consciousness the divine truth which was obscured by sin.[327] It is thus the inherent destiny of the Church to unfold itself, its inner authenticity, forever moving forward in self-discovery, self-actualization and self-completion in Christ, its head; as a fallen humanity, the Church succumbs to historical vicissitudes, it submits itself to continuous auto-examination in the struggle of self-purification and renewal, in self-amelioration and self-adaptation to the needs of the times.[328] In synthesis, the development of the Church is continuous, changing in form, being modified in content; but the Church still remains the same in its fundamental conceptions.

It is hoped that it became evidently clear from the very beginning of this theologico-juridic curriculum that, notwithstanding the Fall, human nature was not deprived of its christological ontology; it retained its essential qualities of rationality, conscientiousness and sociability; it never lost its potentiality of becoming morally what it is ontologically. This position comes in confrontation with the doctrine of some patristic Fathers and jurists who cherished a pessimistic perception of human nature. The fundamental presupposition of the present study does not, and cannot, allow, by force of logic, the envisaging of law as curtailment, subjugation, suppression, a tool in the hands of a "God's anointed" intended to crush a humanity capable of nothing but *malitia* and *cupiditas*. Only a sick mind would conceive of law in this manner. Law, states Demosthenes, is a gift of

---

[327] Cf *Lumen Gentium* n.4, p. 17; *Ad gentes divinitus*, n.4, pp. 588-589.

[328] *Lumen gentium*, n.48, p.79.

Philosophy of Law
103

God, *donum Dei;* or as Cynus Pistoriensis defines it, "inventio et donum Dei."[329] And that is how we perceive law in its crude essence; in this manner *a fortiori* we apprehend ecclesiastical law.

Saint Thomas Aquinas furnishes us with an extensive exposition on law in general. According to him "a law is nothing else but a dictate of practical reason emanating from the ruler who governs a perfect community."[330] In Thomistic philosophy, law is presented as the disclosure of human consciousness; law is the result and reflection of the rationality, conscientiousness, and sociability of human consciousness. "Dictate of practical reason" basically means that law is in essence rationality; indeed it is human consciousness itself searching for the truth, a conscientious consciousness explicating the eternal truth which is within itself in specific circumstances -- "It is from the precepts of the natural law, as from general and indemonstrable principles, that the human reason needs to proceed to the more particular determination of certain matters."[331] Thus the "dictate of practical reason" by its very nature traces its roots in natural law.[332] In this perspective, natural law stands out as the primordial source, the ultimate guide and the only director of a just government. Saint Thomas goes on to say that "it belongs to the notion of human law to be ordained to the common good of the state."[333] Thus, in terms of our thesis, law is conceived of as the driving force of human consciousness, by which it enables itself to explicate its universal inwardness, and thus the human individual unfolds himself into a moral and ethical being. In conclusion, the Thomistic philosophy of law runs counter to the contention

---

[329] *In Digesti Veteris . . .*, prooemium, n. 8, fol. 2 v.

[330] *Summa Theologica*, Ia-IIae, q. 91, art. 1, Resp., *American Ed.*, vol. 1, p.996; cf. ibid., art. 3, resp., p.997; Ia-IIae, q. 90, art. 1, resp., p.993; Ia-IIae, q.97, art. 3, resp., p. 1024.

[331] Ibid., Ia-IIae, q. 91, art.3, resp., loc.cit., vol. 1, p. 997

[332] Ibid., Ia-IIae, q.91, art. 3, resp., loc.cit., vol. 1, p.997; Ia-IIae, q. 91, art. 4, resp., loc.cit., p. 998; Ia-IIae, q. 95, art. 4, resp., p. 1016; IIa-IIae, q. 57, art. 2, ad 2um, loc.cit., vol. 2, p.1432; IIa-IIae, q. 60, art. 5, Resp., p. 1450.

[333] Ibid., Ia-IIae, q. 95, art. 4, ad 2um, loc.cit., p. 1016.

of those who view law as an imposition upon an indomitable human nature. Law in Thomistic theory is essentially a form of real and full human life. Upon this premise, law is thought to be a device for the correction of human behaviour *accidentaliter,* and not *substantialiter.*[334]

Law is the result of the ruler's decision: "dictate of practical reason emanating from the ruler." As the definition stands, Saint Thomas seems to adhere to a conception of a sovereign legislative authority, completely distinct and totally independent of the community itself, with a power of making and unmaking laws, which knows no legal limits, and from which there is no appeal. This interpretation is further corroborated by his adherence to a political theory that considers the ruler to be above the law.[335] Such a contention presupposes a political philosophy which, on the one hand, fosters an incontestable paternalistic form of government and a divinely instituted autocracy, and, on the other hand, denies any socio-political rights to the community, due to its inherent inability to govern itself. It must be said, however, that the Aquinatis does indeed acknowledge *populus* as the primordial source of law; consequently the ruler is perceived as the representative of the community.[336] In another place, he recognizes democracy as the best form of government where "we have law sanctioned by the lords and Commons."[337] In this perspective, law thus appears as being the "dictate of practical reason," emanating ultimately from the community, rather than from the ruler. In short, "populus causa remota, princeps causa proxima est legis." Law is not taken to mean an

---

[334] Ibid., Ia-IIae, q. 95, art. 1, Resp., ad 1um, loc.cit., vol. 1, pp. 1013-1014; Ia-IIae, q. 96, art. 5, Resp., p. 1020: "Secondly, a man is said to be subject to a law as the coerced is subject to the coercer. In this way the virtuous and righteous are not subject to the law, but only the wicked. Because coercion and violence are contrary to the will: but the will of the good is in harmony with the law, whereas the will of the wicked is discordant from it. Wherefore in this sense the good are not subject to the law, but only the wicked."

[335] Ibid., Ia-IIae, q. 96, art. 5, ad 3um, loc. cit., vol. 1, p. 1021

[336] Ibid., Ia-IIae, q. 90, art. 3, Resp., Loc. cit., vol. 1, p. 995: "Now to order anything to the common good, belongs either to the whole people, or to someone who is the viceregent of the whole people."

[337] Ibid., Ia-IIae, q. 95, art. 4, ad 3um, loc.cit., vol. 1, p. 1017.

arbitrary command imposed by a Superior; rather, the concept of law, as the synthesis of l'esprit de corps, the authentic expression of the universal human consciousness, which found its first realization in *Gerousia* of Sparta, in *Areopagus* of Athens, and in *Senatus Populusque Romanus* in Rome, is substantially maintained by Thomistic philosophy.[338]

Keeping with the main stream of the Thomistic philosophy of law, our attempt is to understand the nature of ecclesiastical law. In contrast with *ius canonicum,* which, as earlier stated, pertains to the divine aspect of the Church, *lex ecclesiastica* is here taken to mean the human aspect of the same. The Church, just as much as it is the embodiment of divine revelation, is human consciousness itself enlightened by the Gospel. Ecclesiastical law thus appears, at first hand, as the manifestation of Christian consciousness in its forward march of self-unfolding and therefore of self-discovery; it is the epitome of the active actuality of the christianized l'esprit de corps. Ecclesiastical law is the instrument by which the Church actualizes itself and activates itself towards self-fulfillment in Christ. Ecclesiastical law at the same time reveals what stage the christianized human consciousness has reached in the process of explication of its Christological ontology.

Canon 7 prescribes "A law comes into being when it is promulgated." Law can never be conceptualized in isolation, abstractly; law in its simplest form is actuality, rational actuality; it is a pragmatic reflection of human consciousness of itself, by itself, and for itself. More specifically, law is human consciousness objectified, the objective externality of the fusion of minds into one-mindedness, the genuine expression of the universal inwardness of the human being objectified in l'esprit de corps. Law is objective freedom, reasonableness, insight, and conviction. It is conviction in the most intensive and extensive manner since it constitutes the tangential point at which different minds come into unison, and at which the good of the individual and the good of the community are harmonized

---

[338] In spite of the democratization of modern political life, laws are still looked upon as the expression of the judgment of somebody other than the community itself, although this somebody with legislative powers represents more or less adequately the interests of the community and justly interprets its actual needs.

and protected. Through law and in law, human consciousness becomes at once the subject and object of itself. Thus law is not an arbitrary command imposed by a Superior, nor is it "creatio ex nihilo et ab abrupto." Law is conviction, and, as such, it must be conceived in the bosom of the community. This conviction transforms itself into a law when it reaches the appropriate intensity and universality, so as to appear a genuine pragmatic reflection of l'esprit de corps; and then the legislative authority authenticates and seals its realization. Once the law is conceived of as the making of the community, its observance by the community pertains to the very nature of the law. The immediate rejection of the law by the community is a sign by itself that the law is the conviction of somebody other than that of the community. By the same principle, the force of law intrinsically depends on the observance of the law by the community.[339] With law thus conceptualized, the substantial similarity between law and custom becomes apparent.

Saint Isidore of Seville enumerates the essential qualities of law. A law in order to be valid must be honest, just, possible, according to nature, in consonance with the particular culture, adjusted to the place and time, necessary, useful, clear, intended for the common good.[340] Once it is maintained that law is human consciousness objectified, that is, that the content of the law is l'esprit de corps itself, the living movement within itself, the essentiality of each and every mentioned quality assumes major clarity of comprehension.

"Laws concern matters of the future, not those of the past, unless provision is made in them for the latter by name."[341] No one can ever question the validity of this law; it constitutes a specification of the

---

[339] Ibid., Ia-IIae, q. 97, art. 3, resp., loc.cit., vol. 1, p. 1024.

[340] *Etymologia*, Liber V, cap. 21, n. 1, loc.cit., col. 203":Erit autem lex honesta, justa, possibilis, secundum naturam, secundum patriae consuetudinem, loco, temporique conveniens, necessaria, utilis, manifesta quoque, ne aliquid per obscuritatem in captionem contineat, nullo privato commodo, sed pro communi civium utilitate conscripta"; cf. *Decretum Gratiani*, Pars I, Dist. IV, c.2; IVO CARNOTIENSIS, *Decretum*, Pars IV, cap. 168, loc. cit., coll. 303-304.

[341] Canon 9.

principle of justice. However, our understanding of law suggests a deeper scrutiny of the said canon.

The law has traditionally been understood as a dictate, however rational, emanating from an authority completely independent of the community. The concept of sovereignty of authority and its independence from the community intrinsically necessitates the absoluteness of the law. Stability, stationariness, and perennity are bound to form the characteristics of the law. A *distinctio realis* is thus being placed between law and the observance of the law. In this perspective also, one is inclined to perceive the law as being complete in itself in the act and by the act of promulgation, and existing in the present, whereas its object belongs to the future -- "laws concern matters of the future." Law is said to be born and to die. However, the creation of the law as well as its death depend entirely on the legislative authority.

This traditional position runs counter to the concept of law endorsed in the present dissertation. It has been contended earlier that the content of the law is the spirit itself, the living movement within itself, that law is the objective externality of the universal human consciousness. This position necessarily leads to the understanding that the law owes its creation and existence ultimately to the community. Law cannot be perceived in isolation, abstractly; it does not exist if not in existentiality, in its observance by the community. Only when law is considered as activation, or actualization of human consciousness does it receive actual reality, and its true significance. Since law burgeons from human consciousness, it must by inner necessity assume the characteristics of its primordial source -- "operatio sequitur esse." Law, like human consciousness, is thus forever unfolding, always becoming, in continuous transformation. In this perspective, law is, in essence, its observance by the community; in scholastic terms, there exists *distinctio formalis,* rather than *realis,* between law and the observance of the law. Law can be said to exist partly in the present and partly in the future; being dynamic in nature, like its source, law is always evolving through its observance by the community. Rather than "lex respicit futura," it should be said that "lex respicit seipsam in futurum." The notion of dynamism in the nature of the law can be envisaged in the words of the *Institutiones:* "A law which the state establishes for itself is bound to change either by the consent of the same community or by a subsequent law contrary to the existent law."[342] This same view was cherished also by canon lawyers. Antonius A Butrio remarks that "ius canonicum est mutabile" (Canon law is changeable).[343] Ioannes Andreae is more explicit in his view; he writes: "ius canonicum sub perpetuo motu consistit" (Canon law exist in perennial motion).[344] From the moment of its promulgation, the process of transformation of the law commences through its observance by the community, continually changing with the change of circumstances or ideas. Indeed, as canon 27 prescribes, "custom is the best interpreter of laws." Great contribution to the law in its process of evolution is given by jurisprudence, doctrinal interpretation, dispensation, epikeia, and excusing causes. Law hardly ever dies; it transforms itself. Law, being human consciousness objectified, is a continuum; it emerges from its antecedent law, and enshrines in embryo its subsequent law; changing in form, modified in content, the law remains still the same in its fundamental conception. In this context the rationale of canon 21 stands out more clearly; it reads: "In doubt, the revocation of a previous law is not presumed; rather, later laws are to be related to earlier ones and, as far as possible, harmonized with them." In conclusion, the universal human consciousness, the spirit of the community, externalizes itself in the law, and through the law it actualizes, solidifies, unfolds and evolves itself in view of its ultimate self-fulfillment.

---

[342] *De iure naturali et gentium et civili* 1, 2, §11. "ea vero, quae ipsa sibi quaeque civitas constituit, saepe mutari solent vel tacito consensu populi vel alia postea lege lata".

[343] *In Sextum Decretalium..., De Constitutionibus,* cap. 1, *Licet Romanus,* n. 49, fol. 3r.; cf. *In Librum Quartum Decretalium..., De Consanguinitate et affinitate,* cap. 8, *Non debet,* n. 2, fol. 37 v.

[344] *In Primum Decretalium Librum..., De Consuetudine,* cap. 11, *Cum tanto,* n. 17, fol. 59 v.

Equity, Epikeia and Dispensation

Closely related to the concept of justice and law is the concept of equity. In literature the term assumes so many different nuances as to render it difficult to provide a precise meaning in a given text. In dismissing, however, the minute connotations which have been accumulating since the time of Aristotle and the rhetoricians, it may be feasible to group the different senses of the term under three major headings: equity as principle, as virtue, and as criterion of legal justice.

Equity Understood as Principle and as Virtue

Aristotle who, as far as we know, was the first to discuss the concept of equity, conceives of the term both as principle and as virtue. In reference to equity as principle, he makes the following remark: "When we look into the matter we find that justice and equity are neither absolutely identical nor generally different."[1] Thus he maintains that both justice and equity form merely two aspects of the same ontological truth. In this sense, equity is distinct from and superior to legal justice: "for equity, though superior to one kind of justice (legal), is still just, it is not superior to justice (absolute principle) as being a different genus."[2] In like manner, equity and justice constitute essentially the same virtue; however, in the legal sense, being equitable is different from being just. In fact, the equitable man is "one who chooses and does equitable acts, and is not unduly insistent upon his rights, but accepts less than his share, although

---

[1] *The Ethics of Aristotle*, Trans. J.A.K. Thomson, Middlesex, England, 1976, Bk V, chapter 10, p. 198.

[2] Ibid., p. 199.

he has the law on his side. Such a disposition is equity: it is a kind of justice, and not a distinct state of character."[3]

In the history of Roman law what immortalized the *praetor peregrinus* was his ability to solve cases on the principle of equity -- "praetor naturali aequitate motus "(the praetor's judgment is directed by natural equity).[4] The *praetor peregrinus* in dealing with foreigners could not apply the *ius civile* and the *legis actio* system which were meant to deal with contentious cases among Roman citizens. In adjudicating cases he had to resort to *naturalis aequitas*, which signified natural justice common to all peoples, to *ius gentium*, and to reliance on his own discretion. It is worth noting that ideas, principles and values which formed the basis of jurisprudence of the *praetor peregrinus* from the early times of the Empire found their way gradually in the general jurisprudence of the Roman legal system.

A staunch advocacy of equity in human relations is undoubtedly found in the writings of Cicero. It is not easy, however, to determine what Cicero precisely meant by the term. A twofold significance of equity seems to emerge. In one instance equity is defined as nature. In this sense, the term seems to signify the absolute principle of justice or natural law. As such, it clusters two fundamental and incontestable human rights, "tuitionem sui et ulciscendi ius" (the safeguarding of one's possessions and the defense of one's rights).[5] In another instance, equity is understood as institution, which seems to indicate basically human law; thus, it appears to be an interpretation and implementation of the principle of justice. The institution of equity manifests itself in legitimate usage (*legitima*), expediency (*conveniens*) and custom (*moris vetustate confirmata*).[6] The institution of equity may also assume three different connotations: equity is defined as *pietas* (piety) in matters concerning the gods; *sanctitas* (sanctity) in one's

---

[3] Ibid., p. 200.

[4] Inst., *De hereditatibus quae ab intestato deferuntur*, 3, 1, §9.

[5] *Topica*, cap. 23, n.90, *Opera Omnia*, p. 188.

[6] Ibid.

devotion towards ancestors (*manes*); *iustitia* or *aequitas* proper in matters pertaining to human interactions.[7] In another work Cicero identifies equity as mere institution, distinct from natural law and from legal justice; thus he writes: "Unless equity, trust, and justice proceed from natural justice, and if all these realities are not brought into practice, there would not be one person who would be found just."[8]

In Roman law the term *aequitas* primarily stands for natural law -- *naturalis aequitas*: "It is natural equity that one should not favour himself to the detriment and harm of another."[9] As Modestinus remarks, natural justice and equity should form the basic criteria of legal justice: "Nulla iuris ratio aut aequitatis benignitas patitur, ut quae salubriter pro utilitate hominum introducuntur, ea nos duriore interpretatione contra ipsorum commodum producamus ad severitatem."[10] It is because of its ontological superiority over legal justice that equity takes precedence over the rigour of the law. *Lex, placuit*, in particular, attests to this truth: "It is appropriate that justice and equity prevail in all things rather than the inflexible insistence of right."[11] In the acknowledgement of equity as the

---

[7] Ibid., "Quum autem de aequo et iniquo disseritur, aequitatis loci colligentur. Hi cernuntur bipartito, et natura et instituto. Natura partes habet duas, tuitionem sui et ulciscendi ius. Institutio autem aequitatis tripartita est; una pars legitima est, altera conveniens, tertia moris vetustate confirmata. Atque etiam rursus aequitas tripartita dicitur esse; una ad superos deos, altera ad manes, tertia ad homines pertinere. Prima pietas, secunda sanctitas, tertia iustitia aut aequitas nominatur."

[8] *De Finibus Bonorum et Malorum ad Brutum*, Lib. II, cap. 18, n. 59, *Opera Omnia*, p. 1010. "Nisi aequitas, fides, iustitia proficiscantur a natura, et si omnia haec ad utilitatem referantur, virum bonum non posse reperiri."

[9] Pomponius, L. *Iure naturae*, 206, D., *De diversis regulis iuris antiqui*, 50, 17: "Iure naturae aequum est neminem cum alterius detrimento et iniuria fieri locupletiorem"; cf. Ulpianus, L. *Ait praetor*, 2, §2, D., *De precario*, 43, 26; Inst., *De hereditatibus quae ab intestato deferuntur*, 3, 1, §9.

[10] L. *Nulla iuris*, 25, D., *De legibus senatusque consultis et longa consuetudine*, 1, 3.

[11] Impp. Constantinus et Licinius, L. *Placuit*, 2, C. *De iudiciis*, 3, 1: "Placuit in omnibus rebus praecipuam esse iustitiae aequitatisque quam stricti iuris rationem"; cf. Impp. Diocletianus et Maximianus, L. *Cum res*, 5, C., *Si aliena res pignori data sit*, 8, 15 (16); Impp. Diocletianus et Maximianus, L. *Quotiens*, 3, §1, C., *De donationibus quae sub modo vel condicione vel ex certo tempore conficiuntur*, 8, 54 (55); Paulus, L. *Servitutes*, 20, §2, D., *De servitutibus praediorum urbanorum*, 8, 2; Ulpianus, L. *Et si quis*, 14, §2, D., *De religosis et sumptibus funerum et ut*

full expression of what is just, it was also feasible for the Roman jurist to endorse that "necessity and poverty do not recognize any law."[12] In the study of Roman law a question remains yet to be answered as to whether these terms, equity and justice, each indicate a distinct absolute principle. There are many instances where equity is taken to mean justice, although texts are not lacking in which the term stands for a distinct concept.

In patristic literature the term "equity" assumes both the notion of principle and of virtue. Equity, conceived of as a principle, denotes natural law, the absolute principle of justice. John of Salisbury defines equity as divine law -- "Lex ejus aequitas" (His law is equity)[13] to which legal justice is subordinate, "Aequitatis servus est princeps" (the ruler is the servant of equity).[14] In this sense the term "equity" is used by Saint Ambrose. *Inter alia*, he writes: "Only when public authority is consolidated by equity, is injustice exterminated."[15] In the estimation of Gregory the Great,[16] and of Jonas Aurelianensis,[17] the hierarchical configuration of

---

funus ducere liceat, 11, 7; Paulus, L. *Si quis*, 30, D., *De pecunia constituta*, 13, 5; Tryhoninus, L. *Bona fides*, 31, D., *Depositi vel contra*, 16, 3; Ulpianus, L. *Si ego*, 9, §1, D., *De iure dotium*, 23, 3; Paulus, L. *Gaius seius*, 45, D., *Soluto matrimonio dos quemadmodum petatur*, 24, 3; Paulus, L. *In summa*, 2, §5, D., *De aqua et aquae pluviae arcendae*, 39, 3; Paulus, L. *An eadem causa*, 14, D., *De exceptione rei iudicatae*, 44, 2; Papinianus, L. *Inter eos*, 51, §1, D., *De fideiussoribus et mandatoribus*, 46, 1.

[12] Inst., *De hereditatibus quae ab intestato deferuntur*, 3, 1, §9: "necessitas et paupertas legem non agnoscunt"; Ulpianus, L. *Si autem*, 7(8), §3, D., *De negotiis gestis*, 3, 5; Ulpianus, L. *Sin autem*, 19 (20), ibid; Ulpianus, L. *Divus Pius*, 5, D., *De hereditatis petitione*, 5,3; Paulus, L. *Quaesitum*, 9, D., *De distractione pignorum et hypothecarum*, 20,5; Impp. Arcadius et Honorius, L. *Eos*, 6, §6, C., *De modo multarum quae ab iudicibus infliguntur*, 1, 54; Impp. Diocletianus et Maximianus, L. *Si res tuas*, 8, §1, C., *Ad exhibendum*, 3, 42; Imp. Constantinus, L. *Si quis*, 2, C. *De patribus qui filios distraxerunt*, 4, 43; Impp Severus et Antoninus, L. *Si tempore*, 1, C., *De operis libertorum*, 6, 3.

[13] *Polycraticus* . . . , Liber IV, cap. 2, *Opera Omnia*, col. 514.

[14] Ibid., col. 515.

[15] *De Officiis Ministrorum* . . . , Liber II, cap. 19, n. 95, *Opera Omnia*, Tomus II, pars prior, col. 136. "aequitas imperia confirmet, et injustitia dissolvat."

[16] *Registri Epistolarum Libri Quartuordecim*, Liber V (Indictione XIII), Epistola 54, Ad Universos Regni Childeberti Episcopos, Opera Omnia, Tomus III, P.L., Tomus 77, Parisiis, 1849, coll. 785-786.

[17] *Opusculum de Institutione Regia*, cap. VIII, *Opera Omnia*, Tomus unicus, P.L., Tomus 106, Parisiis, 1851, coll. 296-297.

society is based on divine decree, the law of equity. It seems that, for Alcuin, the term *aequitas* indicates the tangential point of ultimate significance towards which are ordained the spiritual and the temporal orders of things. He writes apropos: "Equity in one's whole life is preserved in the observance of divine worship and in the maintenance of human rights."[18] Although the term equity, defined as principle, leads one to believe that in patristic literature the terms equity and justice are synonymous,[19] this identical similarity of concepts is sometimes found lacking in the same text without any specification of notion.[20]

The virtue of equity, according to Jonas of Orleans, signifies right knowledge and rectitude of behaviour: "Equity is to discern rightly and act accordingly."[21] If such is the definition of equity, there exists no distinction between the virtue of equity and the virtue of justice. As can be expected, unanimity of consent is lacking among the Fathers as to whether equity and justice are identical in meaning,[22] or denote two distinct concepts.[23] Hugo de Sancta Maria seems to define equity as

---

[18] *Dialogus de Rhetorica* . . ., *De Virtutibus, Opera Omnia*, Tomus II, col. 944. "In hac divinitatis cultus et humanitatis jura, et aequitas totius vitae conservatur."

[19] JONAS AURELIANENSIS, *De Institutione Laicali* . . ., Liber II, cap. 24, *Opera Omnia*, col. 218: "Sicut enim aequum est ut qui recte sapit, recte agat, ita iniquum est recte sapere et non recte agere."

[20] SANCTUS AMBROSIUS, *De Officiis Ministrorum* . . ., Liber I, cap. 28, n.130, *Opera Omnia*, Tomus II, coll. 66-67; IOANNIS SARESBERIENSIS, *Polycraticus* . . ., Liber IV, cap. 1, *Opera Omnia*, col. 515.

[21] *De Institutione Laicali* . . ., Liber II, cap. 24, *Opera Omnia*, col. 218. "aequum est ut qui recte sapit, recte agat."

[22] MAGNUS AURELIUS CASSIODORUS, *Variarum Libri Duodecim*, Liber III, Epist. 27, *Opera Omnia*, Tomus I, P.L., Tomus 69, Parisiis, 1865, col. 591; CATULFUS, *Instructio Epistolaris* . . . *Opera Omnia*, col. 1365.

[23] IOANNIS SARESBERIENSIS, *Polycraticus* . . ., Liber IV, cap. 2, *Opera Omnia*, col. 514; IONAS AURELIANENSIS, *Opusculum de Institutione Regia*, cap. IV, *Opera Omnia*, coll. 290-291.

prudence and temperance.[24] The virtue of equity for Saint Ambrose denotes a different connotation from the virtue of justice; equity is described as kindness (beneficentia), generosity (liberalitas), mildness (benignitas), and goodness (bonitas). He thus concludes: "Justice is more lofty, whereas liberality more gracious."[25]

John of Salisbury makes reference to the equity of justice, "justitiae aequitas" (equity of justice),[26] as if to say that the principle of justice is not absolute, but defective and incomplete; justice needs a superior principle, the principle of equity, in order to test its own validity. However, by *justitia* John of Salisbury means *iustitia humana*, legal justice, whereas by *aequitas* he understands *iustitia divina*, *aequitas naturalis*, natural law. In this context, the superiority of equity over justice needs no explanation. A similar reference is found in the *Decretum Gratiani* where equity is endorsed as *mater iustitiae*.[27] As in *Polycraticus* by John of Salisbury, in the *Decretum* the term equity denotes eternal justice, while the term, *justice*, refers to legal justice, whether civil or canonical. In this sense, the validity of justice must be tested by the criterion of equity. It must be said, however, that both in *Decretum*[28] and in *Clementinis*[29] the terms equity and justice are also used indiscriminately to signify eternal justice, natural law.

Among the Decretalists the term equity denotes primarily eternal justice. In this sense, Albericus De Rosate describes equity as "aequitas prima, iustitia primitiva" (primordial justice, primitive justice).[30] Baldus De

---

[24] *Tractatus de Regia Potestate et Sacerdotali Dignitate*, Liber I, cap. 6, Tomus unicus, P.L., Tomus 163, Parisiis, 1854, col. 948.

[25] *De Officiis Ministrorum..*, Liber I, cap. 28, n. 130, *Opera Omnia*, Tomus II, pars prior, col. 66. "justitia mihi excelsior videtur, liberalitas gratior."

[26] *Polycraticus* . . . , Liber IV, cap. 1, loc. cit., col. 514.

[27] Pars II, Causa XXV, q. 1, c. 16, II pars: " . . . considerata tamen rationis equitate, ut que mater iusticiae est in nullo ab ea dissentire inveniatur . . . ."

[28] Pars II, Causa XI, q. 3, c. 90, VII pars, Gratianus, §1.

[29] *Clementinarum Liber V*, Tit. XI, *De Verborum Significatione*, cap. 2.

[30] *Dictionarium* . . . , v. *aequitas*, p. 31.

Equity, Epikeia and Dispensation

Ubaldis qualifies equity by the attribute "natural" -- "aequitas naturalis"[31] -- and defines it as dictate of natural reason, "dictamen naturalis rationis."[32] By the term equity, Antonius A Butrio understands reason, in its pure sense,[33] natural equity (*aequitas naturalis*)[34] natural law.[35] In like manner Hostiensis conceives of equity.[36] Needless to say, the qualification added to *aequitas* -- *prima, primitiva,* or *naturalis* -- is used in contradistinction to legal equity. Ioannes Andreae, in stating that "we often witness that the dictates of equity contradict those of strict right,"[37] does nothing but express the universal awareness that legal justice not rarely comes into open confrontation with the principle of equity.

The very belief in a principle expects the implementation of the principle in human behaviour. A principle is said to turn into a virtue when the principle, already contained in germ in human consciousness, is explicated for the fulfillment of the same. Thus the just person is the actualization of the principle of justice. Once it has been laid down that the terms, equity and justice, indicate one and the same principle, it stands to reason that in like manner both terms are used to signify the same virtue. This identification of terms is not necessarily so according to

---

[31] *In Decretalium Volumen...*, *Super Secundo Decretalium, De Causa Possessionis, et Proprietatis,* cap. 5, *Pastoralis,* n. 12, fol. 179r; loc.cit., *De Probationibus,* cap. 10, *Per tuas,* n. 2, fol. 209r; *Consiliorum...*, Vol. I, cons. 232, n.1, fol. 67v; loc. cit., Vol. IV, cons. 19, n. 3, fol. 8r.

[32] *In Decretalium Volumen...*, *Super Secundo..., De Causa Possessionis, et Proprietatis,* cap. 5, *Pastoralis,* n. 12, fol. 179r.

[33] *Super Prima Primi...*, Tomus Primus, *De Consuetudine,* cap. 11, *Cum tanto,* n. 54, fol. 85v: "nam aequitas, et ratio idem sunt"; cf. ibid., n.55.

[34] *Super Prima Primi...*, Tomus Primus, Lib. I, *De Constitutionibus,* prooemium, n. 8, fol. 9r.

[35] *Super Secunda Primi Decretalium Commentarii Tomus Secundus,* Venetiis, 1578, *De Officio Delegati* cap. 26, *Quaerenti,* n. 4, fol. 41v: "Nota 3 ius canonicum insequi aequitatem."

[36] *In Primum Decretalium..., De Translatione Episcopi vel Electi,* cap. 2, *Inter Corporalia,* n. 32, fol. 82v.

[37] *In Primum Decretalium..., De Consuetudine,* cap. 11, *Cum tanto,* n. 43, fol. 61v. "saepe videmus, quod ratio aequitatis est contraria rationi stricti iuris."

Aristotle, as indicated earlier. The equitable man is one who "is not unduly insistent upon his rights, but accepts less than his share, although he has the law on his side."[38] For Aristotle being equitable means being sympathetic.[39] In this sense too, Albericus De Rosate seems to understand the meaning of equity as virtue. Equitableness is an attitude which is not extremely concerned with one's own right; it is a reasonable *modus operandi* which endeavours to mitigate one's rightful claims with leniency: "Equity is a rational way of thinking which entails both convenience and harshness";[40] thus it is "quoddam temperamentum recedens ex causa" (a certain moderate consequence of the cause).[41] In another place, however, Albericus conceives of equity as the virtue of fortitude in enduring want, and of temperance amidst abundance.[42]

Among civilists, Azo is prime in his treaty on the subject. In his exposition the concept of equity stands out first as the germination of eternal wisdom in the human heart -- "quis ex corde suo inveniat";[43] thus equity is understood as natural law, natural wisdom, common also to the uncultured.[44] In this context too, equity signifies divine positive law.[45] Equity thus conceived constitutes the fundamental criterion for human justice; consequently, human law is nothing other than interpretation and

---

[38] *Ethics*, Bk V, chap. 10, p. 200.

[39] Ibid., Bk VI, chap. 11, p. 219.

[40] *Dictionarium* . . . , v. *Aequitas*, p. 31 "Aequitas est rationabilis modus continens in se convenientiam et rigorem."

[41] Ibid.

[42] Ibid., v. *Iustitia*, p. 414: "Iustitia est aequitas tolerandi inopiam, et temperantiam habere in abundantia."

[43] *Summa Institutionum*, Liber IV, *De Officio Iudicis*, p. 382, col. 1.

[44] *Ad Singulas Leges XII* . . . , Liber I, tit. 14, *De Legibus et Constitutionibus*, n. 2, p. 39; *Summa Super Codicem*, Liber I, *Incipit Materia ad Codicem*, p. 1, col. 2; *Summa Institutionum*, Liber I, *De Iure Naturali Gentium et Civili*, p. 348, col. 2.

[45] *Summa Super Codicem*, Liber I, *Incipit Materia ad Codicem*, p. 2, col. 1; *De Summa Trinitate et Fide Catholica ut Nemo publice contendere audeat*, p. 3, col. 1.

Equity, Epikeia and Dispensation 117

application of equity.[46] Antonius De Tremolis, in the manner of Azo, uses the term to mean the eternal wisdom enscribed in human consciousness; he considers, in fact, human conscience as the *locus* of equity -- "forus conscientiae est forus boni et equi" (the forum of conscience is a forum of good and equity).[47] For Placentinus, equity is reason itself.[48] The exposition by Cynus Pistoriensis on the subject is more elaborate. He endorses the identity of concept between equity and justice. As such, equity "is the soul not yet explicated in the law";[49] for this reason, "equity lays hidden in its occult aims, and it is only through the chiseling of it, as it were, by the wise, and by their debates that equity is smoothed, clarified, and explicated into a specific law."[50] It seems that the view of Cynus on equity correlates in substance with the central idea of the present study; it is indeed inferred by Cynus that human consciousness is charged by inner necessity to unfold, explicate and actualize the glimmer of eternal truth which it received at the moment of its creation. Thus human law for Cynus is nothing other than the endeavour of human consciousness to realize this inner destiny -- "Ius est aequitas in praeceptis redacta" (Law is equity expressed in norms).[51]

---

[46] *Summa Institutionum*, Liber I, *De Iure Naturali Gentium et Civili*, p.348, col. 2; *Summa Super Codicem*, Liber I, *Incipit Materia ad Codicem*, p. 1, col. 2.

[47] Quoted by Ubertus De Bonacurso, *Preludia et Exceptiones*, Lugduni, 1522, fol. 109r.

[48] *In Summam Institutionum* . . . , Liber I, Tit. I, *De Iustitia et Iure*, p. 1.

[49] *In Digesti Veteris* . . . , Rubrica I, *De Iustitia et Iure*, n. 4, fol. 3r. "est anima non formata in ius."

[50] *In Codicem Commentaria*, Liber I, Tit. 14, *De Legibus et Constitutionibus Principum*, n. 9, fol. 25r. "aequitas enim latebat in suis occultis finibus, et per elimationes et disputationes prudentum elimatur et reducitur in speciem iuris."

[51] *In Digesti Veteris* . . . , Rubrica I, *De Iustitia et Iure*, n. 4, fol. 3r.

The term, equity, among civilists is taken to mean virtue, as well. However, there is great discrepancy as to what the concept precisely entails. It seems that the prevailing consensus of authors defines equity as *benignitas* (kindness) and *clementia* (clemency).[52] Iacobus De Ravanis believes that equitableness sometimes conflicts with goodness.[53] Cynus seems to make a distinction between goodness and equitableness.[54] Pileus Modicensis adopts the expression *benignitas equitatis*,[55] a phrase which infers that the virtue of equity does not necessarily include goodness.

The acknowledgement of equity as the absolute principle of justice leads to the question on the relation between equity and legal justice. This issue, per se, has already been addressed in some length in our study on natural law. It appeared then quite clearly that equity, understood as eternal justice, constitutes the foundation of human justice, the rectification of an unjust law, the correction of abuse of political power. A confirmation of this position is found in the Aristotelian statement: "Thus justice and equity coincide, and although both are good, equity is superior. What causes the difficulty is the fact that equity is just, but not what is legally just: it is a rectification of legal justice."[56] Upon this presupposition, human law by intrinsic necessity assumes the nature of interpretation, implementation, and adaptation of natural law at a particular stage of the humanization process of human consciousness. For clarity's sake, however, it seems imperative to re-iterate briefly our understanding on how human law reflects natural law.

"Nil in temporali lege iustum quod ab aeterno non derivetur." The intrinsic dependency of human law on eternal justice cannot be missed in the Augustinian dictum. Jurists, both canonical and civilist, classify *aequitas*

---

[52] CYNUS PISTORIENSIS, *In Codicem Commentaria*, Liber I, Tit. 14, *De Legibus et Constitutionibus Principum*, n. 9, fol. 25r.

[53] Ibid.

[54] *In Digesti Veteris* . . . , Rubrica I, *De Iustitia et Iure*, n. 5, fol. 3r.

[55] *Quaestiones Aureae*, Romae, 1560, Quaestio 29, n. 7, p. 44.

[56] *Ethics*, Bk V, chap. 10, p. 199.

Equity, Epikeia and Dispensation

into *non scripta* and *scripta*.[57] This twofold classification is based on mere fact, regardless of whether equity is applied by the legal system as a remote or as a proximate norm in the pursuance of eternal justice. *Aequitas* is defined as *non scripta* since it is not found written in the codification; it is only inscribed in the human heart,[58] as Cynus describes it: "anima non formata in ius" (the soul not yet explicated in law). *Aequitas non scripta* may thus be recognized as the remote norm of justice in the accomplishment of legal justice. *Aequitas scripta* indicates nothing other than mere fact that the legal system has resorted explicitly and proximately to the principle of equity due to its own inherent deficiency.

It is the Christian conviction that the eternal wisdom has been translated and transposed into human consciousness in the act of creation. It has been laid down as the fundamental assumption of the present study that the germination of the eternal wisdom implanted in the human being is human consciousness itself; it is thereby the inherent destiny of human consciousness, as individual reality as well as the esprit de corps, to unfold, explicate, and actualize this glimmer of eternal truth in itself to become more of itself. In becoming morally what it is ontologically, human consciousness is forever discovering itself, evolving itself, unfolding itself, forever becoming more humanized, explicating its intrinsic authenticity. The eternal truth enshrined in human consciousness is the spirit of God, a vivifying principle, complete in itself; it is thus an inner force leading human consciousness in the authentication of itself in order that the implanted divine truth may become human consciousness; and thus human consciousness reflects more genuinely its *causa formalis*, Christ. This means

---

[57] BALDUS UBALDI, *In Decretalium Volumen . . . , Super Primo Decretalium, De Constitutionibus*, cap. 1, *Canonum*, n. 18, fol. 10v; *Super Secundo Decretalium, De Causa Possessionis,et Proprietatis*, cap. 5, *Pastoralis*, n. 12, fol. 179r; ALBERICUS DE ROSATE, *Dictionarium . . . ,* v. *aequitas*, p. 31; AZO, *Summa Institutionum*, Liber IV, *De Officio Iudicis*, p. 382, col. 1; CYNUS PISTORIENSIS, *In Codicem Commentaria*, Liber I, Tit.14, *De Legibus et Constitutionibus Principum*, n. 6, fol. 24 v.

[58] BALDUS UBALDI, *In Decretalium Volumen, Super Secundo Decretalium, De Causa Possessionis, et Proprietatis*, cap. 5, *Pastoralis*, n.12, fol. 179r: "licet aequitas non sit scripta, ex solo tamen dictamine naturalis rationis debet servari."

that eternal wisdom, while complete in itself, and fully actual in human consciousness, exists *in potentia* in respect to self-fulfillment of the same.

The study so far accomplished reaches the following conclusion:

1. equity appears to be at once cause and effect of the ongoing process of humanization;
2. characteristic of its *modus operandi* is its spontaneity in human behaviour;
3. the superiority of equity over legal justice cannot be ignored[59] without nefarious results for social justice;
4. equity can truly be defined as "anima non formata in ius," namely l'esprit de corps, and it should find its fullest expression for the time in the legal system;
5. human law is by nature the implementation of equity -- "Ius est aequitas in praeceptis redacta";[60]
6. thus, *aequitas non scripta*, per se, does not enjoy the force of law in the juridic sense.[61]

Natural law and human consciousness constitute one and the same substance; yet they are two distinct components. It is in the nature of human consciousness to implement natural law within itself in the pursuit of ever becoming more rational, conscientious and social. These essential qualities direct human consciousness into the full expression of itself as a social being. In this context the legal system is thus envisaged as the

---

[59] ALBERICUS DE ROSATE, *Dictionarium* . . ., v. *Ius*, p. 412; AZO, *Ad Singulas Leges XII* . . ., Liber III, Tit. 1, *De Iudiciis*, lex 8, n. 1, p. 167; Liber V, Tit. 17, *De Repudiis, et Iudicio de Monilibus Sublato*, lex 1, n.3, p. 406; CYNUS PISTORIENSIS, *In Codicem Commentaria*, Liber III, Tit. 1, *De Iudiciis*, n. 1, fol. 129r; Liber IV, Tit. 18, *De Constituta Pecunia*, n. 1, fol. 209v; *In Digesti Veteris* . . ., Rubrica XIV, *De Officio Praetoris*, n. 5, fol. 13v; HENRICUS DE SEGUSIO, *In Primum Decretalium* . . ., *De Transactionibus*, cap. 11, *Ex parte tua*, nn. 9-13, fol. 181v; *In Secundum Decretalium Librum Commentaria*, Venetiis, 1581, *De Ordine Cognitionum*, cap. 2, *Cum dilectus*, n. 16, fol. 37r; *De Exceptionibus*, cap. 9, *Apostolicae Sedis*, n. 5, fol. 145r; *In Quintum Decretalium* . . ., *De Sententia Excommunicationis*, cap. 32, *Cum illorum*, n. 7, fol. 114v.

[60] CYNUS PISTORIENSIS, *In Digesti Veteris* . . ., Rubrica I, *De Iustitia et Iure*, n. 4, fol. 3r,; cf. ALBERICUS DE ROSATE, *Dictionarium* . . ., v. *Iustitia*, p. 414.

[61] BALDUS UBALDI, *In Decretalium Volumen* . . ., *Super Primo Decretalium, De Constitutionibus*, cap.1,*Canonum*,n.18,fol.10v;ALBERICUSDEROSATE,*Dictionarium*. . .,v.*Aequitas*,p.31.

reflection of the individual human consciousness burgeoning into the esprit de corps in the pursuance of ever becoming a genuine reflection of natural law. This contention demonstrates that the distinction between equity and legal justice exists from the very nature of things; it shows that the subordination of legal justice to equity arises from inner necessity; it points to the innate deficiency of legal justice; it explains the reason for the discrepancy and conflict which not rarely arise between equity and legal justice.

The evolutionary nature of human consciousness is not only responsible for the limitedness of legal justice, but it hinders the human mind from acquiring a perfect notion of equity, according to the axiom: "Quidquid accipitur per modum recipientis accipitur" (What is comprehended, according to the ability of the recipient is comprehended). Human consciousness conceives of justice in terms of the Roman definition: "Iustitia est constans et perpetua voluntas ius suum cuique tribuens" (Justice is the constant and perpetual volition to give one his or her right). The Roman definition is an excellent one when considered metaphysically, outside the socio-political spectrum. *Ius suum* in the present stage of humanization is primarily perceived as a sacrosanct personal prerogative emanating from, or sanctioned by, state sovereignty. The evangelical notion of *ius suum* is particularly encountered in the Sermon on the Mount,[62] and in the parable of the vineyard.[63] Strange as it might seem, the evangelical understanding of justice, or equity, is aptly summarized in the Marxist axiom: "From each according to his ability, to each according to his needs."[64] The Gospel signals the ultimate goal which human consciousness is destined to pursue in the explication of divine justice enshrined in it. In the final stage of the humanization of human consciousness, when human consciousness becomes the authentic reflection of eternal wisdom engraved upon it, and thus the Gospel teaching is explicated into human

---

[62] Matt. V: 1-17.

[63] Matt. XX: 1-16.

[64] *Critique of the Gotha Programme*, Revised Translation, New York, 1973, p. 10.

consciousness in the most intensive and extensive manner, it is then that equity and legal justice become one norm of truth.

In juridic literature two definitions of equity are given. One of them stands in opposition to the above exposition. It reads: "Aequitas est iustitia dulciore misericordiae temperata" (Equity is justice mitigated by the gentle spirit of mercy).[65] Needless to say, the term, *iustitia*, is here taken to mean legal justice; thus, equity is defined as legal justice mitigated by mercy. This distortion of the concept of equity as natural justice cannot go unnoticed. Equity perceived in this manner loses its primordial meaning of natural right, and assumes the connotation of kindness, compassion, commiseration, mercy, sympathy, and pity. This means that relaxation of the law assumes the nature of a favour granted out of benevolence of the Superior, rather than an acknowledgement and endorsement of one's human dignity and uniqueness as a fundamental and inalienable right. Consequently, with this definition a dichotomy is suggested between natural law and legal justice. Such a concept of equity presupposes a philosophy that acclaims political authority, which originally belonged to the people, to be a reality essentially distinct and independent of the community itself. In this context, political authority does not consider itself as the synthesis of l'esprit de corps, as the emergence of human consciousness in the concretization of its inherent universality, but rather acclaims itself as distinct, by reason of origin and nature, from the community; thus it presents itself as the exclusive source of justice. This definition of equity could find any justification only in a theocratic condescending form of government, so dear to Medieval Churchmen, the source of the dictatorial characteristic of the legal system which crippled the humanization process for many centuries. Another remark refers to the subjectivism of the definition, concentrating merely on the legal justice without the least consideration to objective actuality; its self-centredness does not allow any commitment in the search for truth, for natural justice. Moreover, the said definition, as we shall see

---

[65] HENRICUS DE SEGUSIO, *In Primum Decretalium* . . . , *De Transactionibus*, cap. 11, *Ex parte tua*, n. 9, fol. 181v; cf. IOANNIS ANDREAE, *In Primum Decretalium* . . . , *De Transactionibus* . . . , cap. 11, *Ex parte*, n. 5, fol. 278r; ALBERICUS DE ROSATE, *Dictionarium* . . . , v. *Aequitas*, p. 31; v. *ius* p. 412; v. *iustitia*, p. 414

later on, does not comprise all circumstances where equity can and ought to be applied.

Another definition of equity, to which we subscribe, reads as follows: "Equity is a convenient mode of action which, in things being equal, attends to equal rights and considers different goods in an equal manner."[66] No allusion is made in this definition to the absolute paternalism of the political authority with its arrogant condescending approach towards the individual as a mere recipient of favours. Political authority is thus presented as being essentially human consciousness itself in its ongoing process of humanization. The complete disregard for legal justice in this definition implicitly vouches for the subordination of the legal justice to natural law. This definition attests to the most deeply felt endeavour of human consciousness in search of the ultimate truth; thus the main emphasis is placed on actual objectivity which finds its intrinsic validity in eternal justice. Equity is thereby understood as "fairness," rather than as sympathy, kindness, and pity; equity is wisdom in placing all circumstances in their right perspective, on their own merits, and in reaching a tangential point between the good of the individual and that of the community. Moreover, the aforesaid definition is sufficiently basic to comprise all circumstances when equity should be applied.

Equity as Fundamental Criterion of Legal Justice

Legal justice and divine justice are distinct; yet the former flows from the latter. Thus the subordination of legal justice to equity, which is eternal justice itself, emerges from the very nature of legal justice. The inferiority of the legal justice is the result of its inherent imperfection and limitedness. The indispensability of equity in the legal system can never be

---

[66] AZO, *Summa Institutionum*, Liber I, *De Iusticia et Iure*, p. 348, col.1: "Equitas est rerum convenientia que in paribus causis paria iura desiderat et omnia bona coequiparat"; cf. *Ad Singulas Leges XII* . . . , Liber III, Tit.1, *De Iudiciis*, Lex 8, n. 1, p. 167; PLACENTINUS, *In Summam Institutionum* . . . , Liber I, Tit. I, *De Iustitia et Iure*, p. 1; CYNUS PISTORIENSIS, *In Codicem Commentaria*, Liber I, Tit. 14, *De Legibus et Constitutionibus Principum*, n. 9, fol. 25r; IOANNIS SARESBERIENSIS, *Polycraticus* . . . , Liber IV, cap. 2, col. 514.

over-estimated. The involvement of equity may be perused in three dimensions, namely, as mitigation, as rectification, and as substitution of legal justice.

Equity as Mitigation of Legal Justice

Under this heading equity is not taken to mean a test which should be applied to actual laws, such that if these were not conformable to natural law they ought to be amended. The subject of the dependency of human law on natural law for its own validity has been the subject of previous study. The present exposition presupposes that the human law is just. Equity as mitigation of legal justice thereby implies that the variability of the law lies in the nature of things with which it is concerned, rather than in itself. When this variability concerns the validity of the law itself, the matter becomes the exclusive competence of the legislative authority. "Only we (public authority) have the right and duty to decide which belongs to equity and which pertains to strict law."[67]

Legal justice resorts to equity in order to protect itself from itself. Human consciousness, realized in a socio-political spirit, is cognizant of the fact that justice for the sake of justice does not reveal the real nature of human consciousness; it is rather a travesty of justice. Equity is the measure of equilibrium between the universal inwardness of the individual human consciousness and its outward realization in the ethical world. The degree of application of equity in the legal system registers at what stage human consciousness has thus far arrived in its process of humanization. In reference to this contention goes the adage, "Summum ius, summa iniuria," or as Hostiensis phrases it, "Omne quod est nimium, vertitur in vitium" (In being in excess anything turns into a fault).[68] Modestinus was preoccupied

---

[67] Imp. Constantinus, L. *Inter*, 1, C., *De legibus et constitutionibus principum et edictis*, 1, 14:
"Inter aequitatem iusque interpositam interpretationem nobis solis et oportet et licet inspicere";
cf. AZO *Ad Singglequlas Leges XII* . . . , Liber I, Tit. 14, *De Legibus et Constitutionibus*, n. 2,
p. 39, "Si ergo ipsi erraverunt nimis dure constituendo in iure, soli principi licet
interpretationem facere"; CYNUS PISTORIENSIS, *In Codicem Commentaria*, Liber I, Tit. 14, *De Legibus et Constitutionibus Principum*, n. 6, fol. 24 v.

[68] *In Tertium Decretalium Librum Commentaria*, Venetiis, 1581, *De Testamentis*, cap. 15, *Requisisti*,

Equity, Epikeia and Dispensation 125

lest justice in the cause of truth alienates itself.[69] In resorting to equity, human consciousness demonstrates its endeavour, its constant self-discernment and self-scrutiny, in order that it may indeed unfold itself, its inherent genuineness, through its own laws, and thus approach the ultimate truth. "Equity," remarks Hostiensis, "is more concerned with truth than in dallying with subtilities."[70] This premise leads to the conclusion that, in principle, there should be no conflict between law and equity.[71] In case of conflict, the norm stands that equity prevails over the law. *Lex, Placuit*, reads apropos: "It seems to us fit that justice and equity should be upheld in all things in opposition to the inflexible insistence of right."[72] This norm was acknowledged and endorsed not only by civilists,[73] but also by canonists.[74] Reference has already been made to the classification of

---

n. 8, fol. 77v.

[69] L. *Nulla iuris*, 25, D., *De legibus senatusque consultis et longa consuetudine*, 1, 3: "Nulla iuris ratio aut aequitatis benignitas patitur, ut quae salubriter pro utilitate hominum introducuntur, ea nos duriore interpretatione contra ipsorum commodum producamus ad severitatem."

[70] *In Quartum Decretalium . . . , De Eo, qui duxit in Matrimonium, quam polluit per Adulterium*, cap. 5, *Cum haberet*, n. 11, fol. 20 v. "magis insistit veritati, quam subtilitati."

[71] CYNUS PISTORIENSIS, *In Codicem Commentaria*, Liber IV, Tit. 18, *De Constituta Pecunia*, n. 1, fol. 209 v: "ubi est eadem ratio aequitatis, idem ius esse debet"; cf. HENRICUS DE SEGUSIO, *In Primum Decretalium . . . , De Translatione Episcopi vel Electi*, cap. 2, *Inter corporalia*, n. 32, fol. 82 v.

[72] Impp. Constantinus et Licinius, L. *Placuit*, 2, C., *De iudiciis*, 3, 1: "Placuit in omnibus rebus praecipuam esse iustitiae aequitatisque quam stricti iuris rationem"; cf. Paulus, L. *In omnibus*, 90, D., *De diversis regulis iuris antiqui*, 50,17: "In omnibus quidem, maxime tamen in iure aequitas spectanda est"; cf. notam 11.

[73] AZO, *Brocardica Aurea*, Neapoli 1568, Rubrica 71, *De Iustitia et Iure atque Aequitate*, fol. 152r; *Summa Institutionum*, Liber IV, *De Officio Iudicis*, p. 382, col. 1; *Ad Singulas Leges XII . . .*, Liber III, Tit. 1, *De Iudiciis*, Lex 8, n. 2, p. 167; Liber V, Tit. 17, *De Repudiis, et Iudicio de Monilibus sublato*, Lex 1, n. 3, p. 406; CYNUS PISTORIENSIS, *In Codicem Commentaria*, Liber III, Tit. 1, *De Iudiciis*, n. 1, fol. 129r; *In Digesti Veteris . . .*, Rubrica XIV, *De Officio Praetoris*, n. 5, fol. 13v; PILEUS MODICENSIS, *Quaestiones Aureae*, qu. 29, n. 8, p. 45.

[74] HENRICUS DE SEGUSIO, *In Primum Decretalium . . . , De Transactionibus*, cap. 11, *Ex parte tua*, n. 10, fol. 181v; *In Secundum Decretalium . . . , De Ordine Cognitionum* cap. 2, *Cum dilectus*, n. 16, fol. 37r; *De Exceptionibus*, cap. 9, *Apostolicae Sedis*, n. 5, fol. 145r; *Quintum Decretalium . . . , De Sententia Excommunicationis*, cap. 32, *Cum illorum*, n. 7, fol. 114v;

equity into *aequitas non scripta* and *aequitas scripta*. By *aequitas non scripta* it is meant natural law; Azo terms this type of equity *Rudis*, common to all humans, since it is engraved in the human heart.[75] *Aequitas scripta* is that which is explicitly endorsed by legal justice -- "quae in corpore iuris est collocata" (which is found in the code of law).[76] It is understood, however, that the principle announced in *lex, Placuit*, is only applicable to *aequitas scripta*.[77] According to Albericus, *aequitas scripta* does not *a priori* prevail over the law; its superiority can only be upheld when the law sanctions something in general, and equity prescribes something in particular, or when both law and equity establish something in general or in particular, but not when the law deals with the matter in particular, and equity in general.[78]

In the category of *aequitas scripta*, the following *Regulae Iuris in VI°* may be included. However, in the understanding of Albericus these *Regulae Iuris* prescribe the matter in general:

1. Nemo potest ad impossibile obligari (R.I.6).
2. Odia restringi et favores convenit ampliari (R.I.15).
3. In poenis benignior est interpretatio facienda (R.I.49).
4. Non debet aliquis odio alterius praegravari (R.I.22).
5. Qui prior est tempore potior est jure (R.I.54).

IOANNES ANDREAE, *In Primum Decretalium* . . . , *De Consuetudine*, cap. 11, *Cum tanto*, n. 43, fol. 61v; ALBERICUS DE ROSATE, *Dictionarium* . . . , v. *Aequitas*, p. 31; ANTONIUS A BUTRIO, *In Librum Quintum Decretalium Commentarii Septimus Tomus*, Venetiis 1578, *De Sententia Excommunicationis*, cap. 32, *Cum illorum*, n. 29, fol. 127r.

[75] *Ad Singulas Leges XII* . . . , Liber I, Tit. 14, *De Legibus et Constitutionibus*, n. 2, p. 39; Liber III, Tit. 1, *De Iudiciis*, Lex 8, n. 3, p. 167; *Summa Institutionum*, Liber IV, *De Officio Iudicis*, p. 382, col. 1; *Summa Super Codicem*, Liber I, *Incipit Materia ad Codicem*, p. 1, col. 2.

[76] *Ad Singulas Leges XII* . . . , Liber I, Tit. 14, *De Legibus et Constitutionibus*, n. 4, p. 39.

[77] AZO, *Summa Institutionum*, Liber IV, *De Officio Iudicis*, p. 382, col. 1; *Ad Singulas Leges XII* . . . , Liber I, Tit. 14, *De Legibus et Constitutionibus*, n. 4, p. 39; Liber III, Tit. 1, *De Iudiciis*, lex 8, n. 4, p. 167; HENRICUS DE SEGUSIO, *In Primum Decretalium* . . . *De Transactionibus*, cap.11, *Ex parte tua*, n. 10, fol. 181v; BALDUS DE UBALDIS, *In Decretalium Volumen* . . . , *Super Secundo Decretalium*, *De Restitutione Spoliatorum*, cap. 11, *Gravis*, n. 8, fol. 184v.

[78] *Dictionarium* . . . , v. *Aequitas*, p. 31.

6. Locupletari non debet aliquis cum alterius iniuria vel iactura (R.I.48).
7. Quae a iure communi exorbitant nequamquam ad consequentiam sunt trahenda (R.I.28).
8. Cum sint partium iura obscura reo favendum est potius quam actori (R.I.16).
9. Non licet actori quod reo licitum non existit (R.I.32).

Ubertus De Bonacurso[79] and Bagarotus[80] offer an exhaustive casuistic as to when equity should be applied in Court.

Explicit mention of equity is made in the Code of canon law where a clear distinction is indicated between equity and charity.[81] Equity is thus conceived of as a rightful claim of the individual rather than the virtue of magnanimity on the part of the Superior. The adjective is sometimes used in lieu of the noun, such as, "equitable fashion,"[82] "equitable solution,"[83] "equitable manner,"[84] "good and equitable."[85] The Code seems to attest to three different types of equity: equity in general,[86] natural equity,[87] canonical equity.[88] The qualifications, "natural" and "canonical" are used only to distort the basic concept. In reality, these two different types of equity signify the same ontological truth, natural law engraved in human

---

[79] *Preludia et Exceptiones*, foll. 9v., 61r., 96r.-v., 109r.

[80] *Tractatus de Reprobationibus Testium*, Lugduni, 1549, nn.2,7, 10, 24, 25, p.4; *Tractatus Perutilis de Exceptionibus, Dilatoriis, et Declinatoriis Iudicii*, nn. 2, 8,9, 10,11, 19, 20, 27, 40, 41, 46, 49, 53, 58, 61, 62, 77, foll. 100v. 101v.

[81] Cf. canons 686, §3; 702, §2; 1148, §3.

[82] Canon 1346.

[83] Canons 1446, §2; 1733, §1, 2.

[84] Canon 1580.

[85] Canon 1718, §4.

[86] Cf. canons 221, §2; 686, §3; 702, §2.

[87] Cf. canons 271, §3; 1148, §3.

[88] Cf. canon 1752.

consciousness. "Canonical equity" is natural equity endorsed by the Code -- a qualification which is utterly meaningless. "Canonical equity" is meant to indicate natural equity enlightened and inspired by Evangelical truth; in that case, however, not only equity, but the canonical codification in whole and in every single canon, by its very nature, should reflect human consciousness, enlightened and imbued by the Gospel truth, in implementing its inherent divine law in the pursuance of becoming morally what it is ontologically.

Equity as Rectification of Legal Justice

The limitedness of legal justice requires that it resort to equity as rectification of its own laws. This reality also implies the subordination to and dependency of the legal justice on divine justice. In this sense, Hostiensis[89] and Antonius A Butrio[90] define equity as relaxation of the law. Azo qualifies it as *exceptio*,[91] *interpretatio*,[92] *dispensatio*,[93] *excusatio*.[94] In principle, all these terms can rightfully be attributed to equity. However, each of these terms denotes a specific juridic concept which in law must be maintained. The use of the word, "rectification," is intentional for better clarity. Thus equity, as rectification of legal justice, comprises *epikeia*, interpretation and dispensation.

---

[89] *In Quintum Decretalium* . . . , *De Sententia Excommunicationis*, cap. 32, *Cum illorum*, n. 7, fol. 114v.

[90] *In Librum Quintum* . . . , *De Sententia Excomnunicationis*, cap. 32, *Cum illorum*, n. 29, fol. 127r.

[91] *Ad Singulas Leges XII* . . . , Liber III, Tit. 1, *De Iudiciis*, lex 8, n.3, p. 167: "exceptiones sunt de aequitate."

[92] Loc. cit., Liber I, Tit. 14, *De Legibus et Constitutionibus*, nn. 4, 5, P. 39.

[93] Loc. cit., Liber III, Tit. 1, *De Iudiciis*, Lex 8, n. 4, p. 167.

[94] *Brocardica Aurea*, Rubrica 81, *De Necessitate et Paupertate*, fol. 165v.

Epikeia

It appears from the "Ethics" of Aristotle that the Greek legal system recognized equity as rectification of its laws. The notion of equity as *epikeia* given by Aristotle is as valid today as it was in Classical Greece: "So when the law states a general rule, and a case arises under this that is exceptional, then it is right, where the legislator owing to the generality of his language has erred in not covering that case, to correct the omission by a ruling such as the legislator himself would have given if he had been present there, and as he would have enacted if he had been aware of the circumstances."[95]

In the *Corpus Iuris Civilis* the endorsement of equity as *epikeia* was a *fait accompli*. In the analysis of the Roman codification two basic reasons stand out in justification of *epikeia*: one reason resides in the nature of the law itself, the other is found in the application of the law to particular circumstances. It is in the nature of the law that its aim be directed towards the ordinary, the usual, and the general. "Laws are instituted for the common good, and not for the private good";[96] "Laws are not established because of incidents which very rarely take place";[97] "Laws do not concern themselves with rare cases but rather with matters which frequently and easily occur."[98] The Roman legislator was fully conscious that the generality of the aim was the very imperfection of the law and that this generality in particular actuality might cause conflict between the intended justice and the absolute principle of justice. To overcome this difficulty it was necessary to resort to equity. Thus the jurisprudence of

---

[95] *Ethics*, Bk V, chap. X, p. 199; cf. THOMAS AQUINAS, *Summa Theologica*, IIa-IIae, q. 60, art. 5, ad 2um, *American Ed.*, vol. II, p. 1450.

[96] Ulpianus, L. *Iura*, 8, D., *De legibus senatusque consultis et longa consuetudine*, 1, 3. "Iura non in singulas personas, sed generaliter constituuntur."

[97] Celsus, L. *Ex his*, 4, ibid. "Ex his, quae forte uno aliquo casu accidere possunt, iura non constituuntur."

[98] Celsus, L. *Nam*, 5, ibid. "Nam ad ea potius debet aptari ius, quae et frequenter et facile, quam quae perraro eveniunt."

epikeia finds its raison d'être in the following laws: "In the execution of law it is imperative that equity be upheld in all matters";[99] "Nulla iuris ratio aut aequitatis benignitas patitur, ut quae salubriter pro utilitate hominum introducuntur, ea nos duriore interpretatione contra ipsorum commodum producamus ad severitatem."[100] *Epikeia* was an excellent tool in the hands of the *praetor*, his use of this principle helped ensure the immortality of Roman law.[101] The Roman philosophy on *epikeia* can be summarized in one single phrase: "Necessity and poverty recognize no law."[102]

The Aristotelian concept of *epikeia* as interpretation of the law finds approval in canon law. Indeed, *epikeia* is in essence interpretation, not of the letter of the law, but of its spirit, of *mens legislatoris*. This concept is emphasized by Gregory IX in *Liber X*: "Expressions are to be understood according to the proper meaning of words since speech should relate faithfully to the matter in question, and not the matter to speech";[103] Pope Gregory insists that one should be concerned not with the words expressed but with the will and intention of the person concerned. The intention should not be subordinate to the words, but rather the words

---

[99] Paulus, L. *In omnibus*, 90, D., *De diversis regulis iuris antiqui*, 50, 17. "In omnibus quidem, maxime tamen in iure aequitas spectanda est."

[100] Modestinus, L. *Nulla iuris*, 25, D., *De legibus senatusque consultis et longa consuetudine*, 1. 3.

[101] Inst., *De legitima adgnatorum successione*, 3, 2, §3a: " . . . donec praetores, paulatim asperitatem iuris civilis corrigentes sive quod deestadimplentes, humano proposito alium ordinem suis edictis addiderunt . . . "; §7 " . . . quod iterum praetores imperfecto iure corrigentes non in totum sine adminiculo relinquebant . . . sed nos nihil deesse perfectissimo iuri cupientes nostra constitutione sanximus . . . ."

[102] Cf. Inst. *De hereditatibus quae ab intestato deferuntur*, 3, 1, §9: "necessitas aut paupertas non habet legem"; Ulpianus, L. *Si autem*, 7(8), D., *De negotiis gestis*, 3, 5, §3; Ulpianus, L. *Sin autem*, 19(20) ibid; Ulpianus, L. *Divus Pius*, 5, D., *De hereditatis petitione*, 5, 3; Paulus, L. *Quaesitum*, 9, D., *De distractione pignorum et hypothecarum*, 20, 5; Impp. Arcadius et Honorius, L. *Eos*, 6, C., *De Modo multarum, quae ab iudicibus infliguntur*, 1, 54, §6; Impp. Severus et Antoninus, L. *Si tempore*, 1, C. *De operis libertorum*, 6, 3; Imp. Constantinus, L. *Si quis*, 2, C., *De patribus qui filios distraxerunt*, 4, 43.

[103] Liber V, Tit. 40, *De Verborum Significatione*, cap. VI. "Intelligentia dictorum ex causis est assumenda dicendi, quia non sermoni res, sed rei est sermo subiectus."

ought to be at the service of one's intention. This means that the words are taken to mean instruments with which human will and intention are manifested.[104] *Epikeia* is in essence dispensation, and may correctly be defined as *iuris relaxatio, excusatio*. This statement, however, needs clarification. *Epikeia* is a dispensation, not from the spirit of the law, but from the letter of the law, since in *epikeia* it is presumed that *mens legislatoris* concurs in the relaxation of the letter of the law due to particular circumstances. In this context *epikeia* may also be termed *licentia praesumpta*. On the other hand, *epikeia* differs from dispensation in the strict sense since in the application of *epikeia* it is the individual subject who takes upon himself the responsibility of waiving with the observance of the law, whereas in the case of dispensation the one who grants it must have authorization to do so. The following is the definition of *epikeia* commonly given by canonical authors: "*Epikeia* is a benign interpretation of the law in accordance with what is equitable and good. It interprets the mind of the legislator as having made a clause of exemption in the prescription of law for a particular case due to extraordinary circumstances."[105]

Epikeia is humanness itself since it is an indication that legal justice acknowledges the presence of the individual human being within its system and that the member has his own personal needs. By means of *epikeia* an equilibrium is maintained between the good of the individual and the good of the community. *Epikeia*, per se, militates against the absolutism of the law. A legal system, which allows *epikeia* in the observance of its laws,

---

[104] Ibid., cap. XV. "... quod iuxta eundem Gregorium non debet aliquis considerare verba, sed voluntatem et intentionem, quum non intentio verbis, sed verba intentioni debeant deservire."

[105] Cf. REIFFENSTUEL, ANACLETUS, *Ius Canonicum Universum*, Parisiis, 1889, vol. I, Liber 1, Tit. 2, *De Constitutionibus*, para.15, *De Interpretatione Legum, sive Constitutionum*, n. 378, p. 183: "Epikeia est benigna legum interpretatio secundum aequum et bonum, declarans casum aliquem particularem ex mente legislatoris ob suas circumstantias speciales sub lege universaliter lata non esse comprehensum"; FERRARIS, LUCIUS, F., *Prompta Bibliotheca Canonica, Iuridica, Moralis, Theologica*, Lutetiae Parisiorum, 1865, Tomus V, v. *Lex*, art. 5, n. 41, col. 91; SCHMALZGRUEBER, FRANCISCUS, *Ius Ecclesiasticum Universum*, Romae, 1843, Tomus I, Pars 1, parsI, Tit. 2, para. 7, n. 49, pp. 217-218.

proves itself to be the expression of a civilized esprit de corps. Only a dictatorial political system, which is insecure and weak, does not recognize the right of its members to decide in particular circumstances how best to observe the law according to one's rationality and conscientiousness, without losing sight of the common good.

Interpretation

Under this heading the term "interpretation" is not understood in a broad sense as to be equivalent to *epikeia*, namely, *iuris relaxatio*, *excusatio*; it is understood rather in a strict sense; hence the departure of the concept of interpretation from *epikeia*. Interpretation, in the strict sense, means the literal reading of the law, whereas *epikeia* is the understanding of the spirit of the law, that is, the mind of the lawgiver.[106] In this sense, interpretation does not equal dispensation.

Authentic interpretation of the law, which is the subject of canon 16, §1,2, is not the concern of the present theme. Our attention is centered upon the doctrinal interpretation of law, which forms the subject-matter of canons 17 and 18. The legislator in these canons recognizes the purport of the community in the life of the law, in its evolution and transformation, in order that it may ever more genuinely express the mind of l'esprit de corps. The legislator, as it were, places the law in the hands of his subjects that through them it may undergo a crisis of growth. In this manner, the law, which by reason of origin, is an authentic expression of the universal human consciousness through the legislator, by that very reason turns back to its source in order to form an integral part of the same consciousness. Thus we basically understand canon 17: "Ecclesiastical laws are to be understood according to the proper meaning of the words

---

[106] FERRARIS, L. F., *Prompta Bibliotheca* . . . , Tomus V, v. *Lex*, art. 5, n. 42, col. 91: "In hoc autem differt epicheia ab interpretatione legis, quod per interpretationem interpretantur verba legis, quando sunt obscura, et ambiguum sensum reddunt; per epicheiam vero interpretatur mens legislatoris, ubi constat de universali verborum sensu, dubitatur autem de mente legislatoris, utrum nempe is talem casum particularem, ob certas circumstantias, voluerit, vel potuerit comprehendere sub generali locutione legis." Cf. REIFFENSTUEL, A., *Ius Canonicum* . . . , vol. I, Liber 1, Tit. 2, para. 15, n. 379, p. 183.

Equity, Epikeia and Dispensation

considered in their text and context. If the meaning remains doubtful or obscure, there must be recourse to parallel places, if there be any, to the purpose and circumstances of the law, and to the mind of the legislator." Canon 18 sanctions: "Laws which prescribe a penalty, or restrict the free exercise of rights, or contain an exception to the law, are to be interpreted strictly."

It is evidently clear that the ecclesiastical legislator, in canons 17 and 18, is placing the institution of interpretation within the spectrum of equity. The *mens legis* of these canons is that equity be always maintained and safeguarded from the absolutism of legal justice. Indeed, this *ratio iuris* can also be envisaged in the Roman laws, *Nulla iuris*,[107] and *Semper*.[108] One of the essential qualities of the law, as pointed out earlier, is clarity. Without prejudice to the provision of canon 17, the centuries old axiom, "lex dubia, lex nulla," or "In dubio, libertas," still holds its validity in the interpretation of the canon. Indeed, this axiom should be recognized as *aequitas Scripta* since it forms the prescription of canon 14: "Laws, even invalidating and incapacitating ones, do not oblige when there is a doubt of law."

Canon 18 aims at the preservation of equity in opposition to the rigour of law in three different spheres of legal activity: criminal imputability; exercise of one's rights; exception to the law. Azo remarks: "The Gospel should dominate the mind of the judge through-out the legal proceedings."[109] In our belief, this golden rule must be maintained in any kind of interpretation of the law, whether judicial, executive, or doctrinal. A genuine interpretation of the Gospel is the *Regula Iuris*, "Nemo potest ad impossibile obligari" (R.I.,6). In a previous publication,[110] we have

---

[107] Modestinus, L., *Nulla iuris*, 25,D., *De legibus senatusque consultis et longa consuetudine*, 1, 3: "Nulla iuris ratio aut aequitatis benignitas patitur, ut quae salubriter pro utilitate hominum introducuntur, ea nos duriore interpretatione contra ipsorum commodum producamus ad severitatem."

[108] Gaius, L. *Semper*, 56, D., *De diversis regulis iuris antiqui*, 50, 17: "Semper in dubiis benigniora praeferenda sunt."

[109] *Summa Institutionum*, Liber IV, *De Officio Iudicis*, p. 382, col. 1. "praesentia evangeliorum debet esse apud iudicem a principio iudicii usque ad finem."

[110] *The Endorsement of Human Dignity in the Jurisprudence of the Sacred Roman Rota in the XVI-*

demonstrated that, both in the Rota jurisprudence and in canonical and civilist literature, preference was given to the Respondent over the Plaintiff: "reus est praeferendus"; "actore non probante, reus absolvitur." *Regula Iuris* also dictates: "What is denied to the respondent is not permitted to the plaintiff."[111] Pileus synthesizes the traditional doctrine on the subject in this manner: "In all cases the judge should be more disposed to absolve than to condemn."[112] Preference to the position of the *reus* turns even into leniency in criminal imputability; thus *Regula Iuris* prescribes: "In poenis benignior est interpretatio facienda" (R.I.,49). The prescription of canon 1313, §1,2, has its *ratio iuris* in this *Regula Iuris*.

Laws which restrict the free exercise of rights are strictly interpreted. No one can ever question the justification of this law; it cuts right into the heart of the issue of human dignity; it implies the natural right of the individual's freedom to master his own destiny. The *Regula Iuris*, "Odia restringi et favores convenit ampliari" (R.I.15), not rarely may be of assistance in the application of this law. This said, however, we do not accept the concept of right in an absolute manner; the concept of right is contingent upon the stage of human consciousness; it clarifies a par with gradual explication of human consciousness of its inherent authenticity.

The third strict interpretation refers to laws, either found in the Code itself or outside, which constitute an exception to the common law. The universal conviction of today's society is that all members are equal in the eyes of the law. Laws containing an exception to the general rule are thereby considered as a breach with the wholesomeness of the esprit de corps. On the one hand, legal justice is bound to acknowledge and endorse personal needs flowing from one's uniqueness; on the other hand, a favour

---

XVII Centuries, in *The Jurist*, 42(1982) 2, pp. 481s.

[111] R.I.32, in VIº: "non licet actori quod reo licitum non existit"; cf. R.I. 11: "Cum sint partium iura obscura reo favendum est potius quam actori."

[112] *Quaestiones Aureae*, qu. 29, n. 8, p. 45: "proniores enim universi debent esse iudices ad absolvendum quam ad condemnandum"; cf. n.7, p.44; HENRICUS DE SEGUSIO, *In Primum Decretalium . . . , De Transactionibus*, cap. 11, *Ex parte tua*, n.11, fol. 181v; ALBERICUS DE ROSATE, *Dictionarium . . .* , v. *Aequitas*, p. 31.

Equity, Epikeia and Dispensation   135

granted to one may be burdensome to another individual or to the community at large.[113] Upon the aforesaid presupposition, one can easily peruse the rationale behind the prescriptions of canon 36, §1, (on administrative acts), of canon 77 (on privileges), and of canon 92 (on dispensation), that in case of doubt in the meaning of the words entailed therein a strict interpretation is to be given. In this manner, the ultimate aim of equity is attended to in retaining an equilibrium between the good of the individual and the good of the community. The following *Regulae Iuris* may help clarify the *ratio iuris* of canon 18 which prescribes that laws containing an exception to the law are to be interpreted strictly:

"Non debet aliquis odio alterius praegravari" (R.I., 22);

"Locupletari non debet aliquis cum alterius iniuria vel iactura" (R.I.48);

"Quae a iure communi exorbitant nequaquam ad consequentiam sunt trahenda" (R.I.,28);[114]

"In argumentum trahi nequeunt quae propter necessitatem aliquando sunt concessa" (R.I.,78);

"Quod alicui gratiose conceditur trahi non debet ab aliis in exemplum" (R.I.,74).

Dispensation

Another institution, besides *epikeia*, which flows intrinsically from the concept of equity is dispensation. This premise *a priori* runs counter to the understanding of dispensation as a wound inflicted upon the law, *vulnus legis*,[115] or violation of the law, *violatio iuris*.[116] A total dismissal of

---

[113] Pars II, Causa XXV, q.1, c. 16, II pars. This conflict of interests is pointed out in the *Decretum Gratiani*: "Valet ergo, ut ex premissis colligitur, sancta Romana ecclesia quoslibet suis privilegiis munire, et extra generalia decreta quedam speciali beneficio indulgere, considerata tamen rationis equitate, ut que mater iusticiae est in nullo ab ea dissentire inveniatur, ut privilegia videlicet, que ob religionis, vel necessitatis, vel exhibiti obsequii gratiam conceduntur, neminem relevando ita divitem faciant, ut, multorum detrimenta non circumspiciendo, in paupertatis miseriam nonnullos deiciant."

[114] Cf. Paulus, L. *Quod vero*, 14, D., *De legibus senatusque consultis et longa consuetudine*, 1, 3; Iulianus, L. *In his*, 15, ibid.

[115] ALBERICUS DE ROSATE, *Dictionarium* . . ., v. *Dispensatio*, p. 189.

[116] BALDUS DE UBALDIS, *In Decretalium Volumen* . . ., *Super Primo Decretalium, De Electione et Electi Potestate*, cap. 59, *Si alicuius*, n. 7, fol. 91v.

dispensation in a legal system can only be cherished by a political philosophy fostering absolute sovereignty of the legal justice. Such a political creed implicitly entails a total denial of the eternal truth and justice. One is faced at this point with a predicament: dispensation, like *epikeia*, signals a paradox in the context of human consciousness as the embodiment of equity; dispensation registers a humanized human consciousness which still functions at a stage of mediocrity. This statement certainly needs explanation. On the one hand, it takes a developed human consciousness to acknowledge and appreciate dispensation as an essential component of legal justice. The endorsement of dispensation indicates at what stage human consciousness has arrived in the process of its own humanization. The emerging universal awareness of the dignity and uniqueness of the human being necessitates the indispensability of dispensation in the legal system. The institution of dispensation presupposes a legal system which has outgrown its own insecurity and inflexibility, and which is capable of maintaining an equilibrium between the good of the individual and that of the community.[117] Indeed, the institution of dispensation, like *epikeia*, reveals the inherent imperfection and limitedness of the human law,[118] but, at the same time, it is through dispensation that the legal system adroitly posits eternal justice into practice. "To dispense," states Hostiensis, "is to discern prudently between different matters and to decide whether a relaxation of the law in a particular case is expedient";[119] in other words, the Superior must decide whether the vigour

---

[117] *Summa Theologica*, Ia-IIae, q. 97, art. 4, ad lum, *American Ed.*, p. 1025: "When a person is dispensed from observing the general law, this should not be done to the prejudice of, but with the intention of benefitting, the common good."

[118] Ibid., Resp., p. 1025: "Now it happens at times that a precept, which is conducive to the common weal as a general rule, is not good for a particular individual, or in some particular case, either because it would hinder some greater good, or because it would be the occasion of some evil."

[119] *In Primum Decretalium . . . , De Renunciatione*, cap. 10, *Nisi cum pridem*, n. 78, fol. 93r. "Dispensare enim est diversa discrete pensare, et in animo, an relaxatio iuris expediat, versare."

Equity, Epikeia and Dispensation

of the law should give way to equity: "the judge in his discernment should peruse prudently and evaluate what benefits mostly the Church, namely, whether to follow the rigour of the law or to let the exercise of equity prevail."[120] On the other hand, it takes a fully developed human consciousness to do away with many laws which for their part often require dispensation. The existence of dispensation denotes a human consciousness which still needs a gamut of laws in order to function properly.

Canon 85 defines dispensation as "the relaxation of a merely ecclesiastical law in a particular case." The definition of dispensation is self-explanatory. However, this definition concerns itself with the nature of the thing, the mere actuality, leaving open to discussion the question of the right of the subject to ask for dispensation and the obligation of the Superior to grant it. In civil law, as Baldus De Ubaldis points out, the term *indulgentia* is used in lieu of *dispensatio*.[121] Baldus himself defines dispensation as *mera gratia*.[122] For Hostiensis dispensation denotes *clementia*,[123] whereas Antonius A Butrio understands dispensation as *indulgentia*.[124] This nomenclature insinuates by itself a condescending attitude of the Superior in the granting of dispensation vis-à-vis a supplicatory demeanour on the part of the petitioner -- a contention which we strongly rebut. Our refutation rests on two main reasons, namely, the existence of a cause in the granting of dispensation, and the limitedness of the human law.

---

[120] Loc. cit., *De Filiis Presbiterorum*, cap. 5, *Veniens*, n. 6, fol. 115r. "iudex in lance mentis suae discrete pensat et ponderat quid magis ecclesiae expedit, scilicet, sequi rigorem iuris, vel ei aequitatis dispensationem praeferre."

[121] *In Decretalium Volumen . . . , Super Secundo Decretalium, De Iudiciis*, cap. 4, *At si clerici*, n. 10, fol. 153v.

[122] Ibid., *De Appellationibus*, cap. 60, *Cum cessante*, n. 7, fol. 304r.

[123] *In Primum Decretalium Librum . . . , De Electione et Electi Potestate*, cap. 32, *Cum dilectus*, n. 2, fol. 58r.

[124] *Super Prima Primi Decretalium . . . , De Translatione Praelatorum*, cap. 4, *Licet*, n. 7, fol. 155v.

Canon 90, §1, reads: "A dispensation from an ecclesiastical law is not to be given without a just and reasonable cause, taking into account the circumstances of the case and the importance of the law from which the dispensation is given; otherwise the dispensation is unlawful and, unless given by the legislator or his Superior, it is also invalid." In the canon a principle is laid down that no law can be dispensed without an existing cause: a dispensation granted without reason is unlawful when given by the legislator or his Superior and invalid if given by an inferior to the legislator. Authors who conceive of dispensation as *indulgentia, gratia*, and *clementia* are the same ones who insist on the existence of a cause in the granting of dispensation.[125] Hostiensis emphatically maintains that "a dispensation granted without a just cause, is not dispensation at all but dissipation of the law."[126] The dependency of dispensation on the cause is such that once the cause ceases to exist, dispensation loses its validity. "Once the cause of dispensation is removed, the dispensation loses its valid reason to be."[127] Canon 93 prescribes apropos: "A dispensation capable of successive applications ceases in the same way as a privilege. It also ceases by the certain and complete cessation of the motivating reason."

The principle announced in canon 90, §1, together with canon 93, that there must be a reason for the granting of dispensation, proceeds from the fundamental assumption that human law, in order to be just, should

---

[125] BALDUS DE UBALDIS, *In Decretalium Volumen* . . . , *Super Secundo Decretalium, De Appellationibus*, cap. 60, *Cum cessante*, n.7, fol. 304r; HENRICUS DE SEGUSIO, *In Primum Decretalium* . . . , *De Electione et Electi Potestate*, cap.19, *Cum nobis*, n. 20, fol. 47r; eod. Tit., cap. 54, *Dudum*, n. 45, fol. 76v; *De Renunciatione*, cap. 10, *Nisi cum pridem*, n. 75, fol. 92v; *In Tertium Decretalium* . . . , *De Voto et Voti Redemptione*, cap. 1, *De Peregrinatione Votis*, n. 6, fol. 124v; AZO, *Brocardica Aurea*, Rubrica 81, *De Necessitate et Paupertate*, fol. 165v; ALBERICUS DE ROSATE, *Dictionarium* . . . , v. *Dispensatio*, pp. 188, 189; ANTONIUS A BUTRIO, *Super Prima Primi Decretalium* . . . Tomus I, *De Electione*, cap.44, *Nihil*, n. 10, fol. 140v; *In Sextum Decretalium Volumen* . . . , *De Aetate et Qualitate, et Ordine Praeficiendorum*, cap. 1, *Permittimus*, nn. 8, 9, fol. 76r.

[126] *In Primum Decretalium Librum* . . . , *De Renunciatione*, cap. 10, *Nisi cum pridem*, n. 78, fol. 93r. "dispensatio sine causa facta, non dispensatio, sed potius dissipatio dici debet."

[127] BALDUS DE UBALDIS, *In Decretalium Volumen* . . . , *Super Primo Decretalium, De Electione et Electi Potestate*, cap. 59, *Si alicuius*, n. 8, fol. 91v. "Sublata causa dispensationis tollitur dispensatio."

accord with eternal justice -- "Nil in temporali lege iustum quod ab aeterno non derivetur." Human law thus appears as a reflection, expression, and implementation of eternal truth, and the law-giver automatically assumes the role of interpreter of the divine Will, rather than that of the ultimate source of law. For this precise reason, the legislator becomes subject to the law which he himself has enacted, hence the political theory which maintains "legislator sub lege." It stands to reason, therefore, that the legislator has no absolute authority over his own laws, and that neither he nor his Superior can lawfully grant dispensation without a cause proportionate to the gravity of the law.[128] Thus we cannot concur with the contention of Antonius A Butrio that the Roman Pontiff needs no motivating reason to lawfully grant a dispensation.[129] This leads to the conclusion that the ecclesiastical dispenser is not acting out of magnanimity of heart, but, as an interpreter of the divine Will, he is to see to it that his law be a true interpretation, rather than a hindrance, of divine justice. The existence of a cause proportionate to the gravity of the law imposes upon the dispenser an obligation to grant dispensation.

Granted the existence of a cause is a *conditio-sine-qua-non* for the validity or lawfulness of dispensation, reason forces one to perceive the cause as the source of the individual's right to petition and be granted dispensation. Azo seems to adhere to this position when he states "one deserves exemption whenever necessity calls for it."[130] Henricus De Segusio maintains that whenever there is a reason the person has a right to the granting of dispensation (debita est dispensatio), and therefore the superior sins in not granting it (praelatus peccat non dispensando).[131] Albericus De

---

[128] According to the Aquinatis, "If however he grant this permission without any such reason, and of his mere will, he will be an unfaithful or an imprudent dispenser," *Summa Theologica*, Ia-IIae, q. 97, art. 4, Resp., American Ed., p. 1025.

[129] *In Librum Tertium Decretalium Commentarii Quintus Tomus*, Venetiis, 1578, *De Voto, et Voti Redemptione*, cap. 5, *Non est*, n. 4, fol. 149r.

[130] *Brocardica Aurea*, Rubrica 81, *De Necessitate et Paupertate*, fol. 165v. "propter necessitatem aliquem mereri excusationem."

[131] *In Primum Decretalium Librum . . .*, *De Renunciatione*, cap. 10, *Nisi cum pridem*, nn. 75,76, fol. 92v; *De Transactionibus*, cap. 11, *Ex parte tua*, n.4, fol. 181v.

Rosate, while agreeing with Hostiensis, nevertheless interprets the petition as mere supplication, rather than a right enjoyed by the petitioner;[132] this is a position which goes beyond our comprehension. Antonius A Butrio distinguishes between *dispensatio debita* and *dispensatio non debita*: the former arises from a cause, and thereby constitutes a right; the latter is devoid of a motivating reason, and hence it denotes mercy on the part of the dispenser.[133] We cannot subscribe to this position since as Hostiensis points out, "that dispensing from the law without a just cause is nothing other than breaking the law." Moreover, the dispenser, in granting dispensation without a reason, is placing himself above the law, as the ultimate source of justice, whereas he is a mere interpreter of the eternal Will. Thus Hostiensis concludes: "Also the Roman Pontiff should never grant a dispensation without a sufficient cause."[134] Our understanding of the right of the individual in being granted dispensation can be summarized as follows: the legislator or his Superior in relaxing the law is subordinating himself to reason, to that same truth and justice which forms the source and aim of the law; it is that same motivating reason which entitles the individual to the right to be exempted from the said law; by that same reason, as well, the dispenser is bound in conscience to waive the law.

Law must be just to be valid. The limitedness of the human law to implement *in integro* eternal justice, *a priori* posits the same law as cause of injustice, not in the universality of things, but in their specifics. Law is law only in the sphere of existentialism. What is actual is real, true, and rational, and only in actuality does the law come into being, and its justice be attained. In particular circumstances, when the law contradicts itself as

---

[132] *Dictionarium* . . . , v. *Dispensatio*, p. 189: "Licet ex causis praedictis dispensatio sit debita, et peccet praelatus non dispensando . . . tamen subditi non habent ius petendi, nisi forte supplicando."

[133] *In Sextum Decretalium Volumen* . . . , *De Electione, et Electi Potestate*, cap. 14, *Licet canon*, n. 10, fol. 47r: "Dicit tamen, quod ubi dispensatio est debita, ius est: quia executiva iustitiae . . . si vero sit permissa non debita, tunc non est ius, sed misericordia."

[134] *In Secundum Decretalium Librum* . . . , *De Sententia et Re Iudicata*, cap. 19, *In causis*, n. 7, fol. 166v. "sine causa non debet etiam Summus Pontifex dispensare."

a reflection of eternal justice, alienates itself from itself, becomes reason by itself not to be, a reason which entitles the subject to the right not to observe the law, that same law *ex sese* calls for its own dispensation. The competent authority is thus expected to recognize the injustice of the law in specific actuality by the nature of the law itself; indirectly the same authority is acknowledging human dignity as superior to the law.

From the foregoing presentation one can appreciate the prescriptions of canons 87, §1, 2; 88, and 91. An exception, however, is made with laws which define the constitution of institutes, and juridical acts (canon 86), and those which deal with judicial proceedings and penalties (canon 87, §1). Apart from penal laws, all these types of law do not concern the well-being of the individual person if not indirectly and remotely. Although penal laws cannot be dispensed with, there are causes contemplated in Canon Law, and principles in the understanding of the human act, which either excuse or diminish the person's imputability towards crime.

Dispensation, like *epikeia*, pertains as an integral part to the concept of equity. In both cases the endeavour is basically the same, namely, to retain an equipoise between the good of the individual and the good of the community.[135] The common good must be alive and active, but the private good must likewise be fully and vividly developed. Only if both aspects are present in their full vigour can l'esprit de corps be considered structured and truly organized. It must be said, however, that in dispensation and in *epikeia* a disruption in the intensity of l'esprit de corps, albeit minimal, is caused, a certain amount of disquilibrium is registered in the global harmonization. Individual human consciousness is itself realized only as a part of a concrete whole; its self-awareness is drawn to the fullest from common life in and with others; it only finds its true inherent universal content in and with the community; in the social setting it is at once its full self and realization of universal mind. Albericus De Rosate insists that dispensation "should not be taken as a norm."[136] Indeed, if circumstances

---

[135] Dispensation and *epikeia* are essentially the same thing: both signify relaxation of the law in a particular case. They differ only in that in *epikeia* the person takes upon himself the responsibility which would otherwise belong to one invested with such an authority.

[136] *Dictionarium* . . . , v. *Dispensatio*, p. 190. "non est pro regula assumenda."

frequently necessitate the relaxation of the law, whether by dispensation or by *epikeia*, the validity of the law becomes automatically questionable. In such instances there is nothing intrinsically wrong with the law; it is simply becoming useless. It is precisely the forward march of human consciousness in the discovery of itself, in its own unfolding, in its own humanization, that provokes this crisis in the law, and finally renders it obsolete. In fact, Henricus De Segusio reminds us that "laws too are abrogated by non-observance of the same."[137] On the other hand, the law-giver has to see to it that abuses do not creep in which might jeopardize the normal and gradual development of human consciousness. To this end, he establishes in canon 18 that laws which contain an exception to the law are to be interpreted strictly, a prescription which finds its application in canon 92: "A strict interpretation is to be given not only to a dispensation in accordance with canon 36, §1, but also to the very power of dispensing granted for a specific case."

Aequitas as Substitution of Legal Justice

It is pointed out in the *Corpus Iuris Civilis* that the law concerns itself not only with actuality but also with possibility,[138] thus Azo remarks: "In law not only those matters which *de facto* exist, but also those matters which may occur should be brought into consideration; one should however distinguish between those matters which have more recurrence and those which hardly take place."[139] This notwithstanding, as Aristotle remarks, the

---

[137] *In Quintum Decretalium . . . , De Privilegiis et excessibus Privilegiatorum*, cap. 6, *Si de Terra*, n.2, fol. 80r. "Sed et leges per desuetudines abrogantur."

[138] Paulus, L. *Legavi*, 25, D., *De Liberatione Legata*, 34, 3; Gaius, L. *In quantitate*, 73, §I, D., *Ad Legem Falcidiam*, 35, 2; Terentius Clemens, L. *Si non voluntate*, 32, D., *Qui et a quibus manumissi liberi non fiunt et ad Legem Aeliam Sentiam*, 40, 9; Celsus, L. *Si Quis ab alio*, 13, D., *De re iudicata et de effectu sententiarum et de interlocutionibus*, 42, 1; Ulpianus, L. *Qui tabulas*, 27, D., *De Furtis*, 47, 2.

[139] *Brocardica Aurea*, Rubrica 19, *De Legum Figmentis*, fol. 60v: "in iure inspiciuntur non tantum ea quae sunt. sed ea quae contingere possunt, distingue autem an circa ea quae plerunque contingant et facile contingere possunt an vix et raro in primo casu intelligitur ista Rubrica";

law not rarely falls short of its objective. Law is right and just in the generality of cases, but not necessarily so in particular circumstances. Ioannes Andreae considers the limitedness of the law more as pertaining to the nature of the thing than being a mere fact -- "it is never expedient, neither it is ever possible for the law to take into consideration all eventual cases."[140] The inherent deficiency of the law justifies *epikeia*. Our present discussion, however, concentrates on a more serious fault in the legal justice; the law itself is lacking. Thus, in the first instance, when equity is applied as rectification of legal justice, the law reveals its limitedness; in the second instance, when equity is called for as substitution of legal justice, it is the legal system itself which manifests its restrictive capacity to implement eternal justice. For this reason, Baldus De Ubaldis concludes: "When there is no express provision of the law for a particular case, recourse should be made to the unwritten equity."[141]

The Roman legal system recognized its deficiency in this regard: "haec aequitas suggerit, etsi iure deficiamur" (this what equity postulates, although the law is lacking).[142] *Ius honorarium* was partly equity in substitution for legal justice.[143] The *praetor peregrinus* and the *praetor urbanus*, each in his own sphere of jurisdiction, were commissioned to make up for the lack of law by resorting to common wisdom, natural justice, and

---

cf. UBERTINUS DE BOBIO, *Solennis Tractatus de Positionibus*, Lugduni, 1549, n. 1, fol. 187r.

[140] *In Secundum Decretalium Librum Novella Commentaria*, Venetiis, 1581, *De Feriis*, cap. 5, *Conquestus*, n. 10, fol. 56r. "nec expedivit, nec potuit lex omnes casus exprimere."

[141] *In Decretalium Volumen . . . , Super Secundo Decretalium, De Causa Possessionis, et Proprietatis*, cap. 5, *Pastoralis*, n. 12, fol. 179r. "ubi deficit ius scriptum recurritur ad aequitatem etiam non scriptam."

[142] Paulus, L. *In summa*, 2, §5, D., *De aqua et aquae pluviae arcendae*, 39, 3; cf. Inst., *De legitima adgnatorum successione*, 3, 2, §3a; Impp. Diocletianus et Maximianus, L. *Si res tuas*, 8, §I, *Ad exhibendum*, 3, 42.

[143] Papinianus, L. *Ius autem*, 7, §1, D., *De iustitia et iure*, 1, 1: "Ius praetorium est, quod praetores introduxerunt adiuvandi vel supplendi vel corrigendi iuris civilis gratia propter utilitatem publicam.quod et honorarium dicitur ad honorem praetorum sic nominatum"; cf. Marcianus, L. *Nam*, 8, D., eod. tit., Paulus, L. *Ius pluribus*, 11, D., eod tit., Ulpianus, L. *Et si quis*, 14, §2, D., *De religiosis et sumptibus funerum et ut funus ducere liceat*, 11, 7; Inst., *De legitima adgnatorum successione*, 3, 2, §3a, §7.

ius gentium in solving contentious cases. To these one may add the arbiter whose decision was sanctioned by the Roman law. Once the contestants had mutually promised to abide by the arbiter's decision, he was free to apply fundamental principles of justice or *ius gentium* -- "in viri boni arbitrium" (in the judgment of the just man)[144] -- in reaching a decision.

Never did the Roman legal system doubt of its own limitations in attaining the fulfillment of justice. Neither did the Church. In substitution of law, civilists and canonists, following in the footsteps of the *praetor Romanus*, resorted to equity in order that in similar circumstances eternal justice be attended as far as it is humanly feasible -- "nemini enim debet iustitia denegari" (justice should be denied to no one).[145] In order to remedy this legal vacuum, the fundamental premise had to be brought back into the foreground, namely the essence of law, which is "right reason," *recta ratio*; thus, "In cases where the same reason occurs, the same law should be applied."[146] Once law is defined as right reason, equity is to be upheld in lack of *ius scriptum*, since equity and right reason signify one and the same thing -"Nam aequitas, et ratio idem sunt" (equity and reason are one and the same thing);[147] both reflect ultimately divine justice -- "nam naturalis iustitia, et aequitas idem sunt" (for natural justice and equity signify the same thing).[148] This argumentation leads to the

---

[144] Imp. Iustinianus, L. *Super rebus*, 15, C., *De contrahenda emptione*, 4, 38; cf. Ulpianus, L. *Nonnumquam*, 82, D., *De iudiciis: ubi quisque agere vel conveniri debeat*, 5, 1; Gaius, L. *Si merces*, 25, D., *Locati conducti*, 19, 2; Ulpianus, L. *Si quis arbitratu*, 43, D., *De verborum obligationibus*, 45, 1; Pomponius, L. *furioso*, 9, D., *De re iudicata et de effectu sententiarum et de interlocutionibus*, 42, 1.

[145] HENRICUS DE SEGUSIO, *In Primum Decretalium* . . . , *De Officio Iudicis Ordinarii*, cap. 2, *Si sacerdos*, n. 4, fol. 159r.

[146] AZO, *Ad Singulas Leges XII* . . . , Liber VI, Tit. 28, *De Liberis Praeteritis vel ex Hereditatis*, Lex 1, n. 3, p. 494: "ubi enim eadem ratio, idem ius"; cf. Liber VIII, Tit. 37, *De Rebus Litigiosis*, Lex 1, n. 3, p. 644; HENRICUS DE SEGUSIO, *In Primum Decretalium Librum* . . . , *De Translatione Episcopi vel Electi*, cap. 2, *Inter corporalia*, n. 32, fol. 82v; *In Secundum Decretalium Librum* . . . , *De Testibus et Attestationibus*, cap. 15, *In causis*, n.1, fol. 87r; IOANNES ANDREAE, *In Tertium Decretalium Librum Novella Commentaria*, Venetiis, 1581, *De Censibus, Exactio, et Procuratio*, cap. 23, *Procurationes*, n. 2, fol. 211v.

[147] ANTONIUS A BUTRIO, *Super Prima Primi Decretalium* . . . , Tomus I, *De Consuetudine*, cap. 11, *Cum tanto*, n. 54, fol. 85v.

[148] BALDUS DE UBALDIS, *In Decretalium Volumen* . . . , *Super Secundo Decretalium, De Causa*

conclusion that "the same law should be applied insofar as the reason is identical; and whenever the application of equity is justified, the law should conform."[149] While the principle is retained that "unwritten equity does not enjoy the force of law,"[150] legal justice is nevertheless forced to make recourse to equity because of its own deficiency; thus, the legal justice is bound to call for the *illatio iuridica*; hence, the juridical principle, "de similibus ad similia est procedendum" (between similarities illation is in order).[151]

The above presentation helps one to peruse the rationale of canon 19 which prescribes "If on a particular matter there is not an express provision of either universal or particular law, nor a custom, then, provided it is not a penal matter, the question is to be decided by taking into account laws enacted in similar matters, the general principles of law observed with canonical equity, the jurisprudence and practice of the Roman Curia, and the common and constant opinion of learned authors." The prescription of canon 19 reveals at what stage human consciousness has arrived in its process of Christianization. In other words, if indeed human consciousness had actualized itself into the right reason implanted in itself so as to fulfill in the most intensive and extensive manner the Gospel truth, there would not have been the need of ordinances intended to

---

Possessionis, et Proprietatis, cap. 5, *Pastoralis*, n. 12, fol. 179r.

[149] HENRICUS DE SEGUSIO, *In Primum Decretalium . . . , De Translatione Episcopi vel Electi*, cap. 2, *Inter corporalia*, n. 32, fol. 82v: "ubi eadem ratio, idem ius . . . et ubi eadem aequitas idem ius"; cf. CYNUS PISTORIENSIS, *In Codicem Commentaria*, Liber IV, Tit. 18, *De Constituta Pecunia*, n. 1, fol. 209v; AZO, *Brocardica Aurea*, Rubrica 29, *De Similibus et Contrariis, Simile ex Lege et eadem ratio equitatis est*, foll. 82v-83r.

[150] BALDUS DE UBALDIS, *In Decretalium Volumen . . . , Super Primo Decretalium, De Constitutionibus*, cap. 1, *Canonum*, n. 18, fol. 10v: "aequitas non scripta non habet vim legis."; cf. CYNUS PISTORIENSIS, *In Codicem Commentaria*, Liber I, Tit. 14, *De Legibus et Constitutionibus Principum*, n. 9, fol. 25r; ALBERICUS DE ROSATE, *Dictionarium . . . , v. Aequitas*, p. 31.

[151] Gaius, L. *Illud*, 32, D., *Ad Legem Aquiliam*, 9, 2; cf. AZO, *Ad Singulas Leges XII . . .*, Liber VIII, Tit. 37, *De Rebus Litigiosis*, lex 1, n. 3, p. 644; *Brocardica Aurea*, Rubrica 29, *De Similibus et Contrariis*, fol. 82v.

dictate, direct, and govern human consciousness in minute fashion -- a necessity which demonstrates a state of mere dawn of self-awareness. Human consciousness, however, is far from being morally what it is ontologically, far from being in unison with its universal inwardness, far from standing on its own inner strength. Human consciousness still requires outward direction in almost every step taken in the direction of self-explication. No legal justice, including canonical legislation, is ever capable of producing a legal dossier which can substitute for the inefficiency of human consciousness. The Church, as any human institution, must make recourse to equity, alas, with due caution lest equity be maneuvered into iniquity.

Thus canon 19 prescribes that *illatio iuridica* can be applied in all cases with the exception of penal matters. This exception falls in line with the content of canon 18 which states that laws prescribing a penalty are to be interpreted strictly. It relates also to the *Regula Iuris*, 15, in VI°: "Odia restringi et favores convenit ampliari." It is worth noting that no mention is made as to whether *illatio iuridica* could be made to matters constituting an exception to the norm. Canon 18 apropos dictates that laws which contain an exception to the law are to be interpreted strictly. One may also be reminded of the following *Regulae Iuris* in VI°: "In argumentum trahi nequeunt quae propter necessitatem aliquando sunt concessa"(R.I., 78); "Quod alicui gratiose conceditur trahi non debet ab aliis in exemplum"(R.I..,74); "Quae a iure communi exorbitant nequaquam ad consequentiam sunt trahenda"(R.I.,28).[152] Neither do we believe that equity can be administered through recourse to laws which restrict the free exercise of rights (cf. canon 18) -- "Odia convenit restringi." "The question is to be decided by taking into account laws enacted in similar matters." Thus, *illatio iuridica*, as it appears from the text, can only be made to laws contained in the Code of canon law. This prescription, however, does not prohibit recourse to laws found in canonical tradition

---

[152] IOANNES ANDREAE, *In Tertium Decretalium Librum . . . , De Censibus, Exactio et Procuratio.*, cap. 23, *Procurationes*, n. 2, fol. 211v: "Licet ubi est eadem ratio iuris communis, idem ius censeatur, non tamen ubi est eadem ratio privilegii, est idem privilegium, nisi a principe impetretur."

(canon 6, §2), and laws enshrined in the *Corpus Iuris Civilis*, if they clarify, or simply confirm, the law resorted to, as canonical jurisprudence testifies from early times down to our age. In lack of laws concerning similar matters such a recourse becomes compelling by necessity. In similar circumstances one may even resort to *ius gentium*. As earlier indicated, *ius gentium* was taken to mean *ius naturale* by Hostiensis,[153] Baldus De Ubaldis,[154] and Antonius A Butrio.[155] According to Albericus De Rosate such a recourse can also be made to *ius civile* since human law traces its roots to *ius naturale*.[156] Hostiensis points out apropos: "Canon law is not subordinate to the laws of the state; on the contrary, one should assist the other."[157] We fully concur with this stand, provided that *ius gentium* and *ius civile* do not contradict equity enlightened and strenghtened by the evangelical truth.

Canon 19 also directs one in search of justice to the general principles of law observed with "canonical" equity. General principles of law are to be understood to include the general norms contained in Book One of the Code as well as those endorsed by canonical tradition. Let it be remembered that the Code forms, to some extent, a synthesis of Christian experience throughout the centuries. For, although in every step forward a new concept of justice emerges, a higher and richer concept than that which preceded, it is also in the nature of the humanization of human

---

[153] *In Primum Decretalium Librum* . . . , *De Summa Trinitate, et Fide Catholica*, cap. 1, n. 32, fol. 6r: "naturalis ratio item ius gentium."

[154] *In Decretalium Volumen* . . . , *Super Secundo Decretalium, De Sententia et Re Iudicata*, cap. 11, *Consanguinei*, n. 3, fol. 280v: "ius gentium, quod idem est, quod aequitas."

[155] *Super Prima Primi Decretalium* . . . , Tomus I, Liber I, *De Constitutionibus*, Prooemium, n. 8, fol. 9r: "Hoc iure sunt universales gentes post peccatum: quod modicum distat ab aequitate naturali ideoque quandoque appellatur naturale . . . et hoc ideo, quia naturali ratione inductum."

[156] *Dictionarium* . . . , v. *Ius*, p. 411: "in qua significatione potest etiam ius civile et praetorium dici naturale."

[157] *In Quintum Decretalium* . . . , *De Privilegiis et Excessibus Privilegiatorum*, cap. 2, *Sicut*, n. 10, fol. 79v. "Non enim subest legi humanae lex canonica, sed econtra unum tamen ius semper altero adiuvatur."

consciousness that what each generation has brought forward as knowledge and spiritual creation, the next generation inherits. Whatever principles are appealed to -- not necessarily juridical -- ought to be understood and applied in consonance with canonical equity, namely in the spirit of evangelical truth. The study so far accomplished had precisely this objective, to show that the human consciousness in its totality forms a cycle returning upon itself -- "quia in interiore homine habitat veritas." In following the Lord's teaching, human consciousness at once moves inwardly, towards its authentic self, wherein the first (subjective freedom, crude being) becomes the last, and the last (objective freedom, being essence) becomes first; thus the result is at the same time the principle: the fulfillment of right reason.

The Juridical Concept of Custom

In colloquial language, terms such as habit, culture, tradition, usage are often used to indicate custom. *Consuetudo* is the Latin word for custom, and which is derived from *conuesco* or *consuefacio*.[1] Synonymous terms are also found in Latin; *mos, usus, habitus,* are words usually adopted in lieu of *consuetudo*.[2] Although there are certain similarities between these terms and the concept of *consuetudo*, in juridic nomenclature the term, *consuetudo*, entails a connotation of its own with far reaching consequences in the moral and ethical realms of human consciousness.

The present study on custom is based on the twofold classification of custom fostered by St. Isidore of Seville: custom of fact, and custom of law. Custom of fact is understood as being rationality itself; thus by its very nature, it cannot conflict with divine law, whether natural or positive; by its own virtue, custom of fact binds in *foro conscientiae*. Custom of law is in essence custom of fact sanctioned by public authority; thus it is said to be reasonable, and as such, binds in *foro externo*.

Custom of Fact

By custom of fact Saint Isidore understands a mere attitude (*habitus*) usage (*mos, usus*) of long duration: "Tradition is a custom of lengthy

---

[1] HENRICUS DE SEGUSIO, *In Primum Decretalium. . . , De Consuetudine*, cap. 1, *Consuetudines*, n. 1., fol. 29r: "Et dicitur consuetudo, quasi communis assuetudo quia ex communi usu venit"; CYNUS PISTORIENSIS, in *Codicem Commentaria*, Lib. VIII, Tit. 53, *Quae sit longa consuetudo*, n. 7. fol. 521v; BALDUS UBALDI PERUSINUS, *In Decretalium Volumen . . . , Super Primo Decretalium, De Consuetudine*, cap. 8, *Cum dilectus*, n. 3. fol. 58r.

[2] Cf. FACCIOLATUS, JACOBUS-FORCELLINUS, AEGIDIUS, *Totius Latinitatis Lexicon*, Patavii, 1827, Tomus I, v. *Consuetudo*, p. 755.

duration consisting of a long series of (similar) acts.";[3] "it is called "custom" because it is common usage."[4] But custom of fact entails more enterprise on the part of human consciousness than mere repetition of actions.

Custom is, in essence, actuality, realization of the collective spirit, the animating spirit of individual human consciousnesses coming together and fusing themselves into one-mindedness. Custom reveals most genuinely the universal inwardness of human consciousness. Custom, like law, is simply inconceivable outside the realm of existentiality. Custom may indeed be defined as *usus,* but conscious, rational and responsible *usus.* The Latin term, *consuetudo (consuesco),* more so than its English equivalent, clusters the idea of togetherness, solidarity, conformity, unison, one-mindedness. It therefore necessarily presupposes a communal reality; it is indeed the direct product and the most genuine and spontaneous expression of *l'esprit de corps.* Custom, thus being the spirit in actuality, must of its nature be perennial, but perennially evolving. The qualities of consistency and of continuance of behaviour form an integral part of the concept; thus custom may also be defined as *habitus,* in opposition to precariousness, coincidence, unpredictability, inconsistency. But the spirit, alive and rational, is in a perennial process of self-discovery; custom, the spirit itself, the movement of the spirit within itself, does not signify determinism, mere repetition of actions; being the spirit itself, custom is fully and vividly developing, always becoming, passing over into a higher mode of consciousness.

---

[3] *Etymologiarum Libri XX,* Liber V cap.3, n.3, *Opera Omnia,* Tomus III, loc. cit. Col. 199: "Mos autem longa consuetudo est de moribus tracta tantumdem."
According to Ulpianus, "mores sunt tacitus consensus populi, longa consuetudine inveteratus," *Tituli ex Corpore Ulpiani,* §4, in *Institutionum et Regularum Iuris Romani Syntagma,* Lipsiae, 1880, p. 310.
Facciolatus, J. -- Forcellinus, Ae. define *mos:* "Institutum consuetudine usuque firmatum, sive bonum sive malum sit," *Totius Latinitatis Lexicon,* Tomus III, v. *mos,* p. 149.
For Albericus De Rosate *mos* indicates custom of fact: "mos est quod solitum est fieri, vel mos est longa consuetudo tracta de moribus." Positive laws emanate from *mores:* "mores leges faciunt, et omne ius legibus et moribus constat . . . plus est nobilitas morum, quam dignitas generis . . . Maiora sunt damna morum quam rerum temporalium," *Dictionarium. . . ,* v. *mos,* p. 494.

[4] Ibid, n. 4, col. 199; "vocata autem consuetudo, quia in communi est usu."

The Juridical Concept of Custom

Custom needs to be considered as plain rationality. If custom were to be understood simply as *usus,* the beast would by far exceed the human being in this respect. There is nothing more deterministically consistent than the actions of the beast. In the reality of custom, there is more profundity of commitment than mere exercise or repetition of actions, however constant and longeval they may be. The Isidorian definition, "vocata est consuetudo, quia in comuni usu est," is applicable to beasts as well as humans. A similar definition does not do justice to the rational and conscientious universality of human nature; indeed, it equates and degrades the universal inwardness of human consciousness to the herd instinct. Custom is actuality, but a rational actuality arising from inner conviction of which the beast is devoid. By definition, custom is human consciousness explicating itself, realizing its inherent universality, objectifying its rationality, conscientiousness, and sociability. Thus custom and community constitute an interlocked reality. Saint Isidore defines community in this manner: "By the term *populus* is understood an aggregate of persons coming together by the bond of law and common consent."[5] Custom is the will of the people in actuality, as Cynus Pistoriensis remarkably points out: "The tacit consent of the community, and not mere practice, is the cause of custom,"[6] custom stands out primordially as mentality, communal mentality, and the spontaneity of its manifestation reveals the reality of *l'esprit de corps* as being human consciousness itself; it is the most genuine, direct, immediate, and proximate revelation of the collective spirit. *L'esprit de corps,* which is nothing other than the tangential point, the synthesis, and the epitome of human awareness of its ontology, has a mind and will partly of its own; as such, it is *recta ratio* of itself; thus it has the ability to function as a knowing, intelligent, willing and responsible agent; its acts are truly *actus humani.* It becomes apparent that it is in the nature of *l'esprit de corps* that customs exist.

---

[5] Loc. cit. Liber. IX, cap. 4, n.5, col. 349: "populus est coetus humanae multitudinis, juris consensu et concordi communione sociatus."

[6] *In Codicem Commentaria,* Lib. VIII, Tit. 53, *Quae sit longa consuetudo,* n.7., fol. 521 r: "usus non est causa consuetudinis, sed tacita voluntas populi."

There exists an interdependence between the collective spirit and the individual member, between the individual human consciousness and custom. This results from the nature of the community which should not be envisaged as a substantial entity in and by itself, a rational actuality in and by itself, a distinct mind imposing itself upon individual wills. On the contrary, the individual human consciousness is the creator, the ultimate reality, the primary source, and the finality of *l'esprit de corps,* and consequently, of custom. The individual human consciousness *per se,* is in and for itself, and has nothing apart from itself; it yearns for nothing outside itself; its object is inwardness itself; it relates to objective externality, not by dependency on it, not by blind compulsion, but simply because it is attracted to the actual rationality reckoned in the reality of itself. In other words, through its own sociability the individual human consciousness suspends itself from itself, negates itself, only to come back to itself more conscious of itself, more rational, more conscientious, and more universal. In this manner, selfhood finds its absolute reason for being, its fulfillment, in absolute freedom. Thus the spirit emerging outside itself, objectifies itself in a collegial spirit, expressing itself in diverse dimensions, particularly in custom, only to return to itself more true and real to its ontological nature. Thus custom emanates from the ontology of human nature; it is the end result of the rationality, conscientiousness and sociability of human consciousness. The life of the individual human consciousness is a perennial cycle of being itself and being otherness. Human consciousness, in explicating its universal inwardness, suspends itself in order to move outside itself, thus extending itself beyond itself, and reaches a phase where it converges with other individual consciousness, and thus finds the full realization of itself within itself. In so doing, human consciousness reaches a further development of what it is implicitly; it moves to a higher mode of being; it enters into a new phase of self-actualization: a new quasi-creation of itself in otherness, forming a collective spirit with others in perpetuity. Thus *l'esprit de corps* is created. Although intrinsically anchored in the individual human consciousness, the collective spirit has a life and longevity of its own. On the other hand, *l'esprit de corps,* being the universal inwardness of human consciousness in

The Juridical Concept of Custom

actuality, by its very nature is destined to evolve; it is constantly becoming, perennially unfolding, objectifying its ontological nature, disclosing its true inner self.

Custom, which has been defined as the genuine, direct and immediate manifestation of the life of the collective spirit, by inner necessity must assume the characteristics of its proximate cause, which are consistency, continuity, and longevity. However, by the same token, custom must also submit itself to the destiny of the spirit, the law of development. Thus perpetuity, as a quality of custom, should not be understood in an absolute manner; it does not inspire perennity and irreversibility of actions; longevity of custom does not signify irrevocability. Custom, while anchored in the past, reaches out into the future.

In conclusion, custom, from an ontological point of view, is rationality itself, *recta ratio*. As such, it cannot contradict divine law, whether it be considered as natural law or divine positive law; thus custom, ontologically speaking, binds in conscience. Existentially, custom signals at what stage human consciousness has arrived in the process of its own self-realization.

Custom of Law

Custom of law has the same nature and characteristics as custom of fact with the difference, however, that custom of law is a juridic institution. In the establishment of custom of law, *l'esprit de corps* ratifies with sanction the actuality of its mentality. In binding itself to itself, it imposes the explication of itself as a moral and ethical obligation on the individual human consciousness. In light of what has been stated earlier, custom of law should not be considered as an imposition by an external agent since there only exists *distinctio formalis* between the individual human consciousness and the collective human consciousness. Therefore, like custom of fact, custom of law finds its beginning in the universal inwardness of human consciousness. As juridic institution, custom must find its roots in *iustitia aeterna,* the reflection of which is the eternal law enshrined in the human heart. Thus custom of law not only reveals human consciousness corresponding to the stage of its own humanization, but also requires for its validity those same essential qualities expected in the law in justification of its existence. Therefore, custom has to be honest, just, possible, according to nature, necessary, useful, clear, intended for the common good.[7] A more comprehensive exposition on custom of law is left for a later part of this study. At this point we acknowledge custom of law as custom of fact to be not only rational, but also reasonable.

Custom in Roman Law

Athens before Draco, Sparta before Licurgus, and Rome before Numa Pompilius, were said to have been ruled mostly by custom. One may surmise that the force of custom started to diminish in the life of the community with Solon in Athens, with Licurgus in Sparta, and with the enactment of *Lex duodecim tabularum* by the *decemviri* in Rome. It is generally maintained by scholars, however, that all positive laws in these civilizations were ultimately founded upon, and continued to be valid in virtue of, the custom of the people.

The general introduction to the study on custom was prompted by analysis of the Roman codification on the subject. Cicero finds the essence of custom identical to that of law. He defines law and custom as *recta ratio*. It has been pointed out earlier that *recta ratio* for Cicero denotes the eternal law inscribed in the human heart.[8] Pomponius assures us that the Roman legal system initially functioned on *mores* and *consuetudines*.[9] It must be remembered that after the supreme power had passed from the people to the emperor, the theory of popular sovereignty remained in the Roman political philosophy. This political ideology helps explain the part played by custom as source of law, and how law continued to be valid in

---

[7] JOANNES ANDREAE, *In Primum Decretalium Librum* . . . , *De Consuetudine*, cap *Nunc.* n. 13, fol. 62v.

[8] *De Legibus*, Lib. I, cap. 15, n. 42, loc. cit. p. 1207.

[9] Pomponius, L. *Necessarium* 2, §1, 4, 5, 12, D., *De origine iuris et omnium magistratuum et successione prudentium*, 1, 2.

virtue of the custom of the people. The general principle that custom can create law is recognized in numerous texts of *Corpus Iuris Civilis*.[10]

In Roman philosophy of law, custom was basically conceived of as actuality; its essence was its existentiality; thus custom is nothing else but *mos, usus* in its crude being -- "the written code of laws traces its origin to unwritten norms which were in vigour."[11] But this actuality is a conscious and rational one, intrinsically flowing from human consciousness. Ulpianus[12] and *Institutiones*[13] define custom as *consensus*. Julianus conceives of custom as *iudicium populi* (the judgment of the people).[14] Hermogenianus understands custom as *tacita civium conventio* (tacit agreement of the citizens).[15] For Celsus, custom originating from error is not custom at all; custom to be true to itself must be reason itself.[16] The concepts of custom cherished by these Roman jurists enable one to envisage in the nature of custom human consciousness explicating its ontological

---

[10] Julianus, L. *De quibus*, 32 *De legibus senatusque consultis et longa consuetudine*, 1, 3: "De quibus causis scriptis legibus non utimur, id custodiri oportet, quod moribus et consuetudine inductum est . . . §1. Inveterata consuetudo pro lege non immerito custoditur, et hoc est ius quod dicitur moribus constitutum. nam cum ipsae leges nulla alia ex causa nos teneant, quam quod iudicio populi receptae sunt, merito et ea, quae sine ullo scripto populus probavit tenebunt omnes," cf. Ulpianus, L. *Diuturna*, 33, D., eod. Tit; Paulus, L., *Immo*, 36, D., eod. Tit; Callistratus, L. *Nam*, 38, D., eod. Tit; Celsus, L. *Quod*, 39, D., eod. Tit; Modestinus, L., *Ergo*, 40, D., eod. Tit,; Pomponius, L. *Necessarium*, 2, §12, D., *De origine iuris et omnium magistratuum et successione prudentium*, 1, 2; Inst., *De iure naturali et gentium et civili*, §9, 1, 2; Imp. Alexander, L. *Praeses*, 1, C., *Quae sit longa consuetudo* 8, 52 (53); Imp. Constantinus, L. *Consuetudinis*, 2, C., eod. Tit; Impp. Leo et Anthemius, L. *Leges*, 3, C., eod,Tit.

[11] Inst. *De iure naturali et gentium et civili*, §9, 1,2: "Ex non scripto ius venit, quod usus comprobavit"; cf. Celsus, L. *Ex his*, 4, D., *De legibus senatusque consultis et longa consuetudine*, 1, 3; Celsus L. *Nam*, 5,D., eod. Tit.

[12] *Tituli ex Corpore Ulpiani*, §4, in *Institutionum et Regularum Iuris Romani Syntagma*, edidit Rudolphus Gneist, Lipsiae, 1880, p. 310: "Mores sunt tacitus consensus populi, longa consuetudine inveteratus."

[13] *De iure naturali et gentium et civili*, §9, 1, 2: "nam diuturni mores consensu utentium comprobati legem imitantur."

[14] L. *De quibus*, 32, §1, D., *De legibus senatusque consultis et longa consuetudine*, 1, 3.

[15] L. *Sed et ea*, 35, D., *De legibus senatusque consultis et longa consuetudine*, 1. 3.

[16] L. *Quod*, 39, D., *De legibus senatusque consultis et longa consuetudine*, 1,3.

nature, unfolding its inherent universality, realizing itself in a rational, conscientious, and social body. Custom, ultimately, is the genuine manifestation of the existence of *l'esprit de corps*, as well as its pure intention and will.

The Roman legal system insisted upon longevity as a constitutive element in the realization of custom as juridic institution. Emperor Constantine decreed apropos: "A custom or usage of long duration enjoys no small authority."[17] In order that custom be acknowledged and endorsed as a legal binding force, its perpetuity, moreover, had to be characterized by consistency and uninterruptedness of behaviour: "Laws are not enacted because of matters which very seldom arise";[18] "Law should concern itself not with matters of rare occurrence, but rather with those matters of frequent and easy recurrence";[19] "Those matters have juridical value which are confirmed by a long lasting custom and observed for many years";[20] "A custom of long duration and tenaciously observed is similar to the law, and enjoys the same force."[21]

---

[17] L. *Consuetudinis*, 2, C., *Quae sit longa consuetudo*, 8, 52 (53): "Consuetudinis ususque longaevi non vilis auctoritas est"; cf. Imp. Alexander, L. *Praeses*, 1, C., eod, tit,; Julianus, L. *De quibus*, 32, §1, D., *De legibus senatusque consultis et longa consuetudine*, 1, 3; Ulpianus, L. *Diuturna*, 33, D., eod, tit; Hermogenianus, L. *Sed et ea*, 35, D., eod. tit; Celsus, L. *Nam*, 5, D., eod. tit,; Callistratus, L. *Nam imperator*, 38, D., eod, tit,; Inst,. *De iure naturali et gentium et civili*, §9, 1, 2; Ulpianus, *Tituli ex Corpore Ulpiani*, §4, in *Institutionum et Regularum* . . . p. 310.

[18] Celsus, L. *Ex his*, 4, D., *De legibus senatusque consultis et longa consuetudine*, 1, 3: "Ex his, quae forte uno aliquo casu accidere possunt, iura non constituuntur."

[19] Celsus, L., *Nam*, 5, D., *De legibus senatusque consultis et longa consuetudine*, 1, 3: "nam ad ea potius debet aptari ius, quae et frequenter et facile, quam quae perraro eveniunt."

[20] Hermogenianus, L. *Sed et ea*, 35, D., *De legibus senatusque consultis et longa consuetudine*, 1, 3. "Sed et ea, quae longa consuetudine comprobata sunt ac per annos plurimos observata."

[21] Impp. Leo et Anthemius, L. *Leges*, 3, C., *Quae sit longa consuetudo*, 8, 52 (53): "Leges quoque ipsas antiquitus probata et servata tenaciter consuetudo imitatur et retinet."

Custom in Ecclesiastical Codification

"Custom" in law, "Tradition" in dogma, are terms adopted to indicate Christian charisma. They signify the inherent ability of Christian consciousness to express itself, to disclose itself in a most spontaneous and genuine manner. Canon 750 prescribes that tradition forms an integral part of the deposit of faith. Following the main stream of thought so far expounded, custom ought to be defined in canon law as Christian consciousness itself. Custom is envisaged as the spontaneous and constant emergence of the authenticity of the Church -- a church which has previously been conceptualized as being, in essence, human consciousness itself.

Patristic literature understood custom in this light, and endorsed it as proof of the apostolicity of the Church. Saint Augustine in no ambiguous terms adheres to this perception of custom in the following statement: "In these matters, about which Sacred Scriptures have made no definite pronouncement, the custom of the people of God and the traditions of our ancestors are to be retained as law."[22] Saint Eusebius Hieronymus, in defense of the institution of Confirmation as a sacrament, resorts to the tradition of the Church in addition to Scripture, in his discussion of the subject. He writes apropos: "For many other observances of the Churches, which are due to tradition, have acquired the authority of the written laws, as for instance the practice of dipping the head three times in the laver . . . and there are many unwritten practices which have their place through reason and custom. So you see we follow the practice of the Church, although it may be clear that a person was baptized before the Spirit was

---

[22] *S. Aurelii Augustini Epistolae*, Classis II, *Epistola Casulano presbytero* Epist. XXXVI, cap. 1, n. 2, *Opera Omnia*, Tomus II, P.L., Tomus 33, Parisiis, 1844, col. 136: "In his enim rebus de quibus nihil certi statuit Scriptura divina, mos populi Dei, vel instituta majorum pro lege tenenda sunt."; cf. *De Diversis Quaestionibus LXXXIII Liber Unus*, loc.cit., n. 1, col. 21: "Consuetudine autem jus est quod aut leviter a natura tractum aluit, et majus fecit usus, ut religionem; et si quid eorum quae ante diximus, a natura profectum, majus factum propter consuetudinem videmus: aut quod in morem vetustas vulgi approbatione perduxit."

invoked."[23] In the same light, custom is perceived by Saint Basil: "Of the beliefs and practices whether generally accepted or publicly enjoined which are preserved in the Church some we possess derived from written teaching; others we received delivered to us in a mystery by the tradition of the apostles; and both of these in relation to true religion have the same force. And these no one will gainsay; no one, at all events, who is even moderately versed in the institutions of the Church."[24] According to Saint Basil, the eternal truth reveals itself in history in a mysterious way, "in mysterio tradita"; or rather, divine Revelation emanates from a redeemed human consciousness in a spontaneous manner. In the Christian vision, custom thus appears as a manifestation of human consciousness being enlightened, vivified, and energized by the Spirit at Pentecost; it stands out as the gradual self-unfolding of the universal Christian consciousness, the constant disclosing of its inherent authenticity; thus custom signals the stage at which Christian consciousness has arrived in the process of self-fulfillment.

Ivo Carnotensis, like Saint Isidore, concentrates more on the legal aspect of custom. His treatise, in fact, relies heavily on Roman legal texts and on the writings of Saint Isidore. The doctrine of Ivo on the subject is well summarized in his statement "All that which has been endorsed by ancient practice should be observed in all its integrity."[25] This contention places Ivo in complete accord with the other Fathers. It seems safe to say

---

[23] *Dialogus contra Luciferianos, Mos Ecclesiarum in manuum Impositione*, n.8, *Opera Omnia*, Tomus II, P.L., Tomus 23, Parisiis, 1865, col. 172: "Nam et multa alia quae per traditionem in Ecclesiis observantur, auctoritatem sibi scriptae legis usurpaverunt, velut in lavacro ter caput mergitare . . . multaque alia scripta non sunt, quae rationabilis sibi observatio vindicavit. Ex quo animadvertis nos Ecclesiae consuetudinem sequi, licet ante advocationem Spiritus constet aliquem baptizatum."

[24] *Liber De Spiritu Sancto*, cap. 27, n.66, *Opera Omnia*, Tomus, IV, P.G., Tomus 32, Parisiis, 1857, col. 187; "Ex asservatis in Ecclesia dogmatibus et praedicationibus, alia quidem habemus e doctrina scripto prodita; alia vero nobis in mysterio tradita recepimus ex traditione apostolorum: quorum ultraque vim eamdem habent ad pietatem; nec iis quisquam contradicet: nullus certe, qui vel tenui experientia noverit quae sint Ecclesiae instituta."

[25] *Decretum*, Pars IV, cap. 199, loc. cit., col. 309:"Omnia quae usus antiquitatis statuit, in omnibus intemerata serventur."

that Ivo adheres to the twofold classification of custom, cherished by Saint Isidore, into custom of fact (*consuetudo facti*),[26] and custom of law (*consuetudo iuris*).[27] As earlier remarked, such a distinction is purely juridical since, philosophically speaking, custom, whether of fact or of law, is in essence *recta ratio* -- "ratio quae consuetudinem suasit" (the reason conducive to custom);[28] whenever custom contradicts right reason is no custom at all.[29] Custom of law is nothing other than custom of fact ratified by public authority; hence it binds in the ethical realm. In this sense, custom is defined as "jus quoddam moribus institutum" (a specific law established by tradition).[30]

The theme in *Decretum Gratiani* is mere reiteration of doctrine as presented by Saint Isidore and Ivo Carnotensis, however with greater clarity. The distinction between custom of fact and custom of law is maintained by Gratianus.[31] In reference to custom of fact,[32] Gratianus analyzes custom in the two phases of human consciousness: in the state of nature, and in the state of grace. In the state of nature, custom appears as instrinsically flowing from the nature of human consciousness: "It is by virtue of customary law, which is of a later date than natural law, that

---

[26] Ibid, Pars IV, cap 194, col 308," Nam diuturni mores consensu utentium approbati legem imitantur"; cf. cap. 201, col. 309; cap. 10, pars XVI *Ex concilio Triburiensi*, col. 903.

[27] Ibid, Pars IV, cap. 200, col. 309.

[28] Ibid, Pars IV, cap 201, col. 309.

[29] Ibid, Pars IV, cap 202, col. 309.

[30] Ibid, Pars IV, cap 200, col. 309.

[31] *Decretum Gratiani*, Pars I, Dist. I, c.5. Gratianus:" apparet quod consuetudo partim est redacta in scriptis partim moribus tantum utentium est reservata. Quae in scriptis redacta est, constitutio sive ius vocatur; quae vero in scriptis redacta non est, generali nomine, consuetudo videlicet, appellatur."

[32] Ibid, Pars I, Dist. I, c.4: "mos autem est longa consuetudo, de moribus tracta tantumdem."

human beings coming together started to form a community."³³ Custom is thus acknowledged primarily as the result of human sociability. In the state of grace, custom assumes major significance in the process of humanization of human consciousness. In the redeemed world, custom is the realization of human consciousness which, enlightened and vivified by the Spirit, proceeds more adroitly in unfolding itself gradually explicating its ontological nature, its genuine universal inwardness.³⁴ It is *a fortiori* ascertained that the christianized human consciousness must abide by its own customs.³⁵ The definition of custom of law³⁶ in the *Decretum* is taken *verbatim* from Saint Isidore.³⁷

Juridic Analysis of Custom

The term "custom" is reserved in this study to denote human behaviour, in opposition to the concept of usage which is applicable to the doings of the beast.³⁸ Custom is taken to mean the exclusive product of

---

[33] Ibid, Pars I, Dist. VI, c.3, Gratianus, §1. "Jus vero consuetudinis post naturalem legem exordium habuit, ex quo homines convenientes in unum ceperunt simul habitare."

[34] Ibid., Pars I, Dist, XI, c.5: "Ecclesiasticarum institutionum quasdam scripturis, quasdam vero apostolica traditione per successores in ministerio confirmatas accipimus; quasdam vero consuetudine roborata approbavit usus, quibus par ritus et idem utriusque pietatis debetur affectus . . . Si enim attenderimus consuetudines ecclesiae non per scripturas a Patribus traditas nichil estimare, quantum religio detrimenti sit latura, intentivum despicientibus liquido constabit. Unde hec et alia in hunc modum non pauca, nisi tacita ac mistica traditione a Patribus ecclesiastico more ac reverentiori diligentia sunt in ministeriis observata magis silentio, quam publicata scripto?"

[35] Ibid., Pars I, Dist. XI, c. 7: "In his rebus, de quibus nihil certi statuit divina scriptura, mos populi Dei et instituta maiorum pro lege tenenda sunt. Et sicut prevaricatores legum divinarum, ita contemptores consuetudinem ecclesiasticarum cohercendi sunt"; cf. Pars I, Dist. X, c.4.

[36] Ibid., Pars I, Dist, I, c.2; "Omne autem ius legibus et moribus constat."

[37] Ibid., Pars I, Dist. I, c. 5; cf ISIDORUS, *Etymologiarum* . . . , lib. V, cap. 3, n.3, loc.cit., col. 199; IVO CARNOTENSIS, *Decretum*, Pars IV, cap, 200, loc. cit., col. 309.

[38] The term "custom," in a broad sense, indicates a fixed perpetration of actions which may proceed from instinct as Antonius A Butrio points out: "Dic, si attendatur consuetudo, prout est facti, ut est genus, comprehendit in se omnem usum, sive a ratione, sive a consensu, sive assensu appetitivo, aut instinctu, naturae impulsu; hoc modo animalia dicuntur habere

The Juridical Concept of Custom 161

the human mind, founded upon human deliberation for its origin and continuance. It implies the actualization of the inherent rationality, conscientiousness, and sociability of human nature, the unfolding of human consciousness itself at a particular stage of its own humanization process. The term "custom" is normally understood in this sense by juridical authors. For Hostiensis, in fact, custom is not merely *usus*, but *usus rationabilis*.[39] Cynus similarly contends that "it is not the mere practice, but the tacit will of the people which is the cause of custom."[40] Baldus De Ubaldis, when considering custom in the strict sense, insists upon reason as being the essence of custom: "Reason is said to be the garment of custom without which custom is cold and naked."[41] The most emphatic assurance on the nature of custom comes from Antonius A Butrio in the following statements: "Causa efficiens immediata (consuetudinis) est consensus"

---

consuetudinem," *Super Prima Primi Decretalium . . . , De Consuetudine*, cap. 11, *Cum tanto*, n.45, fol. 84r; cf. ibid. n.21, fol. 78v; loc. cit., *De Consuetudine*, cap. 9, *Cum consuetudinis*, n.2, fol. 76r. In juridical literature the term not rarely assumes this connotation. Cynus writes a propos: "Quidam dicunt, quod consuetudo et usus in nihilo differunt" (*In Codicem Commentaria*, Lib. VIII, tit. 53, *Quae sit longa consuetudo*, n.7, fol. 521r). In this context Baldus De Ubaldis seems to understand custom when he writes: "consuetudo est altera natura" (*Consiliorum, sive Responsorum . . .* , Vol. III, Cons. 284, n.3, fol. 79r), or "ratio non est de substantia consuetudinis" (*In Decretalium volumen . . . , Super Secundo Decretalium, De Appellationibus*, cap.66, *Dilecti*, n.2, fol. 307v).

[39] *In Primum Decretalium Librum . . . , De Consuetudine*, cap. 10, *Ex parte*, n.9, fol. 31v; cf. JOANNES ANDREAE, *In Primum Decretalium Librum . . . , De Consuetudine*, cap. *Nunc*, n.2, fol. 62v; ALBERICUS DE ROSATE, *Dictionarium . . .* , v. *Consuetudo*, p. 140.

[40] *In Codicem Commentaria*, Lib. VIII, tit. 53 *Quae sit longa consuetudo*, n.7, fol. 521 r: "usus non est causa consuetudinis, sed tacita voluntas populi."; cf. *In Digesti Veteris Libros . . .* , Rubica III, *De Legi. et sena. et long. consu.*, n.1, fol. 7r; JOANNES ANDREAE, *In Primum Decretalium Librum . . . , De Consuetudine*, cap. *Nunc*, n. 14, fol. 63 r; AZO *Summa Super Codicem*, Lib. VIII, *Que sit longa consuetudo*, P. 325, col.l.

[41] *In Decretalium Volumen . . . , Super Secundo Decretalium, De Probationibus*, cap. 2, *Sicut*, n. 7, fol. 201r: "ratio est vestimentum consuetudinis, alias consuetudo est frigida et nuda."; cf. *Super Primo Decretalium, De Consuetudine*, cap. 8, *Cum dilectus*, n.3., fol. 58r; ibid., cap. 11, *Cum tanto*, n. 23, fol. 60r; ibid., *De Electione et Electi Potestate*, cap. 50, *Cumana*, n. 45, fol. 85v.

(reason is the proximate efficient cause of custom);[42] "Ex hoc consensu surgit vinculum consuetudinis" (the bond of custom arises from this consent).[43] The term "custom" in the juridical analysis assumes more a profound dimension than "id quod solitum est fieri";[44] it reveals human nature as alive, dynamic, conscious of itself, explicating its inherent authenticity of, by, and to itself.

The twofold classification of custom -- custom of fact and custom of law -- is maintained in the present exposition. However, another equally fundamental distinction should be endorsed for a correct and all-embracing understanding of custom. Custom is thus also subdivided into private and public custom. Private custom, *per se*, is outside the concern of the present study. A contrast between private and public custom seems, nevertheless, expedient for greater clarity of the theme.

Consuetudo privata is also defined as *consuetudo patrisfamilias* -- "Sic paterfamilias consuevit facere" (the *paterfamilias* is accustomed to act in this manner)[45] or as *consuetudo specialissima*.[46] Private and public custom share the same source, namely human consciousness. They differ from each other by reason of the two dimensions in which human consciousness expresses and realizes itself. Private custom emanates from individual human consciousness; it denotes the rational activity of the

---

[42] *Super Prima Primi Decretalium . . . , De Consuetudine*, cap. 11, *Cum tanto*, n. 12. fol. 77v.

[43] Ibid., n. 14, fol. 77v; cf. n. 16, fol. 80 v; n. 50, fol. 85r.

[44] ALBERICUS DE ROSATE, *Dictionarium . . .* , v. *Mos*, p. 494.

[45] ANTONIUS A BUTRIO, *Super Prima Primi Decretalium . . . , De Consuetudine*, cap. 11, *Cum tanto*, n. 21, fol. 78v: "Secunda est consuetudo privata ratione inducta. Et haec duplex, quaedam est privata, et personalis: et haec est illa, quam dicimus. Patrisfamilias est haec consuetudo, cuius finis est praesumere, et ea utitur ius ad praesumendum de actibus suis: sicut dicamus. Paterfamilias. sic consuevit facere"; cf. JOANNES ANDREAE, *In Primum Decretalium Librum . . . , De Consuetudine*, cap. *Nunc*, n.6, fol. 62 v; HENRICUS DE SEGUSIO, *In Primum Decretalium . . . , De consuetudine*, cap. 8, *Cum dilectus*, n. 12, fol. 31r; *In Secundum Decretalium . . . , De Confirmatione utili, vel inutili*, cap. 5, *Ad nostram*, n.l. fol. 208v.

[46] HENRICUS DE SEGUSIO, *In Primum Decretalium . . . , De Consuetudine*, cap. 8, *Cum dilectus* n. 12, fol. 31r.

human person, otherwise known as *habitus*.[47] There seems to be divergency of opinions whether private custom could enjoy a juridical validity with respect to *ius publicum*. Joannes Andreae[48] and Antonius A Butrio[49] deny such a possibility, a position which is contradicted by Baldus De Ubaldis[50] and Hostiensis.[51] The former contention seems to us more plausible if we want to be coherent with the fundamental conceptualization of custom. Nonetheless, private custom has juridical significance in matters pertaining to *ius privatum*. Private custom constitutes the basis for the institution of prescription[52] as Antonius A Butrio points out: "The practices observed by

---

[47] The definition of *habitus* here understood does not relate to the one given by Aristotle (Meta. V,20), which is found, per se, in the nature of things. *Habitus* in the present context stands for human behaviour founded upon human deliberation for its origin and continuance.
In reference to *consuetudo privata* Antonius A Butrio writes: "consuetudo potest considerari tripliciter. Uno modo pro ipso habitu in homine bono et malo ex actibus et operationibus generato: et haec est facti. Unde dicimus. Hic habet consuetudinem delinquendi: talis est consuetudo Patrisfamilias,"*Super Prima Primi Decretalium . . . , De Consuetudine*, cap 11, *Cum tanto*, n. 20, fol. 80v.

[48] *In Primum Decretalium Librum . . . , De Consuetudine*, cap. *Nunc*, n.6, fol. 62 v: "quia sicut lex est, vel fuit praeceptum populi . . . Sic et consuetudo . . . et per hoc, quod dicit, Populi, excludit consuetudinem privati, vel patrisfamilias quae ius non inducit."

[49] *Super Prima Primi Decretalium . . . , De Consuetudine*, cap 11, *Cum tanto*, n. 12, fol. 77v: "Potest tamen inducere in suis actibus consuetudinem, quae non habet vim legis, sed solum declarat suos actus ex consuetudine primi. Sic est, quando dicimus, consuetudo patrisfamilias attenditur."

[50] *Consiliorum, Sive Responsorum . . .* , Volumen IV, Cons. 289, n.l., fol. 62 v: "consuetudo etiam penitus privatae personae iure publico tribuere potest."

[51] *In Secundum Decretalium . . . , De Confirmatione utili, vel inutili*, cap. 5. *Ad nostram*, n.l. fol. 208v.

[52] F. Lucius Ferraris defines prescription as follows: "Praescriptio magis proprie sumpta idem est ac exceptio peremptoria, per quam possessor bonae fidei post decursum certi temporis a lege definiti, potest repellere dominum rem suam pristinam repetentem, vel antiquo suo jure uti volentem, opponendo ei continuatam possessionem talis rei, vel juris bona fide factam tempore a lege definito ad praescribendum, seu peremptorie excipiendum, per quam possessionem talem rem, vel jus fecit suum,"*PromptaBibliotheca. . .*Tomus VII, v. *Usucapio, seu Praescriptio*, col. 1441. Custom differs from *stylus curiae* (cf. canon 19). The difference between the two is given by Cynus Pistoriensis: "Stilus est ius quoddam non scriptum, usibus introductum, ab uno iudice stillatum. Et in hoc ultimo differt a consuetudine, quoniam consuetudo est ius introductum usibus plurium, ut a populo," In *Codicem Commentaria*, Lib. VIII, Tit. 53, *Quae sit longa consuetudo*, n.

the *paterfamilias* include also customs of private nature which are acknowledged by law to endorse particular rights. Such private customs are usually defined as prescriptions or right to ownership acquired by length of possession."[53] It also forms the criterion for juridical presumptions.[54]

Custom and habit are essentially of the same nature; they both signify a constant pattern of behaviour resultant of the intellect and will. They nevertheless differ from each other: whereas habit denotes the rational activity of individual human consciousness, custom proceeds from a collective human consciousness. Custom is a sign that human consciousness in being rational is at once being social. Human consciousness finds in custom the explication of its universal inwardness. Custom is the movement of *l'esprit de corps* within itself; it is the very reality of the life of a collective spirit. Custom, more than mere conformity or solidarity, reveals one-mindedness, the essential oneness of human consciousness; it is the explication of the universal inwardness of human consciousness. In short, it may be concluded that whereas the individual human consciousness is *causa efficiens proxima* in the formation of a habit, it turns out to be *causa efficiens remota* in the establishment of custom. In custom, the *causa efficiens proxima* is the collective body which in juridic literature is termed *populus* -- "consuetudo consensu populi tacito nititur et fulcitur" (custom is

---

7. fol. 521v; cf. ANTONIUS A BUTRIO, *Super Prima Primi Decretalium* . . . , *De Consuetudine*, cap. 11, *Cum tanto*, n.45, fol. 84r.

[53] *Super Prima Primi Decretalium* . . . , *De Consuetudine*, cap. 11, *Cum tanto*, n. 45, fol. 84r: "consuetudo patrisfamilias . . . comprehendit etiam in se consuetudinem privatam, quae iure est ordinata ad quaerenda iura particularia, quam iam appellamus praescriptionem, et usucapionem."

[54] ANTONIUS A BUTRIO, *Super Prima Primi Decretalium* . . . , *De Consuetudine*, cap. 11. *Cum tanto*, n. 21, fol. 78v: "patrisfamilias est haec consuetudo cuius finis est praesumere, et ea utitur ius ad praesumendum de actibus suis: sicut dicamus. Paterfamilias.sic consuevit facere"; cf. ibid, n. 12, fol. 77v. HENRICUS DE SEGUSIO, *In Primum decretalium librum* . . .,*De Consuetudine*, cap. 8, *Cum dilectus*, n. 12, fol. 31 r: "Item est specialissima, secundum quam in dubiis iudicatur, et haec praesumptionem inducit, cui statur, nisi, forte contra probetur, haec est consuetudo patrisfamilias." JOANNES ANDREAE, *In Primum Decretalium Librum* . . . , *De Consuetudine*, cap.8, *Cum dilectus*, n.7, fol. 57v.

The Juridical Concept of Custom 165

caused and upheld by the tacit consent of the people).[55] The distinction between private and public custom is fundamentally based on this reality. When custom has the collective human consciousness as the *causa efficiens proxima*, it is defined as public, *consuetudo publica*. It is precisely because of its origin and nature -- emanating from and at once being the reality of collective human consciousness -- that custom of fact has the potentiality of becoming custom of law.[56] The basic similarity of custom with the law is that both gather all members in a common bond and considers them all equal.[57]

Public custom constitutes the main concern of the present study. In this section, the study on public custom concentrates on its two aspects or stages, that of being custom of fact, and being custom of law. In the former perception, custom appears as being essentially rationality, *recta ratio*, and makes itself felt in the realm of individual morality. In the later perspective, custom becomes, in addition, reasonable, and functions in the ethical sphere.

---

[55] CYNUS PISTORIENSIS, *In Digesti Veteris Libros* . . . ,Rubrica III, *De Legi, et Sena. et long. consu.*, n.1, fol. 7r; n.11, fol. 7v; *In Codicem Commentaria*, Lib. VIII, tit. 53, *Quae sit longa consuetudo*, n.7, fol. 521 r; BALDUS DE UBALDIS, *In Decretalium Volumen* . . . , *Super Primo Decretalium, De Consuetudine*, cap. 11 *Cum tanto*, n. 23, fol. 60 r; AZO, *Summa Super Codicem*, Lib. VIII, *Que sit longa consuetudo*, pp. 324-325; HENRICUS DE SEGUSIO, *In Primum Decretalium Librum* . . . , *De Consuetudine*, cap. 1, *Consuetudines*, n.1, fol. 29r; ibid., cap 10, *Ex parte*, n. 9, fol. 31v; ANTONIUS A BUTRIO, *Super Prima Primi Decretalium* . . . *De Consuetudine*, cap. 11, *Cum tanto*, n. 16, fol. 77v; n. 21, fol. 78v.

[56] ANTONIUS A BUTRIO, *Super Prima Primi Decretalium* . . . , *De Consuetudine*, cap. 11, *Cum tanto*, n. 21, fol. 78v: "quaedam (vocatur) publica communi ratione . . . quia in usu exigitur pars populi, et eius consensus . . . Stricte tamen sumendo praescriptio opponitur consuetudini: quia differunt ex parte finis: consuetudo ordinatur in finem quaerendi ius ut publicum certae personae non appropriatum, praescriptio autem ordinatur in finem quaerendi ius privatum rerum corporalium, aut incorporalium."
It is worth noting the following contention by Antonius on the subject: "praescriptio autem, quia odiosa, est restringenda . . . consuetudo, tanquam favorabilis, non est restringenda, sed dilatanda," *Super Secunda Primi Decretalium* . . . , Tomus II, *De Officio Archidiaconi*, cap.10, *Dilecto*, n. 44. fol. 19r.

[57] ANTONIUS A BUTRIO, *Super Secunda Primi Decretalium* . . . , Tomus II, *De Officio Archidiaconi*, cap. 10, *Dilecto*, n. 44. fol. 19 r: "Consuetudo enim se habet ad ius, ut commune, et universale."

Custom of Fact

The conceptualization of custom as rationality prompts three related issues. Custom, flowing from the collective spirit, indeed being *l'esprit de corps* in action, expresses itself in a continuum. Custom, the living movement of the spirit within itself, more than being static, is by nature dynamic; it is in the process of becoming. Custom, conceived of as rationality itself, must by inner necessity correlate to divine law, natural and divine positive law.

Custom has been defined as being fundamentally the movement of *l'esprit de corps* within itself. Characteristic of human consciousness, whether as individual or collective reality, is its consistency in evolving itself in self-disclosure and self-actualization. Custom, which is the spirit in its externality, is bound to reveal genuinely and clearly the nature of human consciousness. Thus it is in the nature of custom that it reflects the consistency of the collective spirit within itself in the ongoing process of self-explication. For no other reason does juridical philosophy require that constancy and uninterruptedness of behaviour be considered as essential components in the formation of custom.[58] The explanation of the subject by the Aquinatis helps clarify more the theme: "Wherefore by actions also, especially if they be repeated, so as to make a custom, law can be changed and expounded; and also something can be established which obtains force of law, in so far as by repeated external actions, the inward movement of the will, and concepts of reason are most effectually declared; for when a thing is done again and again, it seems to proceed from a deliberate judgment of reason."[59] For Hostiensis, custom is a rational practice endorsed by a legitimately prescribed duration, or by a duration which is immemorial. This practice must not be interrupted by contrary act, or

---

[58] It must be said that these qualities must be present also in order that private custom -- *praescriptio, usucapio* -- acquire juridical validity.

[59] *Summa Theoloqica*, Ia-IIae, q. 97, art. 3. Resp., *American Ed.*, vol 1, p. 1024.

antagonize the right reason by frequent contrary acts. This usage must be adopted generally by all concerned.[60]

The immediate conceptualization of custom postulates the idea of entrenchment in the past with strong resistance to change and progress. However, if indeed custom is to be perceived, and rightly so, as the human consciousness in actuality, the notion of constancy and of uninterruptedness should not be conceived in an absolute manner. Custom is other than irreversibility of attitude which, *per se*, savours of instinctualistic determinism. Constancy and uninterruptedness, as essential qualities of custom, should therefore be understood within the context of the inherent consistency of human consciousness to evolve, unfold, and explicate itself. These qualities merely signify a relative concept since it is in the nature of custom, as it is with law, to evolve, transform itself, and turn into a higher mode of human expression apace with the forward march of human consciousness in its process of humanization. At a stage when *lex, Non omnium*[61] is verified, custom, *ipso facto*, becomes *contradictio in terminis*; it loses its intrinsic validity; it is no longer the genuine expression of the human mind; it changes from *actus humanus* into *actio hominis*, and thereby it must be abolished.

A crucial question arises as to whether custom could antagonize divine law, natural or divine positive law. Customs have emerged in the history of peoples and communities which were the product of a primitive mind. A classical example is slavery which later developed into serfdom, and has found its third stage of transformation in proletarianism. Custom,

---

[60] HENRICUS DE SEGUSIO, *In Primum Decretalium librum . . . De Consuetudine*, cap. 10, *Ex parte*, n. 9 fol. 31v: "Quid est consuetudo?" His answer is: "usus rationabilis competenti tempore confirmatus, nullo actu contrario interruptus, frequenti actu, seu contradictorio iudicio, vel quod non extet memoria inductus, usuque communi utentium approbatus."; cf. JOANNES ANDREAE, *In Primum Decretalium Librum . . . De Consuetudine*, cap. *Nunc*, n.2, fol. 62v; ALBERICUS DE ROSATE, *Dictionarium . . .*, v. *Consuetudo*, p. 140; BALDUS DE UBALDIS, *In Decretalium Volumen . . ., Super Primo Decretalium, De Constitutionibus*, cap. 6, *Cum omnes*, n. 59, fol. 15r; ANTONIUS A BUTRIO, *Super Prima Primi Decretalium . . .*, Tomus I, *De Consuetudine*, cap, 11, *Cum tanto*, n. 16, fol. 80v; n. 50, fol. 85r.

[61] Julianus, L. *Non omnium*, 20, D., *De Legibus senatusque consultis et longa consuetudine*, 1, 3: "Non omnium, quae a maioribus constituta sunt, ratio reddi potest."

remarks Ivo Carnotensis, can be a source of evil. Injustice, fraud, and altercations may find their way insidiously and have a grasp over the community under the pretext that "sic solitum fieri."[62] It goes without saying that canonists and civilists always maintained the incontestable superiority of divine law over human law and custom.[63] Therefore a statement by Cynus Pistoriensis serves as a premise for the theme on the relation of custom to divine law. He writes: "Natural reason always resists that which is contrary to it, and never succumbs to anything";[64] thus Ivo Carnotensis concludes: "Once the truth is known, custom must give way to truth." [65]

Canon 24, §1, prescribes: "No custom which is contrary to divine law can acquire the force of law." It is evident that the canon understands custom as *consuetudo facti*. In other words, no *consuetudo facti* can ever become *consuetudo iuris* if it militates against divine law -- natural or

---

[62] *Decretum*, Pars IV, cap. 203, loc. cit., col. 309: "Mala consuetudo, quae non minus quam perniciosa corruptela vitanda est, quae nisi citius radicitus evellatur, in privilegiorum jus ab impiis assumitur, et incipiunt praevaricationes, et variae praesumptiones celerrime non compressae, pro legibus venerari et privilegiorum more perpetuo celebrari."

[63] *Decretum*, Pars I, Dist. VIII, II pars, Gratianus: "Dignitate vero ius naturale simpliciter prevalet consuetudini et constitutioni. Quecumque enim vel moribus recepta sunt, vel scriptis comprehensa, si naturale iuri fuerint adversa, vana et irrita sunt habenda," cf. IVO CARNOTENSIS, *Decretum*, pars IV, cap. 204, loc. cit., col. 309; HENRICUS DE SEGUSIO, *In Primum Decretalium Librum* . . . *De Consuetudine*, cap. 10, *Ex parte*, n.10, fol. 32r; ibid., *De Electione et Electi Potestate*, cap. 23, *Bonae memoriae*, n. 14, fol. 51r; JOANNES ANDREAE, *In Primum Decretalium Librum* . . . , *De Consuetudine*, cap. 10. *Ex parte*, nn. 1, 2, fol. 58v; ibid., cap.11, *Cum tanto*, nn. 1,2, 11, fol.59v., n. 46, fol. 61v; CYNUS PISTORIENSIS, *In Codicem Commentaria*, Lib. I, Tit. 2, *De Sacrosancta Ecclesia*, n. 1, fol. 6r; ibid., Lib. VIII, Tit. 53, *Quae sit longa consuetudo*, n.l. fol. 520r; BALDUS DE UBALDIS, *In Decretalium Volumen* . . . , *Super Secundo Decretalium, De Probationibus*, cap. 2, *Sicut*, n. 2., fol. 200v; *Consiliorum, sive Responsorum* . . . , vol. V, cons. 349, n. 3, fol. 87v; ANTONIUS A BUTRIO, *Super Prima Primi Decretalium* . . . , Tom. I, *De Consuetudine*, cap. 11, *Cum tanto*. n. 1., fol. 77v, n.25, fol. 79r., n.14, fol. 80r; *Super Prima Secundi Decretalium* . . . , Tom III, *De Iuramento Calumniae*, cap. 5, *Caeterum*, n. 7. fol. 80v; ibid., *De Iudiciis*, cap.8, *Clerici*, n. 11, fol. 13v; *In Librum Tertium Decretalium* . . . Tom. V, *De his quae fiunt a maiori parte capituli*, cap.1, *Cum in cunctis*, n.11. fol. 66r.

[64] *In Codicem Commentaria*, Lib. VIII, Tit. 53, *Quae sit longa consuetudo*, n.l. fol. 520r: "naturalis ratio semper omni suo contrario resistit, et numquam cedit."

[65] *Decretum*, Pars IV, cap. 208, loc. cit. col. 310: "veritate manifestata, cedat consuetudo veritati."

The Juridical Concept of Custom

divine positive law. It is worth noting that the present theme relates closely with the central idea of the global dissertation that human consciousness is natural law in its existentiality, and that this eternal law has as its immanent destiny the gradual disclosure of itself. Thus the theme on custom intrinsically proceeds from an earlier exposition on the nature of natural law. As a summary, it may be re-stated that natural law reaches the full dimension of its existentiality the moment that human consciousnesses, as separate entities, actualize their universal inwardness in a collective consciousness. Custom thus appears as the crude reality of *l'esprit de corps* itself and of its inherent destiny to unfold itself. Upon this assumption, the ontological nature of custom is divine law itself. In this sense, custom contrary to divine law is *contradictio in terminis*. In answer, therefore, to canon 24, §1, it must be said that *consuetudo facti* contrary to divine law not only does not enjoy *ius ad rem* to become *consuetudo iuris*, but, more fundamentally, it is no custom at all; it deserves the qualification of *usus*, *actio hominis*, a beastly doing.

Granted that custom is human consciousness explicating its inner authenticity which, if ever fully explicated, would most genuinely implement the eternal truth in itself, it becomes even more difficult to explain the fact that customs have existed, and do exist which come in open confrontation with eternal justice. Prior to solving this dilemma, it must be emphasized that the ever-development of custom within itself does not entail self-contradiction. It is worth re-iterating that custom, being the movement of the collective spirit within itself, by inner necessity moves forward. Human consciousness, and likewise custom, is constantly in the process of becoming, of transforming itself into a higher and more perfect mode of self-expression. In so doing, it does not contradict itself, and less still negates itself, nor is it revealing a multifarious aspect of eternal wisdom, since there is no other but one truth and one justice. Custom in its own self-development merely demonstrates that human consciousness explicates what it has always been implicitly *ab initio*.

A classification of custom fostered by Hostiensis helps clarify the aforesaid problem. This classification is based on the criterion of the extensiveness of custom. Hence custom is classified into *generalissima*, *generalis*, *specialis*, and *specialissima*.⁶⁶ By *generalissima* Hostiensis understands a universal custom, "as it is the custom among Catholics to look towards the East when praying."⁶⁷ *Consuetudo generalis* is meant to be a custom existing within a province.⁶⁸ *Consuetudo specialis* refers to a custom which emerges in a city or a particular place.⁶⁹ At this point, *consuetudo generalissima* constitutes our main concern. However, for a better comprehension of its nature, it is incumbent to envisage *consuetudo generalissima* in light of the twofold dimension of human consciousness; thus we peruse *consuetudo generalissima* first as human consciousness in its state of nature, then as human consciousness absorbed in the mystery of Redemption.

In the state of nature, *consuetudo generalissima* stands for the universal human consciousness; it is human consciousness in the most intensive and extensive mode of its existentiality; it is the most integral embodiment of the universal human spirit at a particular stage of its humanization process. In this sense, *consuetudo generalissima* is a true revelation of the eternal wisdom being actualized in the burgeoning of human consciousness. One is reminded apropos of a statement of Joannes Andreae "non est verisimile totum mundum errare" (it is not likely that the whole world errs on the same thing).⁷⁰ Indeed it is our conviction that the denial of the prerogative of inerrancy in *consuetudo generalissima* denotes the refusal of accepting human consciousness as the reflection of divine wisdom. Thus *consuetudo generalissima* by its very nature cannot contradict divine law, natural and divine positive law. Because of its intrinsic validity,

---

[66] *In Primum Decretalium Librum* . . . , *De Consuetudine*, cap.8, *Cum dilectus*, nn. 9, 10, fol. 31r; cf. JOANNES ANDREAE *In Primun Decretalium Librum* . . . , *De Consuetudine*, cap.8, *Cum dilectus*, n.7. fol. 57v.
An understanding of *consuetudo specialissima*, known also as *consuetudo patrisfamilias*, has been given in a previous section of this study.

[67] Ibid., n.9, fol. 31r: "ut est consuetudo inter omnes catholicos versus Orientem orare."

[68] Ibid., n.10, fol. 31r.

[69] Ibid.

[70] *In Primum Decretalium Librum* . . . , *De Consuetudine*, cap. 11, *Cum tanto* n. 42, fol. 61r.

it stands as a fundamental criterion of justice in human legislation; indeed, human laws are bound to conform themselves to it in order to attest to their own validity.

In the state of grace, *consuetudo generalissima* appears as the Pentecostal Spirit being actualized in human consciousness; it reveals the Church, human consciousness christianized, in the process of self-unfolding, self-discovery, and self-explication; it forms part of the *magisterium fidelium* to which reference is made in canon 750: "the ordinary and universal *magisterium*, which is manifested by the common adherence of Christ's faithful under the guidance of the sacred *magisterium*." This custom is essentially "ecclesial," and consequently by intrinsic necessity cannot run counter to divine law. For this same reason, a refusal in accepting its prerogative of inerrancy implies, *a priori*, the denial of the Church itself. Upon this assumption, no ecclesiastical law can abrogate or derogate an "ecclesial" custom, but rather an ecclesiastical legislation should conform to it.

In conclusion, the classification into custom of fact and custom of law loses all significance as far as *consuetudo generalissima* is concerned. Being human consciousness in its entirety, it has, by its very nature, the force of law, and binds in conscience as well as in the ethical realm. This cannot be maintained with respect to other public customs of lesser comprehensiveness, since they are particular in nature, and therefore they do not represent human consciousness in its entirety. It is this condition that renders them liable to error, and this predicament posits them subject to the regulation of the legal authority. The classification into custom of fact and custom of law proceeds precisely from this subordination of particular customs to the law. This reality leads us directly to the question of the relationship between a particular custom and the law. In this perspective, custom may turn out to be *consuetudo praeter legem*, *consuetudo contra legem*, or *consuetudo secundum legem*. Since our main objective is custom in the Code of Canon Law, we intend to concentrate solely on this subject.

Custom in the Code of Canon Law.

The two classifications of custom, equally fundamental, are retained in the Code of Canon Law. A distinction is thus made between custom of fact and custom of law, and between private custom and public custom. Needless to say, the ontological concept of custom as *recta ratio* is maintained. Not any custom, however, constitutes *ius consuetudinarium*. Custom of fact "ordinatur ad creandum ius" (ordained to create laws),[71] but it is not *ius* itself. A custom besides being rational, namely in harmony with divine law, must also be reasonable, that is abiding with the norms laid down by the Code, in order to be endorsed as custom of law, thereby enjoying the force of law. Canon 24, §2, requires that a custom, whether contrary to or apart from canon law, must be reasonable in order to obtain the force of law. The Code refrains from giving a definition of reasonableness of custom. The said canon does say, however, that "a custom which is expressly reprobated in the law is not reasonable." Thus one may concur with Hostiensis that "unless it is expressly reprobated by the law, custom is to be upheld as reasonable."[72] We believe that in being reasonable a custom implies more than being not expressly reprobated. Hostiensis finds difficulty with his previous statement since he charges the judge to decide on whether a custom is reasonable or not.[73] He, in fact,

---

[71] ANTONIUS A BUTRIO, *Super Prima Primi Decretalium* . . . , Tom. I, *De Consuetudine*, cap. 11, *Cum tanto*, n. 45, fol. 84r.

[72] *In Primum Decretalium Librum* . . . , *De Consuetudine*, cap. 10. *Ex parte*, n. 12, fol. 32r:"nisi a iure expresse reprobetur, semper rationabilis" ; cf. JOANNES ANDREAE, *In Primum Decretalium Librum* . . . , *De Consuetudine*, cap. 11, *Cum tanto*, n. 26, fol. 60r: "hic rationabilis dicitur omnis consuetudo, quae non obviat canonicis institutis, vel quam ius sustinet etiam contra canones"; ANTONIUS A BUTRIO, *Super Prima Primi Decretalium* . . . , Tom. I, *De Consuetudine*, cap. 11, *Cum tanto*, n. 14, fol. 80r; ALBERICUS DE ROSATE, *Dictionarium* . . . , v. *Consuetudo*, p. 140.

[73] Ibid., n. 11, fol. 32r: "utrum autem sit rationabilis, vel non, relinquo iudici, cum nec regula posset tradi."

requires that a custom should not be onerous[74] and that it ought to be laudable.[75] Antonius A Butrio expects a custom to be honest, possible, convenient, congruous, and fostering the common good.[76] If by reasonableness are understood all the said qualities, the view of Isidorus on the objective of law and custom is more specified, that is, "which aligns with religion, concurs with discipline, and fosters the salvation of souls."[77] Custom, flowing right from human consciousness, by inner necessity, should manifest the endeavour of the collective human consciousness in unfolding its inherent authenticity, sometimes even against positive law. Thus an ecclesiastical custom must have as its objective "bonum possibile et melius" (the possible good and the better). A custom with a lofty purpose, whether it is confirmed by legitimate prescription or not, ought to be considered as being a favourable thing; thus it should be interpreted not strictly, but in a broad sense.[78]

The Code does not, and could not, ignore the fundamental and inalienable right of the Christian community to introduce a custom, for in so doing the ecclesiastical authority would be denying the very existence of the common priesthood, and therefore of the Church itself. On the other hand, custom of fact needs the authentication of the ecclesiastical legislator for the transition from its natural standing to the legal realm. This requirement results from the fact that public authority forms a constitutive component in the nature of a socio-political community -- so with the

---

[74] *In Secundum Decretalium Librum..,. De Sententia, et Re Iudicata*, cap. 8, *Cum causa*, n. 1. fol. 158v.

[75] Ibid., n.2, fol. 158v; cf. CYNUS PISTORIENSIS, *In Codicem Commentaria*, Lib. VIII, Tit. 53, *Quae sit longa consuetudo*, n. 7, fol, 521v.

[76] *Super Prima Primi Decretalium* . . . , Tom. I, *De Consuetudine*, cap. 11, *Cum tanto*, n. 14, fol. 80r; *Super Prima Secundi Decretalium* . . . , Tom III, *De Iuramento Calumniae*, cap. 5, *Caeterum*, n.7, fol. 80v.

[77] *Etymologiarum Libri XX*, Lib.V, cap.3, n.4, loc.cit., col. 199: "quod religioni congruat, quod disciplinae conveniat, quod saluti proficiat"; cf. *Decretum gratiani*, Pars I, Dist. I, c.5, §2.

[78] ANTONIUS A BUTRIO, *Super Secunda Primi Decretalium* Tom., II, *De Officio Archidiaconi*, cap. 10, *Dilecto*, n. 44, fol. 19r: "utrum consuetudo melioris propositi sit firmata necne, . . . consuetudo, tanquam favorabilis, non est restringenda, sed dilatanda."

Church. In reference to the subject, canon 23 prescribes: "A custom introduced by a community of the faithful has the force of law only if it has been approved by the legislator . . ."[79] It is in the nature of the Church that the common priesthood and ministerial priesthood constitute one interlocked reality. The nature of the Church is such that it would be against its very essence, had a dichotomy been established between authority and community. In the reality of custom of law, the two aspects of the Church, common priesthood and ministerial priesthood, converge into objectification of the collective spirit to the full. In custom of law, the authoritative apostolicity approves, confirms, and endorses human consciousness in the ultimate evangelical realization of itself.

In the Code no mention is made of the classification of custom into *generalissima*, *generalis*, *specialis*, and *specialissima*. A general principle is laid down which distinguishes custom as private and public. A custom introduced by a community "capable at least of receiving a law"[80] is said to be public; otherwise it is a private custom. The question however remains to determine which communities in the Church qualify according to the prescription of Canon 25. It can be sustained with utmost certainty that any juridical, moral person, whether public or private, the norms for which are found in the chapter on juridical persons,[81] is entitled to introduce a public custom. Excluded from this category seem to be private associations of the faithful not recognized in the Church ad norman canonis 299, §2,3.

In synthesis, therefore, a community capable of receiving a law and a public authority capable of enacting laws form constitutive components in the formation of custom of law. Another component equally essential must

---

[79] In spite of the prescription of canon 23, an objection can still be raised as to whether in canon law custom of fact is indeed totally devoid of any juridical significance and legal force. Reference is made to this point in canon 19. The question arises as to whether the term refers to custom of law only, or to custom of fact as well. One may argue that the term includes both instances of custom since "si lex non distinguit, nec nos distinguere debemus." Moreover, the rationale of canon 19 has as its ultimate objective equity which can be found as pronounced also in custom of fact.

[80] Canon 25.

[81] Cf. canons 113-123.

The Juridical Concept of Custom

concur in the formation of custom of law; hence, canon 24, §2, prescribes: "A custom . . . cannot acquire the force of law unless it is reasonable." Reasonableness of custom is nothing other than adaptation of the same to the norms of canon law, which norms vary in respect to the relation of custom to the law. In light of this juridical reality, it is incumbent to analyse custom in its three different stances: as existing apart from the law (*praeter legem*), as contradicting the law (*contra legem*), as concurring with the law (*secundum legem*).

Consuetudo praeter legem

Consuetudo praeter legem is *consuetudo conditrix* par excellence,[82] "productiva de nullo ad aliquid" (producing something out of nothing)[83] since it exists in total lack of positive law. Isidorus gives the following definition of this type of custom: "Custom is a certain type of law established through practice; it has the force of law once the written law is lacking."[84] It is a law with full juridical purport, albeit not written, and as such, it should be recognized and observed. "Consuetudo est altera lex, et pro lege servatur" (custom is a certain type of law; thus it enjoys the force of a law).[85] Canon 19 of the present Code understands custom in this

---

[82] AZO, *Summa Super Codicem*, Lib. VIII, *Que sit longa consuetudo*, P. 324, col. 2; JOANNES ANDREAE, *In Primum Decretalium librum* . . ., *De Consuetudine*, cap. 11, *Cum tanto*, n. 42, fol. 61r.

[83] BALDUS DE UBALDIS, *In decretalium volumen* . . ., *Super Primo Decretalium, De Consuetudine*, cap. 11, *Cum tanto*, n. 25, fol. 60r.

[84] *Etymologiarum libri XX*, Lib. V. cap.3, n.3, loc. cit., col. 199: "Consuetudo autem est jus quoddam moribus institutum, quod pro lege suscipitur, cum deficit lex"; cf. IVO CARNOTENSIS, *Decretum*, Pars IV, cap. 200, loc. cit., col. 309.

[85] ANTONIUS A BUTRIO, *Super Secunda Primi Decretalium* . . ., Tom. II, *De Arbitris*, cap. 4, *Dilecti*, n. 7. fol. 136v; cf. *Super Prima Primi Decretalium*. Tom. I, Lib. I, *De Constitutionibus, prooemium*, n.9, fol. 9r; *De Consuetudine*, cap. 11, *Cum tanto*, n. 50, fol. 84v; *In Librum Tertium Decretalium* . . . Tom.V, *De Sepulturis*, cap. 7, *De uxore*, n.6. fol. 117r; HENRICUS DE SEGUSIO *In Primum Decretalium Librum* . . ., *De Consuetudine*, cap. 8, *Cum dilectus* n.8, fol. 31r; *In Secundum Decretalium Librum* . . ., *De Sententia, et Re Iudicata* cap. 8, *Cum causa*, n.2. fol. 158v; JOANNES ANDREAE, *In Primum Decretalium Librum* . . ., *De Consuetudine*, cap. *Nunc*, n. 13, fol. 63r; ALBERICUS DE ROSATE, *Dictionarium* . . ., v. *Iuris*, p. 403; AZO, *Summa Super*

context, namely on a par with positive law. It was the common consensus of old jurists that the non-observance of custom constitutes, in the manner of the law, a transgression liable to penalty. *Decretum Gratiani* is explicit and insistent on this point: "In those matters upon which Sacred Scriptures have made no definite pronouncement, the custom of the people of God and the traditions of our ancestors are to be retained as law. Thus those who disobey the customs of the Church must be punished in the same manner as if they have transgressed the divine law."[86]

What makes a custom specifically *praeter legem* is the very lack of positive law. By virtue of canon 23, such a custom nonetheless needs the approval of the legislative authority to be what it is, namely, custom of law. Since it is *praeter legem*, it stands to reason that the approval is found in the tacit consent of the said authority according to the adage "Qui tacet, consentire videtur" (the one who remains silent is presumed to consent).[87] A difficulty arises regarding the prescription of canon 24 §2: "A custom which is expressly reprobated in the law is not reasonable." This prescription turns into *contradictio in terminis* in reference to *consuetudo praeter legem*: a custom opposing a reprobatory law is by that very fact *consuetudo contra*, and not *praeter, legem*.

Codicem, Lib. VIII, *Que sit longa consuetudo*, p. 324, col. 2; *Summa ad Pandectas*, Papiae, 1506, *De Legibus et Senatus consultis et Longa Consuetudine*, p. 385, col.2; CYNUS, *In Digesti Veteris Libros* . . . , Rubrica *III, De Legi. et sena. et long. consu.*, nn. 1, 3, 11, fol. 7r-v; *In Codicem Commentaria*, Lib. VIII, Tit. 53, *Quae sit longa consuetudo*, n. 1. fol. 525v; BALDUS DE UBALDIS, *In Decretalium Volumen* . . . , *Super Primo Decretalium, De Consuetudine*, cap. 11, *Cum tanto*, n 25, fol. 60r; n.44, fol. 61r; *Super Secundo Decretalium, De Appellationibus*, cap. 21, *Quaestioni*, n.4, fol. 292v; *Consiliorum, sive Responsorum* . . . , Cons. 58, n.8, fol. 14r.

[86] Pars I, Dist, XI, c. 7: "In his rebus, de quibus nihil certi statuit divina scriptura, mos populi Dei et instituta maiorum pro lege tenenda sunt. Et sicut prevaricatores legum divinarum, ita contemptores consuetudinum ecclesiasticarum cohercendi sunt"; cf. HENRICUS DE SEGUSIO, *In Secundum Decretalium Librum* . . . , *De Appellationibus*, cap. 21, *Quaestioni*, n.1, fol. 176v: "sunt enim transgressores consuetudinis, sicut et legum transgressores puniendi"; BALDUS DE UBALDIS, *In Decretalium Volumen* . . . , *Super Primo Decretalium, De Constitutionibus*, cap. 6, *Cum omnes*, n.25, fol. 14r.

[87] R.I. 43, in VI°. It differs from its Roman source which reads: "Qui tacet, non utique fatetur: sed tamen verum est eum non negare," Paulus, R.I. 142,D., *De Diversis regulis iuris antiqui*, 50, 17. The Roman *Regula Iuris* is more revealing of equity than the canonical one.

The Juridical Concept of Custom 177

A custom besides being reasonable, must endure for a certain length of time in order to have its purport in canon law. The required term of years is a criterion dependent upon the reasonableness of the custom,[88] but it is the time factor in which custom finds its perfection, as Baldus De Ubaldis remarks: "that custom assumes legal force only through a prescribed time."[89] Roman law gave great importance to the longevity of a custom.[90] However it always remained a debatable issue as what was specifically meant by the term *longaevitas*.[91] The Code solved the quandary with the prescription of canon 26: a custom which "is apart from the canon law, acquires the force of law only when it has been lawfully observed for a period of thirty continuous and complete years."

Consuetudo contra legem

In contrast with *consuetudo praeter legem*, which stands by itself, indeed in substitution of positive law, *consuetudo contra legem* by its very nature presupposes an existing law. The existence of law renders ambiguous the nature of the custom. On one hand, it assumes the nature of interpretation, albeit contradictory with the law; on the other hand, interpretation, as the word itself implies, cannot go against the law -- this would be *contradictio in terminis*.

The Roman legal system never lost sight of the fact that the power of government ontologically and historically resided in the people. The institution of *consuetudo contra legem* may suggest this consciousness on the part of the Roman legislator. But the endorsement of *consuetudo contra*

---

[88] HENRICUS DE SEGUSIO, *In Primum Decretalium Librum* . . . , *De Consuetudine*, cap. 10, *Ex Parte*, n.9. fol. 31v: "Bene dixi rationabilis, sic enim praescribi potest."

[89] *In Decretalium Volumen..*, *Super Secundo Decretalium, De Probationibus*, cap. 2, *Sicut*, n.7, fol. 201r: "tempus praescriptum est perfectio consuetudinis."

[90] Imp. Constantinus, L. *Consuetudinis*, 2, C., *Quae sit longa consuetudo*, 8, 52, (53); Ulpianus, L. *Diuturna*, 33, D. *De legibus senatusque consultis et longa consuetudine*, 1, 3.

[91] Cf. AZO, *Summa Super Codicem*, Lib. VIII, *Que sit longa consuetudo*, p. 324, col.2; *Summa ad pandectas, De Legibus et Senatus consultis et longa consuetudine*, p. 385, col.2.

legem has more significance in its relation to the law. It brings about an equilibrium between the sovereignty of the law and the will of the community. The absolutism of the law is thus checked, and the power of collective human consciousness is strongly felt by its existence. But most importantly it questions the validity of the law either because it does not reflect eternal justice or because it does not correspond to the actual exigencies of *l'esprit de corps*. Antonius A Butrio, in fact, considers custom precisely in this light. He states: "consuetudo est instrumentum: quo iustitia (legalis) regulatur, in ipsa insistere oportet."[92] Baldus De Ubaldis ascertains even more strongly: "Custom must first remove a contrary law in order that it establishes itself. It is necessary that a previous practice be removed first in order that a contrary practice be introduced in its stead, such as it happens that an illness must be overcome before health is restored."[93] *Consuetudo contra legem* was traditionally understood as interpretation of the law, indeed a remedial interpretation. It was defined as *correctiva* (correcting),[94] *reformans* (reshaping), or *emendans* (emending).[95] Cynus Pistoriensis sums up the traditional doctrine exquisitely when he points out: "take note that custom . . . sometimes corrects . . . but to interpret is to correct according to the proper significance of the matter . . . and therefore insofar as it corrects, it also interprets."[96]

---

[92] *Super Prima Primi Decretalium* . . ., Tom. I, *De Consuetudine*, cap. 11, *Cum tanto*, n.6, fol. 80r.

[93] *In Decretalium Volumen* . . ., *Super Primo Decretalium, De Consuetudine*, cap, 11, *Cum tanto* n. 44. fol. 61r: "consuetudo primo removet legem contrariam, secundo statuit consuetudinem, oportet primum habitum removeri prius, quam contrarius habitus subintroducatur, sicut oportet, quod primo removeatur aegritudo, quam introducatur sanitas."

[94] HENRICUS DE SEGUSIO, *In Primum decretalium Librum* . . ., *De Consuetudine*, cap. 8, *Cum dilectus*, n. 8, 12, fol. 31r; JOANNES ANDREAE, *In Primum Decretalium Librum* . . ., *De Consuetudine*, cap. 8, *Cum dilectus*, n.7. fol. 57v.

[95] BALDUS DE UBALDIS, *In Decretalium Volumen* . . ., *Super Primo Decretalium, De Consuetudine*, cap. 11, *Cum tanto*, n. 23, fol. 60r.

[96] *In Codicem Commentaria*, Lib. VIII,Tit. 53, *Quae sit longa consuetudo*, n.2, fol 525v: "Secundo nota quod consuetudo . . . quandoque corrigit . . . sed interpretari est corrigere, secundum propriam significationem . . . et ideo sicut corrigit, ita interpretatur."

The Juridical Concept of Custom 179

A custom contrary to the law necessarily implies non-observance of the law. It has earlier been contended that observance of the law pertains to the essence of the law, a view cherished by Gratianus: "Transgressors may not be penalized for the non-observance of laws which although legitimately promulgated have not been approved by common observance."[97] It is precisely on this assumption that the non-observance of the law not only questions the validity of the law, but it also intrinsically implies the repealing of the law in part or in whole: "Nam per desuetudinem inumbratur lex" (a law is eclipsed by non-observance).[98] But a juridical institution, which has the power of repealing a law, is a law in itself; thus *consuetudo contra legem* is more than mere interpretation. Having thus the force of a law, a custom can repeal part of the provisions of law (derogat),[99] or abolish the law in its entirety (abrogat); thus Hostiensis: "Leges per desuetudines abrogantur" (Laws are abrogated by non-observance).[100] Needless to say, a custom contrary to a law repeals the law partially or wholly only if it is subsequent to the law since a subsequent, contrary law repeals a *consuetudo praeter legem*.

The same criteria required by the Code for *consuetudo praeter legem* stand also for *consuetudo contra legem*. By virtue of canon 23, the approval

---

[97] *Decretum*, Pars I, Dist.IV, c.6, IV pars: "Hec etsi legibus constituta sunt, tamen quia communi usu approbata non sunt, se non observantes transgressionis reos non arguunt"; cf. ibid., c.3, Gratianus: "Sicut enim moribus utentium in contrarium nonnullae leges hodie abrogatae sunt, ita moribus utentium ipsae leges confirmantur . . . "

[98] *In Primum Decretalium Librum* . . . , *De Consuetudine*, cap. 8, *Cum dilectus*, n. 10, fol. 31r.

[99] CYNUS PISTORIENSIS, *In Digesti Veteris Libros* . . . , Rubrica III, *De legi. et sena. et long. consu.* n. 11, fol. 7v; AZO, *Ad Singulas Leges XII* . . . , Lib. VIII, Tit. 53, *Quae sit longa consuetudo*, lex 2, n.6, p. 672. HENRICUS DE SEGUSIO, *In Primum Decretalium Librum* . . . , *De Consuetudine*, cap.8, *Cum dilectus*, n. 12, fol. 31r.

[100] *In Quintum Decretalium Librum* . . . , *De Privilegiis et Excessibus Privilegiatorum*, cap. 6, *si de terra*, n. 2. fol. 80r; cf. *In Primum Decretalium Librum* . . . , *De Consuetudine*, cap. 8, *Cum dilectus*, n.8. fol. 31r; CYNUS PISTORIENSIS, *In Digesti Veteris Libros* . . . , Rubrica III, *De Legi. et Sena. et Long. Consu.*, n.2, fol. 7r: "sicut lex scripta tollitur per aliam legem ita lex per consuetudinem contrariam abrogatur"; ibid., n. 7. fol. 7v; AZO, *Ad Singulas Leges XII* . . . , Lib. I, Prooemium, n. 16, p.2: "Tollitur enim lex per desuetudinem, sicut et fit per consuetudinem"; *Summa Super Codicem*, Lib. VIII, *Que sit longa consuetudo*, p. 324, col. 2. JOANNES ANDREAE, *In Primum Decretalium Librum* . . . , *De Consuetudine*, cap. 11, *Cum tanto* n. 42, fol. 61r.

of the legislator is a requisite for its legal validity. The general presumption is that a custom which is not explicitly reproved in the law,[101] enjoys the approval of the legislator. By reason of reasonableness three types of custom emerge, which are: simply contrary, prohibited, and reprobated. A reprobated custom is the only one which is not reasonable and therefore can never be prescribed.[102] Simply contrary and prohibited customs are reasonable, differing however from each other by reason of the period required for legal recognition. Canon 26 prescribes a period of thirty continuous and complete years for a simply contrary custom, whereas for a contrary custom prohibited in advance by the law, the canon demands that the custom be of a hundred years' standing, or exceed human memory.

Consuetudo secundum legem

"Optima enim est legum interpres consuetudo" is a well-known statement of Paulus[103] which found its way in the *Corpus Iuris Canonici*.[104] Canon 27 simply repeats the dictum: "Custom is the best interpreter of laws," a definition which refers to *consuetudo secundum legem*. The observance of the law reveals the intent of the law. The way a law has been observed is the right understanding of the law concerned. Unlike *consuetudo contra legem*, this type of custom is interpretation in its entirety,[105] but its ability may nonetheless assume different connotations. It

---

[101] Canon 24, §2.

[102] Ibid.

[103] Paulus, L. *Si de interpretatione*, 37, D., *De legibus senatusque consultis et longa consuetudine*, 1, 3.

[104] *Decretum Gratiani*, Pars I, Dist. IV, c.3, Gratianus: "Leges instituuntur, cum promulgantur, firmantur, cum moribus utentium approbantur"; C. 8, X, *De Consuetudine*, 1, 4; R.I. 45, in VI°.

[105] BALDUS DE UBALDIS, *Consiliorum, sive Responsorum* . . . , Vol. III. Cons. 48, n.3, fol. 13v; *In Decretalium volumen* . . *Super Primo Decretalium, De Consuetudine*, cap. 11, *Cum tanto*, n. 23, fol. 60r; AZO, *Ad Singulas Leges XII* . . . , Lib. III, Tit. 9, *De Litis Contestatione*, n. 10, pp. 182-183; HENRICUS DE SEGUSIO, *In Primum Decretalium Librum* . . . , *De Consuetudine*, cap.8, *Cum dilectus* n. 12, fol. 31r; ibid., *De Rescriptis* cap.28, *Non nulli*, n. 10. fol. 22v; *In Secundum Decretalium Librum* . . . , *De Fide Instrumentorum*, cap.6, *Inter dilectos*, n.8, fol. 114v; JOANNES

may determine or clarify what is ambiguous in the law, as Hostiensis remarks: "It is the characteristic of custom to interpret a dubious law."[106] One may phrase it differently: "Clarificat quod non potest lex per se ipsam determinare praecise" (custom can clarify what the law itself cannot define accurately); in this sense, as Cynus ascertains: "interpretari est corrigere" (to interpret is to correct).[107] *Consuetudo secundum legem* highlights the intrinsic relationship between law and observance of the law, the interlocked reality of public authority and community. This type of custom is a demonstration that it is the community that shapes the law, for the law is ultimately the product of the spirit of the community.

Conclusion

No custom has binding force in the ethical realm unless it is approved by the legislative authority. The legal involvement seems, at first hand, a curtailment of the free and spontaneous devolvement of *l'esprit de corps*. Custom of fact normally obtains its legal endorsement according to the prescriptions of the Code. The Code, nevertheless, contemplates an instance where the legislator may intervene personally in the development of *l'esprit de corps* by shortening the term of years required by law.[108]

Public authority pertains to the nature of human consciousness; hence the legal endorsement is imperative in order that a custom posit itself as a binding force of the community. The central idea of the Hegelian theory helps us understand the dynamics of the collective human consciousness in the formation of custom. In the Hegelian perspective, custom presents itself as a dialectical process of human consciousness. The human consciousness

---

ANDREAE, *In Primum Decretalium Librum* . . . , *De Consuetudine*, cap.8, *Cum dilectus*, n. 7. fol. 57v; ibid. cap.11, *Cum tanto*, n.42, fol. 61r.

[106] *In Primum Decretalium Librum* . . . , *De Consuetudine*, cap. 8, *Cum dilectus*, n. 8. fol. 31r: "est ista una virtus consuetudinis, scilicet interpretandi ius dubium."

[107] *In Codicem Commentaria*, Lib. VIII, Tit. 53, *Quae sit longa consuetudo*, n.2.fol. 525v.

[108] Canon 26.

divides itself into two extremes, community and public authority, in view of reaching a synthesis. The collective human consciousness suspends itself into otherness created by the same human consciousness within itself. This it does in the pursuit of ultimate self-discovery. Custom is for the collective human consciousness what the law is for the legislator; it manifests *l'esprit de corps* alive, aware of itself, functioning at a stage of its humanization process. However, in custom, the collective spirit suspends itself in otherness of itself by transfering its own consciousness, custom, to public authority in order that custom may come back to its source as the full and authentic product of the human consciousness. In other words, it is the community which provides the material (custom of fact), but it is the legislative authority which gives it the binding force (custom of law). Thus custom of fact reaches its perfection with the approval of the legislative authority. At this stage, however, this perfection is merely ontological; custom of law is merely a principle, a norm. But a custom cannot be fully real and actual, cannot reach its ultimate significance unless it goes back to the community, observed by the community.

Custom is other than savage resistance to change; illustration of this is found in canons 5 and 28; the former deals with customs existing at the time of the promulgation of the Code, the latter concerns future customs. A change in whole or in part of a custom is brought about by non-observance of the same custom, by the emergence of a different custom, or by the enactment of a conflicting law according to the prescription of canon 28. A custom by the very fact that it emanates directly from human consciousness itself, shares the same destiny as its source; it must change, transform itself, move to a higher mode of expression.

The Concept of Public Authority

The Understanding of Public Authority in Roman Law

Cicero was the forerunner of a political theory on public authority which permeated Western civilization throughout the *ancien régime,* until it received its *coup de grace* in the French Revolution. In perusing his writings, one cannot miss his antagonism towards a democratic government. He could not conceive of an authority ultimately deriving from *populus.* In the footsteps of Aristotle, he maintained: "The very inequality is unjust since it allows no degrees of rank."[1] He could not see Athens be ruled by the mob, rather than by the areopagus.[2] Thus it seems safe to say that in the Ciceronean political philosophy public authority stands out as a reality essentially distinct from, and a sovereignty absolutely independent of, *populus.* It has been established in a previous study on the nature of law that Cicero nevertheless maintained the subordination of human justice to an eternal law which is found implanted in the human heart; therefore, any arbitrariness on the part of the ruler in the enactment of his laws is antithetical to the Ciceronean position. Thus Cicero takes exception to the statement of Ulpianus, "Quod principi placuit, legis habet vigorem" (the wish of the ruler has the force of law)[3] if taken in an absolute manner.

---

[1] *De Re Publica,* Lib. I, cap. 27, n. 43, loc.cit., p.1178: "ipsa aequabilitas est iniqua, quum habet nullos gradus dignitatis."

[2] Ibid.

[3] Ulpianus, L. *Quod principi,* l, D., *De constitutionibus principum,* 1. 4.

In the *Corpus Iuris Civilis,* Law, with the exception of the *senatus consultum,* is acknowledged as deriving its authority ultimately from *populus*. The emperor is acclaimed the source of law but only because the people, by their own legislative act, endowed him with such power, created him, as it were, as its synthesis and epitome. Ulpianus, writing in the second century A.D., ascertains that the emperor's will is law only because *populus* transferred its innate right to the emperor.[4] Justinian, the great spokesman of Roman law in the sixth century writes: "All power and authority of the Roman people were transformed unto the emperor."[5] However, the Christian influence is apparent in the same text of Justinian. God has subjected all laws to the emperor whom He has given to the community as a living law: "it is the will of God that we rule the empire -- an authority bestowed on us by the divine majesty -- and sustain the structure of the common weal."[6] Justinian tries, but fails, to reconcile the two seemingly opposing theories on the origin and nature of public authority; thus his view on the matter remains vague, indeed ambiguous.

The question was already being debated among Roman jurists as to whether the emperor, once instituted the sole source of law, was thereby exempted from his own law. Ulpianus could not perceive how political sovereignty in its own doing could subject itself to itself; thus he concludes: "Princeps legibus solutus est" (the ruler is exempt from his own laws).[7] This juridical position of the ruler, enables him, to dispense from

---

[4] Ibid., "Quod principi placuit, legis habet vigorem: utpote cum lege regia, quae de imperio eius lata est, populus ei et in eum omne suum imperium et potestatem conferat."

[5] Imp. Justinianus, L. *Deo auctore,* 1, §7, C., *De Veteri iure enucleando et auctoritate iuris prudentium qui in digestis referuntur,* 1, 17: "omne ius omnisque potestas populi Romani in imperatoriam translata sunt potestatem"; Inst., *De iure naturali et gentium et civili,* §6, 1, 2; Julianus, L. *De quibus* 32, §1, D., *De legibus senatusque consultis et longa consuetudine,* 1,3: "quare rectissime etiam illud receptum est, ut leges non solum suffragio legis latoris, sed etiam tacito consensu omnium per desuetudinem abrogentur."

[6] Imp. Justinianus, L. *Deo auctore,* 1, C., *De veteri iure enucleando et auctoritate iuris prudentium qui in digestis referuntur,* 1, 17: "Deo auctore nostrum gubernantes imperium, quod nobis a caelesti maiestate traditum est . . . et statum rei publicae sustentamus . . ."

[7] Ulpianus, L. *Princeps,* 31, D., *De legibus senatusque consultis et longa consuetudine,* 1, 3.

his own laws,[8] to bestow privileges and honours, and grant pardon for crimes.[9] For emperors, Theodosius and Valentinianus, however, political sovereignty should not be perceived in an absolute manner. They seem to infer that human authority is subject to a supreme principle of justice, to which human justice should be subordinate and by which it should abide. The prince is bound by his own laws, for his authority is drawn from the authority of the law -- "De auctoritate iuris nostra pendet auctoritas" (our authority derives from the authority of the law).[10] The law, for its part, draws its authority from *recta ratio,* which is nothing other than natural law, as the *Institutiones* point out: "Divi autem principes non passi sunt talem contra naturam iniuriam sine competenti emendatione relinquere . . . "[11] In this second hypothesis, a link is thus retained between the sovereignty of the ruler and the supremacy of the people; between the ruler and his subjects there exist basic continuity and mutuality of obligations. The community suspends itself and transfers itself into otherness, to be ruled and directed towards its own inner destiny which is the full development of itself; thus it creates public authority as its own self out of itself. It becomes apparent that public authority is limited and conditioned by its origin, nature, and finality. In positing the legislator above the law the first hypothesis necessarily leads to an alternative conclusion: it either fosters an authority which recognizes no boundary to its nature, and thus the most brutal despotism would be in order, or it subordinates the legislator to a superior and absolute principle of justice. In the latter case, legislative authority, by force of reason, must subject itself to its own law, which must reflect the absolute principle of justice for its own intrinsic validity; thus, in ultimate analysis, "de auctoritate iuris nostra pendet

---

[8] Imp. Justinianus, L. *Si imperialis,* 12, §5, C., *De Legibus et constitutionibus principum et edictis* 1, 14; Imp. Constantinus, L. *Inter* 1, loc.cit.

[9] Ulpianus, L. *Princeps,* 31, D., *De legibus senatusque consultis et longa consuetudine* 1,3; Ulpianus, L. *Quod principi,* 1, §2, D., *De constitutionibus principum* 1,4.

[10] Impp. Theodosius et Valentinianus, L. *Digna vox,* 4, C., *De legibus et constitutionibus principum et edictis,* 1, 14.

[11] Inst. *De hereditatibus quae ab intestato deferuntur,* §15, 3, 1.

auctoritas'' (our authority derives from the authority of the law). The ruler, stripped of any arbitrary power in legislating, is rather conceived of as an interpretor of the absolute principle of justice, ministering to the community. In spite of the denial of legislative absolutism, there is not a contradiction in acknowledging the right of the legislative authority to dispense from the law, to bestow privileges, and to grant pardon for crime, if these activities are perceived within the context of the subordination of the law to equity, as expounded earlier.[12]

The Concept of Authority in the Judeo-Christian Religion

The world-historical importance and significance of the Jewish Religion is its concept of God as a Supreme Being beyond space, and time. His essence is being, and a pure being. Anything outside Yahweh is nothingness without him. Everything, which is not He, is contingent, subordinate to him in essence and existence. Humans are regarded as individual creatures without pretense of being participants in the divinity. All other creatures are seen devoid of spirit, intellect and will. An essential distinction is laid down between divine supremacy and human sovereignty. Only Yahweh is the supreme and exclusive authority. In the Ancient Near East, and indeed in all ancient cultures, the cultic position of the monarch constituted the basis and the source of power by which he governed; it expressed ritually his position between gods and humans, for the power of kingship was perceived as the will of the gods. The king was the reincarnation of the divinity. Among the Israelites, the concept of royal power differed notably and sharply. Monarchy, on principle, was conceived as rejection of God's sovereignty. "But Yahweh said to Samuel, Obey the voice of the people in all that they say to you, for it is not you they have rejected; they have rejected me from ruling over them . . . they deserted

---

[12] Imp. Justinianus, L. *Si imperialis*, §12, 5, C., *De legibus et constitutionibus principum et edictis.*, 1, 14.

me and served other gods."[13] The Jewish king was not the descendant of the Gods; he had no ichor in his veins, as the pagan king claimed to have. He was rather a charismatic leader, possessing the gift by divine election proclaimed through a prophetic oracle, and thus became the anointed one. Yahweh could anytime reject him for his disobedience, as He did with Saul and others.

The Greek notion of God as existing in the speculative idea or in beauty itself expressed in marble, or metal, and in physical human strength and proportion is repudiated once and for all in the Pure One assuming a splendid and sinless humanness. The Word became flesh as the fulfillment of times; the *causa formalis* became a historic reality; thus it became more abundantly clear that Christ is also the *causa finalis* of creation: "There is only Christ: he is everything and he is in everything";[14] "that he would bring everything together under Christ, as head, everything in the heavens and everything on earth."[15] The Lord repeats Yahweh's admonition to the Israelites: "You know that among the pagans the rulers lord it over them, and their great men make their authority felt."[16] And He introduced a concept of authority unknown in the history of political science: "Anyone who wants to be great among you must be your servant, and anyone who wants to be first among you must be your slave, just as the Son of Man came not to be served but to serve, and to give his life as a ransom for many."[17] The Lord's concept of authority formed the fundamental premise of the apostolic teaching on social and political matters. In his first letter, Saint Peter reiterates the supreme authority of God: "You are slaves of no one except God."[18] In the Pauline letter to the Colossians, the absolute

---

[13] 1 Sam. 8: 7 - 8; cf. 11-18.

[14] Col. 3: 11; cf. 1:15 - 20.

[15] Eph. 1:10.

[16] Matt. 20:25.

[17] Mat. 20: 26-28.

[18] 1 Pet. 2:16.

supremacy of God is further clarified in its externalization in the *Unio Hypostatica*. It was the will of God from eternity that Christ be "the first-born of all creation, for in him were created all things in heaven and on earth . . . all things were created through him and for him . . . and he holds all things in unity";[19] hence all creation is subject to the authority of the Son of Man who came not to be served but to serve. Upon this premise, Saint Paul categorically repudiates the Aristotelian contention that it is a law of nature that humans are classified into those capable of the higher level, and others who belong to a lower level of socio-political stratification: "In that image there is no room for distinction between Greek and Jew, between the circumcised or the uncircumcised, or between barbarian and Scythian, slave and free man. There is only Christ: he is everything and he is in everything."[20]

In the writings of both Apostles, one can easily envisage their preoccupation that a socio-political upheaval might ensue. Christianity has a great potential for breaking right through the very foundations of social structure. The danger was therefore imminent, since Christian solidarity antagonized *a priori* the socio-political configuration of society. On the other hand, the Apostles were cognizant of the fact that the Christian spirit must abide by the law of nature to enter into actual reality in a generally valid and conscious manner, starting with the inner conviction of human conscience. Christianity is the antithesis of human authority which exists only as compulsion par excellence. The human consciousness looks upon authoritative power as a chain, as something suppressing its separate existence for its own sake, and hence hates the ruler, obeys only with secret malice, and stands ever ready to burst out in rebellion. In opposition, Christianity is essentially the interiorization of human consciousness, revitalization of itself within itself; this process leads to exteriorization of itself in otherness in view of its own self-fulfillment. The Christian spirit must first excite the Christians to become strong in themselves, to develop

---

[19] Col. 1: 15-17

[20] Col. 3: 11, cf. 1 Cor. 12: 13; Gal. 3: 27 - 28.

and assert their christological individuality, that is their authentic humanness. Christ, it has been stated earlier, is the *causa formalis* of human nature, and hence the christological ontology of human consciousness. Christianity is nothing other than the revitalization of the impulse of the human spirit within itself to break through the bonds, the shell of naturalness, of sensuousness, of crude being, of estrangement from itself, and to arrive at deeper consciousness of itself. It is in the nature of the Christian reality that human conviction and insight must correspond to the stage at which human consciousness has arrived in the christolization process of itself. In the unfolding process of itself, the universal human spirit, which is history itself, must abide by its inherent law of development, the law of graduation. The human spirit is therefore prone to resist any imposition which disturbs its innate momentum of transformation of itself. Conscious of this reality, the Apostles took care to lay down the fundamentals for revitalization of the christological ontology of the human spirit through catechesis. Thus the Apostles, while rejecting any pretence of the ruler as the re-incarnation of the deity, nevertheless acknowledged and endorsed civil authority, in its metaphysical conceptualization, as a reflection of divine wisdom and justice. Saint Paul ascertains that all authority derives from heaven and is therefore valid and sacred. In unison with this doctrine, Saint Peter exhorts thus the Christians: "For the sake of the Lord, accept the authority of every social institution: the emperor, as the supreme authority, and the governors as commissioned by him to punish criminals and praise good citizenship. God wants you to be good citizens, so as to silence what fools are saying in their ignorance. You are slaves of no one except God, so behave like free men, and never use your freedom as an excuse for wickedness. Have respect for everyone and love for our community; fear God and honour the emperor."[21] Similarly, Saint

---

[21] 1 Pet. 2: 13 - 17

Paul in his admonition to Titus[22] and to Timothy[23] teaches respect and obedience to civil authority.

This apostolic stand is not, by any means, a pragmatic approach based on mere expediency, convenience, and compromise which savours of opportunism and submissiveness. It is rather a profound understanding of the ontology of the universal human consciousness. Notwithstanding the mediocre stage at which the human spirit found itself at the time in the process of its inherent christolization, the aim of the Apostolic teaching was to exhort Christians to individually live the fruition of this same process as found established in the Gospel. In the context of an *ad hoc* situation, and in spite of it, Paul sublimates the socio-political relationship of master and slave to a community of love and understanding, to an inter-personal relationship fully human, to a fusion of minds into oneness.[24] Christianity could never condone slavery, for slavery destroys the very foundation of the human *consortium* of which Christianity is the epitome. The situation of slavery has not been solved even in our times: the purport of the parable of the vineyard[25] has not as yet been grasped to the full by the universal human consciousness. The modern mind looks with dismay and horror at slavery, not being aware that, in the proletarian system, only shape and form have changed, but the reality remains substantially the same. Modern society still functions on the Aristotelian premise of class discrimination; human exploitation is alive and stringent as in the time of slavery and serfdom; the rabble still prostitutes itself as an amount of energy, and bows to those who exploite it; it still believes in the divine nature of the monarch. In spite of these odds, Christianity never desists from enlightening human consciousness of its inherent authenticity, which is consciousness of itself in the image of Christ. This it does by taking into consideration the present ability of the human spirit to know itself.

---

[22] Tit. 3: 1-2

[23] 1 Tim. 2: 1-2

[24] Col. 3: 22-24; 4:1.

[25] Matt. 20: 1-16.

Concept of Authority in Patristic Literature

"Since all government comes from God, the civil authorities were appointed by God, and so anyone who resists authority is rebelling against God's decision, and such an act is bound to be punished."[26] In the syllogism of Paul, the conclusion is his, but not the premise. This is apparent from the literary point of view, since Paul takes it for granted that the doctrine of the divine institution of authority is known and accepted by his readers acquainted with the Book of Proverbs; "By me monarchs rule and princes issue just laws; by me rulers govern, and the great impose justice on the world."[27] The Pauline doctrine forms the central idea of patristic literature on the subject.

Reference to the patristic teaching on the subject has already been made in a previous study dealing with human law. This reference, however brief, was imperative for a better understanding of the law, since law and authority form one interlocked reality; one intrinsically necessitates the other. Some repetition is therefore expected for the sake of clarity.

Upon the Pauline premise that all authority descends from divine authority, a distinctive and fundamental principle had to be set down, namely that authority and community are two essentially distinct entities, although one intrinsically necessitates the other, and as such, they should be perceived and studied. The Roman theory that the community is the ultimate source of authority is *a priori* discarded in the patristic contention. Human authority is perceived as a divine mandate, a commitment directly assigned by God to the one in power, as Theophilus of Antioch phrases it: "For in a kind of way his government is committed to him by God."[28]

---

[26] Rom. 13: 1-2.

[27] Prov. 8: 15 - 16.

[28] *To Autolycus*, Bk I, chap. 11, *The Ante-Nicene Fathers*, Trans. Marcus Dods, Vol. II, Grand Rapids Michigan, 1975, p. 92.

The assumption of the divine institution of authority does not *a priori* entail the belief in the naturalness of human authority. No general consensus, in fact, was reached in the patristic literature on the score. Saint Augustine seems to be of the opinion that authority indeed belongs to the essence of human nature.[29] Gregory the Great makes it very clear that the manner in which society is stratified is a reflection of the celestial hierarchy. In his presentation, it follows that authority is as natural as it is divine, and it is intended by divine consent to keep peace and to foster charity among humans.[30] In another *opus*, however, he realizes a basic equality to exist among humans, which nevertheless allows a certain variety among individuals by reason of personal abilities.[31] In the same *Libri Morales*, he seems to retract from his original position in considering human authority divinely willed as a curtailment to human rebelliousness: "Subjects sometimes act as beasts and for this reason they must be controlled by fear."[32] Sanctus Optatus De Milevis, according to whom discrimination of classes was intended by God, seems to adhere[33] to this belief in the naturalness of authority.

---

[29] *Expositio Quarundam Propositionum*. . ., loc. cit., col. 2083: "Cum enim constemus ex anima et corpore, et quamdiu in hac vita temporali sumus, etiam rebus temporalibus ad subsidium degendae hujus vitae utamur; oportet nos ex ea parte, quae ad hanc vitam pertinet, subditos esse potestatibus, id est, hominibus res humanas cum aliquo honore administrantibus."

[30] *Registri Epistolarum*. Lib. V; Epist. 54, loc. cit., coll. 785 - 786: "Ad hoc dispensationis divinae provisio gradus diversos et ordines constituit esse distinctos, ut dum reverentiam minores potioribus exhiberent, et potiores minoribus dilectionem impenderent, una concordiae fieret ex diversitate contextio, et recte officiorum gereretur administratio singulorum . . . coelestium militiarum exemplar nos instruit, quia dum sunt angeli, et sunt archangeli, liquet quod non sunt aequales, sed in potestate et ordine, sicut nostis, differt alter ab altero . . . Hinc etenim pax et charitas mutua se vice complectuntur, et manet firma concordiae in alterna, et Deo placita dilectione sinceritas."

[31] *Moralium Libri, sive Expositio in Librum B. Job*, Pars IV, Lib. XXI, cap. 15, n.22, *Opera Omnia*, Tomus II, P.L. Tomus 76, Parisiis, 1878, col. 203: "Nam, ut praefati sumus, omnes homines natura aequales genuit, sed variante meritorum ordine, alios aliis dispensatio occulta postponit."

[32] Ibid., n. 23, col. 204: "ex qua parte bestiales sunt subditi, ex ea etiam debent formidini jacere substrati"

[33] *De Schismate Donatistarum* . . . , Lib.III, cap..3,loc. cit.,,coll.999 - 1000.

Prevalent among the Fathers seems to be the view that civil authority, albeit of divine origin, is not natural. Human authority is the result of sin; it is there to curb human corruption. Saint Ambrose writes apropos: "To indiscreet persons the wise become as rulers to guide by their power the foolishness of the crowd which they rule under the guise of power, when they bring unwilling subjects to obey those who are more wise and to submit to the laws."[34] According to Saint Irenaeus, human authority is imposed by God because of human restless conduct, murder, avarice, and growing viciousness among humans.[35] In the writings of the Fathers, the general idea of authority, whether civil[36] or ecclesiastical[37] is essentially that of terror. John of Salisbury is very explicit in his concept of civil authority: "quamdam carnificii repraesentare videtur imaginem."[38] In the

---

[34] *Letters, Letter to Simplicianus,* 54 (37), loc. cit., p. 288; cf. *Letter to Valentinian,* (21), 9, ibid. p. 54.

[35] *Against Heresies,* Bk. 5, chap. 24, n.2, loc. cit., p. 119: "For since man, by departing from God, reached such a pitch of fury as even to look upon his brother as his enemy, and engaged without fear in every kind of restless conduct, and murder, and avarice; God imposed upon mankind the fear of man, as they did not acknowledge the fear of God, in order that, being subjected to the authority of men, and kept under restraint by their laws, they might attain to some degree of justice, and exercise mutual forbearance through dread of the sword suspended full in their view"; cf. HONORIUS AUGUSTODUNENSIS, *Summa Gloria de Apostolico et Augusto,* cap. V, *Opera Omnia,,* Tomus Unicus, P.L., Tomus 172, Parisiis, 1854, col. 1266; HINCMARUS RHEMENSIS, *De Divortio Lotharii* . . . , Quaestio VI. loc.cit., col. 757; ISIDORUS, *Sententiarum Libri* . . . , Lib. III, cap. 47, n.1, loc.cit., col. 717: "Inde et in gentibus principes, regesque electi sunt, ut terrore suo populos a malo coercerent, atque ad recte vivendum legibus subderent"; S. BERNARDUS, *De Consideratione Libri Quinque ad Eugenium Tertium,* Lib. IV, cap. 3, n.7, *Opera Omnia,* Tomus I, P.L., Tomus 182, Parisiis, 1862, col. 776; JOANNIS SARESBERIENSIS, *Polycraticus* . . . ,Lib. IV, cap. 3, loc. cit., col. 516.

[36] IRENAEUS, *Against Heresies,* Bk 5, chap. 24, n.2, loc. cit., pp 119- 120 AMBROSE, *Letters, Letter to Simplicianus,* 54 (37), loc. cit., p. 288; HONORIUS AUGUSTODUNENSIS, *Summa Gloria* . . . , cap IV, cap. V,,loc. cit., coll. 1264, 1266; PETRUS DAMIANUS, *Opusculum Quinquagesimum Septimum -- De Principis Officio,* cap. II, *Opera Omnia,* Tomus Posterior, P.L.,Tomus 145, Parisiis, 1867, col. 821; *Sermo in Dedicatione Ecclesiae,* (Sermo LXIX) loc.cit., col. 900; ISIDORUS, *Sententiarum Libri* . . . , Lib. III, cap. 47, n. 1, loc. cit., col. 717; JOANNIS SARESBERIENSIS, *Polycraticus* . . . lib. IV, cap. 3, loc. cit.,, col. 516.

[37] HONORIUS AUGUSTODUNENSIS, *Summa Gloria* . . . , cap. IV, loc.cit., col. 1264; S. BERNARDUS, *De Consideratione Libri* . . . , Lib. IV, cap. 3, n.7, loc. cit., col. 776.

[38] *Polycraticus* . . . , Lib. IV, cap. 3, loc.cit., col. 516.

opinion of Optatus De Milevis, the king is to be feared -- "Qui post Deum ab hominibus timebatur" (who after God is the most feared by man).[39] All this notwithstanding, Irenaeus assures us that "Earthly rule, therefore, has been appointed by God for the benefit of nations, and not by the devil."[40] We believe it would not be far from the mark if the following two conclusions were deduced from the teaching of the Fathers on the nature of authority: 1) the fostering of a concept of divine dictatorship, similar to the pagan conceptualization of divinity, which contradicts the Lord's teaching on the fatherhood of God; 2) the pessimistic view of the patristic outlook on the redeemableness of human nature to overcome its own mediocrity.

In fairness to Saint Paul it must be admitted that no mention is made in his letters on the form of authority. In the Patristic literature, autocracy is acclaimed as the sole, valid form of government. Absolute sovereignty was for many centuries a *fait accompli:* any other form of government seems to have been beyond human comprehension. Ecclesiastical authority showed adamant hesitation in recognizing any form of government other than the traditional autocracy; for many years democratization of authority was frowned upon as anti-biblical and anti-Christian. Two factors, one historical and the other doctrinal, have contributed to the belief in absolute monarchy as the sole, valid form of ruling. In the Roman empire and later in the Sacred Roman empire down to the rise of modern States, authority was invested *in integro* in one single person. The Fathers knew of no other model than the *de facto* absolute monarchism. From the theological and historical points of view, civil and ecclesiastical authorities were perceived as two inseparable entities, sometimes even as two aspects of the same reality, since both find their source in God. The turbulent relationship between Church and State, beginning with the Peace of Constantine down to the secularization of the State, stems from this very fundamental assumption that God is the source of human authority. It was for ever a

---

[39] *De Schismate Donatistarum* . . . , Lib III, cap. 3, loc. cit., col. 1003.

[40] *Against Heresies*, Bk. 5, chap 24, n.2, loc. cit., p. 120.

heated debate academically and politically which of the two, Church or State, is the direct and proximate embodiment of divine authority. The subject *per se* surpasses the scope of the present paper. One may nevertheless mention, among others, Isidore,[41] Hincmarus Rhemensis,[42] Petrus Damianus,[43] Honorius Augustodunensis,[44] Sanctus Bernardus,[45] Joannis Saresberiensis,[46] who endorse the supremacy of Church authority over the secular one, whereas Optatus De Milevis,[47] Catulfus,[48] and Hugo

---

[41] *Sententiarum Libri Tres*, Lib. III, cap. 51, n. 6., loc. cit., coll. 723-724- "Cognoscant principes saeculi Deo debere se rationem reddere propter Ecclesiam, quam a Christo tuendam suscipiunt. Nam sive augeatur pax et disciplina Ecclesiae per fideles principes, sive solvatur, ille ab eis rationem exiget, qui eorum potestati suam Ecclesiam credidit."

[42] *Ad Proceres Regni . . .*, cap.9, loc. cit., col. 997: "Et ideo, quia res ecclesiasticas divino judicio tuendas et defensandas suscepit, consensu ejus, electione cleri ac plebis, et approbatione episcoporum provinciae, quisque ad ecclesiasticum regimen absque ulla venalitate provehidebet."

[43] *Sermo in Dedicatione Ecclesiae*, loc.cit., col. 900: "Felix autem, si gladium regni cum gladio jungat sacerdotii, ut gladius sacerdotis mitiget gladium regis, et gladius regis gladium acuat sacerdotis. Isti sunt duo gladii, de quibus in Domini passione legitur . . . Tunc enim regnum provehitur, sacerdotium dilatatur, honoratur utrumque, cum a Domino praetaxata felici confoederatione junguntur."

[44] *Summa Gloria . . .*, cap. IV, loc. cit., col 1264: "Qui Constantinus Romano pontifici coronam regni imposuit, et ut nullus deinceps Romanum imperium absque consensu apostolici subiret imperiali auctoritate censuit." Ibid., col. 1265: "ergo rex a Christi sacerdotibus, qui veri Ecclesiae principes sunt, est constituendus; consensus tamen laicorum requirendus: igitur quia sacerdotium jure regnum constituat, jure regnum sacerdotio subjacebit." Ibid., cap. V, col. 1266: "unde et in Evangelio cum discipuli dixissent Domino: Ecce duo gladii hic (Luc. 22), hic verba horum sua auctoritate roboravit, quia ad regimen Ecclesiae in praesenti vita duos gladios necessarios praemonstravit."

[45] *De Consideratione Libri Quinque . . .*, Lib. IV, cap.3., n.7, loc. cit., col. 776: "Uterque ergo Ecclesiae et spiritualis scilicet gladius, et materialis; sed si quidem pro Ecclesia, ille vero et ab Ecclesia exserendus: ille sacerdotis, is militis manu, sed sane ad nutum sacerdotis, et jussum imperatoris."

[46] *Polycraticus . . .*, Lib. IV, cap. 3., loc. cit., col. 516: "Hunc ergo gladium de manu Ecclesiae accipit princeps, cum ipsa tamen gladium sanguinis omnino non habeat. Habet tamen et istum, sed eo utitur per principis manum, cui coercendorum corporum contulit potestatem, spiritualem sibi in pontificibus auctoritate reservata."

[47] *De Schismate Donatistarum . . .*, Lib. III, cap.3, loc. cit., col. 999: "non enim respublica est in Ecclesia, sed Ecclesia in republica est, id est, in imperio Romano: quod Libanum appellat Christus in Canticis Canticorum."

[48] *Instructio Epistolaris . . . ,loc.* cit., col. 1364: "Memor esto ergo semper, rex mi, Dei regis tui cum timore et amore, quod tu es in vice illius super omnia membra ejus custodire, et regere, et rationem reddere in die judicii, etiam per te; et episcopus est in secundo loco, in vice Christi tantum est. Ergo considerate inter vos diligenter, legem Dei constituere super populum Dei, quod Deus tuus dixit tibi, cujus vicem tenes."

De Sancta Maria,[49] vouch for the subordination of ecclesiastical authority to secular power. There is a strong reason to believe that the conceptualization of authority by the Fathers was based on the theology of the Petrine Chair. One may even speculate that the increasing autocracy of the civil power reinforced the doctrine of absolute Petrine supremacy because of the perceived intimacy between Church and State. The conclusions reached by Optatus De Milevis and by John of Salisbury, which are repulsive to human consciousness at this further stage of humanization, conform well to the patristic thesis. Optatus De Milevis thus concludes: "Whoever is above human beings, is compared almost to God,"[50] and John of Salisbury maintains: "Imago quaedam divinitatis est princeps" (the prince is somehow an image of the divinity).[51]

The doctrine of the direct and immediate bestowal of authority by God upon one single person was further emphasized by the pessimistic view of human nature espoused by some of the Fathers. Civil authority is there to curb the evil in humankind. Thus Saint Irenaeus writes: "God imposed upon mankind the fear of man, as they did not acknowledge the fear of God, in order that, being subjected to the authority of men, and kept under restraint by their laws, they might attain to some degree of justice, and exercise mutual forbearance through dread of the sword suspended full in

---

[49] *Tractatus de Regia Potestate* . . . , Lib. I, cap. 3, loc. cit., col. 942: "Verumtamen rex in regni sui corpore Patris omnipotentis obtinere videtur imaginem, et episcopus Christi. Unde rite regi subjacere videntur omnes regni ipsius episcopi, sicut, Patri Filius deprehenditur esse subjectus, non natura, sed ordine, ut universitas regni ad unum redigatur principium."

[50] *De Schismate Donatistarum* . . . , Lib.III, cap. 3., loc. cit., col. 1003: "quidquid est supra homines, jam quasi Deus est."

[51] *Polycraticus* . . . , Lib. VIII, cap. 17, loc. cit., col. 778; cf. Lib IV, cap. 1, col. 513.

their view."[52] A similar idea is succinctly expressed by Honorius Augustodunensis: "Those who rebel against the law of God and do not take heed of authority of the Church must be punished by the civil authority."[53] From the premise that authority is divinely instituted to restrain the rebelliousness of human nature, the logical sequence implies that in disobeying civil ordinances one also sins against God's anointed, the king. Magnus Aurelius Cassiodorus remarks apropos: "Subjects can sin against God and the King."[54] A threat of excommunication was launched against those who violated the ordinances of the monarch,[55] or who undermined or conspired against royal dignity.[56] Obedience to the monarch was unconditional, although some Fathers took exception to this position; thus Jonas Aurelianensis writes: "The king must rule justly; in ruling devoutly, justly and compassionately, he deserves to be called a king; but if he discards these qualities of leadership, he loses the royal title,"[57] with whom concurs Ratherius Veronensis,[58] and Joannis Saresberiensis.[59]

---

[52] *Against Heresies*, Bk. 5, chap. 24, n. 2, loc. cit., pp. 119-120.

[53] *Summa Gloria* . . . , Cap. V, loc.cit., coll. 1266-1267: "Necesse est enim ut hos regalis potestas subigat gladio materiali, qui legi Dei rebelles non possunt corrigi stola sacerdotali."

[54] *In Psalterium Expositio,* Pars Prima, *Expositio in Psalmum 50,* vers. 5, *Opera Omnia,* Tomus Posterior, P.L., Tomus 70, Parisiis, 1847, col. 361: "De populo si quis erraverit, et Deo peccat, et regi."

[55] REGINO PRUMIENSIS, *De Ecclesiasticis Disciplinis et Religione Christiana Libri Duo,* Lib. II, cap. 300, *Opera Omnia,* Tomus unicus, P.L., Tomus 132, Parisiis, 1853, col. 342: "Si quis potestati regiae, quae non est juxta Apostolum nisi a Deo, contumaci et inflato spiritu contradicere vel resistere praesumpserit, et ejus justis et rationabilibus imperiis secundum Deum et auctoritatem ecclesiasticam ac jus civile obtemperare noluerit, anathematizetur."

[56] Ibid, Lib. II, cap. 299, col. 342: "Si quis contra regiam dignitatem dolose ac callide et perniciose agere comprobatus fuerit, nisi dignissime satisfecerit, anathematizetur."

[57] *Opusculum de Institutione Regia,* Cap. III, loc. cit., col. 287: "Rex a recte regendo vocatur; si enim pie, et juste, et misericorditer regit, merito rex appellatur; si his caruerit, nomen regis amittit."

[58] *Praeloquiorum* . . . , Tit. II, n. 5, loc. cit.,col. 222.

[59] *Polycraticus* . . . , Lib. VIII, cap. 17, loc. cit., col. 778.

The teaching of Gregory the Great is generally held responsible for the theory of absolute and arbitrary authority of the ruler which prevailed both in the Middle Ages and later. The pope believed in absolute powers of the sovereign, but with well-determined qualifications, so as to safeguard the community from any tyrannical form of government. It was far from the mind of the pope to foster a doctrine which savours of arbitrariness of legal authority. In the context of the above accusation, Gregory would have contradicted the Pauline premise of the divine institution of authority, discarded *a priori* the doctrine of the subordination of human authority to divine justice, and denied its finality which is meant to lead the subjects to the beatific vision. The premise of Gregory's dissertation seems to be found in the following admonition: "Subjects and prelates are to be admonished differently: the former that subjection crush them not, the latter that superior place elate them not: the former that they fail not to fulfil what is commanded them, the latter that they command not more to be fulfilled than is just: the former that they submit humbly, the latter that they preside temperately . . . Let the former learn how to order their inward thoughts before the eyes of the hidden judge; the latter how also to those that are committed to them to afford outwardly examples of good living."[60] In his teachings, Gregory's concern is to retain an equilibrium between tyrannical despotism and anarchism.[61] The pope admonishes the subjects not to condemn authority,[62] not to imitate bad rulers,[63] not to become bold because of the crimes perpetrated by those in authority,[64] but in all

---

[60] *Regulae Pastoralis Liber,* Tertia Pars, cap. IV, *Opera Omnia,* Tomus III, P.L., Tomus 77, Parisiis, 1849, col. 54: "Aliter admonendi sunt subditi, atque aliter praelati. Illos ne subjectio conterat, istos ne locus superior extollat. Illi ne minus quae jubentur impleant, isti ne plus justo jubeant quae compleantur. Illi ut humiliter subjaceant, isti ut temperanter praesint . . . Illi discant quomodo ante occulti arbitri oculos sua interiora componant, isti quomodo etiam commissis sibi exempla bene vivendi exterius praebeant."

[61] Ibid., *Moralium Libri* . . . , Pars V, Lib. XXV, cap. 16, n. 36, loc.cit., col.345.

[62] *Regulae Pastoralis Liber,* Tertia Pars, cap.IV, loc. cit., col. 55.

[63] Ibid.

[64] Ibid., *Moralium Libri* . . . , Pars IV, Lib.XXII, cap. 24, n. 55, loc.cit., col. 248.

instances to show reverence to the ruler.[65] It cannot be denied that in some instances Gregory expects from the subjects total submissiveness to the point of one's self-degradation.[66] These instances, however, should not be perused except within the global context. Just as much as Gregory is insistent on respect and obedience to authority, he inculcates the grave responsibility of the ruler in the administration of justice. The pope emphatically reminds the one in power that he is not ruling beasts, but humans, and that he should not seek personal glory but the good of all.[67] The true leader is the one who does first himself what he expects from others.[68] The pope recognizes that the community as well as the ruler can be a source of corruption: one can influence the other into delinquency.[69] It is the utmost responsibility of the ruler to be of good example to his subjects,[70] for he is responsible not only for his own personal sins,[71] but

---

[65] *Regulae Pastoralis Liber*, Pars III, cap. IV, loc. cit., col. 55.

[66] Ibid., col. 56: "Qui etsi quando pro infirmitate sese abstinere vix possunt, ut extrema quaedam atque exteriora praepositorum mala, sed tamen humiliter loquantur, quasi oram chlamidis silenter incidunt . . . Facta quippe praepositorum oris gladio ferienda non sunt, etiam cum recte reprehendenda judicantur. Si quando vero contra eos vel in minimis lingua labitur, necesse est ut per afflictionem poenitentiae cor prematur"; cf. *Moralium Libri* . . . , Pars V, Lib. XXV, cap. 16, n. 37, loc. cit., col. 345.

[67] *Moralium Libri* . . . , Pars IV, Lib. XXI, cap. 15, n. 23, loc. cit., col. 204: "Nequaquam ergo praepositi ex hoc quaesito timore superbiunt, in quo non suam gloriam, sed subditorum justitiam quaerunt. In eo enim quod metum sibi a perverse viventibus exigunt, quasi a non hominibus, sed brutis animalibus dominantur, quia videlicet ex qua parte bestiales sunt subditi, ex ea etiam debent formidini jacere substrati."

[68] *Regulae Pastoralis Liber*, Pars III, cap. IV, loc.cit., col. 55.

[69] *Moralium Libri* . . . , Pars V, Lib. XXV, cap. 16, n. 35, loc. cit., col. 344: "Certum vero est quod ita sibi invicem et rectorum merita connectantur et plebium, et saepe ex culpa pastorum deterior fiat vita plebium, et saepe ex plebium merito mutetur vita pastorum."

[70] Loc. cit., Pars IV, Lib. XXII, cap. 24, n. 56, col. 249.

[71] Loc. cit., Pars V, Lib. XXV, cap. 16, n. 35, col. 344.

also for the sins of those who follow him in his crime.[72] Thus he concludes: "Holy men when they govern do not attend to the power of orders with which they are invested; they are rather conscious of the same condition they share with others. They do not enjoy ruling over people; instead, they take delight in being of good example to others."[73]

The universal human consciousness at its present stage of self-emancipation cannot tolerate supreme power being invested in one person. Modern States are generally structured on the principle of balance of powers. The patristic contention that the sovereign was accountable to God alone, particularly when he was placed above the law,[74] was a distinct concept, but closely related to the theory of absolute sovereignty. It seems to us, however, that, once authority is placed within the context of the Redemptive mystery, the contention which stands for the non-accountability of the sovereign towards his subjects antagonizes the Pauline doctrine of the inter-dependence of all the members in the Mystical Body of Christ.[75] This said, there is nothing farther from the truth than the imputation to the patristics of an irresponsible authority. It was far from the mind of any of the Fathers to foster a capricious, arbitrary, unprincipled, and less still despotic, autocracy.

Once the sovereign is acclaimed the representative of God, who derives his authority directly from God, in whom supreme power resides, who must be obeyed in the name of God, and who is accountable to God

---

[72] *Regulae Pastoralis Liber,* Pars III, cap. IV, loc. cit., col. 54: "Scire etenim praelati debent, quia si perversa unquam perpetrant, tot mortibus digni sunt, quot ad subditos suos perditionis exempla transmittunt."

[73] *Moralium Libri . . . ,* Pars IV, Lib. XXI, cap. 15, n. 22, loc. cit., col. 203: "Sancti autem viri cum praesunt, non in se potestatem ordinis, sed aequalitatem conditionis attendunt, nec praeesse gaudent hominibus, sed prodesse."

[74] OPTATUS DE MILEVIS *De Schismate Donatistarum . . . ,* Lib. III, cap. 3, loc.cit., col 1001: "cum super imperatorem non sit nisi solus Deus"; MAGNUS AURELIUS CASSIODORUS, *In Psalterium Expositio,* Pars Prima, *Exp. in Psalmum 50,* vers. 5., loc. cit., col. 361: "quando rex delinquit, soli Deo reus est, quia hominem non habet qui ejus facta dijudicet"; HINCMARUS RHEMENSIS, *De Divortio Lotharii . . . ,* Quaestio VI, loc. cit., col. 757: "rex est, et nullorum legibus vel judiciis nisi solius Dei subjacet."

[75] 1 Cor. 12: 12 - 26.

alone, it appears a consonant conclusion that the ruler is not bound to obey his own laws. This is, in fact, the conclusion reached by John of Salisbury. The reason John gives is that the prince acts out of love for justice, rather than out of fear of punishment, and that he prefers the common good over his personal interests.[76] Optatus De Milevis[77] and Magnus Aurelius Cassiodorus[78] do not discuss explicitly the issue. However, no conclusion could be reached from their writings other than the one cherished by John of Salisbury. This view did not enjoy unanimity of consensus among the Fathers. In adherence to the latter opinion, Saint Ambrose writes: "An emperor passes laws which he first of all keeps."[79] Saint Isidore likewise insists that the ruler is the first to obey his own laws.[80] Hincmarus Rhemensis seems to share the same view in his statement: "The emperor should issue laws which he himself must first obey."[81] To this school seems to belong Sedulius Scotus.[82]

The latter hypothesis seems to trace its validity to two fundamental criteria, which are: the subordination of human authority to divine authority; the inherent dependency of human law on eternal justice. It must be admitted that this view, in positing the ruler subject to his own laws, does not intrinsically infer his accountability to his subjects. The

---

[76] *Polycraticus..*, Lib. IV, cap.2. loc.cit., col. 515: "Princeps tamen legis nexibus dicitur absolutus, non quia ei iniqua liceant, sed quia is esse debet, qui non timore poenae, sed amore justitiae aequitatem colat, reipublicae procuret utilitatem, et in omnibus aliorum commoda privatae praeferat voluntati"; cf. ibid., cap.7, col. 527.

[77] *De Schismate Donatistarum* . . . , Lib. III, cap.3, loc.cit., col. 1001.

[78] *In Psalterium Expositio*, Pars Prima, *Exp. in Psalmum 50*, vers. 5, loc. cit., col. 361.

[79] *Letters, Letter to Valentinian*, (21), 9, loc.cit., p. 54.

[80] *Sententiarum Libri Tres*, Lib. III, cap. 51, nn. 1, 2, loc. cit., col. 723.

[81] *De Divortio Lotharii* . . . , Quaestio 5, loc.cit., col. 754: "Leges enim imperator ferat, quas primus ipse custodiat."; However, he seems to contradict himself in *Quaestio VI*, ibid., col. 757, in his statement "rex est, et nullorum legibus vel judiciis nisi solius Dei subjacet."

[82] *Liber de Rectoribus* . . . , cap.II, loc. cit., col. 295: "Qui apicem regiae dignitatis, Domino praestante, ascenderit, oportet ut se ipsum primum regat, quem divina dispositio alios regere ordinavit."

contention that the ruler is bound by his own laws does not necessarily exclude the absolute sovereignty of the ruler; hence, it can logically be maintained that he is accountable to God alone. "For when the king sins," remarks Magnus Aurelius Cassiodorus, "he is accountable only to God since no human being is empowered to adjudicate his actions."[83] Whatever might be the conclusions reached from the premise on absolute sovereignty, the patristic teaching never did foster an arbitrary, capricious, and unscrupulous sovereignty.

The office of ruling in the patristic literature assumed a theological dimension, which rendered human authority subordinate to divine justice, as well as a moral dimension, which bound the ruler in conscience to administer his authority in justice and truth, and therefore made him accountable to God. That human law must have its roots in eternal justice for its intrinsic validity is unanimously endorsed by the Fathers. For Saint Irenaeus there is no reason for the establishment of human authority other than the correction and benefit of the subjects, and the preservation of justice.[84] He also realizes that it can easily turn into iniquitous and impious tyranny.[85] The king is there, states Theophilus of Antioch, "not to be worshipped, but to judge justly."[86] In a letter to emperor Valentinian, Saint Ambrose makes this point very clear: "I would not want your law to be above the law of God."[87] Saint Augustine writes apropos: "For anybody, who thinks that also in matters of conscience he is subject to the authority of those who are invested with some power in temporal affairs, falls in a

---

[83] *In Psalterium Expositio,* Pars Prima, *Exp. in Psalmum 50,* vers. 5, loc. cit., col. 361: "Nam quando rex delinquit soli Deo reus est, quia hominem non habet qui ejus facta dijudicet."

[84] *Against Heresies.,* Bk. 5, chap. 24, n. 3, loc. cit., p. 120.

[85] Ibid.

[86] *To Autolycus,* Bk I, chap. 11, loc.cit., p. 92.

[87] *Letters, Letter to Valentinian,* (21), 9. loc.cit., p. 54.

more serious error."[88] No State can survive without justice, which for its part traces its origin to eternity, and leads to eternity.[89] St. Augustine is known for saying: "In the absence of justice, what is sovereignty but organized brigandage?"[90] The doctrine of Saint Isidore retains in substance the Augustinian philosophy on the subject.[91] The main characteristics of kingship are justice and piety, and the more sublime of the two is piety.[92] The following statement summarizes the entire view of Isidore on the subject: "Authority, when it derives from God, is a good thing. It is there that evil may be restrained, not to let anyone rashly perpetrate evil. There is nothing worse than having the liberty to sin from one's authority, and nothing more distasteful than having the power to commit evil."[93] Sedulius Scotus admonishes the king that he should first control himself before he controls others, and that his administration of justice should be based on reason.[94] The glory of God, not his personal gratification, should be persued in the execution of justice.[95] Sedulius conceives of sovereignty devoid of justice in the manner of Saint Augustine: "What are unjust monarchs if not the leading brigands of the earth, ferocious as lions, fierce

---

[88] *Expositio quarumdam . . . 72.* loc.cit., col. 2084: "Item si quis sic se putat esse subdendum, ut etiam in suam fidem habere potestatem arbitretur eum qui temporalibus administrandis aliqua sublimitate praecellit; in majorem errorem labitur."

[89] *De Vera Religione,* n. 58, loc. cit., col. 148.

[90] *The City of God,* Bk. IV, chap. 4, loc.cit., p. 195.

[91] *Sententiarum Libri Tres,* Lib. III, cap. 49, nn. 2,3,4, loc. cit., coll. 720-721.

[92] *Etymologiarum . . . ,* Lib. IX, cap. 3, n.5, loc.cit., col. 342: "Regiae virtutes praecipuae duae, justitia et pietas; plus autem in regibus laudatur pietas; nam justitia per se severa est."

[93] *Sententiarum Libri Tres,* Lib. III, cap. 48, n. 5, loc. cit., coll. 718 - 719: "Potestas bona est, quae a Deo donante est, ut malum timore coerceat, non ut temere malum committat. Nihil autem pejus quam per potestatem peccandi libertatem habere; nihilque infelicius male agendi facultate."

[94] *Liber de Rectoribus . . . ,* Cap.II, loc. cit., col. 295.

[95] Ibid., col. 296: "per justas vindictas non propriae victoriae sed legi Dei studeat ut metuatur."

as bears."[96] Jonas Aurelianensis states in a nutshell: "With justice the state stands firm, whereas with injustice the state is destroyed."[97] Only in governing according to equity and justice can royal ministry bring about peace and harmony in society.[98] Joannis Saresberiensis defines the monarch "aequitatis servus" (the servant of equity).[99] John makes a clear distinction between a true prince, worthy of the name, and a tyrant;[100] a prince abusive of his authority turns indeed into a despot;[101] "The tyrant is the image of perversity; in many instances he should be killed."[102] The authority of the prince enjoys its rightfulness only insofar as it stems from divine justice.[103] Not *odium personae*, but justice should be the motive of the prince in inflicting penalties.[104]

It has been pointed out earlier that the question of whether the sovereign is bound or not by his own laws does not necessarily imply his accountability to his subjects. The advocacy of absolute sovereignty rather posits the ruler *de facto,* if not *de iure,* in a position of non-accountability to anyone; thus the issue will ever remain a theoretical one. The theory of

---

[96] Ibid., Cap. VIII, loc. cit., col. 305: "Quid sunt autem impii reges, nisi majores terrarum latrones, feroces ut leones, rabidi ut ursi?"

[97] *De Institutione Laicali . . . ,* Lib.II, cap. 24, loc. cit., col. 218: "Per justitiam quippe stabilitur regnum, et per injustitiam evertitur."

[98] *Opusculum de Institutione Regia,* Cap. IV, loc. cit., coll 290-291: "Regale ministerium specialiter est populum Dei gubernare et regere cum aequitate et justitia, et ut pacem et concordiam habeant studere"; cf. ibid, Cap. VIII, col. 296.

[99] *Polycraticus . . . ,* Lib. IV., cap.2, loc. cit., col. 515.

[100] Ibid., Lib. VIII, cap. 17, col. 777.

[101] Ibid., col. 778.

[102] Ibid: "tyrannus pravitatis imago, plerumque etiam occidendus."

[103] Ibid., Lib. IV, cap. 2, col. 514: "nec in eo sibi principes detrahi arbitrentur, nisi justitiae suae statuta praeferenda crediderint justitiae Dei, cujus justitia, justitia in aeternum est, et lex ejus aequitas."

[104] Ibid., col. 515:"Nam sicut lex culpas persequitur sine odio personarum, ita et princeps delinquentes rectissime punit, non aliquo iracundiae motu, sed mansuetae legis arbitrio."

absolute sovereignty as envisaged by the Fathers does not, by any means, foster an arbitrary and irresponsible political authority. It appears to us extremely difficult to hold that the general teaching of the Fathers, was responsible for an unbridled government, characteristic of the *ancien regime*, when they perceived the office of ruling as a divine mandate, a vocation, a divine mission, for which the one in charge has one day to answer, if not to another human being, to the supreme divine Judge. Saint Justin writes: "Every man will pay the penalty of his misdeeds in the everlasting fire, and that every one will give an account in proportion to the powers he received from God."[105] After his admonition to the ruler, Saint Irenaeus concludes that "the just judgment of God . . . passes equally upon all."[106] Saint Ambrose reminds Simplicianus that, although king David was not subject to his own laws, he was found guilty in the eyes of God.[107] God's judgment over the ruler's response to duty is assured by Cassiodorus,[108] Isidorus,[109] Catulfus,[110] Hrabanus Maurus,[111] and Hincmarus.[112] The premise holding the subordination of human authority to divine justice, unanimously endorsed in the patristic literature, by itself *a priori* implies this conclusion; consequently it necessarily excludes the particularity of arbitrariness in the concept of authority. Regardless of whether or not the ruler is subject to his own laws, since his authority is subordinate to divine authority, he must govern according to the laws which he enacts, which are said to reflect divine justice. Clement of Alexandria

---

[105] *The First Apology*, Chap 17, loc. cit., p. 52.

[106] *Against Heresies*, Bk 5, Chap. 24, n.3, loc.cit., p. 120.

[107] *Letters, Letter to Simplicianus*, 54 (37), loc.cit., p. 295.

[108] *In Psalterium Expositio*, Pars I, *Exp. in Psalmum 50*, vers. 5, loc. cit., col. 361.

[109] *Sententiarum Libri Tres*, Lib. III, cap. 48, n.6, loc. cit., col. 719.

[110] *Instructio Epistolaris* . . . , loc. cit., col. 1364.

[111] *De Universo Libri* . . . , Lib. XVI, cap. 3, loc. cit., col. 446.

[112] *De Divortio Lotharii* . . . , Quaestio VI, loc. cit., col. 757; *ad Proceres Regni* . . . , cap. 9, loc.cit., coll 996-997.

succinctly phrases the patristic teaching on the subject in the following statement: "He is a king who governs according to the laws."[113]

In the patristic premise, legal authority and the community were endorsed as two entities essentially distinct from each other. Whatever political philosophy one may cherish, the metaphysical inseparability of the two realities cannot be ignored. This presupposition results in the equally fundamental principle of inverse proportion; the progression of one intrinsically entails the regression of the other. The insistence of Paul on the divine institution of authority does not *per se* militate for absolute sovereignty, and therefore it does not necessarily deny the community as the ultimate source of authority. In the democratic ideology, the Pauline doctrine still retains its full purport. The patristic understanding of the Pauline doctrine was diametrically opposite; accordingly the gap in their teaching between the inter-relatedness of the legal authority and the community became more pronounced, the position of the sovereign was rendered more solidified, the excellence of his person was hilariously extolled by some, and his legal powers were intensified to the extremes. The community, by inverse proportion, was curtailed in its inherent ability of self-expression and self-explication, since it was alleged to be, by nature, in a state of self-helplessness. This political philosophy placed the community as an irreversibly passive recipient, thus necessitating a paternalistic form of government, or, as Saint Ambrose puts it, it has to be ruled by the wise man,[114] who was thus by reason of heredity. In addition to this state of helplessness there were the voices of some who believed in an irresistible proclivity of human nature to self-destruction. It was, therefore, imperative for its own survival that the community must live by

---

[113] *The Miscellanies*, Bk I, chap. 24, loc. cit., vol. I, p. 456.

[114] *Letters, Letter to Simplicianus*, 54 (37), loc.cit., p. 288

the sword.[115] Authority, in fact, was commonly defined simply as *gladius, gladius materialis -- gladius spiritualis.*[116]

The general presumption by the Fathers was that the ruler is a wise and saintly person who is divinely charged to lead his subjects to the beatific vision. If, however, the ruler turns out to be the personification of evil, the community is to be blamed. God in His infinite justice allows the subjects to suffer at the hands of a ruthless leader as punishment for their sins, as Gregory the Great phrases it: "The disposition of the ruler depends on the merit of the subjects."[117]

As a conclusion, it is safe to say that the patristic teaching on the nature of authority reached unanimity of consensus in the following main points: 1. public authority is divinely instituted; 2. it is clearly implied that not only the essence but also the form of government, that is, absolute sovereignty, is of divine origin; 3. this authority proceeds directly and proximately from God; 4. the community and public authority are two realities essentially distinct; 5. the community is envisaged as being, by nature, a passive recipient, incapable of acting on its own virtues.

The *Patristica* moves into two opposing streams of thought on the question of the naturalness of public authority. The first opinion maintains that public authority is the result of sin; therefore, it is divine, but not natural. This stand results from a pessimistic outlook on human nature, a corrupt nature which requires the threat of the sword in order to protect

---

[115] Isidorus, *Sententiarum Libri Tres*, Lib. III, cap. 47, n. 1, loc. cit., col. 717: "Inde et in gentibus principes, regesque electi sunt, ut terrore suo populos a malo coercerent, atque ad recte vivendum legibus subderent."

[116] PETRUS DAMIANUS, *Opusculum Quinquagesimum* . . . , cap. II, loc. cit., col. 821; *Sermo in Dedicatione* . . . , loc.cit.,col. 900; SANCTUS BERNARDUS, *De Consideratione Libri* . . . , Lib. IV, cap. 3, n. 7, loc. cit., col. 776; HONORIUS AUGUSTODUNENSIS, *Summa Gloria* . . . , Capp. IV, V, loc. cit., coll. 1264, 1266; JOANNIS SARESBERIENSIS, *Polycraticus* . . . , Lib. IV, cap. 3, loc. cit., col. 516.

[117] *Moralium Libri* . . . , Pars V, Lib XXV, cap. 16, n. 35, loc. cit., col. 344: "secundum meritum plebium disponuntur corda rectorum."; cf. ibid., n. 34, col. 343; SAINT AUGUSTINE, *The City of God*, Bk. V, chap. 19, loc. cit., p. 288; Bk. XIX, chap. 15, loc. cit., p. 223; SANCTUS ISIDORUS, *Sententiarum Libri Tres*, Lib. III, cap. 48, n. 11, loc. cit., col. 720: "Reges quando boni sunt, muneris est Dei, quando vero mali, sceleris est populi"; HINCMARUS RHEMENSIS, *De Divortio Lotharii* . . . , Quaestio VI, loc. cit., col. 758.

itself from self-destruction.[118] A contrary view, equally prevalent among the Fathers, believes that human nature, although weakened by sin never did lose its intrinsic goodness. In this hypothesis, authority is not perceived as an imposition upon the human will corrupted by sin, a curtailment to human rebelliousness, but rather as an institution intrinsically stemming from the sociability of human nature.[119] This latter view is in complete unison with the conceptualization of human consciousness as expounded in these papers. Our understanding of public authority is magisterially synthesized in the statements of two great Doctors of the Church, Saint Augustine who states: "Every part which is not in agreement with its whole is foul,"[120] and John of Salisbury who reiterates the same concept with greater clarity: "All matters are found in the head (of state), and thus the

---

[118] SILVESTER II, *Epistola XI ad Monasteria Stabulense* . . . , loc. cit., coll. 282 - 283; IRENAEUS, *Against Heresies*, Bk 5, chap. 24, n.2, loc. cit., pp. 119-120; OPTATUS DE MILEVIS, *De Schismate Donatistarum* . . . , Lib. III, cap. 3, loc. cit., coll 1001 - 1002; FLACCUS ALBINUS, *Dialogus de Rhetorica* . . . , loc. cit., coll. 920- 921; SAINT AMBROSE, *Letters, Letter to Simplicianus*, 54 (37) loc. cit., p. 288; ISIDORUS, *Etymologiarum* . . . , Lib. V, cap. 20, n.1, loc. cit., col. 202; *Sententiarum Libri Tres*, Lib. III, cap. 47, nn. 1, 3, loc. cit., col. 717; HINCMARUS RHEMENSIS, *De Divortio Lotharii* . . . , Quaestio VI, loc. cit., col. 757; HONORIUS AUGUSTODUNENSIS, *Summa Gloria* . . . , Cap. V, loc. cit., col. 1266..

[119] SAINT AUGUSTINE, *The Good of Marriage*, chap. 1, loc. cit., p. 9; *De Genesi ad Litteram* . . . , lib. IX, cap. 9, loc. cit., col. 398; *De Libero Arbitrio* . . . , Lib. I, cap. 6, nn. 14, 15, loc. cit., col. 1229; *Expositio Quarumdam Propositionum* . . . , LXXII, loc. cit., coll. 2083-2084; *The City of God*, Bk 19, chap. 12, loc.cit.,p. 215; GREGORIUS MAGNUS, *Moralium Libri* . . . ,Pars IV, Lib. XXI, cap. 15, n. 22, loc. cit., col. 203; *Registri Epistolarum* . . . , Lib. V, Epist. 54, loc. cit., coll. 785-786; MAGNUS AURELIUS CASSIODORUS, *Variarum Libri* . . . , Lib.III, Epist. 17, loc.cit., col. 585; ibid., Lib. IV, Epist. 33, col. 630; CATULFUS, *Instructio Epistolaris* . . . , loc. cit., col. 1364; SEDULIUS SCOTUS, *Liber de Rectoribus* . . . , Cap. II, loc.cit., coll 295-296; JONAS AURELIANENIS, *Opusculum de Institutione Regia*, Capp. III, IV, VIII, loc. cit., 287,290, 296-297; *De Institutione Laicali* . . . , Lib. II, cap. 24, loc. cit., col. 219; HUGO DE S. MARIA, *Tractatus de Regia Potestate* . . . Lib. I, capp. 2, 3, 6, loc. cit., coll. 942-943, 948; JOANNIS SARESBERIENSIS, *Polycraticus* . . . , Lib. IV, cap.1, loc. cit., coll. 513-514.

[120] *Confessionum Libri Tredecim*, Lib.III, cap. 8, n. 15, *Opera Omnia*, Tomus I, P.L., Tomus 32, Parisiis, 1845, col. 689: "Turpis enim omnis pars est suo universo non congruens."

head subordinates all members to itself so that in moving in the right direction they follow the decision of the ruler's sound mind."[121]

Concept of Authority by Juridical Authors

The patristic doctrine on civil authority is re-iterated in its substantiality by the juridic school. The question as to whether civil authority pertains to the natural order of things is not explicitly dealt with by jurists. However, one may surmise from the general content of their writings that authority indeed proceeds from *l'esprit de corps,* as the epitome of the universal inwardness of the individual human consciousness. This understanding can be deduced in particular from the writings of Azo,[122] Hostiensis,[123] and Albericus De Rosate, who in beauty of style gives the rationale for the establishment of public authority: "in order that the solidarity of human society under the guidance of justice may be blessed with a safe tranquillity of peace."[124]

The divine provenance of authority is retained by jurists. The statement of Antonius A Butrio -- "the imperial authority was handed down from the divine majesty"[125] speaks for the juridical tradition.[126] This view

---

[121] *Polycraticus* . . . , Lib. IV, cap. 1, loc. cit., col. 513: "sensus universos in capite collocavit, et ei sic universa membra subjecit, ut omnia recte moveantur, dum sani capitis sequuntur arbitrium."

[122] *Summa Super Codicem,* Lib. I, *Incipit materia ad Codicem,* p. 1, col. 2.

[123] *In Primum Decretalium* . . . , Prooemium, *Gregorius Episcopus,* n.6, fol. 3v., ibid., *De Maior. et Obedientia,* cap.6, *Solitae,* n.3, fol. 170v.

[124] *Dictionarium* . . . , v. *Lex,* p. 422: "ut proinde humanae societatis conciliatio, tuta pacis tranquillitate sub custodia iustitiae laetaretur."; ibid., "finis quem intendit lex humana, est pax humani generis."

[125] *In Sextum Decretalium* . . . , *De Supplenda Negligentia Praelatorum,* cap. 2, *Grandi,* n. 10, fol. 72v: "imperium a coelesti maiestate traditum est."

[126] HENRICUS DE SEGUSIO, *In Primum Decretalium* . . . , *De Translatione Episcopi vel Electi,* cap. 1, *Cum ex illo,* n. 4, fol. 81v; *In Secundum Decretalium* . . . , *De iudiciis,* cap. 13, *Novit,* n. 1, fol. 5v; CYNUS PISTORIENSIS, *In Codicem* . . . , Lib. I, Tit. 14, *De Legibus et Constitutionibus Prin.,* n. 6, fol. 26r; ibid., Lib. I, Tit. 2, *De Sacrosancta Ecclesia,* n.3, fol. 6r; *In Digesti Veteris* . . . , Rubrica IV, *De Constitutionibus Principum,* n. 1, fol. 8r.

is expressed by Baldus De Ubaldis, in envisaging the act of ruling as being the explicit will of God: "What the emperor does, seems to be done by God."[127] Others manifest this belief within the context of law. *Decretum Gratiani* endorses the divine origin of authority in this perspective: "Whoever disobeys the laws of the emperor which are enacted in accordance with the divine truth receives severe punishment."[128] Azo in similar vein states: "God promulgates laws through the mouths of princes."[129] Baldus De Ubaldis quotes Bartolus A Saxoferrato as saying that he is heretic who denies the Roman emperor as monarch.[130] The law, in the estimation of Cynus Pistoriensis, recognizes the emperor as a divine person, since the empire proceeds from God: "The emperor is divine and always celestial . . . his laws are said to be divine."[131] Cynus is so wrapped up in the divine power of the emperor that he believes the

---

[127] *In Decretalium Volumen . . . , Super Primo Decretalium, Prooemium,* cap. *Rex pacificus,* n. 5, fol. 5r: "quod facit imperator, videtur facere ipse Deus."; cf. ibid., n. 16, fol. 5r.

[128] Pars I, Dist IX, c. I, §1: "Quicumque legibus imperatorum, que pro Dei veritate feruntur, obtemperare non vult, acquirit grande supplicium."

[129] *Ad Singulas Leges* XII . . . , Lib. I, Tit. 1, *De Summa Trinitate, et Fide Catholica,* Lex 1, n. 6, p. 5: "Deus enim leges promulgavit per ora principum."; cf. *Summa Super Codicem,* Lib. I, *Si contra ius vel utilitatem publicam vel per mendacium fuerit aliquod rescriptum. vel postulatum vel impetratum,* p. 13, col. 2; HENRICUS DE SEGUSIO, *In Secundum Decretalium . . . , De Iureiurando,* cap, 30, *Nimis,* n. 3, fol. 137r; JOANNES ANDREAE, *In Secundum Decretalium . . . , De Iureiurando,* cap. 30, *Nimis,* n.2, fol. 199r; ALBERICUS DE ROSATE, *Dictionarium . . . ,* v. *Lex.* p. 422: "legis enim latores eas proferendi a Deo licentiam acceperunt scilicet leges proferendi et ideo dicuntur per ora principum divinitus promulgatae."

[130] *In Decretalium Volumen . . . , Super Primo Decretalium, De Maioritate, et Obedientia,* cap. 6, *Solitae,* n. 6, fol. 131v: "Dicit Bar . . . quod si quis diceret Imperatorem Romanorum non esse monarcham, esset haereticus, quia diceret contra determinationem ecclesiae." Baldus rebuts such a contention: "dic quod non esset haereticus, quia non dicit, quod Deus non potuerit perficere, sed quod non praefuerit. nec ista est quaestio de spiritualibus, sed de temporalibus. puniendus est tamen gladio materiali."

[131] *In Digesti Veteris . . . ,* Rubrica IV, *De Constitutionibus Principum,* n. 1, fol. 8r: "Imperator divinus est, et celestis semper . . . leges suae dicuntur divinae."

emperor has the power to absolve from perjury,[132] and that one can take an oath in the name of the emperor.[133] The emperor, as in pagan Rome, is thus exalted to the throne of divinity. The view of Cynus does not impress, in the least, Antonius A Butrio who makes a sharp distinction between the anointing of the monarch and that of the bishop. Only in the latter case does true consecration take place.[134] Hostiensis accepts the Pauline premise, "all authority derives from God," only in a broad sense.[135] Joannes Andreae clarifies Hostiensis' view with the remark that, strictly speaking, only the laws enacted by the Roman Pontiff ought to be considered divinely promulgated, "who alone is the general vicar of Christ"[136] Cynus ridicules canonists who maintain that all laws, whether civil or canonical, are divinely promulgated. He argues: either laws directly and proximately emanate from God, and this is absolutely not true with regards to civil laws, or they proceed indirectly and remotely from God, a principle without any significance to the case in point since it is applicable to creation as a whole.[137] It is for this reason that he concludes: "Iustitiae author est Deus, iuris imperator"[138] -- the emperor is the source of law which, however, traces its intrinsic validity to divine justice.

From this brief presentation on the divine provenance of public authority, it appears sufficiently clear that autocracy is held by the juridic

---

[132] *In Codicem Commentaria*, Lib. I, Tit. 22, *Si contra ius vel utilitatem publicam*, etc., n. 5, fol. 40r.

[133] *In Digesti Veteris* . . . , Rubrica IV, *De Constitutionibus Principum*, n.2, fol. 8r.

[134] *Super Prima Primi Decretalium* . . . , Tomus I, *De Electione*, cap. 34, *Venerabilem*, n. 14, fol. 132r.

[135] *In Primum Decretalium* . . . , *De Translatione episcopi vel Electi*, cap. 1, *Cum ex illo*, n. 4, fol. 81v: "largo tamen modo omnis potestas a domino Deo est."

[136] *In Secundum Decretalium* . . . , *De iureiurando*, cap. 30, *Nimis*, n. 2, fol. 199r: "qui solius est Christi vicarius generalis."

[137] *In Codicem Commentaria*, Lib. VII, Tit, 33, *De Praescriptione longi temporis decem vel viginti anno*, n.2, fol. 444v.

[138] *In Digesti Veteris* . . . , Rubrica I, *De Justitia et Jure*, n.4, fol. 3r.

school as the sole form of government. Some authors go to the extremes of emphasizing the absolute sovereignty of the emperor. For Baldus De Ubaldis, "the emperor is the source of justice"[139] in absolute manner.[140] Albericus De Rosate acclaims the emperor the living law -- "lex animata est Imperator in terra."[141] It goes without saying that such a position comes in conflict with the political theory which recognizes the community as the ontologically and historically primordial source of authority. Some authors, while believing in the divine institution of autocracy, ascertain that authority once resided in the people;[142] thus they consider its divine provenance as a mere historical datum, but not stemming from the nature of the thing itself. No explanation is given, however, for these two conflicting data. In others, no mention is made of the authority of the people, inferring, perhaps, that this was never the case. Human consciousness through its self- unfolding gave solution to the quandary.

"The emperor is lord of the world in respect to universal jurisdiction

---

[139] *Consiliorum, sive Responsorum* . . . , Vol. III, Cons. 359, n. 5, fol. 101v: "Imperator est fons iustitiae."

[140] *Consiliorum, sive Responsorum* . . . , Vol. V, Cons. 300, n. 2, fol. 75v: "Imperator est dominus mundi, quo ad omnimodam iurisdictionem, et potestatem supremam"; loc. cit., vol. III, Cons. 370, n.5, fol. 105r: "potuit imponere legem, quam voluit"; loc. cit., vol. I, Cons. 328, n. 7, fol. 102v: " Quicquid tamen agitur supra legem, absoluta potestas est, nec est subditorum corripere"; *In Decretalium Volumen* . . . , *Super Primo Decretalium, De Constitutionibus,* cap. 1, *Canonum,* n. 71, fol. llv: "plenitudini potestatis nihil resistit."

[141] *Dictionarium* . . . , v. *Lex,* p. 421.

[142] AZO, *Summa Super Codicem,* Lib. I, *De Legibus et Constitutionibus, Principum et Edictis,* p.8, col. 2; loc. cit., Lib. VIII, *Que sit longa consuetudo,* p. 324, col. 2; *Ad Singulas Leges* XII. Lib. I, Tit. 14, *De Legibus et Constitutionibus,* lex 4, *Digna vox,* n. 15, p. 40:; CYNUS PISTORIENSIS, *In Digesti Veteris* . . . , Rubrica III, *De legi. et sena. et long. consu.,* n. 14, fol. 7v; ibid., Rubrica XIV, *De Officio Praetoris,* n. 6, fol. 13 v; ibid; Rubrica I, *De Jurisdictione omnium iudicum,* n.2, fol. 26v; PLACENTINUS, *In Summam Institutionum* . . . , Lib.I, Tit. II, *De Iure Naturali Gentium, et Civili,* p.3; JOANNES ANDREAE, *In Primum Decretalium* . . . , *De Constitutionibus, Translatio,* n. 11, fol. 12v; ibid., *De Consuetudine,* cap. 11, *Cum tanto,* n. 42, fol. 61r; ANTONIUS A BUTRIO, *Super Prima Primi* . . . , Tomus I, Lib. I, *De Constitutionibus,* cap. 3, *Translato,* n. 18, fol. 12v.

and supreme authority."[143] Absolute sovereignty signifies the full concentration of the legislative, coercive and administrative powers in the person of the sovereign. The ruler was thus acclaimed the sole law-giver who could enact laws, interpret or correct, abrogate, change or derogate a law.[144] A custom could only be introduced with his permission.[145] The prince is the one who can grant dispensation and bestow privileges.[146] Emphasis, however, was rather put on the coercive power of the sovereign; the threefold authority was, in fact, coined *gladius materialis* -- "The ruling power consists in the power of the sword."[147] In judiciary matters, the sovereign was the supreme judge, and no judge could annul his sentence, but himself.[148] Whereas there was unanimity of consensus regarding the legislative and coercive powers of the sovereign, a discrepancy of opinion existed among jurists concerning the administrative powers of the monarch. The universal recognition of him as "totius mundi dominus" was a *fait accompli*. Correlative to this belief stood the

---

[143] BALDUS DE UBALDIS, *Consiliorum, sive Responsorum* . . . , Vol. V, Cons. 300, n. 2, fol. 75v: "Imperator est dominus mundi quo ad omnimodam iurisdictionem, et potestatem supremam."

[144] PILEUS MODICENSIS, *Quaestiones Aureae*, Romae, 1560, Quaestio 43, *An sententia appellationis per Imperatorem lata parte non citata valeat*, n. 1, p. 91; AZO, *Summa Super Codicem*, Lib. I, *Incipit Materia ad Codicem*, p. 1, col. 2; ibid., Lib. I, *De Legibus et Constitutionibus Principum et Edictis*, p. 9, col. 1; *Ad Singulas Leges XII* . . . , Lib. I, Tit. 14, *De Legibus et Constitutionibus*, n. 2, p. 39; PLACENTINUS, *In Summam Institutionum* . . . , Lib. I, Tit. II, *De Iure Naturali Gentium, et Civili*, p. 3; HENRICUS DE SEGUSIO, *In Secundum Decretalium* . . . , *De Probationibus*, cap. 12, *Ad nostram.*, n. 1, fol. 82r.

[145] BALDUS DE UBALDIS, *Consiliorum, Sive Responsorum* . . . , Vol. IV, Cons. 401, n. 3, fol. 92r; CYNUS PISTORIENSIS, *In Digesti Veteris* . . . , Rubrica III, *De Legi. et Sena. et long. Consu.*, n. 14, fol. 7v. Clarification on the subject is given in the preceding paper.

[146] CYNUS PISTORIENSIS, *In Digesti Veteris* . . . , Rubrica II, *Quod quisque iuris in alterum statuerit, ut ipse eodem iure utatur*, n. 18, fol. 31v.

[147] CYNUS PISTORIENSIS, *In Digesti Veteris* . . . , Rubrica I, *De Iurisdictione omnium Judicum*, n. 2, fol. 23r: "Imperium consistit in gladii potestate."; ANTONIUS A BUTRIO, *Super Prima Secundi Decretalium* . . . , Tom. III, *De Iudiciis*, cap. 13, *Novit*, n. 72 fol. 20v; HENRICUS DE SEGUSIO, *In Primum Decretalium* . . . , *De Maioritate et Obedientia*, cap. 6, *Solitae*, nn. 2, 13, foll. 170 v.-171r; *In Secundum Decretalium* . . . , *De Iudiciis*, cap. 13, *Novit*, n. 1, fol. 5v.

[148] PILEUS MODICENSIS, *Quaestiones Aureae*, Quaestio 43, *An sententia appellationis per Imperatorem lata parte non citata valeat*, nn.1, 3, pp. 92-93.

presumption that the actions of the sovereign, being God's anointed and representative, were beyond reproach.[149] Upon these premises, some, like Antonius A Butrio[150] voiced the opinion that land, cattle, and material wealth of the subjects were ultimately the sole possession of the sovereign. Cynus rebuts such a preposterous claim on behalf of the sovereign; the emperor is "totius mundi dominus" only in the sense that he enjoys supreme jurisdictional and administrative powers, without having any right over his subjects' patrimony.[151]

In the footsteps of the *Patristica*, the juridical school, in advocating the theory of absolute sovereignty, never did imply irresponsible and capricious high-handedness of the ruler. The subordination of human authority to divine justice formed the *cardo* of the canonical and civilist philosophy of law. At the head of the juridic school, one may place *Decretum Gratiani:* "Whoever disobeys the laws of the emperor, which are enacted against the will of God, receives a great reward."[152] While they inordinately exalted the majestic figure of the emperor, authors never did recognize the sovereign as the absolute source of justice; the ruler too is subject to divine law in the execution of his office. Cynus defines the sovereign as, "servus Dei" (servant of God);[153] as such, he is subject to

---

[149] PILEUS MODICENSIS, loc. cit., n. 3, p. 92: "nec enim verisimile est principem Romanum quicquam illicite agere."

[150] *In Sextum Decretalium . . . , De Supplenda Negligentia Praelatorum,* cap. 2, *Grandi,* n. 10, fol. 72v: "Imperator est dominus mundi . . . et omnia sua esse intelliguntur"; cf. BALDUS DE UBALDIS, *In Decretalium Volumen . . . , Super Primo Decretalium,* Prooemium, cap. *Rex pacificus,* n. 6, fol. 5r; *Super Secundo Decretalium, De Mutuis Petitionibus,* cap. 12, *Cum venisset,* n. 7, fol. 158v.

[151] *In Codicem Commentaria,* Lib. VII, Tit. 37, *De Quadriennii Praescriptione,* n. 4, fol. 445v; Lib. I, Tit. 19, *De Precib. Imperatori offerend. etc.,* n. 12, fol. 36v.

[152] Pars I, Dist. IX, c. 1. §1: "Quicumque ergo legibus imperatorum, que contra voluntatem Dei feruntur, obtemperare non vult, acquirit grande premium."

[153] *In Codicem Commentaria,* Lib. I, Tit. 19, *De Precib. Imperatori offerend. etc.,* n. 10, fol. 36r.

The Concept of Public Authority

natural and divine positive law.[154] The prince is thus expected to act according to the dictates of his own conscience;[155] consequently, "the one who is invested with supreme power has to abide by the rule of absolute honesty and supreme equity."[156] It follows from this assumption that the ruler is bound to observe *ius gentium*.[157] He is even expected to fulfill the contractual obligations arising from agreements with his own subjects.[158] According to Azo, the ruler is bound to observe the laws of the land since "at the installation the ruler takes an oath that he will observe his own laws."[159] His administration of justice should be mainly directed to the

---

[154] CYNUS PISTORIENSIS, Loc. cit., nn. 9, 10, fol. 36r; HENRICUS DE SEGUSIO, *In Secundum Decretalium, De Probationibus*, cap. 12 *Ad nostram*, n. 1, fol. 82r; PLACENTINUS, *In Summam Institutionum* . . . , Lib. I, Tit. II, *De Iure Naturali Gentium, et Civili*, p. 3; AZO, *Summa super Codicem*, Lib. I, *Si contra ius vel utilitatem publicam vel per mendacium fuerit aliquod rescriptum vel postulatum vel impetratum*, p. 13, col. 2; ibid., Lib. IV, *De Usuris*, p. 141, col. 2; BALDUS DE UBALDIS, *Consiliorum, Sive Responsorum* . . . , Vol. I, cons. 267, n. 9, fol. 59v; cons. 328, n. 7, fol. 102v; vol. V, cons. 457, n. 5, fol. 122r.

[155] BALDUS DE UBALDIS, *Consiliorum, Sive Responsorum* . . . , Vol. I, cons. 327, n.2, fol. 101r; cons. 326, n. 6, fol. 100v. We find the view of Cynus repulsive: "princeps est supra legem, adeo secundum conscientiam suam iudicare potest, quia semper praesumitur incorruptibilis. Et est praesumptio pro eo, quod facit quod iuste faciat, ita quod non admittitur probatio in contrarium," *In Codicem Commentaria*, Lib. I, Tit. 19, *De Precib. Imperatori offerend. etc.*, n. 11, fol. 36v. Such a position not only confronts the canonical and civilist doctrine on authority, but also constitutes the radix of the most unscrupulous and brutal despotism.

[156] BALDUS DE UBALDIS, *Consiliorum Sive Responsorum* . . . , Vol. IV, cons. 19, n. 3, fol. 8r: "qui enim tenet supremam potestatem, debet observare summam honestatem, et summam aequitatem tanquam regula."

[157] CYNUS PISTORIENSIS, *In Codicem Commentaria*, Lib. I, Tit. 19, *De Precib. Imperatori offerend. etc.*, n. 12, fol. 36v: "Imperator non potest rescribere contra ius gentium, cum iura gentium sint immutabilia."

[158] BALDUS DE UBALDIS, *Consiliorum, sive Responsorum* . . . , Vol. I, cons. 271, n. l, fol. 81v; cons. 327, n. 9, fol. 101v; CYNUS PISTORIENSIS, *In Codicem Commentaria*, Lib. I, Tit. 14, *De Legibus et Constitutionibus Prin.*, n. 7, fol. 26r.

[159] *Brocardica Aurea*, Rubrica 31, *De Rescriptis seu Privilegiis*, fol. 85v: "in principio suae creationis iurat, se observaturum leges"; cf. *Ad Singulas Leges XII* . . . , lib. I, Tit. 14, *De Legibus et Constitutionibus*, lex 4, *Digna vox*, n. 18, p. 40; PILEUS MODICENSIS, *Quaestiones Aureae*, Quaestio 43, *An Sententia appellationis per Imperatorem lata parte non citata valeat*, n. 2, p. 92: "Cum ergo nihil horum possit facere Imperator, multo minus iuris ordinem perturbando."

defense of the Church, the poor, and the weak.[160] Clemency should be the golden rule whenever justice calls for punitive action on a subject of his. "It is better," remarks Albericus De Rosate, "to render account for being merciful than for being harsh." [161] Civil authority, states Azo,[162] is not endowed with the prerogative of infallibility. Already in *Decretum Gratiani* there is attested the inadmissibility of blind obedience and unconditional compliance to public authority.[163] Doctrine maintained, and history testifies, that an unworthy ruler can and ought to be deposed.[164] It was this very doctrine on the subordination of civil authority to divine justice that induced many Christian writers to place civil authority also subject to Church authority.

The traditional Christian doctrine of the subordination of human authority to the divine, and of human law as the reflection of eternal wisdom, should imply the conclusion that the ruler is bound by laws which he enacts. Clear as it might seem, not all authors concur with this syllogism. Cynus believes that the prince is above the law; he is said to judge according to his own conscience which is presumed *(praesumptio iuris*

---

[160] BALDUS DE UBALDIS, *In Decretalium Volumen* . . . , *Super Primo Decretalium, De Electione et Electi Potestate*, cap. 34, *Venerabilem*, n. 11, fol. 78v.

[161] *Dictionarium* . . . , v. *Ius*, p. 412,: "Melius est de misericordia quam de severitate reddere rationem"; cf. CYNUS PISTORIENSIS, *In Codicem Commentaria*, Lib. V. Tit. 4, *De nuptiis*, n. 3., fol. 294r; HENRICUS DE SEGUSIO, *In Primum Decretalium* . . . , *De Maioritate et Obedientia*, cap. 17, *Humilis doctrina*, n. 7. fol. 175v.

[162] *Ad Singulas Leges XII* . . . , Lib. I, Tit. 14, *De Legibus et Constitutionibus*, n. 1, p. 39: "quod illi qui iura composuerunt, homines fuerunt, et quod errare potuerunt. Imo et hoc aliter esse non potuit: quia omnium habere memoriam, et in nullo penitus peccare, divinitatis potius est quam humanitatis."

[163] Pars I, Dist. IX, c.1, §1; cf. BALDUS DE UBALDIS, *Consiliorum sive Responsorum* . . . , Vol. III, cons. 371, n.1, fol. 105v. "et potest esse ex parte subditorum iustitia resistendo, si ex parte domini sit iniusta, et notoria violentia."

[164] HENRICUS DE SEGUSIO, *In Primum Decretalium* . . . ,*De Electione et Electi Potestate*, cap. 34, *Venerabilem*, n. 22, fol. 60v.

et de iure) to be incorruptible.[165] *Decretum Gratiani*,[166] and other canonists and civilists[167] never doubt of the sincerity of the sovereign, but insist that he should govern according to the law since his conscience is as liable to error as any other human conscience. In the perspective of the latter view, the rationale for the existence of a just cause in the granting of dispensation stands out more logically and clearly.[168]

The Concept of Public Authority in Thomas Aquinas

The doctrine on legal authority found an excellent exponent in Saint Thomas Aquinas. The Aquinatis presented a philosophy on the subject which by far surpassed the common doctrine of his contemporaries. The conceptualization of authority by Saint Thomas with its logical sequences correlates adequately with the proposed understanding of civil authority by human consciousness at this particular stage of its own humanization process.

The Angelic Doctor concurs *in integro* with the Christian tradition on the divine institution of legal authority; thus, in unison with the traditional

---

[165] *In Codicem Commentaria*, Lib. I, Tit. 19, *De Precib. Imperatori offerend.* etc., n. 11, fol. 36v; cf *In Digesti Veteris* . . . , Rubrica II, *Quod quisque iuris in alterum statuerit, ut ipse eodem iure utatur*, nn. 18, 19, fol. 31v; BALDUS DE UBALDIS, *Consiliorum, sive Responsorum* . . . , Vol. I, cons. 328, n. 7, fol. 102v; ALBERICUS DE ROSATE, *Dictionarium* v. *lex*, p. 425. Although Albericus does say that Lycurgus, the great Lacedemonian law-giver never enacted a law which he himself did not observe, ibid., p. 422.

[166] Pars I, Dist. IX, c. II: "Justum est, principem legibus obtemperare suis. Tunc enim iura sua ab omnibus custodienda existimet, quando et ipse illis reverentiam prebet. Principes legibus teneri suis, nec in se convenit, posse damnare iura, que in subiectis constituunt. Justa est enim vocis eorum auctoritas, si quod populis prohibent, sibi licere non patiantur."

[167] AZO, *Ad Singulas Leges XII* . . . , Lib.I, Tit. 14, *De Legibus et Constitutionibus*, Lex 4, *Digna vox*, n. 14, p. 40; PILEUS MODICENSIS, *Quaestiones Aureae*, Quaestio 43, *An sententia appellationis per Imperatorem lata parte non citata valeat*, nn 1, 3, pp. 92, 93; HENRICUS DE SEGUSIO, *In Quintum Decretalium* . . . , *De Privilegiis, et excessibus Privilegiatorum*, cap. 20, *Petistis*, n.4, fol. 86r.

[168] ANTONIUS A BUTRIO, *Super Prima Primi Decretalium* . . . , Tom. I, *De Electione*, cap. 44, *Nihil*, n. 10, fol. 140v: "Item, quod omnis dispensatio, etiam a iure, debeat fieri cum causa." ALBERICUS DE ROSATE, *Dictionarium* . . . , v. *Dispensatio*, pp. 188, 190.

teaching, he maintains that disobedience to authority is a mortal sin.[169] This position, however, does not restrict the Aquinatis to envisaging authority as intrinsically flowing from the nature of human consciousness. "Man is bound to obey secular princes in so far as this is required by the order of justice."[170] For this reason, he maintains, and rightly so, that the institution of authority would have existed also in the state of innocence.[171] Within the context of this premise, it is not difficult for Saint Thomas to acknowledge the social community as the primordial source of authority.[172] In consequence, he defines legal authority as representation and delegation of the primordial source, as "someone who is the viceregent of the whole people."[173] From these basic ideas, the Aquinatis could not but advocate democracy of government which most outstandingly reveals authority as stemming from human consciousness itself, as the product of the universal inwardness of the individual human consciousness.

The subordination of public authority to the order of justice is so pronounced in the Thomistic presentation that the law appears as a dictate of right practical reasoning.[174] Thomas even sustains that in the remitting of punishment of a guilty person, public authority, absolute sovereignty not excluded, cannot lawfully act without the consent of the injured party, and after taking into consideration the common good.[175] This rule holds true also in the granting of dispensation.[176] John of Salisbury in no ambiguous

---

[169] *Summa Theologica*, IIa-IIae, q. 105, art. 1. Resp., loc. cit., vol. 2, p. 1647.

[170] Loc. cit., IIa - IIae, q. 104, art. 6, ad 3um, vol. 2, p. 1646.

[171] Loc. cit. Ia, q. 96, art. 4, Resp., vol. 1, pp. 488-489.

[172] Loc. cit., Ia-IIae, q.90., art. 3, Resp., vol. 1, p. 995.

[173] Ibid.

[174] Loc. cit., Ia-IIae, q. 91, art. 1, Resp., vol. 1, p. 996.

[175] Loc. cit., IIa-IIae, q. 67, art. 4, Resp., vol. 2, p. 1485.

[176] Loc. cit., Ia-IIae, q. 97, art. 4, Resp., vol. 1, pp. 1024-1025.

terms advocates the elimination of the tyrant, also with violence.[177] Thomas does not propose the destruction of an unjust ruler, but he certainly postulates disobedience to his unjust laws,[178] and, if necessary, he justifies a political upheaval.[179]

In the Thomistic dissertation, there is a major point which conflicts with the present-day understanding of public authority. Saint Thomas follows the opinion of those who contend that an absolute ruler is not bound by his own laws. It must be pointed out that the ruler's supremacy over the law is restricted by Saint Thomas to coercive powers.[180] However, in light of this contention, it seems contradictory to insist at the same time that the ruler cannot lawfully grant pardon for a crime without taking into consideration the consent of the injured party and the common good.[181] Moreover, the arbitrary nature of the above qualification exposes the Thomistic contention to a serious objection: once a principle of this nature is reckoned as valid, it ought to be applied to the universality of cases concerning the legislative and administrative powers, as well. The traditional doctrine on absolute sovereignty never did make any distinction between the three spheres of power in reference to the point in question.

The Concept of Public Authority in the Context of the Present Study

The Christological ontology of human nature has been laid down as the central idea of the themes so far expounded. The *unio hypostatica* was placed from the start as the *causa formalis* and *causa finalis* in the creation of human consciousness, whether it is reckoned as individual or universal reality. Human consciousness in its forward march in self-discovery and

---

[177] *Polycraticus* . . . , Lib. VIII, cap. 17, loc. cit., col. 778.

[178] Loc. cit., IIa-IIae, q. 104, art. 6, ad 3um, vol. 2, p. 1646.

[179] Loc. cit., IIa-IIae, q. 42, art. 2, ad 3um, vol. 2, p. 1366.

[180] Loc.cit., Ia-IIae, q. 96, art. 5, ad 3um, vol. 1, p. 1021.

[181] Loc. cit., IIa-IIae, q. 67, art. 4, Resp., vol. 2, p. 1485.

self-explication is following its inner destiny of returning back to its foundation, to Christ as its *causa formalis* and *finalis,* to that prototype and truth on which it was featured and on which it depends for its ultimate significance and self-completion. Thus, in the pursuance of its immanent self-unfolding, human consciousness does not move outward as if into externality, into something which is not already implicitly contained; it unfolds by moving inwardly, into its essential authenticity, which is nothing other than a germ of the eternal law of justice, truth, and wisdom. In this eternal law, everything is clustered which forms the gamut of experiences of which human consciousness is capable in the natural and supernatural order of things. In returning upon itself, human consciousness is unfolding itself and explicating its ontology, its christological nature, the all-inclusive and unchanging model of human consciousness. This has been the perspective of our understanding of public authority, which can be summarized in the following manner: the source of public authority is the universal human consciousness which emerges from the universal inwardness of the individual human consciousness, which for its part is a reflection of Christ, the divine Wisdom incarnate.

Public authority should not be seen in isolation, abstractly, but as a reality forming part of the one, sole, human spectrum. The objective of these paragraphs is first to illustrate that public authority is the individual human consciousness objectified. It has been stated earlier that human consciousness is composed of three essential components -- rationality, conscientiousness, and sociability -- which taken together form the universal inwardness of the human being. Because of these qualities, the individual human consciousness sees others similar as itself, and itself as them in a free unity or universal substance of rationality and conscientiousness; in other words, being by nature social, the human being exists by inner necessity as a unitary member of the universal consciousness. In the social world, the individual human consciousness actually passes to the fruition of itself; it explicates its universal inwardness in the most intensive and extensive manner. This means that the individual human consciousness is only realized, only finds its true universal content, in and with the order of society. The community is thus defined as the universal inwardness of the individual objectified, the absolutely accomplished realization of human consciousness as a rational, conscientious and social being. It is by force of nature that just as much as there is no community without human beings, there are no human beings without a community in actuality.

It is in the nature of human consciousness to contradict its individuality, to move out from crude being, and to enter into a higher stage of existence, which is the realm of profound solidarity, of one-mindedness. From this renunciation and transformation of the individual human consciousness emerges *l'esprit de corps*, a universal spirit which clarifies itself in the socio-political community. *L'esprit de corps,* although intrinsically dependent on the existence of the individual members, has a life partially of its own, and is endowed with a consciousness of its own; it knows itself and wills itself. This universal human consciousness needs by its very nature an expression of itself as an actuality, as an existing objectivity; it requires a unifying force within itself to solidify itself. Public authority is born out of this inner necessity of *l'esprit de corps*. Public authority is thus the objectivization and epitome of the communal spirit which has formed itself, knows itself, and wills itself. In ultimate analysis, it may be concluded that the individual human consciousness, by virtue of its universal inwardness, converges into the realization of public authority. In conclusion, the existence of human consciousness forms a cycle returning upon itself: the realization of itself must ultimately result in the institution of public authority which, as another self, helps its causative self to unfold itself, and reaches the fruition of itself.

From the above exposition on the origin and nature of public authority, it follows that legal authority stems from human nature, and assumes a form appropriate to the stage at which it finds itself in the process of its own awareness and self-realization. Upon this premise, one has to concur with Aquinas in envisaging the institution of public authority independently of the Fall. In consonance with the same premise, one has to adhere to the Roman theory which acknowledged and endorsed *populus* as the primordial source of authority both metaphysically and historically; indeed, we proceed further, and reckon the individual human consciousness as *causa causae* since in it alone "lex insita est"; and this law is the reflection of the Incarnate Word. Within the same context, the democratic government stands out as the most genuine expression of *l'esprit de corps*, and fundamentally, of the universal inwardness of the individual human consciousness. In enacting laws, the legislator assumes the role of interpreter and minister of the community. His substantial task consists in rendering actual what is timely in and by itself, that is, the will of *l'esprit de corps*: its needs, inclinations, desires, and aspirations. Contrary to what was traditionally understood by sovereignty -- to lord it over the subjects as in the case of absolute sovereignty, or the modern totalitarian state -- public authority is the executioner of a purpose which forms a stage in the forward march of the universal human consciousness. This conceptualization of authority leads to the conclusion that the legislator is thus bound by the laws he enacts. Moreover, once law is defined as *recta ratio,* by this very same reason the legislator must submit himself to his own laws. In light of these two presuppositions, it is required also of the legislator that he act by reason of a just cause in granting dispensation and privileges, and in pardoning a guilty person of a crime, provided the injured person consents and the common good is safeguarded.

The present exposition on authority appears, at first hand, in contradiction to the Christian Tradition on the divine institution of authority: all authority descends from God rather than ascends from the people. In the pursuance of a solution, it is just to first ask whether authority comes from God proximately and directly, or remotely and indirectly. The theme is *per se* based on this alternative question.

The adherence to the first hypothesis of direct and proximate provenance of authority from God necessitates an *a priori* dismissal of our understanding of authority. The traditional Christian contention rejected, by force of logic, any claim by the community to be the source of authority. A fundamental premise was therefore laid down that community and public authority are two essentially distinct entities. A logical sequence necessitated the acknowledgement of absolute sovereignty as the sole, valid form of government. In this context it was appropriate to believe that the sovereign is God's anointed, God's representative, through a quasi-consecration. Logically subsequent to this contention, public authority was perceived as an imposition upon the community which by some was looked upon as a herd of wild beasts. Democratization of authority was the last thing in the minds of Christian authors. The present state of affairs posits a dilemma to Christian Tradition -- that is, whether in a democratic state authority still comes from God.

There is one authority since God is one. Human authority proceeds remotely and indirectly from God, that is, through Christ once God has from eternity bestowed on him all authority in heaven and on earth. Before his ascension to the Father, the Lord uttered: "All authority in heaven and on earth has been given to me."[182] The Lord's statement should not be taken to mean a *hic et nunc* bestowal of authority, but rather a solemn declaration that he enjoyed divine authority throughout his terrestrial life. This statement of the Lord assumes further depth of comprehension if the christological ontology of human nature be brought into focus. Once Christ has been acknowledged as the *causa formalis* and *finalis* of human consciousness, the divine authority of the Lord must be perceived to transcend time and to precede creation, and it must be endorsed as the immediate source of human authority, whether civil or ecclesiastical. Christ, as *causa formalis* of human consciousness, is the source of civil authority; as *causa finalis,* he is the source of ecclesiastical authority.

Civil authority descends from Christ indirectly and remotely through mediation of the divine law inscribed in every human consciousness. Human consciousness by virtue of this same divine law must unfold itself in accordance with its *causa formalis,* and it thus approaches Christ, its *causa finalis.* Civil authority, which is an immanent creation of human consciousness, must by inner necessity develop apace with human consciousness in its forward march of self-explication in Christ; indeed, it registers at what stage human consciousness has arrived in the realization of its *causa formalis.* Human consciousness, in response to its inner destiny, gradually objectifies itself in public authority in the spirit of the Gospel, leading to the implementation of the Lord's command: "Anyone who wants to

---

[182] Matt. 28:18; Lk. 24:9-10; Jn. 3:15.

be great among you must be your servant, and anyone who wants to be first among you must be your slave, just as the Son of Man came not to be served but to serve, and to give his life as a ransom for many."[183] Civil authority, as all other dimensions of human consciousness, finds its ultimate aspiration in Christianity.

The Concept of Ecclesiastical Authority

The christocentric understanding of creation necessarily promotes the ontological identity of Church and human family as considered in its pure state; the existing distinction and difference are merely "contingential," or accidental, a fact caused by sin. However sharp may appear the antithesis, human family and Church are said to proceed from God. In our understanding they are said to emanate from the idea and spirit of Christ as prototype of human consciousness. In this latter context, we envisage civil and ecclesiastical authorities as stemming from Christ as their unmediate source of justice, and in Christ they share the same finality of pursuit. The ultimate aspiration of both societies is to converge into self-completion designed by the Gospel. Precisely because it was imbued with the Holy Spirit at Pentecost, the Church signals this finality. Being herself subject to the inherent law of self-discovery and self-unfolding in Christ, the Church nonetheless is the perpetuation of Christ in history. Being the sole possessor of the *Magisterium*, she remains forever the embodiment of Christ as *causa finalis* of human consciousness. Within this context, one can see more clearly the reason why ecclesiastical authority emanates in a direct and proximate manner from the Lord Himself, her head: "You did not choose me, no, I chose you; and I commissioned you to go out and to bear fruit, fruit that will last";[184] "I confer a kingdom on you, just as my Father conferred one on me."[185] Pentecost is an irrefutable illustration of

---

[183] Matt 20:26-28; Lk 22:25-27; Mk 9:35; Jn 13:4-15.

[184] Jn. 15:16.

[185] Lk. 22:29.

the direct provenance of ecclesiastical authority from God through Christ.[186]

It has always been the incontestable doctrine of the Church, based on Scripture, that the chair of Peter by divine right should be occupied by one person; in him universal and supreme authority resides. Canon 332, §1, reads: "The Roman Pontiff acquires full and supreme power in the Church when, together with episcopal consecration, he has been lawfully elected and has accepted the election . . . " The autocratic form of authority, albeit somewhat mitigated, is also found in the office of Bishop with regard to his own diocese.[187]

The subject of the jurisdictional supremacy of the pope, as one would expect, was high on the agenda of canonical literature. "The Pope is not only a bishop," writes Baldus De Ubaldis, "but supreme over all bishops and others whomever the mind can think of. To him is given the fullness of the keys and total freedom of authority. This authority is defined as absolute supremacy over all the restrictions of canon law and over any other restrictive ordinance, with the exception of Evangelical and Apostolic laws. When the Pope writes by virtue of his supreme authority nobody can oppose him unless his writing goes against grace." [188] Some authors in their zeal to exalt papal supremacy fall into ridicule; thus they deny what they affirm. Joannes Andreae, to mention one, states: "As long as the Pope lives, he is called lord, and can change a square into a circle."[189] It is a different

---

[186] Acts 2:1-4.

[187] Canons 375, §1; 381, §1.

[188] *In Decretalium Volumen . . . , Super Primo Decretalium,* Prooemium, cap. *Gregorius,* nn. 11, 14, fol. 3r: "(Papa) non solum est episcopus sed culmen episcoporum, et caeterorum, quos intellectus potest imaginari, cui data est clavium plenitudo, et summa libera potestas, quae appellatur potestas absoluta ab omnibus vinculis canonum, et ab omni regula arctativa, praeterquam ab evangelica, et apostolica . . . quando Papa scribit de plenitudine potestatis nihil potest opponi, quod annihilet gratiam."

[189] *In Secundum Decretalium . . . , De Iudiciis,* cap. 12, *Cum venissent,* n. 7, fol. 8v: "quandiu papa vivit, dominus dicitur, et potest mutare quadrata rotundis."; cf. BALDUS DE UBALDIS, *In Decretalium Volumen . . . , Super Primo Decretalium, De Postulatione Praelatorum,* cap. 4, *Bonae memoriae,* n. 15, fol. 64r: "Papa a nullo dependet, et sicut se habet sol in planetis, ita Papa in ecclesiis"; ANTONIUS A BUTRIO, *Super Prima Secundi Decretalium . . . ,* Tom. III, *De Iudiciis,*

story, however, when these same authors discuss in detail what plenitude of jurisdiction really entails. That the pope is subordinate to none[190] is a generalization which certainly needs clarification. In the administration of his jurisdiction, he is verily subject to divine, natural and positive, law.[191] The Chair of Peter is there to preserve, consolidate, and animate the deposit of faith handed down to the Church by the Lord Himself, and never to formulate a faith. The pope is not above, but in the Church; thus he is liable to heresy because of which he would be condemned, excommunicated, and deposed.[192] The subordination of papal jurisdiction is also extended to

---

cap. 12 *Cum venissent*, n. 9, fol. 17r: "Papa potest quicquid vult de potestate absoluta"; HENRICUS DE SEGUSIO, *In Primum Decretalium Librum . . . De Translatione Episcopi vel Electi*, cap. 3, *Quanto personam*, n. 12, fol. 84r: "Et breviter (papa) excepto peccato quasi omnia de iure potest, ut Deus"; ibid., *De Authoritate, et Usu Pallii*, cap. 4, *Ad honorem Dei*, n. 7, fol. 86r.

[190] JOANNES ANDREAE, *In Quintum Decretalium Librum . . . , De Sententia Excommunicationis*, cap. 44, *Inquisitioni*, n. 5, fol. 145r.

[191] BALDUS DE UBALDIS, *In Decretalium Volumen . . . , Super Secundo Decretalium, De Iureiurando*, cap. 18, *Quanto*, n. 5, fol. 252r: "Nam quod dicitur, quod Papa omnia potest, debet intelligi clave discretionis non exorbitante a divinis regulis, et naturalibus praeceptis"; Ibid., *Super Primo Decretalium*, Prooemium, cap. *Gregorius*, n. 11, fol. 3r; ANTONIUS A BUTRIO, *In Librum Tertium Decretalium. . . ,* Tom. V, *De Voto, et Voti Redemptione*, cap. 7, *Magnae* n. 10, fol. 150v; *Super Prima Primi Decretalium . . . ,* Tom. I, *De Consuetudine*, cap. 4, *Quanto*, n. 18, fol. 71r; HENRICUS DE SEGUSIO, *In Primum Decretalium Librum . . . , De Consuetudine*, cap. 4, *Quanto*, n.4. fol. 29v; ibid., *De Authoritate, et Usu Pallii*, cap. 4, *Ad honorem Dei*, n. 7. fol. 86r; JOANNES ANDREAE, *In Secundum Decretalium Librum. . . , De Iudiciis*, cap. 12, *Cum venissent*, n. 7, fol. 8v; *In Tertium Decretalium Librum. . . , De Voto, et Voti Redemptione*, cap. 7, *Magnae*, n. 5, fol. 171r.

[192] HENRICUS DE SEGUSIO, *In Primum Decretalium Librum . . . , De Maioritate et Obedientia*, cap. 16, *Cum inferior*, nn. 6,7, 175r: " Papa quantumcunque delinquat a nemine iudicatur, vel condemnatur, cum et immediate omnes homines subsint ei . . . excepto crimine haereseos, in quo nemini est parcendum."; ibid., *De Electione et Electi Potestate*, cap. 6, *Licet*, n. 16, fol. 39r; JOANNES ANDREAE, *In Primum Decretalium Librum . . . , De Electione*, cap. 6, *Licet*, n. 25, fol. 75v; ibid., *De Maioritate et Obedientia*, cap. 17, *Cum inferior* n. 2, fol. 270r; *In Tertium Decretalium Librum . . . , De Concess. Praeben. et Ecclesiae non Vacan.*, cap.4, *Proposuit*, n.14, fol. 50v; In *Quintum Decretalium Librum . . . De Sententia Excommunicationis*, cap. 44, *Inquisitioni*, n.5, fol. 145r; ANTONIUS A BUTRIO, *Super Prima Primi Decretalium. . . ,* Tom. I, *De Electione*, cap. 6, *Licet*, n. 30, fol. 98r; *Super Prima Secundi Decretalium . . . ,* Tom. III, *De Iudiciis*, cap. 12, *Cum venissent*, n. 9, fol. 17r; *In Librum Tertium Decretalium . . . ,* Tom. V, *De Voto et Voti Redemptione*, cap. 7, *Magnae*, n. 10, fol. 150v; ibid., *De Baptismo*, cap. 3, *Maiores*, n. 11. fol. 196r; *In Librum Quintum Decretalium . . . ,* Tom VII, *De Haereticis*, cap. 4, *Fraternitatis*, n. 2, fol. 4lr.

Apostolic Tradition.[193] Unless he is teaching *ex cathedra* on faith and morals, the pope, as any other mortal, is not immune from error and other human weaknesses. "The Pope," remarks Hostiensis, "sometimes errs or can be led astray."[194]

The supreme and universal authority of the Roman Pontiff, termed by the Decretalistae *plenitudo clavium*, incorporates three spheres of activity, namely legislative, coercive, and administrative. A brief explanation on each of these aspects seems useful.

"Any law which the Pope promulgates, God is said to be promulgating of whom the Pope is the vicar."[195] The illiterate tends to generalize and to over-simplify things. Every generalization savours of dogmatism, necessarily entails inexactitude, and indicates superficiality of comprehension. The statement of Hostiensis is valid only in its generality. This is not to say that the Roman Pontiff is not the official and rightful interpreter of divine law.[196] Indeed, ecclesiastical law is by its very nature a manifestation, expression, and implementation of a faith. In promulgating disciplinary laws, the supreme legislator is doing nothing other than explicating the *causa formalis* in view of the fulfilment of the *causa finalis*, that is, acknowledging the stage of development at which the christianized human consciousness has arrived in the process of its own christolization.

---

[193] BALDUS DE UBALDIS, *In Decretalium Volumen* . . . , *Super Primo Decretalium*, Prooemium, cap. *Gregorius*, n.11, fol. 3r.

[194] HENRICUS DE SEGUSIO, *In Tertium Decretalium Librum* . . . , *De Reliquiis, et Veneratione Sanctorum*, cap. 1, *Audivimus*, n. 15, fol. 173r: "Papa quandoque fallit, et fallitur."; cf. *In Primum Decretalium Librum* . . . , *De Aetate et Qualitate Ordinandorum*, cap. 4, *Eam te*, n. 4, fol. 106r: "(papa) quandoque per nimiam importunitatem non concedenda concedit"; *In Tertium Decretalium Librum* . . . , *De Religiosis Domibus ut Episcopo sint subiectae*, cap. 6, *Constitutus*, n. 10, fol. 137v: "dominus Papa debet (sive saltem ipsum decet) servare mundas manus suas, quamvis sit supra legem."

[195] HENRICUS DE SEGUSIO, *In Secundum Decretalium Librum* . . . , *De Iureiurando*, cap 30, *Nimis*, n. 2, foll. 136v-137r: "Quid iuris promulgat Papa, Deus, cuius vicarius est, intelligitur promulgare"; cf. JOANNES ANDREAE, *In Secundum Decretalium Librum* . . . , *De Iureiurando*, cap. 30, *Nimis*, n. 2, fol. 199r.

[196] ANTONIUS A BUTRIO, *Super Secunda Secundi Decretalium..*, Tom. IV, *De Iureiurando*, cap. 31, *Nimis*, n. 4, fol. 91r; HENRICUS DE SEGUSIO, *In Secundum Decretalium Librum* . . . , *De Iureiurando*, cap. 30, *Nimis*, n.2, fol. 137r.

In light of the Augustinian premise, civil law, to be true to itself, must be the embodiment of eternal justice; ecclesiastical law must furthermore be the realization of that same justice incarnate. More so than civil law, ecclesiastical law clarifies the divine law engraved in human consciousness in the pursuance of its own explication in Christ. In this light, one can see more clearly the reason why ecclesiastical law should bind in conscience. All this being said, the statement of Hostiensis, that laws promulgated by the Supreme head of the Church are thought to be enacted by God, must be understood in a very broad sense. "Merely ecclesiastical laws," which form the content of Canon 11, are traditionally acknowledged as being fundamentally human laws. In the light of the present study, the supreme authority, being at once the direct continuity of the Lord's authority, and the synthesis of the universal christianized human consciousness, in enacting "merely ecclesiastical laws," does nothing other than actualize this same collective spirit, the Church, at a particular developmental stage of self-discovery. In ultimate analysis, ecclesiastical laws are not to be considered as "merely ecclesiastical laws," as if to denote merely human laws enacted by ecclesiastical authority, but rather as laws emanating ultimately from a christianized human consciousness.

In judicial matters the pope is the supreme judge in the Church;[197] as the saying goes, "Roma locuta est, causa finita est" (Once Rome has spoken, the case is closed). Juridically speaking, in word and action the pope is accountable to nobody, the Ecumenical Council being no exception.[198] Thus, in perpetration of a crime, he does not incur the penalty prescribed by law.[199] In such a case, states Antonius A Butrio, the

---

[197] BALDUS DE UBALDIS, *In Decretalium Volumen . . . , Super Primo Decretalium, De Rescriptis*, cap. 14, *Pastoralis*, n. 12, fol. 36r: "Papa est iudex iudicum. . . unde nemini subalternatur, nisi se submittat ex iusta causa."

[198] JOANNES ANDREAE, *In Tertium Decretalium Librum . . . , De Concess. Praeben. et. Ecclesiae non Vacan.*, cap.4, *Proposuit*, n. 14, fol. 50v; *In Quintum Decretalium Librum . . . , De Sententia Excommunicationis*, cap. 44, *Inquisitioni*, n. 5, fol. 145 r.

[199] HENRICUS DE SEGUSIO, *In Primum Decretalium Librum . . . , De Maioritate et Obedientia*, cap. 16, *Cum inferior*, n. 6, fol. 175r; JOANNES ANDREAE, *In Primum Decretalium Librum . . . , De Maioritate et Obedientia*, cap. 17, *Cum inferior*, n. 2, fol. 270r; ANTONIUS A BUTRIO, *Super Prima Secundi Decretalium . . .* , Tom III, *De Iudiciis*, cap. 12, *Cum venissent*, n. 9, fol. 17r.

pope would be judge in his own criminal case.[200] Contrary to this common view, Huguccio, with whom Baldus De Ubaldis seems to concur, maintains that the Roman Pontiff should be removed on account of a notorious infamous crime.[201] As pointed out earlier, the crime of heresy constitutes the exception to the above general rule, in which case, according to Antonius A Butrio, the pope would have to submit himself to the judgment of the Ecumenical Council.[202] Never was there any doubt among jurists on the pope's authority to excommunicate any member of the Church, bishops and monarchs included.[203] Joannes Andreae believes that the pope would be acting *ultra vires* if he were to deprive the Church of bishops, since in such a case he would be changing the general state of the Church.[204] By virtue of his supreme authority, the pope can grant pardon to any penalty incurred.[205] It was debated, however, among the Decretalists whether the pope could redeem one from the crime of perjury.[206]

It was well established in canonical literature that the supreme

---

[200] *Super Prima Secundi Decretalium* . . . , Tom. III, *De Iudiciis*, cap. 12, *Cum venissent*, n. 9, fol. 17r: "in causa delicti proprii dic quod potest esse iudex in causa propria: quia a nemine iudicatur, excepta haeresi."

[201] BALDUS DE UBALDIS, *In Decretalium Volumen* . . . , *Super Primo Decretalium, De Rescriptis*, cap. 25, *Olim ex literis*, n. 32, fol. 47r. "Papa potest removeri propter notorium crime enorme." Cf. HENRICUS DE SEGUSIO, *In Primum Decretalium Librum* . . ., *De Electione et Electi Potestate*, cap. 6, *Licet*, n. 16, fol. 39r., who contradicts Huguccio.

[202] *In Librum Quintum Decretalium* . . . , Tom. VII, *De Haereticis*, cap. 4, *Fraternitatis*, n. 2, fol. 41r.

[203] ANTONIUS A BUTRIO, *Super Prima Secundi Decretalium* . . . , Tom III, *De Dilationibus*, cap. 4, *Exposuit*, n. 19, fol. 88r.

[204] *In Primum Decretalium Librum* . . . , *De Officio Legati*, cap. 4, *Quod translationem*, n. 9, fol. 240r.

[205] HENRICUS DE SEGUSIO, *In Primum Decretalium Librum* . . . , *De Electione et Electi Potestate*, cap. 54, *Dudum*, n. 36, fol. 76r.

[206] Cf. CYNUS PISTORIENSIS, *In Codicem Commentaria*, Liber I, Tit. 22, *Si contra ius vel utilitatem publicam, etc.*, n. 5, fol. 40r.

legislator is not bound by his own laws.[207] For reasons already stated, we cannot subscribe to this general consensus. This issue does not in itself entail the question of accountability. Thus, while we ascertain that the Roman Pontiff is subject to the law which he enacts, we nevertheless maintain the traditional doctrine that "Roma a nemine iudicatur" (the Roman Pontiff is judged by no one) in matters pertaining to faith and morals, with the exception of heresy. If not juridically, the pope is nonetheless, in a mystical manner, accountable to the whole Church in consonance with the Pauline doctrine of the unfathomed inter-dependency of all members in the Mystical Body of Christ.[208] The reality of this mystery is applied to him as a member of the Church, but more so as head of the Church. In this context too he is bound to obey his own laws.

"Whenever it is a question of positive law, The Roman Pontiff, who is above the law, can render an act no longer sinful."[209] The statement of Antonius A Butrio needs clarification. Reference has been made earlier to the three modes of expression of the one law, natural, divine positive, and human law. No instance is contemplated by authors whereby the supreme head of the Church can dispense from the primary dictates of natural law, or from an article of faith.[210] In reference to divine positive law, the

---

[207] HENRICUS DE SEGUSIO, *In Secundum Decretalium Librum* . . . , *De Confirmatione Utili, vel Inutili*, cap. 5, *Ad nostram*, n. 1, fol. 208v; *In Tertium Decretalium Librum* . . . , *De Concessione Praebendae*, cap. 5, *Quia diversitatem*, n. 9, fol. 36r; ibid., *De Religiosis Domibus ut Episcopo sint Subiectae*, cap. 6, *Constitutus*, n. 10, fol. 137v; ANTONIUS A BUTRIO, *Super Prima Primi Decretalium* . . . , Tom. I, *De Consuetudine*, cap. 5, *Cum inter*, n. 18, fol. 72r; *In Librum Tertium Decretalium* . . . , Tom. V, *De Concessione Praebendae*, cap. 4, *Proposuit*, n. 7, fol. 49v., *In Librum Quintum Decretalium* . . . , Tom. VII, *De Excessibus Praelatorum*, cap. 8, *Sicut*, n. 13, fol. 81r.

[208] 1 Cor. 12:12-26.

[209] ANTONIUS A BUTRIO, *In Librum Tertium Decretalium* . . . , Tom. V, *De Voto, et Voti Redemptione*, cap. 7, *Magnae*, n. 10, fol. 150v: "Ubi ex lege positiva est, quia super illam est (Romanus Pontifex) possit facere peccatum non esse peccatum."

[210] HENRICUS DE SEGUSIO, *In Primum Decretalium Librum* . . . , *De Renunciatione*, cap. 11, *Post translationem*, n. 18, fol. 94v; *In Secundum Decretalium Librum* . . . , *De Restitutione Spoliatorum*, cap. 9, *Literas*, n. 3, fol. 54r; *In Tertium Decretalium Librum* . . . , *De Statu Monachorum, et Canonicorum Regularium*, cap. 6, *Cum ad monasterium*, n. 29, fol. 134r.

The Concept of Public Authority

authority of the Roman Pontiff in granting dispensation is acknowledged, however only from certain precepts which are not prohibitive injunctions,[211] and provided a just cause is present under pain of invalidity.[212] Thus a cause must precede the granting of dispensation from vows,[213] and from oath.[214] The integrity of faith being safeguarded, the Roman Pontiff *a fortiori* enjoys the power to dispense from laws enacted by the Apostles.[215] It goes without saying that the Roman Pontiff can dispense from laws enacted either by himself, his predecessors, or by an Ecumenical Council.[216] Antonius A Butrio believes that the will of the pope suffices in

---

[211] HENRICUS DE SEGUSIO, *In Primum Decretalium Librum* . . . , *De Transactionibus* cap. 11, *Ex parte tua*, n. 4. fol. 181v; *In Tertium Decretalium Librum* . . . , *De Concessione Praebendae*, cap. 4, *Proposuit*, n. 12, fol. 35r; *In Quintum Decretalium Librum* . . . , *De Simonia*, cap. 46, *Mandato*, n. 10 fol. 27v; ANTONIUS A BUTRIO, *In Librum Quartum Decretalium* . . . , Tom. VI, *Qui Filii sint Legitimi*, cap. 13, *Per venerabilem*, n. 59, fol. 54v; *In Librum Quintum Decretalium* . . . , Tom. VII, *De Usuris*, cap. 4, *Super eo* n. 2, fol. 62r.

[212] ALBERICUS DE ROSATE, *Dictionarium* . . . , v. *Dispensatio*, p. 189: "Dispensatio facta sine causa in his, quae sunt iuris divini, non tenet, etiam in foro contentioso"; "Dispensationi etiam Papali fiendae, sine iusta causa non est multum innitendum" (ibid., p. 188); ANTONIUS A BUTRIO, *In Librum Quartum Decretalium*, Tom. VI, *Qui Filii sint Legitimi*, cap. 13, *Per venerabilem*, n. 6, fol. 49v: "Et sic patet, quod Papa etiam non dispensat sine causa: quia homo est, et peccare potest sicut alius, licet a nemine iudicetur"; HENRICUS DE SEGUSIO, *In Tertium Decretalium Librum* . . . , *De Concessione Praebendae*, cap. 4. *Proposuit*, n. 12, fol. 35r.

[213] ANTONIUS A BUTRIO, *Super Secunda Secundi Decretalium* . . . , Tom IV, *De Fide Instrumentorum*, cap. 7, *Quod super*, n. 3, foll. 61v - 62r: "Nota 2. quod in absolutione voti absolvens debet attendere utilitatem finis voti, et salutem animae voventis"; *In Librum Tertium Decretalium* . . . , Tom. V, *De Clericis Coniugatis*, cap. 6, *Cum olim*, n.7, fol. 19r; HENRICUS DE SEGUSIO, *In Tertium Decretalium Librum* . . . , *De Concessione Praebendae*, cap. 4, *Proposuit*, n. 12, fol. 35r.

[214] BALDUS DE UBALDIS, *In Decretalium Volumen* . . . , *Super Secundo Decretalium, De Iureiurando*, cap. 18, *Quanto*, n. 5, fol. 252r; HENRICUS DE SEGUSIO, *In Tertium Decretalium Librum* . . . , *De Concessione Praebendae*, cap. 4, *Proposuit*, n. 12, fol. 35r.

[215] HENRICUS DE SEGUSIO, *In Primum Decretalium Librum* . . . , *De Renunciatione*, cap. 11, *Post translationem*, n. 18, fol. 94v; *In Tertium Decretalium Librum* . . . , *De Concessione Praebendae*, cap. 4, *Proposuit*, n. 12, fol. 35r; ANTONIUS A BUTRIO, *Super Secunda Primi Decretalium* . . . , Tom. II, *De Bigamis*, cap. 2, *Super eo*, n. 5, fol. 11v.

[216] ANTONIUS A BUTRIO, *Super Secunda Primi Decretalium* . . . , Tom. II, *De Bigamis*, cap. 2, *Super eo*, n. 5, fol. 11v; HENRICUS DE SEGUSIO, *In Primum Decretalium Librum* . . . , *De Pactis*, cap. 4, *Cum pridem*, n. 5, fol. 177v., *In Tertium Decretalium Librum* . . . , *De Concessione Praebendae*, cap. 4, *Proposuit*, n. 12. fol. 35r.

the granting of dispensation from ecclesiastical laws -- "Adverte, hoc verum de honestate, in Papa est speciale, ut sola voluntas ad validitatem dispensationis sufficiat pro causa."[217] Albericus De Rosate[218] and Hostiensis[219] hold contrary opinions. In light of what has been discussed earlier on the nature of dispensation, we cannot but subscribe to the latter opinion, which requires the existence of a reason, at least, for liceity.

The theory which advocates the legislator to be above the law tries to find its argument in the granting of dispensation of the same law.[220] In other words, it is because he is above the law that the pope has the power to dispense from ecclesiastical laws. In that case, the promoters of this theory fail to indicate the reason for the authority of the pope to dispense from certain precepts of divine positive law.

If the words of Antonius A Butrio on the authority of the pope -- "potest de nihilo aliquid facere" (who can make anything out of nothing)[221] -- were given full purport, the administrative powers of the pope would have savoured of fully-fledged despotism. Indeed authors were not lacking who viewed the Church's wealth and the property of the faithful as the sole possession of the pope; consequently, he could dispose of anything in the Church -- "omnia disponere tanquam dominus." Thus the pope enjoyed the fundamental right to alienate ecclesiastical possessions, and give to one what belongs to another.[222] These views stirred a

---

[217] *In Librum Quartum Decretalium* . . . Tom. VI, *Qui Filii sint Legitimi,* cap. 13, *Per venerabilem,* n. 6, fol. 49v.

[218] *Dictionarium* . . . , v. *Dispensatio,* p. 188.

[219] *In Secundum Decretalium Librum* . . . , *De Sententia et Re Judicata,* cap. 19, *In causis,* n. 7, fol. 166v: "sine causa non debet etiam summus Pontifex dispensare."

[220] ANTONIUS A BUTRIO, *In Librum Tertium Decretalium* . . . , Tom. V, *De Concessione Praebendae,* cap. 4, *Proposuit,* n. 7, fol. 49v; HENRICUS DE SEGUSIO, *In Tertium Decretalium Librum* . . . ,*De Concessione Praebendae,* cap. 5, *Quia diversitatem,* n. 9, fol. 36r.

[221] Ibid.

[222] BALDUS DE UBALDIS, *In Decretalium Volumen* . . . , *Super Primo Decretalium, De Renunciatione,* cap. 4, *Admonet,* n. 4. fol. 94v.

vehement reaction in Joannes Andreae who circumscribed papal authority to plain administration, and reminded the pope that he had better act and judge rightly "quia sibi terribilius est, quam parti" (for it will be more harsh the divine judgment on him than on his subject).[223] Historical vicissitudes helped clarify these views. In canon 1273 the pope is defined as supreme administrator and steward of all ecclesiastical goods.[224]

Conclusion

It was beyond the expectations of the present study to cover the different dimensions of authority, both civil and ecclesiastical. The theme was limited to the concept of authority as such. The relationship of authority to human consciousness constituted our exclusive concern. It was shown, hopefully clearly, that authority does not exist as an institution in, by, and for itself, an externality imposed on human consciousness, but rather as an emanation of the same. Civil authority is the revelation of human consciousness returning upon itself in order to find itself, its authentic self, created in the image of Christ. In resolving itself of itself, human consciousness becomes more its own cognition of itself, it clarifies itself to itself as rationality, conscientiousness, and sociability; it knows itself as such, it epitomizes itself, passes into another self in order to come back more fully to itself; thus it evermore explicates its universal inwardness. This other self is nothing other than public authority which is at once manifestation, expression, and actualization of human consciousness, and a force of unification and direction towards Christ, the finality of

---

[223] *In Secundum Decretalium Librum, De Iudiciis*, cap. 12, *Cum venissent*, n. 7, fol. 8v; "... nec ipse, nec alius praelatus est dominus ... Unde nec papae licet alienare ... nec successio locum habet in ecclesia Dei ... caveat tamen, quod iuste iudicet, quia sibi terribilius est, quam parti."

[224] Canon 1256: "Under the supreme authority of the Roman Pontiff, ownership of goods belongs to that juridical person which has lawfully acquired them." By ecclesiastical goods is meant either goods which belong to a moral person, collegial or non-collegial (canon 115,§2) or constitute the very substance of a juridical entity lawfully established in the Church (canon 115,§3). The Roman Pontiff can dispose of these ecclesiastical goods only whenever these juridical persons desist to exist.

human consciousness. Authority is there to actualize and accomplish what is timely in and by itself -- the needs, desires, and aspirations of *l'esprit de corps* at a particular stage in its humanization process.

Unlike civil authority, ecclesiastical authority proceeds from the Lord Himself, as *causa formalis* as well as *causa finalis* of human consciousness. It is precisely for this reason that the ultimate aspiration of human consciousness is found in Christianity. While being anchored in the perennity of the Gospel truth, the Church as integral part of humanity, indeed being human consciousness itself, by inner necessity must move forward in self-authentication. The role of ecclesiastial authority is to see to it that human consciousness reaches its finality, so vividly delineated in Scriptures, by rendering itself in conformity with its *causa formalis*. Civil authority emerges from the nature of human consciousness, which was created in the image of Christ; thus civil authority descends indirectly and remotely from Christ, through the human consciousness. Ecclesiastical authority proceeds directly and proximately from Christ in order to vitalize, facilitate and bring to completion the christological ontology of human consciousness. Ecclesiastical authority, like civil authority, accomplishes what is timely, appropriate and beneficial for the christianized human consciousness at a particular stage in the process of its humanization; it is there to revitalize, enhance, and invigorate what is contained in human consciousness *ab initio,* that glimmer of truth engraved in the human heart. Being the Church human just as much as it is divine, the unfolding cognizance of ecclesiastical authority of itself signals at the same time the stage which human consciousness, imbued with the Spirit of Pentecost, has reached in the revelation of itself, that is, the christolization of itself.

Personhood as Endorsed in the Code of Canon Law

The advent of Christendom marked the emergence of the human being as an immortal and unique creation in antithesis to the pantheistic conceptualization of the human soul by primitive religions.[1] The human person, being endorsed as the image of the divine by the Judeo-Christian religion, is *a priori* conceived of as a creation of supreme worth, titular of innate and irreducible rights. Being thus endowed with a spiritual-immortal soul, the human person is presented as being, by nature, a rational, conscientious, and social creature. The Church, as the epitome and re-enforcement of the christological nature of human personhood, strives in the new Code to endorse and heighten human dignity in accordance with these three prerogatives of human personhood. "For the human person deserves to be preserved; human society deserves to be renewed. Hence the pivotal point of our total presentation will be man himself, whole and entire, body and soul, heart and conscience, mind and will."[2] Thus we try to examine in the Christian spectrum the human person who by reason of his very nature belongs to the *Ecclesia* in a mystical and real sense.

Rationality

"God has regard for the dignity of the human person whom He Himself created; man is to be guided by his own judgment and he is to

---

[1] This fact is acknowledged by Carl J. Jung: "It was the great and imperishable achievement of Christianity that, in contrast to these archaic systems which are all based on the original projection of psychic contents, it gave to each individual man the dignity of an immortal soul," *The Practice of Psychotherapy*, New York, 1954, p. 105.

[2] *Guadium et spes*, n. 3, p. 201.

enjoy freedom."[3] Endowed with a spiritual soul, the human person is a conscious creation. While the human being is the culmination of the cosmic wisdom, he is also the participant in the absolute, transcendent, and eternal values. "For its part, authentic freedom is an exceptional sign of the divine image within man. For God has willed that man be left" in the hand of his own counsel "so that he can seek his Creator spontaneously, and come freely to utter and blissful perfection through loyalty to Him. Hence man's dignity demands that he act according to a knowing and free choice. Such a choice is personally motivated and prompted from within. It does not result from blind internal impulse nor from mere external pressure."[4] The prerogative of rationality enables the human individual to stand alone among equals. In verity, the human mind is a microcosmos in its own merits, the reason to be for every human individual is his uniqueness. Therefore each individual life takes on a corresponding absolute uniqueness in its existential significance.

But the uniqueness of human consciousness has more profound significance than when considered in its existential spectrum. Human consciousness finds its ultimate and absolute reality in being itself, that is in explicating its inner freedom. It is that innate ability of human consciousness to acknowledge its own actions as its own personal creation, that power which enables human consciousness to choose between possibilities of action, which is known in psychology as psychological freedom.[5] Gemelli defines this human prerogative in the following manner: "La capacita' che ha un uomo di rispondere di una azione. Essa dipende da una caratteristica inerente alla nostra natura umana e che fa sì che l'atto che noi compiamo sia ritenuto e giudicato come propriamente nostro: la liberta."[6] Upon this psychological freedom is based moral freedom, which is

---

[3] *Dignitatis humanae*, n. 11, p. 690.

[4] *Gaudium et spes*, n. 17, p. 214.

[5] ZAVALLONI, ROBERTO, *La Liberta' Personale*, Milano, 1956, p. 246.

[6] GEMELLI, AGOSTINO, *La Responsabilita' nelle Azioni Umane dal Punto di Vista della Psicologia e della Psichiatria*, Milano, 1944, pp.228-229.

the ability of the human person to discern between good and evil, to decide whether to obey or to rebel. "Essere libero, in senso morale, vuol dire essere in grado di scegliere fra il bene e il male, fra la conformita' e l'opposizione alla legge morale. Abbiamo dunque due accezioni ben distinte della liberta' la *liberta' psicologica,* o liberta' di scelta nel senso fondamentale della parola, e la *liberta' morale.* Quest' ultima presuppone la prima, ma non viceversa."[7] It is precisely because of this inner freedom, which is consciousness itself, that Christian philosophy maintains that justice is based on internal morality. By its own virtue, human consciousness charges itself with the responsibility of its own deeds before its Creator and before others similar. Thus *actus humanus,* in antithesis to *actio hominis,* is considered by Christian philosophy as the pivotal point in the understanding of human imputability. Saint Thomas Aquinas writes apropos: "Est autem homo dominus suorum actuum per rationem et voluntatem: unde et liberum arbitrium esse dicitur facultas voluntatis et rationis. Illae ergo actiones proprie humanae dicuntur, quae ex voluntate deliberata procedunt."[8] On the Aquinatis assumption, the human act is not to be confused with instinctive and inadvertent action. By *actus humanus* is meant a free, deliberate act that marks the human individual as a moral agent, an act resulting from the will acting freely, with antecedent knowledge of the end or purpose, and accompanying advertence. Thus, whatever evolves in *foro externo* must have for its validity a foundation in *foro conscientiae.* It must be said, however, that because of the rationality of the human mind every human act is presumed in *foro externo* as the result of due deliberation: "Quilibet actus semper praesumitur recte gestus."[9]

---

[7] ZAVALLONI, R., loc. cit.

[8] *Summa Theologica,* Ia IIae, qu. 1, art. 1, vol. 6, Romae 1895, p.6.

[9] C. Cum, 46; c. *Frater vester,* 47, D.L; *Dictum Gratiani,* c.12, c.l,qu.4;c. *Sicut noxius,* 1 X, *De Praesumptionibus,* II, 23; c. *Si vero,* 4, X, *De Sententia Excommunicationis,* V, 39; c. *Sicut tenor,* 15, X, *De Regularibus et Transeuntibus ad Religionem,* III 31; canon 1321, §3: "Where there has been an external violation, imputability is presumed, unless it appears otherwise."

In conclusion, the uniqueness of human consciousness, expressing itself in complete inner freedom, makes of itself master of its own destiny, absolutely intangible, supreme, and even resistible to its own Creator. Redemption remains forever inconsequential without the concurrence of the human *fiat*.

In line with the aforesaid philosophy on human consent, canon 11 prescribes that "merely ecclesiastical laws bind those who were baptized in the Catholic Church or received into it, and who have a sufficient use of reason . . ." When it concerns, however, personal commitment, whether spiritual or temporal, use of reason does not suffice. The intention of the person concerned must intervene for the validity of one's own action. By intention is meant knowledge of the object being desired with free deliberation. Canon 126 is indeed a logical sequence of this presupposition: "An act is invalid when performed as a result of ignorance or of error which concerns the substance of the act, or which amounts to a *conditio sine qua non*; otherwise it is valid, unless the law provides differently. But an act done as a result of ignorance or error can give rise to a rescinding action in accordance with the law."[10]

For this same reason, no sacrament can validly be administered to an adult unless preceded by the intention of the recipient to receive the sacrament.[11] Religious vows emitted in an institute of consecrated life or society of apostolic life lack moral and juridical value unless they proceed

---

[10] Deceit and error are two distinct realities which often concur together. A person errs without being deceived; therefore error is bound to materialize without being the result of deceit; philosophically speaking, error can be apprehended as a concept on its own merits. This cannot, however, be said about deceit. Essentially deceit is a cause; whereby, deceit, as a concept and as a reality, intrinsically depends on its effect, which is the error in the victim. In brief, one may conclude that although deceit and error are two concepts very akin, and not rarely concur as "cause-effect," error may subsist on its own both as a concept and as a reality, while this cannot be upheld about deceit -- there is no deceit unless error is successfully provoked in the mind of the victim.

[11] Cf. canon 865, §1, 2 (baptism); canon 889,§2; 891 (confirmation); canon 914 (Eucharist); canons 987, 989 (penance); canons 1006, 1007 (anointing of the sick); canon 1026 (ordination); canons 1057, §1,2; 1095, n. I (marriage).

from human consent as defined above.[12] Human enterprise of whatever nature -- contract, donation, testament -- enjoys binding force only insofar as it is the product of due deliberation. No crime is imputable to a person unless it implies a morally imputable violation of the law by reason of malice or of culpability.[13] Criminal externality of behaviour finds its intrinsic validity exclusively in internal morality, that is to say it must essentially be a mortal sin.

The cause of human dignity is further fostered by the Church's concern in protecting human deliberation against external forces bent to diminish its fullness. The Church, thus committed to the human cause, must ensure that commitments of serious and grave nature be undertaken out of a sense of personal conviction rather than assumed by reason of moral or physical coercion.[14] The gist of the Church's doctrine on this score is found in canon 125,

§1 "An act is invalid if performed as a result of force imposed from outside on a person who was quite unable to resist it."

§2 "An act performed as a result of fear which is grave and unjustly inflicted, or as a result of deceit, is valid, unless the law provides otherwise. However, it can be rescinded by a court judgment, either at the instance of the injured party or that party's successors in law, or ex officio."

In certain serious matters the law indeed provides otherwise, and hereby the human act is by law null and void in the following instances:

"A vow made as a result of grave and unjust fear or of deceit is by virtue of the law itself invalid" (canon 1191, §3).

"An oath extorted by deceit, force or grave fear is by virtue of the law itself invalid" (canon 1200, §2).

---

[12] Cf. canons 656, n. 4; 657, §1.

[13] Cf. canons 1321, §1; 1322; 1323, n.2; 696, §1. Canon 1348 constitutes, to some extent, an exception to this natural law. One may take exception to the prescription of canon 1348 for the fact that it empowers the Ordinary to inflict penal remedies on the person who has been found not guilty of a crime.

[14] *Dignitatis humanae*, n. 1, p. 675.

"If the freedom of an election has in any way been in fact impeded, the election is invalid by virtue of the law itself" (canon 170).

"A vote is therefore invalid if, through grave fear or deceit, someone was directly or indirectly made to choose a certain person or several persons separately" (canon 172,§1, n.1).

"A resignation which is made as a result of grave fear unjustly inflicted, or of deceit, or of substantial error, or of simony, is invalid by virtue of the law itself" (canon 188).

"A marriage is invalid which was entered into by reason of force or of grave fear imposed from outside, even if not purposely, from which the person has no escape other than by choosing marriage" (canon 1103).

"A person contracts invalidly who enters marriage inveigled by deceit, perpetrated in order to secure consent, concerning some quality of the other party, which of its very nature can seriously disrupt the partnership of conjugal life" (canon 1098).

One can also read the mind of the Church on the score in the establishment of the impediment of abduction and detention with the purpose of marriage (canon 1089).

There are however other instances which by nature of the thing itself do not allow the Church to secure the desired freedom for human deliberation with the force noted in the measures mentioned above. The Church nevertheless seeks to attain this end by certain laws, particularly when it involves *forum internum sacramentale*. One can witness the concern of the Church on the matter in the following issues: freedom of the faithful in choosing a confessor (canon 991); freedom of seminarians in approaching any confessor (canon 240, §1); freedom of seminarians in the choice of spiritual director deputed by the Bishop (canons 239, §2; 246, §4); freedom enjoyed by religious regarding the sacrament of penance and the direction of conscience (canon 630, §1); religious Superiors can hear the confession of their subjects only if the religious spontaneously approach them (canon 630, §4). The same law applies to the director and assistant director of novices, and the rector of a seminary or of any other institute of education (canon 985). Religious Superiors can in no way induce their subjects to make a manifestation of conscience to them (canon 630, §5).

The Christian philosophy on human consent as previously expounded is self-explanatory in the adjudication of human imputability. The Code nonetheless takes pains to specify the doctrine in serious issues pertaining to *forum externum*. Instances of this are encountered in the following canons:

"It is never lawful for anyone to force others to embrace the catholic faith against their conscience" (canon 748, §2; cf. canon 787, §2).[15]

"If a witness refuses to take an oath, he or she is to be heard unsworn" (canon 1562, §2).

"For a person to be ordained, he must enjoy the requisite freedom. It is absolutely wrong to compel anyone, in any way or for any reason whatsoever, to receive orders . . . " (canon 1026).

The belief of the Church in the inherent freedom of the human mind becomes more apparent in the question of penalties. As in all other human circumstances, internal or external causes may eliminate or debilitate one's discretionary faculty in criminal behaviour; thus one's criminal imputability may accordingly be adjudicated as non-existent, or at least diminished. Canon 1323 enumerates the instances when the law totally ignores one's liability to penalty. It is worth noting that these *causae excusantes* from criminal liability, rather than implement the Christian philosophy on human deliberation, do indeed vouch for the humaneness of the law towards the criminal. Even when it is clearly established that one's liability cannot be excused by virtue of canon 1323, there are still other instances contemplated in canon 1324, §1, in which one's imputability is said to be diminished. In view of these *causae minuentes,* the law sees to it that the penalty be either mitigated or replaced by a penance.

Mindful of her sacred vocation in the advocacy and safeguarding of the dignity of the human person, the Church becomes more insistent on personal conviction based on the full awareness of the responsibilities to be

---

[15] Loc. cit., n. 4, p. 682.

assumed when it involves a state of life. In these circumstances the Church requires a maturity of the discretionary and critical faculties in the candidate proportionate to the responsibilities entailed therein. It may be said that the Church, in so doing, indeed protects the person from the institution, however sacred and sublime it may be. This is particularly true when it involves the marital state, priesthood, and religious life. In this respect one may mention the following norms:

> Discretionary judgment concerning the essential matrimonial rights and obligations to be mutually given and accepted (canon 1095, n.2);
>
> diriment and impedient impediment of age in entering marriage (canon 1083, §1,2);
>
> thorough information on priestly life to be given to seminarians (canon 247, §2);
>
> maturity required in the candidate to the priesthood (canons 241,§1;1029);
>
> prescribed age is laid down for the priesthood and the diaconate (canon 1031, §1, 2,3,4);
>
> degree of maturity is expected in the candidate to religious profession (canons 642; 721, §3);
>
> age prescribed for the novitiate under pain of invalidity (canon 643, §1, n.1).

Conscientiousness

"Conscience is the most secret core and sanctuary of a man. There he is alone with God, whose voice echoes in his depths."[16] "Man perceives and acknowledges the imperatives of the divine law through the mediation of conscience. In all his activity a man is bound to follow his conscience faithfully, in order that he may come to God, for whom he was created."[17]

---

[16] *Gaudium et spes*, n. 16, p. 213.

[17] *Dignitatis humanae*, n. 3, p. 681.

To be rational is to be moral. The conscious soul is in essence a conscientious soul. The human soul is rational and conscientious because it was created spiritual, bearing the imprint of eternal truth. By its very nature the human soul transcends immediacy and crude being, enters into the profundity of itself and discloses itself to itself, and comes to perceive ever increasingly the unchanging truth within itself: "God, who probes the heart, awaits him there."[18] In consequence of sin, the knowledge of truth by the soul within itself was obscured, but never deleted. It is the destiny of the fallen soul to slowly regain the primordial wisdom. In doing so it directs itself to its foundation, and in this return it approaches the authenticity of itself. It is precisely because of this innate destiny that revelation is bound to unfold the dignity of fallen humanity in its full dimensions. Thus, even as one is a conscious and responsible creature, so one is also a moral creature, bound to respond to the dictates of conscience.

Conscience in its pure state is known in scholastic philosophy as *synderesis,* a term denoting the capacity of the soul to grasp by itself the primary moral truths imprinted in itself, itself being the image of the divine created. But by conscience is also meant that inherent capacity of the human soul to draw logical conclusions in virtue of its rational ability and to apply them to different situations as they occur -- an ability which is commonly defined as moral freedom to do good or evil. In reaching a decision the soul binds itself by itself, that is by the moral principles inherent to its nature. "Authentic freedom is an exceptional sign of the divine image within man. For God has willed that man be left "in the hand of his own counsel" so that he can seek his Creator spontaneously, and come freely to utter and blissful perfection through loyalty to Him."[19]

It may be said that by reason of the spiritual nature of the human soul the human person is the responsibility of the Church. By virtue of the *votum baptismi* at least, the unbaptized belongs to the Church and is

---

[18] *Gaudium et spes,* n. 14, p. 212

[19] Loc. cit., n. 17, p.214; cf. *Dignitatis humanae,* n.3, p.680.

entitled to the Church's solicitude for his or her spiritual well-being. The Code instructs the diocesan Bishop to approach with dignity and concern both the baptized non-Catholic (canon 383, §3) and the non-baptized (canon 383, §4) so that through the Christian manifestation of God they may increasingly grasp their personal eschatological fulfillment.

The human soul is unique by reason of its origin and nature. It is Catholic dogma that God creates each individual human soul, which thereby enjoys distinctive individuality and is unique in its self-fulfillment. It follows therefore that the human conscience is likewise uniquely committed in the search of the objective truth, and uniquely assertive in assuming the responsibility of its own judgments. This characteristic of human conscience should not be confused with misinformed conscience which easily lends itself to subjectivism in total disregard to objective truth. The ultimate destiny of the human soul is to come to know itself, its true self, through the ever increasing knowledge of the perennial truth of which it is the bearer.

The characteristic of uniqueness of human conscience thus entails the right to be excused because of invincible ignorance, or because of physical or moral impossibility -- "nemo potest ad impossibile obligari."[20] It is by reason of the distinctiveness of human conscience that dispensation from the law constitutes an integral part of the concept of justice. By dispensation is meant "the relaxation of a merely ecclesiastical law in a particular case."[21] The belief of the Church in the uniqueness of human conscience is especially envisaged in canon 1195 which prescribes: "A person who has power over the matter of a vow can suspend the obligation of the vow for such time as the fulfillment of the vow would affect that person adversely," and in canon 1203 which establishes: "Those who can suspend, dispense or commute a vow have, in the same measure, the same power over a promissory oath . . . "

---

[20] R. I. 6, in VI°.

[21] Canon 85; cf. canons 87, §I, 2; 88.

Sociability

"By his innermost nature man is a social being, and unless he relates himself to others he can neither live nor develop his potential."[22] Thus "in the use of all freedoms, the moral principle of personal and social responsibility is to be observed."[23]

The human being is a social creature. It is in the nature of the human person to live and relate to other fellow humans in justice and peace. Sociability is as constituent an element as rationality and conscientiousness are in human nature. In the analysis of the two previous characteristics of the human mind, rationality and conscientiousness, the individual human consciousness was appreciated in itself and by itself, and also in its relation to its Creator. In this context the human person was acknowledged and endorsed as a moral consciousness, whereas within the spectrum of sociability the same consciousness assumes the ethical dimension of its being. The sociability of human consciousness is indeed a reality without which rationality and conscientiousness cannot explicate their individual intrinsic potentiality. This truth is nowhere as clearly attested as in the Judeo-Christian religion in which the dependence of the human individual on his Creator and, subordinately to it, the fraternal consortium of the human person with fellow humans are maintained as to form the synthesis of individual human existence -- "ad Deum per fratrem."

The twofold prerogative, rationality and conscientiousness, highlights the spiritual dimension of human consciousness, whereas the social reality stresses the temporal aspect of the same. The dignity of the human person demands the conviction that these three prerogatives be accepted as one interlocked reality lest the cause of humanity be reduced into futility. There was never a time when the Church denied the dignity of the human person as a spiritual being. It is a different story, however, when it came to endorse this same dignity of the human person as a social being, as

---

[22] *Gaudium et spes*, n. 12, p. 211.

[23] *Dignitatis humanae*. 7, p. 686.

history amply testifies. The Church in Vatican Council II confesses her former deficiencies in this matter: "In the life of the People of God as it has made its pilgrim way through the vicissitudes of human history, there have at times appeared ways of acting which were less in accord with the spirit of the Gospel and even opposed to it."[24] Through the influence of Roman and seigneurial systems the Church managed to dissect, as it were, the human personality into two separate spheres: the spiritual reality and the temporal reality of human existence. In so doing she ignored the holistic conceptualization of the human person, and thus entertained a limited understanding of human dignity. In this manner, the Church managed to rationalize her non-involvement in the cause of the individual against the social injustice of the *ancien régime*. The sociability of the human person is nothing else than the acceptance and adequate understanding of personhood, without which the concept of human dignity becomes highly susceptible to subjective interpretation. Only in the appreciation and growing knowledge of human personhood can the universal human consciousness grasp its own inherent dignity in its entirety and endorse it with due justice.

With the emergence of personhood in human awareness, the intimate relationship between the natural and supernatural order of things appears more clearly. It has been stated earlier that the human person is the measure of all things since he forms a microcosmos in himself, a synthesis of the spiritual and the temporal. Thus one may claim that the knowledge of the uncreated and the created and their inter-relatedness develops on a par with the unfolding of the human consciousness by itself within itself. Since human consciousness is becoming increasingly aware of itself as the ultimate convergence of the natural and supernatural orders, it is likewise feasible to interpret that the humanization of human consciousness, whether universal *esprit de corps* or distinctive individual reality apprehended, leads, by its very nature, to the christianization of the same; by force of logic,

---

[24] Loc. cit., n. 12, p. 692. It would have been more historically correct were the words "Church authority" used in lieu of "People of God." The common priesthood emerged from ecclesial serfdom only since Vatican Council II.

the christianization of the Christian consciousness, whether as a community or individual and ultimate reality, has the end in view of the full actualization of its humaneness. This position is further solidified when Christ is visualized as the centrifugal and centripetal point of this ongoing process of the humanization of human consciousness.

The Church is gradually growing into this awareness. Canon 327 testifies to the Church's awareness of the intimacy that exists between the natural and supernatural orders. Talking about Lay associations of the faithful, the canon states that Christ's faithful "should especially esteem those associations whose aim is to animate the temporal order with the Christian spirit, and thus greatly foster an intimate union between faith and life." Indeed, harmony exists by nature between the two orders; therefore, the Church's mission is to animate, energize, evolutionize, rather than revolutionize, what is implicitly entailed in the human spirit, that is, its christological nature. The same idea can be envisaged in canon 787, §1, which insists that the evangelization of peoples must always take into account the native character and culture of the people.

The discovery of human personhood enables one to bring into focus the intimate relationship of the natural and supernatural orders within the individual human consciousness itself. Thus one is in a position to realize that psychological maturity and Christian maturity cannot be presented as two separate experiences, but they rather form one and the same phenomenon in human development. It is an undeniable historical truth that the Church has shown through the centuries keen interest in the education of the human mind in its entirety. The Church insists on the right to establish and govern universities precisely because she firmly believes that institutes of higher studies "serve to promote the deeper culture and fuller development of the human person, and to complement the Church's own teaching office."[25] The new Code assigns particularly canons 793 to 821 to Catholic education. There are other canons worth quoting in confirmation of the Church's belief in the holistic formation of human personality. Canon 217 states that Christ's faithful "have the right to a christian education,

---

[25] Canon 807.

which genuinely teaches them to strive for the maturity of the human person and at the same time to know and live the mystery of salvation."
The same idea is brought up again in canon 795: "Education must pay regard to the formation of the whole person, so that all may attain their eternal destiny and at the same time promote the common good of society. Children and young persons are therefore to be cared for in such a way that their physical, moral and intellectual talents may develop in a harmonious manner, so that they may attain a greater sense of responsibility and a right use of freedom, and be formed to take an active part in social life." This doctrine is further inculcated in the formation of seminarians[26] and religious.[27] Liturgical feast days are celebrated in the Church as worship to the Almighty; thus the faithful are obliged to assist at the Eucharist and abstain from work. However, canon 1247 also points out that the Lord's day serves as "due relaxation of mind and body."

The analysis of the nature of the Church so far accomplished may be recapitulated into one major conclusion, which in its turn leads to two subsequent ones: the intimacy of the Church with human nature finds its roots in the creation of Christ as the first born of the human family regardless of the Fall. This position makes of the Church the ultimate expression of the dignity of human personhood. In consequence of the intimacy between the Church and human nature, the human person, the image of Christ, is by this very fact titular of rights in the Church as far as natural law is concerned. Upon this theological assumption the Church is able to see herself as the promoter and defender, *par excellence*, of the dignity of the human being based on social justice. The awareness of the Church of this commitment is stated in clear terms in canon 747, §2:

> "The Church has the right always and everywhere to proclaim moral principles, even in respect of the social order, and to make judgments about any human matter in so far as this is required by fundamental human rights or the salvation of souls."

---

[26] Cf. canons 234, §1,2; 241, §1; 244; 245, §1; 239,§3; 279,§3.

[27] Cf. canons 652, §2; 660, §1.

The commitment of the Church to social justice falls first and foremost upon those who are called to be ministers of the Word in the Church. In the catechetical formation of Christ's faithful, the clergy, in particular, are to set out the teaching of the magisterium on the dignity and freedom of the human person, on people's social obligations and the ordering of temporal affairs according to the plan established by God (canon 768, §2). To this aim, the teaching of the magisterium and the solicitude of the Church on social justice should form part of the academic curriculum for those who are being prepared for the sacred ministry (canon 256, §2).

The Church to be true to herself must practice what she preaches. Indeed, as history amply testifies, the Church from the beginning directed her apostolate also towards human want through charitable organizations. The Code insists on this inherent right of the Church.[28] Canon 287, §1, expects the clergy to work in the cause of the human individual by fostering "among people peace and harmony based on justice."[29] The pastor, in particular, by word[30] and action[31] must see to it that the dignity of the human person always prevails in all instances of human experience. One may also mention that in the new Code the Papal Legate too is charged with the task "to promote whatever may contribute to peace, progress, and the united efforts of peoples" (canon 364, n.5). The Code also reminds religious institutes of their vocation in giving collective testimony of charity; it is the obligation of the institute to help out of its own resources in the financial burden of the Church and to succour the poor (canon 640). Needless to say, the Christian belief in human dignity was kept alive through the centuries through charitable institutions mostly run by religious. Christ's faithful are not exempt from this sacred commitment. They too have the obligation "to promote social justice and, mindful of the

---

[28] Canon 1254, §2.

[29] Cf. §2.

[30] Canon 528, §1.

[31] Canon 529, §1.

Lord's precept, to help the poor from their own resources" (canon 222,§2). Manifestation of Christian charity is expected also from juridical persons erected in the Church according to the prescription laid down by canon 1285.

Truly, "God has willed that man be left in the hand of his own counsel."[32] However this counsel must relate to that law implanted by God in the human soul by virtue of which, in the use of one's personal freedom, one is expected to observe the moral principle of personal and social responsibility. Human sociability, which expresses itself in respect for the rights of others and one's duty towards others, is nothing but the realization of the human creature being conscientious in the ethical sphere. Canon 223, §1, may rightly be defined as *lex fundamentalis* of the canonical codification on the subject of social justice. It reads: "In exercising their rights, Christ's faithful, both individually and in associations, must take account of the common good of the Church, as well as the rights of others and their own duties to others." A specification of this fundamental law is found in canon 128 which dictates: "Whoever unlawfully causes harm to another by a juridical act, or indeed by any other act which is deceitful or culpable, is obliged to repair the damage done."[33] In line with the concept of sociability based on moral principles, canon 1204 prescribes that, if a person in taking an oath acts deceitfully, the oath should be interpreted in accordance with the intention of the person in whose presence the oath is taken.

The theme of social justice as so far presented in the Code has been dealt with in its generality. Thus the presentation remains superficial and vague unless a thorough analysis of the Code on the score is undertaken. It is an arduous enterprise which we intend to exemplify. A presentation of

---

[32] *Gaudium et spes*, n.17, p. 214.

[33] Canon 1062, §2, deals with another social obligation for the reparation of damages arising from a promise of marriage.
Surprisingly enough the Code has to remind religious bodies that a member who becomes insane during the period of temporary vows cannot be dismissed from the institute (canon 689, §3), or who contracted an infirmity, whether physical or psychological through the negligence of the institute or because of work performed in the institute (canon 689, §2).

the canons on the theme is thereby listed according to the different fundamental human rights.

Right to Life

Latae sententiae excommunication is inflicted on the one who procures abortion (canon 1398).

Penalties are inflicted on those who commit murder, abduct, imprison, mutilate or gravely wound a person (canon 1397).

Marriage is invalid between the person because of whom the murder was perpetrated and the murderer of his or her spouse (canon 1090, §1,2; canon 1078, §2, n.2).

They are irregular for the reception of Sacred Orders who have committed, or positively co-operated in, homicide or abortion (canon 1041, n.4); who have gravely and maliciously mutilated themselves or others, or attempted suicide (canon 1041, n.5).

The right of the spouse together with the children to end cohabitation with the other spouse who threatens physical or spiritual harm (canon 1153,§l).

An oath taken to harm others, to antagonize public good, or endanger eternal salvation is by its very nature null and void (cf.canon 1201,§2).

Right to Embrace the Faith

All humans have the right to embrace the Catholic faith and keep it (canon 748,§1).

Right to Freedom of Conscience

No person is to be forced in any way to embrace the Catholic faith (canon 748,§2).

Right to Privacy

Every person has the right to protect his or her privacy (canon 220).

The sacramental seal of confession is directly and indirectly inviolable for the confessor himself, the interpreter and those who come to a knowledge of sins from a sacramental confession (canon 983, §1,2).

"A confessor who directly violates the sacramental seal, incurs a *latae sententiae* excommunication reserved to the Apostolic See; he who does so only indirectly is to be punished according to the gravity of the offence" (canon 1388, §1).

"Interpreters and the others mentioned in canon 983, §2, who violate the secret, are to be punished with a just penalty, not excluding excommunication" (canon 1388, §2).

All knowledge obtained in sacramental confession by the confessor is inadmissible in the ecclesiastical court even with the permission of the penitent. The same holds true for the interpreter and those whose knowledge was acquired from sacramental confession (canon 1550, §2, n.2).

The confessor is absolutely forbidden to use knowledge acquired in confession to the detriment of the penitent, even when all danger of disclosure is excluded (canon 984, §1). Nor can a religious Superior avail himself of knowledge acquired in sacramental confession for the purpose of external governance (canon 984, §2).

Religious Superiors have no right whatever to induce their subjects to make a manifestation of conscience to them (canon 630, §5).

Rector of the seminary or of any other institute of education, novice master and his assistant are banned from hearing confessions of their students unless the latter spontaneously approach them in individual cases (canon 985).

In admission of seminarians to Sacred Orders or in their dismissal from the seminary, the spiritual director and confessors are excluded from voting (canon 240, §2).

No one is obliged to exhibit documents if there is danger of violating a secret which is to be observed (canon 1546, §1).

Right to Good Reputation

The good reputation which a person enjoys is a right to be respected by all (canon 220).

A just penalty is to be inflicted upon the one who injures the good name of another or calumniously denounces an offence to an ecclesiastical Superior (canon 1390, §2).

A *latae sententiae* interdict is inflicted on one who falsely denounces a confessor of *solicitatio ad turpia,* of which mention is made in canon 1387 (canon 1390, §1).

In any preliminary investigation regarding a criminal act, the Ordinary must take care that such an inquiry does not call into question anyone's good name (canon 1717, §2).

"The accused person is not bound to admit to an offence, nor may the oath be administered to the accused" (canon 1728, §2) -- *"nemo tenetur prodere seipsum."*

They are exempt from giving testimony in an ecclesiastical court who by giving evidence fear a loss of personal reputation (canon 1548,§2,n.2).

No one is obliged to exhibit documents whenever personal reputation is jeopardized (canon 1546, §1).

In court proceedings, when the evidence given puts at risk the reputation of others, the judge can bind witnesses, experts and the parties and their advocates or procurators by an oath of secrecy (canon 1455, §3).

The obligation of observing a *latae sententiae* penalty which has not been declared may be suspended in whole or in part because of the good name of the offender if the case is not notorious in the place (canon 1352,§2).

The protection of the good name of the offender may allow that the petition for remission of a penalty or the remission itself be made public (canon 1361, §3).

Endorsement of this fundamental right is found in the codification on legitimacy. "Children who have been adopted in accordance with the civil law are considered the children of that person or those persons who have adopted them" (canon 110; canon 1140).

Children who are conceived of a putative marriage are legitimate (canon 1137).

Children are presumed legitimate born at least 180 days after date the marriage was celebrated, or within 300 days from the date of the dissolution of conjugal life (canon 1138, §2).

"Illegitimate children are legitimated by the subsequent marriage of their parents, whether valid or putative, or by a rescript of the Holy See" (canon 1139; cf. canon 1161, §1).

Right to Protect Oneself from Grave Burden

They are exempt from giving testimony in an ecclesiastical court who by giving evidence fear dangerous harassment or some other grave evil arising for themselves, their spouse or their relatives (canon 1548, §1).

No one is obliged to exhibit documents which cannot be communicated without danger of harm mentioned in canon 1548, §2, n.2 (canon 1546, §1).

A privilege which causes an inconvenience for others is lost if lawful prescription intervenes (canon 82).

"If dispensation from an oath would tend to harm others and they refuse to remit the obligation, only the Apostolic See can dispense the oath" (canon 1203).

Right to Assume a State of Life

"All Christ's faithful have the right to immunity from any kind of coercion in choosing a state in life"(canon 219).

"All can contract marriage who are not prohibited by law" (canon 1058).

A Catholic enjoying the necessary qualifications required by universal law and the laws of the institute may be admitted to an institute of consecrated life (canon 597, §1).

A Catholic male, having the necessary qualifications as requested by the Code of canon law, has the right to present himself as a candidate to sacred ministry (canons 241, §1; 1024; 1025, §1,2).

Right to Obtain Personal Documents

Anyone has the right to receive an authentic written or photostat copy of documents, which are of their nature public, concerning one's own personal status (canon 487, §2).

Right to Just Remuneration

"Administrators of temporal goods:
1. in making contracts of employment, are accurately to observe also, according to the principles taught by the Church, the civil laws relating to labour and social life;
2. are to pay to those who work for them under contract a just and honest wage which will be sufficient to provide for their needs and those of their dependents" (canon 1286).

"Lay people who are pledged to the special service of the Church have the right to a worthy remuneration befitting their condition, whereby, with due regard also to the provisions of the civil law, they can becomingly provide for their own needs and the needs of their families. Likewise, they have the right to have their insurance, social security and medical benefits duly safeguarded"(canon 231, §2; cf. canon 1274,§3).

"Married deacons who dedicate themselves full-time to the ecclesiastical ministry deserve remuneration sufficient to provide for themselves and their families . . . " (canon 281, §3).

If someone is removed from an office on which that person's livelihood depends, the competent ecclesiastical authority is to ensure that the person's livelihood is secure for an appropriate time, unless this has been provided for in some other way (canon 195).

The diocesan Bishop is to ensure that the priests in his care are provided with adequate means of livelihood and social welfare in accordance with the law (canon 384).

Clerics deserve the remuneration that befits their condition, taking into account both the nature of their office and the conditions of time and place. It is to be such that it provides for the necessities of their life and for the just remuneration of those whose services they need (canon 281,§1).

"Suitable provision is likewise to be made for such social welfare as clerics may need in infirmity, sickness or old age" (canon 282, §2).

The diocesan Bishop must see to it that before the incardination of a cleric the provisions of law concerning the worthy support of the cleric are observed (canon 269, n.1).

The diocesan Bishop, in granting permission to his cleric to exercise the ministry elsewhere, must first ensure that the rights and duties of the cleric are determined by written agreement with the diocesan Bishop who will host the cleric (canon 271, §1).

A pastor, who has been removed and is not suitable to occupy another office, is given a pension in so far as the case requires this and the circumstances permit (canon 1746).

The Vicar forane is to ensure that pastors of his district do not lack spiritual and material help. When they die, he is to ensure that their funerals are worthily celebrated (canon 555, §3).

If a removed pastor, because of sickness, cannot be transferred elsewhere from the parochial house without inconvenience, the Bishop is to leave to him the use, even the exclusive use, of the parochial house for as long as this necessity lasts (canon 1747, §2).

Religious Superiors are to give the members entrusted to them opportune assistance in their personal needs (canon 619).

"No religious house is to be established unless it is prudently foreseen that the needs of the members can be suitably provided for" (canon 610,§2).

Right to Equality Among Spouses

"Each spouse has an equal obligation and right to whatever pertains to the partnership of conjugal life" (canon 1135).

"Spouses are to have a common domicile or quasi-domicile. By reason of lawful separation or for some other just reason, each may have his or her own domicile or quasi-domicile" (canon 104).

Right of the Spouse and Children to Financial Support by the Other Spouse After Separation or Dissolution of Marriage

"In the judgment of nullity of marriage the parties are to be reminded of the moral, and also the civil, obligations by which they may be bound, both towards one another and in regard to the support and upbringing of their children" (canon 1689)

In case of separation while the bond of marriage remains, provision is always, and in good time, to be made for the due maintenance and upbringing of the children (canon 1154).

In cases of Pauline Privilege, "in the light of the moral, social and economic circumstances of place and person, the local Ordinary is to ensure that adequate provision is made, in accordance with the norms of justice, christian charity and natural equity, for the needs of the first wife and of the others who have been dismissed" (canon 1148, §3). This norm holds true also in cases of Petrine Privilege.

Except in a case of necessity, permission of the local Ordinary is required to assist at a marriage of a person for whom a previous union has created natural obligations towards a third party or towards children (canon 1071, §1, n.3).

One's Rights in Ecclesiastical Courts

Three different types of cases may be considered under this heading:

cases of contentious nature, defence against administrative decrees, cases of criminal liability.

Prior to discussing the specific rights of the person acknowledged by the Church on the matter, the Code of canon law lays down the following fundamental norms:

"Any person, baptised or unbaptised, can plead before a court. A person lawfully brought to trial must respond" (canon 1476).

The poor has the right to free legal aid, known as *gratuitum patrocinium* (canons 1649, §1, n.3; 1464).

The party in the case may object to any officer of the tribunal for reasons mentioned in canon 1448, §1,2, and the persons in question are to be changed (canons 1449, §1-4; 1450).

One's Rights in Foro Contentioso

"A party is always entitled, within ten canonical days, to have recourse, based upon stated reasons, against the rejection of a petition . . ." (canon 1505, §4).

In a trial the parties may submit to the judge propositions upon which a party is to be questioned (canon 1533).

"If a party or a witness refuses to testify before the judge, that person may lawfully be heard by another, even a lay person, appointed by the judge, or asked to make a declaration either before a public notary or in any other lawful manner" (canon 1528).

If a judgment was given against a party who, in accordance with canon 1593, §2, was lawfully absent, the sentence is vitiated by remediable nullity (canon 1622, n.6).

If the right of defence was denied to one or other party, the sentence is vitiated by irremediable nullity (canon 1620, n.7).

Whenever it concerns minors in a contentious trial, the judge is *ex officio* to appoint a legal representative for the minor who lacks one (canon 1481, §3).

"If the judge considers that the rights of minors are in conflict with the rights of the parents, guardians or curators, or that these cannot sufficiently protect the rights of the minors, the minors are to stand before the court through a guardian or curator assigned by the judge" (canon 1478, §2).

"In cases concerning spiritual matters and matters linked with the spiritual, if the minors have the use of reason, they can plead and respond without the consent of parents or guardians; indeed, if they have completed their fourteenth year, they can stand before the court on their own behalf; otherwise, they do so through a curator appointed by the judge" (canon 1478, §3).

One's Right of Defence Against Administrative Decrees

In such matters canon 36, §1, constitutes a fundamental norm in the interpretation of an administrative act: "An administrative act is to be understood according to the proper meaning of the words and the common manner of speaking. In doubt, a strict interpretation is to be given to those administrative acts which concern litigation or threaten or inflict penalties, or restrict the rights of persons, or harm the acquired rights of others, or run counter to a law in favour of private persons; all other administrative acts are to be widely interpreted."

"A person who contends that he or she has been injured by a decree, can for any just motive have recourse to the hierarchical Superior of the one who issued the decree. The recourse can be proposed before the author of the decree, who must immediately forward it to the competent hierarchical Superior" (canon 1737, §1).[34]

The person making recourse always has the right to the services of an advocate or procurator. An advocate is to be appointed *ex officio* if the person does not have one and the Superior considers it necessary (canon 1738).

---

[34] Canon 1733,§1: "When a person believes that he or she has been injured by a decree, it is greatly to be desired that contention between that person and the author of the decree be avoided, and that care be taken to reach an equitable solution by mutual consultation, possibly using the assistance of serious-minded persons to mediate and study the matter. In this way, the controversy may by some suitable method be avoided or brought to an end."

If a pastor is removed from office, he has the right to oppose the decree of removal by way of contention. The Bishop cannot proceed with the intended removal unless he subscribes to the prescription of canon 1745.

In transfer from one parish to another the pastor has the right to oppose the Bishop's decree in writing (canon 1749). The Bishop cannot proceed with the transfer without having abided by the prescription of canon 1750.

Both in removal or transfer of a pastor the prescription of canon 1747 is to be applied, always observing canonical equity (canon 1752).

The Right of One Accused of a Criminal Act

In case of criminal liability, if the Ordinary believes the matter should proceed by way of an extra-judicial decree, the accused has the right to be notified of the allegation and the evidence, and be given an opportunity for defence (canon 1720, n.1).

"In a penal trial the accused must always have an advocate, either appointed personally or allocated by the judge" (canon 1481, §2).

The accused has the right to engage an advocate (canon 1723,§1). If the accused refuses, the judge himself is to appoint an advocate before the joining of the issue, and this advocate will remain in office for as long as the accused has not engaged an advocate (canon 1723, §2).

"In the argumentation of the case, whether done in writing or orally, the accused person or the advocate or procurator of the accused, always has the right to write or speak last" (canon 1725).

In case of dismissal on crimes mentioned in canons 1397, 1398, 1395, the religious has the right to be presented with the accusation and the evidence together with the right of defence against the accusation and evidence (canon 695, §2).

In case of dismissal for reasons enumerated in canons 695 and 696, the religious always retains the right to communicate directly with the supreme Moderator of the institute (canon 698).

The decree of dismissal of a member from a religious institute has no effect unless it is confirmed by the Holy See, if the institute is of pontifical right, or by the Bishop in whose diocese is located the religious house, if the institute is of diocesan right. For validity the decree must indicate the right of the person dismissed to have recourse to the competent authority within ten days of receiving notification of the decree (canon 700).

In case of dismissal of a religious for reasons mentioned in canon 696,§1, the religious is to be warned by the major Superior in writing, or before two witnesses, with an explicit caution that dismissal will follow unless the member reforms. The reasons for dismissal are to be clearly expressed and the member is to be given every opportunity for defence.

The religious is entitled to another warning to be given after an interval of, at least, fifteen days (canon 697, §1).

At the request of the Supreme Moderator with the consent of the council, exclaustration of a member of an institute of pontifical right can only be imposed by the Holy See, or by a diocesan Bishop if the institute is of diocesan right (canon 686, §3).

Respect Shown Towards the Penalized Person

In addition to the question of human dignity in matters concerning criminal liability are the following canons which illustrate that alongside justice Christian charity should be uppermost in similar dealings. Justice devoid of Christian charity is bound to express itself in a streak of vengeance, as the latin axiom goes " *summum ius summa iniuria.*" Justice without Christian charity inspires the degradation of human dignity. The Church therefore sees to it that justice be tempered by sincere and rightful humaneness. We believe that by reason of his own nature the human person is entitled to this humaneness and equity. Thus the Code lays down the following norms:

> "Whenever the offender had only an imperfect use of reason, or committed the offence out of fear or necessity or in the heat of

passion or with a mind disturbed by drunkenness or a similar cause, the judge can refrain from inflicting any punishment if he considers that the person's reform may be better accomplished in some other way" (canon 1345).

"If a law is changed after an offence has been committed, the law more favourable to the offender is to be applied" (canon 1313, §1).

The sixteenth year of age is required for penal liability (canon 1323,n.1).

The penalty prescribed in the law or precept must be diminished, or a penance substituted in its place whenever any of the conditions enumerated in canon 1324, §1, are present.

Whenever one of the conditions mentioned in canon 1324, §1, is verified, the offender is not bound by a *latae sententiae* penalty (canon 1324, §3).

In danger of death a penalty prohibiting the reception of the sacraments or sacramentals is suspended (canon 1352, §1).

"Each year documents of criminal cases concerning moral matters are to be destroyed whenever the guilty parties have died, or ten years have elapsed since a condemnatory sentence concluded the affair. A short summary of the facts is to be kept, together with the text of the definitive judgment" (canon 489, §2).

One of the tasks of the Vicar forane is to show a particular solicitude for those clerics who experience personal problems (canon 555, §2, n.2).

The same solicitude and charity ought to be shown by religious Superiors in helping their insubordinate members to return and persevere in their vocation (canon 665, §2).

"In imposing penalties on a cleric, except in the case of dismissal from the clerical state, care must always be taken that he does not lack what is necessary for his worthy support" (canon 1350, §1).

In case of dismissal from the clerical state, the Ordinary is to provide in the best way possible if the cleric is truly in need (canon 1350, §2).

In case of imposed exclaustration of a member of an institute either of pontifical or of diocesan right, equity and charity are to be observed (canon 686, §3).

Although in case of leaving or of dismissal from a religious institute one cannot claim remuneration for work done in the institute (canon 702,§1), the institute, nonetheless, is to show equity and evangelical charity towards the ex-religious (canon 702, §2).

Canon 618 insists that religious Superiors ought to show reverence for the human person in the use of their authority. This admonition is in itself an affront; it reveals at what stage the institutional charisma of Christian perfection finds itself in the process of self-discovery and self-explication. In truth, the universal Christian consciousness finds itself in the same dilemma. It would have been most appropriate were the reverence for the human person announced in explicit terms by the Code for all the faithful in a Christian perspective rather than being expressed in a contractual connotation by canon 223, §1. A similar norm would have indeed constituted the *lex Legum* of the whole codification on social justice.

Conclusion

This historiosophy of human consciousness -- as we envisage it -- unfolds in three distinct periods of development. These are savagery, civilization, humanization. A human community without laws to govern itself is either operating in a stage of savagery, or has reached the pinnacle of its own humanization. A society, in which the law forms the axis of all social interactions, bespeaks of its own civilization. A community in a stage of savagery, because it knows of no law, emphatically needs the law; it is a lawless society in which the rule of the fittest prevails; such a group only entails the components of the herd; it is the most authentic expression of the subjective and instinctualistic freedom of human consciousness, at least in the case of the fittest. This said, we do not believe that human consciousness ever experienced such debased existence -- pure, crude being. Civilization marks the second phase of development when the human will submits itself to the law at the risk of its own subjective freedom. Human will tries to reach a *modus vivendi* between its own subjective freedom and the subjective freedom of others through a common norm. In spite of this ethical communion of minds, law will ever remain an imposition on the human will, a curtailment -- a civilized human will is a bridled will.

The increasing accumulation of laws in the governance of a society marks in direct proportion its progress achieved from the stage of savagery, or at least from its primitivism. On the other hand, the accumulation of laws in a society must bring in its trail the escalation of the indispensability of the positive law which in its turn leads, in various degrees, to the idolization of the same. As history testifies, the sovereignty of the law, besides being a major factor in the rise of national imperialism, may easily end in despotism. A civilized society, as commonly understood, indeed manifests a psycho-social, psycho-political and psycho-spiritual infantilism of *esprit de corps*. It goes without saying that the need of a detail instruction reveals either the inexperience, the immaturity or the mental deficiency of the one being instructed. This truth is valid in the case of a society which finds itself "robotised" by its own laws due to its own self-helplessness, the Church not being an exception. In the final phase, that of humanization, society liberates itself from itself, for it is no longer in want of the laws of its infancy. In this situation the minimum of laws is required in the pursuance of its own development. Needless to say, the full attainment of the humanization of human consciousness is a myth.

Nevertheless, a society in its evolution, by virtue of its inner destiny, moves constantly to a lesser self-dependency on the law. The same must be said with respect to Church legislation. The stage of humanization thus registers, ontologically speaking, the fulfillment of the absolute objective freedom of human consciousness. Freed from inner estrangement and entanglement, the human mind reaches out and operates out of its own inner authentic freedom. In short, it lives the evangelical ideal to the full.

No civilization is worthy of its name, we believe, which does not find its source and aim in the "christianization" of human consciousness. The concept of civilization must be formulated on the rationality, conscientiousness and sociability as constituting three essential qualities of human consciousness. It is further necessary that an equipoise be maintained among them. The endorsement of one with the exclusion of the other two results in degradation of human dignity. Thus, the insistence on the exclusivity of the rationality of the human being postulates rationalism, positivism, or empiricism, which in their respective forms foster atheism; the belief in conscientiousness with the denial of the rest likely leads to manichaeism and spiritualism -- such were the Paulicians, Bogmils, Cathari and Albigenses; the exclusive indoctrination of the sociability of human consciousness has given sufficient evidence of its nefarious results; political totalitarianism or authoritarianism of the state is usually the outcome. The monumental achievement of Christianity was that it discovered these three essential qualities in human consciousness and endorsed the equipoise between them. Thus it may be said that human consciousness can discover no point in its aspiration of explicating its inherent authentic nature that is not already enshrined in the teaching of the "Word made flesh."

The Person as Member of the Common Priesthood

The search for self-identity is the phenomenon of our age. Its impact is deeply felt in all aspects of life, both private and public. Human rights, women's liberation, responsible parenthood, parent-child relationship, and many other issues, are the outcome of a new outlook on the meaning of individual human identification, which in turn has provoked a threatening crisis of authority and order. The twentieth century witnessed almost from its commencement a steady acceleration of human individualization expressed and nurtured, at first, by social and political malcontent. The social conflicts, with the rise of Labour Unions in the mid-nineteenth century down to the present-day coups d'etat in almost every part of the globe, two world-devastating wars, and skirmishes constantly happening in different parts of the world, constitute an authentic syndrome of human consciousness in search of itself.

The present world-wide phenomenon traces its origin to the French Revolution, the philosophy of which is found rooted in the memorable three-word motto, "Liberté, egalité, fraternité." In the turmoils of the eighteenth and nineteenth centuries, the individual sought personal identification by means of and through the group. "Fraternité" and "egalité" were intended as a presupposition of the desired "liberté," that is the full expression of one's potentialities, and consequently self-actualization. The desired socio-political aim of the French upheaval has not as yet been attained. The old aspirations and yearnings of human consciousness in the explication of itself are not in the least satiated. It must be said, moreover, that the French Revolution could never completely satisfy the human mind, for its philosophy failed to bring the person in touch with the core of his own being. Of course, that was not the intention of the Revolution. The human being, in spite of the amelioration of social condition still feverishly seeks himself in the deepest strata of his own being. The ever-growing interest in psychology attests to this stark truth.

Although interest in psychology had been steadily growing, particularly since the late nineteenth century, the human individual had to learn the hard way, sometimes with horrendous mistakes and disappointments. With the turn of the century, the human consciousness seems to have desisted from pursuing the intended individualization through the group, in line with the creed of the French Revolution and of the Labour Unions, and to have turned its attention to a new philosophy. Human consciousness decided to find itself and be itself by losing itself in complete oblivion in the herd instinct. The Russian Revolution which ushered in present-day Communism, the Spanish Civil War, Hitler's Germany and Mussolini's Fascism had aimed at this idea, resulting in carnage of millions of human souls.

After the Second World War fiasco, the reason for dismissal of the theory of the herd instinct as an end in itself was compelling. The human mind saw for itself that one's absolute surrender to a national totalitarian supremacy led it to a stage of brutal savagery. Thus human consciousness turned its attention to the search for its own self-identification by committing itself by itself beyond national boundaries.

The dignity of the human person became the universal post-war outcry. The metaphysical understanding of human personality became more sacred than the state itself and bound to no national or political configuration. Thus the spectacle of "l'uomo universale" testifies that the universal human consciousness is emerging from the tribal understanding of itself, that of national imperialism, into a deeper awareness of its inherent universality, that of pure and simple humanity. The cosmological figure of the human person is today acknowledged, at least in principle, by many State-constitutions. The "Universal Declaration of Human Rights" issued by the General Assembly of the United Nations on December 10th, 1948, constitutes the *magna charta* in the gradual realization of "l'uomo universale," an image of human dignity pivoted on natural law. Indeed, it is our firm belief that this universal movement will eventually lead to the revival of natural law, the recognition of which will necessarily imply its supremacy over the authority of the State as the sole source of justice. Human laws will retain their binding force insofar as they rightly interpret natural law in particular exigencies.

The identification of the human person accepted in this perspective, if not controlled with adequate measures based on psychological, civic and ethical criteria, will in all certainty enhance self-idolization, and consequently end in self-atrophy. Self-idolization clusters in itself self-complacency which can never be fully attained if not in the delusional world. Frustration, therefore, dereliction and total psychological alienation are bound to tarnish human behaviour and curb the human pursuit of self-actualization.

This instinctualistic and materialistic frame of mind offers a major setback in the implementation of ultimate human aspiration, which is the gradual unfolding of its christological nature. The awareness of self-actualization, its growth and completion require a constant striving toward maturity on the lines of ideals, principles and values formulated by Christian religion. Some are unable to grasp even the common standards of morality, others fall back because of pressure required by such standards. The whole concept of human dignity, if not properly featured on the eschatological dimension of human existence, will eventually turn into an avenue of delinquency, corruption, and chaos both for the individual and for society at large. Freud contributed, to a considerable extent, to instilling in the minds of many this false understanding of human actualization. In the present stage of human maturation, in order that human self-development may not be degraded into "laissez-aller," there ought to be an authority external to the individual human consciousness which provides a corps of directives of human conduct and attitude.

The human mind operating on a materialistic premise will always fall short of its self-actualization. Human consciousness, seemingly frustrated in attaining the desired self-fulfillment, is in search of another avenue of self-satisfaction which is known to be easily attainable. Thus the human individual, as Karl Marx remarks, obtained freedom from human dependence; he shattered the patriarchal social pattern of the "ancien regime," only to achieve in the bourgeois society "personal independence founded on material dependence";[1] "personal power (has) changed into material power";[2] "both his power over society and his association with it (are) carried in his pocket."[3] The human mind projecting its own self into a creature outside itself automatically alienates itself from itself; by identifying itself with an external object, it loses its own basic identity. Since the object replacing the self signifies social power, human consciousness obscures its inherent sociability; a socio-psychological autism is likely to ensue; it creates a "Robinson Crusoe" image of itself which is antithetical to its own nature.

Thus the process of humanization of human consciousness is not, in the least, immune to hazards and errors. Life struggle is felt more compelling and challenging than ever before since the individual now faces life on his own. Day by day one is bound to renew and replenish one's stamina to cope maturely with the humdrum of daily life. The foundations of a new society established on the equality and uniqueness of the individual human being are being laid down in our times. With the opening of a new era in human emancipation, however, human decisions are beset with imminent dangers which, if not confronted properly, may result in the most serious dilemmas that the human person has ever faced -- "nimia fiducia calamitati solet esse."

The Church in Vatican Council II groomed herself for this global human scenario. The Church, cognizant of the demands and dangers which this gigantic evolution creates for the human individual, initiated Vatican Council II with the sole intent of facilitating the universal human pursuit of evangelical enlightenment. The Conciliar Fathers in their message to humanity wrote apropos: "It is far from true that because we cling to Christ we are diverted from earthly duties and toils. On the contrary, faith, hope, and the love of Christ impel us to serve our brothers, thereby patterning ourselves after the example of the Divine Teacher, who "came

---

[1] *Grundrisse*, Trans. by D. McLellan, London, 1972, p. 67.

[2] Ibid., p. 66.

[3] Ibid.

not to be served but to serve." Hence, the Church too was not born to dominate but to serve . . . As we undertake our work, therefore, we would emphasize whatever concerns the dignity of man, whatever contributes to a genuine community of peoples . . . the Church is supremely necessary for the modern world if injustices and unworthy inequalities are to be denounced, and if the true order of affairs and of values is to be restored, so that man's life can become more human according to the standards of the Gospel."[4]

Vatican Council II appears as a towering milestone in the history of the Church. One of its paramount contributions is the impetus given by the Council to the revitalization of the common priesthood. Granted this acknowledgement, the Council is far from being a *creatio ex nihilo,* a unique event without precedent. There is nothing in the ongoing process of the human consciousness which emerges *ex abrupto.* Human consciousness, whether in its state of nature or in its state of grace, contains *ab initio,* albeit implicitly, all that is explicated in its own evolution. The being always points forward to a phase of self-unfolding higher and richer than the one preceding it, but the idea, the *causa formalis,* remains the basis, all-inclusive and unchanging; thus the result (*causa finalis*) is the principle (*causa formalis*). Each generation inherits the principles, values, ideas, and aspirations of its predecessor, interprets and transforms them according to the stage at which the human consciousness has arrived in its humanization process; thus every generation contains in embryo the one succeeding it. This is what we call the inner destiny of human consciousness. The Vatican reform cannot be perused and explained, if not in this perspective.

The reality and theology of the common priesthood are not the novel discovery of Vatican Council II. The existence of the common priesthood is a dogma proclaimed unmistakably in the Sacred Scriptures and uninterruptedly endorsed by the Fathers of the Church.[5] Saint Peter teaches

---

[4] *Message to Humanity, issued at the Beginning of the Second Vatican Council by its Fathers, with the Endorsement of the Supreme Pontiff,* Abbott Translation, pp. 4-6.

[5] DABIN, PAUL, *Le Sacerdoce Royal des Fidèles dans les Livres Saints,* Paris, 1941; *Le Sacerdoce Royal des Fidèles dans la Tradition ancienne et moderne,* Paris, 1950.

that the redeemed human family is a chosen race, a royal priesthood, a holy nation, a people set apart.[6] Saint Paul in his letters mentions the gifts of God being distributed among the believers.[7] The Church from the start was fully conscious that the Spirit of the Lord activates the individual member for the building up of the Mystical Body, not only mystically, but also ministerially.[8] The social awareness and concern of the early Christians is witnessed to, particularly in the institution of the diaconate.[9] The best compliment the early Christians received from a Roman emperor was that of Julianus the Apostate (361-363) who openly confessed: "It is shameful to us (pagans) that no beggar should be found among the Jews, and that the impious Galilaeans should support not only their own poor, but ours also, while these last appear destitute of all assistance from ourselves."[10] Since time immemorial hospitals, orphanages, guilds, schools, and other charitable organizations were erected in the bosom of the Church;[11] these reveal a common priesthood fully alive, truthful to itself, conscious of being a community of faith and action in the service of the human being. The charism of *diakonia* exercised by the common priesthood in the pastoral sphere persisted, needless to say, throughout the centuries, down to our times. The Council, *per se,* did nothing other than energize and foster the pastoral charism of the common priesthood which, since the apostolic age,

---

[6] 1 Pet. 2:9

[7] Rom. 12:4-8; 1 Cor. 12: 4-11.

[8] EASTWOOD, CYRIL, *The Royal Priesthood of the Faithful,* London, 1963, pp.56-57, 59-61, 66-70, 73-75, 181.

[9] Acts 6:1-6

[10] KEIGHTLEY, THOMAS, *History of the Roman Empire,* New York, 1848, p.341.

[11] C.,*De episcopis et orphanotrophis et brephotrophis et xenodochiis et asceteriis et monachis et privilegio eorum et castrensi peculio et de nuptiis clericorum vetitis seu permissis,* 1, 3; KURTSCHEID, BERTRANDUS, *Historia Iuris Canonici -- Historia Institutorum,* Romae, 1951, pars I, chap.23, pp.94-98; pars II, chap.17, pp.219-220, 222; pars III, chap.15, pp.306-308; DE ANGELIS, SERAPHINUS, *De Fidelium Associationibus,* Neapoli, 1959, vol 1, pp.2-3; BURCKHARDT, JACOB, *The Age of Constantine the Great,* Trans. Moses Hadas, New York, 1967, pp.310,321.

never did lose its vitality, and which accommodated itself to the needs of the times.

The activity of the common priesthood in the cultic sphere was much less pronounced. Down to the eve of the Second Vatican Council its activity in this regard was curtailed to a state of passivity, ignorance, total dependency, and indolence. In spite of this, however, the charism of the common priesthood was never dormant, as can be witnessed by the existence, throughout the centuries, of confraternities and other associations of the faithful with a cultic aim.

The common priesthood never failed to make itself felt as an essential component through its *diakonia* in the life of the Church. It must be said, however, that the general spectrum of the stratification of the Church down to the eve of Vatican Council II was similar to the one characteristic of the *ancien regime* in which the theocratic-descending form of government looked at the individual as a mere recipient of favours with no autonomous function within the community. The seigneurial ideology of the Church could not see the faithful as other than passive recipients, as Friedrich Herr remarks: "The Church of the latter Middle Ages was becoming completely institutionalized and completely clerical: the laity were regarded as little more than serfs, as slaves even, 'instruments' whose function was to yield willing obedience. (It is interesting that this word 'instrument', used by Aristotle with reference to slaves, is still retained, for example, by Catholic Action, to describe the distinctive role of the laity)."[12] In the Second Vatican Council, the Church saw herself being transformed from a system of absolute monarchism and extreme hierarchical stratification into a model of *communio* between the ministerial priesthood

---

[12] *The Intellectual History of Europe*, Trans.Jonathan Steinberg, New York, 1966, pp.274-275; cf. GUITTON, JEAN, *The Church and the Laity*, Trans. Malachy Gerard Carroll, Montreal ,Canada, 1965, p.38: "The gap which, by the Middle Ages, divided the clergy from the laity, because of the hierarchical structure of the Church and because of the feudal structure of society, became an abyss at the time of the Reformation. An attempt to fill in that abyss has begun only in our times with the Second Vatican Council"; MOHLER, JAMES A., *The Origin and Evolution of the Priesthood*, Staten Island, N. Y. 1970, pp.105-107, 111-112, 115, 119; EASTWOOD, C., *The Royal Priesthood . . . ,pp.81-82,* 87-90, 103.

The Person as Member of the Common Priesthood

and the common priesthood. This transformation gave the lead to the charism of the common priesthood to bloom in all its magnitude.

With the rejuvenation commenced by Vatican Council II, the holistic reality of the Church, the people of God, has been reinstalled to its pristine and authentic significance. In this light, the Church is presented in *Lumen gentium:* "Christ the Lord, High Priest taken from among men" (cf. Heb. 5:1-5), "made a kingdom and priests to God his Father" (Apoc. 1:6; cf. 5:9-10) out of this new people. The baptized, by regeneration and the anointing of the Holy Spirit, are consecrated into a spiritual house and a holy priesthood. Thus through all those works befitting Christian men they can offer spiritual sacrifices and proclaim the power of Him who has called them out of darkness into His marvelous light (cf. 1 Pet. 2:4-10). Therefore all the disciples of Christ, persevering in prayer and praising God (cf. Acts 2:42-47), should present themselves as living sacrifices holy and pleasing to God (cf. Rom. 12:1). Everywhere on earth they must bear witness to Christ and give an answer to those who seek an account of that hope of eternal life which is in them (cf. 1 Pet. 3:15).[13] A synthesis of this theology is found in canon 204, §1,: "Christ's faithful are those who, since they are incorporated into Christ through baptism, are constituted the people of God. For this reason, they participate in their own way in the priestly, prophetic and kingly office of Christ. They are called, each according to his or her particular condition, to exercise the mission which God entrusted to the Church to fulfill in the world." The holistic image of the Church is further clarified in juridical terms in canon 208. This canon maintains in unequivocal terms that the *ecclesia,* as a holistic reality, is uniquely based on a genuine equality of dignity and action of all who are reborn in Christ. Thus the canon states: "Flowing from their rebirth in Christ, there is a genuine equality of dignity and action among all of Christ's faithful. Because of this equality they all contribute, each according to his or her own condition and office, to the building up of the Body of Christ."

The genuine equality of dignity and action which makes of every baptized an active participant in the Royal priesthood of Christ, does not,

---

[13] N.10, pp.26-27.

in any way, deny the twofold classification of priesthood in the Church. The common priesthood and the ministerial priesthood are interrelated so as to form one interlocked reality. "Each of them in its own special way is a participation in the one priesthood of Christ."[14] Nevertheless, "they differ from one another in essence and not only in degree."[15]

What the Council insists upon is that it pertains to the intrinsic nature of the common priesthood, together with the ministerial priesthood, to carry out the *mandatum divinum* in the building up of the Body of Christ and in the christianization of the human family. The right to equality of dignity equally entails the obligation to action. A certain degree of psychological, spiritual and doctrinal maturity is expected in the common priesthood. In this manner, all the more the sense of belonging ingrained in individual Christian consciousness enables one to become morally what one is ontologically through rebirth in Christ; in like manner the individual Christian may assume the ecclesial responsibilities which ensue from one's own personal condition and from the office entrusted to him or her by the Church. The Decree, *Ad gentes divinitus,* in fact, makes the following remark: "The Church has not been truly established, and is not yet fully alive, nor is it a perfect sign of Christ among men, unless there exists a laity worthy of the name working along with the hierarchy. For the gospel cannot be deeply imprinted on the talents, life, and work of any people without the active presence of laymen. Therefore, even in the very founding of a Church, the greatest attention is to be paid to raising up a mature Christian laity."[16] A statement of emperor M. Aurelius Antoninus, "A man then must stand erect, not be kept erect by others,"[17] suits the Christian of the Vatican era who must assume personal responsibility as a conscious,

---

[14] Loc. cit., n. 10, p. 27.

[15] Ibid., cf. canons 205; 207, §1.

[16] n. 21, pp. 610-611 cf. *Lumen gentium,* nn. 9-17, pp. 24-37; nn. 30-38, pp. 56-65; *Apostolicam actuositatem,* pp. 489-521; *Sacrosanctum concilium,* pp. 137-178; *Gaudium et spes,* pp. 199-308; *Unitatis redintegratio,* pp. 341-366.

[17] *The Thoughts of the Emperor M. Aurelius Antoninus,* Trans. by George Long, New York, III, p. 61.

intelligent and active participant in the life of the Church. "Each individual layman must stand before the world as a witness to the resurrection and life of the Lord Jesus and as a sign that God lives. As a body and individually, the laity must do their part to nourish the world with spiritual fruits (cf. Gal. 5:22), and to spread abroad in it that spirit by which are animated those poor, meek, and peacemaking men whom the Lord in the gospel calls blessed (cf. Mt. 5:3-9)." In a word, "What the soul is to the body, let Christians be to the world."[18]

In the post-conciliar era, the Church has slowly introduced the faithful into the core of her liturgical and pastoral activity. In the new Code of canon law a repertoire of rights and duties is found aimed to specify the *capacitas agendi* of the faithful, appropriate to the stage of maturation which the universal Christian consciousness has so far attained in its psychological, social, political, intellectual and spiritual segments. The present juridical status of the faithful is a realization of the concept that each individual member is a "living and active part" in the Church. The status of the faithful is so vital that one's contribution not only interrelates with, but also implements and completes, and in some instances also substitutes for, the ministerial priesthood. Only when it involves the powers of Sacred Orders does the Christian participate as a recipient. Thus, in the whole spectrum of the Church's activity as delineated in the new Code of canon law, "the member who fails to make his proper contribution to the development of the Church must be said to be useful neither to the Church nor to himself."[19] The Code, moreover, perpetuates the vision cherished by Vatican Council II that whatever the lay apostolate accomplishes in any level of the Church's activity has its dimension in the *Ecclesia;* thus, the Church is indeed the *locus operandi* for the Christian, from where he or she can reach out to all humans (canon 204, §1).

Canon 96 enshrines the source and the gist of the *capacitas agendi* of the faithful. The canon states: "By baptism one is incorporated into the

---

[18] *Lumen gentium*, n. 38, p. 65.

[19] *Apostolicam actuositatem*, n. 2, p. 491 cf. n.6, p. 496.

Church of Christ and constituted a person in it, with the duties and the rights which, in accordance with each one's status, are proper to Christians, in so far as they are in ecclesiastical communion and unless a lawfully issued sanction intervenes."

The redemptive death of Christ which happened but once in history is renewed in the actual administration of baptism. The human person through the sacramental death and resurrection with the Lord enters into the sphere of His saving activity; the actual mystery of redemption becomes the property of the soul in view of the ultimate glorification. Baptism was willed by the Lord as the gateway of Christian life and foundation of the discipleship.[20] In juridical terms, through baptism one becomes a juridical person, *capacitas essendi,* titular of rights and duties.

In accordance with individual condition and status, one enjoys the *capacitas agendi*, a juridical capacity of partaking actively in the sacramental, liturgical and pastoral life of the Church. However, canon 96 goes on to say that, although one is acknowledged as *capacitas essendi* by virtue of baptism, one's *capacitas agendi* may be curtailed due to lack of full communion with the Catholic Church or due to an inflicted sanction. Canon 96 does not, in any way, deny the dogmatic truth on the source and nature of the common priesthood. Baptism must remain the pivotal point in the conceptualization and realization of the common priesthood subsisting in the Christian Church. However, canon 96 points out that baptism by itself does not suffice for the full realization of the common priesthood, as far as the Catholic Church is concerned. Indeed, there exist realities which curtail the common priesthood from attaining the fullness of self-expression. It is in this context that the *capacitas agendi* of the faithful is *normally* understood in the Code of canon law.

---

[20] *Lumen gentium,* n.7, p.20; nn. 10, 11, pp. 27-28; *Sacrosanctum concilium,* n. 14, p. 144; *Apostolicam actuositatem,* n. 3, p. 492; *.Unitatis redintegratio,* n. 22, p. 364.

Rights in General of the Common Priesthood

Under this heading are grouped the rights which are basic to the *capacitas agendi* of the common priesthood.

Fundamental to all the rights enumerated in the following paragraphs is the right of the faithful to receive the integrity and unity of the faith to be believed. This sacred commitment weighs primarily on the Bishop[21] who is bound to shepherd his flock with great solicitude[22] towards holiness by his personal Christian life, by constant instruction, and by the celebration of the sacraments.[23]

Consequential to the above fundamental right are the following prerogatives of the faithful:

"Christ's faithful are at liberty to make known their needs, especially their spiritual needs, and their wishes to the Pastors of the Church" (canon 212, §2).

"They have the right, indeed at times the duty, in keeping with their knowledge, competence and position, to manifest to the sacred Pastors their views on matters which concern the good of the Church. They have the right also to make their views known to others of Christ's faithful, but in doing so they must always respect the integrity of faith and morals, show due reverence to the Pastors and take into account both the common good and the dignity of individuals" (canon 212, §3).

Ancillary to these last is canon 1222, §2, according to which the Bishop, in giving permission for a particular church to be used for a secular purpose, must be sure that the good of souls would not be harmed by the said transfer.

---

[21] Canons 386, §2; 392, §1, 2.

[22] Canon 383, §1.

[23] Canons 387, 386, §1.

Right of the Faithful to Christian Education

The tremendous urgency for religious instruction caused by the awakening of the common priesthood, can hardly be over-estimated. The vitality of the desired lay apostolate necessarily presupposes a well-instructed laity. One of the major concerns of the Council was precisely the religious education and formation of the faithful, first in its catechetical stage and later in a more scientific manner. The new Code sees to it that the prospect of the Council should be implemented in all desired levels.

The content of canons 217 and 229, §1, serve as an introduction to the theme. Canon 217 prescribes: "Since Christ's faithful are called by baptism to lead a life in harmony with the gospel teaching, they have the right to a christian education, which genuinely teaches them to strive for the maturity of the human person and at the same time to know and live the mystery of salvation" (cf. canon 213). Acknowledgement of the same right is encountered in canon 229, §1: "Lay people have the duty and the right to acquire the knowledge of christian teaching which is appropriate to each one's capacity and condition, so that they may be able to live according to this teaching, to proclaim it and if necessary to defend it, and may be capable of playing their part in the exercise of the apostolate."

Therefore the need for catechesis, especially to the young, requires no explanation (canon 774, §1), particularly when it involves the reception of individual sacraments (canon 843, §2). Parents are the first catechetical instructors of their own children. "Because they gave life to their children parents have the most serious obligation and the right to educate them. It is therefore primarily the responsibility of christian parents to ensure the christian education of their children in accordance with the teaching of the Church" (canon 226, §2; cf. canons 774, §2; 1136; 793, §1, 2). Consequently, it weighs on the parents, and on those who take their place, "to send their children to those schools which will provide for their catholic education. If they cannot do this, they are bound to ensure the proper catholic education of their children outside the school" (canon 798). For this reason "Parents must have a real freedom in their choice of schools" (canon 797).

The right of the faithful to Christian instruction entails at the same time the right of the Church "to establish and to direct schools for any field of study or of any kind and grade" (canon 800, §1). She also insists that "Christ's faithful are to promote catholic schools, doing everything possible to help in establishing and maintaining them" (canon 800, §2), or to strive to secure that civil laws "provide a religious and moral education in the schools that is in accord with the conscience of the parents" (canon 799; cf. canon 797).

The appropriate formation of the laity in sacred sciences also occupied the attention of the Council.[24] The lawful freedom of inquiry and of expression nurtures the ecclesial maturation of the faithful, enhances one's sense of identity, and invigorates one's feeling of usefulness in the life of the Church. Obedience to the magisterium should not reflect ignorance, apathy, passivity and infantile reverence, but responsible, intelligent, knowledgeable, active and willful endeavour of the human mind for the truth.[25] Imbued with the required knowledge, the Christian more readily feels himself or herself an integral part of the Church. Thus the faithful "have the right to acquire that fuller knowledge of the sacred sciences which is taught in ecclesiastical universities or faculties or in institutes of religious sciences, attending lectures there and acquiring academic degrees" (canon 229, §2). The topic is taken up again in the section on Catholic universities (canon 811, §1, 2). As a correlation to this right is the prerogative of the faithful to involve themselves in the investigation of truth and to be allowed just freedom of expression. Thus canon 218 prescribes: "Those who are engaged in fields of sacred study have a just freedom to research matters in which they are expert and to express themselves prudently concerning them, with due allegiance to the magisterium of the Church" (cf. canon 386, §2).

---

[24] *Gaudium et spes*, n. 62, p. 270.

[25] Ibid, n. 43, p. 244.

Right of the Faithful to Receive the Sacraments

In spite of her many deficiencies and distortions of vision which crept into the ecclesiastical government, never did the Church ignore or deny this right to the faithful. Perhaps, the old adage, *sacramenta propter homines,* genuinely testifies to the traditional and uninterrupted attitude of the Church in this line of sacred duty. It stands to reason, therefore, that no spectacular innovations can be expected in the new codification.

Canon 843, §1, constitutes the premise of the present theme. It states: "Sacred ministers may not deny the sacraments to those who opportunely ask for them, are properly disposed and are not prohibited by law from receiving them" (cf. canon 213).

Thus, the faithful who are "not forbidden by law may and must be admitted to holy communion" (canon 912). On Sundays and on each holy day they are entitled to *missa pro populo,* to be celebrated by the diocesan Bishop (canon 388, §1-4) and by the pastor (canon 534, §1, 3).

In the sacrament of penance the penitent with rightful disposition has the right to the absolution of his or her sins (canon 980). It is a serious obligation on the part of those who are in the care of souls to provide for the hearing of confessions of the faithful who reasonably request confession, and to arrange for confessions on days and times convenient to the faithful (canon 986, §1). "In an urgent necessity, every confessor is bound to hear the confessions of Christ's faithful, and in danger of death every priest is so obliged" (canon 986, §2).

With regard to the sacrament of Confirmation, the obligation falls first on the diocesan Bishop who "is bound to ensure that the sacrament of confirmation is conferred upon his subjects who duly and reasonably request it" (canon 885, §1).

The right to marry has been mentioned in a previous presentation (canon 1058).

Finally, there is the right of the faithful to receive the Anointing of the Sick which is normally accompanied by the Viaticum. The Code insists rather on the obligation of the pastor to administer the sacrament to those in need of it: "All priests to whom has been committed the care of souls, have the obligation and the right to administer the anointing of the sick to those of the faithful entrusted to their pastoral care. For a reasonable cause, any other priest may administer this sacrament if he has the consent, at least presumed, of the aforementioned priest" (canon 1003, §2).

The Involvement of the Faithful in the Liturgical Life of the Church

The radical revision in liturgy brought about by the Constitution, *Sacrosanctum Concilium,* can hardly be fully appreciated. It is not an overexaggeration to maintain that the liturgical role of the faithful in the pre-Vatican Church did not proceed beyond that of a stranger or of a silent spectator. In contrast to this state of affairs, the Constitution took as its central theme the dogmatic truth that the active involvement of the faithful in the liturgical life of the Church flows from the nature itself of the common priesthood.[26] Upon this assumption, and in implementation of it, the Constitution saw to it that the faithful grew from passive bystanders into full participants, capable of experiencing intelligently, actively and fruitfully the worship of the Church.[27] Of paramount importance also was the revision of the liturgical complexus in a manner that allowed liturgical celebration to adapt itself to the native genius of a particular culture.[28]

The liturgical evolution did not end with the implementation of the said Constitution. The post-Vatican Church went beyond what seems to have been the prospect of the Constitution. The *Motu proprio, Ministeria quaedam,* in its revision of minor orders brought forth a further advancement of the laity's role in the liturgy. In substitution of minor orders and the subdiaconate, the ministries of lector and of acolyte were

---

[26] *Sacrosanctum concilium,* n. 14, p. 144.

[27] Ibid., n. 11, p. 143.

[28] nn. 37-40, pp. 151-152; nn. 116-119, pp. 172-173.

instituted into which the layman may be installed.[29] With the institution of "Extraordinary ministers of communion" women were allowed to participate in the distribution of holy communion. It is also worth noting that the Constitution, *Lumen gentium*,[30] and the Decree, *Apostolicam actuositatem*,[31] specified that the faithful may substitute for the priest in providing sacred services to the brethren in faith when extraordinary circumstances call for it.

"The sanctifying office is exercised principally by Bishops" (canon 835,§1) who by divine institution are constituted priests of sacred worship (canon 375,§1). The office of sanctification itself belongs to the whole body, the Church. The faithful, by reason of their baptism, share in the priestly adoration of the Church, "for in one spirit we were all baptized into one body, whether Jews or gentiles, whether slaves or free; and we were all given to drink of one spirit. For the body is not one member, but many."[32] Thus the faithful, with the reception of baptism, receive a twofold *mandatum* of sanctification: through personal holiness the baptized enriches the Mystical Body itself as well as imbues and perfects the universal human consciousness with the spirit of the gospel in its ongoing process of humanization. "All Christ's faithful, each according to his or her own condition, must make a wholehearted effort to lead a holy life, and to promote the growth of the Church and its continual sanctification" (canon 210). "They have also, according to the condition of each, the special obligation to permeate and perfect the temporal order of things with the spirit of the gospel. In this way, particularly in conducting secular business and exercising secular functions, they are to give witness to Christ" (canon 225, §2).

The doctrine of the universal priesthood of the faithful is intrinsically related to the doctrine of the unifying nature of the liturgical

---

[29] AAS, LXIV (1972) pp. 531-532, art. 5, 6, 3.

[30] n. 35, p. 62.

[31] n. 1, p. 490.

[32] 1 Cor. 12:13-14.

celebrations. Liturgy, as the public official service of the Church, pertains to the whole body of the Church, the ministerial priesthood and the common priesthood united into one inseparable reality. Liturgy manifests and at the same time solidifies the wholeness of the Church. Despite their hierarchical character, liturgical celebrations are the most authentic expression of the oneness of the Church. Thus even when the physical presence of the common priesthood is lacking, the moral presence of the same still forms an integral part of the liturgical action so as to be the full and genuine expression of the Church through her ordained priest in the sanctification at once of herself and that of the human race. Apropos canon 837, §1, teaches: "Liturgical actions are not private but are celebrations of the Church itself as the 'sacrament of unity', that is, the holy people united and ordered under the Bishops. Accordingly, they concern the whole body of the Church, making it known and influencing it. They affect individual members of the Church in ways that vary according to orders, role and actual participation." It is precisely because of this dogmatic presupposition regarding the ecclesial reality of the Church's sanctifying office that "the other members of Christ's faithful have their own part in this sanctifying office, each in his or her own way actively sharing in liturgical celebrations, particularly in the Eucharist" (canon 835, §4). Consequential to this truth, "since liturgical matters by their very nature call for a community celebration, they are, as far as possible, to be celebrated in the presence of Christ's faithful and with their active participation" (canon 837, §2).

Thus baptism entitles the faithful to take part in the sacramental, liturgical, and pastoral life in Christ, an office which proceeds from the one Spirit and rests upon faith in the one Spirit (canon 836). "Incorporated into the Church through baptism, the faithful are consecrated by the baptismal character to the exercise of the cult of the Christian religion. Reborn as sons of God, they must confess before men the faith which they have received from God through the Church."[33] Special mention is made by the Code on the sanctifying office enshrined in the family (canon 835, §4),

---

[33] *Lumen gentium*, n. 11, p. 28; cf. n. 7, p. 20.

the domestic church,[34] which stands as a "special gift among the People of God"[35] and in which "Christianity pervades a whole way of life and ever increasingly transforms it";[36] hence "Christian husbands and wives are co-operators in grace and witnesses of faith on behalf of each other, their children, and all others in their household."[37]

The Rite forms the basic and determining factor of one's participation in the liturgical life of the Church. Through the reception of baptism one automatically belongs to an autonomous ritual Church. By Rite is meant a complexus of discipline and rituals proper to an autonomous ritual Church in union with the See of Rome. The Rite may be defined as a particular expression of the faith while retaining the uniformity in essentials and in faith with the Catholic dogma. Therefore, once our attention is concentrated on the Code of canon law of the latin Rite, the following exposition is directed to the rights and duties of the faithful belonging to this Rite.

Fundamental to the present theme is canon 214 which reads: "Christ's faithful have the right to worship God according to the provisions of their own rite approved by the lawful Pastors of the Church." Correlative to this rite stands the obligation of the diocesan Bishop to provide for the spiritual needs of the faithful of a different rite in his diocese either by means of priests or parishes of the same rite, or by an episcopal Vicar (canon 383, §2).

In the choice of Rite, any candidate for baptism who is fourteen years of age has the right to be baptized in the Rite of any autonomous ritual Church, in which case the person belongs to the Church which he or she has chosen (canon 111, §2). In case of children under the age of fourteen the prescription of canon 111, §1, must be observed: "Through the reception of baptism a child becomes a member of the latin Church if the

---

[34] *Apostolicam actuositatem*, n. 11, pp. 502-503; *Lumen gentium*, n.11, p.29.

[35] *Lumen gentium*, n. 11, p. 29.

[36] Ibid., n. 35, p. 61.

[37] *Apostolicam actuositatem*, n. 11, p. 502; cf. *Lumen gentium*, n.41, p. 69.

parents belong to that Church or, should one of them not belong to it, if they have both by common consent chosen that the child be baptised in the latin Church: if that common consent is lacking, the child becomes a member of the ritual Church to which the father belongs." After the reception of baptism one is allowed to move from one autonomous ritual Church to another according to the norms laid down in canon 112, §1: "1. those who have obtained permission from the Apostolic See; 2. a spouse who, on entering marriage or during its course, has declared that he or she is transferring to the autonomous ritual Church of the other spouse; on the dissolution of the marriage, however, that person may freely return to the latin Church; 3. the children of those mentioned in nn. 1 and 2 who have not completed their fourteenth year, and likewise in a mixed marriage the children of a catholic party who has lawfully transferred to another ritual Church; on completion of their fourteenth year, however, they may return to the latin Church."

When it comes to the liturgical participation of the faithful, the Code places emphasis on the responsibility of the pastor. Canon 528, §2, gives a precise sketch of how the liturgical life of the parochial community should evolve. The Eucharist is to be upheld as the centre of the parochial life in all its segments since it is the source and aim of all the other sacraments. Canon 899, §2, teaches apropos: "In the eucharistic assembly, the people of God are called together under the presidency of the Bishop or of a priest authorised by him, who acts in the person of Christ. All the faithful present, whether clerics or lay people, unite to participate in their own way, according to their various orders and liturgical roles." Therefore, "Christ's faithful are to hold the blessed Eucharist in the highest honour. They should take an active part in the celebration of the most august Sacrifice of the Mass; they should receive the sacrament with great devotion and frequently, and should reverence it with the greatest adoration . . . " (canon 898). Although canon 928 allows certain freedom in the choice of language in celebrating Mass, we cannot see how the desired intelligent and active participation of the faithful in sacred liturgy could be attained unless the vernacular be adopted. Indeed, we believe the use of the vernacular in sacred liturgy, Mass not being excluded, intrinsically follows from the right of the faithful to participate in the liturgy, especially when the subsequent canons are brought into consideration. Finally, in fulfilling his office the pastor is to see to it that the faithful entrusted to his care are led to a prayerful life, and are encouraged to an intelligent and active participation in sacred liturgy (canon 528, §2).

As earlier indicated, the ministries of lector and acolyte were established by the *Motu proprio, Ministeria quaedam,* in view of major active participation of the faithful in the liturgy. In the pursuance of the intended aim, the new Code provides several canons concerning these ministries as well as other circumstances where the faithful, though not installed as ministers, may function in that capacity.

In reference to the ministries of lector and acolyte, canon 230, §1, establishes: "Lay men, whose age and talents meet the requirements prescribed by decree of the Episcopal Conference, can be given the stable ministry of lector and of acolyte, through the prescribed liturgical rite . . . " This norm, however, does not restrict others among the faithful from assuming a temporary assignment of lector in liturgical functions (canon 230, §2). Moreover, any of the faithful may be entrusted with other roles, such as commentator, cantor, master of ceremonies, which form part of the liturgical action (canon 230, §2). The Code contemplates also situations where the necessity of the Church warrants that lay persons, although they are not installed in the ministries, may supply certain functions proper to the said ministries. Thus they may "exercise the ministry of the word, preside over liturgical prayers, confer baptism and distribute Holy Communion, in accordance with the provisions of the law" (canon 230, §3). It is worth noting that the extraordinary minister, whether installed acolyte or not (canon 910, §2), may, if the need arises, carry the Viaticum to the sick (canon 911, §2). Moreover, "in special circumstances the minister of exposition and deposition alone, but without the blessing, is an acolyte, and extraordinary minister of holy communion, or another person deputed by the local Ordinary, in accordance with the regulations of the diocesan Bishop" (canon 943). Of great liturgical and pastoral importance is the prescription of canon 1248, §2, in instances when the priest is not available to sanctify Sunday or a holy day with the celebration of the Eucharist. In similar circumstances, the Christian community takes over and celebrates together a liturgical function as prescribed by the local Bishop. During this para-liturgy Holy Communion may also be distributed. Hence the canon: "If it is impossible to assist at a eucharistic celebration, either because no sacred minister is available or for some other grave reason, the faithful are strongly recommended to take part in a liturgy of the Word, if there be such in the parish church or some other sacred place, which is celebrated in accordance with the provisions laid down by the diocesan Bishop; or to spend an appropriate time in prayer, whether personally or as a family or, as occasion presents, in a group of families" (cf. canon 230, §3). Ancillary to the topic is the permission granted to a priest who is blind or suffering from some other infirmity to be assisted by a properly instructed lay person (canon 930, §2). In case of a blind priest, the assistant may say the prayers, read the Gospel, and direct the priest through the Eucharistic prayer. Great reservation is shown by the Code when it comes to preaching by the laity in a church or oratory. This role should be allowed only by exception, in determined circumstances, and in accordance with the provisions laid down by the Episcopal Conference. It is never permissible that the laity deliver a homily (canon 766).

Mention has been made in canon 230, §3, that a lay person may be deputed by the Church to administer baptism. It must be reminded that this delegation is necessary only *ad liceitatem* since baptism administered by a lay person -- even unbaptized -- is always valid once the matter and form and the right intention are observed (cf. canon 861, §2).

The canonical form of marriage is retained *in integro* by the new Code (canon 1108, §1). However, by virtue of canon 1112, §1, a lay person can be delegated by the Bishop to assist at marriages, provided the consent is given in the presence of two witnesses. Such a delegation is feasible only when priests or deacons are not available, and if the Episcopal Conference has given its prior approval and the permission of the Holy See has been obtained.

In the new codification, lay persons are empowered to administer certain sacramentals in accordance with the liturgical books and subject to the judgment of the local Ordinary (canon 1168).[38]

The faithful are encouraged, in certain circumstances, to take part in the liturgy of the hours with the clergy (canon 1174, §2).

The reading of the above-mentioned canons illustrates the resuscitation of the common priesthood in the liturgical life of the Church. The present role of the faithful demonstrates a transformation from a condition of passivity and total dependency to a mature and responsible involvement in the office of sanctification. However limited might appear to some the present role of the common priesthood in the liturgical life of the Church, it is a serious obligation that this limited involvement be preceded by appropriate preparation of the one who volunteers for such services. Hence canon 231, §1, instructs: "Lay people who are pledged to the special service of the Church, whether permanently or for a time, have a duty to acquire the appropriate formation which their role demands, so that they may conscientiously, earnestly and diligently fulfil this role."

As a last commentary on the subject, there remain two fundamental rights of the faithful which may appear to some superfluous. Be that as it may, the Code insists on the prerogative of the faithful to have a free and gratuitous entrance to a church during sacred functions (canon 1221). The faithful, the poor not excluded (canon 1181), are entitled to a Church funeral according to the norms of law (canon 1176, §1).

The Involvement of the Common Priesthood in the Pastoral Life of the Church

Every action of the Church is at once liturgical and pastoral. In her adoration to God, the Church edifies the human family and enables it to direct itself to its eschatological goal. In her service to the human person, the Church worships God through her profound solidarity and solicitude for the one who was created in the image of his Son -- "I tell you solemnly,

---

[38] *Sacrosanctum concilium*, n. 79, p. 162. Cf. SIMONS, THOMAS G., *Blessings: A Reappraisal of their Nature,Purpose, and Celebration*, Saratoga, CA., 1981, pp. 78-79.

in so far as you did this to one of the least of these brothers of mine, you did it to me."[39] In Christian mysticism, liturgy and apostolate are merely dimensions of the same reality, expressions of the twofold divine commandment, love of God and love of neighbour. Liturgy indicates human dependency on God; apostolate expresses human solidarity and interrelatedness through Christ in the Spirit; they cannot be implemented if not simultaneously and in their entirety. The distinction commonly adopted between liturgy and apostolate reflects rather mere external emphasis, since the Christian life is in essence the expression of both. In this theological spectrum, the sanctifying office of the universal priesthood of believers should be understood as being both liturgical and pastoral in essence. It is thereby the right and duty of the baptized to actively participate in the pastoral life of the Church. "The member who fails to make his proper contribution to the development of the Church must be said to be useful neither to the Church nor to himself."[40] Thus the Council insists that "training for the apostolate should start with a child's earliest education. In a special way, however, adolescents and young adults should be initiated into the apostolate and imbued with its spirit. This formation must be perfected throughout their whole lives in keeping with the demands of new responsibilities. It is evident, therefore, that those who have the obligation to provide for Christian education also have the duty to provide for formation in the apostolate."[41]

By virtue of its sanctifying office, the common priesthood, under the guidance of ecclesiastical authority, partakes of the ordinary and universal magisterium (canon 750). Through holiness of personal life and by word, the faithful contribute to the building up of the Mystical Body (canons 210, 759). But by reason of their baptism and confirmation, their personal life becomes also "martyrion" for the world. They have "the special obligation

---

[39] Mt. 25:40.

[40] *Apostolicam actuositatem*, n.2, p.491; cf. n. 6, p. 496.

[41] Ibid., n. 30, p. 518; cf. nn.24-25, pp.513-515; *Lumen gentium*, n.37, pp. 64-65; *Christus Dominus*, n. 17, pp. 409-410.

to permeate and perfect the temporal order of things with the spirit of the Gospel. In this way, particularly in conducting secular business and exercising secular functions, they are to give witness to Christ" (canon 225, §2; cf. canon 227). However, in this regard, "they are to heed the teaching of the Church proposed by the magisterium, but they must be on guard, in questions of opinion, against proposing their own view as the teaching of the Church" (canon 227). To the world they present themselves as heralds of the Kingdom to come, since they "have the obligation and right to strive so that the divine message of salvation may more and more reach all people of all times and all places" (canon 211). "Whether as individuals or in associations . . . , this obligation is all the more insistent in circumstances in which only through them are people able to hear the Gospel and to know Christ" (canon 225, §1).[42] Thus, "they can also be called upon to cooperate with Bishops and priests in the exercise of the ministry of the word" (canon 759).

The sanctifying office of the faithful is responsible to the universal Church (canons 209, §2; 529, §2). "Because the whole Church is of its nature missionary and the work of evangelisation is to be considered a fundamental duty of the people of God, all Christ's faithful must be conscious of the responsibility to play their part in missionary activity" (canon 781), by promoting and supporting apostolic action by their own initiative (canon 216). A specification of this commitment is "the obligation to provide for the needs of the Church, so that the Church has available to it those things which are necessary for divine worship, for apostolic and charitable work and for the worthy support of its ministers" (canon 222, §1). In like manner, the promotion of priestly and religious vocations falls upon the whole Christian community "so that the needs of the sacred ministry are sufficiently met in the entire Church" (canon 233, §1).

As pointed out earlier in this paper, the charism of the common priesthood throughout the centuries expressed itself in charitable organizations and associations with cultic aim, according to the needs of

---

[42] *Christus Dominus*, n.30, 1), p.418; *Lumen gentium*, n.33, p. 59; *Apostolicam actuositatem*, nn.1-2, pp. 490-492.

the time.[43] Vatican Council II inculcated the right of the faithful to establish, or to subscribe to, similar associations. It calls for prudence and discretion, however, in the erection of new ones in order to avoid useless multiplicity of groups with the same goals, with a resulting dissipation of energy.[44] Thus the Code decrees that "Christ's faithful may freely establish and direct associations which serve charitable or pious purposes or which foster the Christian vocation in the world, and they may hold meetings to pursue these purposes by common effort" (canon 215).[45]

As canon 298, §1, points out, distinct from associations of Christ's faithful are institutes of consecrated life and societies of apostolic life. Life consecrated through the profession of evangelical counsels in a society erected with a formal decree of the competent ecclesiastical authority (canon 579) is not the prerogative of the ministerial priesthood; it pertains to the life and holiness of the People of God (canon 207, §2) and in its juridical status it rather forms an integral part of the charism of the common priesthood. These associations are grouped under three categories: religious institutes (canon 607, §2), secular institutes (canon 710) societies of apostolic life (canon 731, §1).

The Role of the Faithful in the Diocese

Canon 209, §2, states that the faithful are to carry out their responsibilities also towards the particular Church to which they belong. By particular Church here is meant the diocese or its equivalent (canon 368).[46] "A diocese is a portion of the people of God, which is entrusted to a

---

[43] Under the term common priesthood are also included Religious Congregations, and individual religious who of their own accord established similar institutions.

[44] *Apostolicam actuositatem*, n.19, p.510; *Lumen gentium*, n.37, p.65.

[45] In reference to associations of Christ's faithful, the Code dedicates canons 298-329. Among these associations are included the third Orders secular (canon 303).

[46] Canon 296 treats the participation of the faithful in the pastoral activities of a personal prelature. Little can be said on the matter. Their contribution has to be clarified by way of agreement with the prelature and in accordance with the statutes of the same.

Bishop to be nurtured by him . . . " (canon 369). It follows therefore that the promotion of lay apostolate falls principally upon the Bishop; in fact, "he is to insist on the faithful's obligation to exercise the apostolate according to the condition and talents of each. He is to urge them to take part in or assist various works of the apostolate, according to the needs of place and time" (canon 394, §2). "He must in a very special way foster vocations to the various ministries and to consecrated life, having a special care for priestly and missionary vocations" (canon 385). The clergy likewise are asked to nurture in the faithful that spirit of commitment towards the Church and the world which was instilled in them in baptism (canon 275, §2).

Bearing in mind the missionary nature of the Church, baptism and confirmation designate us, each according to his or her condition, to the realization of that same purpose. This does not mean that all baptized are called to exercise public ministries in the Church. A public ministry, understood in the strict sense, may be defined as a specific service performed by one who has been stably deputed by the pastors of the Church to further a spiritual purpose. This call presupposes in the person the charisma proper to the particular service. The ministry, to be true to itself, must be rendered gratuitously to the community and graciously received by the same.[47]

This is not to say that the universal ministry of the faithful loses its spontaneity and its diversity of expression. Ministry is the unfolding of the Christian charisma through the work of the Spirit. Ministries emerge straight from the core of Christian consciousness in the most unstructured and spontaneous manner in response to the needs of time and place. Whatever is done for the love of God and of neighbour is indeed a true and valid ministry. Throughout the entire history of the Church, great souls have accomplished colossal work in the cause of the human person long before the reality of "ministry of the faithful" caught the attention of the

---

[47] THOTTUMKAL, THOMAS, *People's Ministry*, Edmonton, Alberta, 1983, p. 8. The diversity of ministries is almost indeterminable. Ministries can be directed to all human needs. The flourishing of the ministries depends only at what stage of self-awareness the Christian community has arrived. Several types of ministries are mentioned by the author; cf. pp. 15-17.

ecclesiastical authorities. These men and women were deputed by nobody; they simply lived their Christian vocation to the utmost of their human potentiality.

The apostolate in the entire diocese evolves under the direction and vigilance of the local Ordinary (canon 394, §1). Spiritual activity of whatever nature performed or undertaken in public form by the faithful is thereby subject to the authority of the Bishop who is ultimately responsible for the spiritual welfare of the diocese (canons 369; 381, §1). Nonetheless, the Code pays special attention to certain matters which ought to be the prime responsibility of the Bishop. A similar activity is the teaching of sacred sciences which by the new law requires a mandate from the local Ordinary (canons 229, §3; 812).[48] Publications of the faithful which touch upon matters of faith and morals must first receive the approval of the competent ecclesiastical authority (canon 823, §1). An even stricter norm is enforced whenever it concerns the publication of Sacred Scriptures (canon 825, §1, 2). Pastoral action in the area of social communication has been given a priority by the Vatican Council.[49] It is a ministry in which the faithful are encouraged to give their contribution (canon 822, §2, 3). Nevertheless, because of the serious repercussions which this ministry might have on faith and morals, canon 823, §1, requires the diligent vigilance of the Bishop. Lay ministry becomes also subject to the supervision and governance of the ecclesiastical authority (canons 323, §1; 305, §1), when it organizes itself as an association, and presents itself as part of the People of God (canon 299, §1).

The role of the faithful in the pastoral life of the diocese has assumed a great impetus in Vatican Council II, particularly in matters pertinent to the constitutional configuration of the Church. The Code, faithful to the conciliar mandate, endeavours to introduce the laity into areas of responsibility traditionally reserved to the clergy. These areas cover the administrative, as well as the judicial, powers of the Church.

---

[48] A distinction must be made in this regard between the seminary professor (canon 253, §1) and those who teach sacred sciences in Catholic schools and universities.

[49] *Inter mirifica*, PP-319-331

In the governance of the diocese, a series of opportunities is encountered where the Bishop can avail himself of the resourcefulness of the common priesthood. The following are instances when the laity may, or ought to, assist in matters of a pastoral nature:

In the pastoral care of those who are called to married life, the Code proposes that the Bishop, if need be, should seek the experience and expertise of men and women who can assist him more effectively in this pursuit (canon 1064).

It is also stipulated that due to penury of priests or deacons in certain parts of the world, saving the prescription of canon 1112, §1, "a suitable lay person is to be selected, capable of giving instruction to those who are getting married, and fitted to conduct the marriage liturgy properly" (canon 1112, §2).

The general involvement of the laity in the pastoral field is more appreciated in its participation in the diocesan pastoral council, the aim of which "is to study and weigh those matters which concern the pastoral works in the diocese, and to propose practical conclusions concerning them" (canon 511). Whenever this council is established in the diocese (canon 511) lay people are to be assigned as members along with clerics and religious (canon 512, §1).

The presence of the laity is expected, in the capacity of members, in the celebration of the diocesan synod;[50] they are to be selected according to the prescription of canon 463, §1, n.5. The Bishop, moreover, is empowered to invite other lay persons to assist as members in the synod (canon 463, §2).

The Code contemplates the participation of the laity in plenary (canon 437, §1) and provincial (canon 440, §1) councils. The presence of the laity as members in these particular councils, with consultative vote, can easily be perused in canon 443, §4, 5. It is also suggested that the Episcopal Conference may invite lay persons to attend the plenary council

---

[50] Canon 460 -- The diocesan synod is an assembly of selected priests and other members of Christ's faithful of a particular Church which, for the good of the whole diocesan community, assists the diocesan Bishop, in accordance with the following canons.

as guests; the Bishops may likewise invite them to attend the provincial council (canon 443, §6).

The intervention of the faithful is further witnessed in the financial administration of the diocese. In each diocese a finance committee is to be established to which at least three lay persons are to be appointed as members by the Bishop (canon 492, §1). The authority of the Bishop is, in certain financial matters, subject to consultation, or even consent, of the finance committee. The consultation with the finance committee must precede the decision reached by the Bishop in the following instances: in the appointment of the financial administrator of the diocese (canon 494, §1); in the reduction of obligations which ensue from legacies (canon 1310, §2); in carrying out acts of administration which, in the light of the economic situation of the diocese, are of major importance (canon 1277); in the levying of a moderate tax on public juridical persons subject to his authority (canon 1263); in determining which acts go beyond the limits and procedures which concern the ordinary administration of juridical persons, if the statutes do not mention such acts (canon 1281, §2). The consent of the finance committee is requested by law in order that the Bishop may alienate goods which belong to the diocese itself (canon 1292, §1). The same consent is required before the Bishop may grant permission for the alienation of goods which belong to juridical persons subject to his authority, in accordance with the prescription of canon 1292, §1. An annual report on the administration of ecclesiastical goods, which come under the supervision of the diocesan Bishop, must be passed by the same to the finance committee for examination. Any contrary custom is reprobated (canon 1287, §1). In each diocese, a financial administrator is to be appointed by the Bishop, and he can be selected from among the laity (canon 494, §1, 2). The laity can likewise be appointed administrators of public juridical persons (canon 1279, §2; 1282).

The most astounding deliberation reached by Vatican Council II in the acknowledgement of the common priesthood consists, in our belief, in the involvement of the laity in the exercise of ecclesiastical jurisdiction.[51] Thus canon 129, §2, establishes: "lay members of Christ's faithful can co-operate in the exercise of this same power in accordance with the law." In conjunction with this constitutional norm, one notes the definition of ecclesiastical office which differs from the one given by the 1917 Code.[52] "An ecclesiastical office is any post which by divine or ecclesiastical disposition is established in a stable manner to further a spiritual purpose" (canon 145, §1). The Code, in no ambiguous terms, allows the laity to hold an ecclesiastical office in which ecclesiastical jurisdiction is exercised. Hence, canon 228, §1, prescribes: "lay people who are found to be suitable are capable of being admitted by the sacred Pastors to those ecclesiastical offices and functions which, in accordance with the provisions of law, they can discharge."

An ecclesiastical office can be exercised either in *via administrativa,* or in *via iudiciali.* As far as *via administrativa* is concerned, the Code refrains from being specific in determining which ecclesiastical offices the laity may validly occupy. It is safe to say that the laity is banned from an ecclesiastical office when of its very nature it requires sacred Orders, or when there is an express prohibition laid down by the Code. The offices of chancellor and of notary of the diocesan curia, for instance, can be offered to lay persons (canons 482, §1; 483, §2). A lay person appointed to conduct marriages, as prescribed in canon 1112, §2, may be considered to hold ecclesiastical office. In *via iudiciali,* the issue is assumed by the Code in more detail. In ecclesiastical tribunals, the laity may be assigned as auditors (canon 1428, §2, 3), assessors (canon 1424), promotor of justice and defender of the bond (canon 1435), and, with the permission of the Episcopal Conference, also one of the college of judges (canon 1421, §2).

---

[51] Cf. canon 129, §1.

[52] Canon 145, §1.

Conclusion

Vatican Council II emerged as the fruition of the christianized humanization of human consciousness. The ecclesiastical authority had no other choice but to accept the stage of maturation which the common priesthood had reached, and allowed it into more participation in the pastoral, and more so, in the liturgical life of the Church. The rightful and active role of the common priesthood in the ecclesial reality was sealed by the *Motu proprio, Catholicam Christi Ecclesiam,* January 6, 1967, with the erection of the "Council for the Laity" in the Roman curia.[53] A statement by the American Bishops issued on the occasion of the fifteenth anniversary of the consiliar Decree, *Apostolicam actuositatem,* seems appropriate since it harbours a prophetic vision: "While focusing on the laity, we wish to address the whole Church. We affirm the vision of the Second Vatican Council and the importance it gives to the laity. We look forward to what is still to come under the guidance of the Holy Spirit, making the Church more and more the perfect image of Christ. We also acknowledge that these continuing developments may require new concepts, new terminology, new attitudes, and new practices. In prayerful dialogue with all our sisters and brothers we are prepared to make those changes which will aid in building the Kingdom."[54] Without ignoring their commitment to the active, intelligent, and responsible participation in the Liturgical life of the Church, the faithful should never desist in permeating and perfecting the temporal order with the spirit of the Gospel.[55] Imbued with this spirit, the common priesthood is charged with the sacred duty of defending the fundamental and inalienable human rights against social and political injustices. The *visio beatifica,* the ultimate purpose of human existence, can be attained only through human inter-relatedness, solidarity, and reciprocity

---

[53] AAS, 59 (1967) I, 26-27.

[54] *Called and Gifted: The American Catholic Laity -- Reflections of the American Bishops commemorating the Fifteenth Anniversary of the Issuance of the Decree on the Apostolate of the Laity,* November 13, 1980, p.2, National Conference of Catholic Bishops, Washington, D.C.

[55] Canon 225, §2.

in Christ. It is precisely for this reason that the ultimate aspiration of human consciousness is found in Christianity.

The Parochial Community

Nowhere does the Church verify itself, identify itself, and complete itself more profoundly than in a parochial community. In this community the Church of Christ truly exists and functions.[1] The Church as a parochial community forever explicates its christological nature so that its spirit permeates the human family, and invigorates it in the pursuance of its own eschatological humanization. The parochial community is the Church in miniature, for it enshrines the essential components of Christ's Mystical Body; although ministerial priesthood and common priesthood are distinct realities, one intrinsically necessitates the other, one must complement and fulfill the other.[2]

History testifies to this fundamental conceptualization of a parochial community. The concept of parish as the synthesis of ministerial priesthood and common priesthood emerges first from the etymology of the word, *parochia* (portion, section).[3] The term, "diocese,"[4] was hardly used in ecclesiastical documents of the first Christian millennium, but rather the

---

[1] *Sacrosanctum Concilium*, n. 42, p. 152 ". . . parishes set up locally under a pastor who takes the place of the bishop are the most important: for in a certain way they represent the visible Church as it is established throughout the world."

[2] *Apostolicam actuositatem*, n. 10, pp 500 - 501.

[3] ALBERICUS DE ROSATE BERGOMENSIS, *Dictionarium Iuris tam Civilis, quam Canonici*, Venetiis, 1573, v. *Parochia*, p.562: "Parochia graece, latine divisio seu partitio dicitur"; cf. FERRARIS, LUCIUS, *Prompta Bibliotheca Canonica, Juridica, Moralis, Theologica . . .* , Tomus VI, Parisiis, 1865, v. *Parochia*, n. 3, col. 32.

[4] Concilium Carthaginense, (a. 421), Tit. X, *Sacrorum Conciliorum Nova, et Amplissima Collectio a Joanne Dominico Mansi*, Tomus IV, Florentiae, 1760, col. 450; Concilium Bracarense III, (a. 572), can. 1, *Mansi*, Tomus IX, Florentiae, 1763, col. 838.

word *parochia* was indiscriminately adopted to denote diocese[5] as well as parish.[6] The concept of parish, however, stems from a more profound reality than mere etymology; it devolved historically from the theological significance of a diocese. In a society highly concentrated in rural population, as was Medieval Europe, the size of a European city could not afford more than one cathedral, and perhaps two more churches. It was thus feasible for a bishop to be in direct and complete charge of the pastoral care of the city, but certainly not of rural areas. It seems that soon after the Peace of Constantine the pastoral care among the rural population was a priority on the Church's agenda. Already by the time of the Council of Antioch I (a. 341), the institution of *chorepiscopi*, rural bishops who came under the jurisdiction of the bishop in the city, was a

---

[5] *Canones Apostolorum*, Gentiano Herveto Interprete, (a. 52?), cann. 13, 14 *Mansi*, Tomus I, Florentiae, 1759, col. 31; *Canones Apostolorum Sanctorum*, Dionysio Exiguo Interprete, cann. 14, 15, loc. cit., col. 52; Concilium Antiochenum I, (a. 341), cann. 3, 9, 18, 21, *Mansi*, Tomus II, Florentiae, 1759, coll. 1310-1318; Concilium Vernense, (a.755), can. 3, *Mansi*, Tomus XII, Florentiae, 1766, col. 580; Concilium Arelatense VI, (a.813), can. 17, *Mansi*, Tomus XIV, Venetiis, 1769, col. 61; Concilium Meldense, (a. 845), cann. 50, 51, loc. cit., col. 830; Concilium Troslejanum, (a. 909), cap. 6, *Mansi*, Tomus XVIII, Venetiis, 1773, col. 280; *Hettonis Capitulare*, capp. 13, 18, *Patrologiae Cursus Completus accurante J.P. Migne*, Series Latina, Tomus 105, Parisiis, 1851, Series Secunda, coll. 765-766; HINCMARUS RHEMENSIS, *Capitula ad Presbyteros Parochiae Suae*, cap. 16, *Mansi*, Tomus XV, Venetiis, 1770, col. 479; *Decretum Gratiani* ,I pars, Dist. 92, cc. 4, 5, 6; ALBERICUS DE ROSATE, *Dictionarium* . . . , v. *Parochia*, p. 562; FERRARIS, L., *Prompta Bibliotheca* . . . , v. *Parochia*, n. 7, col. 33.

[6] Concilium Agathense, (a. 506), cap. II, cann. 21, 49, 53, *Mansi*, Tomus VIII, Florentiae, 1762, coll. 328 - 334; Concilium Vasense III, (a. 529), cann. 1, 2, loc. cit., coll. 726 - 727; Concilium Vernense (a. 755), can. 7, *Mansi*, Tomus XII, col. 581; Concilium Arelatense VI, (a. 813), can. 10, *Mansi* Tomus XIV, col. 60; Concilium Ravennense, (a. 877), Statutum XVIII, *Mansi*, Tomus XVII, Venetiis, 1772, col. 340; Concilium Troslejanum, (a. 909) cap. VI, *Mansi*, Tomus XVIII, col. 280; Concilium Lateranense III, (a. 1179), can. 3, *Conciliorum Oecumenicorum Decreta*, curantibus Josepho Alberigo, Josepho A. Bossetti Perikle, P. Joannou Claudio Leonardi, Paulo Prodi, Ed. III, Bologna, 1973, p. 212; Concilium Lateranense V, (a 1512-1517), Sessio IX, *Bulla de Reformatione Curiae*, loc. cit., p. 617; Concilium Tridentinum, (a. 1545 - 1563), Sessio XXI, *Decretum de Reformatione*, cann. 4, 7; Sessio XXII, *Decretum de Observandis et Vitandis in Celebratione Missarum;* Sessio XXIV, *Decretum de Reformatione*, can. 13, loc. cit., pp. 729, 731, 737, 767-768; *Capitulare Theodulfi Episcopi Aurelianensis ad Parochiae Suae Sacerdotes*, can. 14, *Mansi*, Tomus XIII, Florentiae, 1767, col. 998; HINCMARUS RHEMENSIS, *Capitula Archidiaconibus Presbyteris Data*, cap. VII, *Ut Parochias Rusticanas confundere vel dividere non praesumant, et ut Ecclesias omnes, Capellasque illis subjectas describant*, Opera Omnia, Tomus Prior, P. L., Tom. 125, Parisiis, 1879, col. 802; AMULUS, *Epistola Prima ad Theodboldum Ep. Lingonensem*, cap. VII, P. L., Tom. 116, Parisiis, 1879, col. 82; *Capitula Herardi*, capp. 29, 76, Series Secunda, P.L.,Tom. 121, Parisiis, 1852 coll. 766, 769; c. 4, C. IX, q. 2; c. 1, C. XIII, q. 1.

fait accompli.⁷ More often, however, particularly in the later centuries, the bishop reached the rural population through the *presbyteri*.⁸ They were the bishop's personal representatives, assigned to churches located in these areas, and subject to reassignment at his discretion.⁹

In ecclesiastical documents, prior to the Council of Trent, emphasis was placed more on the pastoral than on the juridical aspect of the parish. In the earliest of these documents three realities appear to have been the essential components in the formation of a parish:
1. the assignment of a priest to the pastoral care;
2. a Christian community;
3. the construction of a church with the right to have a baptismal font (*ecclesia baptismalis*).

The Christian community, under the leadership of the bishop's representative, gathered in the parochial church, as the *ecclesia filialis* of the cathedral, to express in some real and full sense its unity with the entire diocese with the bishop at its head.¹⁰ This concept of parish was

---

[7] Concilium Antiochenum I, can. 10, *Mansi*, Tomus II, Florentiae, 1759, col. 1311: "Ii qui sunt in vicis vel pagis, qui dicuntur chorepiscopi, etiamsi episcopi ordinationem manuumve impositionem acceperint, visum est, ut suum modum sciant, et sibi subjectas ecclesias administrent, earumque cura et solicitudine gerenda contenti sunt . . ."; cf. Concilium Chalcedonense, (a. 451), can. 17, *De Paroeciis Rusticis, Conciliorum Oecumenicorum Decreta* . . . p.95.

[8] Concilium Arelatense VI, (a. 813), can. 10, *Mansi*, Tomus XIV, Venetiis, 1769, col. 60; Concilium Triburiense, (a. 895), can. 14, *Mansi*, Tomus XVIII, Venetiis, 1773, col. 140; Concilium Troslejanum, (a. 909), cap. VI, loc. cit., col. 280; HINCMARUS RHEMENSIS, *Capitula Archidiaconibus* . . ., Cap. VII, loc. cit., col. 802; c. 3, *Ad audientiam*, X, *De Ecclesiis Aedificandis vel Reparandis*, III, 48.

[9] REIFFENSTUEL, ANACLETUS, *Ius Canonicum Universum*, Vol. IV, Parisiis, 1889, Lib. III, Tit. 29, n. 3, p. 590: "Pro quo sciendum, quod licet olim curam animarum totius dioecesis solus episcopus per sacerdotes pro suo libitu missos, et ad nutum amovibiles administrarit, assignatis cuivis laboranti sacerdoti iis sustentationis mediis, quae episcopus pro tali judicaverat sufficientia, ut propterea tota dioecesi merito diceretur parochia . . ."; FERRARIS, L., *Prompta Bibliotheca* . . ., Tomus VI, v. *Parochia*, n. 7, col. 33.

[10] Concilium Aquisgranense II, (a. 836), Cap. II, *De Vita et Doctrina Inferiorum Ordinum*, can. 5, *Mansi*, Tomus XIV, Venetiis, 1769, coll. 680-681: "Presbyterorum vero qui praesunt ecclesiae Christi, et in confectione divini corporis, et sanguinis consortes cum episcopis sunt, ministerium esse videtur, ut in doctrina praesint populis, et in officio praedicandi, nec in aliquo desides inventi appareant. Item ut de omnibus hominibus, qui ad eorum ecclesiam pertinent, per omnia

retained substantially throughout history[11] in spite of later inclusion of juridical elements in the conceptualization of the parish.

In canonical legislation, the parochial ministry reckoned as the extension of the episcopal office appeared as early as Concilium Antiochenum I (a. 341).[12] *Capitulare Theodulfi* (a. 797) recognizes these priests as helpers of the bishop in his ministry, as doctors and as leaders of the people of God -- "nostri ministerii adjutores . . . populo Dei doctores et ductores."[13] Concilium Aquisgranense II, (a. 836), acknowledges

---

curam gerant, scientes se pro certo reddituros rationem pro ipsis in die judicii, quia cooperatores oneris nostri esse procul dubio noscuntur . . . "; AMULUS, *Epistola Prima ad Theodboldum* . . . , Cap. VII, loc. cit., col. 82: "Unaquaeque plebs in paroechiis et ecclesiis, quibus attributa est, quieta consistat; ubi sacrum baptisma accipit, ubi corpus et sanguinem Domini percipit, ubi missarum solemnia audire consuevit, ubi a sacerdote suo poenitentiam de reatu, visitationem in infirmitate, sepulturam in morte consequitur . . . "; CHRODEGANGUS, *Regula Canonicorum*, Capp. 32, 33, 34, 36, 44, 71, 73, 74, 78, 79, P.L., Tomus 89, coll. 1072 - 1090.

[11] C.1, *In ecclesiis*, X, *De Capellis Monachorum et Aliorum Religiosorum*, III, 37; c. 32, *Quum singula, De Praebendis et Dignitatibus*, III, 4, in VI°; c. *Presbyteri, De Capellis Monachorum*, III, 18, in VI°; Concilium Tridentinum, Sessio XXII, *Decretum de Observandis et Vitandis in Celebratione Missarum;* Sessio XXIV, *Decretum de Reformatione*, can. 18, *Conciliorum Oecumenicorum Decreta* . . . , pp. 737, 770; FERRARIS, L., *Prompta Bibliotheca* . . . ,Tomus VI, v. *Parochia*, n. 18, coll. 35-36: "Parochialis ecclesia dicitur, quae habet jus consistens in cura animarum parochianorum, ipsis sacramenta ministrans, et proprium habens rectorem, seu parochum."

[12] Can. 24, *Mansi*, Tomus II, col. 1318: "Recte habet, ut ea quae sunt ecclesiae, ecclesiae serventur cum omni bona conscientia, et fide in omnium praesidem et judicem Deum: quae etiam administrari convenit cum judicio, et potestate episcopi, cui est omnis populus creditus, et eorum animae quae in ecclesiam conveniunt . . . "; cf. Concilium Carthaginense (a. 419), Tit. VII, *De Reconciliandis Infirmis, Mansi*, Tomus IV, Florentiae, 1760, col. 425; Concilium Bracarense III, (a. 572), can.1, *Mansi*, Tomus IX, Florentiae, 1763, coll. 838-839; Concilium Vernense (a. 755) cann. 3, 7, *Mansi*, Tomus XII, coll. 580, 581; Concilium Arelatense VI, (a. 813), can. 17, *Mansi*, Tomus XIV, col. 61; Concilium Romanum, (a. 853), cann. 8, 24, *Mansi*, Tomus XIV, Venetiis, 1769, coll. 1003, 1006; Concilium Ravennense (a. 877), Statutum XVIII, *Mansi*, Tomus XVII, col. 340; Concilium Troslejanum, (a. 909), cap. VI, *Mansi*, Tomus XVIII, col. 280.

[13] *Mansi*, Tomus XIII, (additio): coll. 1006 - 1007: "Dilectissimi fratres, sanctissimi consacerdotes, et nostri ministerii adjutores . . . et sitis populo Dei doctores et ductores in omni exemplo bono, ut populus Dei utrumque et per vestram sanctam conversationem et devotam praedicationem erudiatur in laudem et in gloriam sancti nominis Domini nostri Jesu Christi, et in salutem sempiternam animarum vestrarum . . . Dei sacerdotes, qui populo Dei praeesse debent et gubernare ecclesias Christi"; cf. *Capitula Herardi*, capp. 39, 72, 76, Series Secunda, P.L., Tomus 121, coll. 767, 769; CHRODEGANGUS, *Regula Canonicorum*, cap. 78, *ut Presbyteri inconsulto Episcopo non constituantur in Ecclesiis, vel de Ecclesiis expellantur ab aliquo*, P.L. Tomus 89,

The Parochial Community

them as equal sharers with the bishop, especially in the celebration of the Eucharist -- "in confectione divini corporis, et sanguinis consortes cum episcopis sunt."[14] With the publication of the *Decretales Gregorii IX*, the juridical connotation of the parochial ministry became more pronounced. Gradually, the idea that the bishop's power abided in the parochial pastor gave way to the subordination of the latter to the former.[15] This change brought in its trail more stability of office,[16] which was further developed by the Council of Trent.[17] Down to the 1917 Code, a twofold classification of stability of office was still maintained: *parochus amovibilis, parochus inamovibilis*.[18] Stability of office is requested by the present Code[19] with the elimination, however, of the right to irremovability.[20]

In the gamut of the Church's legislation, whether particular[21] or

---

col. 1090.

[14] Cap. II *De Vita et Doctrina Inferiorum Ordinum*, can. 5, loc. cit., coll. 680 - 681.

[15] C.1, *In ecclesiis*, X, *De Capellis Monachorum et Aliorum Religiosorum*, III, 37: "ut ex solius episcopi arbitrio tam ordinatio eius quam depositio, et totius vitae pendeat conversatio"; cf. c. 32, *Quum singula, De Praebendis et Dignitatibus*, III, 4,in VI°; c. *Presbyteri, De Capellis Monachorum*, III, 18, in VI°.

[16] It cannot be denied that attempts were made by certain earlier councils to secure the stability of priests in their respective ministry, as can be witnessed in Concilium Vernense (a. 755), can. 12, *Mansi*, Tomus XII, col. 528.

[17] Sessio XXIV, *Decretum De Reformatione*, can. 13, *Conciliorum Oecumenicorum* . . . , p. 768: "Mandat sancta synodus episcopis pro tutiori animarum eis commissarum salute, ut distincto populo in certas propriasque parochias unicuique suum perpetuum peculiaremque parochum assignent, qui eas cognoscere valeat, et a quo solo licite sacramenta suscipiant."

[18] Canon 454, §2.

[19] Canon 522

[20] *Christus Dominus*, n. 31, pp. 419 - 420.

[21] Concilium Carthaginense (a. 419). Tit. 7, *De Reconciliandis Infirmis, Mansi*, Tomus IV, col. 425; Concilium Agathense, (a. 506) Cap. II, can. 21. *Mansi*, Tomus VIII, col. 328; Concilium Vasense III, (a. 529), cann. 1,2; loc. cit., coll. 726 - 727; Concilium Bracarense III, (a. 572), can. 1. *Mansi*, Tomus IX, col. 838; Concilium Vernense (a. 755), cann. 3, 7, *Mansi*, Tomus XII, coll. 580, 581; Concilium Aquisgranense II, (a. 836), Cap. II, *De Vita et Doctrina Inferiorum Ordinum*, can. 5, *Mansi*, Tomus XIV, coll. 680 - 681; Concilium Meldense, (a. 845) can. 48, loc. cit., col. 830.

universal,[22] the parochial community has been generally conceived of as being exclusively cultic. This is not to say that reference was never made to works of apostolate and of charity to be performed by the parochial community. A portion of the *decimae*, the oldest institution in the juridical formation of the parish, was intended to assist the poor.[23] Particular councils, though few in number, insisted upon the obligation of the parochial community in caring for the poor, the widows, and the orphans.[24] Amulus was one of the few canonical authors who envisaged the activity of the parochial community in its twofold dimension. After concentrating on the cultic aspect of the parish, he writes: "Each individual parochial community is to see to it that orphans, widows, the needy, and travellers benefit by the generous donations of goods which God has bestowed on its members, that it must be prompt in exercising hospitality, and that it takes care that goods be administered wisely for its own benefit and for the sake of others rather than having these goods wasted through banquets, drunkenness and enterprises only sought by worldly people."[25] Thus with

---

[22] C. 3, *Ut quisque*, X, *De Vita et Honestate Clericorum*, III, 1; c. 3, *Ad audientiam*, X, *De Ecclesiis Aedificandis vel Reparandis*, III, 48; Concilium Tridentinum, Sessio XXI, *Decretum de Reformatione*, can. 4; Sessio XXIV, *Decretum de Reformatione*, can. 13, *Conciliorum Oecumenicorum Decreta* . . . , pp. 729,767.

[23] Concilium Moguntinum I, (a. 847), cap. 10, *Mansi*, Tomus XIV, col. 906; Concilium Lateranense V, (a. 1512 - 1517), Sessio IX, *Bulla Reformationis Curiae*, *Conciliorum Oecumenicorum Decreta* . . . , p. 617.

[24] Concilium Moguntiacum (a. 813), can. 8, *Mansi*, Tomus XIV, col. 67; Concilium Arelatense VI, (a. 813), can. 17, loc. cit., col. 61; Concilium Moguntinum I, (a. 847), cann. 7, 10, loc. cit., coll. 905, 906.

[25] *Epistola Prima ad Theodboldum Ep. Lingonensem*, Cap. VII, P.L., Tomus 116, col. 82: "ibi itaque unaquaeque plebs pupillis et viduis, pauperibus et peregrinis, de facutatulis quas Deus tribuit eleemosynarum largitionem exhibeat, hospitalitatis officia impendat, et quodcunque comessationibus et ebrietatibus et quaestu hominum vanorum consumere solebat, in istiusmodi suis et proximi salubribus utilitatibus expendat"; cf. REGINO PRUMIENSIS, *De Ecclesiasticis Disciplinis et Religione Christiana Libri Duo*, Lib. II, can. 421, Tomus Unicus, P.L., Tomus 132, Parisiis, 1853, col. 364: "Placuit nobis et nostris fidelibus ut presbyteri suos parochianos admoneant ut et ipsi hospitales, ut nulli iter facienti mansionem denegent, et ut omnis occasio rapinae tollatur, nihil charius vendant transeuntibus nisi quanto in mercato vendere possunt."

few exceptions, the overriding mass of canonical literature[26] down to the 1917 Code concerned itself with the cultic aspect of the parish: the ministerial priesthood was there with the sole purpose of administering the sacraments and performing other religious functions, with the common priesthood to benefit from them. The parochial comunity, for all intents and purposes, was conceived of as a community of souls, rather than of human beings in their holistic reality -- a conceptualization which provoked the centuries old dictum "cura animarum," rather than "cura personarum."

It was not illiteracy and ignorance of the Latin language alone which impeded the common priesthood from actively participating in the liturgical life of the Church; the ecclesiastical legislation expressly vetoed such participation as can be witnessed in *Capitula Herardi*.[27] Thus, in the life of the parish, since the pastoral dimension was hardly acknowledged, and the liturgical life was the sole prerogative of the ministerial priesthood, the parochial community down to Vatican Council II was a highly paternalistic community in which the pastor took upon himself complete responsibility; and the faithful in turn assumed an insignificant role which necessarily led to a puerile and lackadaisical approach toward their own reality as an essential and living component of the parochial community. The nomenclature itself, "*plebs*," which was often used in reference to the

---

[26] REIFFENSTUEL, A., *Ius Canonicum* . . . , Vol. IV, Lib III, Tit. 29, n. 3, p. 590; FERRARIS, L., *Prompta Bibliotheca* . . . , Tomus VI, v. *Parochia*, n. 3, col. 31; n. 18, coll. 35-36; SCHMALZGRUEBER, F., *Ius Ecclesiasticum Universum*, Tomus III, Pars II, Romae, 1844, Pars III, Tit. 29, para. 1. n. 2, p. 645; n. 8, p. 647; GIGNAC, Jos., N., *Compendium Iuris Canonici*, Quebeci, 1901, Lib. I, *De Personis*, n. 516, pp. 343-344.

[27] Cap. 24, col. 766: "De mulieribus ac laicis, ut ad altaria non accedant, et ut sacramenta et panes sanctorum, exceptis quae offerunt, non tangant"; cap. 82, col. 769: "Ut laici infra cancellos non stent, et ut oblatio populo foris septa recipiatur"; cap. 136, col. 774: "Laicus non debet in ecclesia publice lectionem recitare, nec alleluia, sed psalmos et responsoria" -- P. L., Series Secunda, Tomus 121; cf. *Hettonis Capitulare*, cap. 16, P. L., Series Secunda, Tomus 105, col. 765.

faithful[28] is sufficiently indicative of how little the ability of the common priesthood was appreciated.

The parochial church constituted the third essential component in the theologico-juridical concept of a parish. In early documents the parochial church, *"ecclesia,"*[29] was frequently used to designate the whole parochial *compositum*. In the parish, chapels *(capellae)* and oratories *(oratoria)*[30] existed, but it was the parochial church which stood as sign of the Christian community in a particular area. The parochial church formed the binding force and the point of convergence of the ministerial priesthood and the common priesthood. The parochial community finds the full expression of its reality and its ultimate significance in its sacramental and liturgical life. In these early documents, it becomes apparent that the parochial community can express its full cultic dimension in no other church than the parochial church, *qua ecclesia filialis* of the cathedral.[31]

---

[28] Concilium Bracarense III, (a. 572), can. 1, *Mansi*, Tomus IX, col. 838; Concilium Barcinonense, (a. 599), can 3, *Mansi*, Tomus X, Florentiae, 1764, col. 483; Concilium Romanum, (a.853), cann. 8, 16, Mansi, Tomus XIV, Coll. 1003, 1005; AMULUS, *Epistola Prima ad Theodboldum* . . . , cap. VII, P.L., Tomus 116, col. 82; *Capitula Herardi*, cap. 39, P.L., Series Secunda, Tomus 121, col. 767; c. 5, C. IX, q. 2; C. 1., C. XIII, q. 1; c. 45, C. XVI, q. 1; c. 3, *Ut quisque*, X, *De Vita et Honestate Clericorum*, III, 1.

[29] Concilium Bracarense III, (a. 572), can. 1., *Mansi*, Tomus IX, coll. 838-839; Concilium Moguntiacum (a. 813), can. 29, *Mansi*, Tomus XIV, col. 72; Concilium aquisgranense II, (a. 836), loc.cit., cap. II, *De Vita et Doctrina Inferiorum Ordinum*, cann.5, 6, loc. cit., coll. 680 - 681; Concilium Moguntinum, (a. 847) cann. 7, 10, 11, loc. cit., coll. 905-906; Concilium Triburiense, (a. 895) can. 14, *Mansi*, Tomus XVIII col. 140, *Capitulare Theodulfi* . . . , (a.797), Additio, *Mansi*, Tomus XIII, col. 1007; *Capitula Herardi*,(+ 870) capp. 48, 49, 72, 79, P.L., Series Secunda, Tomus 121, coll. 767, 769; c.1, *In ecclesiis, X, De Capellis Monachorum et Aliorum Religiosorum*, III, 37.

[30] Concilium Agathense, (a. 506), cap. II, can. 21, *Mansi*, Tomus VIII, col. 328; Concilium Moguntinum I (a. 847), cap. 11, *Mansi*, Tomus XIV, col. 906; HINCMARUS RHEMENSIS, *Capitula Archidiaconibus* . . . , cap. VII, *Ut Parochias Rusticanas confundere vel dividere non praesumant, et ut Ecclesias Omnes, Capellasque illis subjectas describant, Opera Omnia*, Tomus Prior, P.L., Tomus 125, col. 802, (740); *Epistula Paschalis II ad Florentinos Clericos, Mansi*, Tomus XX, col. 1052.

[31] Concilium Agathense, (a. 506), cap. 11, can. 21, *Mansi*, Tomus VIII, col. 328; Concilium Vernense, (a. 755), can. 7, *Mansi* Tomus XII, col. 581; Concilium Aquisgranense II, (a. 836), cap.II, *De Vita et Doctrina Inferiorum Ordinum*, can. 5, *Mansi*, Tomus XIV, col. 680; Concilium Meldense, (a. 845), can. 48. loc. cit., col. 830; *Capitulare Theodulfi* . . ., (a. 797). cann. 14, 45, *Mansi*, Tomus XIII, coll. 998, 1006; AMULUS, *Epistola Prima ad Theodboldum* . . .,(a. 853), cap. VII, P.L., Tomus 116, col. 82; cc. 4,5, C.IX q.2; *Epistula Paschalis II ad Florentinos Clericos,*

These three realities -- common priesthood, ministerial priesthood, the parochial church -- for many centuries formed the sole essential components of the parish. The term *plebs*, used to identify the parish, demonstrates by itself that the parish was considered as being fundamentally a community. Although the territorial boundary was first enjoined by Pope Dionysius (a. 268-274) in his letter to Bishop Severus,[32] it was not until the ninth century that the parish began to be circumscribed by territorial boundaries.[33] Parishes without fixed boundaries were still in existence in the sixteenth century.[34] The territorial circumscription became universal law with the Council of Trent.[35] Undue emphasis on the principle of territoriality, however, was responsible for the transformation of the conceptualization of parish as a Christian community into an ecclesiastical district in which the Christian community resides.[36]

Mansi, Tomus XX, col. 1052; *Concilium Tridentinum*, (a.1545 -1563), Sessio XXI, *Decretum de Reformatione*, can. 4, *Conciliorum Oecumenicorum Decreta* . . ., p. 729; Sessio XXII, *Decretum de Observandis et Vitandis in Celebratione Missarum*, loc. cit., p. 737; Sessio XXIV, *Decretum de Reformatione*, can. 13, loc. cit., p. 768.

[32] C. 1, C. XIII, q. 1: "Ecclesias singulas singulis presbiteris dedimus; parrochias et cimiteria eis divisimus, et unicuique ius proprium habere statuimus, ita videlicet, ut nullus alterius parrochiae terminos aut ius invadat, sed unusquisque terminis suis sit contentus, et taliter ecclesiam et plebem sibi commissam custodiat . . ."

[33] Concilium Triburiense (a. 895). can. 14, *Mansi*, Tomus XVIII, col. 140; HINCMARUS RHEMENSIS, *Capitula Archidiaconibus* . . . cap. VII, *Opera Omnia*, Tomus Prior, P.L., Tomus 125, col. 802; *Capitula Herardi*, cap. 30, Series Secunda, P.L., Tomus 121, col. 766.

[34] Concilium Tridentinum (a. 1545-1563), Sessio XXIV, *Decretum De Reformatione*, can. 13, *Conciliorum Oecumenicorum* . . ., p. 768.

[35] Ibid. "In his quoque civitatibus ac locis, ubi parochiales ecclesiae certos non habent fines, nec earum rectores proprium populum, quem regant, sed promiscue petentibus sacramenta administrant: mandat sancta synodus episcopis pro tutiori animarum eis commissarum salute, ut distincto populo in certas propriasque parochias unicuique suum perpetuum peculiaremque parochum assignent, qui eas cognoscere valeat, et a quo solo licite sacramenta suscipiant . . ."

[36] REIFFENSTUEL, A., *Ius Canonicum* . . ., Vol. IV. Lib. III, Tit. 29, n. 3., p. 590; FERRARIS, L., *Prompta Bibliotheca* . . ., Tomus VI, v. *Parochia*, n. 3, coll. 31-32; n. 16, col. 35. Franciscus Schmalzgrueber retains the communitarian conceptualization of parish, although he recognizes that by the term, parish, the parochial district, is also frequently meant, *Ius Ecclesiasticum* . . ., Tomus III, Pars II, Pars III, Tit. 29, para. 1, n. 2, p. 645. It is worth noting that *parochiae gentilitiae*, personal parishes, existed side by side with territorial parishes. Cf, FERRARIS, L., ibid, n. 17, col. 35.

Another element which found its way into the juridical formation of the parish was the right of the pastor to live on the resources of the parish. Saint Paul acknowledges this right of the clergy.[37] Since rural parishes initially did not enjoy autonomy, as they were viewed as mere stations of the cathedral church, it was natural that all offerings and contributions by the faithful were placed in possession of the bishop who distributed them according to the various needs of individual churches. There is evidence, however, that by the fifth century parochial churches enjoyed the right to endowment.[38] In a letter of Pope Gelasius I (a. 492-496) to Archdeacon Justine the right to ownership by the parochial church is acknowledged, but the administration of the same was reserved to the bishop who would then distribute the proceeds accordingly: one part for the bishop, one for the maintenance of the clergy, one for the maintenance and repair of churches, and one for the poor.[39] In addition to land property and donations, *decimae*[40] (tithes) and *primitiae*[41] (first produce of the year) were other sources of revenue[42] which were likewise distributed

---

[37] I Cor. 9: 13.

[38] Concilium Carthaginense (a. 419) Titt, XXXI, XXXIX, *Mansi* Tomus IV, coll. 430, 432; Concilium Carthaginense (a. 421), Titt. IX, X, loc. cit., col. 450; Concilium Agathense, (a. 506), cap. II, cann. 49, 53, *Mansi*, Tomus VIII, col. 333; Concilium Moguntiacum, (a. 813), can. 41, *Mansi*, Tomus XIV, col. 74; Concilium Lateranense V, (a. 1512-1517), Sessio IX, *Bulla Reformationis Curiae, Conciliorum Oecumenicorum Decreta* . . . , p. 617; Concilium Tridentinum, Sessio XXI, *Decretum de Reformatione*, can. 7. loc. cit., p. 731; c. 1, (Gratianus) c. XIII, q. 1; c. 3, *Ad audientiam*, X, *De Ecclesiis Aedificandis vel Reparandis*, III, 48.

[39] C. 23, C. XII, q. 2; cf. Concilium Moguntinum I (a. 847), cap. 10, *Mansi*, Tomus XIV, col. 906.

[40] REIFFENSTUEL, A., *Ius Canonicum* . . . , Vol. IV, Lib. III, Tit. 30, n. 2, p. 593: "Decimae ad proposítum bene definiuntur, quod sint 'decima pars omnium fructuum et proventuum juste acquisitorum, Deo in recognitionem universalis, supremique dominii debita, atque Ecclesiae ministris solvenda."

[41] Loc. cit., §IX, n. 171, p. 635: "Per Primitias intelliguntur, primi fructus, qui ex terra et humo gignuntur, puta, agrorum, vinearum, hortorum, arborum, etc . . . Qui primi et optimi fructus ex praecepto divino olim offerebantur Domino in signum recognitionis et gratitudinis debitae."

[42] Concilium Moguntiacum (a. 813). can. 41, *Mansi*, Tomus XIV, col. 74; Concilium Arelatense VI, (a. 813), cann. 9. 20, loc. cit., coll. 60, 62; Concilium Moguntinum I, (a. 847), capp. 10, 11, loc. cit., col. 906; concilium Ravennense, (a. 877), Statutum XVIII, *Mansi*, Tomus XVII, col. 340; Concilium

according to the Gelasian regulation.[43] By the sixth century, however, a gradual decentralization in the administration of revenues had commenced. In the Council of Lyons II (a. 567) the pastor is presented as the one in charge of the finance of the parish.[44] *Capitula Herardi*, in the ninth century, explicitly charges the pastor with this responsibility under the surveillance of the bishop.[45] Hincmarus Rhemensis, a contemporary of Herardus, voiced the concern about human greed in the administration of parishes: "The Bishop should visit his parishes not in quest of material profit but for the purpose of instructing his people."[46]

From this process of decentralization, the parish emerged at long last as a juridical person, and as a benefice. By virtue of enjoying the right to endowment, the parish developed into a juridical person[47] and the pastor became its *curator natus*.[48] With the institution of *decimae* and *primitiae*,

---

Triburiense, (a. 895), can. 14, *Mansi*, Tomus XVIII, col. 140; Concilium Troslejanum (a. 909) cap. VI., loc. cit., col. 280; Concilium Tridentinum, (a. 1545-1563), Sessio XXI, *Decretum de Reformatione*, can. 4, *Conciliorum Oecumenicorum Decreta* . . . , p. 729; Sessio XXIV, *Decretum de Reformatione*, can, 13, loc. cit., p. 767; *Capitulare Theodulfi* . . . , (a. 797), can. 14, *Mansi*, Tomus XIII, col. 998; *Hettonis Capitulare*, (a. 802 -822), cap. 15, P.L., Series Secunda, Tomus 105, col. 765; AMULUS, (a. 853), *Epistola Prima ad Theodboldum* . . . , cap. VII, P. L., Tomus 116, col. 82; CHRODEGANGUS, *Regula Canonicorum*, cap. 75, *De Decimis Dividendis*, P.L., Tomus 89, col. 1089; *Capitula Herardi*, (+ 870), capp. 32, 35, P.L., Series Secunda, Tomus 121, col. 766; c. 45, C. XVI, q. 1; C.I. (gratianus), C. XIII, q. 1.

[43] Concilium Moguntinum (a. 847), cap. 10, *Mansi*, Tomus XIV, col. 906; HINCMARUS RHEMENSIS, (a. 852), *Capitula Quibus de Rebus*, cap. 16, *Mansi*, Tomus XV, col. 480; CHRODEGANGUS, *Regula Canonicorum*, Cap. 75. De Decimis Dividendis, P.L., Tomus, 89, col. 1089.

[44] Concilium Lugdunense II, can. 5, *Mansi*, Tomus IX, col. 788; cf. Concilium Moguntinum I, (a. 847), capp. 10, 11, *Mansi*, Tomus XIV, col. 906; Concilium Ravennense, (a. 877), Statutum XVIII, *Mansi*, Tomus XVII, col. 340; Concilium Triburiense, (a. 895), can. 14, *Mansi*, Tomus XVIII, col. 140.

[45] Cap. 35, Series Secunda, P.L., Tomus 121, col. 766: "ut decimae et fideliter a populis dentur, et canonice a presbyteris dispensentur, et annis singulis rationem suae dispensationis episcopo vel suis ministris reddant."

[46] *Capitula Archidiaconibus Presbyteris* . . . , cap. II, *Opera Omnia*, Tomus Prior, P.L., Tomus 125, col. 801: "ut parochias non occasione victus, sed instructionis causa circumeant."

[47] Canon 515, §3; canon 113, §2.

[48] Canon 1182 (1917); can. 532 (1983).

the parish was transformed into a benefice,[49] and the pastor was placed as the sole beneficiary.[50] Two factors, however, seem to have contributed significantly to the establishment of the parochial benefice: the introduction of territorial circumscription by which it was determined more precisely who were those bound by the law of *decimae* and *primitiae*;[51] and the replacement of these by *iura stolae*.[52] In the new Code, the parish retains its juridical personality, but has lost its character of a benefice.

The juridical configuration of the parish remained substantially the same down to the eve of Vatican Council II. The parish in the 1917 Code was essentially perceived as a territorial section,[53] operating as an insular cell within the perimeter of a larger estate. Too much emphasis on its juridical personality rendered the parish as an entity too distant and aloof from the parish church and the parochial community. The parish as benefice contributed considerably to the disruption of the presbyteral unison intended to the building-up of the parochial community. The curate was assistant to the person of the pastor,[54] rather than associate pastor assigned to the parish. The position of the pastor was, furthermore,

---

[49] FERRARIS, L., *Prompta Bibliotheca* . . . , Tomus I, Parisiis, 1866, v. *Beneficium*, Art. I, n. 6, col. 1083: "Beneficium ecclesiasticum, de quo hic est sermo, est jus perpetuum percipiendi fructus ex bonis ecclesiasticis ratione spiritualis officii personae ecclesiasticae auctoritate Ecclesiae constitutum."

[50] 1917 Code, canon 463, §1.

[51] REIFFENSTUEL, A., *Ius Canonicum* . . . , Volumen IV, Lib. III, Tit. 29, n. 3, p. 591: "Praeter divisionem parochiarum divisa sunt etiam bona mere ecclesiastica, prius soli dispensationi episcoporum commissa, assignatis cuivi parochorum suae parochiae decimis, una cum reliquis juribus parochialibus."

[52] Canon 463, §1, (1917 Code).

[53] Canon 216, §1: "Territorium cuiuslibet dioecesis dividatur in distinctas partes territoriales: unicuique autem parti sua peculiaris ecclesia cum populo determinato est assignanda, suusque peculiaris rector, tanquam proprius eiusdem pastor, est praeficiendus, pro necessaria animarum cura."
Cf. FANFANI, LUDOVICUS I., *De Iure Parochorum ad Normam Codicis Iuris Canonici*, Taurini-Romae, 1924, pp. 2,3. In the manner of Schmalzgrueber, the author distinguishes between the material (parochial district), and formal (parochial community) understanding of parish.

[54] Canon 476, §1 (1917 Code).

solidified with the institution of irremovability from office, as sanctioned in canon 454, §2, of the 1917 Code. The autocratic stratification of the parish was even more evidenced when the pastor's authority was compared with the role of the faithful who were, for all intents and purposes, a *qualite négligeable*.

With this brief historical survey of the evolution of the juridical configuration of the parish, one can really appreciate the reform brought about by Vatican Council II. The juridical elements, which have infiltrated through the centuries into the formation of the parish, have obscured, even distorted, the theological and mystical significance of the parish. The aim of the Council was to distill the nature of the parish, and, in so doing, to humanize the parish as it existed in its primordial stage. Thus with Vatican Council II started the transformation of the parish from an impersonal juridical entity into a true community of persons.

The conciliar Decree, *Christus Dominus*, laid down, in our belief, the foundation stone for the revival of authentic conceptualization of the parish. The Decree defines the parish as a "certain part of the diocese."[55] Thus the definition of the parish depends fundamentally on that of the diocese: "A diocese is that portion of God's people which is entrusted to a bishop to be shepherded by him."[56] In this perspective, the parish is therefore conceived of as a "certain part" of that portion of God's people. This understanding of parish is even more explicitly established by the Constitution, *Sacrosanctum Concilium*, which defines the parish as a "grouping of the faithful."[57] In this manner, the principle of territoriality has consequently been eliminated as a constitutive element in the juridical concept of the parish. This does not mean that the traditional territorial arrangement should not remain normative. The principle of territoriality has its pragmatic validity; it is conducive to better efficiency and expediency of

---

[55] n. 30, p. 418.

[56] *Christus Dominus*, n. 11, p. 403; canon 369.

[57] n. 42, p. 152.

organization and of functioning.[58] With the conciliar revision, the parish is no longer perceived as a distinctive territorial section to which a determined populace is assigned, an impersonal juridical entity, a product of human imagination, a matter of convenience, but a true community of persons: "A parish is a certain community of Christ's faithful stably established within a particular Church, whose pastoral care, under the authority of the diocesan Bishop, is entrusted to a parish priest as its proper pastor."[59] With the Vatican reform, the parish has resumed its pristine state as the Church in miniature, essentially composed of the ministerial priesthood and the common priesthood and as a continuum of the diocese; the faithful are that very portion of the people of God, and the office of the pastor is the extension of the bishop's office -- "who takes the place of the bishop."[60] The parochial church, the mystical replica of the cathedral church, becomes the sign of the common priesthood and of the ministerial priesthood as individual, mystical realities (*sanctificans et sanctificatum*), as well as the point of their convergence into the one Church of Christ; it rises as a symbol of the eschatological finality of each of its members. The restoration of the concept of diocese as being essentially people of God, and thereby the wholesome reality of the same, has redeemed the parochial community from its insular existence into the full life of the diocese, a process which reveals in a most pronounced manner the place and role of the parochial community in the full life of the diocese and ultimately in the mystery of the Church itself.[61] From this ecclesial self-awareness, the parochial community can easily see itself reaching out, and identifies itself with the human family as such.

The humanization of the parish with the subsequent diminution of the principle of territoriality has further important ramifications in the general spectrum of the apostolate. Rather than being perceived as an exception,

---

[58] Canon 518.

[59] Canon 515, §1.

[60] *Sacrosanctum Concilium*, n. 42, p. 152.

[61] Canon 529, §2; *Apostolicam Actuositatem*, n. 10, pp. 501-502.

The Parochial Community

quasi-parishes, as defined in canon 516, §1, and personal parishes as defined in canon 518 -- traditionally known as *parochiae gentilitiae*[62] -- are endorsed by the new Code as in consonance with the fundamental concept of diocese. In this new vision of diocese -- parish, the adaptation of team ministry in charge of different parishes becomes feasible.[63]

The abolition, or at least the reform, of the benefice system sanctioned by the conciliar Decree, *Presbyterorum Ordinis*, played an important part in the rejuvenation of the parish.[64] The issue, although it directly concerned the ministerial priesthood, had nonetheless profound bearing on the parish at large. This reform may be perceived as another contributing factor in the enactment of canon 517, §1, on team ministry, a datum which stands as a sign of the collegiality of the ministerial priesthood, and as evidence of participation in the offices of teaching, sanctifying and ruling. Proximately adjacent to the revision of the benefice system was the abolition of the irremovability of office of pastor enjoined by the conciliar Decree, *Christus Dominus*.[65] Thus the ministerial priesthood within the context of the parish was purified from two archaic elements which had aggravated to a large extent the distortion of the primordial concept.

---

[62] FERRARIS, L., *Prompta Bibliotheca* . . ., Tomus VI, v. *Parochia*, n. 17, col. 35: "Pluribus in locis adsunt parochiae, quae non distinguuntur per domos materiales, et per determinatos districtus locorum, sed per populos, seu familias, et istae vocantur parochiae gentilitiae earumdem familiarum, ita ut etsi eaedem familiae commorentur in districtu alterius parochiae, subsunt nihilominus jurisdictioni suae parochiae gentilitiae."

[63] Canon 517, §1.

[64] n. 20, p. 573: "The chief emphasis should be given to the office which sacred ministers fulfill. Hence the so-called benefice system should be abandoned or at least it should be reformed in such a way that the beneficiary aspect, that is, the right to revenues accruing to an endowed office, will be treated as secondary, and the main consideration in law will be accorded to the ecclesiastical office itself. From now on such an office should be understood as any function which has been permanently assigned and is to be exercised for a spiritual purpose," *Ecclesiae Sanctae*, AAS, 58 (1966) 762, n.8; canons 1272, 281.

[65] n. 31, pp. 419-420; *Ecclesiae sanctae*, AAS, 58 (1966) 768-769, n. 20; canons 522, 1740 - 1752.

The office of associate pastor has assumed nuances which exceed the expectations of the 1917 Code. In the present Code more emphasis is given to the mutual co-operation and the sharing of concerns between the pastor and the associate-pastor; although always under the pastor's authority, any project undertaken must proceed from common counsel and effort.[66] Such a harmonious co-responsibility in decision making and performance clearly reveals the collegial nature of the presbyterate in the reality of the parochial community. It is also worth noting that with the elimination of the principle of territoriality as a constitutive element, it is now feasible for an associate pastor to be appointed to a number of parishes at the same time.[67] Such an appointment demonstrates, as does team ministry, the holistic nature of the diocese as fostered by Vatican Council II.

Toward a Further Understanding of the Parochial Community in Light of the Teaching of Vatican Council II.

Ministerial priesthood and common priesthood form the two essential components in the reality of the Mystical Body of Christ. Authoritative ministry is commonly attributed, and rightly so, to the ministerial priesthood, whereas charisma constitutes the nature of common priesthood. Their mutual correlation and their interdependence are such that one intrinsically necessitates the other. The ministerial priesthood has no reason to be if not in view of the ultimate fulfillment of the Christian community. Outside this perspective, authoritative ministry is likely to turn into mere domination and mundane supremacy. Common priesthood, on the other hand, needs authoritative ministry for the continuity of its apostolicity. Without authoritative ministry, the charism of the common priesthood runs the risk of being reduced to pure subjectivism and fanaticism. Authoritative ministry must, by its very nature, be incorporated into the life of the faith community as its indispensable means and instrument for self-actualization

---

[66] Canon 545, § 1.

[67] Canon 545, § 2.

The Parochial Community

and self-completion as the Mystical Body of Christ. Although the concept of ministry in the early Church appears to have been vague and unique to individual communities, there is no evidence anywhere in the New Testament that elders, prophets, and teachers were not in operation in these communities. Apart from the reality of leadership, it is the Catholic dogma that the powers of Order are the sole prerogative of the ministerial priesthood. The sacraments of the Eucharist, Penance, Confirmation, and Anointing of the Sick, need sacred Ordination in the minister in order to produce sanctifying grace in the recipient.

The assumption of ministry and charism as characteristics of the ministerial priesthood and common priesthood respectively can only be upheld in principle and in general terms. Both realities intermingle in both the ministerial priesthood and common priesthood: ministry ultimately is charisma just as much as charisma is ministry. The role of the priest and that of the faithful converge ultimately in the one ministry of Christ in a variety of ways: in directing, animating, guiding, inspiring and succouring. An essential distinction, however, should not be missed between the priest and the faithful, between ordained ministry and charismatic ministry. It is only in the priestly ministry handed down through Sacred Ordination that sacred power and authority reside.

The parish should not be acknowledged solely as a juridical entity historically evolving from the diocese since the early times of the Church. However its importance may be assessed in the stratification of the diocese, the parish by its nature expresses a theological reality. The parochial community enshrines the unbroken chain of apostolic succession in the authoritative ministry through sacred ordination, and specifically in the appointment of the pastor by the legitimate ecclesiastical authority for the service of the community; it is also itself the continuity of apostolicity. In brief, the parochial community is a continuum of the diocese; it is indeed an authentic reflection of the Church of Christ. As has been expounded earlier, the Church, being in essence natural law transposed and translated into human consciousness, is by its very nature *koinonia, diakonia, martyrion,* to itself and to the human family. The parochial community, to be true to itself, should likewise bear the same characteristics.

The Parochial Community is Koinonia

The parish is indeed a community in itself, but not by itself and for itself. Its polarity must evidently be found first in the concept of fellowship, of inter-personal relationship, of active, conscious, and responsible inter-communication and inter-dependence of all its members.[68] The reality of fellowship or discipleship, however, assumes its validity from the universal ecclesial community, the Mystical Body of Christ, specified through the diocesan dimension, and it ultimately reaches out and correlates with the human family itself.

Because of the intimacy between the Church and the human family founded and centered in Christ as their finality, the parochial community is at once a faith community and the human family itself. It is the christological nature of human consciousness that induces the parochial family to recognize itself and to explicate itself in the realm of naturalness. This faith community by its own consciousness of being an integral part of the Mystical Body acknowledges and endorses the supreme worth of human nature; its very being helps its own members to understand that the human being by the fact of being human has the fundamental right to the concern, solicitude, and succour of the parochial community.

A tendency lurks in our times which tries to reduce the Gospel teaching on Christian salvation to the problem of changing social and political structures. It is a serious error to simplify the Evangelical message to a mere socio-political ideology. By so doing, this movement is at the same time ignoring the eschatological dimension of human existence, and thus inserting a materialistic connotation into the Christian message.

It is equally a serious distorting of the Evangelical message, however, to deny the intimate connection between the proclamation of the Gospel and socio-political issues which prompt human integrity and liberation. In

---

[68] In order that the parochial community may indeed become a unison of minds, canon 524 suggests that, in the appointment of a pastor, the bishop, if he deems it appropriate, should consult some priests and faithful.

the holistic conceptualization of the human being as presented in the Gospel, and as far as it is comprehended by human consciousness at the present stage of its own humanization, Christian consciousness can no longer argue that the liberation of the human person from social and political alienation does not form an integral part of the Christian aspiration. The absorption of the human individual into the mystery of salvation, by all means, entails interiorization of the heart, mind and spirit. But this inner re-vitalization by its inner destiny must explicate itself within the context of the human community. To maintain that conversion and Christian perfection can be accomplished independently of the human community is to reject the very nature of the Church as taught by the Catholic Tradition. Nowhere in the Gospel is the human person not perceived in his totality and complexity, which includes the economic, social, and political dimensions of his existence. Vatican Council II, particularly in the Constitution, *Gaudium et Spes,* apodictically discards the concept of an apolitical Church. According to this Constitution, the renewal of the human soul in view of the *parousia* and the promotion of social justice constitute the most fundamental objectives of the Christian message[69] in modern times. The inter-relatedness between the process of humanization of human consciousness and the manifestation of the Kingdom has been the subject also of papal Encyclicals.[70] One cannot acquire an indepth understanding of canons 747, §2, 225, §2, 528, §1, without having first studied the doctrine of Vatican Council II and of these papal Encyclicals on the subject.

Before it relates to the human family, the parochial community must identify itself with the universal Church through the diocese. Within this *complexus,* particularly under the authority of the bishop,[71] the parish

---

[69] N. 26, pp. 225-226.

[70] *Rerum Novarum,* May 15, 1891, *Acta Leonis XIII,* Tom. XI, (1892) 97-148; *Quadragesimo anno,* May 15, 1931, AAS, 23 (1931) 177-228; *Mater et Magistra,* May 15, 1961, AAS, 53 (1961) 401-464; *Pacem in Terris,* April 11, 1963, AAS, 55 (1963) 257 - 304; *Populorum Progressio,* March 26, 1967, AAS, 59 (1967) 257-299; *LaboremExercens,* September 14, 1981, AAS, 73 (1981) 577-647.

[71] Canons 515 §1; 519.

activates, evolves and develops. The parochial community, thus being in direct and proximate correlation with the human family, on one hand, and an integral part of the Mystical Body of Christ on the other, enables the individual Christian consciousness to find in the most intensive-extensive manner the purposefulness and meaningfulness of its own existence -- that of rationality, conscientiousness, and sociability -- which by its inner destiny must unfold into eschatological self-fruition.

Christ has been posited in these papers as the centrifugal and centripetal force of the Church and creation. This same central idea must be valid in the conceptualization of the parish as *koinonia*. Nowhere can this idea be apprehended so indisputably true and real as in the Eucharist. Thus the celebration of the Eucharist is at once the symbol and epitome of the parish as human community and as ecclesial community.[72]

The Parochial Community is Diakonia

The concept of *koinonia* necessarily entails the concept of *diakonia*. The ecclesial community, indeed any true human community, can only be kept alive through the magnanimous service of all towards others. The Aristotelian classification of humans into those born to rule and those born to serve is *a priori* antithetical to the Christian assumption on the nature of community. The concept of *diakonia* will ever remain paradoxical in an aristocratic stratification of the Christian community.

The concept of *diakonia* at the present stage of christolization of the christianalized human consciousness is thought to be based on three criteria, which are: the principle of subsidiarity, the principle of co-responsibility, the principle of legitimate diversity. The criterion of subsidiarity calls for the mitigation of autocracy, the decentralization of basic authority, from which intrinsically follows the principle of co-responsibility. The concept of subsidiarity is antinomous to autocracy, but neither is it synonymous with democracy; it can very well be implemented

---

[72] This point needs more elaboration and clarification. I deal more extensively with the subject in my lecture on the Eucharist. Cf. *Sacrosanctum Concilium*, n. 42. p. 153.

within the hierarchic structure of a community, and in various degrees. In more specific terms, the concept of subsidiarity does not conflict with, and less still does it reject, the existence of leadership. The term itself -- subsidiarity, *subsidium* -- presupposes a superior authority since it indicates auxiliary, supplementary, and adjunct collaboration with authority. In practice, it all depends on the basic security, self-assurance, and maturity of the authority concerned. The concept of co-responsibility must therefore always be understood in the light of the principle of subsidiarity. It goes without saying that the implementation of both principles -- subsidiarity and co-responsibility -- demands as prerequisite a psychological and spiritual formation in the one who is asking for personal involvement in the service of the Christian community.

The criterion of legitimate diversity may appear, at first, contradictory with the concept of *koinonia,* which inspires harmony, conformity, uniformity, and one-mindedness. The principle of legitimate diversity would be a paradox in this perspective if the Christian community were conceptualized as a homogenous group, a throng devoid of *esprit de corps,* a mere gathering of humans functioning at a level of bare existence. Indeed, it is the nature of the Pentecostal Spirit that allows, and more so endorses, the charismatic diversity in unity. The prophetic mission of the ministerial priesthood consists precisely in this, that it tries to read, and accept the Spirit of God working through the common priesthood, which reveals itself in diversified and spontaneous charisms corresponding to the needs of the time.

As earlier indicated, the ministerial priesthood and common priesthood join into one interlocked reality in forming the parochial community; both, clergy and faithful, each in their own particular way, contribute to the realization of one-mindedness in Christ. The ministerial priesthood with its office of teaching, sanctifying, and governing nurtures the common priesthood in the pursuance of its own realization.[73] The common priesthood makes effective the service given by its response to its own sanctification, and in its assistance to the ministerial priesthood in the

---

[73] Canon 519.

formation and solidification of the *koinonia* in its anthropological and eschatological dimensions.[74] A brief exposition on the role of the pastor, and of the faithful, each within the context of *diakonia,* may clarify more their respective contributions to the building up of the parochial community.

The Office of Pastor in the Context of Diakonia

The ministerial priesthood is actualized in accentuated form in the office of the parochial pastor. This ministry is the focal reality with which the parochial community identifies, and in which it finds its unity in itself, with the diocese, and with the universal Church. For this reason, the parochial community enjoys the innate right to an authoritative ministry in order to ensure and enhance its apostolicity.[75] The pastor is thus said to be the *didaskalos,* the teacher of the good news, the witness, the guarantor, and the animator of the apostolicity of the parochial community.

The institutional aspect of the office of pastor should not be interpreted as socio-political leadership by way of mandate from the community, in accordance with modern understanding of civil government. On the other hand, this ministry should not infer absolutism of authority as much as inspire insensitivity to the rights and needs of the faithful. Authoritative ministry is charismatic just as much as it is institutional. Ordained ministry is charismatic in the sense that it is a prophetic role, and as such, *pneuma hegemonikon,* charisma of leadership. The pastor's role is that of an overseer who makes sure that all needs are met, all services are rendered, and all ministries are carried out in due manner. His role is to facilitate communication between himself and the faithful entrusted to his care, to exhibit willingness and readiness to encourage all members to active participation in the life of the community, to support and animate any type of *diakonia* corresponding to the needs of the community, and to

---

[74] Canon 228.

[75] Canon 212, §3.

motivate and stimulate the charisms which solidify and enrich the *koinonia*. The task of the pastor is to live the Gospel himself, to proclaim and to interpret the Good News of the Kingdom to present circumstances. The pastor is there to lead each and every member of the community by way of direction, admonition, comfort, animation, and inspiration.[76] This he does, in particular manner, through preaching, catechetical formation, counseling, and in the celebration and administration of the sacraments.[77] More so now than ever before, the prophetic task of the pastor much reach out to the human personhood in all its entirety. The Code, in canon 529, §1, directs the pastoral activity of the pastor also to works of social welfare and human development. The pastor thus stands out as the official prophet in the community, and the driving force of the community in the explication of its own christological nature. Most of all, he is the minister *par excellence* of the sacraments. This is the most serious responsibility of the pastor to see to it that the parochial community is being nourished by those very tools which the Lord has established for the building up of His Mystical Body, and for the salvation of every individual in the community. To this aim, Canon 528, §2, points out that the Eucharist and penance ought to be of major concern in his ministry.

The Faithful in the Context of Diakonia

In the service to itself and to others outside itself the parochial community moves more towards being itself; it acquires more awareness of itself as actuality of the universal inwardness of human consciousness; it recognizes the best of itself, and reaches out into the awareness of itself with the global human family. *Diakonia* is the only valid source from which the parochial community receives the stimulus towards self-identification and self-actualization.

---

[76] Canon 529, §1.

[77] Canons 519, 528, §1, 2.

For many centuries the faithful were forced into a state of passivism which resulted in infantile dependency upon the pastor, indifferentism, and uninvolvement leading towards the denial of their own ecclesial consciousness as an alive, active, constitutive element of the Church. The gradual emancipation of the common priesthood, initiated by Vatican Council II, had to have profound and proximate bearing upon the parochial community, as such, and upon the individual member. Any member who does not actively participate in the pastoral and liturgical life of the community is not only useless to the community, but also to himself; no human can live in isolation. What the individual member does to the community, whether civil or ecclesiastical, he is doing to himself; in rendering service, the person is actually becoming at once more humanized, more christianized, more authentic. The participation of the faithful in the pastoral and liturgical life of the parish has been discussed in the exposition on the common priesthood in general. As a reminder, it suffices here to quote the teaching of the conciliar Decree, *Apostolicam Actuositatem:* "As sharers in the role of Christ the Priest, the Prophet, and the King, the laity have an active part to play in the life and activity of the Church. Their activity is so necessary within church communities that without it the apostolate of the pastors is generally unable to achieve its full effectiveness . . . Strengthened by active participation in the liturgical life of their community, they are eager to do their share in the apostolic works of that community."[78] Charisms are manifestations of Pentecost perpetuating itself in history. Being one with the universal Church through the diocese, the parochial community is, by its very nature, a means by which the different charisms of the common priesthood, under the direction of the ministerial priesthood, are identified, genuinely expressed, authentically actualized, and developed, for the building-up of the Mystical Body of Christ and of the human family at large. Nowhere is the sense of belonging to the Church felt to be so real, so close, so alive to the faithful as in the parochial community. And the parochial *koinonia* can be experienced in its plenitude in no other manner than in its actualization as *diakonia*. And *diakonia* can

---

[78] N. 10, p. 500.

never reach its profound significance unless it is directed to the fundamental dignity of the human person.

Diakonia is itself prophetic charisma since it accommodates itself to the needs of time and place. By its very nature, it is spontaneous, manifold in self-expression, and forever evolving. It is the universal inwardness of the christianized human consciousness in action; it is the rationality, conscientiousness, and sociability of the human being in actuality. Its very nature discards any human speculation regarding the manner in which it emerges and develops. Whereas the institution of ministries for the liturgical life of the community[79] is endorsed by the present Code, no mention is made regarding the pastoral life of the same. From the juridical point of view it seems that the diverse pastoral activities of the faithful ought to be considered ministries only in the broad sense. In this sphere of activity, the spontaneity of the charism is left untouched, without, however, ignoring the right and duty of the pastor to supervise these under-takings. Three instances, however, are mentioned in the Code where the faithful may exercise their *diakonia,* and these are: the pastoral council;[80] the finance committee;[81] a parish entrusted to the faithful.[82]

It is commonly understood that new forms of ministries should result from the community's own decision as to what its needs are and how these are best met. In law, however, a distinction is made between diakonia, and "ministries." Etymologically and in actual fact, both terms signify service, and are an answer to an urgent and concrete need expressed by the community. But the term "ministries" assumes in the Code a specific connotation. Thus the juridical term "ministry" retains fundamentally the concept of *diakonia,* whereas the term *diakonia* does not qualify as "ministry" in the juridical sense. The term "ministry," which is adopted exclusively in the Code to refer to the sacral life of the community, entails

---

[79] The liturgical ministries of the faithful have been pointed out in the preceding paper.

[80] Canon 536, § 1,2.

[81] Canon 537.

[82] Canon 517, §2.

certain characteristics not found in the concept of *diakonia*. By itself *diakonia* is not self-authenticating; thus it needs an official recognition, and requires that the person be designated and installed in that particular ministry by the ecclesiastical authority and received by the community in full confidence. The sense of being called and being sent to exercise a particular service is thus verified in the minister. In this sense, the juridical concept of "ministry" differs substantially from *diakonia*. In accordance with canon 145, §1, "ministry" should be defined as an ecclesiastical office.

The Parochial Community is Martyrion

The parochial community, manifesting itself in gratuitous service, stands out as the most authentic and irreversible solidarity of all believers in the one Head. Life in the community introduces and integrates the individual into the full participation in the salvific mission of the Church. "Offering an obvious example of the apostolate on the community level is the parish, inasmuch as it brings together the many human differences found within its boundaries and draws them into the universality of the Church."[83] In this perspective, the dynamism of the parochial community may be reckoned as being a converging force. On the other hand, the active participation in the life of the parochial community places the individual in close contact with all the members; it introduces the person to the different segments of human want; it opens up a vision which surpasses the perimeters of the community itself, into a universal and fundamental solidarity of all humans; it is a proof by itself that Christianity knows no boundaries or limitations. Through the parochial community the faithful come in direct and close contact with humanness itself as a sacred and sublime creation. Thus the parochial community is a centrifugal, just as much as it is a centripetal, force. Through *diakonia* exercised especially in social and charitable activities the parochial community is *martyrion* to itself and to the World; indeed, it is a force which by its nature explicates

---

[83] *Apostolicam actuositatem*, n. 10, p. 501.

the wholeness of the human person -- one's total humanness in an eschatological dimension.

The tangential point of the twofold dimension -- sacramental and pastoral -- of the parochial community is the parish church which stands out as the mystical replica of the cathedral church, the converging point of the diocese. In the parish church the three sacraments of Christian initiation are celebrated. In the parish church the person enters into the Christian community through baptism. With the reception of baptism the Lord engrafts the person into his sacred Mystical Body; thus in the act of engrafting the person is at once absorbed into the mystery of Redemption and immersed more fully into human nature of which Christ is the *causa formalis;* thus with one's reception of baptism Christ explicates himself more intensively and extensively as *causa finalis* of human nature. In view of this aim, the baptized is confirmed, strengthened, and vivified with the same Spirit of the Lord in the parish church that he may more adroitly reach out to the world as herald of the Mystery. At the proper time, the baptized approaches the Eucharist, the source and aim of all the sacraments, the force of unity of the Christian community. The baptized together with the brethren in faith celebrates the Memorial of the Lord's sacrifice, and partakes of the one meal: "As this broken bread was scattered upon the mountain tops and after being harvested was made one, so let Thy Church be gathered together from the ends of the earth into Thy Kingdom, for Thine is the glory and the power through Jesus Christ forever."[84] The parish church thus stands out as a real sign that the parochial community is truly alive, witnessing to itself and to others that Christ is indeed the focal point of creation, the human being in particular.

---

[84] *The Didache* or *Teaching of the Apostles,* chap. 9. Trans. Francis X. Glimm, *The Fathers of the Church,* New York, 1947, p. 179.

Episcopal Conference in the Life of the Church

The Bishops went into Vatican Council II with the firm intent of regaining what was theirs *ex iure divino*, and which they had lost through the passage of time. The outcome, as one might say, was that they divorced "Roma" only to marry "Conferentia." Frequent complaints have been voiced against the subsequent restriction of the episcopal powers caused by the infiltration of authority by the Episcopal Conference in the governance of the diocese.

However justified may be the complaint, the Episcopal Conference constitutes the realization of the ongoing process of the Church in self-discovery, self-purification and self-actualization. The Episcopal Conference signals the ecclesial spirit in its endeavour to explicate its inherent nature, what it truly is: community, communio, one-mindedness of the many in the Spirit.

The Episcopal Conference finds its roots in the event of Pentecost. Indeed it is the perpetuation of the salvific mission by the messianic gift ever present in history. It manifests and endorses the intrinsic validity of the Episcopal College in self-subsistence, beyond the diocesan stratification of the Church; it confirms and solidifies the communal nature of the Episcopal College. One can appreciate the juridical significance of the Episcopal Conference only if it is placed in the theological spectrum of the *Ecclesia* starting from Pentecost.

Theology of the Episcopal Conference

Creation of the human race finds its ultimate meaning in the mystery of Pentecost. The messianic gift's intent was to purify, intensify and perfect the individual member with its fortifying virtue. The spirit of God made itself visible in parted tongues, as it were, of fire and sat upon every one of them.[1] The messianic spirit, accommodating itself to individual idiosyncrasies, brings about, nonetheless, interiorization of the same leading to objective, absolute freedom. From the transformation thus registered, emerges the exteriorization of the human self in a bond of unity and profound solidarity with other humans of the same faith. Thus, in the phenomenon of Pentecost the human mind regained its primordial authentic freedom in the establishment of one-mindedness in unison with legitimate individual diversity. Baptized with the Holy Spirit at Pentecost the Apostolic College emerged as one, solid, alive, dynamic, compact group into the sphere of salvific action. Filled with the Holy Spirit, "they began to speak with different tongues, according as the Holy Spirit gave them to speak."[2] Thus the Church, the new creation, emerged from its cradle essentially as a community in testimony of the one Spirit, the Spirit of truth rooted in charity. The collegiality of the episcopal order finds its roots precisely in the one-mindedness of the pentecostal group. The intrinsic continuity of succession makes of the Episcopal College and the Apostolic College one interlocked reality in which the *thesaurus fidei* resides and is perpetuated. For this reason the infallible *magisterium* is the prerogative of the Episcopal College.

The event of Pentecost is forever a reality, as the present is. The compactness of the pentecostal group makes itself felt in the bond of the College of Bishops, which, scattered throughout the world, exercises the authentic magisterium in the offices of teaching, sanctifying and ruling.[3] The collegial nature and meaning of the episcopal order finds its crystallization in the ecumenical council. The Bishops sitting with their head fulfill in a solemn form the divine mandate. Thus in this supreme hierarchical assembly the Church proves to be static in nature, for it maintains its bond of unity with the Apostolic College and preserves the

---

[1] Acts II,1.

[2] Acts II,4.

[3] Canons 752; 1008.

genuine doctrine of Christ, while submitting itself to continuous auto-examination and renewal in the struggle of self-actualization and self-adaptation to the needs of the times.[4] This bond of unity in the episcopal order is evident, albeit in a lesser degree, in plenary and provincial councils.[5] The pentecostal nature of the Episcopal College finds its true and authentic expression also in the establishment of two new institutions. In the post-Vatican Church we witness a further confirmation of the collegial nature of the episcopal order in the Synod of Bishops[6] and in the Episcopal Conference.[7]

History of the Episcopal Conference

The origin of the Episcopal Conference can be traced back to certain meetings of neighbouring Bishops whose aim was the promoting of coordinated pastoral activity, although not on a juridical basis. The Code of 1917 for the first time in the history of the Church legislation accepts and promotes this reality, without giving it the name "Episcopal Conference," and demands that the Bishops of a province should meet in this way at least once every five years for consultations about pastoral activities in their diocese and about the agenda concerning the next provincial council.[8] However, the prototype of the Episcopal Conference was launched by the plenary council of Latin America in 1899. From it emerged a program aimed at the study and coordinated solutions of common problems. After World War I, France, Spain, and the United States followed suit. Particularly after

---

[4] *Lumen gentium*, n. 22.

[5] Canons 439-446.

[6] Canon 342.

[7] Canon 447.

[8] Canon 292.

World War II national and even supranational Episcopal Conferences were created or approved by the Holy See.[9]

The subject was taken up by Vatican Council II. The Decree, *Christus Dominus,* describes the Episcopal Conference as "a kind of council in which the bishops of a given nation or territory jointly exercise their pastoral office by way of promoting that greater good which the Church offers mankind, especially through forms and programs of the apostolate which are fittingly adapted to the circumstances of the age."[10] The Decree also takes pains in establishing fundamental norms on the structure and functioning of the Episcopal Conference which form the substratum of the new codicial legislation.[11] It must be said, however, that in the conciliar document the nature and aim of the Episcopal Conference do not go beyond the idea of a gathering for mere consultation, in which "the insights of prudence and experience have been shared and views exchanged."[12] Moreover, the insistence of the Council for these meetings, "as supremely opportune"[13] seems to indicate mere advocacy, rather than imposition. It was only with the promulgation of the *Motu Proprio, Ecclesiae Sanctae,* that the establishment of the Episcopal Conference became obligatory.[14] During the intervening time between the Vatican Council and the publication of the new Code of Canon Law the Holy See saw to it that the juridical position of the Episcopal Conference becomes solidly established by recognizing its authority over that of the individual Bishop. The Holy See by leaving the execution of ordinances to the discretion of the Episcopal Conference did indeed curtail the growing autonomy of the episcopal office. This policy

---

[9] Cf. LETTMANN, REINHARD *Episcopal Conferences in the New Canon Law,* in *Studia Canonica,* XIV (1980), pp.347-348.

[10] n. 38, 1.

[11] Ibid.

[12] n. 37.

[13] Ibid.

[14] AAS, vol. LVIII, 6 Augustii 1966, art. 41, §1, p. 773.

paved the way to the new codification, in which the preponderance of power entrusted to the Episcopal Conference over the individual Bishop, is a *fait accompli*.

The Episcopal Conference may be seen as a curtailment of the episcopal office in the governance of the diocese. One may even speculate whether the Episcopal Conference might have been adopted as a tool to curb the restoration of the Bishop's authority in the diocese, regained in Vatican Council II. Such a speculation can only be justified if we deny the collegiality of the episcopal order as the theological basis of the Episcopal Conference.[15] Such a speculation seems to us an oversimplification and even misinterpretation of the working of the Spirit commenced in Vatican Council II. The Episcopal Conference is nothing other than the authentic expression of the growing consciousness of the Church in the universality of the episcopal order; it is the acknowledgement and endorsement by the Church of the ecclesial identity of the episcopal office. The Episcopal Conference emerges in the new codification on a par with this growing consciousness. It seems imperative, therefore, to present a cursory exposition on the rights and duties of the Bishop towards the universal Church in the new Code of Canon Law.

The Vatican Model of the Church in Antithesis to the Manorial Model of the Medieval Church

The feudal or manorial model, enforced particularly by Gregory the Great,[16] nurtured extreme compartmentalization of the ecclesial configuration, thus constructing a mosaic of particular Churches in the *civitas Dei*. The juridical concept of the diocese rooted in the system of manor was strictly territorial, and thereby barricaded from its sister-dioceses. The diocese was considered as an administrative, independent, self-sufficient and seclusive estate. As an organic unity each particular

---

[15] LETTMANN, R., *Episcopal Conferences* . . . p. 350.

[16] CLEBSCH, WILLIAM A., *Christianity in European History*, New York,1979, pp. 110-111, 115-116, 118-119.

Church was accountable only to the Apostolic See, and any connection which it might have had with the rest of christendom was through the Roman See. The compartmentalization of the Church on the lines of the manorial system provoked for centuries the universal feeling that the solicitude of the whole Church, as such, was the sole concern of Rome. That profound sense of solidarity and reciprocity was lacking among the particular Churches. Of course, ecumenical, plenary and provincial councils took place throughout the history of the Church down to our times. Some *vinculum iuridicum* existed between the Metropolitan diocese and its suffragan. Apart from this scanty relationship, one could hardly envisage in the pastoral and juridical life of the Church the bond of unity between particular Churches, especially between the diocese and the rest of christendom. The manorial model, which seems to have accommodated the needs of the Medieval Church, nonetheless brought with it disruption in the organic unity of the Church.

This is not to say that from early times particular Churches, or dioceses, did not exist. But the fact that it was realized that each of the local Churches was a local realization of Christ's Church did not stop the early Christians from being fully aware of the essential bonds that tied all these Christian communities together. These bonds enhanced not only the preservation and encouragement of the spirit of *communio,* but they were actualized in several forms, particularly through mutual hospitality, letters of communion, and financial aid.[17]

With the model of communio fostered by Vatican Council II the particular Churches emerge as living members in communion with each other, not only from the theological and spiritual points of view, but also on the pastoral and juridical levels. The Vatican model illustrates conformity of faith as well as *consortium* of the global apostolate. The organic unity of all the Churches into one Church of Christ is procured through direct and close commitment of the particular Churches to each other. The idea of compactness, the belief in *unita fortius,* as fostered by

---

[17] KURTSCHEILD, BERTRANDUS, *Historia Iuris Canonici -- Historia Institutorum*, Romae, 1951, pp. 12-20.

this model, instills a sense of concern, loyalty, co-responsibility, and sacrifice, in the particular Church towards the Church as a whole. The decree, *Ad gentes divinitus*, teaches apropos: "In virtue of this communion, individual Churches carry a responsibility for all the others. They make their needs known to one another, and keep one another mutually informed regarding their affairs. For the extension of the Body of Christ is the duty of the whole College of Bishops."[18]

In the "estate" model the territorial boundaries formed an essential element in the conceptualization of the diocese. In the Vatican model the territorial element loses much of its conditioning and seclusive quality, and the diocese is merely conceptualized as "that portion of God's people which is entrusted to a bishop to be shepherded by him."[19] Thus the concept of diocese assumes a personalistic, rather than manorial aspect, and assumes a more pastoral, than juridical, dimension. So far, the apostolate was delineated in the context of the estate, or manorial assumption, while henceforth the territorial predicament should comply with the exigencies of the apostolate which is universal as is the Church itself.[20]

The Episcopal College as Viewed by the Medieval Church and by Vatican Council II

The manorial model did not, and could not dispense with the nature of the episcopal office as instituted by the Lord Himself. It did, however, stress the territorial element in the conceptualization of the episcopal jurisdiction. The territorial circumscription constituted the substratum, as

---

[18] n.38.

[19] *Christus Dominus*, n. 11; canon 369.

[20] *Christus Dominus*, n.22: "These requirements, then, demand a proper determination of the boundaries of dioceses and a distribution of clergy and resources which is reasonable and in keeping with the needs of the apostolate. All these things will truly benefit not only the clergy and Christian people directly involved, but also the entire Catholic Church. Concerning diocesan boundaries, therefore, this most sacred Synod decrees that, to the extent required by the good of souls, a fitting revision of diocesan boundaries be undertaken prudently and as soon as possible." Cf. n.23.

well as restricting predicament, in the understanding of the episcopal office and in its relation to the *Ecclesia*. The bond of unity between the Bishop and the diocese was such as to be compared with the bond of matrimony; it entailed the qualities of unity and indissolubility. Hence one finds in canonical literature "matrimonium spirituale initum ab episcopo cum sua dioecesi,"[21] although polygamy was tolerated if the Bishop happened to have "ichor" running in his veins. The extreme circumscription of the episcopal office to the diocese was the philosophy still maintained in the Code of 1917.[22] Suffice it to say that juridically speaking, the ecclesial identity of the Bishop evaporated into thin air the moment he stepped out of his territory. The Bishop and the diocese were conceived of as such an organic unity that the concept of the bishopric apart from that of the diocese was from the juridical point of view simply inconceivable. It appeared that only by virtue of the *missio canonica* to govern a local Church did the Bishop share membership with the rest of the episcopate. It must be said that the theology on the collegiality of the episcopal order was uninterruptedly maintained throughout history. However, the manorial model, by focusing on the intimate relationship of the Bishop with the diocese, eclipsed the ecclesial dimension of the episcopal office.

Another consequence of the manorial model was the juridical relationship between the local Ordinary and the faithful. In keeping with the system this relationship was centered on the territorial criterion. The Bishop was not the shepherd of a portion of God's people, but rather a ruler, or better still a vassal, of a domain within which lived Christ's faithful; thus a feeling of immediate, direct and personal communicability could never be nurtured between the Bishop and his flock.

The model of *communio* fostered by Vatican Council II implies a revival of the collegial reality of the ministerial priesthood so characteristic of the early Church. Great emphasis is given by the Council to the principles of solidarity, reciprocity and subsidiarity on all levels of the

---

[21] Decretum, Pars II, Causa XXI, qu.2, *Sicut in unaquaque*, c. IV; REIFFENSTUEL, ANACLETUS, *Ius Canonicum*, Parisiis, 1889, vol. I, Lib. I, Tit. VII, *De Translatione Episcopi*, §II, pp. 383-387.

[22] Cf. canon 329, §1.

Church's activity which in turn nurture a universal feeling of togetherness and one-mindedness and promote coordinated pastoral activity.

The Council insists on the collegiality of the episcopal order. The college of Bishops is an ecclesial reality subsisting beyond and above the local Churches. The Council teaches that "by virtue of sacramental consecration and hierarchical communion with the head and other members of the college, a bishop becomes a part of the episcopal body."[23] In this statement lies the essence of the episcopal office which consists in the membership of the College of Bishops with the Roman Pontiff at its head. It is worth noting that no mention is made of the Bishop's assignment to a particular Church. Thus it is the collegial, rather than the local or particular, reality that is fundamental in the conceptualization of the episcopal office. Willy Onclin, in fact, insists that "the bishops are legitimate heads of particular churches only as members of the college of bishops and in communion with this college and its head."[24] In the conciliar doctrine the reality of the college does not derive from a conglomeration of bishoprics with their locally restricted authority to a particular Church, but rather this reality subsists on its own as a collegial directive body. Thus the essence of the episcopal order is no longer intimately linked with the concept of *missio canonica* and with the concept of *territorialitas*. "As members of the body of bishops which succeeds the college of Apostles, all bishops are consecrated not just for some one diocese, but for the salvation of the entire world."[25] In this theology the qualities of irremovability and of territoriality lose much of their traditional purport in the concept of *missio canonica*, and the Bishop's assignment to a particular Church assumes the nature of *diakonia* in its pure sense.

---

[23] *Christus Dominus*, n.4.

[24] *Collegiality and the Individual Bishop*, in *Concilium -- Theology in the Age of Renewal*, vol. 8, *Pastoral Reform in Church Government*, New York, 1965, p. 83, footnote 4; cf. JIMENEZ-URRESTI, TEODORO, *The Ontology of Communion and Collegial Structures in the Church*, eodem loco, pp. 10-13.

[25] *Ad gentes divinitus*, n. 38; cf. n. 19, n.30; *Christus Dominus*, n. 6, n.3; *Lumen gentium*, n. 22, n. 23, n. 24.

The Theologico-juridical Understanding of the Episcopal College in the New Code of Canon Law

The new Code is a faithful implementation of the Vatican doctrine on the nature of the episcopal order. A comparative glance at the presentation of the theme between the old and the new Code of Canon Law is sufficiently illustrative of the radical change of vision brought about by Vatican Council II. In the Code of 1917 the theme, *De clericis in specie*, concentrated first on the Roman Pontiff, then on ecumenical councils and cardinals, followed by a long list of dignitaries and offices of the Roman Curia. Down at the bottom of the list, in a separate chapter, came the office of Bishop and his subordinates. In the new Code, in the section on the supreme authority of the Church, chapter I is entitled "The Roman Pontiff and the College of Bishops." Before dealing with these two realities separately, the Code lays down the *status quaestionis* to the doctrine in canon 330; "The Roman Pontiff, the successor of Peter, and the Bishops, the successors of the Apostles, are united together in one." Chapter II is dedicated to the Synod of Bishops, whereas the cardinal comes fourth in line. Another significant point to consider is the chapter on Bishops. Article I of this chapter focuses on the episcopal office, *qua talis*, independently of its relationship with the diocese. Whereas the Bishop of a diocese is the topic of article II.

In line with the Vatican vision the College of Bishops forms an interlocked reality with the chair of Peter.[26] It subsists on its own inherent nature apart from the diocesan stratification of the Church.[27] For this reason chapter II of part II, section I entitled "The Supreme Authority of the Church," is exclusively dedicated to the Episcopal College. "The Bishops by virtue of their sacramental consecration and hierarchical

---

[26] Canon 333, §2.

[27] This actuality can also be envisaged in canon 1372 which reads: "A person who appeals from an act of the Roman Pontiff to an Ecumenical Council or to the College of Bishops, is to be punished with a censure." Cf. canons 752, 337, §3.

communion with the head of the College and its members" form the Episcopal College.[28] Very significant is canon 332, §1, which illustrates the intrinsic relatedness of the chair of Peter with the Episcopal College. The elected Pope cannot acquire *ius in re* of supreme authority in the Church unless he is first consecrated Bishop. Implicitly this prescription of the Code entails that one cannot occupy the chair of Peter unless he first becomes a member of the Episcopal College. In like manner, the Bishop partakes of this supreme authority only through the episcopal consecration and hierarchical communion with the head of the College and its members.[29]

The College of Bishops, being of divine institution, "in union with its head and never without its head,"[30] is the embodiment of divine authority which enshrines in itself the offices of sanctifying, of teaching and of ruling.[31] By virtue of this prerogative the College is "subject of supreme and full power over the universal Church."[32]

"The office of preaching the Gospel to the whole Church has been committed principally to the Roman Pontiff and to the College of Bishops."[33] This *magisterium* enjoys the quality of infallibility, when the College as teacher and judge of faith and morals, sits in solemn form in an Ecumenical Council.[34] The College retains its infallible magisterium also when "the Bishops, dispersed throughout the world but maintaining the bond of union among themselves and with the successor of Peter, together

---

[28] Canon 336.

[29] Canons 375, §2, 1; 835, §1.

[30] Canon 336.

[31] Canon 375, §2.

[32] Canon 336.

[33] Canon 756, §1.

[34] Canons 337, §1; 749, §2; 341, §1.

with the same Roman Pontiff authentically teach matters of faith or morals, and are agreed that a particular teaching is definitively to be held."[35]

The oneness of the College retains still its authentic *magisterium* when the Bishops, scattered throughout the world, teach on faith or morals, even if they do not intend to proclaim it with a definitive act.[36] On such matters the Episcopal College can also issue decrees for the universal Church once these matters are introduced or freely accepted by the Roman Pontiff.[37]

The Code makes it clear that this authentic *magisterium* is to be found in every individual episcopal office,[38] whenever a number of Bishops simultaneously carry out the office of preaching together in respect of a number of different Churches,[39] or gathered together in Episcopal Conference: "Whether they teach individually, or in Episcopal Conferences . . . Bishops in communion with the head and the members of the College, while not infallible in their teaching, are the authentic instructors and teachers of the faith for Christ's faithful entrusted to their care . . . "[40] One may thus easily recognize the Episcopal Conference as a particular manifestation of that bond existing between the Apostolic College and the Episcopal College, and as a specific expression of the Episcopal College. Thus the Episcopal Conference by its very nature may be said to be a continuum of the authentic *magisterium* of the Church in a specific locality.

We are cognizant of the objection raised in Vatican Council II as to whether the collegiality of the episcopal order should be the theological

---

[35] Canon 749, §2.

[36] Canons 752; 337, §2.

[37] Canon 341, §2; 754.

[38] Canon 375, §1,2.

[39] Canon 756, §2.

[40] Canon 753.

basis of the Episcopal Conference.[41] The present paper so far has aimed at the advocacy of the Episcopal Conference being a continuum of the episcopal collegiality. The ultimate answer to this question centers on the theological understanding of episcopal collegiality. In a purely physical definition, the term collegiality has a numerical connotation; it rather connotes collectiveness, a mere collection of views agreeing on a particular subject. Such a definition cannot be upheld in the theological comprehension of the episcopal collegiality in which the *magisterium* resides. The nature of the College is the very immanence of the Pentecostal Spirit which vivifies indivisibly and entirely both the College as a whole and each member of the same College. The ontological nature of the episcopal collegiality is exclusively spiritual; thus it essentially stands for one-mindedness, bond, communion, moral togetherness, conformity. Only in this perspective of the collegiality of the episcopal order should the *magisterium* be understood. Since the episcopal collegiality is not collectiveness of ideas, any classification of the *magisterium* has to be qualitatively, rather than quantitatively, apprehended. Only by reason of the intention of the episcopal collegiality is a classification of the *magisterium* feasible, that is infallible *magisterium*, and *authentic magisterium*. Ontologically speaking, the collegiality and magisterium resides also in that Bishop who happens to be the only one alive.

If we adhere to the view that authentic collegiality can be attributed only to the entire body of Bishops assembled under and with its head, one must conclude that it is only in an Ecumenical Council that the Episcopal College can exercise its *magisterium*. Outside the Ecumenical Council the College cannot enjoy the prerogative of infallibility as endorsed by canon 749, §2, since it lacks the physical participation of the entire episcopate and the active presence of the Roman Pontiff. For the same reason, the College is deprived of its authentic *magisterium* sanctioned in canon 752. On the contrary, the moral presence of the entire episcopate and of the head of the College is as real and actual as the physical presence of the same.

---

[41] Cf. LETTMANN, R., *Episcopal Conferences* . . . pp. 350-352.

The reality of the Episcopal College, as an entity in itself, has larger dimensions than being the titular of supreme authority over the universal Church. The truth that it enshrines is rooted in charity. The communal nature of the episcopal order entails concern, sharing and sacrifice, in short, commitment by the members of the College, globally and individually, towards the needs of the universal Church in all segments of her activity. Thus canon 1271 requests from all Bishops their readiness for the cause of the Church: "By reason of their bond of unity and charity, and according to the resources of their dioceses, Bishops are to join together to produce those means which the Apostolic See may from time to time need to exercise properly its service of the universal Church."[42] The overall direction and coordination of missionary activity of the Church pertains to the Roman Pontiff as well as to the College of Bishops;[43] thus the Bishops in their particular dioceses must show a special solicitude for missionary activity especially by initiating, fostering, and sustaining missionary activities in their own particular Churches,[44] and as sponsors of the universal Church they see to it that their faithful concur financially to national or universal initiatives of the Church.[45]

The activity of the College, as a unified force, goes beyond the precincts of the Catholic Church, and reaches the ecumenical enterprise commenced by Vatican Council II. The Code, in fact, acknowledges the ecumenical initiative as the responsibility of the entire College of Bishops just as much as it is of the Apostolic See.[46]

As participants in the supreme and full authority over the universal Church, "all Bishops, but only Bishops, who are members of the College of

---

[42] Canon 337,§3:"It belongs to the Roman Pontiff to select and promote, according to the needs of the Church, ways in which the College of Bishops can exercise its office in respect of the universal Church in a collegial manner."

[43] Canon 782, §1.

[44] Canon 782, §2.

[45] Canon 1266.

[46] Canon 755, §1.

Bishops, have the right and the obligation to be present at an Ecumenical Council with a deliberative vote."[47] Once "the office of preaching the Gospel to the whole Church has been committed principally to the Roman Pontiff and to the College of Bishops,"[48] it follows that the Bishop has the innate right to preach anywhere in the Church, unless expressly forbidden by another local Bishop.[49] The same universality of the episcopal order entitles the Bishop to validly and licitly administer the sacrament of Confirmation also outside his diocese in accordance with the prescriptions of canon 886, §1. On the same presupposition the universal jurisdiction of the Bishop to hear confessions is acknowledged unless in a particular case the local Bishop has refused.[50] His authority to confer sacred orders everywhere is recognized in canon 1017, however with prior permission of the diocesan Bishop, *ad liceitatem*.[51]

Episcopal Conference as Juridical Person

The preceding exposition was intended to present a theological rationale for the existence of the Episcopal Conference as a constitutional institution in the post-Vatican Church. Our attention is now directed to the canons of the new Code by which the Church implements the said theology. We plan to study, from the juridical point of view, the institution in six different dimensions: the Episcopal Conference *in se*; the Episcopal Conference in relation to the Holy See; the Episcopal Conference in relation to the universal Church; the Episcopal Conference in relation to the diocese; the Episcopal Conference and Religious Superiors; the Episcopal Conference and Ecumenism.

---

[47] Canon 339, §1.

[48] Canon 756, §1.

[49] Canon 763.

[50] Canon 967, §1.

[51] Canon 1017.

Nature and Purpose of the Episcopal Conference

It is the sole prerogative of the Holy See to establish, suppress, or alter Episcopal Conferences.[52] Once it is lawfully established the Episcopal Conference enjoys juridical personality by virtue of the law itself.[53]

Canon 447 defines the Episcopal Conference: "a permanent institution, namely, an assembly of the Bishops of a country or of a certain territory, exercising together certain pastoral office for Christ's faithful of that territory. By forms and means of apostolate suited to the circumstances of time and place, it is to promote, in accordance with the law, that greater good which the Church offers to all people."

As stated earlier, the Bishops sitting in conference form a continuum of the universal episcopal collegiality to that portion of the people of God assigned to them by the Apostolic See.[54] Upon this theological *suppositum* is founded the authority of the Episcopal Conference to issue general decrees, in accordance, however, with the prescription of canon 455, §1. It is because of this integrality of the Episcopal Conference with the whole College of Bishops that the faithful are bound to adhere to the instructions and teaching of the Episcopal Conference.[55]

The Episcopal Conference must have its own statutes which have to be reviewed by the Apostolic See.[56] The major concern of the statutes is to lay down norms regarding membership,[57] the right to vote,[58] plenary

---

[52] Canon 449, §1.

[53] Canon 449, §2.

[54] Canon 753.

[55] Canons 753, 754.

[56] Canon 451.

[57] Canons 448, §1; 450, §1, 2.

[58] Canon 454, §1, 2.

meetings of the Conference,[59] the permanent committee of Bishops,[60] the general secretary of the Conference,[61] and other offices and commissions,[62] the election of the President who by law is also the president of the permanent committee.[63]

By virtue of canon 395, §2, an obligatory attendance is imposed on those members who enjoy deliberative vote in accordance with the prescription of canon 450, §1.[64] The Episcopal Conference is a collegial moral person and, as such, it functions. Canon 455 lays down two basic norms of how the Episcopal Conference shall act in reaching a decision and in issuing general decrees: two-thirds of the votes are required of those who have the right to deliberative vote in cases where the universal law so prescribes or by special mandate of the Apostolic See;[65] unanimity of votes is prescribed by law in all other issues[66] according to the prescription of canon 119,n.3. Canon 455, §4, goes on to say that in these latter cases the competence of each Bishop remains intact.[67] As in all other laws,[68] the decrees of the Conference are to be promulgated, and in the manner

---

[59] Canons 451, 453.

[60] Canons 451, 457.

[61] Canons 451, 458, n.l.

[62] Canons 451, 775, §3.

[63] Canon 452, §1.

[64] Canon 454, §1, determines the members who by law have a deliberative vote. Auxiliary Bishops and other titular Bishops do not, *per se*, enjoy right to membership. This holds true also for the papal Legate (canons 450, §2; 454, §2). If they are admitted as members, the statutes shall determine whether they have a deliberative or consultative vote. They have only consultative vote in the making or changing of the statutes (canon 454, §2).

[65] Canon 455, §2, 1; cf. *Christus Dominus*, n. 38. 4).

[66] Canon 455, §4.

[67] If a member, who has a deliberative vote in the Conference, was not present for the meeting, he is still free to act against the decision of the Conference.

[68] Canon 7.

determined by the Conference.⁶⁹ However, any decree issued by the Conference has no binding force unless it is first reviewed by the Apostolic See.⁷⁰

Ecclesiastical Province and Ecclesiastical Region

Apart from the Episcopal Conference, but within the territory of the same, the Code contemplates two other assemblies of Bishops, namely ecclesiastical province and ecclesiastical region. Thus it may be said that the Episcopal Conference is composed of ecclesiastical provinces, whenever it is feasible, which on their part may be further grouped into ecclesiastical regions.

It belongs to the Apostolic See alone, after consultation with the Bishops concerned, to establish, suppress, or alter ecclesiastical provinces.⁷¹ Once an ecclesiastical province is established, it is endowed with a juridical personality by virtue of the law itself⁷² with a certain defined territory.⁷³ In the new legislation there are no longer exempt dioceses, but individual dioceses and other particular Churches, which exist within the territory of an ecclesiastical province, must belong to that ecclesiastical province.⁷⁴ The Code acknowledges the authority of the Metropolitan, and of the provincial council, if there happens to be one, over the ecclesiastical province, taking into account, however, the prescriptions of the law.⁷⁵

The purpose of the ecclesiastical province is defined by canon 431, §1, which is "to promote, according to the circumstances of persons and

---

[69] Canon 455, §2, 3.
[70] Canons 455, §2; 456.
[71] Canon 431, §3.
[72] Canon 432, §2.
[73] Canon 431, §1
[74] Canon 431, §2.
[75] Canon 432, §1.

place, a common pastoral action of various neighbouring dioceses, and the more closely to foster relations between diocesan Bishops." To the provincial Bishops' meeting the Code entrusts the task of determining taxes for the execution of rescripts from the Apostolic See,[76] the offerings on the occasion of the administration of the sacraments and sacramentals, unless the law prescribes otherwise,[77] and also Mass stipends.[78]

In spite of its juridical personality, the provincial Bishops' meeting is, *per se*, a consultative body. If, however, it decides to act collegially, the prescription of canon 119, n. 2, must be observed. How often the provincial meeting should be held, is left to the discretion of the Bishops concerned. However, the purpose of the provincial assembly, as defined in canon 431, §1, necessitates a certain degree of stability and continuity. And this cannot be verified unless the Bishops meet, at least, once a year.[79]

"If it seems advantageous, especially in countries where there are very many particular Churches, the Holy See can, on the proposal of the Episcopal Conference, join together neighbouring provinces into ecclesiastical regions."[80] The purpose of the ecclesiastical region, in line with that of the ecclesiastical province, is to enable the Bishops of the region to meet for consultations about pastoral activities in their diocese, and to study and coordinate programs of pastoral issues concerning the region.[81]

Unlike the ecclesiastical province, the ecclesiastical region does not by law enjoy juridical personality.[82] The Code makes it clear that the ecclesiastical region should not interfere or in any way assume the powers

---

[76] However these taxes must first be approved by the Holy See.

[77] Canon 1264.

[78] Canon 952, §1.

[79] By recourse to canon 453.

[80] Canon 433, §1.

[81] Canon 434.

[82] Canon 433, §2.

given to Episcopal Conferences, unless the Holy See has granted some of these powers.[83] The ecclesiastical region remains essentially a consultative body to be convened at the discretion of the Bishops concerned. However, the same holds true for the ecclesiastical region as that which has been pointed out earlier regarding the convocation of the ecclesiastical province.

Plenary Council

A council celebrated within the territory of an Episcopal Conference is called plenary council. The necessity or usefulness of its convocation is left to the discretion of the Episcopal Conference having first sought the approval of the Apostolic See.[84] "It is the responsibility of the Episcopal Conference: 1. to convene a plenary council; 2. to choose a place within the territory of the Episcopal Conference for the celebration of the council; 3. to elect from among the diocesan Bishops a president of the plenary council, who is to be approved by the Apostolic See;[85] 4. to determine the order of business and the matters to be considered, to announce when the plenary council is to begin and how long it is to last, and to transfer, prorogue and dissolve it."[86]

Besides diocesan Bishops, coadjutor and auxiliary Bishops, only "titular Bishops who have been given a special function in the territory, either by the Apostolic See or by the Episcopal Conference" have deliberative vote.[87] The Episcopal Conference has the right to invite as

---

[83] Canon 434.

[84] Canon 439, §1.

[85] By "Bishop" here is meant also one who is equivalent to a diocesan Bishop ad normam canonis 450, §1.

[86] Canon 441.

[87] Canon 443, §1.

guests to the council any priest, religious, lay person, and even any of the separated Brethren.[88]

Episcopal Conference and Holy See

From the reading of the previous section the reader ought to have noticed the authority of the Apostolic See over the Episcopal Conference. Suffice it to say that all decrees of the Conference need the warrant of the Holy See for their valid promulgation. Moreover, the minutes of each plenary meeting are to be submitted by the president of the Conference to the Apostolic see for information.[89] Another restriction concerns the territory of jurisdiction. It is the Holy See alone which, after consultation with the diocesan Bishops concerned, decides on the territory of greater or less extent, and lays down special norms for each case.[90] Besides the territoriality, the content of jurisdiction is taken care of, as well. Canon 459, §2, forbids the Episcopal Conference to undertake actions or affairs which have an international character before it first consults with the Apostolic See.

These injunctions may appear as vestiges of traditional paternalism if we were to consider the Episcopal Conference merely as an expedient for practical needs, despite its juridical personality. If, on the other hand, we see the Episcopal Conference grounded in the collegial dimension of the episcopal order, the Holy See assumes pivotal significance in the life of the Episcopal Conference; the Apostolic See appears, in this perspective, the *ligamen* between the Episcopal Conference and the entire Church, the knot that binds all Episcopal Conferences into the one and only Episcopal College, the substratum of the authentic magisterium enjoyed by the individual Episcopal Conference.

---

[88] Canon 443, §6.

[89] Canon 456.

[90] Canon 448, §2.

Besides the hierarchical relationship just mentioned, there is another communication between the Episcopal Conference and the Apostolic See which implements, to some extent, the Church's consciousness of its inherent collegiality and the ecclesial identity of the episcopal order. In order to make more firm and effective the bond of unity of the universal College of Bishops with its head, the principal task of the papal Legate is "to foster close relations with the Episcopal Conference, offering it every assistance."[91] This same pursuit is also reckoned in the election of Bishops by the Episcopal Conference to the Synod of Bishops.[92]

Another indication of this communal reality between the two institutions may be apprehended in the task of the Episcopal Conference in presenting every three years a list of priests who are suitable for the episcopate, to the Apostolic See.[93] In the appointment of a diocesan Bishop or of a coadjutor Bishop, the papal Legate must, among other persons, consult with the president of the Episcopal Conference.[94] In the establishment of personal Churches,[95] and of personal prelatures[96] the Holy See intends to consult first the Episcopal Conference before reaching a decision. Therefore, one must acknowledge some degree of co-responsibility being conferred on the Episcopal Conference by the Apostolic See.

Episcopal Conference and Ecclesia

The relationship between the Episcopal Conference and the entire Church is still in its initial phase of development. Very few canons, in fact, are directed by the new Code to the subject, and they concentrate rather

---

[91] Canon 364, n.3.

[92] Canon 346, §1.

[93] Canon 377, §2.

[94] Canon 377, §3.

[95] Canon 372, §2.

[96] Canon 294.

on the relationship of the Episcopal Conference with the neighbouring ones. Canon 459, §1, explores the whole theme: "Relations are to be fostered between Episcopal Conferences, especially neighbouring ones, in order to promote and defend whatever is for the greater good." For this reason the general secretary of the Conference has to see to it that, on the direction of the Conference at a plenary meeting or of the permanent committee of Bishops, acts and documents issued by the same are delivered to neighbouring Episcopal Conferences.[97] The Episcopal Conference, in previous consultation with the Holy See, may undertake actions or affairs of international character.[98] In our belief, the most illustrative canon which shows the intimate link of the Episcopal Conference with the whole Church is canon 792 which imposes upon the Episcopal Conference the charge "to establish and promote means by which those who come to their territory from the missions, for the purpose of work or study, are to be given a fraternal welcome and helped with suitable pastoral care."

Episcopal Conference and Diocese

The Episcopal Conference assumes its ultimate significance in its relationship with the diocese. The Pentecostal Spirit, which is ever present in the Church, makes itself manifest in the Episcopal Conference. As on the day of Pentecost the one and eternal Spirit of God parted over each member of the Apostolic College, the same parting of the Spirit is verified in the Episcopal Conference, through which it vivifies, activates and solidifies that portion of Christ's faithful in the building-up and consolidation of the Mystical Body. While the Episcopal Conference is the Spirit adapting itself to the needs of the faithful in a given circumstance and conditions, it is at the same time a dynamic force of the Mystical Body in its self-explication, self-unification, and growth in charity.

---

[97] Canon 458, n. 2.

[98] Canon 459, §2.

From this theological *suppositum*, flows the authority of the Episcopal Conference to enact general decrees. We have already alluded to the fact that the exercise of such an authority is subject to the provision of common law, namely that "the Episcopal Conference can make general decrees only in cases where the universal law has so prescribed, or by special mandate of the Apostolic See, either on its own initiative or at the request of the Conference itself."[99] The faithful, in communion with their authentic instructors and teachers of the faith, are thereby "obliged to observe the constitutions and decrees which lawful ecclesiastical authority issues for the purpose of proposing doctrine or of proscribing erroneous opinions."[100]

We intend to present the theme on the juridical bearing of the Episcopal Conference on the governance of the particular diocese under the following headings: clergy; sacraments; liturgy; pastoral activity; judiciary; administration; diocesan synod.

Clergy

Under this sub-heading we include all that which concerns the formation, rights and duties of the clergy, and the two colleges of priests. It is the responsibility of the Episcopal Conference to draw up the Charter of Priestly Formation.[101]

> An inter-diocesan seminary needs the approval of the Episcopal Conference, besides that of the Holy See, if its erection is intended for the whole of its territory.[102]
>
> It is the right and duty of the Episcopal Conference to issue norms on the spiritual formation and doctrinal instruction for candidates to

---

[99] Canon 455, §1; cf. §2, 4.

[100] Canon 754; cf, canon 753.

[101] Canon 242, §1.

[102] Canon 237, §2.

the permanent diaconate. It is up to the Conference to determine the manner of how the three years of formation should evolve.[103]

Norms can be enacted by the Episcopal Conference on the ecclesiastical dress of clerics.[104]

The Episcopal Conference is charged with the responsibility of taking care of all clerics in its territory in what concerns their social security.[105] The upkeeping of a Bishop after his resignation becomes the responsibility of the Episcopal Conference, bearing in mind, however, that the primary obligation falls on the diocese which he served.[106]

The Episcopal Conference is to see to it that norms be enacted with which the diocesan Bishop avails himself in providing for the appropriate maintenance and residence of the priest after his resignation from office of pastor.[107]

The Code insists that as a general norm the pastor should be appointed for an indeterminate period of time, and that only by decree of the Episcopal Conference allowing this, can the diocesan Bishop appoint him for a specified period of time.[108]

The Episcopal Conference is to see to it that norms be issued which assist the diocesan Bishop in approving the statutes of the senate of priests.[109] "The Episcopal Conference can determine that the

---

[103] Canon 236, n. 2.

[104] Canon 284.

[105] Canon 1274, §2.

[106] Canon 402, §2.

[107] Canon 538, §3.

[108] Canon 522.

[109] Canon 496.

functions of the college of consultors be entrusted to the cathedral chapter."[110]

Sacraments

With the exception of Eucharist and Anointing of the Sick, the Episcopal Conference has involvement in the administration of all the other sacraments.

Baptism

The provisions of the Episcopal Conference are to be observed in the administration of baptism whether it is conferred by immersion or by pouring.[111]

In the case of an adopted child the Episcopal Conference is to see to it that norms are issued regarding the registration of the child's natural parents in accordance with canon 877, §1 and 2.[112]

Confirmation

The age for the Sacrament of Confirmation can be determined by the Episcopal Conference.[113]

The Episcopal Conference may decide whether the records of Confirmation should be kept in the parochial archive.[114]

---

[110] Canon 502, §3.

[111] Canon 854.

[112] Canon 877, §3.

[113] Canon 891.

[114] Canon 895.

Penance

It is expected that some criteria be formulated by the Episcopal Conference which will enable the diocesan Bishop to determine in which cases of necessity general absolution should be imparted.[115]

Norms are to be enacted by the Episcopal Conference regarding the confessional.[116]

Sacred Orders

"Episcopal Conferences may issue a regulation which requires a later age for the priesthood and for the permanent diaconate."[117]

Marriage

"The Episcopal Conference may establish a higher age for the lawful celebration of marriage."[118]

Taking into consideration the local customs and civil laws, the Episcopal Conference is to enact laws on promise of marriage whether this be unilateral or bilateral.[119]

"The Episcopal Conference is to lay down norms concerning the questions to be asked of the parties, the publication of marriage

---

[115] Canon 961, §2.

[116] Canon 964, §2. There is a proviso, however, in the canon which states "that confessionals, which the faithful who so wish may freely use, are located in an open place, and fitted with a fixed grille between the penitent and the confessor."

[117] Canon 1031,§3. The Code prescribes twenty-fifth year of age for priesthood (canon 1031,§1); twenty-fifth year of age for permanent diaconate for the unmarried candidate (canon 1031§2), thirty-fifth year of age for married candidates (canon 1031, §2).

[118] Canon 1083,§2. Thus it may be said that the Episcopal Conference is empowered to establish an impedient impediment.

[119] Canon 1062, §1.

banns, and the other appropriate means of enquiry to be carried out before marriage."[120]

"The Episcopal Conference can draw up its own rite of marriage, in keeping with those usages of place and people which accord with the Christian spirit."[121]

With the prior permission of the Holy See, the Episcopal Conference can permit the diocesan Bishop to delegate lay persons to assist at marriages whenever priests or deacons are not available.[122]

As far as mixed marriages are concerned, it is the responsibility of the Episcopal Conference to prescribe the manner in which the declarations and promises on the part of the Catholic party are to be made, and to determine how they are to be established in the external forum, and how the non-Catholic party is to be informed of them.[123]

With regards to the canonical form in mixed marriages, it is for the Episcopal Conference to establish norms whereby the dispensation from canonical form may be granted in a uniform manner.[124]

The Episcopal Conference may prescribe the manner in which the registration of marriages ought to be done.[125]

Liturgy

This sub-title includes an assortment of subjects in which the Episcopal Conference has some involvement in decision making.

---

[120] Canon 1067.

[121] Canon 1120: This rite is to be reviewed by the Holy See, and it is without prejudice to the law that the person who is present to assist at the marriage is to ask for and receive the expression of the consent of the contracting parties."

[122] Canon 1112, §1.

[123] Canon 1126.

[124] Canon 1127, §2.

[125] Canon 1121, § 1.

Sacred Times

With the prior approval of the Apostolic See, the Episcopal Conference may suppress certain holy days of obligation or transfer them to a Sunday.[126]

"The Episcopal Conference can determine more particular ways in which fasting and abstinence are to be observed. In place of abstinence or fasting the Episcopal Conference can substitute, in whole or in part, other forms of penance, especially works of charity and exercise of piety."[127]

It is the responsibility of the Episcopal Conference to prescribe norms regarding abstinence from meat, or from some other food on Fridays.[128]

Liturgical Books

"It pertains to Episcopal Conferences to prepare vernacular translations of liturgical books, with appropriate adaptations as allowed by the books themselves and, with the prior review of the Holy See, to publish these translations."[129]

Liturgy of the Hours

It is left to the discretion of the Episcopal Conference to decide

---

[126] Canon 1246, §2.

[127] Canon 1253.

[128] Canon 1251.

[129] Canon 838, §3.

which parts of the liturgy of the Hours should be recited by the permanent deacons.[130]

Lay Ministries

The Episcopal Conference is to see to it that requirements are prescribed for the instalment of lector and acolyte on lay men.[131]

Preaching by Lay Persons

Provisions are to be laid down by the Episcopal Conference in respect to preaching by lay persons in churches or oratories without prejudice to the prescription of canon 767, §1.[132]

Altar

The Episcopal Conference may allow that a worthy and solid material, other than a single natural stone, be used as *mensa altaris*.[133]

Shrines

The approval of the Episcopal Conference is necessary for a shrine to be recognized as national.[134]

The Episcopal Conference alone is competent to approve the statutes of a national shrine.[135]

---

[130] Canon 276, §2, n.3.

[131] Canon 230, §1.

[132] Canon 766.

[133] Canon 1236, §1.

[134] Canon 1231.

[135] Canon 1232, §1.

Pastoral Activity

This sub-heading contains the involvement of the Episcopal Conference in catechetical instruction, social communication, and associations of the faithful.

Catechesis

"The Episcopal Conference may establish a catechetical office, whose principal purpose is to assist individual dioceses in catechetical matters."[136]

With the approval of the Apostolic See the Episcopal Conference may publish catechisms for its territory.[137]

Catechumenate

"It is the responsibility of the Episcopal Conference to establish norms concerning the arrangement of the catechumenate, determining what should be done by catechumens and what should be their prerogatives."[138]

It is the prerogative of the Episcopal Conference to issue particular norms on the instruction to be scheduled at various stages of the catechumenate and on the rite itself.[139]

---

[136] Canon 775, §3.

[137] Canon 775, §2.

[138] Canon 788, §3.

[139] Canon 851, n.l.

Schools

It is for the Episcopal Conference to issue general norms concerning the formation and education in the Catholic religion in schools.[140]

Whenever it is feasible and appropriate the Episcopal Conference is to take care to have within its territory a suitably located university or at least faculty, in which the various disciplines, while retaining its own scientific autonomy, may be researched and taught in the light of Catholic doctrine.[141]

The Episcopal Conference has the duty and the right of seeing to it that in Catholic universities the principles of Catholic doctrine are faithfully observed.[142]

Where it is possible, the Episcopal Conference is to provide for the establishment of institutes for higher religious studies, in which are taught theological and other subjects pertaining to Christian culture.[143]

Social Communication

"It is for the Episcopal Conference to lay down norms determining the requirements for clerics and members of religious institutes to take part in radio and television programmes which concern catholic doctrine or morals."[144] The same prescription holds true also for the faithful: "In expounding Christian teaching on radio or television, the provisions of the Episcopal Conference are to be observed."[145]

---

[140] Canon 804, §1.

[141] Canon 809.

[142] Canon 810, §2.

[143] Canon 821.

[144] Canon 831, §2.

[145] Canon 772, §2.

The Episcopal Conference has the duty and the right to ensure that in writings or in the use of the means of social communication there should be no ill effect on the faith and morals of Christ's faithful.

The Episcopal Conference has also the duty and the right to demand that where writings of the faithful touch upon matters of faith and morals, these be submitted to its judgment.

Likewise, it is the right and duty of the Episcopal Conference to condemn writings which harm true faith or good morals.[146]

The Episcopal Conference may draw up a list of censors, competent to give a judgment about books, to be available to diocesan curias; it may even establish a commission of censors whom the local Ordinary can consult.[147]

Sacred Scripture

Books of the sacred Scriptures and the publication of their translation need, at least, the approval of the Episcopal Conference.[148]

Associations of the Faithful

The Episcopal Conference is the sole authority to establish public associations of the faithful which by their very establishment are intended for work throughout the whole nation.[149]

For grave reasons the Episcopal Conference can suppress these national associations established by it.[150]

---

[146] Canon 823, §2.

[147] Canon 830, §1.

[148] Canon 825, §1.

[149] Canon 312, §1, n.2.

[150] Canon 320, §2.

The Episcopal Conference is competent to issue a formal decree by which a private association of the faithful acquires a juridical personality.[151] For the same reason the Episcopal Conference shall approve the statutes of the same.[152]

The Judiciary

In this section are grouped the canons which deal with tribunals, arbitration, and office for equitable solutions.

Tribunals

In cases concerning the nullity of marriage the competence of the tribunal can be decided on the place where the plaintiff has a domicile, provided that both parties live within the territory of the same Episcopal Conference.[153]

Whenever it is impossible to constitute a college of judges, the Episcopal Conference can, for as long as the impossibility persists, permit the Bishop of first instance to entrust cases to a sole clerical judge.[154]

"The Episcopal Conference can permit that lay persons also be appointed judges."[155]

With the prior approval of the Holy See, the Episcopal Conference

---

[151] Canon 322, §1.

[152] Canon 322, §2.

[153] Canon 1673, n.3.

[154] Canon 1425, §4.

[155] Canon 1421, §2. However only one lay person is permitted to join the college of judges.

must constitute a tribunal of second instance whenever a single tribunal of first instance has been erected for several dioceses.[156]

"Apart from the cases mentioned in para. 1, the Episcopal Conference can, with the approval of the Apostolic See, constitute one or more tribunals of second instance."[157]

"In respect of the second instance tribunals mentioned in para. 1-2, the Episcopal Conference, or the Bishop designated by it, has all the powers that belong to a diocesan Bishop in respect of his own tribunal."[158]

Arbitration

Norms may be established by the Episcopal Conference in what concerns agreements, mutual promise to abide by an arbiter's award, and arbitral judgments which the parties are to use in case they have not chosen any.[159]

Office for Equitable Solutions

"The Episcopal Conference can prescribe that in each diocese there be established a permanent office or council which would have the duty, in accordance with the norms laid down by the Conference, of seeking and suggesting equitable solutions."[160]

---

[156] Canon 1439, §1. An exception is made by the canon when the several dioceses are all suffragans of the same archdiocese.

[157] Canon 1439, §2.

[158] Canon 1439, §3.

[159] Canon 1714.

[160] Canon 1733, §2.

Administration

Under this heading are included canons dealing with parochial registers, benefices, administration of ecclesiastical goods, monetary collections, amalgamation of funds.

Parochial Registers

The Episcopal Conference may prescribe registers, other than those of baptisms, of marriages and of deaths, to be added to the parochial archive.[161]

Benefices

"In those regions where benefices properly so called still exist, it is for the Episcopal Conference to regulate such benefices by appropriate norms, agreed with and approved by the Apostolic See."[162]

Administration of Goods

"It is for the Episcopal Conference to determine what are to be regarded as acts of extraordinary administration."[163]

It is the responsibility of the Episcopal Conference to establish the maximum sum permissible in the alienation of goods for its region.[164]

"It is the duty of the Episcopal Conference, taking into account the local circumstances, to determine norms about the leasing of

---

[161] Canon 535, §1.

[162] Canon 1272.

[163] Canon 1277.

[164] Canon 1292, §1.

ecclesiastical goods, especially about permission to be obtained from the competent ecclesiastical authority."[165]

Collections

"The Episcopal Conference can draw up rules regarding collections, which must be observed by all, including those who from their foundation are called and are mendicants."[166]

Amalgamation of Funds

The Code suggests an amalgamation of various diocesan funds. This can be achieved within the diocese, by association of various dioceses, or forr13 the whole territory of the Episcopal Confe ence.[167]

Diocesan Synod

It is prescribed by canon 467 that "the diocesan Bishop is to communicate the text of the declarations and decrees of the synod to the Metropolitan and to the Episcopal Conference." Needless to say, the submitting of the text does not entail confirmation by the Episcopal Conference.[168] By no means does canon 467 insinuate that the diocesan Bishop is in any way accountable to the Episcopal Conference in the celebration of the synod. The gesture endorsed by the canon rather signifies the collegiality of the episcopal order, and helps consolidate the bond of unity among the dioceses within the territory of the Episcopal Conference.

---

[165] Canon 1297.

[166] Canon 1265, §2; cf. canon 1262.

[167] Canon 1274, §4.

[168] Cf. canon 466.

Conclusion

As the reader might have already gathered, the canons dealt with in the section, "the Episcopal Conference and the diocese," concern, in the majority of cases, issues which can be solved or settled by one act of execution. If this was the case, the Episcopal Conference could have in a few plenary meetings complied with all the demands required of it by the Code and would have withdrawn by now in a stage of lethargy. By reason of its nature and aim the Episcopal Conference is far more than being a mere executive body of canon law. The canons listed in this section form only a minor portion of the rationale for the presence of the Episcopal Conference in the life of the Church. This institution is meant to be, by its very nature, means for mutual consultation, a source of mutual support, a center for deeper understanding of and confrontation with pastoral issues and social problems, a coordinating instrument in the accomplishment of the Church's mission to itself and to the world. The Episcopal Conference is, first and foremost, an integral part of the *magisterium*.

Episcopal Conference and Institutes of Consecrated Life

The intent of the Spirit is to use the Episcopal Conference as a tool in the explication of itself in the whole Mystical Body. Thus the Episcopal Conference has to reach also that segment of the Christian community characterized by a consecrated life to the Evangelical counsels. For this reason, canon 708 insists that between the major religious superiors and the Episcopal Conference there shall exist coordination and cooperation of motivation and endeavours.[169] And when it comes to plenary council the

---

[169] Cf. *Perfectae Caritatis*, n.23.

major superiors, whether male or female, of religious institutes and societies of apostolic life, are to be invited by the Episcopal Conference.[170]

Episcopal Conference and Ecumenism

The decree on ecumenism, *Unitatis redintegratio*, concludes with this marvelous statement: "This most sacred Synod urgently desires that the initiatives of the sons of the Catholic Church, joined with those of the separated brethren, go forward without obstructing the ways of divine Providence and without prejudging the future inspiration of the Holy Spirit."[171] This spontaneous and far-reaching attitude of Vatican Council II towards the separated brethren is the concern first of the Episcopal College dispersed throughout the world.[172] The "Secretariat for Promoting Christian Unity" published a *Directorium*, on May 14, 1967, whereby it empowered the institution of diocesan ecumenical commissions authorized by and under the supervision of the Episcopal Conference or of the Bishop himself.[173] A similar document was published on August 28, 1969, by the "Secretariat for non-Believers."[174]

In the restoration of unity among Christians the Code follows the dictates of Vatican Council II. Canon 755, §2, reads apropos: "It is a matter likewise for Bishops and, in accordance with the law, for Episcopal Conference, to promote this same unity and, in line with the various needs and opportunities of the circumstances, to issue practical norms which accord with the provisions laid down by the supreme authority of the Church." The Decree, *Unitatis redintegratio*, had already endorsed the authority of the Episcopal Conference in issuing norms concerning

---

[170] Canon 443,§3,n.2. Their number is to be determined by the Episcopal Conference.

[171] n. 24.

[172] *Christus Dominus*, n.16,(f); *Unitatis redintegratio*, n.8; canon 755,§1.

[173] AAS, 59, 1967, n.3, p. 575.

[174] AAS, 60, 1968, pp. 692-704.

communicatio in sacris.¹⁷⁵ It is for the Episcopal Conference to lay down guiding principles, to translate general principles to practical cases and to adjust undertakings which gradually take place in the region. For this reason, the Directory, *Ad totam Ecclesiam*, requested that a commission of Bishops for ecumenical affairs be erected within each national Conference of Bishops.¹⁷⁶ The aim of this commission is "to give guidance in ecumenical affairs and determine concrete ways of acting in accordance with the Decree on ecumenism and with other ordinances and legitimate customs."¹⁷⁷

In certain ecumenical issues the Episcopal Conference takes over the responsibility and authority of the local Bishop. An instance of this is the granting of permission that versions of the Scriptures may be prepared and published by Catholics in collaboration with our separated brethren.¹⁷⁸ It also belongs exclusively to the Episcopal Conference to decide on cases of cooperation between a Catholic seminary on the one hand and a non-catholic seminary or a non-denominational university on the other. The Program of Priestly Formation issued by the same should include general rules on this type of cooperation and what part the clerical students may take in these ventures.¹⁷⁹

In other issues the ecumenical commitment falls equally on the Episcopal Conference and the diocesan Bishop. The growth of harmony among Christians through dialogue and consultation on a territorial and

---

¹⁷⁵ AAS, 57 (1965) n.8, p. 98.

¹⁷⁶ AAS, 59 (1967) n.7, p. 577.

¹⁷⁷ The English translation in this section on ecumenism is taken from Vatican Council II -- *The Conciliar and Post Conciliar Documents*, edited by Austin Flannery, O.P., Vol. I, Lesminster, 1980 -- *Ad totam Ecclesiam*, n. 7, p. 486. The commission of bishops, if possible, should be assisted by a permanent secretariat and by experts (Ibid.) The tasks of the commission are enumerated in nn.6 and 8 of the Directory (Eng.Ed., pp. 485-486).

¹⁷⁸ Canon 825, §2.

¹⁷⁹ *Spiritus Domini*, AAS, 62 (1970) n.84, P. 719; n. 93, p. 723.

diocesan basis should advance through the initiative of both authorities.[180] However, it is also their responsibility to exercise pastoral vigilance in order to keep the dialogue on appropriate lines lest dangers of indifferentism and proselytism creep in.[181] It belongs to the diocesan Bishop, or to the Episcopal Conference, to decide when grave and pressing needs do occur in order that other Christians, in whose Churches penance, the Eucharist and anointing of the sick are not valid, may receive these sacraments.[182] Neither the local Ordinary nor the Episcopal Conference shall issue norms in this matter unless the competent authority of the non-catholic Church or ecclesial community concerned has been consulted.[183] In this manner, the Catholic Church would not be accused of fostering proselytism. The Episcopal Conference, as well as the individual Bishop, should take pains to promote ecumenism in institutes of advanced learning, including the seminary.[184]

Conclusion

We believe the ongoing process of the identification of episcopal office should be envisaged in the spectrum of the universal ecclesial spirit. The aim of the spirit's destiny is to discover itself, understand and comprehend itself, to explicate itself. Its inner destiny is to turn back to its foundation, to return to its primordial origin and truth on which it depends. This seems to be the central idea underlying the aspirations of the Church in Vatican Council II. As part of the human nature, which groans and travails in pain in the process of self-amelioration, it is the inherent

---

[180] *Unitatis redintegratio*, AAS, 57 (1965) n.4, pp. 94-95,96; *Ad totam Ecclesiam*, AAS, 59 (1967) n.2, pp. 574-575; n.27, p. 584; canons 383, §3; 755, §2.

[181] *Ad totam Ecclesiam*, loc. cit., n. 28, p. 584.

[182] Canon 844, §4; cf. *Unitatis redintegratio*, loc. cit., n.8, p. 98; *Ad totam Ecclesiam*, loc. cit., n. 55, p. 590; *Dans ces derniers temps*, AAS, 62 (1970) n. 7, p. 187.

[183] Canon 844, §5; *Ad totam Ecclesiam*, loc. cit., n. 42, p. 587.

[184] *Spiritus Domini*, AAS, 62 (1970) nn. 65, 66, pp. 705-706; n. 79, pp.717-718.

destiny of the Church to move on in the quest of her own maturation towards authentic Christianity. In no ambiguous terms the Church acknowledges her human element liable to deficiencies, and feels the need of growth. "Christ summons the Church, as she goes her pilgrim way, to that continual reformation of which she always has need, insofar as she is an institution of men here on earth. Therefore, if the influence of events or of the times has led to deficiencies in conduct, in Church discipline, or even in the formulation of doctrine (which must be carefully distinguished from the deposit itself of faith) these should be appropriately rectified at the proper moment."[185]

The emergence of the Episcopal Conference as a powerful tool in the unification and solidification of the Church may bear indeed the imprint of human drama characterized by individual interests, selfish needs and senseless passions of concern, fear, and anxiety. This reminds us of the Hegelian interpretation of history that the spirit has plenty of time to explicate itself gradually because it is outside of time, it is eternal. What seems to be a tremendously integrated expense of subjective, individual interests interrelating antagonistically with each other, is the very tool by which the world spirit accomplishes its end, to come to itself and to contemplate itself as actual reality.[186] Translating this idea into a theological perspective, God makes known his will to mankind through the events of humans well entrenched in and estranged by their selfish interests -- an obscure text indeed written in cryptic language, which, when one seeks to decipher it, appears, *prima facie*, a dossier filled with errors, gaps, and contradictions.

The Episcopal Conference signals the growing consciousness of the Church of the ecclesial configuration of the episcopal office; it is a specific actualization of the universality of the episcopal college. By means of the Episcopal Conference the authority of the Bishop moves out beyond the

---

[185] *Unitatis redintegratio*, n. 6.

[186] HEGEL, GEORG, WILHELM, FRIEDRICH, *Selections from the Philosophy of History*, Trans. by Carl J. and Paul W. Friedrich, in *The Philosophy of Hegel*, edited with an Introduction by Carl J. Friedrich, New York, 1954, p. 16.

territorial limits of his jurisdiction and reaches out into the *Ecclesia*. In his participation in the Episcopal Conference the individual Bishop actualizes the dogmatic truth that through consecration he has become a member of that college to which the Lord has entrusted, in union with the Roman Pontiff, supreme and full power over the universal Church[187] by fulfilling the offices of sanctifying, teaching and ruling[188] so as to form an uninterrupted, intrinsic succession of the Apostolic College.[189] Therefore, rather than being a means of curtailment, the Episcopal Conference is, in essence, the expression of the collegial nature of the episcopal office.

---

[187] Canon 336.

[188] Canon 375, §2.

[189] Canon 330.

Diocesan Consultors -- Senate of Priests

In the diocese of the post-Vatican Church another college of priests emerged which, together with the diocesan consultors, assists the Bishop in fulfilling his duties to that portion of the people of God which is the diocese. This new college of priests is known as council of priests or senate of priests.

By reason of their juridical nature and purpose there is no distinction between these two juridical colleges, for both by nature are consultative bodies established as assistants to the Bishop in the governance of the diocese. On the other hand, they form two colleges essentially distinct from each other, each upholding a specific nature with well-determined competence. Both assume the nature of senate of the Bishop. However, while the senate of priests must fully represent the *presbyterium*, we cannot attribute, *per se*, this qualification to the college of diocesan consultors. For this reason, the council of priests, on principle, ought to be conceived of as an elected body. This juridical truth does not apply to the college of diocesan consultors freely appointed by the Bishop, although he has to choose them from among the members of the senate of priests. In reference to competence there are substantial differences between the two colleges. In some matters, it is the council of priests with which the Bishop has to consult, in others it is the college of diocesan consultors. In some areas, the college of diocesan consultors is accredited the power of deliberation, while this seems not feasible for the council of priests. Once the See is vacant, the council of priests automatically lapses, and all the responsibility of the diocese falls in the hands of the diocesan consultors.

This general introduction leads us to the analysis of the nature and competence of the individual college. We shall first deal with the senate of priests.

Council of Priests

One cannot appreciate the juridical significance of the priestly senate without first attending to its theological assumption. This theology is endorsed particularly by the Conciliar Decree on the ministry and life of priests, *Presbyterorum ordinis*. The juridical significance of the senate of priests finds its roots in the undivided oneness of the ministerial priesthood, which the Church has believed and taught from the beginning. The Decree, *Presbyterorum ordinis*, does nothing else but confirm this theology: "All priests, together with the Bishop, so share in one and the same priesthood and ministry of Christ that the very unity of their consecration and mission requires their hierarchical communion with the order of Bishops."[1] The accomplishment of the Vatican Council was its bringing to fuller realization this dogmatic truth through the advocacy of a closer and amicable relationship of the Bishop with his priests, that he "should regard priests as his brothers and friends,"[2] and through deeper awareness in the Bishop of the priest's rightful standing in the fulfillment of Christ's ministry. Thus, "the Bishop should regard them (priests) as necessary helpers and counsellors in the ministry and in the task of teaching, sanctifying, and nourishing the People of God . . . He should gladly listen to them, indeed, consult them, and have discussions with them about those matters which concern the necessities of pastoral work and the welfare of the diocese."[3] Thus, the Decree concludes: "In order to put these ideals into effect, a group or senate of priests representing the presbyterium should be established. It is to operate in a manner adapted to modern circumstances and needs and to have a form and norms to be determined by law. By its counsel, this body will be able to give effective

---

[1] N.7.

[2] Ibid.

[3] Ibid.

assistance to the Bishop in his government of the diocese."[4] By virtue of the *Motu proprio, Ecclesiae Sanctae*, on August 6, 1966, the council of priests became an institution in the Church.[5] The nature of this council is well defined in canon 495 §1 which reads: "In each diocese there is to be established a council of priests, that is, a group of priests who represent the presbyterium and who are to be, as it were, the Bishop's senate." In this statement two essential components are considered: the priestly senate is a representative body; it is the Bishop's senate. In different canons the Code takes pains to explicate and actualize these two juridical realities.

In order that this council be truly representative of the clergy, the Code appeals to two important norms which are found in canons 499 and 498. The first norm concerns itself with the structure of the council. Canon 499 prescribes that the statutes should see to it that as far as it is feasible the *presbyterium* be well represented in the council. Such a representation can be achieved if the election procedure is based on the criterion of the different ministries established in the diocese, and on the criterion of geographical districts. For a number of dioceses the criterion of personnel seems to be the most acceptable; the clerical body is thus classified into groups according to the years of ordination, and from each individual group a certain number of priests is elected to the council. The second norm stipulates the right of those who have active and passive voice in the election. Titular to such a right are all priests incardinated in the diocese, and indeed all priests "who are living in the diocese and exercise some useful office there." In the latter category no discrimination is made between incardinated and not incardinated, between diocesan clergy and priest members of institutes of consecrated life.[6] Canon 498 §2 goes on to say that statutes may even acknowledge this right to priests who have domicile or quasi-domicile in the diocese.

---

[4] Ibid.

[5] AAS, LVIII, 1966, n. 15, P. 766.

[6] Canon 498, §1.

Pertinent to the subject of representation is canon 497 which forces us to modify the initial presupposition of representation. Indeed the canon mitigates the fundamental democratic nature of the council by imposing on the council ex-officio membership and free appointments to the council by the Bishop. It may be said that for the valid establishment of the council only half of the members need be elected. And this half should not be taken as a numerical quantity, but rather as an approximation, since the canon clearly states "about half are to be freely elected." In such a case, one may rightly ask whether the council really represents the *presbyterium*.

The second essential component of the council is that it serves as the Bishop's senate -- a senate which has no semblance, in any shape or form, to the gerousia of Sparta, the areopagos of Athens, or the senate of modern democratic states. The council of priests is a consultative body which the Bishop is expected to hear before he reaches a decision on matters well defined in the Code of Canon Law.[7] "The council of priests can never act without the diocesan Bishop."[8] It is the Bishop who convenes the council, presides over it, determines the agenda or accepts items proposed by its members.[9] "He alone can make public those things which have been decided in accordance with §2."[10]

Canon 500 §2 indicates that there are some matters specified by the Code in which the Bishop requires the consent of the council. In similar circumstances the council thus turns into a deliberative body, a moral collegial person. However, we are not aware of any canon in the Code which requires the consent of the priestly senate in order that the Bishop may act validly.

The precarious nature of the senate and its total dependency on the person of the Bishop is well envisaged in two instances: it can always be dissolved either because its members fail to fulfil the office entrusted to

---

[7] Canon 500, §2.

[8] Canon 500, §3.

[9] Canon 500, §1.

[10] Canon 500, §3.

Diocesan Consultors -- Senate of Priests 373

them or because they gravely abuse the office consigned;[11] it ceases the moment the See becomes vacant.[12]

Besides its nature, canon 495 §1 indicates the purpose of the senate of priests. The canon reads: "The council's role is to assist the Bishop, in accordance with the law, in the governance of the diocese." The Code in different canons determines the matters in which the senate of priests can be of help to the Bishop, and therefore he cannot validly act without consulting it. Thus the Bishop must consult the senate of priests:

1. in the establishment of the pastoral council in each parish.[13]
2. in the erection, suppression or notable alteration of parishes.[14]
3. in the granting of permission for the building of a church.[15]
4. in the granting of permission for a church to be used for secular, but not unbecoming, purposes.[16]
5. in prescribing regulations concerning offerings received from the faithful for some parochial function, and remuneration of persons who fulfil these functions.[17]
6. in levying taxes on public juridical persons subject to his authority for the needs of the diocese.[18]

---

[11] Canon 501, §3: "If the council of priests does not fulfil the office entrusted to it for the welfare of the diocese, or if it gravely abuses that office, it can be dissolved by the diocesan Bishop, after consultation with the metropolitan; in the case of a metropolitan see, the Bishop must first consult with the suffragan Bishop who is senior by promotion. Within a year, however, the diocesan Bishop must reconstitute the council."

[12] Canon 501, §2.

[13] Canon 536, §1.

[14] Canon 515, §2.

[15] Canon 1215, §2.

[16] Canon 1222, §2.

[17] Canon 531.

[18] Canon 1263.

7. in deciding whether a synod should be held in his diocese.[19]

The instances just mentioned are prescribed by law as to when the Bishop has to convene the council and consult it. It does not thereby follow that the senate should be disregarded in other matters. Such a policy would be against the *mens juridica* expressed in canon 495, §1: "The council's role is to assist the Bishop, in accordance with the law, in the governance of the diocese, so that the pastoral welfare of that portion of the people of God entrusted to the Bishop may be most effectively promoted." Canon 500, §2 insists that "the diocesan Bishop is to consult it in matters of more serious moment." Liberty is also envisaged for anyone to propose matters for the agenda.[20]

Although no mention is made of how often the council should be convened, and granted that the Bishop is the one who convenes the council and prepares the agenda, the prescriptions of canons 495, §1, and 500, §1,2 remain meaningless unless the council enjoys a certain degree of stability and continuity. On the other hand, to recognize the council as a permanent institution would seem to go against the intention of the Code, since its convocation is left to the discretion of the Bishop. Ultimately, it depends on the judgment of the individual Bishop to perceive the validity of this institution and thereby avail himself of its potential resources.

Ancillary to the main theme are two topics worth mentioning. The first concerns the removal and transfer of pastors. In the procedure for their removal or transfer, the Bishop is to discuss the matter with two pastors before he reaches a decision. The senate of priests may be asked by the Bishop to designate a stable group of pastors whom the Bishop may approach on these matters, e.g., the Personnel Board.[21] The second deals with the right and obligation of the council of priests to participate in particular councils: in case of a diocesan synod, all members of the council

---

[19] Canon 461, §1.

[20] Canon 500, §1.

[21] Canons 1742, §1; 1750.

are obliged to attend;[22] when it concerns a provincial council two of its members shall participate, designated in a collegial manner.[23] In both cases, the members enjoy consultative vote.[24]

College of Diocesan Consultors[25]

In some sense one may consider the college of diocesan consultors as an offshoot of the medieval cathedral chapter of canons. The Code of 1917 presents this college as a substitute of the cathedral chapter whenever it was not feasible, in the judgment of the local Ordinary, to institute or revive the former cathedral chapter.[26] In lieu of the cathedral chapter the college of diocesan consultors was thus acknowledged as the senate of the Bishop.[27]

In the new Code of Canon law it is not expressly stated that this college constitutes a senate of the Bishop. However, from the reading of the canons pertinent to this institution, this college has all the characteristics of a senate, indeed of a moral collegial person, more so than the senate of priests. As a senate, the college of diocesan consultors has the Bishop as its president.[28] This college indeed functions as a senate when the Code requires that the Bishop shall consult it "in carrying out acts of administration which, in the light of the financial situation of the

---

[22] Canon 463, §1, n.4.

[23] Canon 443, §5.

[24] Canons 466; 443, §5.

[25] Canon 502, §4: "Unless the law provides otherwise, in a vicariate or prefecture apostolic the functions of the college of consultors belong to the council of the mission mentioned in can. 495, §2."

[26] Canon 423.

[27] Canon 427.

[28] Canon 502, §2.

diocese, are of major importance."[29] A similar counsel is requested from the college by the Bishop in the appointment and removal of the financial administrator.[30] It must be said that this college enjoys even greater juridical powers in the governance of the diocese than the senate of priests. In certain matters it becomes a collegial moral person in the full juridical sense, that is, with a deliberative vote. This happens particularly in acts of extraordinary administration, as determined by the Episcopal Conference, in which case the Bishop needs the consent of the college.[31] Likewise, in alienation of goods, whether the goods pertain to juridical persons subject to the diocesan Bishop or belong to the diocese itself, the Bishop needs the consent of the college.[32] In the administration of the diocese, the authority of the diocesan administrator is even more curtailed by the vote of the diocesan consultors. The administrator, in fact, needs the consent of the college in order to remove the chancellor and the other notaries,[33] to issue dismissorial letters,[34] to grant excardination, incardination, or permission to move to another particular church.[35]

It is worth noting that in the new Code the college of diocesan consultors is a different institution from the cathedral chapter, and that the former took over what were the prerogatives of the latter in the old Code. Only by decree of the Episcopal Conference can the cathedral chapter take the place of the college of diocesan consultors.[36]

---

[29] Canon 1277.

[30] Canon 494, §1, 2.

[31] Canon 1277.

[32] Canon 1292, §1.

[33] Canon 485.

[34] Canon 1018, §1, n.2.

[35] Canon 272.

[36] Canon 502, §3.

To conclude, in every diocese there ought to be two bodies: the council of priests and the college of diocesan consultors. Both are institutions endowed with stability and continuity. The question however arises as to whether the diocesan consultors should be approached on a constant basis in all other matters not contemplated in the Code, as the Bishop wishes. In such a case one encounters two senates simultaneously functioning in the diocese. Such a configuration would establish in the governance of the diocese the idea of the double chamber -- the house of representatives and the senate -- as it is found in civil government.

It must be admitted that the Decree, *Christus Dominus*, acknowledges the college of diocesan consultors among the collaborators of the Bishop, as much as the senate of priests, in the governance of the diocese.[37] Moreover, an objection cannot be validly raised against the simultaneous functioning of these two senates as simply senseless redundancy since the diocesan consultors are at the time of appointment members of the priestly senate.[38] Canon 502 §1 insists that the diocesan consultors should be selected from among the members of the council of priests. This does not, however, necessarily mean that the diocesan consultors must always be members of the priestly senate at the same time. It well may happen, and it frequently does, that the duration of office in the priestly senate does not coincide with that of the diocesan consultor. Particular statutes of the priestly senate may prescribe a much shorter period than the term of office of five years requested by canon 502 §1 for the diocesan consultor. Therefore, one cannot rightly conclude that by reason of the members themselves these two colleges form one and the same senate. Apart from the time factor, the diocesan consultors may well be selected from among the members of the council of priests who were freely appointed to the priestly senate by the Bishop.[39] One may judge that, because of this appointment of diocesan consultors, the college itself loses much of its

---

[37] n. 27.

[38] Canon 502, §1.

[39] Canons 502, §1; 497, n.3.

validity. Precisely because of these ambiguities we firmly believe that the college of consultors can and must be convened only in matters expressly stated in the law; in all other matters the Bishop has the senate of priests on which he is asked to rely and in which he should have full trust in the governance of the diocese.

The college of diocesan consultors differs from the senate of priests in that it is not an elected body, and therefore does not, *per se*, represent the presbyterium, and in that in some matters it has the power to deliberate. But the most striking difference between the two is their relationship to the person of the Bishop for their individual existence. The senate of priests totally depends on the person of the Bishop so as to be, as it were, his shadow. With his withdrawal from the diocese, the senate of priests ceases completely, whereas with the withdrawal of the Bishop the college of diocesan consultors emerges in full potential and absorbs all the powers of the priestly senate. Canon 501 §2 reads: "When the See is vacant, the council of priests lapses and its functions are fulfilled by the college of consultors."

With the death of the Bishop, the governance of the diocese becomes the responsibility of the college of consultors. In absence of an auxiliary Bishop in the diocese, the college of consultors must as soon as possible notify the Apostolic See of the death of the Bishop.[40] With the vacancy of the See it becomes the right and duty of the college of consultors to appoint a diocesan administrator,[41] despite the fact that there might be one or more auxiliary Bishops in the diocese.[42] It is the sacrosanct prerogative

---

[40] Canon 422.

[41] Canon 421, §1: "Within eight days of receiving notification of the vacancy of an episcopal see, a diocesan Administrator is to be elected by the college of consultors, to govern the diocese for the time being, without prejudice to the provisions of can. 502, §3."

[42] Canon 419: "While the see is vacant and until the appointment of a diocesan Administrator, the governance of the diocese devolves upon the auxiliary Bishop. If there are a number of auxiliary Bishops, it devolves upon the senior by promotion. If there is no auxiliary Bishop, it devolves upon the college of consultors, unless the Holy See has provided otherwise. The one who thus assumes the governance of the diocese must without delay convene the college which is competent to appoint a diocesan Administrator." This norm does not apply when there is a

of the college to choose the priest or Bishop whom it wishes, according to the prescriptions of canon 119. The same responsibility falls upon the diocesan consultors whenever the see is impeded, abiding, of course, by the requirements of canon 413, §1, 2.[43] Upon his election the diocesan administrator is bound to make the profession of faith in the presence of the college.[44] Removal of the diocesan administrator is reserved to the Holy See.[45] But whenever the diocesan administrator is removed, resigns or dies, the right to elect another devolves always to the diocesan consultors in accordance with canon 421.[46] In case of resignation, the diocesan administrator is to submit it to the college without requiring acceptance by the college.[47] The college of consultors is involved also in the canonical possession of the diocesan Bishop[48] and in the appointment of the coadjutor

---

coadjutor Bishop (canon 403,§3) or an auxiliary Bishop with special faculties (canon 403, §2). Either one takes the place of the diocesan Bishop whenever he is absent or impeded (canon 405, §2).

Strange as it might seem, the auxiliary Bishops are deprived of any voice in the election of the diocesan administrator, unless they also belong to the college of diocesan consultors. It is the auxiliary Bishop senior by promotion alone who, by virtue of canons 419 and 502, §2, has the right to vote in the election.

The college of diocesan consultors may elect any priest in accordance with canon 498, §1, 2. However, there is nothing in the Code which impedes the college from choosing a priest or an auxiliary Bishop from another diocese.

[43] Canon 502, §2: "The diocesan Bishop presides over the college of consultors. If, however, the see is impeded or vacant, that person presides who in the interim takes the Bishop's place or, if he has not yet been appointed, then the priest in the college of consultors who is senior by ordination."

[44] Canon 833, n.4.

[45] Canon 430, §2.

[46] Canon 430, §2.

[47] Canon 430, §2.

[48] Canon 382, §3: "A Bishop takes canonical possession of his diocese when, personally or by proxy, he shows the apostolic letters to the college of consultors, in the presence of the chancellor of the curia, who makes a record of the fact. This must take place within the diocese. In dioceses which are newly established he takes possession when he communicates the same letters to the clergy and the people in the cathedral church, with the senior of the priests present making a record of the fact."

Bishop.[49] The canonical possession of each consists in the presentation of the apostolic letters of appointment to the college of consultors. The same norm likewise holds true when the diocesan Bishop is totally impeded. The coadjutor Bishop or the auxiliary Bishop, in similar cases, must submit to the college of consultors the apostolic letters of appointment.[50]

Interestingly enough, mention is not made in the Code of the college's participation in either the diocesan synod or the provincial council. By virtue of canon 502, §1, the members of the college of consultors are at the time of appointment members of the senate of priests; thereby what is prescribed in canon 463, §1,n.4, regarding the diocesan synod, and in canon 443, §5, regarding provincial council, in reference to the senate of priests is, by the very nature of things, applicable to members of the college of diocesan consultors. As pointed out earlier, the term of office in both colleges does not necessarily coincide. In practice, therefore, the above explanation does not hold true. It may well happen that some or none of the members of the college of consultors are members of the priestly senate, and consequently they would be deprived of the right, nor would they have any obligation, to participate either in the diocesan synod or provincial council.

The last point to be mentioned concerns the college of diocesan consultors in the presentation of names to the Holy See for the appointment of a diocesan Bishop or a coadjutor Bishop. Canon 377, §3, imposes the obligation on the papal Legate to approach some members of the college on the score.

Thus we terminate our canonical exposition on the nature and aim of the two priestly colleges which are conceived by the new Code of Canon Law as appropriate and efficient tools for the diocesan Bishop in his

---

[49] Canon 404, §1: "The coadjutor Bishop takes possession of his office when, either personally or by proxy, he shows the apostolic letters of appointment to the diocesan Bishop and the college of consultors, in the presence of the chancellor of the curia, who makes a record of the fact."

[50] Canon 404, §3: "If the diocesan Bishop is wholly impeded, it is sufficient that either the coadjutor Bishop or the auxiliary Bishop show their apostolic letters of appointment to the college of consultors, in the presence of the chancellor of the curia."

shepherding of the people of God. It remains to add some personal views on the subject.

Two major topics hold our attention. Both concern the process of transformation of the Church's configuration from the traditional seigneurial model of stratification to the model of *communio*. The first issue relates to the establishment of the senate of priests in relation to the process of democratization in the Church in opposition to the extreme monarchism of the past. The second theme concentrates on the validity of the existence of two priestly colleges in the diocese.

The introduction of the senate of priests into the governing process of the diocese revives the centuries-old theological question of the hierarchical distinction between the *episcopoi* and *presbyteroi* as a premise to the present discussion. The issue in its historical context will ever remain vague and inconclusive. Apparently, the *episcopoi-presbyteroi* concept may include two alternative meanings of hierarchical structure: either the monarchic figure of the *episcopos* with the fullness of the priesthood, surrounded by a college of *presbyteroi* who partake of this same priesthood in a lesser degree; or the collegial configuration of a group of *episcopoi-presbyteroi* exercising the full ministry together under the leadership of an apostle or his delegate. We have no intention of re-opening the question as such, which, *per se*, pertains to the domain of systematic theology. The doctrine on the superior powers of the priesthood bestowed on the Bishop alone has been sanctioned by the Council of Trent[51] and re-affirmed by Vatican Council II.[52] The humanization of the Church, however, brings to the general awareness the fact that the principles of co-responsibility and subsidiarity in the juridical and pastoral fields do not deny or in any way obscure or diminish the lofty priesthood of the Bishop. The Council, having this in mind, nevertheless insists that "all priests, together with the Bishop, so share in one and the same priesthood and ministry of Christ that the very unity of their consecration and mission requires their hierarchical

---

[51] Sessio XXIII, *De Ordine*, canon 7, *The Teaching of the Catholic Church*, edited by Karl Rahner, Trans. by Geoffrey Stevens, Mercier Press, 1967, n. 639, p. 346.

[52] *Lumen gentium*, n. 21; *Christus Dominus*, n.15; *Sacrosanctum concilium*, n. 41.

communion with the order of Bishops."[53] The failure to delegate goes against the whole strong direction of the Council. The more insecure the leader, the heavier his iron hand falls upon his subjects.

Hence the question: does the establishment of the senate of priests indicate a move towards the democratization of the ecclesial spirit in the ministerial priesthood? A faint sign of democratic spirit was registered in certain powers conferred by the 1917 Code on the cathedral chapter, or the diocesan consultors, as the case might have been,[54] and the council of administration.[55]

But neither the cathedral chapter, or the college of diocesan consultors in the 1917 Code, nor the college of diocesan consultors in the 1983 Code represents the presbyterate, the membership of each of these bodies being based on free conferral by the Bishop. It is the senate of priests which truly represents the presbyterium, the membership of which depends on election by the priests themselves. Some hesitation may be voiced in recognizing the emergence of the democratic spirit in the institution of the senate of priests. The juridical nature of the senate, its automatic cessation with the vacancy of the see, the threat of its dissolution by the Bishop, the very existence of the college of diocesan consultors, all serve to demonstrate how vague and precarious still is the democratic spirit in Church governance. In spite of these objections, the senate of priests nevertheless appears to us as a sign of democratization of the ecclesiastical hierarchy, particularly when one adverts to the senate functioning on a steady program of frequent convocations.

The second question, which is closely related to the first, seeks an explanation for the presence of the two priestly colleges in the direction of the modern diocese. The very institution of the senate of priests brings into question the validity of the college of diocesan consultors. The first objection raised against the college of diocesan consultors is its membership

---

[53] *Presbyterorum Ordinis*, n.7.

[54] Canon 423.

[55] Canons 391, §1; 1532, §2,3; 1541, §2, n.2,3; 435, §1.

based on free conferral. The appointment by the Bishop may cause some to question its objectivity, whether its counsel or consent is being requested. Moreover, the senate of priests could have easily taken over the responsibilities of the diocesan consultors in compliance with the axiom "non sunt multiplicanda entia sine necessitate." In this manner the process of democratization would have been further explicated. But the *multiplicatio entium* seems to satisfy certain emotional needs still lingering in the Church, needs which indeed reveal lingering paternalism and a degree of fear of democracy. The *multiplicatio entium* seems to indicate the nostalgic predilection of the Church for the caste system, the classification of the clergy into *clero alto* and *clero basso,* between patricians and plebeians. The college of diocesan consultors, and more so when this college is absorbed by the cathedral chapter,[56] bears the vestiges of the aristocratic system. This belief is more solidified when one realizes that in some matters the college of diocesan consultors is empowered with deliberative vote, whereas this is never feasible for the senate of priests. Moreover, the Code contemplates the dissolution of the priestly senate; no such possibility is to be found in the Code in reference to the college of consultors. One may speculate on the reason for such discrimination. It may be suggested that the Code is confident that no abuses will ever infiltrate the college of consultors once they are freely appointed. But the stipulation also indicates certain basic mistrust in the senate of priests. There is no reason why, with the vacancy of the see, the senate of priests should cease. There is no solid argument why, *sede vacante*, the senate of priests should not take over the responsibilities of the diocese, in lieu of the diocesan consultors, if not for this lack of basic trust in the ordinary *presbyterium* among whom, it is thought, there are plenty of tongues that move and few minds that think.

    The existence of the diocesan consultors seems to be a hangover from the "ancien regime" where few participated in governing power. Nonetheless, the introduction of the senate of priests in the direction of the diocese signals the beginning of a new era in the Church.

---

[56] Canon 502, §3.

Ecumenism in the Code of Canon Law

The ecumenical movement is a sign and reality of the Church's ongoing process of self-discovery. The Catholic Church in Vatican Council II emerged from a stage of extreme institutionalism into a consciousness of universality. Ecumenism signals maturation and transformation on the part of the Catholic Church from a condition of self-absorption into an attitude of reciprocity, trust, esteem, respect and love for other Christian Churches and ecclesial communities. The Catholic Church is now in a position to acknowledge that truly Christian elements and endowments do indeed exist in other Christian communities, that the mystery of salvation is operative outside her visible boundaries.[1] The quest for unity places her in the full realization that "whatever is truly Christian is never contrary to what genuinely belongs to the faith."[2] While still retaining in full consciousness her own intrinsic reality, the Catholic Church in the ongoing process of self-discovery is able to see new horizons, longs for fresh air, and feels the need of nourishment "from the treasures of the many traditions, past and present, which are alive in other Churches and ecclesial communities; such are the treasures found in the liturgy, monasticism and mystical tradition of the Christian East; in Anglican worship and piety; in the evangelical prayer and spirituality of Protestants."[3]

The ecumenical initiative helps bring about a clarity of position to the Catholic Church never feasible in the old pattern of self-absorption. In

---

[1] *Unitatis redintegratio*, AAS, 57 (1965) n. 3, p.93; n.4, p.96; nn.14-18, pp.101-104; nn.22,23, pp.105-106.

[2] The English translation in this paper, unless otherwise notified, is taken from *Vatican Council II -- The Conciliar and Post Conciliar Documents*, edited by Austin Flannery, O.P., Vol. I, Lesminster, 1980; n.4, p.458.

[3] *Spiritus Domini, Directory Concerning Ecumenical Matters: Part Two: Ecumenism in Higher Education*, n.70, p.520; cf. AAS,62 (1970) n.70, p.710.

an attitude of humility and repentance she can now look back, in true sincerity of heart, at her own deficiencies of the past in moral conduct, in discipline and theological exposition of dogma.[4] In this manner the Catholic Church is more able to examine her own faithfulness to Christ and discern her self-identity. She realizes that the quest for Christian unity runs the danger of futility unless it finds its roots in renewal in truth and charity, "and in interior conversion to personal holiness.[5]

The ultimate aim of the ecumenical movement is the restoration of complete communion of faith and sacramental life of all who believe in the Triune God and confess Jesus Christ, God made man, as Lord, mediator between God and the human being, source and centre of the ecclesial community.

In spite, however, of the initiatives and activities in ecumenical endeavour, the Decree, *Unitatis redintegratio,* made it emphatically clear that ecumenism is essentially and exclusively a convergence of minds in one faith. It is false ecumenism when it savours of proselytism, compromise, or conversion. The Catholic Church cannot compromise in what she believes to be the deposit of faith handed down from the Apostles and the Fathers. "For it is through Christ's Catholic Church alone, which is the universal help towards salvation, that the fullness of the means of salvation can be obtained."[6] Precisely for this same reason individual admission into the Catholic Church not only "is of its nature distinct from ecumenical action,"[7] but it ensues from that fullness of the means of salvation which subsists in the Catholic Church. Moreover, "It is well known that the

---

[4] *Unitatis redintegratio,* AAS, 57 (1965) n.6, pp. 96-97; cf. *Pauli Papae VI et Athenagorae Patriarchae Constantinopolitani Declaratio Communis,* AAS, 58 (1966) pp. 20-21.

[5] *Unitatis redintegratio,* AAS, 57 (1965), n.4, p.94; n.6, pp. 96-97; nn.7,8, pp.97-98. "This change of heart and holiness of life, along with public and private prayer for the unity of Christians, should be regarded as the soul of the whole ecumenical movement, and merits the name "spiritual ecumenism," n.8, p.460. Cf. *Ad totam Ecclesiam, Directorium ad ea quae a Concilio Vaticano Secundo de re oecumenica promulgata sunt exsequenda,* AAS, 59 (1967) n.2, p.575.

[6] *Unitatis redintegratio,* n. 3, p. 456; cf. n.2, p. 454.

[7] *Unitatis redintegratio,* n. 4, p. 457.

Catholic Church attaches a decisive importance to the traditional teaching about the necessity of the ministerial priesthood connected with the apostolic succession, and the conditions in which it exists."[8] In the ecumenical enterprise the Catholic Church cannot betray herself, but she neither intends to betray others; she does not approach other Churches and ecclesial communities with the intention of converting them from their perfidious errors. The drive of ecumenism must lie, not in futile efforts towards the accommodation, and less still proselytization of other Christian believers to the Catholic faith, but in the maintenance of a kind of inner, candid discontent in all the participants in the face of the very highest Christian achievement. The concern and preoccupation of the ecclesiastical authority in upholding the integrity and purity of Catholic dogma for the faithful needs no clarification. It would be sheer naiveté to ignore the weighty ecclesiological and sacramental differences existing between Catholic and Protestant faiths, such as, interpretation of revealed truth,[9] the teaching authority of the Church,[10] the eucharistic mystery in its fullness,[11] the doctrine on the other sacraments particularly that of sacred orders.[12] Frivolous or imprudent zeal, bent on the facile accommodation of a free-spirited mentality, is totally alien to the authenticity of the ecumenical movement as envisaged by the Catholic Church; it surely will have tragic repercussions. "Nothing is so foreign to the spirit of ecumenism as a false irenicism which harms the purity of Catholic doctrine and obscures its genuine and certain meaning."[13]

---

[8] *Dans ces derniers temps,* n.4, p.504; cf. AAS, 62(1970) n.4, p. 186.

[9] *Unitatis redintegratio,* AAS, 57 (1965) n.19, p. 104.

[10] Loc. cit., n. 21, p. 105.

[11] Loc. cit., n. 22, p. 106.

[12] Ibid.

[13] Loc. cit., n. 11, p. 462; n. 24, p. 470; cf. *Ad totam Ecclesiam,* AAS, 59 (1967) n. 2, pp. 574-575; *Dans ces derniers temps,* AAS, 62 (1970) n. 8, p. 187.

Holy See

The ecumenical commitment, to be true to itself, must evolve under the leadership of the responsible ecclesiastical authorities. Needless to say, the Roman Pontiff enjoys supreme and universal authority in ecumenical affairs.[14] Together with the Supreme Pontiff the same responsibility for the whole universal Church falls upon the college of Bishops.[15]

The supreme and universal jurisdiction of the Roman Pontiff is implemented through the *Secretariat for the Promotion of the Unity of Christians*.[16] The papal legate carries on this authority in his task with the Bishops of particular churches in fostering the ecumenical cause.[17] Furthermore, the Directory, *Ad totam Ecclesiam*, insists that the Commission of Bishops for ecumenical affairs established within the Episcopal Conference must maintain relations with the Holy See.[18] The diocesan commission for ecumenical affairs is expected to follow the directions issued from time to time by the *Secretariat for the Promotion of the Unity of Christians*.[19]

---

[14] *Unitatis redintegratio*, AAS, 57 (1965) nn.8, 9, p. 98; *Ad totam Ecclesiam*, AAS, 59 (1967) n.2, p. 574.

[15] Canon 755, §1.

[16] *Regimini Ecclesiae*, AAS, 59 (1967) nn.92-95, pp. 918-919. The following are the Instructions issued by the Secretariat: *Ad Totam Ecclesiam*, May 14, 1967, AAS, 59 (1967) pp. 574-592; *Dans ces derniers temps*, January 7, 1970, AAS, 62 (1970) pp. 184-188; *Spiritus Domini*, April 16, 1970, AAS, 62 (1970) pp. 705-724; *Reflections and Suggestions Concerning Ecumenical Dialogue*, August 15, 1970, Flannery (ed.) pp. 535-553; *In quibus rerum circumstantiis*, June 1, 1972, AAS, 64 (1972) pp. 518-525; *nota su alcune interpretazioni* October 17, 1973, 65 (1973) pp. 616-619; *Ecumenical Collaboration at the Regional National and Local Levels*, typis Polyglottis Vaticanis, 1975.

[17] Canon 364, n. 6.

[18] AAS, 59 (1967) n.8,(g), p.578.

[19] *Ad totam Ecclesiam*, AAS, 59(1967)n.6, (b), p.576.

Episcopal Conference

On the regional level, the authority is assumed by the Episcopal Conference.[20] The Decree, *Unitatis redintegratio,* had already endorsed the authority of the Episcopal Conference in issuing norms concerning *communicatio in sacris.*[21] It is for the Episcopal Conference to lay down guiding principles, to translate general principles to practical cases and to adjust undertakings which gradually take place in the region. For this reason, the Directory, *Ad totam Ecclesiam,* requested that a commission of Bishops for ecumenical affairs be erected within each national Conference of Bishops.[22] The aim of this commission is "to give guidance in ecumenical affairs and determine concrete ways of acting in accordance with the Decree on ecumenism and with other ordinances and legitimate customs."[23] In certain ecumenical issues the Episcopal Conference takes over the responsibility and authority of the local Bishop. An instance of this is the granting of permission that versions of the Scriptures may be prepared and published by Catholics in collaboration with our separated brethren.[24] It also belongs exclusively to the Episcopal Conference to decide on cases of cooperation between a Catholic seminary on the one hand and a non-Catholic seminary or a non-denominational university on the other. *The Program of Priestly Formation* issued by the same should include general rules on this type of cooperation and what part the clerical students may take in these ventures.[25] In other issues the ecumenical commitment falls equally on the Episcopal Conference and the diocesan Bishop. The growth of

---

[20] Canon 755, §2.

[21] AAS, 57(1965), n.8, p.98.

[22] AAS, 59(1967) n.7, p.577.

[23] *Ad totam Ecclesiam,* n.7, p. 486. The commission of Bishops, if possible, should be assisted by a permanent secretariat and by experts (Ibid). The tasks of the commission are enumerated in nn.6 and 8 of the Directory (Eng.Ed., pp. 485-486).

[24] Canon 825, §2.

[25] *Spiritus Domini,* AAS, 62 (1970) n.84, p.719; n.93, p.723

harmony among Christians through dialogue and consultation on a territorial and diocesan basis should advance through the initiative of both authorities.[26] However, it is also their responsibility to exercise pastoral vigilance in order to keep the dialogue on appropriate lines lest dangers of indifferentism and proselytism creep in.[27] It belongs to the diocesan Bishop, or to the Episcopal Conference, to decide when grave and pressing needs do occur in order that other Christians, in whose Churches Penance, the Eucharist, and Anointing of the Sick are not valid, may receive these sacraments.[28] Neither the local Ordinary nor the Episcopal Conference shall issue norms in this matter unless the competent authority of the non-Catholic Church or ecclesial community concerned has been consulted.[29] In this manner, the Catholic Church would not be accused of fostering proselytism. The Episcopal Conference, as well as the individual Bishop, should take pains to promote ecumenism in institutes of advanced learning, including the seminary.[30]

Local Ordinary

Apart from the above mentioned matters, the local Ordinary remains the legitimate and sole authority in the diocese in matters ecumenical. He is to encourage his faithful to join in prayer for unity with other Christians. Indeed, all ecumenical activities in the diocese should be under his supervision and guidance.[31] With his approval, ecumenical gatherings and

---

[26] *Unitatis redintegratio*, AAS, 57(1965)n. 4, pp.94-95, 96; *Ad totam Ecclesiam*, AAS, 59 (1967) n.2, pp.574-575; n.27, p.584; canons 383, §3; 755, §2.

[27] *Ad totam Ecclesiam*, AAS, 59 (1967) n.28, p.584.

[28] Canon 844, §4; cf. *Unitatis redintegratio*, AAS, 57(1965) n.8, p. 98; *Ad totam Ecclesiam*, AAS, 59 (1967), n.55, p.590; *Dans ces derniers temps*, AAS, 62 (1970) n. 7, p. 187.

[29] Canon 844, §5; *Ad totam Ecclesiam*, AAS, 59(1967) n.42, p.587.

[30] *Spiritus Domini*, AAS, 62 (1970) nn.65,66, pp.705-706; n.79, pp.717-718.

[31] *Ad totam Ecclesiam*, AAS, 59(1967) n.32,p.585. Canon 383, §3: "He is to act with humanity and charity to those who are not in full communion with the Catholic Church; he should also foster ecumenism as it is understood by the Church."

services may take place either in a Catholic Church or in any other Christian Church.[32] An effective means and instrument for the Bishop to accomplish his ecumenical duties is the diocesan council, commission or secretariat[33] for Christian unity which the Directory, *Ad totam Ecclesiam*, earnestly desires to be established in the diocese.[34] The same Directory enumerates several functions which the diocesan commission is expected to perform.[35] However, of all its assignments the following four seem to be the major ones: 1) promotion of ecumenical activity programmed by the Episcopal Conference or by the local Ordinary or Ordinaries;[36] 2) assistance to other ecumenical institutions and enterprises in the diocese;[37] 3) discussion with other Christian Churches or ecclesial communities on the theology and practice of baptism in its ecumenical dimension;[38] 4) discussion on and participation in enterprises concerning social issues, such as, education, morality, peace, social justice, human dignity, family, etc.[39] Of extreme usefulness to the diocesan commission in the pursuance of its objective is the Instruction, *Ecumenical Collaboration at the Regional, National and Local Levels*. It may be of great help in matters touching social issues,[40] and pastoral commitments.[41] To foster the cause of

---

[32] Loc. cit., n. 36, (b), p.586.

[33] The diocesan ecumenical commission should include, besides the clergy, religious and lay persons, loc. cit., n.5, p.576.

[34] loc.cit., n.3, p.484.

[35] Loc.cit., n.6, pp.576-577.

[36] Loc.cit., n.3, p.575.

[37] Loc.cit., n.4, pp.575-576.

[38] Loc. cit., nn.16,17,18,pp.580-581.

[39] Loc.cit.,n.6,(e),p.576;n.33,p.585; *Spiritus Domini*, AAS,62(1970),n.69(c),(e), pp.708-709; n.75, (c), p.713.

[40] Cf. (g), (h),(i),(j),(k), pp.13-15, (e,II,III) p.26.

[41] Cf. (c),(d),(e),(f),pp.10-13.

Christian unity, the new Code, moreover, leaves it to the discretion of the Bishop to decide whether representatives of other Christian Churches or ecclesial communities should be invited as observers to the synod.[42]

The Code of Canon Law

It goes without saying that the new Code of Canon Law is the law for the universal Latin Church.[43] This premise however does not entail an *a priori* abrogation of previous documents of the Holy See. On the contrary, save the prescription of canon 6, canons 20 and 21 should be applied also in reference to these documents. In the majority of issues the Code retains the same legislation endorsed by these documents. There are instances, however, when one has to resort to these earlier documents either as substitution whenever an express provision in the Code is lacking,[44] or as a clarification of the codicial law if need be.[45] The Decree on ecumenism, *Unitatis redintegratio*, will ever remain *fons codicis primarius*. "*Servatis de iure servandis de quibus supra*," the Directories on ecumenism, *Ad totam Ecclesiam*[46] and *Spiritus Domini*,[47] still retain its binding force, both of which entail implementation of the conciliar Decree, and even further development of guidelines featured in the spirit of the same Decree.[48] To

---

[42] Canon 463, §3. In our opinion, by virtue of canon 443, §6, non- Catholics may be invited to particular councils (plenary or provincial), if this is judged expedient by respective ecclesiastical authorities.

[43] Canon 1.

[44] Canon 19.

[45] Canon 17.

[46] *Directory Concerning Ecumenical Matters: Part One*.

[47] *Directory Concerning Ecumenical Matters: Part Two: Ecumenism in Higher Education*

[48] Other instructions were issued by the same Secretariat as clarification and re-enforcement of the directives laid down by the Directory. These are *Dans ces derniers temps, Reflections and Suggestions concerning Ecumenical Dialogue, In quibus rerum circumstantiis, nota su alcune interpretazioni*.

these one may add the Instruction on *Ecumenical Collaboration at the Regional, National and Local Levels*. This Instruction was never intended by the Secretariat to be as "a set of directives or prescriptions endowed with authority in the juridical sense of the word."[49] Nevertheless "it sets out orientations . . . which have the weight of the experience and insights of the Secretariat."[50] In our opinion, unless it does not oppose the new law in a particular matter, its intrinsic and integral validity ought to be maintained.

Different Dimensions of Ecumenism

The ecumenical reality assumed from the start diverse dimensions which, for lack of better specification, may be divided into ecclesiological, sociological, educational, and spiritual aspects. We shall present a brief exposition on each of these aspects.

Ecclesiological Aspect

The ecclesiological dimension of the ecumenical movement essentially consists in an approach based on dialogue. This dialogue is primarily directed to a closer collaboration on the level of thought and action. The ecumenical approach aims first at the elimination of ancient prejudice and bigotry on both sides, and engenders an attitude of sympathy, friendliness and openness motivated by purity of intention and animated by a spirit of truth and fairness. The historic encounters of Pope Paul VI with different heads of Christian Churches[51] were meant for the restoration of mutual

---

[49] p.2.

[50] Ibid.

[51] Encounter of Pope Paul VI with Patriarch Athenagoras I, on December 7,1965, AAS, 58(1966) pp.20-21; encounter of Pope Paul VI with Archbishop Michael Ramsay, on March 22, 1966, AAS, 58 (1966) pp.286-288; encounter of Paul VI with the Supreme Patriarch of the Armenians, Vasken I Catholicos, on May 12, 1970, AAS, 62(1970) pp.416-417; encounter of Paul VI with Shenouda III, Pope of Alexandria and Patriarch of the See of St. Mark, on May 10, 1973, AAS, 65 (1973)

understanding, esteem, respect, and true Christian charity among the members of the respective Churches. Gathered in prayer or discussion, in an attitude of humility and repentance, each in his own way, discerns his faithfulness to Christ and his commitment to humanity. The dialogue fosters discussion and analysis which in turn lead to a truer knowledge and greater appreciation of the doctrine and spirituality of the participants. Priority is given, in fact, by the Directory, *Spiritus Domini,* to the idea of the Catholic clergy forming a relationship with ministers of other denominations "for the purpose of getting to know each other better and of solving pastoral problems by a joint Christian effort."[52] Simple as it might sound, a dialogue based on trust, esteem, and charity enables us to discover new ways of overcoming the differences which still exist.

Efficient means and instruments for Christian unity are the councils of Churches and Christian councils which are blossoming in many parts of the Christian world.[53] These councils are to be found on all levels ranging from parochial to national, and even supranational.[54] Because of the multiplicity and diversity of these councils, an attempt to approach them in a classified manner is almost impossible. They differ from each other by reason of their individual history, constitution, or operation. Whatever the case may be, these councils nevertheless express the unity already existing among the Christian Churches and ecclesial communities, which by itself serves as an effective Christian witnessing. But they are also instrumental in advancing the desired unity among Christians. They prove to be the *locus operandi* where local conversations are initiated on theological questions,

---

pp.299-301; encounter of Paul VI with Archbishop Frederick Donald Coggan, Archbishop of Canterbury, on April 29, 1977, AAS, 69 (1977) pp. 286-289; encounter of Pope John Paul II with Patriarch Demetrius I, on November 30, 1979, AAS 71 (1979) pp.1599- 1604; encounter of Pope John Paul II with Archbishop of Canterbury Runcie, on May 29, 1982, AAS, 74 (1982) pp. 924- 926.

[52] n. 78, P. 526.

[53] In reference to the difference existing between councils of Churches and Christian councils confer Instruction, *Ecumenical Collaboration at the Regional, National and Local Levels,* 4, (d), pp. 20-21.

[54] Loc.cit., 4, (b), pp. 18-19.

and initiatives are undertaken on social issues. Sharing of insights, joint exploration of possible collaboration in areas of social justice, human development, and general welfare, public statements on public or private morality are at the same time ways and means which most effectively bring Christians together. The Catholic Church since Vatican Council II calls upon the faithful to participate in the ecumenical movement not only on personal initiative, but also as particular Churches under the guidance of the Bishop, or several Churches conjointly under the Episcopal Conference.[55] The *Secretariat for Promoting Christian Unity* commends this participation "both in matters of social and human concern, and even more in support of Christian testimony in the field of mission."[56]

Sociological Aspect

The growing ecumenical consciousness and endeavour will unmistakably fall short of its pursuit if kept on the purely conceptual level and not brought to the level of action. Differences, however fundamental in dogma, ecclesiology, and structure, should not hinder Christians from joining forces in carrying out duties for the common good of humanity. In Christian doctrine the human being is acclaimed as of supreme worth, and the fundamental human rights are endorsed as sacred, inviolable, and irreducible. Any Christian Church and ecclesial community, worthy of the name, cannot fail to perceive the importance and necessity of united effort in the cause of humanity. This convergence of forces should be actualized not only in word, but most of all in positive and constructive action in every sector of social life. The Decree, *Unitatis redintegratio,* earnestly advocates this cooperation among Christians. "It should contribute to a just appreciation of the dignity of the human person, to the promotion of the blessings of peace, the application of Gospel principles to social life, and the advancement of the arts and sciences in a truly Christian spirit. It

---

[55] Loc. cit. 6, (i) p 28.

[56] Loc. cit., 5, (a), p. 22.

should use every possible means to relieve the afflictions of our times, such as famine and natural disasters, illiteracy and poverty, lack of housing, and the unequal distribution of wealth. Through such cooperation, all believers in Christ are able to learn easily how they can understand each other better and esteem each other more, and how the road to the unity of Christians may be made smooth."[57] The Directory, *Ad totam Ecclesiam,* charges the ecumenical diocesan commission with the task of promoting ecumenical enterprise in the cause of human welfare, such as, education, morality, social and cultural matters, learning and arts.[58] The Instruction, *Ecumenical Collaboration at the Regional, National and Local Levels* is indeed a pragmatic ensemble of how this ecumenical collaboration can evolve in different sectors of social life on behalf of the human cause.[59] This practical course of joint action will not only help in the pursuit of Christian unity, but it will also vouch for common social values, principles and ideals, it will show to the world that believers in Christ do indeed care, respect and love fellow human beings.

Educational Aspect

The educational aspect of ecumenism here means instruction in ecumenism. The Decree, *Unitatis redintegratio,* insists that Catholics should become fully instructed in the authentic teaching both of their Church and of the separated Christian Churches and ecclesial communities.[60] Particular mention is made of the necessary instruction and formation of seminarians in order that they acquire a truly ecumenical mentality.[61] The Directory, in part one, refers to the need for the faithful to gain a truer knowledge and

---

[57] n. 12, p. 463.

[58] AAS, 59 (1967) n.6, (e), p.576.

[59] pp.13-15, 26.

[60] AAS, 57 (1965) n.9, p.98.

[61] Loc. cit., n.10, p.99.

a more just appreciation of the teaching and religious life of their Church and of the other communions involved in the dialogue.[62] Moreover, it charges the ecumenical diocesan commission to help and foster instruction on the subject to clergy, laity, and seminarians.[63]

It is, however, in part two that the Directory concentrates fully and treats exhaustively the subject of ecumenism.[64] It takes pains to lay down basic principles, directives, and orientations in the promotion and advancement of ecumenical knowledge in all institutions of advanced learning, particularly seminaries and theological faculties.[65]

All theological training, *per se*, has relation to the ecumenical movement. The aim of every theological course is the deepening of faith, spirituality and doctrine in the student as well as true knowledge and appreciation of other Christian believers without resorting to polemics. In this manner the student will be in a position to understand carefully and assess impartially both the concordance and dissension in theological themes among Christians. "In every branch of theology the ecumenical standpoint should make for consideration of the link between the subject and the existing mystery of the unity of the Church."[66] The Directory highly recommends that ecumenism be treated as a separate question which may be presented either as a special course of lectures or as the theme of some lectures.[67] Various ways and means are pointed out by the Directory which

---

[62] *Ad totam Ecclesiam*, AAS, 59 (1967) n.2, p.575.

[63] Loc. cit., n.6,(g), p.576.

[64] *Spiritus Domini*, AAS, 62 (1970) pp.705-724.

[65] Loc.cit.,n.67,p.706; n.76,pp.714-715; n.79,(d)(e),p.718, n.84,p.719; n.90,pp.721-722. With regard to the classification of institutes of higher studies in the Code of canon law, cf.canons 809, 810,§1,814,815,821.

[66] Loc. cit., n.73, p. 521.

[67] "Ecumenism should embrace these aspects: (a) those elements of the Christian heritage both of truth and of holiness which are found in common in all Churches and Christian communities, though they are sometimes given different theological expression; (b) the spiritual treasury and wealth of doctrine which each Christian community has for its own, and which can lead all Christians to a deeper understanding of the nature of the Church; (c) whatever in matters of faith causes dissension and division, yet can stimulate a profounder examination of the word of

adroitly serve the enhancement of ecumenical dialogue among students in higher studies, such as courses or lectures,[68] work-shops on ecumenical themes or on social issues,[69] meetings and associations for study, exchange of students,[70] availability of journals, reviews and articles on the theme.[71] All these resources should be available to the clergy, religious and laity.[72] The clergy, in particular, should be exposed to the ecumenical movement, and kept informed of the latest development in the field; indeed, they should actively participate, according to their individual capacity, in its realization.[73]

In spite of the insistence of the Directory that students of higher studies should be acquainted with the ecumenical dialogue, no reference is made on the subject in the new Code of canon law in the section on Catholic universities and other institutes of higher studies and on ecclesiastical universities and Faculties.[74] Again, serious concern is given by the Directory on the doctrinal, spiritual and pastoral formation of seminarians in the ecumenical movement.[75] The document even suggests

---

God, aimed at manifesting what in proclaiming truth are real contradictions and what only seem to be," n. 72, pp. 520-521.

[68] AAS, 62 (1970) n.69, p.707.

[69] Loc.cit., n.69, (c), p.708.

[70] Ibid.

[71] Loc. cit., pp. 708-709.

[72] Loc. cit., n. 78, pp. 716-717.

[73] "In carrying out the established policy of pastoral training for the clergy through clergy councils, special institutes, retreats, days of recollection or pastoral discussion, bishops and religious superiors are earnestly exhorted to make sure that the necessary care is devoted to ecumenism, and also to bear in mind these particular points.
. . .
Theology faculties, seminaries and other seats of learning can make a great contribution to ecumenical effort both by arranging courses of study for clergy doing pastoral work and by urging their own teaching staff to take a ready share in studies and courses organized by others," n. 78, pp. 525-526.

[74] Canons 807-821.

[75] AAS, 62 (1970) n.79, (a-e), pp. 717-718.

"occasional exchange of teachers, mutual recognition of certain courses, various kinds of federation, affiliation to a university."[76] Moreover, it enjoins the Episcopal Conference to insert in the *Program of Priestly Formation* general norms regarding the cooperation between Catholic seminaries and those of other denominations,[77] or to decide on the amalgamation of Catholic educational institutes and seminaries with institutions of other denominations.[78] This objective is not pursued by the new Code of Canon Law. Canon 252 fails to include ecumenism among the subjects to be given in the theological curriculum to seminarians -- at least, not specifically. Perhaps, vague reference to the subject is made in canon 256, §1.[79]

The Directory envisages ecumenism as a special branch of study.[80] This aim can best be achieved with the erection of institutes or centres for advanced ecumenical studies.[81] Interconfessional institutes,[82] or amalgamation of such institutes[83] are considered as feasible by the Directory. These institutions may serve as the appropriate centre for dialogue and study among theologians. Scholars of this calibre will be of great service to the Church in her ecumenical commitment at the local, regional, and national levels.[84]

---

[76] n. 90, P. 531.

[77] AAS, 62 (1970) n. 84, p. 719.

[78] Loc. cit., n. 93, p. 723.

[79] *The Program of Priestly Formation* issued by the Canadian Episcopal Conference scarcely deals with the subject (cf. 54,55), whereas the one issued by the Episcopal Conference of U.S.A. treats the topic extensively (nn. 270-305, pp.67-75).

[80] AAS, 62 (1970) n.75, pp.713-714.

[81] Loc. cit., n.86, p.720. Four types of institutions are suggested.

[82] Loc. cit., n. 87, pp.720-721.

[83] Loc.cit., n.88, p.721; cf. n.92, pp.722-723.

[84] Loc. cit., n. 77, pp.715-716; cf. *Unitatis redintegratio*, AAS, 57 (1965) n. 11. p. 99. There are several publications of joint study on different ecumenical themes by Catholics and other

Spiritual Aspect

The spiritual aspect of ecumenism has already been presented in brief. The essence of ecumenism is renewal of personal holiness of the Christian, as the Decree, *Unitatis redintegratio,* points out: "This change of heart and holiness of life, along with public and private prayer for the unity of Christians, should be regarded as the soul of the whole ecumenical movement, and merits the name, "spiritual ecumenism."[85] Following the same line of thought, the Directory, *Ad totam Ecclesiam,*[86] gives further specification on the different forms of public prayer for Christian unity and on the days and time when these prayers are most suitably held. It established the Week of Prayer for Christian Unity[87] and pointed out other days, festivities, and particular occasions when such public prayer is most fitting.[88] Besides prayers which can be said during the celebration of the Eucharist,[89] votive Mass can be said for the said aim according to the liturgical norms.[90]

The Decree, *Unitatis redintegratio,* ventures even further in its pursuit. It postulates that Catholics come together for common prayer with their separated brethren.[91] Thus we come to the question of *communicatio in spiritualibus* with our separated Christian brethren. However, before we proceed in our exposition, two fundamental distinctions should be kept in

---

Christian Churches. These are available from United States Catholic Conference Publications, Washington, D.C.

[85] n. 8, P. 460.

[86] AAS, 59 (1967) n.21, p. 581.

[87] The week from 18-25 January, loc. cit., n. 22 (a), p. 582.

[88] Loc. cit., n. 22, (a-c), p. 582.

[89] Loc. cit., n. 24, p. 583.

[90] Ibid.

[91] AAS, 57(1965) n.4, p.94; cf. *Ad totam Ecclesiam,* AAS, 59 (1967) n.25, p. 583.

mind which have always constituted the premise of the relations between the Catholic Church and the separated Christian Churches and ecclesial communities and which are repeatedly inculcated by the documents. A distinction must be made between our separated Christian Churches by reason of the validity of Sacred Orders. By reason of participation in worship, a distinction must be endorsed between *communicatio in spiritualibus* and *communicatio in sacris*.

The Decree, *Unitatis redintegratio,* reiterates the traditional belief of the Catholic Church in the validity of the ministerial priesthood and of the Eucharist in the Eastern Churches separated from Rome. "These Churches, although separated from us, yet possess true sacraments, above all -- by apostolic succession -- the priesthood and the Eucharist, whereby they are still joined to us in closest intimacy."[92] Moreover, there is a very close communion between the two Churches, Catholic and Orthodox, in matters of faith, despite the differences in theological expression of doctrine.[93] The Council furthermore acknowledges the rich liturgical and spiritual heritage of the Eastern Churches which ought to be a source of spiritual nourishment to the Catholic faithful.[94] For this reason, all the more "It is the Council's urgent desire that every effort should be made toward the gradual realization of this unity."[95] It must be pointed out, however, that other separated Christian Churches of the West stand on equal footing as the Orthodox Church with regards to the validity of the sacraments and the orthodoxy of doctrine.

Unfortunately, such a stand cannot be upheld when it concerns the Protestants on the whole. The most fundamental difficulty in this regard, as the Decree indicates, is the weighty differences existing among Protestants themselves.[96] As a group, in their relationship with the Catholic Church

---

[92] n. 15, P. 465; cf. Decree, *Orientalium Ecclesiarum*, AAS, 57 (1965), nn. 24-29, pp.83-85; *Ad totam Ecclesiam*, AAS, 59 (1967) nn.39,40, p.587.

[93] *Unitatis redintegratio*, AAS 57 (1965) n. 17, p. 103.

[94] Loc. cit., n. 15, p. 102.

[95] n. 18, p. 467.

[96] AAS, 57 (1965) n.19, p. 104.

they offer major discrepancies in that the absence of the sacrament of Orders is characteristic of Protestantism;[97] thus they lack the eucharistic mystery in its fullness, they believe in the subjective interpretation of revealed truth,[98] and therefore reject the teaching authority of the Church; each denomination has an individual acceptance of the number and nature of the sacraments.

The wish of the Council is that a certain sharing in prayer, appropriate to the present state, be allowed among the Catholic faithful and other Christians.[99] The Directory, *Ad totam Ecclesiam,* saw to it that basic guidelines be given on the sharing of this spiritual activity.[100] Not rarely it may appear quite difficult to discern in practical cases the difference between *communicatio in spiritualibus* and *communicatio in sacris.* For this reason, the Directory endeavours to clarify the two concepts. "*Communicatio in spiritualibus* is used to cover all prayer offered in common, common use of sacred places and objects."[101] Whereas *communicatio in sacris* is participation either in liturgical worship, that is, "worship carried out according to the books, prescriptions or customs of a church or community, celebrated by a minister or delegate of such church or community, in his capacity as minister of that community,"[102] or in the sacraments of another church or ecclesial community.[103]

Ecumenical feeling and mutual regard is solidified and enhanced when Christians come together in prayer, particularly when it is intended for the restoration of unity. Ecumenical prayer groups are flourishing on diocesan

---

[97] Loc. cit., n.22, p. 106.

[98] Loc. cit., n. 21, p. 105.

[99] Loc. cit., n. 8, p. 98.

[100] AAS, 59 (1967) nn.25-29, pp. 583-584.

[101] n. 29, p. 493.

[102] nn. 30, 31, P. 493.

[103] n. 30, p.493.

and parochial levels everywhere.[104] It would be very interesting in itself and extremely useful to ecumenism to conduct a survey on the development of these individual groups, ranging from gatherings, in which Scripture and prayers are the format, to more organized para-liturgies. Moreover, the Directory envisages joint retreats organized for students in higher studies, provided that local and personal circumstances are respected and the liturgical norms observed.[105]

Under the heading of *communicatio in spiritualibus* the Directory, *Ad totam Ecclesiam,* includes the common use of sacred places and objects. The new Code, in canon 933, gives permission to a Catholic priest, "for a good reason, with the express permission of the local Ordinary and provided scandal has been eliminated," to celebrate the Eucharist in a place of worship belonging to a separated Christian community. However, the Directory proceeds even further. It allows the local Ordinary to grant permission that our separated brethren of any denomination may use Catholic buildings, churches and cemeteries to carry out their religious rites.[106] Moreover, Eastern separated brethren may also use our sacred objects necessary for their religious rites.[107] It even imposes the obligation on the authorities of Catholic schools, hospitals, and other institutions of social nature to offer every facility to Orthodox priests and Protestant ministers in order that they may exercise sacramental and spiritual functions to their own faithful in dignified and reverent conditions.[108]

Communicatio in sacris is of a more delicate nature since it entails major involvement of Catholics with separated Christians in the sharing of the means of grace. And therefore more proximate is the danger of indifferentism and false irenicism. Thus the concern of the Catholic Church

---

[104] *Ecumenical Collaboration . . .* , (a), p. 9.

[105] *Spiritus Domini,* AAS, 62 (1970) n.69, (d), p. 709.

[106] *Ad totam Ecclesiam,* AAS, 59 (1967) nn.52, 53, pp. 589-590; nn.61, 62, p. 592; cf. *Orientalium Ecclesiarum,* AAS, 57 (1965) n.28, p. 84; *Ecumenical Collaboration . . .* , (d), pp. 11-12.

[107] Loc. cit., n. 52, pp. 589-590.

[108] Loc.cit., nn.53,54, p.590; nn.62,63, p.592.

in the matter is understandable. It is worth recalling the definition of *communicatio in sacris* as given by the Directory. The concept includes two spiritual realities, namely participation in divine worship as officially prescribed by the respective Christian Church or community, and participation in the sacraments administered by an official minister of a particular Church. The Decree, *Unitatis redinteqratio,* lays down two basic criteria on the subject: first, this type of ecumenical sharing should not be considered as a means to be used indiscriminately for the restoration of unity among Christians; second, whenever this liturgical worship takes place, it must be borne in mind that the unity of the Church ought to be expressed and that the Christian participants really share in the means of grace.[109] Nowhere does the distinction between the Orthodox faith and the Protestant faith appear more stringent, in the eyes of the Catholic Church, than in *communicatio in sacris.* The Decree on ecumenism, in fact, concludes: "Therefore some worship in common (*communicatio in sacris*), given suitable circumstances and the approval of Church authority, is not merely possible but is encouraged."[110] We do not see why the same attitude should not be applied to other Christian Churches which retain the apostolic succession of the ministerial priesthood.

In reference to liturgical worship, in the strict sense, which does not entail sacramental sharing, there are norms which cannot be ignored without detriment to the ecumenical spirit. Of these norms some concern the faithful, others the clergy.

For a just reason, Catholics may attend an Orthodox liturgical service, or Orthodox a Catholic liturgical celebration. In both instances, the participants are allowed to take part in the prayers and rubrics of the Church in which they are guests.[111] With the permission of the local Ordinary they are also permitted to read lessons at the liturgical service.[112] The same holds true with the participation of Catholics in a

---

[109] AAS, 57 (1965) n.8, p. 98; cf. *Ad totam Ecclesiam,* AAS, 59 (1967) n. 38, p. 586.

[110] n. 13, P. 465.

[111] *Ad totam Ecclesiam,* AAS, 59 (1967) n.50, p. 589.

[112] Ibid.

Protestant service, provided that there is nothing at variance with the Catholic doctrine.[113] These same principles govern the manner in which Protestants may assist Catholic liturgical celebration.[114] In both cases the permission of the Local Ordinary and the consent of the authorities of the community concerned are required.[115] Relevant to the subject are two codicial norms: one regards the imparting of blessings to non-Catholic; the other treats of funerals to be performed for non-Catholics. Canon 1170 establishes: "While blessings are to be imparted primarily to Catholics, they may be given also to catechumens and, unless there is a prohibition by the Church, even to non-Catholics." Canon 1183, §3, states: "Provided their own minister is not available, baptized persons belonging to a non-Catholic Church or ecclesial community may, in accordance with the prudent judgment of the local Ordinary, be allowed Church funeral rites, unless it is established that they did not wish this."[116]

With regard to the participation of clergy in liturgical service the Directory prescribes a protocol which has to be observed whenever the Orthodox clergy attend Catholic liturgy and vice versa. "Regarding participation in ceremonies which do not call for sacramental sharing the following should be observed:

1. In ceremonies carried out by Catholics, an oriental clergyman who is representing his Church should have the place and the liturgical honors which Catholics of equal rank and dignity have.
2. A Catholic clergyman present in an official capacity at an Orthodox service can, if it is acceptable to his hosts, wear choir dress or the insignia of his ecclesiastical rank.

---

[113] Loc. cit., n. 59, pp. 591-592.

[114] Ibid.

[115] Loc. cit., n. 56, p. 591.

[116] The Congregation for the Doctrine of the Faith allows funeral Mass being publicly celebrated for a non-catholic provided that the name of the defunct is not mentioned since such a mention presupposes full communion with the Catholic Church -- *Decretum de Missa publice celebranda in Ecclesia Catholica pro aliis christianis defunctis*, AAS, 68 (1976) III, p.622.

3. There should be meticulous regard for the outlook of the clergy and faithful of the Eastern Churches, as well as for their customs which may vary according to time, place, persons and circumstances."[117]

These same principles are valid in liturgical celebrations when Catholic clergy and Protestant ministers take part whether the celebration is carried out by Catholics or Protestants.[118]

The question of ecumenism reaches its crucial point when *communicatio in sacris* involves sacramental sharing. At this point, the issue assumes its full dogmatic dimension and hinges upon the validity of the ministerial priesthood. One can appreciate the concern of the Catholic Church when it comes to the sharing of the sacraments with our separated brethren. One realizes that nothing can be expected in matter of compromise when it comes to fundamental realities. Convergence is feasible but not when it concerns the deposit of faith. Therefore, one should not be surprised to find a long dossier of rules and regulations on the subject matter. An exposition of these norms on each sacrament appears useful for a better understanding of the Catholic approach at the present stage of ecumenical development.

Baptism

The validity of baptism administered outside the boundaries of the Catholic Church is a *fait accompli*. The Decree, *Unitatis redintegratio*, endorses the traditional doctrine of the Catholic Church that baptism validly conferred constitutes the sacramental bond of unity of all Christians. "For men who believe in Christ and have been properly baptized are put in some, though imperfect, communion with the Catholic Church."[119] Indeed, as the Directory points out, baptism is the foundation of the ecumenical movement.[120] Upon this dogmatic premise the same Directory prescribes

---

[117] N. 51, p. 498.

[118] AAS, 59 (1967) n.60, p. 592; n. 37, p. 586.

[119] N. 3, P. 455; cf. n. 4, p.458; n. 22, p. 469.

[120] *Ad totam Ecclesiam*, AAS, 59 (1967) n. 11, p. 578.

that "indiscriminate conditional baptism of all who desire full communion with the Catholic Church cannot be approved."[121] It even takes pains to reiterate the traditional doctrine of the Church on the matter and form of baptism, and the faith and intention of the minister.[122] This doctrine is followed *in integro* by the Code.[123]

Difficulty arises when it comes to sponsors. The Directory allows that an Orthodox,[124] or even a Protestant[125] for a just cause[126] may act as

---

[121] N. 14, p. 489. Because of the great number of Christian Churches and ecclesial communities it is rather difficult to know them all. We mention some of them in which baptism is administered validly: African Methodist Episcopal, Amish, Anglican, Assembly of God, Baptists, Church of God, Church of the Nazarine, Congregational, Disciples and Christians, Disciples of Christ, Episcopalian, Evangelical and Reformed Church, Evangelical United Brethren, Lutheran, Methodist, Mormon (The Church of Jesus Christ of Latter-Day Saints) Old Catholics, Orthodox, Polish National, Presbyterian, Reformed Church in America, Seven Day Adventists, United Church of Canada, United Church of Christ.

[122] (a) Concerning *matter* and *form*. Baptism by immersion, pouring or sprinkling, together with the trinitarian formula, is of itself valid. (Cf. CIC Canon 758). Therefore if the rituals and liturgical books or established customs of a church or community prescribe one of these ways of baptizing, doubt can only arise if it happens that the minister does not observe the regulations of his own community or church. What is necessary and sufficient, therefore, is evidence that the minister of baptism was faithful to the norms of his own community or church. For this purpose generally one should obtain a written baptismal certificate with the name of the minister. In many cases the other community may be asked to cooperate in establishing whether or not, in general or in a particular case, a minister is to be considered as having baptized according to the approved ritual.
(b) Concerning *faith* and *intention*. Because some consider that insufficiency of faith or intention in a minister can create a doubt about baptism, these points should be noted: The minister's insufficient faith never of itself makes baptism invalid. Sufficient intention in a baptizing minister is to be presumed unless there is serious ground for doubting that he intends to do what Christians do. (Cf. Response of the Holy Office, 30 January 1833: "It is sufficient to do what Christians do"; Sacred Congregation of the Council. Decrees approved by Pius V, 19 June 1570, cited by the Provincial Council of Evreux, France, 1576).
(c) Concerning the *application of the matter*. Where doubt arises about the application of the matter, both reverence for the sacrament and respect for the ecclesial nature of the other communities demand that a serious investigation of the community's practice and of the circumstances of the particular baptism be made before any judgment is passed on the validity of a baptism by reason of its manner of administration (cf. CIC Canon 737§1). n. 13, pp.488-489.

[123] Canons 869, §1, 2, 3; 861, §2; 864.

[124] *Ad totam Ecclesiam*, AAS,59(1967) n.48, pp. 588-589.

[125] The Directory prescribes that as a general rule a Protestant should not act as sponsor in the baptism of a Catholic. "The reason is that a godparent is not merely undertaking his responsibility for the Christian education of the person baptized or confirmed as a relation or friend -- he is also, as a representative of a community of faith, standing as sponsor for the faith of the candidate," n.57, p.500. Nevertheless, the Directory considers certain cases where exception could be made (ibid).

[126] Blood relation or friendship is accepted by the Directory as just cause, cf. AAS, 59 (1967) n.57, p. 591.

sponsor together with a Catholic sponsor, and then simply as a witness to the baptism, provided that the Catholic education of the person being baptized is assured. The Code reiterates the policy of the Directory on the matter dismissing, however, the requirement of a just cause.[127] Moreover, the Directory allows a Catholic, for the same reasons, to stand as sponsor of baptism for an Orthodox or Protestant.[128] Since the Code fails to mention anything in this regard, the prescription of the Directory is thought to be still in force.

Penance, Eucharist, Anointing of the Sick

The sacraments of Penance, Eucharist, and Anointing of the Sick are discussed *globatim* both by the Directory,[129] and by the Code.[130] Canon 844, §2, treats of the reception of these sacraments by the Catholic faithful from non-catholic ministers, whereas paragraphs 3 and 4 of the same canon concentrate on the reception of these sacraments by non-catholics from Catholic ministers.

"Whenever necessity requires or a genuine spiritual advantage commends it," Catholic faithful may approach a non-catholic minister for the reception of these sacraments provided these are valid in that

---

[127] Canon 874, §2.

[128] AAS, 59(1967) n.48, pp.588-589; n. 57, p. 591.

[129] Loc. cit., n. 42, p. 587; n. 55, p. 590.

[130] Canon 844, §2,3,4.

particular Church.[131] The Code does nothing but repeat the mind of the Directory.[132]

It is worth noting certain guidelines given by the Directory, *Ad totam Ecclesiam,* which, although missing in the Code, have nonetheless bearing on the ecumenical cause. These concern the Eucharist. The first is: "Since practice differs between Catholics and other Eastern Christians in the matter of frequent communion, confession before communion and the eucharistic fast, care must be taken to avoid scandal and suspicion among the Orthodox, created by Catholics not following the Orthodox usage. A Catholic who legitimately communicates with the Orthodox in the cases envisaged here must observe the Orthodox discipline as much as he can."[133] The same norm ought to be applied when Catholics receive the Eucharist from validly ordained ministers of other denominations. Another question regards the attendance at a Eucharistic celebration by Catholics in an Orthodox Church or another Christian Church (endowed with valid priesthood) on Sundays and days of obligation. Canon 844, §2, talks merely of the reception of the Eucharist. Taking into consideration the prescription of canon 6, we do not see why the norm of the Directory should be considered repealed. The Directory allows that "a Catholic who occasionally, for reasons set out below (cf. n. 50) attends the holy liturgy (Mass) on a Sunday or holiday of obligation in an Orthodox Church is not then bound to assist at Mass in a Catholic Church. It is likewise a good thing if on such days Catholics, who for just reasons cannot go to Mass in their own church, attend the holy liturgy of their separated oriental brethren, if this is possible."[134]

In reference to the lawfulness of administering these three sacraments to non-catholics a distinction is made by canon 844 between those whose Churches retain the validity of the said sacraments and those

---

[131] Canon 844, §2.

[132] *Ad totam Ecclesiam,* AAS, 59 (1967) nn. 44,46, p. 588; n.55, p. 590.

[133] n. 45, p. 497.

[134] n. 47, p. 497.

whose Churches or ecclesial communities lack a valid ministerial priesthood.[135] In the former case, discussed in paragraph 3, no conditions are required except that the non-catholic recipient spontaneously asks for them and is properly disposed.[136] In the latter case, dealt with in paragraph 4, the unity of sacramental faith is deficient; therefore, the participation of non-catholics in these sacraments, as a general rule, is forbidden.[137] Hence, the administration of these sacraments is permissible only in danger of death, or in grave and pressing need, and as long as the recipient accepts the Catholic faith in these sacraments, is properly disposed, cannot approach a minister of his own community and spontaneously asks for them.[138]

The Eucharist is the means by which the unity of Christians is brought about and is the ultimate reality.[139] "The Eucharist really contains what is the very foundation of the being and unity of the Church."[140] The concern of the Catholic Church on the abuses, which often lurk in this respect, needs no explanation or apology. The Secretariat has more than once called our attention to prudence and discretion.[141]

A prohibition had already been expressed by the Directory on the participation of Protestants in reading Scripture and preaching during the Catholic celebration of the Eucharist. In like manner, Catholics are not allowed to participate actively during the principal liturgical service of the Word (or Lord's Supper) held by Protestants.[142] With regards to the

---

[135] Cf. *Ad totam Ecclesiam*, AAS, 59 (1967) nn. 39-47, pp. 587-588; nn. 55-56, pp. 590-591.

[136] Cf. *Ad totam Ecclesiam*, loc.cit., nn. 42,44,46, pp. 587-588.

[137] Loc. cit., n. 55, p. 590.

[138] Canon 844, §4; *Ad totam Ecclesiam* AAS, 59 (1967) n. 55, p. 590.

[139] *Unitatis redintegratio*, AAS, 57 (1965) n.2, p. 91; n.4, p.95.

[140] *In quibus rerum circumstantiis*, II, n. 1, p. 554.

[141] Cf. *Dans ces derniers temps*, AAS, 62 (1970) 184-188; *In quibus rerum circumstantiis*, AAS, 64 (1972) 518-525; *Nota su alcune interpretazioni*, AAS, 65 (1973) 616-619.

[142] *Ad totam Ecclesiam*, AAS, 59 (1967) n.56, p. 591.

reception of the Eucharist by those whose Churches lack the validity of the ministerial priesthood, canon 844, §4, allows it only in danger of death and in some grave and pressing need. The Directory understands "grave and pressing need" being actualized "during persecutions and in prisons."[143] The Instruction, *In quibus rerum circumstantiis,* extends the meaning of "urgent need" to "grave spiritual necessity and with no chance of recourse to their own community."[144] Ultimately, it belongs to the local Ordinary to decide whether in these exceptional cases the required conditions are present or not.[145] If cases of this nature occur often, it will be the responsibility of the Episcopal Conference to issue guidelines on when the required conditions are verified in particular cases.[146] The Instruction, *Nota su alcune interpretazioni*, lays down two criteria which cannot be ignored if one really wants to interpret correctly the mind of the Holy See: first, each case has to be examined individually; hence a general regulation cannot be issued which makes a category out of an exceptional case;[147] second, epikeia is not permissible in similar cases.[148]

A prohibition, which is nowhere found in any other document of the Holy See on ecumenism, is found in canon 908. It appears that because of its serious and blatant nature the documents felt no need to inculcate this prohibition. Be that as it may, canon 908 prescribes: "Catholic priests are forbidden to concelebrate the Eucharist with priests or ministers of

---

[143] Loc. cit., n. 55, p. 590.

[144] VI, P. 559.

[145] *Ad totam Ecclesiam*, AAS, 59 (1967) n.55, p. 590; *In quibus rerum circumstantiis*, AAS, 64 (1972) n.6, p. 524; *Nota su alcune interpretazioni*, AAS, 65 (1973) n.6, p. 617.

[146] *In quibus rerum circumstantiis*, loc. cit., n. 6, p. 524; *Nota su alcune interpretazioni* loc. cit., n. 6, p. 618; *Ad totam Ecclesiam*, loc. cit., n. 55, p. 590.

[147] Loc. cit., n. 6, p. 618.

[148] Ibid.

Churches or ecclesial communities which are not in full communion with the Catholic Church."[149]

Confirmation

Very little is being said, indeed can be said, on the sacrament of Confirmation in the ecumenical spectrum. The Directory only states the fact that the sacrament of Confirmation in Eastern separated Churches is conferred the same time as baptism.[150] The fact "that no mention is made of the confirmation in the canonical testimony of baptism" does not give grounds for the sacrament to be administered again conditionally on the one who asks to join the Catholic Church.[151] The same principle should be applied to those converts who belonged to Churches in which Confirmation is validly conferred by reason of validly ordained priesthood. With regard to sponsor of Confirmation the same conditions are required by the Code as those in the sponsor of baptism.[152]

Marriage

The matrimonial legislation of the new Code in reference to ecumenism is primarily based on two *Motu proprio*, *Crescens matrimoniorum*, issued on February 22, 1967,[153] and *Matrimonia mixta*, promulgated on

---

[149] There is nothing to be said on Sacred Orders in particular. However, it is worth mentioning that the simple impediment to ordination -- "children of non-catholics so long as the parents remain in their error" (canon 987, n. 1 of 1917 Code) -- has been changed into "a neophyte (is impeded from receiving Sacred Orders) unless, in the judgment of the Ordinary, he has been sufficiently tested" (canon 1042, n.3).

[150] *Ad totam Ecclesiam*, AAS, 59(1967) n.12, p. 579.

[151] n. 12, P. 488.

[152] Canons 893, 874, §1, n.3. There is no express prohibition in the new Code for a Catholic to be a sponsor of Baptism or Confirmation to a member of a Christian Church in which these sacraments are validly conferred.

[153] AAS,59(1967)165-166.

January 7, 1970,[154] which substituted the Instruction, *Matrimonii sacramentum* of March 18, 1966.[155] Marriage between a Catholic and a non-catholic remains an impediment even in the new codification. It depends on the fact of baptism or its validity whether the impediment is impedient,[156] or diriment.[157] The severity, however, of the prohibition announced in canons 1060 and 1061, §1, of the 1917 Code has long been removed by the *Motu proprio, Matrimonia mixta*. In line with the *Motu proprio*, canon 1125 requires a just and reasonable cause for the granting of the dispensation.

A radical change from the old Code was brought about by the *Motu proprio, Matrimonia mixta,* regarding the conditions to be fulfilled in mixed marriages.[158] The prescriptions of the *Motu proprio* have been followed *in integro* by the Code, in canon 1125. Of great significance to the ecumenical spirit is the promise of the Catholic spouse to do all in his or her power -- rather than "has to"[159] -- in order that all the children be baptized and brought up Catholic.[160] Another great step toward the ecumenical mutual understanding is the non-involvement of the non-catholic party in these promises, who has only to be informed. On what has been stated earlier, that all divinely revealed truth subsists in the Catholic Church, the Catholic party is still bound by divine precept "to declare that he or she is prepared to remove dangers of defecting from the faith."[161] Canon 1128

---

[154] AAS, 62 (1970) 257-263.

[155] AAS, 58 (1966) 235-239.

[156] Canon 1124

[157] Canon 1086, §1.

[158] AAS,62 (1970)nn.4,5,p.261 versus canon 1061,§1 of 1917 Code.

[159] *Matrimonii sacramentum*, AAS, 58(1966)nn.1,2,p.237.

[160] Canon 1126:"It is for the Episcopal Conference to prescribe the manner in which these declarations and promises, which are always required, are to be made, and to determine how they are to be established in the external forum,and how the non-Catholic party is to be informed of them."

[161] Canon 1125, n.l.

enjoins that both the local Ordinary and the pastor assist the Catholic spouse and the children born of a mixed marriage with all the spiritual help needed to persevere in their faith, and to help the spouses to firmly establish a community of life and love. However, the canon lacks that ecumenical spirit coupled with the earnest concern of the Church for the establishment of a sound and healthy familial milieu so vividly expressed by the *Motu proprio, Matrimonia mixta:* "They (the local Ordinary and pastor) shall encourage the Catholic husband or wife to keep ever in mind the divine gift of the Catholic faith and to bear witness to it with gentleness and reverence, and with a clear conscience. They are to aid the married couple to foster the unity of their conjugal and family life, a unity which, in the case of Christians, is based on their baptism too. To these ends it is to be desired that those pastors should establish relationships of sincere openness and enlightened confidence with ministers of other religious communities."[162]

The traditional canonical form is retained also for mixed marriages.[163] However, relaxation of the law is possible in mixed marriages. In a marriage between a Catholic, either of latin rite or of oriental rite, and a non-catholic of Oriental rite the observance of the canonical form is required only *ad liceitatem.* The intervention of a sacred minister is, however, required for validity.[164] By virtue of canon 1127, §2, the local Ordinary may dispense from the canonical form in individual cases of mixed marriages whenever grave difficulties are in the way with the provision that there should always be some public form of ceremony.[165] It is forbidden to

---

[162] N.14, pp. 513-514.

[163] Canons 1108, §1, 1127, §1.

[164] Canon 1127,§1; cf. *Crescens matrimoniorum,* AAS, 59 (1967) p.166; *Matrimonia mixta,* AAS, 62 (1970) n.8, p. 261. Canon 1127, §1,is intended to foster Christian unity with separated Eastern Christians. If "sacred minister" is taken to mean a minister of any Christian community, canon 1127, §1, falls short of its aim. Catholic jurisprudence acknowledges a marriage invalid of two members of the Orthodox Church due to lack of form prescribed by the Orthodox Church *ad validitatem.* If, therefore, "sacred minister" were to be interpreted in a general sense, the harmony which has existed so far between the two Churches would certainly be seriously disrupted. Moreover, a problem would arise in Catholic jurisprudence in such cases.

[165] Cf. *Matrimonia mixta,* loc.cit., n.9, p.261.

have two ceremonies, one Catholic and the other non-Catholic or civil, in which the same matrimonial consent is given, or to have a Catholic and a non-Catholic minister jointly receiving the matrimonial consent.[166]

No reference is made in the Code as to whether non-Catholics could be admitted as witnesses in a Catholic or a mixed marriage.[167] *"Si lex non distinguit, nec nos distinguere debemus."* The Directory granted permission for non-Catholics to stand as witnesses in a Catholic marriage, and Catholics to act as witnesses in a non-Catholic marriage.[168]

In the old Code it was forbidden for a mixed marriage to be celebrated in a church; and if permission was granted for a serious reason, the celebration of the Eucharist was never permissible.[169] In the new Code a mixed marriage in which both parties are baptized, as a general rule, must be celebrated in the parish church;[170] when the non-Catholic party is unbaptized, the marriage may be celebrated in a church or in another suitable place.[171] The celebration of the Eucharist is allowed and even encouraged when both parties are baptized.[172]

Penalties Concerning Ecumenism

Another significant aspect of the Catholic commitment towards Christian unity is the penal codification of the new Code. The new attitude of the Catholic Church towards other Christians has its commencement in

---

[166] Canon 1127, §3; cf. *Matrimonia mixta,* loc.cit.,n.13, p.262.

[167] Cf. canon 1108.

[168] *Ad totam Ecclesiam,* AAS, 59 (1967) n.49, p.589; n.58, p.591.

[169] Canon 1109, §3, of 1917 Code.

[170] Canon 1118, §1.

[171] Canon 1118, §3.

[172] With regard to reception of the Eucharist by the non-catholic party, confer the section on the Eucharist. In our opinion, the celebration of marriage is an occasion when Eucharist can be given to the non-catholic baptized party, *"servatis de iure servandis de quibus supra."*

the memorable encounter of Pope Paul VI with Patriarch Athenagoras I, when they mutually withdrew the excommunications which their Churches had inflicted upon each other in the year 1054.[173]

The issue on penalties is subordinate to the basic question as to whether non-catholics are bound by the disciplinary laws of the Church. The Code of 1917, in canon 87, considered baptized non-catholics subject to the laws of the Catholic Church. A complete reversal is registered in the new Code. By virtue of canon 11, only those who were baptized in the Catholic Church or received into it are considered bound by ecclesiastical law.

In the Code of 1917 Christians baptized outside the Catholic Church and Catholics who publicly abjured their faith were treated alike. In canon 1325, §2, of the old Code they were considered, without any distinction, either heretics or schismatics. The new Code endorses a distinction between them. According to canon 751, only those who publicly defect from their faith should be called and recognized either apostates, heretics or schismatics, as the case may be.

It seems safe to say that non-catholics are not bound by the penal law of the new Code. "*Salvo meliori iudicio,*" an exception should be made on crimes against natural and divine positive laws. Our view is based on the presupposition that the Church finds its roots in the very creation of the human being. Moreover, through the global redemption by Our Lord the human creature, by his very nature, partakes of the salvific powers of Christ. This means that although a person is not acknowledged as member of the visible Church, it is through the same Church -- the perpetuation of the redemptive powers of Christ -- that the redemption of each human being is obtained. In this perspective one is able to see that the mystical reality of the Church surpasses its visible boundaries. Thus, every human being, by reason of being human, is in some, but real, sense member of the Church.

Upon this assumption one may contend that codicial laws -- including penal ones -- which directly endorse natural or divine positive laws, bind

---

[173] AAS, 58 (1966) p.21.

all human beings indiscriminately. Laws of this category are those, for example, contained in canons 1397, 1398, 1071, §1, n.3. It is true, *"leges quae poenam statuunt, strictae subsunt interpretationi,"*[174] but it is equally true that canon 11 refers exclusively to "merely ecclesiastical laws."

As far as ecumenism is concerned, penalties can indeed be inflicted on Catholics who fail in their commitment to the Church. The rationale for the existence of these penalties is theological, rather than juridical. It has been stated earlier that the Catholic Church claims to be the true Church in which the deposit of faith subsists in full. We have also pointed out that the concept of ecumenism is essentially and exclusively convergence; thus, it excludes, *a priori,* compromise and conversion either way. The individual must maintain his or her loyalty to his or her own Church or ecclesial community in spite of the ecumenical movement. On this line of thought one may understand the reason behind the precautions expressed by canon 844, §2-5, regarding *communicatio in sacris,* and the rationale for the grave prohibition entailed in canon 908. On the other hand, however, since the Catholic Church believes herself to be the true Church, conversion to the Catholic faith does not antagonize, and less still contradict, the commitment of the Catholic Church towards the ecumenical movement. By the same token, it is believed, Catholics cannot defect from their faith. Upon the aforesaid assumption one can easily realize why the Catholic Church is still harsh on those who publicly abjure their Catholic faith.[175] Canon 1364, §1, prescribes: "An apostate from the faith, a heretic or a schismatic incurs a *latae sententiae* excommunication . . . " Furthermore, the person is denied church funeral rites[176] and funeral Mass.[177] The marriage of a defected

---

[174] Canon 18.

[175] Cf. canon 171, §1, n.4 (barred from election); canon 316, §1 (denied membership in public association of the faithful); canon 194, §1, n.2 (removed from office); canon 694, §1, n.1 (dismissed from religious life); canon 1364, §1,and 1336, §1, nn.1,2,3 (deprived of clerical rights and privileges); canon 1741, n.1 (a pastor can be removed if he"causes grave harm or disturbances to ecclesiastical communion.")

[176] Canon 1184, §1.

[177] Canon 1185.

Catholic with a Catholic is to be considered, for all intents and purposes, a mixed marriage.[178] In the new Code one finds also indeterminate penalty sanctioned for certain crimes against the unity of the Church. These are: canon 1365: "One who is guilty of prohibited participation in religious rites is to be punished with a just penalty"; canon 1366: "Parents, and those taking the place of parents, who hand over their children to be baptized or brought up in a non-catholic religion, are to be punished with a censure or other just penalty."

The Right to Stand as Plaintiff

By virtue of canon 1476 of the present Code, any person, baptized or unbaptized, can plead before a court. This was not feasible in the Code of 1917. A non-catholic was deprived of the right of standing as plaintiff in an ecclesiastical court. The Holy Office on January 27, 1928, declared that non-catholics could not even submit a petition of nullity of their marriage to an ecclesiastical tribunal.[179] In this respect canon 87 was to be applied in the sense that they were barred by reason of "some obstacle impeding the bond of communion with the Church." The *Promotor iustitiae* used to act on their behalf. In short, the Church today is showing more respect towards human dignity.

Conclusion

Ecumenism pertains, *per se*, to the domain of systematic theology. Nevertheless, the student of canon law must be aware of a growing Christian consciousness that tries to read theology in a historical perspective. Christian consciousness, it is believed, does not flow only from theological premises dogmatically established. It must also result from a

---

[178] Canons 1124;1086,§1;1125. Such a person is not bound by the canonical form (canon 1117), and the local Ordinary has to be consulted before one can assist at his or her marriage (canon 1071, §1, n.4; §2).

[179] AAS, 20 (1928) p.75.

serious reflection upon historical reality. And from this reflection it passes into action. The ecumenical movement is a clear example. The main thrust of the ecumenical dialogue tends to show that action is possible in spite of theological differences. The ecumenical activity of the Church does not flow exclusively as a conclusion from theological premises. It is rather the endeavour of Christian consciousness in responding to the divine inspiration towards Christian unity through reflection, prayer, and action. This approach undertaken by the Church of Vatican Council II presupposes the Church's self-awareness of being broader than a mere institution as traditionally conceived; its true nature comprises more than her visible boundaries; she finds her roots in humanity itself.

"There is but one road that leads to Corinth," but nobody knows what Corinth would look like when we reach it. Ecumenism, apart from being a commitment of the Catholic Church towards unity, is indeed helping the Church to explicate what she enshrines implicitly in herself. The more she reaches out of herself, suspends herself into otherness, the greater the grasp will be of her self-inwardness, of her solid subsistency, as her ultimate and absolute reality. Far from being an effort towards self-accommodation to a stringent, fatalistic urgency, the ecumenical movement is an inner force resulting from candid discontent in the face of the Church's self-purification and intense christolization of herself. Ecumenism is a return of the Church back to her very foundation.

The present division among Christians is of supreme value in the process of unification. There can never be unification unless this reality ensues from purification of those concerned. The Decree, *Unitatis redintegratio,* is aware of the "deficiencies in moral conduct or in Church discipline or even in the way that Church teaching has been formulated."[180] "Perpetua reformatione, qua humanum terrenumque institutum, indiget."[181] Tension caused by dissension is necessary for the betterment of the individual opposing forces; when tension fails, everything

---

[180] AAS, 57 (1965) n.6, p. 97.

[181] Ibid.

becomes static and sterile -- stagnation follows. Dissension helps energize life, potentialities and commitment. Divergency of views calls for self-analysis, self-discernment, and self-purification. This contradiction holds good for the Catholic Church as well as for an other Christian Church or ecclesial community desirous of unity. The main task of the Christian consciousness is to be attentive to where the pulse of history is beating at this moment.

The raison d'être of canon law in the restoration of Christian unity is to guide the dialogue in a manner faithful to the mind of the Church. It is there to help and facilitate a cautious and effective process towards Christian unity. Specifically, its assignment is to help avoid futile activism and imprudent immediatism, lest ecumenism turns from convergence of mind and heart into dishonest compromise or prosyletism. This it does without obstructing the future inspiration of the Holy Spirit.

Bibliography

<u>Sacred Scriptures</u>
Book of Genesis
First Book of Kings
Book of Proverbs
Book of Wisdom
Gospel according to Matthew
Gospel according to Mark
Gospel according to Luke
Gospel according to John
Acts of the Apostles
Letter to the Romans
First Letter to the Corinthians
Letter to the Galatians
Letter to the Ephesians
Letter to the Colossians
First Letter to Timothy
Letter to Titus
First Letter of Peter

Councils

Ecumenical Councils

Concilium Chalcedonense (a. 451), *Conciliorum Oecumenicorum Decreta,* curantibus Josepho Alberigo, Josepho A Rossetti Perikle, P. Joannou Claudio Leonardi, Paolo Prodi, Ed., III, Bologna, 1973.
Concilium Lateranense III (a. 1179), loc. cit.
Concilium Lateranense V (a. 1512 - 1517), loc. cit.
Concilium Tridentinum (a. 1545 - 1563), loc. cit.
Concilium Vaticanum II (A. 1962 - 1965):
    Ad gentes divinitus (Decree on the Church's Missionary Activity)
    Apostolicam actuositatem (Decree on the apostolate of the laity)
    Christus Dominus (Decree on the Bishop's pastoral office in the Church)
    Dei Verbum (Dogmatic Constitution on divine revelation)
    Dignitatis humanae (Declaration on religious freedom)
    Guadium et spes (Pastoral Constitution on the Church in the modern world).
    Inter mirifica (Decree on the instruments of social communication)
    Lumen gentium (Dogmatic Constitution on the Church)
    Orientalium Ecclesiarum (Decree on Eastern Catholic Churches)
    Perfectae caritatis (Decree on the appropriate renewal of the religious life)
    Presbyterorum Ordinis (Decree on the ministry and life of priests)
    Sacrosanctum concilium (Constitution on the sacred liturgy)
    Unitatis redintegratio (Decree on ecumenism)
    Message to Humanity, issued at the Beginning of the Second Vatican Council by its Fathers, with the Endorsement of the Supreme Pontiff.

Bibliography

Particular Councils

Concilium Agathense, (a. 506), *Mansi,* Tomus VIII, Florentiae, 1762.
Concilium Antiochenum I (a. 341), *Mansi,* Tomus II, Florentiae, 1759.
Concilium Aquisgranense II, (a. 836), *Mansi,* Tomus XIV, Venetiis, 1769.
Concilium Arelatense VI, (a. 813), *Mansi,* Tomus XIV, Venetiis, 1769.
Concilium Barcinonense, (a. 599), *Mansi,* Tomus X, Florentiae, 1764.
Concilium Bracarense III, (a. 572), *Mansi,* Tomus IX, Florentiae, 1763.
Concilium Carthaginense, (a. 419) *Mansi,* Tomus IV, Florentiae, 1760.
Concilium Carthaginense, (a. 421), *Mansi,* Tomus IV, Florentiae, 1760.
Concilium Lugdunense II, (a 567), *Mansi,* Tomus IX, Florentiae, 1763.
Concilium Meldense, (a. 845), *Mansi,* Tomus XIV, Venetiis, 1769.
Concilium Moguntiacum, (a. 813), *Mansi,* Tomus XIV, Venetiis, 1769.
Concilium Moguntinum I, (a. 847), *Mansi,* Tomus XIV, Venetiis, 1769.
Concilium Ravennense, (a. 877), *Mansi,* Tomus XVII, Venetiis, 1772.
Concilium Romanum, (a. 853), *Mansi,* Tomux XIV, Venetiis, 1769.
Concilium Triburiense, (a. 895), *Mansi,* Tomus XVIII, Venetiis, 1773.
Concilium Troslejanum, (a. 909), *Mansi,* Tomus XVIII, Venetiis, 1773.
Concilium Vasense III, (a. 529), *Mansi,* Tomus VIII, Florentiae, 1762.
Concilium Vernense, (a. 755), *Mansi,* Tomus XII, Florentiae, 1766.

Sources of Canon Law

Corpus Iuris Canonici -- Decretum Magistri Gratiani,
Ed. Aemilius Friedberg, Graz, 1959.
Corpus Iuris Canonici -- Decretales D. Gregorii Papae IX,
Ed. Aemilius Friedberg, Graz 1959.
*Corpus Iuris Canonici -- Liber Sextus Decretalium D.
Bonifacii Papae VIII*, Ed. Aemilius Friedberg, Graz 1959
Corpus Iuris Canonici -- Clementis Papae V Constitutiones,
Ed. Aemilius Friedberg, Graz, 1959.
Codex a Benedicto XV promulgatus Constitutione Providentissima Mater Ecclesia, anno 1917.
Ecclesiae Sanctae, Litterae apostolicae motu proprio datae,
A A S, 58 (1966) 757-787.
Regimini Ecclesiae, Constitutio apostolica, A A S, 59 (1967) 885-928
Ministeria Quaedam, motu proprio, A A S, 64 (1972) 529-534.
Matrimonii Sacramentum, Instructio S. Congregationis pro Doctrina Fidei,
A A S, 58 (1966) 235-239.
Crescens matrimoniorum, S. Congregatio pro Ecclesia Orientali, A A S,
59 (1967) 165-166.
Matrimonia mixta, motu proprio, A A S, 62 (1970) 257-263.
Ad totam Ecclesiam, Directorium Secretariatus ad Christianorum Unitatem Fovendam, A A S, 59 (1967) 574-592.
Documentum a Secretariatu pro non-Credentibus, A A S, 60 (1968) 692-704.
Dans ces derniers temps, Declaration de Secretariatu ad Christianorum Unitatem Fovendam, A A S, 62(1970) 184-188.
Spiritus Domini, Directorium a Secretariatu ad Christianorum Unitatem Fovendam, A A S, 62 (1970) 705-724.
In quibus rerum circumstantiis, Instructio a Secretariatu ad Christianorum Unitatem Fovendam, AAS, 64 (1972) 518-525.
Decretum de Missa Publice celebranda in Ecclesia Catholica pro Aliis Christianis Defunctis, A S. Congregatione pro Doctrina Fidei, A A S,
68 (1976) 621-622.
Codex a Ioanne Paulo II promulgatus Constitutione Sacrae Disciplinae Leges,

Bibliography 425

die 25 Januarii, 1983.

Sources of Roman Law

Corpus Iuris Civilis -- Institutiones, Ed. Paulus Krueger, Berolini, 1954.
Corpus Iuris Civilis -- Digesta, Ed. Theodorus Mommsen et Paulus Krueger, Berolini 1954.
Corpus Iuris Civilis -- Codex Justinianus, Ed. Paulus Krueger, Berolini 1959.

Patristic Literature

AMBROSIUS, *De Officiis Ministrorum Libri Tres,* P.L., Tomus 16, Parisiis, 1866.
Enarrationes in XII Psalmos Davidicos, P.L., Tomus 14, Parisiis, 1866.
Expositio Evangelii Secundum Lucam Libris X Comprehensa, P.L., Tomus 15, Parisiis, 1866.
Flight from the World, (*De Fuga Saeculi*), Trans. Michael P. McHugh, *The Fathers of the Church,* Washington, D.C., 1972.
Jacob and The Happy Life, (*De Iacob et Vita Beata*), Trans. Michael P. McHugh, *The Fathers of the Church,* Washington, D.C., 1972.
Letter to Irenaeus, Trans. Sr. Mary Melchior Beyenka, *The Fathers of The Church,* New York, 1954.
Letter to Simplicianus, Trans. Sr. Mary Melchior Beyenka, *The Fathers of The Church,* New York, 1954.
Letter to Valentinian, Trans. Sr. Mary Melchior Beyenka, *The Fathers of the Church,* New York, 1954.

AMULUS, *Epistola Prima ad Theodboldum Ep. Lingonensem,* P.L., Tomus 116, Parisiis, 1879.

AURELIUS AUGUSTINUS, *Confessionum Libri Tredecim,* P.L., Tomus 32, Parisiis, 1845.
Contra Faustum Manichaeum Libri Triginta Tres., P.L., Tomus 42, Parisiis, 1841.
De Diversis Quaestionibus LXXXIII Liber Unus, P.L., Tomus 40, Parisiis, 1841.
De Genesi ad Litteram Libri Duodecim, P.L., Tomus 34, Parisiis, 1841.
De Libero Arbitrio Libri Tres, P.L., Tomus 32, Parisiis, 1845.
De Vera Religione Liber Unus, P.L., Tomus 34, Parisiis, 1845.
One Book on the True Religion, Trans. Sr. Mary Inez Bogan, *The Fathers of The Church,* Washington, D.C. 1968.
Epistola Casulano Presbytero, P.L., Tomus 33, Parisiis, 1844.
Expositio Quarumdam Propositionum ex Epistola ad Romanos -- Liber Unus, P.L., Tomus 35, Parisiis, 1845.

In Psalmum CXLV Enarratio, (*Sermo ad Plebem*), P.L., Tomus 37, Parisiis, 1841.

The City of God, Trans. Gerald G. Walsh and Daniel J. Honan, *The Fathers of the Church,* New York, 1954.

The Good of Marriage (*De Bono Coniugali*), Trans. Charles T. Wilcox, *The Fathers of the Church,* New York, 1955.

BASILIUS, *Liber De Spiritu Sancto,* P.G., Tomus 32, Parisiis, 1857.

BERNARDUS CLARAE-VALLENSIS, *De Consideratione Libri Quinque ad Eugenium Tertium,* P.L., Tomus 182, Parisiis, 1862.

Canones Apostolorum, Gentiano Herveto Interprete, Mansi, Tomus I, Florentiae, 1759.

Canones Apostolorum Sanctorum, Dionysio Exiguo Interprete, Mansi, Tomus I, Florentiae, 1759.

Capitula Herardi, P.L., Tomus 121, Parisiis, 1852.

Capitulare Theodulfi Episcopi Aurelianensis ad Parochiae Suae Sacerdotes, Mansi, Tomus XIII, Florentiae, 1767.

CATULFUS, *Instructio Epistolaris ad Beatum Carolum Regem,* P.L., Tomus 96, Parisiis, 1851.

CHRODEGANGUS, *Regula Canonicorum,* P.L., Tomus 89, Parisiis, 1863.

CLEMENT OF ALEXANDRIA, *The Miscellanies,* (*Stromata*), Trans. William Wilson, *Anti-Nicene Christian Library,* Edinburgh, 1880.

EUSEBIUS HIERONYMUS, *Commentariorum in Epistolam ad Galatas Libri Tres,* P.L., Tomus 26, Parisiis, 1866.

Commentariorum in Isaiam Prophetam Libri Duodeviginti, P.L., Tomus 24, Parisiis, 1865.

Dialogus Contra Luciferianos, P.L. Tomus, 23, Parisiis, 1865.

FLACCUS ALBINUS, *Dialogus De Rhetorica et Virtutibus,* P.L., Tomus 101, Parisiis, 1851.

GREGORIUS MAGNUS, *Moralium Libri, sive Expositio in Librum B. Job,* P.L., Tomus 76, Parisiis, 1878.

Registri Epistolarum Libri Quartuordecim, P.L., Tomus 77, Parisiis, 1849.

Regulae Pastoralis Liber, P.L., Tomus 77, Parisiis, 1849.

Hettonis Capitulare, P.L., Tomus 105, Parisiis, 1851.

HILARIUS PICTAVIENSIS, *Tractatus Super Psalmos,* P.L., Tomus 9, Parisiis, 1844.

HINCMARUS RHEMENSIS, *Ad Proceres Regni, pro Institutione Carolomanni Regis et de Ordine Palatii,* P.L,Tomus 125, Parisiis, 1879.

Capitula ad Presbyteros Parochiae Suae, Mansi, Tomus XV, Venetiis, 1770.

Capitula Archidiaconibus Presbyteris Data, P.L.,Tomus 125, Parisiis, 1879.

Capitula Quibus De Rebus, Mansi, Tomus XV, Venetiis, 1770.

De Coercendo et Exstirpando Raptu Viduarum Puellarum ac Sanctimonialium, P.L., Tomus 125, Parisiis, 1879.

De Divortio Lotharii Regis et Tetbergae Reginae, P.L., Tomus 125, Parisiis, 1879.

Expositiones ad Carolum Regem pro Ecclesiae Libertatem Defensione, P.L.,Tomus 125, Parisiis, 1879.

HONORIUS AUGUSTODUNENSIS, *Summa Gloria de Apostolico et Augusto,* P.L., Tomus 172, Parisiis, 1854.

HUGO DE SANCTA MARIA, *Tractatus de Regia Potestate et Sacerdotali Dignitate,* P.L., Tomus 163, Parisiis, 1854.

IOANNIS SARESBERIENSIS, *Polycraticus sive de Nugis Curialium et Vestigiis Philosophorum,* P.L., Tomus 199, Parisiis, 1855.

IONAS AURELIANENSIS, *De Institutione Laicali Libri Tres,* P.L., Tomus 106, Parisiis, 1851.

Opusculum De Institutione Regia, P.L., Tomus 106, Parisiis, 1851.

IRENAEUS, *Contra Haereses Libri Quinque,* P.G., Tomus 7, Parisiis, 1857 *Against Heresies,* Trans. Alexander Roberts and W. H. Rambaut, *Ante-Nicene Christian Library,* Edinburgh,1880.

ISIDORUS, *Etymologiarum Libri XX,* P.L., Tomus 82, Parisiis, 1878. *Sententiarum Libri Tres,* P.L., Tomus 83, Parisiis, 1862.

IVO CARNOTENSIS, *Decretum,* P.L., Tomus 161, Parisiis, 1855.

JUSTINE, ST., *The First Apology,* Trans. Thomas B. Falls, *The Fathers of The Church,* New York, 1948.

LACTANTIUS, *The Divine Institutes,* Trans. Sr. Mary Francis McDonald, *The Fathers of The Church,* Washington, D.C. 1964.

MAGNUS AURELIUS CASSIODORUS, *De Anima,* P.L., Tomus 70, Parisiis, 1847.

In Psalterium Expositio, P.L., Tomus 70, Parisiis, 1847.

Variorum Libri Duodecim, P.L., Tomus 69, Parisiis, 1865.

OPTATUS AFRI. MILEVITANUS, *De Schismate Donatistarum Adversus Parmenianum,* P.L., Tomus 11, Parisiis, 1845.

ORIGEN, *Against Celsus,* Trans. Frederick Crombie, The Ante-Nicene Fathers, Grand Rapids, Michigan, 1979.

PASCHALIS II, *Epistula ad Florentinos Clericos, Mansi,* Tomus XX, Venetiis, 1775.

PETRUS DAMIANUS, *Opusculum Quinquagesimum Septimum -- De Principis Officio,* P.L. Tomus 145, Parisiis, 1867.

Sermo in Dedicatione Ecclesiae, P.L., Tomus 145, Parisiis, 1867.

RABANUS MAURUS, *De Universo Libri Viginti Duo,* P.L., Tomus 111, Parisiis, 1864.

RATHERIUS VERONENSIS, *Praeloquiorum Libri Sex,* P. L., Tomus 136, Parisiis, 1853.

REGINO PRUMIENSIS, *De Ecclesiasticis Disciplinis et Religione Christiana Libri Duo,* P.L., Tomus 132, Parisiis, 1853.

SEDULIUS SCOTUS, *Liber De Rectoribus Christianis ad Carolum Magnum vel Ludovicum Pium,* P.L., Tomus 103, Parisiis, 1851.

SILVESTER II, *Epistola XI ad Monasteria Stabulense et Malmundartense,* P.L., Tomus 139, Parisiis, 1880.

TERTULLIANUS, QUINTUS, SEPTIMIUS, FLORENS, *De Resurrectione Carnis,* P.L., Tomus 2, Parisiis, 1844.

On the Soldier's Chaplet, (De Corona), Trans. Alexander Roberts and James Donaldson, *Ante-Nicene Christian Library,* Edinburgh, 1882.

On The Testimony of the Soul, (De Testimonio Animae), Trans. Alexander Roberts and James Donaldson, *Ante-Nicene Christian Library,* Edinburgh, 1882.

THEOPHILUS OF ANTIOCH, *To Autolycus,* Trans. Marcus Dods, *The Ante-Nicene Fathers,* Grand Rapids, Michigan, 1975.

Decretalists

A. BUTRIO, ANTONIUS, *Decretalium Commentaria*, Venetiis, 1578.
ANDREAE, JOANNES, *Decretalium Novella Commentaria*, Venetiis, 1581
DE ROSATE, ALBERICUS, BERGOMENSIS, *Dictionarium Iuris tam Civilis quam Canonici*, Venetiis, 1573.
DE SEGUSIO, HENRICUS, *Decretalium Commentaria*, Venetiis, 1581
DE UBALDIS, BALDUS, *Consilia, sive Responsa*, Venetiis, 1575.
    In Decretalium Volumen Commentaria, Venetiis, 1595
FERRARIS, LUCIUS, F., *Prompta Bibliotheca Canonica, Iuridica,*
    Moralis, Theologica . . . , Lutetiae Parisiorum, 1865.
GIGNAC, JOS., N., *Compendium Iuris Canonici*, Quebeci, 1901.
REIFFENSTUEL, ANACLETUS, *Ius Canonicum Universum*, Parisiis, 1889.
SCHMALZGRUEBER, FRANCISCUS, *Ius Ecclesiasticum Universum*, Romae, 1843.

Civilists

AZO, *Ad Singulas Leges XII, Librorum Codicis Iustinianei Commentarius*, Parisiis, 1577.
    Brocardica Aurea, Neapoli 1568.
    Summa ad Pandectas, Papiae, 1506
    Summa Institutionum, Papiae, 1506
    Summa Super Codicem, Papiae, 1506.
BAGAROTUS, *Tractatus De Reprobationibus Testium*, Lugduni, 1549.
    Tractatus Perutilis De Exceptionibus, Dilatoriis, et Declinatoriis Iudicii.
CYNUS PISTORIENSIS, *In Codicem Commentaria*, Francoforti ad Moenum, 1578.
    In Digesti Veteris Libros Commentaria, Francoforti ad Moenum, 1578.
GAIUS, *Institutionum Commentarius Primus, Institutionum et Regularum Iuris Romani Syntagma*, ed. Rudolphus Gneist, Lipsiae, 1880.
PILEUS MODICENSIS, *Quaestiones Aureae*, Romae, 1560
PLACENTINUS, *In Summan Institutionum sive Elementorum D. Iustiniani Libri IIII*, Moguntiae, 1535.
UBERTINUS DE BOBIO, *Solennis Tractatus De Positionibus*, Lugduni, 1549.
UBERTUS DE BONACURSO, *Preludia et Exceptiones*, Lugduni 1522.
ULPIANUS, *Tituli ex Corpore Ulpiani, Institutionum et Regularum Iuris Romani Syntagma*, ed. Rudolphus Gneist, Lipsiae, 1880.

Authors

ANTONINUS, M. AURELIUS, *The Thoughts of the Emperor M. Aurelius Antoninus*, Trans. George Long, New York.

AQUINAS, THOMAS, *Opusculum XXXI De Regimine Principum ad Regem Cypri, Sancti Thomae Aquinatis Opuscula Philosophica et Theologica*, ed. A. Michaele De Maria, Tiferni Tiberini 1886.

Summa Theologica, American Edition in Three Volumes, New York, 1947.

ARISTOTLE, *The Ethics*, Trans. J.A.K. Thomson, Middlesex, England, 1976.

The Politics, Trans. T. A. Sinclair, Middlesex, England, 1978.

BURCKHARDT, JACOB, *The Age of Constantine the Great*, Trans. Moses Hadas, New York, 1967.

CICERO, MARCUS, TULLIUS, *De Finibus Bonorum et Malorum ad Brutum*, Opera Omnia, ed. Carolus Fridericus Augustus Nobbe, Lipsiae, 1850.

De Legibus, loc. cit.

De Re Publica, loc. cit.

Rhetoricorum vel De Inventione Rhetorica Libri Duo, loc. cit.

Topica, loc. cit.

CLEBSCH, WILLIAM A., *Christianity in European History*, New York, 1979.

DABIN, PAUL, *Le Sacerdoce Royal des Fideles dans Les Livres Saints*, Paris, 1941.

Le Sacerdoce Royal des Fideles dans La Tradition Ancienne et Moderne, Paris, 1950.

DE ANGELIS, SERAPHINUS, *De Fidelium Associationibus*, Neapoli, 1959.

EASTWOOD, CYRIL, *The Royal Priesthood of the Faithful*, London, 1963.

Ecumenical Collaboration at the Regional National and Local Levels, Typis Polyglottis Vaticanis, 1975.

FACCIOLATUS, JACOBUS -- FORCELLINUS, AEGIDIUS, *Totius Latinitatis Lexicon*, Patavii 1827.

FANFANI, LUDOVICUS, I., *De Iure Parochorum ad Normam Codicis Iuris Canonici*, Taurini-Romae, 1924.

GEMELLI, AGOSTINO, *La Responsabilita' nelle Azioni Umane dal Punto di Vista della Psicologia e della Psichiatria*, Milano, 1944.

GUITTON, JEAN, *The Church and the Laity*, Trans. Malachy Gerard Carroll, Montreal, Canada, 1965.

HERR, FRIEDRICH, *The Intellectual History of Europe*, Trans. Jonathan Steinberg, New York, 1966.

JIMENEZ-URRESTI, TEODORO, *The Ontology of Communion and Collegial Structures in the Church. Conciluim -- Theology in the Age of Renewal*. New York, 1965.

JUNG, CARL G., *The Practice of Psychotherapy*, New York, 1954.

KEIGHTLEY, THOMAS, *History of the Roman Empire*, New York, 1848.

KURTSCHEID, BERTRANDUS, *Historia Iuris Canonici -- Historia Institutorum*, Romae, 1951.

LETTMANN, REINHARD, *Episcopal Conference in the New Canon Law*, Studia Canonica, XIV (1980) 347s.

MARX, KARL, *Critique of the Gotha Programme*, Revised Translation, New York, 1973.

Grundrisse, Trans. D. McLellan, London, 1972.

MOHLER, JAMES, A., *The Origin and Evolution of the Priesthood*, Staten Island, New York, 1970.

ONCLIN, WILLY, *Collegiality and the Individual Bishop, Concilium -- Theology in The Age of Renewal*, New York, 1965.

PLATO, *The Dialogues*, Trans. B. Jowett, New York, 1895.

SENECA, LUCIUS, ANNAEUS, *Ad Aebutium Liberalem De Beneficiis*, London, 1935.

Ad Lucilium Epistulae Morales, Trans. Richard M. Gummere, London, 1930.

Ad Marciam De Consolatione, Trans. John W. Basore, London, 1935.

Ad Neronem Caesarem De Clementia, Trans. John W. Basore, London, 1963.

Ad Novatum De Ira, Trans. John W. Basore, London, 1963.

Ad Serenum De Otio, Trans. John W. Basore, London, 1935.

SIMONS, THOMAS, G., *Blessings: A Reappraisal of their Nature, Purpose and Celebration*, Saratoga, CA., 1981.

THOTTUMKAL, THOMAS, *People's Ministry*, Edmonton, Alberta, 1983.

ZAVALLONI, ROBERTO, *La Liberta' Personale*, Milano, 1956.

INDEX OF SOURCES AND AUTHORS

Acts of the Apostles, 12, 96, 225, 271, 327.
Ad Totam Ecclesiam, 365, 386, 387, 388, 389, 390, 391, 395, 396, 399-403, 405, 406, 408, 409, 410, 411, 414.
Albericus De Rosate, 49, 59, 65, 68, 93-94, 95, 97, 114, 116, 122, 126, 134, 135, 138, 139-140, 141, 145, 147, 150, 161, 162, 167, 172, 175, 209, 210, 212, 216, 217, 231, 232, 299, 300.
Alcuinus, 113.
Alexander the Great, 26
Ambrose, St., 40-41, 75, 86, 88, 91-92, 112, 114, 193, 201, 202, 205, 206, 208.
Amulus, 300, 302, 304, 306, 309.
Antoninus, Emperor, 31-33, 35, 274.
Antonius A Butrio, 47, 49, 51, 60, 76-77, 93, 94, 95, 97, 98, 108, 115, 126, 128, 137, 138, 139, 140, 144, 147, 161, 162, 163, 164, 165, 167, 168, 172, 173, 175, 178, 209, 211, 212, 213, 214, 217, 225, 226, 227, 228, 229, 230-231, 232.
Antonius De Tremolis, 117.
Aquinas, St. Thomas, 20, 21, 23, 61, 69, 72, 73-75, 76, 103-104, 105, 106, 129, 136, 139, 166, 217-219, 237.
Aristotle, 25-26, 109, 116, 118, 129, 163.
Augustine, St., 7-8, 42, 43, 60, 67, 70, 75, 85-86, 87, 89, 118, 157, 192, 202-203, 204, 207, 208.
Azo, 47, 49, 60, 61, 64, 65, 75, 93, 96, 116, 125, 126, 128, 133, 138, 139, 142, 144, 145, 161, 175, 177, 179, 209, 210, 212, 213, 215, 217.
Bagarotus, 127.
Baldus De Ubaldis, 47, 48, 49, 50, 60, 63, 64, 68, 93, 95, 97, 114-115, 126, 135, 137, 138, 143, 144, 145, 147, 161, 163, 165, 167, 168, 175, 176, 177, 178, 180, 210, 212, 213, 214, 215, 216, 217, 225, 226, 227, 228, 229, 231, 232.
Bartolus A Saxoferrato, 210.
Basil, St., 158.
Bernard, St., 193, 195, 207.
Boniface, Pope, VIII, 15.
Burckhardt, Jacob, 271.
Callistratus, 155, 156.
Capitula Herardi, 305, 309.
Cassiodorus, Magnus, Aurelius, 44, 90, 94, 197, 200, 201, 202, 205, 208.
Catulfus, 86, 195, 205, 208.
Celsus, 35, 38, 66, 129, 142, 155, 156.
Chrodegangus, 302, 309.
Chrysippus, 81.
Cicero, 27-28, 39, 53, 59, 66, 67, 68, 82, 83, 110, 154, 183.
Clebsch, William A., 330.
Clementinarum Liber, 114.
Clement of Alexandria, 26-27, 37, 54, 60, 86, 89, 205-206.
Constantine, Emperor, 156.
Council of Trent, 303, 307, 381.
Cresciens Matrimoniorum, 411.

Cynus Pistoriensis, 49,
68, 93, 94, 95, 96, 97,
103, 117, 119, 125, 145,
151, 161, 163, 165, 168,
173, 176, 178, 179, 209,
210, 211, 212, 213, 214,
215, 216, 229.
Dabin, Paul, 270.
Dans ces derniers temps,
386, 387, 389, 409.
De Angelis, Seraphinus,
271.
Decretum Gratiani, 45, 46,
59, 61, 92, 93, 94, 99,
114, 135, 158, 159-160,
168, 176, 179, 180, 210,
214, 216, 217, 237.
Demosthenes, 81.
Dionysius, Pope, 307.
Eastwood, Cyril, 271, 272.
Ecclesiae Sanctae, 371.
**Ecumenical Collaboration
at the Regional National
and Local Levels**, 387,
390, 392, 393, 395.
Eusebius Hieronymus, 42,
75, 157.
Fanfani, Ludovicus, 310.
Ferraris, Lucius, 131,
132, 163, 299, 300, 301,
307, 310, 313.
Flaccus Albinus, 24, 88,
208.
Florentinus, 34.
Gaius, 59, 60, 83, 133,
142, 144, 145.
Gelasius, Pope, I, 308,
309.
Gemelli, Agostino, 236.
Genesis, 3,4.
Gignac, Joseph N., 305.
Gregory, Pope, IX, 130,
237, 303.
Gregory the Great, 112,
192, 198-200, 207, 208.
Guitton, Jean, 272.
Henricus De Segusio, 49,
50, 68, 93, 95, 97, 115,
122, 124, 125, 128, 134,
136, 137, 138, 139, 140,
142, 144, 145, 147, 161,
162, 163, 164, 165, 166,
167, 168, 169-170, 172,
175, 176, 177, 178, 179,
180, 181, 209, 210, 211,
213, 215, 216, 217, 226,
227, 228, 229, 230, 231.
Hermogenianus, 58, 80,
155, 156.
Herr, Friedrich, 272.
Hieronymus, 87.
Hilarius Pictaviensis, 5,
40.
Hincmarus Rhemensis, 44,
87, 88, 193, 195, 200,
201, 205, 207, 208, 300,
301, 306, 309.
Honorius Augustodunensis,
193, 195, 197, 207, 208.
Hugo De Sancta Maria, 113-
114, 195-196, 208.
Huguccio, 229.
Innocent, Pope, III, 98.
**In Quibus Rerum
Circumstantiis**, 387, 409,
410.
Institutiones, 34, 58-59,
79, 83, 84, 91, 108, 110,
112, 130, 155, 156, 185.
Irenaeus, 6, 86, 87, 88,
193, 194, 196, 202, 205,
208.
Isidorus De Sevillia, 45,
59, 87, 88, 90, 99, 106,
149-150, 151, 158-159,
160, 173, 175, 193, 195,
201, 203, 205, 207.
Ivo Carnotensis, 59, 87,
90, 158-159, 160, 168,
175.
Jacobus De Ravanis, 118.
Jimenez-Urresti, Teodoro,
334.
Joannes Andreae, 49, 59,
93, 94, 95, 97, 98, 108,
115, 122, 126, 143, 144,
146, 154, 161, 162, 163,
164, 167, 168, 170, 172,
175, 178, 179, 180-181,
210, 211, 212, 225, 226,
227, 228, 229, 233.
Joannis Saresberiensis,
86, 90, 91, 94, 112, 114,
193, 195, 196, 197, 201,

204, 207, 208-209, 218.
John, St., 5, 224.
Jonas Aurelianensis, 44, 112, 113, 197, 204, 208.
Julianus, 155, 156, 167, 184.
Julianus, The Apostate, 271.
Jung, Carl J., 235.
Justine, St., 205.
Justinianus, 184.
Keightley, Thomas, 271.
Kurtscheid, Bertrandus, 271.
Lactantius, 39, 67, 72.
Lettmann, Reinhard, 329, 330, 338.
Luke, St., 224.
Mark, St., 224.
Marx, Carl, 121, 268-269.
Matrimonia Mixta, 411, 412, 413, 414.
Matrimonii Sacramentum, 412.
Matthew, St., 187, 190, 224.
Ministeria Quaedam, 281-282, 286.
Modestinus, 83, 111, 124, 130, 133, 155.
Mohler, James, 272.
Onclin, Willy, 334.
Optatus Afri. Milevitanus, 88, 91, 192, 194, 195, 196, 200, 201, 208.
Origen, 38.
Papinianus, 83.
Paul, Pope, VI, 392-393.
Paul, St., 2, 3, 6, 7, 10, 11, 19, 20, 21, 36, 187, 188, 190, 191, 194, 200, 211, 230, 271, 308.
Paulus, 59, 60, 80, 111, 112, 130, 135, 142, 155, 180.
Peter, St., 187, 189, 270-271.
Petrus Damianus, 193, 195, 207.
Pileus Modicensis, 118, 125, 213, 214, 215, 217.
Placentinus, 60, 61, 64,
93, 94, 99, 117, 212, 213, 215.
Plato, 1.
Pomponius, 59, 60, 111, 144, 154, 155.
Prosper, Blessed, 21.
Rabanus Maurus, 24, 205.
Ratherius Veronensis, 44, 197.
Regimini Ecclesiae, 387.
Regino Prumiensis, 197, 304.
Reiffenstuel, Anacletus, 131, 132, 301, 305, 307, 308, 310.
Samuel, 187.
Schmalzgrueber, Franciscus, 131, 305.
Sedulius Scotus, 87, 89, 201, 203, 208.
Seneca, 29, 30, 37, 54, 64, 68, 78.
Silvester, Pope, II, 88, 208.
Simons, Thomas G., 288.
Spiritus Domini, 365, 384, 387, 388, 389, 390, 391, 393, 396.
Terentius Clemens, 142.
Tertullianus, 5, 37-38.
Theophilus Antiochenus, 191, 202.
Tryphoninus, 58.
Ubertinus De Bobio, 143.
Ubertus De Bonacurso, 127.
Ulpianus, 22, 34, 58, 65, 66, 67, 68, 69, 80, 111, 112, 129, 142, 144, 150, 155, 156, 177, 183, 184, 185.
Vatican Council, 1, 8, 10, 11, 12, 13, 14, 15, 16, 101, 235, 236, 239, 242, 243, 245, 246, 250, 269-270, 271-272, 273, 274, 275, 276, 279, 281, 282, 284, 288, 290, 293, 297, 299, 303, 311, 312, 313, 317, 322, 328, 329, 332, 334, 363, 364, 370, 377, 382, 384, 385, 386, 387, 388, 389, 391, 394, 395,

399, 400, 403, 405, 409, 418.
Wisdom, 19, 20, 23, 47, 71.
Zavalloni, Roberto, 236, 237.

INDEX OF SUBJECTS

Administration of Goods, 361, 376.
Administrator, Diocesan, 379.
Altar, 355.
Amalgamation of Funds, 362.
Anointing of the Sick, 280-281, 315, 351, 389, 407.
Apostolate of the Laity, 288-291, 292, 293, 294, 304, 355, 358-359.
Authority, 319.
Authority, Public, 183-224.
Baptism, 11, 15, 16, 243-244, 283, 287, 289, 292, 325, 351, 390, 405-407, 412, 414, 415, 417.
Bishop - Local Ordinary, 225, 291-292, 293, 303, 312, 317, 330, 333, 334, 335, 340, 341, 346, 350, 364, 365, 366, 367-368, 369, 370, 372-373, 374, 375-376, 377, 378, 380-381, 388, 389-391, 394, 413.
Capacitas Agendi, 275-276, 277.
Capacitas Essendi, 276.
Catechesis, 278, 356.
Catechumenate, 356.
Chorepiscopi, 300-301.
Christ, 2, 3, 5, 6, 7, 19, 20, 21, 40, 64, 71-72, 73, 78, 79, 99, 119, 187-188, 189, 220, 223, 224, 233, 234, 247, 318, 325.
Church, 10-11, 12, 13-18, 70, 96-102, 144, 171, 173, 174, 194-195, 224, 226, 227, 228, 232, 234, 235, 241-242, 244, 245, 247, 248, 249, 269, 271, 272-273, 275, 276, 299, 316, 317, 324, 327, 331-332, 339, 347-348, 366, 367, 368, 384-385, 386, 396, 415, 418-419.
Church, Parochial, 306, 307, 325, 373.
Churches, Protestant, 400-401, 409.
Churches, Separated Eastern, 400, 402, 403-404, 408, 410-411.
Clergy, 349-351, 371, 393, 396, 397, 404.
Collections, 362, 373.
College of Bishops, 327, 328, 330, 332, 333, 334, 335-336, 337, 338, 339-340, 341, 347, 368.
College of Consultors, 350-351, 369, 375-383.
Committee, Finance, 295.
Communicatio in Sacris, 388, 389-390, 400, 401, 402-403, 404-405, 416.
Communicatio in Spiritualibus, 399, 400, 401, 402.
Communication, Social, 293, 357.
Community, 206, 207.
Community Parochial, 299-325, 373.
Conference, Episcopal, 294-295, 326-268, 376, 387, 388-389, 394.
Confirmation, Sacrament of, 11, 157-158, 280, 289, 292, 315, 351, 411.
Conscience, 49, 243, 244, 251.
Consciousness, Human, 7-11, 13, 14, 20, 23, 30, 53, 54, 55, 56, 57, 58, 62, 65, 69, 70, 71, 72, 73, 77, 78, 79, 82, 84, 100, 102, 103, 108, 115, 119, 120-121, 124, 125, 141, 145-146, 148, 150, 151, 152, 153-154, 155-156, 158, 160, 161, 164-165, 166-167, 169, 178, 181-182, 189, 190, 219-223, 227, 228, 233-234,

236, 238, 245, 247, 264-265, 267, 268, 269, 270, 297, 317.
Contract Social, 23-24.
Council, Ecumenical, 228, 229, 231, 331, 336, 338, 340.
Council, Plenary, 294, 331, 345-346.
Council, Provincial, 294, 295, 331, 375, 380.
Council of Churches, 393-394.
Council, Pastoral, 294, 373.
Courts, Ecclesiastical, 257-259, 359-360, 417.
Crime, 241, 260-263.
Crime-Ecumenism, 414-417.
Custom, 51, 59, 108, 149-182, 213.
Custom of Fact, 166-171.
Custom of Law, 153-165.
Custom, Private, 162-165.
Custom, Public, 165.
Custom, **Generalissima**, 170-171, 174.
Custom, **Contra Legem**, 177-180.
Custom, **Praeter Legem**, 175-177.
Custom, **Secundum Legem**, 180-181.
Decimae, 304, 308, 309, 310.
Decree, Administrative, 259-260.
Depositum Fidei, 17.
Diaconate, Permanent, 350.
Diakonia, 52, 62-63, 65, 68, 271, 272, 318-320, 324, 334.
Dialogue, Ecumenical, 388-389, 396-397.
Dignity, Royal, 197, 200-205, 207, 209-216.
Diocese, 291-292, 299-301, 311, 330-331, 332, 333, 339, 348-349, 363, 382.
Dispensation, 135-142, 218, 231-232, 244.
Documents, Personal, 255.

Ecceitas, 54-55.
Ecumenism, 339, 364-366, 384-419.
Education, Christian, 247-248, 278-279, 395-398.
Election, 240.
Eucharist, 280, 285-286, 287, 315, 318, 325, 351, 386, 389, 399, 401, 407, 408, 409, 410-411, 414.
Freedom, Human, 9-10, 12, 13, 35, 42, 57, 58, 148, 236-237, 239, 240-241, 243, 250, 251, 263, 264.
Heresy, 229, 415, 416.
Illatio Iuridica, 146-147.
Institutes of Consecrated Life, 291, 292, 363-364.
Interpretation, 132-135, 180.
Iura Stolae, 310, 361.
Ius Gentium, 48, 58-62, 81, 144, 147.
Ius Honorarium, 81, 82, 143.
Ius Praetorium, 81, 82.
Jurisdiction, 296.
Justice, 63-70, 85, 86, 87, 109, 110, 111, 112, 114, 115, 116, 117, 118, 121, 123-124, 125, 129, 142-143, 144, 146, 185, 249-250, 390, 394-395.
Koinonia, 52, 53, 54-58, 62, 316-318, 319, 320, 322.
Law, Divine Positive, 17, 39, 48, 49, 73-79, 116, 232, 415.
Law, Human, 18, 51, 52, 79-108, 117, 129, 134, 137, 140-141, 143, 156, 211, 216-217, 264, 268, 342-343, 349.
Law, Civil, 80, 81, 85-96, 147.
Law, Ecclesiastical, 96-108, 227-228.
Law of Creation, 21.
Law of the Sensitive World, 22.
Law of the Spirit, 22s.

Law, Mosaic, 41, 47, 74, 75.
Law, Natural, 17, 22, 23, 27, 28, 29, 30, 32, 33, 35, 39, 42, 43, 45, 46, 47, 50, 51s, 58, 59, 60, 61, 62, 63, 65, 71, 72, 74, 75, 76, 77, 78, 81, 147, 248, 250, 268, 415.
Law in Canonical and Civil Authors, 45s, 230.
Law in Christian Literature, 36s.
Law in **Corpus Iuris Civilis**, 33s.
Legislator, 185, 186.
Legitimacy, 254.
Liturgy, 281-283, 284-285, 288, 289, 304-305, 306, 353, 402, 403, 404.
Liturgy, Books, 354.
Liturgy of the Hours, 354-355.
Magisterium, 100-101, 171, 224, 226, 249, 327, 336-337, 338, 363, 386, 401.
Marriage, 240, 242, 251, 254, 257, 283-284, 287, 294, 352-353, 411-414, 416-417.
Martyrion, 52, 70-73, 289-290, 324-325.
Ministries, 286-287, 292-293, 323-324, 355.
Missio Canonica, 334.
Oath, 231, 239, 251, 254.
Office of Equitable Solution, 360.
Ordination, Sacred, 251, 252, 255, 315, 352, 386, 408, 409, 410.
Organization, Charitable, 290-291.
Parish, 312, 315, 316, 373.
Parochia Gentilitia, 313.
Pastor, 310-311, 320-321, 350.
Pastor, **Amovibilis-Inamovibilis**, 303, 311, 374.
Pastor, Associate, 310, 314.
Penance, Sacrament of, 240-241, 252, 253, 280, 315, 352, 389, 407.
Pentecost, 11, 12, 14, 36, 55, 56, 70, 99, 102, 224-225, 326-327, 348.
Personhood, 12-13, 235-265.
Pontiff, Roman, 211, 225-230, 334, 335, 338, 339, 368, 387.
Possession, Canonical, 380.
Praetor Peregrinus, 110, 143.
Praetor Urbanus, 143.
Priesthood, 242, 381-382, 386.
Priesthood, Common, 266-298, 299, 305, 306, 307, 314, 315, 319-320, 322-324.
Priesthood, Ministerial, 274, 299, 305, 306, 307, 313, 314, 315, 319-320, 333-334, 396, 403, 409.
Priests, 301, 302-303, 370-371.
Primitiae, 308-309, 310.
Profession, Religious, 242, 255.
Province, Ecclesiastical, 343-344.
Publications, 293, 358, 388.
Region, Ecclesiastical, 344-345.
Registers, Parochial, 361.
Remuneration, 255-256.
Reputation, Good, 253-254.
Resignation, 240.
Revolution, French, 266-267.
Right to Privacy, 252.
Rite, 284-285.
Sacrament, 280-281, 325, 386, 401, 408, 409.
Sacrament-Faith, 406.
Sacrament-Intention, 238, 406.

Sacrament-Matter and Form, 406.
Sacramentals, 287-288.
Schools, 357.
See, Apostolic, 346-347, 387.
Seminary, 349-350, 365, 388, 396, 397-398.
Senate of Priests, 350, 369-375, 377, 378, 381, 382, 383.
Shrines, 355.
Synod, Diocesan, 362, 374, 380, 391.
Synod of Bishops, 294, 328, 335, 347.
Times, Sacred, 354.
Tradition, Sacred, 100, 157, 226-227, 386.
Tradition, Priestly, 3, 4, 5, 6, 73.
Tradition, Yahwist, 3, 4, 5, 6, 36, 40, 54.
Unio Hypostatica, 7, 13, 17, 188, 219, 265.
Via Administrativa, 296.
Via Iudicialis, 296.
Vote, 240.
Vow, 231, 238, 239, 244.